KU-044-572

OZU
AND THE POETICS OF CINEMA

bfi
PUBLISHING

PRINCETON
UNIVERSITY
PRESS

DAVID BORDWELL

First published in 1988 by the
British Film Institute
21 Stephen Street
London W1P 1PL

Published in the United States of
America by
Princeton University Press
41 William Street, Princeton
New Jersey 08540

Copyright © David Bordwell 1988

Typeset and printed in
Great Britain by
W. S. Cowell Ltd., Ipswich, Suffolk

British Library Cataloguing in
Publication Data

Bordwell, David, *1947*—

    Ozu and the poetics of cinema.
    1. Japanese cinema films.
    Directing. Ozu, Yasujiro –
    Critical studies
    I. Title
    791.43'0233'0924

    ISBN 0–85170–158–2
    ISBN 0–85170–159–0 Pbk

Library of Congress Cataloging-in-
Publication Data

Bordwell, David.
    Ozu and the poetics of cinema.

    Bibliography: p.
    Includes index.
    1. Ozu, Yasujirō, 1903–1963—
    Criticism and interpretation.
    2. Motion pictures—Aesthetics. I.
    Title. PN1998.3.O98B67 1988
    791.43'0233'0924 88–4164

    ISBN 0–691–05516–5 (Princeton
    University Press)
    ISBN 0–691–00822–1 (Princeton
    University Press: pbk.)

79.
430233   0334681
OZU

For Edward Branigan
Sensei oshiete kureru

CONTENTS

I was still an assistant when I heard him say: 'Someday, I'm sure, foreigners will understand my films.' Then he added with a modest smile: 'Then again, no. They will say, like everybody else, that my films aren't much of anything.'

YUHARU ATSUTA,
assistant and cameraman for
YASUJIRO OZU

Art and Science cannot exist but in minutely organized Particulars.
WILLIAM BLAKE

Preface

This book began, in an unsystematic way, in 1975 with a seminar on 'sparse' cinema. Across several years of teaching, Ozu increasingly became my guide to what cinema is and can be.

So many friends have helped me in the course of my work that I will probably forget to name every one, but among them are certainly my translators Kenji Kitatani, Jamie Hubbard, Reiko Waggoner, and Morio Watanabe. Inez Hedges provided me with a dialogue transcript of *End of Summer*. Kyoko Hirano shared research findings on *Late Spring* and supported my efforts in many other ways. Joseph Anderson, Ben Brewster, Don Kirihara, Akira Miura, Jim O'Brien, and Miriam Silverberg have all enlightened me about Japanese film. Donald Richie, who almost single-handedly introduced Ozu to Western viewers, assisted my work unstintingly. Alan Casebier clarified aspects of Japanese aesthetics for me. John Dower was a magnificent colleague during his years at Madison, and his comments from San Diego on portions of this book have been of crucial help. I have also benefited from rambling, late-night phone conversations with Noël Carroll. Darrell Davis patiently read the first half of the book and helped me patch up a troublesome chapter. The hospitality of Douglas Gomery and Marilyn Moon enlivened my research stays in Washington, as did that of Janet Staiger during visits to Washington Square.

Several institutions and individuals provided generous access to materials: Peter Grilli and David Owens of the Japan Society of New York; Hiroyuki Chujo of Shochiku Films, Tokyo; Eileen Bowser, Jon Gartenberg, Charles Silver and Anne Morra of the Museum of Modern Art; Elaine Burrows of the National Film Archive in London; Gabrielle Claes, Danielle Nicolas, and Jacques Ledoux of the Royal Film Archive of Belgium; Barbara Humphries, David Parker, Emily Sieger, and Paul Spehr of the Library of Congress; Sheila Paige Bayne of the Fulbright Foundation of Belgium; Hiroko Govaers of the Fondation du Japon (Paris); Edith Kramer of the Pacific Film Archive of Berkeley; and Jose Lopez, John Montague, and of course Dan Talbot of New Yorker Films.

I owe a particular debt to the Japan Foundation of London. The generous subsidy which they provided made it possible for this book to be published in its present form. I hope that the result properly honors one of the greatest of all Japanese artists.

In Ozu's earliest surviving film there is a close-up of a ring of college pennants tacked to a wall, with the University of Wisconsin hanging in the central spot. This fortunate shot should stand as my frontispiece. Many of the friends already thanked have been affiliated with Wisconsin. And only the generous support of the Graduate School Research Program of the University of Wisconsin–Madison has permitted this book to be as detailed and comprehensive as it is. A Vilas Humanist grant for 1984–6 enabled me to complete the project. The pennant could also serve as a banner for the Wisconsin Center for Film and Theater Research, which, thanks to the warm professionalism of Maxine Fleckner Ducey and Linda Henzl, remains an idyllic place to work. Marching under the same standard are my colleagues in the Film division of the Department of Communication Arts: Tino Balio, Don Crafton, Vance Kepley, and J. J. Murphy. Their kindness, wit, and *esprit de corps* have been precious to me. Vance also offered helpful suggestions on historical aspects of my argument. Finally there are the students, now many of them professors, who have over the years enthusiastically welcomed Ozu to Madison and who have offered their criticism of ideas first tried out in the classroom: Serafina Bathrick, Matthew Bernstein, Marilyn Campbell, Kathryn C. D'Alessandro, Martha Davis, Kerman Eckes, David Fishelson, Terry Fowler, Peter Lutze, Sue Pearson, Jim Peterson, Kathy Root, Maureen Turim, Diane Waldman, and the late, much-missed Tom Wisniewski.

I am also grateful to the British Film Institute Publishing Department. Ed Buscombe contracted this book, and Geoffrey Nowell-Smith gave me excellent editorial advice on the manuscript. Tony Rayns gave precious last-minute advice about the transliteration of Japanese and Chinese names. Centrally, of course, there are two fellow researchers and friends: Edward Branigan, the most indefatigable reader one could ask for, and Kristin Thompson, who continues to teach me about Ozu.

Introduction

If one had to sum up the conception of Yasujiro Ozu held by most film critics and viewers, something like this would probably emerge: All of his films are fundamentally alike. His constant subject is the Japanese family, his preferred genre the 'home drama'. His plots, revolving around a subtle depiction of character, are as uneventful as ordinary life itself. His camera, always placed about three feet from the floor, registers the low-level viewpoint of a seated Japanese. His films' contemplative resignation to mutability and his purist approach to form preserve the traditions of Japanese art, often evoking the ineffable wisdom of Zen Buddhism. Ozu is, in short, the most Japanese of all directors.

Widespread as these assumptions are, however, many are just false and others badly need qualification. In some cases, the errors arise from not looking closely enough. A few moments' scrutiny of any Ozu film will show, for instance, that he does not typically put his camera at the eye level of a seated person. In other instances, the mistake comes from a failure of contextualization. Stylistic elements are yanked out of their formal systems and reified as typically Ozuian, or even typically Japanese. To avoid this, we must situate Ozu's dramaturgical strategies, his stylistic choices, and his use of genre conventions within Japanese filmmaking practices of his period. Any claims about his debts to traditional arts, for example, must reckon with the way in which such elements are mediated by his situation as a filmmaker living in a turbulent period of history. Finally, all these directions of inquiry require theoretical reflection. What assumptions underlie claims about his work's realism, the camera's anthropocentric point of view, the relation of his films to Zen? What is it to be 'more Japanese' than someone else? What indeed is 'Japaneseness' in this connection? The critic requires a theoretical frame of reference even to pose intelligible questions of close analysis and broad context. Without such a frame of reference, one is led irresistibly back to clichés.

The frame of reference which I propose here is that of a historical poetics of cinema. 'Poetics' refers to the study of how films are put together and how, in determinate contexts, they elicit particular effects. A narrative film exhibits a total form consisting of materials – subject matter, themes – shaped and transformed by overall composition (e.g. narrative structure, narrational logic) and stylistic patterning. The formal options are constrained and constructed by a range of norms arising from formal principles, conventional practices of film production and consumption, and proximate features of the social context. Through the notion of norms, we can make our poetics historical; only by comparison with prevailing standards and practices can we specify the particular workings of one film or a body of films. I also argue, somewhat more polemically, that by starting from the regulative assumption

1

that the filmmaker is a rational, intentional agent, we can put poetics at the center of any study of a film's social context. All this sounds dauntingly abstract, I know, but discussion of these concepts will emerge piecemeal in the course of this study, and the films will illustrate them concretely.[1]*

A historical poetics reveals some fresh arguments about Ozu. Closely scrutinized, his films turn out to be far less alike than people usually think; to have a greater variety of subject and theme than is frequently granted; to be less concerned with psychological verisimilitude than most critics suggest. Placed in a social context, the films are less indebted to Japanese aesthetics and Zen Buddhism than to a vibrant popular culture and, more indirectly, to ideological tensions. Approached as formal constructs and dynamic systems in process, Ozu's works can be seen to engage the spectator on many levels, both narrative and stylistic, in a fashion that is unique in the history of cinema. Thus the theory is used to produce new knowledge of Ozu's work, but from another angle his work becomes an occasion to test the theory itself.

The format of this book reflects an attempt to analyze and explain the functionings of Ozu's films. The first part constitutes a survey. Two orienting chapters sketch out Ozu's career and describe some pertinent contextual norms. More detailed chapters follow; they analyze the materials and formal processes of the works, drawing on examples from Ozu's entire career. The part ends with a wide-ranging discussion of some social and historical functions of the films. The book's second part consists of a chronologically ordered series of critical analyses of all of Ozu's films. This section embodies the theory 'in practice' while affording an antidote to offhand generalization. The discussion of each film is detailed, but for reasons of space each essay has been confined to a few pages. An appendix supplies some quantitative data about the films, and a bibliography lists important sources. I have aimed to make this book a resource for Ozu admirers, but I also contend that these films are of major importance for any thinking about the nature of fictional cinema.

Some housekeeping notes remain. Japanese names are presented in English order, with given name first and family name last. (So: Shiro Kido, not Kido Shiro.) For ease of printing, the transliteration of Japanese words omits all macrons. I refer to recent historical periods by Japanese imperial epochs: the Meiji era (1868–1912), the Taisho era (1912–26), the Showa era (1926–present). Films by Ozu are cited in the text by their most common English titles; the original Japanese titles will be found in the filmography. Literary works and films by other directors are cited by Japanese title first, followed by an English translation; subsequent mentions use the latter title. The shot lists provided within the text employ these abbreviations: *els* (= extreme long shot), *ls* (= long shot), *mls* (= medium long shot), *pa* (plan-américain, or the knees-up framing), *ms* (= medium-shot), *cu* (= close-up); *ET* (= expository title), *DT* (= dialogue title); *fg* (= foreground), *bg* (= background). I have tried to keep footnotes to a minimum, and most are citations rather than amplifications of a point. The bibliography lists works for further reading as well as sources I have found useful in studying these very unconventional films.

---

* Notes are to be found at the end of the volume, beginning on p.379.

Part 1

1
Career

Yasujiro Ozu lived the sort of unassuming life that most people take as their lot. He was born on 12 December 1903 and died of cancer on his sixtieth birthday. The major events of his life would qualify as muted climaxes in his own films: a youthful stint teaching grade school; acquisition of a job in the film industry; the death of his father in 1934; a life with his mother until her death in 1962; and at intervals the summons to serve in the army. Unlike Mizoguchi and Kurosawa, who accompanied their films to international festivals when the West was discovering Japanese cinema, Ozu stayed at home with films felt to be 'too Japanese'. He lived largely, it seems, to make and watch movies, to be with his mother, and to enjoy his friends.

The biographical critic can nonetheless sift out a few nuggets. If we like, we can trace the comedies about rumbustious college boys back to Ozu's notorious conduct in middle school.[1] His growing propensity for beer, whiskey, and *sake* may be embodied in the sodden old men who wander through his late films. The films' characteristic comedy, alternately vulgar and pawky, seems to spring from the shy, teasing man who loved scatological humor. More generally, our critic could find in Ozu's childhood circumstances – a home governed by a doting mother and lacking a busy father – the origins of the breakdown of family unity which many critics take to be at the center of his work.[2]

Yet even if we could strike a mother lode of such data, we should be no closer to understanding the aesthetic and cultural causes, functions, and consequences of Ozu's work. His depiction of the family could just as easily have come from a blissfully happy childhood. (His films would then be depicting the family disunity he most feared.) Or, to paraphrase Sartre on Valéry, Ozu may have loved alcohol, but not every drinker becomes Ozu.[3] The biographical individual is indispensable to the history of the cinema, but not in isolation. The artist's relation to the work is always socially mediated. The 'social construction of Ozu', as we might call this process, has two products: Ozu the director, man of the cinema; and Ozu the citizen, man of Japan.

A Filmmaker's Legend
As a film director, Ozu exists within a network of practices and discourses – aesthetic, industrial, and journalistic. I shall have occasion to return to them throughout this book, but a factor that deserves separate treatment here is what Boris Tomashevsky calls the 'biographical legend'.[4] Some artists have biographies, others don't. A Byron or a Bergman offers us a strong version of the individual's life that functions in two ways: to permit works to come into being, as fulfillments of the legend; and to orient perceivers to them, to favor certain construals and to block others. The film industry can generate a

biographical legend, as Robert Allen has argued in relation to *Sunrise*;[5] or the artist himself can provide one through interviews, writings, and public pronouncements, as Dreyer did.[6] In the latter event, the creation of a biographical legend should not be considered a cunningly contrived display; public discourse will necessarily appropriate a filmmaker's words and acts, turning them to particular ends. Ozu offers a good example. From early in his career, he wrote essays and gave interviews. Two themes seem salient in both Japanese and Western critical discourse. These have significantly affected how viewers contextualize Ozu's work. First there is Ozu the humble craftsman. If Mizoguchi was the obsessed, tormented artist – involved with a gangster's girl, bouncing from studio to studio, wreaking terror on the set – Ozu was the modest artisan, calmly making film after film according to formula. He compared himself to a carpenter, or more often, a tofu-maker. 'I just want to make a tray of good tofu. If people want something different, they should go to the restaurants and department stores.'[7] The critic Tadao Sato notes that, during a party late in his life, Ozu became angry with another filmmaker for maintaining that film was an art of self-expression rather than of rule-governed form.[8] The craftsman analogy can be found in many contemporary accounts eager to link Ozu to an intrinsically Japanese tradition. Here is Shimba Iida: 'The sight of him huddled around a fireplace in a tiny mountain cabin in the Tateshima hills with Kogo Noda as they thrash out the scenario between them gives me the feeling of watching a true Japanese master at work.'[9] Such an image easily slides into the notion of Ozu the Zen artist, the simple toiler who turns out to have the deep secret.

Reinforcing the artisanal theme is the image of Ozu the stubborn conservative. He is said to have made the same film over and over. For the average art-house moviegoer, Ozu's technique is simple, perhaps 'primitive', and resistant to technological change. This is an image that Ozu cooperated in circulating. He came late to talkies because he was a perfectionist and because his cinematographer was devising his own sound-recording system. Ozu announced jokingly: 'I'm going to film the last fade-out of the silent cinema.'[10] As the legend has it, he steadily eliminated dissolves, fades, and camera movements from his style. After the war, he says, people expected that all the foreign movies he saw in Singapore would have changed his work. But no: 'Look at *The Record of a Tenement Gentleman* for yourself: nothing has changed, the same as always. Some people say that Ozu is a really obstinate buzzard.'[11] He came late to color and never adopted widescreen. 'The wide screen reminds me of a roll of toilet paper.'[12] Again, critics have followed his lead and ranked him (with Dreyer and Bresson) as the cinéaste of minimal means. 'Here is a man,' Iida reports, 'who adamantly refuses to change his approach. His adherence to his own original method will permit no outside advice.'[13]

In the artisanal and conservative themes, Ozu's biographical legend – so divorced from his private life that we might rather speak of a 'temperamental' legend – functions to supply a particular 'set' or orientation to the films. In the argument of this book, this orientation plays various roles. For one thing, it will be questioned. This conservative craftsman makes bold, varied, innovative films. I shall argue that Ozu is an experimental filmmaker, quite likely the greatest. The legend can also be put into various historical contexts. We can suggest, for instance, that what seems to be a stylistic conservatism is actually, in the context of 1930s Japanese film, a somewhat 'progressive' rigor. We can see that along with the conservative element there runs an attitude of joking indifference that would be out of place in the discourse of, say, Dreyer. We can notice that the craftsman analogy is much more emphatic after 1949, the years when Ozu would retreat to Kogo Noda's villa to write scripts in seclusion. Before the war, Ozu's working practice looked rather different. We scarcely recognize the traditional artisan in this 1930 portrait of 'James Maki', Ozu's scriptwriting pseudonym:

> James Maki has the smartness of his American father and the delicacy of his Japanese mother. . . . His study has a shelf covered with intricately designed paper, on which sit toys gathered from all over Japan. We worked through the night drinking Japanese wine and Bordeaux from the 1800s and listening to gramophone records of *The Love Parade*. . . . Next day we met at my house, where, fueled by Washington Coffee, Johnny Walker, pickled squid, and tea over rice, we worked further on the gags.[14]

Even the postwar collaboration with Noda devolved into a routine that was hardly ascetic discipline. The pair could consume one hundred bottles of *sake* in three months of script preparation. Recalls Mrs Noda: 'They had to play before they worked.'[15] Analyzing Ozu's poetics of cinema thus requires us to qualify and contextualize the biographical legend, discounting it when it runs afoul of other evidence while still preserving it as a precious clue to the diverse aesthetic and political roles the work could fulfill.

A Japanese Life

Ozu can be constructed not only as a filmmaker but also as a historical individual. In this construct, 'Japaneseness' plays an important part. The claim that he was the most Japanese of directors, echoing throughout the critical literature, can be understood in several ways. If we assume there to be a Japanese 'essence' or national character, Ozu's work somehow seems to transcribe it on film. I am not here concerned to show that this happened. Rather, I want to scan Ozu's life for features which could create an idealized historical individual of wide appeal. Biography thus reenters our inquiry, but only as those aspects of an individual's life which can typify a portion of the populace as a whole.

Nostalgia comes in two main varieties in Japan: longing for one's rural hometown (from which most urban Japanese are only a couple of generations removed) and longing for chic, cosmopolitan Tokyo. Ozu's life was built around the second type. Born and raised in Fukugawa, he was from the start a *shitamachi*, or 'downtown' person. Fukugawa has a mythical status: it is part of plebeian Edo, a neighborhood of small businesses, sushi restaurants, brothels, shipyards, and teeming markets. Here the haiku master Basho had his cottage. Many of Ozu's friends called him a typical *Edokko*, or 'child of Edo' – a free-spending fellow easily lured by fads and slick charm.[16] His father's class position, declining petty bourgeoisie, was typical of the raffish mercantile milieu of Fukugawa. Both his parents came from wealthy noble families, but by the turn of the century his father was running a fertilizer firm. Yasujiro, along with his older brother Shinichi and two younger sisters, lived in Tokyo until 1913, when they went with their mother to live in Matsusaka, a mercantile castle town in Honshu. After Ozu passed some tempestuous years in middle school, failed the entrance exam for Kobe Higher Commercial School, and spent a year as an assistant teacher in a mountain village, he returned to Tokyo in 1923. It would be his home until he died.

Ozu's life spans the six crucial decades of Japan's modernization. He grew to manhood in the period which saw huge industrial expansion, military conquests, and the creation of a westernized urban culture. His was the first generation to assume that men wore business suits, cut their hair short, ate beef and bread, and played baseball. He was shaped by the liberal Taisho era (1912–26), with its expanding bourgeoisie, its reformist optimism, and its passion for education and intellectual debate. He was in Tokyo during the horrific Kanto earthquake of September 1923, which destroyed his father's company along with over a hundred and thirty thousand other buildings. As a young man in the 1930s, he saw his country move toward jingoism, launch a war-based economy, and embark on a fateful policy of military expansion. He spent his thirty-fourth birthday fighting in Nanking; nearly five years later, in 1942, Doolittle's raid struck near the Waseda University that Ozu had portrayed in his college comedies. With thousands of other soldiers he spent the autumn of 1945 as a prisoner of war. With millions of other Japanese, he lived under American occupation, enjoyed the fruits of a new consumer society, and grew old in an economy in which output was doubling every seven years. When Ozu was born, Tokyo had just installed its first electric streetcar. Only a few years after he died, children at play wore gas masks to protect themselves from pollution.

Like other urban Taisho youths, he admired Western culture, especially one form of it. 'Film had a magical hold on me.'[17] Ozu was almost certainly the most cinephiliac major director before the New Wave. Growing up in Matsusaka, he would sneak away from school to see Chaplin, Pearl White, Lillian Gish, and William S. Hart. He welcomed expulsion from the school dormitory, since it gave him more time to go to movies. He boasted that he took his examination for high school solely to get a trip to Kobe to see *The Prisoner of Zenda*.[18] He disdained his nation's cinema, claiming that when he was interviewed for a job at Shochiku, he could recall seeing only three Japanese films.[19] Throughout the 1930s he continued to follow American films. While he and his cinematographer Atsuta were stationed in Singapore in 1943–45, they screened captured prints of *Citizen Kane*, *The Grapes of Wrath*, *Rebecca*, *The Letter*, *The Little Foxes*, *Wuthering Heights*, and other recent Hollywood products. Admirals might plot strategy, but Ozu had a more direct gauge of the enemy's prowess: 'Watching *Fantasia* made me suspect that we were going to lose the war. These guys look like trouble, I thought.'[20] Throughout his life he had a remarkable memory for the movies he saw, recalling dissolves in *The Marriage Circle* (1924) and criticizing Wyler's famous cut-in to Fredric March watching Dana Andrews' phone call in *The Best Years of Our Lives*.[21] The citations of Hollywood throughout his work, from the *Seventh Heaven* poster in *Days of Youth* (1929) to the poster for *The Defiant Ones* in *Ohayo* (1959), spring from his passionate love of American film.

Ozu's working life makes him typical in another way. In the 1920s and 1930s, as he began his career, the characteristic Japanese-style firm began to emerge. It would be a smallish manufacturing or trading enterprise dominated by a paternalistic owner or manager. White-collar workers submitted to a strict regimen and proffered their loyalty to the company in exchange for job security and slow but certain advancement up the ladder. Salarymen educated at the same college or working in the same department formed a *batsu*, a clique of intimates who habitually ate lunch together, went drinking after work, and played golf or mah-jongg on the weekend. Like many middle-class Japanese men of his generation Ozu was a company employee, working steadily for the same firm all his life.

Before the early 1920s, film production was hardly rationalized, but Ozu came to the Shochiku Cinema Company soon after it had embarked upon a modernization program. Under Henry Kotani the firm adopted Hollywood and European technology, division of labor, and scriptwriting techniques. In 1924, Shiro Kido, the son-in-law of one founder of the Shochiku entertainment combine, became head of the Kamata studio and soon established himself as a trend-setting manager. Some aspects of 'Kidoism' will occupy us in the next chapter, but here we should note how Kido created an orderly promotion system for aspiring directors. A promising young man would be made an assistant director and would spend his time working on scripts. If he showed talent, he would start directing short comedies. Then the youth would graduate to features.[22] Ozu followed this pattern, beginning as an assistant cameraman before, in 1926, being promoted to assistant director under Tadamoto Okubo. 'I moved to be near Kamata and studied morning and night.'[23] In 1927, Kido asked Ozu to compose a script for a historical film and then to direct one himself. Returning after a brief stint in the army, Ozu began making comedies. By 1929 he was turning out contemporary-life films in many genres. Except for three loan-outs to other studios in the 1950s, Ozu made all his films for Shochiku, with Kido still at the helm of the firm.

The Kamata studio in the 1920s was an energetic place. Ozu's mentor Okubo was only seven years older than he was; Shimazu, the dean of Shochiku's contemporary-life films, only six. Ozu's contemporaries were Naruse, Hiroshi Shimizu, Tomu Uchida, Heinosuke Gosho, and Torajiro Saito. Each entered Shochiku at around age twenty and was directing by age twenty-five. Ozu also became friends with the scriptwriter Kogo Noda, the actor Tokihiko Okada, cameraman Yoshiyasu Hamamura, and his own cinematographer Hideo Mohara. For a time Ozu and several friends lived together in a rented home in a Kamata neighborhood.[24] These men, and others such as Sadao Yamanaka, formed Ozu's *batsu*. They had their in-jokes, such as the catchphrase 'Winthat Monnet' ('without money'), which Ozu attached to the credits of *Inn in Tokyo*.[25] Like their salaryman equivalents, these young bachelors did not measure company loyalty by the time clock. After a long day on the set, Ozu and his circle would meet to watch new films, to iron out script problems, or to argue about the mission of the cinema. True,

UNIVERSITY OF WINCHESTER LIBRARY

the film industry was a more disreputable business than those firms that attracted college graduates. But with a paternalistic manager, a firmly rationalized regimen for production and promotion, and a clutch of ambitious young men eager to give all for the firm, Kido's Kamata studio remains an example of the white-collar company that emerged between 1925 and the postwar era.

In a sense, then, individual biography creeps back into this account. As a Taisho-educated Tokyoite, as a soldier, as a lover of Western exoticism, as a company employee, Ozu lived in conformity with one ideal of this century's 'ordinary' Japanese. This can be seen in the way that, with few exceptions, his central characters tended to be about the same age as he was when he made the films. We find college graduates and young parents dominating his earliest movies, working fathers and mothers in the mid-1930s films, maturing sons and daughters in the early 1940s work, middle-aged scholars and businessmen in the first postwar films, and old men in the last films. It is, however, a curiously non-individualized biography; the filmmaker's life becomes important only insofar as it is utterly commonplace. This does not, of course, make Ozu a 'typical Japanese', since that 'Japaneseness' is faithful to only one segment of national life. The peasant, the *burukamin* outcast, the political activist, the chauvinist soldier: these too, 'typically Japanese', find no place in this account. Nevertheless, whenever Ozu's postwar characters sit recalling life before or during the war, the scene's force comes not only from the director's experience but also from the way in which that experience exemplifies what millions of other Japanese did and suffered. To an extent unparalleled in Western cinema, this director lives along with his audience.

Phases of a Career

Across thirty-five years, Ozu directed fifty-three feature films, of which thirty-one survive more or less complete. (*I Graduated, But . . .* of 1929 exists only in a few minutes of excerpts, and *A Mother Should Be Loved* of 1934 lacks two reels.) Ozu also filmed a documentary short, *Kagamijishi* (1935), which also survives. Before we look at this output in more detail, it would be convenient to map out stages, phases, or periods. Let us take as a reference point a period outline that traces the public shape of this career.

Apprenticeship (1923–27) Ozu enters Shochiku studios in the summer of 1923 and, with interruptions for military service, works as an assistant cameraman and then an assistant director. For three years he learns how to make shots, write scripts, and plan continuity.

Emergence (1927–30) He directs his first film in 1927, a year after the Showa emperor assumes power. He makes nineteen films, and several receive critical praise. *Young Miss* (1930) ties for second place in the 'modern-life film' category of the annual *Kinema Jumpo* poll.

Fame (1931–40) *Tokyo Chorus* (1931) earns third place in the *Kinema Jumpo* poll. Then, astonishingly, Ozu wins the *Kinema Jumpo* Best Picture award three years running: for *I Was Born, But . . .* (1932), *Passing Fancy* (1933), and *Story of Floating Weeds* (1934). Although his films are not box-office successes, he is a critics' director. An Ozu film appears on each *Kinema Jumpo*

'Best Ten' list during 1935–37. He moves from downtown Fukugawa to a new house in fashionable Takanawa. He begins to have apprentices, and he influences other directors. In 1938, a critic writes that Japan has only two great filmmakers: Sadao Yamanaka and Ozu.[26]

Prestige (1941–45) *Brothers and Sisters of the Toda Family* (1941) is a great popular success, winning Ozu another *Kinema Jumpo* first prize. *There Was a Father* (1942) wins a second place and is widely praised as a national policy film. Ozu is sent to Singapore to make films for the war effort.

Postwar gropings (1946–48) *Record of a Tenement Gentleman* (1947) and *A Hen in the Wind* (1948) do not find popularity or critical acclaim.

Re-emergence (1949–51) With *Late Spring* (1949), Ozu recovers and wins his fifth *Kinema Jumpo* first prize. It is followed by the prestigious *Munekata Sisters* (1950). *Early Summer* (1951) earns yet another *Kinema Jumpo* first place. In May of 1951, Ozu and his mother move again, to the suburb of Kamakura, where both *Late Spring* and *Early Summer* are set.

The Old Master (1952–63) Making one film a year for Shochiku and occasionally loaned out to other studios, Ozu consolidates his position as the firm's most famous director. Older critics still see him as a major force, so *Tokyo Story* (1953) wins a *Kinema Jumpo* first place; *Early Spring* (1956), sixth place; *Late Autumn* (1960), fifth place; and *An Autumn Afternoon* (1962), eighth place. Some critics and younger filmmakers grow restive, accusing Ozu of retreating into a pensive purism and catering to middle-class tastes. Still, honors accumulate. His films win awards from the Ministry of Education and the Emperor (1958), from the National Society of Artists (1959, 1960, 1961), and from the Asian Film Festival (1961). In 1959, he is the first film director to be elected to the National Academy of Art. In 1961 he has a stroke and in spring 1963 he undergoes surgery and cobalt treatments for a malignant tumor on his neck. Later that year he dies in agony. He is awarded posthumous honors by NHK Television, the Film Writers' Association, and the imperial family.

This outline, however useful as a point of reference, does not deal with the films themselves – their materials, form, and style. A sense of the external shape of the filmmaker's career must be complemented by recognition of pertinent aesthetic features of the works.

Certainly some striking continuities make aesthetic periodization unusually difficult. In technical matters, Ozu clung to trusted associates. From 1934 on, Tatsuo Hamada was usually in charge of art direction; Yoshiyasu Hamamura handled the editing of most of the postwar works. Thirty of Ozu's first thirty-five films were shot by the very skilful cinematographer Hideo Mohara (also known as Hideo Shigehara). When he left during *What Did the Lady Forget?*, Ozu simply promoted Yuharu Atsuta (also known as Yushun Atsuta), who had been Mohara's assistant since his first film for Ozu. Atsuta supervised photography for Ozu's subsequent Shochiku films, fourteen in all.

Despite such long-range continuites, critics have usually worked with a period-scheme that distinguishes 'early Ozu' (roughly, his pre-1949 career) from 'late Ozu' (typified by films from *Late Spring* on). One could justify this split on the basis of Ozu's changing use of the splendid Shochiku stable of actors. The prewar films are showcases for the tall and slender Mitsuko Yoshikawa (the mother of *I Was Born, But . . .*), the doughty Choko Iida (Shigehara's wife and the mother in *The Only Son*), the plump, radiant Kinuyo Tanaka (heroine of *Dragnet Girl*), the stolid Takeshi Sakamoto (Kihachi in several 1930s works), the diabolical child star Tokkan Kozo, and the wry, skinny, skew-shouldered, perpetually embarrassed Tatsuo Saito, Shochiku's principal American-style comedy star. The postwar *Record of a Tenement Gentleman* and *A Hen in the Wind* become valedictories for this era, the final appearance of many of Ozu's favorites. After 1948, Setsuko Hara becomes the archetypal Ozu woman, either the bride-to-be or the widow of middle years; the former matinee idol Shin Saburi returns as a middle-aged salaryman; Eijiro Tono portrays the decrepit teacher or the besotted retiree; and now Chishu Ryu, who had previously played everything from walk-on parts to the protagonist of *There Was a Father*, becomes the hard-pressed manager, the retiring professor, or the aging father sunk in drink and memories of youth.

Further warrant for the pre-1948/post-1948 split comes from Ozu's work with scriptwriters. During the first years of Ozu's career, many hands supplied scripts. Kogo Noda was already an accomplished scenarist when he wrote Ozu's first film, *Sword of Penitence* (1927). In 1928, Noda became head of Shochiku's script department and trained most of the firm's scenarists. Noda wrote scripts for some of Ozu's most acclaimed early films – *Life of an Office Worker* (1929), *An Introduction to Marriage* (1930), and *Tokyo Chorus* – but after 1935 he contributed no scenarios for over a decade. At this period Ozu also relied upon Akira Fushimi, who specialized in nonsense comedies and co-wrote *I Was Born, But . . . .* Most important, Tadao Ikeda, one of Shochiku's major scriptwriters, supplied Ozu with several comedies and became his principal scenarist in the crucial decade 1932–42, working on such central films as *Woman of Tokyo* (1933), *Dragnet Girl* (1933), *Passing Fancy*, *Story of Floating Weeds*, *The Only Son* (1936), *Brothers and Sisters of the Toda Family*, and *There Was a Father*. It was to Ikeda that Ozu turned for his first postwar film, *Record of a Tenement Gentleman*. After the anomalous *Hen in the Wind*, written by Ryosuke Saito, Ozu went back to Noda. From *Late Spring* onward, all the films were the product of the Ozu/Noda collaboration. (Ozu did, however, plan to bring Ikeda back to work with Noda on the unfinished *Radishes and Carrots*.) To some extent, the intuitive 'early/late' split in Ozu's career is traceable partly to the change in scenarists.

Critics have, however, made that split into a qualitative one. For a while it was common to judge the late films as more significant, partly because almost no pre-1950 films were available for viewing. Paul Schrader and Donald Richie rest their critical arguments almost completely on the postwar films.[27] In recent years, the inevitable reaction has emerged, led by Noël Burch, who praises the 'unparalleled beauty' of the films of the late 1930s and early 1940s and who condemns the postwar works as examples of 'academic rigidity'.[28] I shall not enter the evaluative debate, since I think that Ozu made excellent films throughout his career. My main concern is to show that although the standard periodization captures important changes in the films, we ought to recognize that in many ways Ozu's development is more complex than the scheme suggests. In any body of films, different factors may develop at different rates; we ought not to expect that all changes in various aspects of the films will tally with each other.

Subject and theme, for instance, do not fall so neatly into the prewar/postwar categories. We might at first glance see the 'early Ozu' as more socially committed. Peopled with day laborers, prostitutes, petty thieves, students, and penurious salarymen, these films often take a broadly critical view of contemporary social conditions. 'Late Ozu', on the other hand, seems to have renounced both class consciousness and social critique. The complacent businessmen of *Equinox Flower* (1958) and *Late Autumn* and the professional families of *Late Spring* and *Early Summer* no longer worry about where their next meal is coming from. Their concern is how to afford cake, or how to raise a child, or who will marry whom. Perhaps the change can be traced to scenarists: did Ikeda emphasize social realism while postwar Noda favored a bourgeois world-view? Whatever the cause, left-wing critics such as Akira Iwasaki find the later Ozu irresponsible.[29] Other writers, such as Schrader, praise the late works for transcending social conflicts and achieving a serene wisdom, an acceptance of life as it is.[30] Yet the basic assumptions shared by both parties seem, under scrutiny, a little oversimplified.

For one thing, many of the prewar works also present a bourgeois or wealthy milieu. *The Lady and the Beard* (1931), *Where Now Are the Dreams of Youth?*, *A Mother Should Be Loved* and other works take place among well-to-do families and professional people. A crucial film in this connection is *What Did the Lady Forget?* (1937), a comedy satirizing Westernized bourgeois professionals. Ozu was aware of the shift from his 'downtown' films:

> I moved the setting from the city to an expensive residential area. About the same time I had moved from Fukugawa to Takanawa; however, this had nothing to do with the movie. I realized that very few directors had worked on the lives of people in these residential areas.[31]

The Toda family in the 1941 film is also quite wealthy. Moreover, while many of Ozu's early films have a strongly critical cast, many – chiefly the nonsense comedies – do not. By contrast, several postwar works take place in working-class surroundings. The neighborhoods of *Record of a Tenement Gentleman* and *A Hen in the Wind* are similar to that of *Inn in Tokyo* (1935). The mah-jongg parlor of *Tokyo Twilight* (1957) might have come straight out of a 1930s film, and the crowded neighborhood of *Tokyo Story* (1953) and the chock-a-block clotheslines of *Ohayo* (1959) recall the milieu of *I Was Born, But . . . .* One can also still find social criticism in the late Ozu, especially in *Early Spring* (1956). More fundamentally, I shall try to show in Chapter 3 that the social criticism in the 1930s films is less severe than it might seem and that it can, under changed social conditions, easily modulate into the satirical or lyrical treatment we find in the later works.

In considering Ozu's representation of social class we are already tracing out another axis of periodization, that of genre. For in the Japanese production system, some genres are identified with the social positions of their characters. With the exception of *Sword of Penitence*, a historical film,

Ozu worked in the *gendai-geki*, the film about contemporary life. His earliest films were mostly *nansensu* ('nonsense') comedies with many prop gags and odd comic asides. He also turned out melodramas such as *That Night's Wife* (1930) and *Beauty's Sorrows*. But he gained his reputation on his *shoshimin-geki* works, films about lower-middle-class life. The *shoshimin-geki* was a Shochiku specialty cultivated by Kido, and Ozu's three *Kinema Jumpo* 'Best One' awards probably encouraged him to persist in the genre. A related genre was that of Kido's beloved 'home drama', centered on family problems. (The categories ingeniously overlap: *I Was Born, But...* is at once a 'salaryman' film, a *shoshimin-geki*, and a home drama.) By the end of the 1930s, however, Ozu was also working in the *burujoa-eiga*, the film of the bourgeoisie. *What Did the Lady Forget?* and *Toda Family* are in synchronization with a broader shift toward upper middle-class life in the Shochiku home drama generally. After the war, Ozu reverts to the *shoshimin-geki* for two works, *Record of a Tenement Gentleman* and *A Hen in the Wind*, before settling into 'bourgeois' films. It is in this slot that Ozu will remain for the rest of his career, with occasional returns to the 'salaryman' genre.

Evidently we cannot neatly project the contours of Ozu's career onto his use of genres. The melodrama *Woman of Tokyo* is quite similar to *Tokyo Twilight*. *Ohayo* is a rough remake of *I Was Born, But...*, while *Floating Weeds* (1959) is a revised and expanded version of *Story of Floating Weeds* (1934). After his serious *shoshimin-geki* of the mid-1930s, Ozu could make the Lubitschian bourgeois comedy *What Did the Lady Forget?*, which in turn looks forward to *The Flavor of Green Tea over Rice*.

One more aspect of aesthetic periodization needs to be considered. The day that Ozu decided to film all his shots from a systematically low camera height is far more important than the day on which the Emperor gave him an award. For this most cinema-conscious of directors, style held a central place. In his youth he reflected long on niceties of technique.[32] Unlike his contemporaries Naruse, Shimazu, and Mizoguchi, once he had found his style he stuck to it. Interviews record his technical preferences. In *I Was Born, But...*, he claimed, he gave up dissolves; in *Woman of Tokyo* 'the composition of the scenes was beginning to be my own style.'[33]

Critics have in turn traced patterns of abjuration, progress, or retreat. Most writers find Ozu steadily winnowing, gradually eliminating punctuation, high angles, camera movements, and other devices. But this is both oversimplified and inaccurate. There are high angles throughout his career, and fades and camera movements persist until *Equinox Flower* (1958). Schrader finds the most marked stylistic differences to lie between the prewar and the postwar works, though this is again too gross a contrast, given the stylistic variety we shall encounter in later pages.[34] Kristin Thompson has proposed a tripartite scheme: the early experiments (1929–33); the mature works (from *Woman of Tokyo* to *Record of a Tenement Gentleman*); and the late period (1949 and after). She emphasizes the overt playfulness of the early films' style and the presence of many devices which Ozu would eventually forgo, such as dissolves-in-place, optically subjective shots, and transitions by close-ups of hands.[35] Burch also grants pivotal significance to *Woman of Tokyo* but subdivides Ozu's 1930s works into a phase of comic experimentation, a phase exhibiting a mastery of Western découpage (epitomized in *That Night's Wife*), a series of trials for future masterworks, and a phase of mature achievement (from *Woman of Tokyo* to *The Only Son*). There follow, in Burch's opinion, the 'plateau/peak' of *Toda Family* and *There Was a Father* (1942), and then, after a brief postwar hiatus, an immediate decline from 1949 onward.

Trying to define stylistic phases confronts us squarely with the overall problem of divergent criteria for period units. Everything depends on what we want to measure. We ought not to expect that changes in, say, camera position will coincide with a new approach to staging or editing. Although Ozu's camera was placed quite low from early in his career, *I Was Born, But ...* does seem to mark the earliest surviving employment of his characteristically low height. But *I Was Born, But ...* does not exploit intermediate cutaway spaces as fully as does *Walk Cheerfully* or *That Night's Wife*, both made two years earlier. And none of these films offers as vivid examples of the graphic match as does *The Lady and the Beard* or even *Days of Youth*, both made still earlier in Ozu's career.

Similarly, if quantitative features of découpage were our interest, we could break Ozu's career into yet other stages. Appendix A shows that Ozu's surviving silent films display a rough uniformity of average shot length (between four and six seconds). With his first sound feature, *The Only Son*, the ASL doubles to nine seconds and steadily increases across the next three films. In the years 1947–57, the ASL drops back to around eight to ten seconds. In the final phase, Ozu's ASL remains eerily uniform at around seven seconds. (This trend starts with his first color film, *Equinox Flower*, as if this new luxury demanded stringency on another front.) Needless to say, such figures become most meaningful with respect to découpage norms in the Japanese cinema as a whole.

We can, I think, point to milestones in the style's development – *Tokyo Chorus, I Was Born, But ..., Woman of Tokyo, The Only Son, What Did the Lady Forget?, Toda Family, A Hen in the Wind, Late Spring, Equinox Flower* – but often on the basis of rather different stylistic features. Part Two of this book will consider stylistic changes across Ozu's career without seeking to create a rigid master scheme. Since Ozu seemed to regard each film as an occasion to recombine elements which he or someone else had already introduced, we ought to expect neither linear evolution nor simple periodization.

The vicissitudes of Ozu's output demonstrate the extent to which it, like his persona as filmmaker and as Japanese, came to embody a set of values. His career thus constitutes a social construct of great significance. Early on, he could have taken many directions, but critics and his studio steered him away from farce and sentimental romance toward comedy and home dramas. He was rewarded for films which sustained the mildly critical humanism of the *shoshimin-geki* genre. After the war, his collaboration with Noda was applauded by middle-aged critics for its respect for Japanese tradition. But these films of the 1950s paved the way for a reaction. Directors like Oshima and Imamura called for a rude cinema which protested against not only their elders' formal elegance but the definition of 'Japaneseness' inherent in it. Ozu came to be identified with an arid rigor and a serenity that was oblivious to the Japan of the Cold War, resurgent capitalism, and the Security Treaty. For the

West, however, discovering Japan's new international power in the 1970s coincided with discovering Ozu, and exactly those values which the Japanese New Wave loathed became the basis of the Ozu cult abroad. He became the 'essentially Japanese' director once more. We shall see throughout this book how his career – his life, his legend, and his films – reveals that the very question of being Japanese is far from simple, and is itself a site of cultural contestation.

Ozu directs Chishu Ryu and Setsuko Hara in *Tokyo Story* (1953)

2
Backgrounds

> The reader of a poem or the viewer of a painting has a vivid
> awareness of two orders: the traditional canon and the
> artistic novelty as a deviation from that canon. It is precisely
> against the background of that tradition that innovation is
> conceived. The Formalist studies brought to light that this
> simultaneous preservation of tradition and breaking away
> from tradition form the essence of every new work of art.
>
> Roman Jakobson, 1935[1]

The poetics of cinema which I am proposing differs from an 'intrinsic' critical
theory in assuming that only against historically significant backgrounds do
particular works achieve salience, for audiences or analysts. In one sense this
is simply a matter of 'putting Ozu's work into context'; but this formulation
usually fails to specify what will count as theoretically significant features of
context. For a filmmaker, the pertinent backgrounds are at least two: the
mode of film production and consumption within which s/he works; and the
formal norms which come to hand. For Ozu, one more background is made
salient by previous critical discussion: those cultural norms identified with
Zen Buddhism and traditional Japanese aesthetics. In this chapter, I will
sketch in these three frames of reference, as each will be important to my
arguments in the chapters to come.

The chapter also treats these norms as 'mediations', a concept that runs
back to Aristotle and that has particular prominence in Marxist theory. For my
purposes, and simplifying considerably, we can treat Ozu's films as lying at
the core of a set of concentric circles. We cannot simply link the outermost
circle – that is, the most broad and general features of Japanese society or
history – to these films. The concentric circles in between represent the more
pertinent and concrete forces impinging on the films – such forces as Ozu's
working situation, the film industry, and the proximate historical circumstances of his milieu. Throughout this book I will be insisting that
contextualizing Ozu's work requires the critic to trace how broad social forces
are warped, refracted, or transformed by the dynamics specific to these
mediating factors. For example, to disclose the relation of Ozu's films to
devices of Japanese poetry, one must recognize how poetic devices were
appropriated by the Japanese film industry as a whole. Thus each mediating
variable, as Erik Olin Wright phrases it, 'shapes the very relationship between
two other variables: Y causes the way in which X affects Z.'[2]

A Commercial Industry

For a poetics of the cinema, filmmaking is a practice – operating within institutions, regulated by tacit assumptions about the nature of the work process and about the decisions that are allotted to people in different roles. What we think of as the 'Ozu' film is strongly affected by the mode of film practice in which he worked.

Ozu entered a vigorous film industry. Japan's two major studios of the 1920s, Nikkatsu and Shochiku, were surrounded by a host of lesser companies, some flourishing, others marginal. During the 1920s, the industry turned out between six and eight hundred features per year. Although this pace slowed to four to six hundred per year during the 1930s, Japan remained the most prolific filmmaking country in the world. Studios maintained this productivity by lengthening and intensifying the working day, using minimal crews, shooting on location, and making the director responsible for overseeing scriptwriting and editing. The major firms had directors, writers, technicians, and stars under contract; they published fan magazines and publicity brochures; they owned theatres and distribution outlets. In certain ways, the Japanese film industry of 1930 was as rationalized as the American film industry of a decade earlier.

Like Hollywood, the industry relied upon tested genres. *Jidai-geki*, or historical films, were typically shot around Kyoto, while *gendai-geki*, films set in contemporary surroundings, were made in and around Tokyo. Smaller studios tended to specialize and were located in one city or another, but the major firms ran a facility in each city. The most popular *jidai-geki* were the *chambara*, or swordfight films, aimed chiefly at urban working-class men, rural audiences, and children. Chapter 1 has already mentioned some popular *gendai-geki* subgenres of the 1920s and 1930s: the *nansensu* comedy (modeled in part on the popular Harold Lloyd films), the female melodrama, the *shoshimin-geki* films about the lower middle class, and the home drama. There were still other varieties of *gendai-geki*, such as the 'salaryman' film, the student film, the *haha-mono* or mother film, the 'hooligan' or street-crook film, and the 'tendency' film (*keiko eiga*) of liberal social protest. Ozu's leanings toward the *gendai-geki* were confirmed by the critical praise which his early comedies and home dramas won. Indeed, critics were well-disposed to the *gendai-geki* film generally, since it was obviously much more 'modern' than the 'feudal' swordfight movie.

It is still very difficult to be precise about Japanese film exhibition of this time. Throughout the period Japan had remarkably few theatres (never more than 2,000), yet film attendance grew from about 120 million in 1926 to almost 230 million in 1937. Audiences were overwhelmingly urban dwellers, familiar with many sorts of films, traditional entertainments like variety shows, and the growing medium of radio. Exhibition practices were inflected by native customs. In the silent era, patrons checked their shoes upon entering the cinema, sat on the floor or on low benches, and favored programs of a length competitive with the extensive running time of live traditional drama.

The most striking aspect of the screening situation was the *katsuben*, or *benshi*, the performer who accompanied the film by playing all the vocal parts and providing a stream of commentary. The *benshi* were enormously popular and sometimes outdrew the film as an attraction. Some points about this unusual performer are pertinent to Ozu and Japanese cinema of the period. First, although historians sometimes claim that the *benshi*'s job was to read the film's intertitles, many *benshi* were poorly educated. It is likely that the *benshi* often improvised in the manner of any skilled oral performer. Secondly, one might expect that the presence of the *benshi* would lead to an elliptical, allusive approach to narrative and visual style, but this seems not to have been the case. As a rule, the Japanese film of the 1920s and early 1930s was as self-contained an aesthetic construct as any film from any country. The *benshi* provided what Don Kirihara has aptly called an 'emotional overlay'. Without the accompaniment, the film was comprehensible but less exciting.[3] Finally, it is likely that the *benshi* were a thorn in the production companies' side. According to some reports, the *benshi* dictated stories and subject matter to studios. Virtually the only unionized film work force, the *benshi* were highly paid. Had the studios wished to keep this picturesque tradition alive, they would not so quickly have sought to introduce sound, or moved as vigorously to quash *benshi*-initiated walkouts and strikes. Eliminating the *benshi* allowed the industry to expand.[4]

In pursuing such expansion, the major firms were again taking foreign companies as their model. The Hollywood cinema in particular exercised a strong influence over the Japanese industry. During World War I, Universal had pioneered American export to Japan, and for several years Universal 'Jewel' and 'Bluebird' titles far outnumbered other firms' products. After the 1923 Kanto earthquake damaged many theatres and Tokyo studios, American films established themselves solidly in the market. Hollywood films became second only to Japanese films in popularity. Shochiku went so far as to take Paramount as partner in owning a major Tokyo theatre. Studios also relied upon U.S. technology – Bell & Howell, Mitchell, Akeley, and Eyemo cameras; American arc and incandescent lighting fixtures; and, until 1938 or so, Eastman raw stock, both negative and positive. Studio executives visited Los Angeles to buy equipment and observe production methods, while back at home scenarists were urged to study Hollywood scripts, and cinematographers counted and timed shots as they watched American films. Hollywood pictures were cited, copied, remade, and even inserted into Japanese ones. In Shimazu's *Tonari no Yae-chan* (*Our Neighbor Miss Yae*, 1934), the protagonists go see a Betty Boop cartoon; in Shimizu's *Hanagata senshu* (*Star Athlete*, 1937), two marching students compare their situation to Gary Cooper's in *Morocco*. This tendency could not have been unwelcome to Ozu, the lifelong fan of Hollywood, and he was to contribute a good number of allusions, quotations, and pastiches of his own.

Broad industrial factors were mediated by Ozu's specific circumstances: Shochiku's suburban *gendai-geki* studio, located at Kamata until 1936, then at Ofuna. Upon its founding, Shochiku sought to be the progressive firm, hiring Japanese who had worked for American studios and making such defiantly 'Western' films as Minoru Murata's *Rojo no reikon* (*Souls on the Road*, 1921). Most of the resultant films were unpopular with the general public.

After the Kanto quake, Shiro Kido became manager of Kamata. Barely thirty when he took over in 1924, Kido set out to change Japanese filmmaking. He promoted a staple product – American-influenced melodramas, home dramas, and comedies. Mixing laughter and tears, the 'Kamata-flavor' film was aimed at an urban female audience. Kido wanted films that, in his words, 'looked at the reality of human nature through the everyday activities of society.'[5] The films might be socially critical, but their criticism was based on the hope that human nature was basically good. People struggle to better their lot, Kido believed, and this aspiration should be treated in 'a positive, warm-hearted, approving way.'[6] With such films as Shimazu's *Nichiyobi* (*Sunday*, 1924), the 'Kamata flavor' was created.

To produce a stream of such items, Kido instituted a training regimen. Besides introducing the promotion policy mentioned in Chapter 1, Kido revived the studio's acting school and established a script 'research center' at which Kogo Noda trained beginners. Noda has recalled that every scriptwriter had to turn out one serious script and three *nansensu* scripts per month.[7] Directors worked just as hard. Between 1924 and 1928, Yasujiro Shimazu, Kamata's most celebrated director, made fifty-eight features, or about one a month. Kido sent his staff out in teams to study new films and to report back with analyses of plot, cinematography, and direction.[8] Directors dealt with Kido without intermediary, and he would approve scripts and finished films, often demanding rewriting or reshooting. Kido's policy of imitating American découpage also encouraged the development of what I shall shortly call the 'piecemeal' style.

Kido's policies favored cooperative work. We have already seen how Shochiku's young staff formed the equivalent of the business company's *batsu*. Camaraderie over *sake* or on the baseball diamond led to collaborations and the exchange of ideas. While Ozu and his friends worked late editing prints,

Shiro Kido and Ozu in the late 1950s

they talked of cinema. They discussed the strong points of Bluebird or Triangle films, American notions of photoplay construction, and matters of technique.[9] (Do you cut during an actor's movement? Do you cut back to a speaking character after a dialogue title?) Ozu recalled that for his first films, he and his writers would go out to Ginza after work, then return home to play records and drink. By morning they would have a story.[10] Ozu and Torajiro Saito would swap gags for their films, the more obscene the better. Uchida's *Kagarinaki zenshin* (*Unending Advance*, 1937) was based on a magazine story by Ozu, and he later obliged Uchida with a salaryman script (apparently never filmed).

With its long hours, intense production schedule, and close and informal ties among peers, Shochiku Kamata/Ofuna had powerful effects on Ozu's career. He would work calmly within the industry, accepting the star system and the approved genres. He would cultivate the humanistic Kido touch. He would use the studio's casual atmosphere to borrow ideas and quickly launch topical projects. He would become a Shochiku house director.

A Decorative Style

It is useful to assume, at least initially, that filmmakers are rational agents acting according to conventions of filmic composition – what I shall call norms. The poetician makes those norms explicit as a way of explaining why films have certain features. This will involve describing a particular film-making practice by virtue of its preferred subjects, themes, genres, styles, and narrative principles. The task will be pursued throughout this book, but because prior work on Ozu has placed great emphasis upon certain narrative and stylistic features of his work, it is worth sketching in some background here.

However one might hope to discover a radically alternative film practice in Japan, the fact is that throughout the 1920s and 1930s, and with very few exceptions (such as Kinugasa's *Kurutta ippeiji* (*Page of Madness*, 1926)), Japanese cinema is solidly based on classical Hollywood dramaturgy and style. Japanese directors learned scriptwriting, shot composition, and continuity editing from Universal films, as well as from the work of Hart, Chaplin, Fairbanks, Lloyd, and Lubitsch. A 1922 film, *Ninin Shizuka* (*The Two Shizukas*), reveals the influence of the *benshi* in its long takes and absence of dialogue titles, but the découpage is resolutely American in its adherence to establishing shots, analytical cutting, angled shot/reverse-shots, smooth matches on action, point-of-view shots, and overwhelmingly correct matches of eyelines and screen direction. By 1928, we find films such as *Fuum Yoshi* (*Yoshi Castle*), whose slick style wholly accepts the norms of Hollywood lighting, staging, camera position, and cutting.

What makes Japanese filmmaking of this period noteworthy is the widespread use of American conventions as a frame for elaborate technical embroidery, even in films by ordinary directors. Japanese filmmakers deviated, in isolated and controlled ways, from classical norms. This is chiefly evident in the use of particular devices which are rare in Hollywood or mainstream European filmmaking. Consider Tomotaka Tasaka's *Ai no machi* (*Town of Love*, 1928). Within the bounds of orthodox framing and editing, we

21

find fast and intricate camera movements, steep high and low angles, handheld shots, soft focus, rack focus, whip pans, split screen, and moving intertitles. One complex tracking shot follows the heroine's struggle to shove a wheelbarrow through a factory yard; although broken by nine intertitles, the single take itself lasts about two and a half minutes. At another point, when the factory boss strikes an old man, the four shots run as follows:

1. (*mcu*) The old man, three-quarters turned away (11 frames).

2. (*mcu*) The boss, three-quarters to us, raising the cane to strike from behind (14 frames).

3. (*ms*) The heroine cries out (15 frames).

4. (*ms*) The cane falls to the ground (12 frames).

Even more flamboyant is the film's climax, when the businessman and the police officer burst into a room (fig. 1). The officer runs into close-up and leaves the other man in the background (fig. 2). After a dialogue title, the camera tracks back as the businessman moves forward (fig. 3), leaving the officer behind. After another title, the officer hurls himself forward (fig. 4) as the camera retreats. Another title, and the businessman advances again (fig. 5). *Town of Love* is not at all extraordinary in its stylistic eclecticism. Japanese silent cinema constitutes a classical practice in that canonized narrative *functions* were served by technical devices, but this system tolerated a greater range of choice with respect to what *devices* were chosen to convey narrative information.

Instead of creating an indigenous cinema wholly out of pre-Meiji narrative traditions, Japanese filmmakers borrowed extensively from popular literature and theatre's reworkings of Western narrative principles and from Hollywood conventions of structure and style. These traditions gave a basic linear unity to the film. With classical construction as a stable point of departure, Japanese directors freely used diverse technical means to fulfill narrative functions or to create momentary expressive or decorative effects. In *Town of Love*, the rapid editing of the boss's attack rhetorically amplifies the violence of the scene and would not be out of place in a French impressionist film of the 1920s. (According to Sato, Gance's *La Roue* was a major influence on Japanese filmmakers of the period.[11]) More abstractly, the alternation of the officer's and the businessman's rush to the foreground functions as a rhythmic elaboration of a simple action. For the sake of expressiveness or ornamen-

1.   *Town of Love*

2.   *Town of Love*

3.   *Town of Love*

4.   *Town of Love*

5.   *Town of Love*

tation, even the ordinary Japanese filmmaker was expected to use technical devices which would momentarily intensify narrative continuity. Many of these devices became as standardized as their equivalents in the West, and throughout this book I will occasionally draw upon norms of Japan's 'decorative classicism' for pertinent comparisons with Ozu's work.

Such devices have an atomistic, unsystematic quality. The filmmaker usually mixes widely different stylistic elements within the same film, as Tasaka does in *Town of Love*. The same eclecticism is evident across careers as well. Very few Japanese directors of the period 1928–39 exhibit an original and consistent style. Shimazu, Heinosuke Gosho, Mikio Naruse, and Sadao Yamanaka – to name only the most famous – vary their styles significantly from film to film. Even Mizoguchi is fairly pluralistic before *Zangiku monogatari* (*Story of the Last Chrysanthemums*, 1939).

Despite such eclecticism, we can trace out general trends across the period. Apart from the straightforward imitation of the Hollywood sound style, such as we find in *Enoken no Kondo Isamu* (*Enoken as Kondo Isamu*, 1935) or in Tojiro Yamamoto's *Tsuzurikata kyoshitsu* (*Composition Class*, 1938), there seem to be three principal tendencies at work during the period when Ozu emerged as a director.[12]

1. The **calligraphic** style. Associated with the *chambara*, this is a flamboyant, frantic style, bristling with energetic figure movement (often conveyed in fast-motion), rapid and discontinuous editing, tight telephoto framings, and above all bravura camera movements (whip pans, fast dollies, bumpy handheld shots). Everything is sacrificed to the expression of dynamic physical action, and the style reaches paroxysmic heights in scenes of swordplay, with men slashing out at us or popping in and out of the foreground. Pioneered by Daisuke Ito, this style can be seen in *Komatsu Riyuzo II* (1930), *Beni komori* (*The Scarlet Bat*, 1931), *Mito Komon* (1932), and *Iwami Jutaro* (1937). It is applied to a modern subject in Uchida's fine *Keisatsukan* (*Policeman*, 1933).

2. The **pictorialist** style. This is associated with urban drama and melodrama, often *shimpa*-derived and set in the Meiji or Taisho periods. Strongly influenced by Sternberg, the pictorialist style emphasizes each shot as a complex composition. Long shots predominate, deep space and deep-focus cinematography are common, decor and lighting create an abstract effect, and figures are typically subordinated to the overall design. To some extent pictorialism reacts against the frenzied calligraphic trend by presenting dense, almost motionless tableaux that invite the spectator to scan the frame. At its limit, the style achieves great opacity, often blocking our vision of faces or gestures. Examples would include Shimazu's *Joriku no dai-ippo* (*First Steps Ashore*, 1932), Murata's *Muteki* (*Steam Whistle in the Mist*, 1934), and Sotoji Kimura's *Ani imoto* (*Older Brother, Younger Sister*, 1936). The most consistent exponent of this tendency is Kenji Mizoguchi in such films as *Maria no Oyuki* (*Oyuki the Virgin*, 1935), *Naniwa ereji* (*Naniwa Elegy*, 1936), *Gion no shimai* (*Sisters of Gion*, 1936), and *Story of the Last Chrysanthemums* (1939).[13]

3. The **piecemeal** style. Associated with the *gendai-geki*, and especially the domestic genres, this style dissects each scene into neat, static shots. Although

23

the spectator may not notice it, there is a great deal of editing, with films having an average shot length of three to five seconds. Unlike the calligraphic trend, this approach avoids exaggerated action, complex camera movements, and dynamic montage. Unlike the pictorialist trend, this style does not rely on opaque shots; each composition is highly legible. This style's closest kin is Hollywood cinema 1917–25, the one-bit-of-information-per-shot approach of Fairbanks, Lloyd, Lubitsch, and William De Mille. There is also a certain playfulness about the style, as unexpected cuts and sudden screen entrances disturb the limpid flow of information. Examples would be *Shingun* (*Marching On*, 1930), Naruse's *Kimi to wakarete* (*Apart from You*, 1933) and *Yogoto no yume* (*Nightly Dreams*, 1933), Gosho's *L'Amour* (1933) and *Izu no odoriko* (*Dancing Girl of Izu*, 1933), Shimazu's *Our Neighbor Miss Yae* (1934), and Shimizu's *Arigato-san* (1935).

All these trends offer the director ways of expressively or decoratively elaborating the narrative point. Yet to isolate them as I have done should not occlude the fact that many films furnish mixed cases. *Town of Love*, for example, fundamentally adheres to the piecemeal style, but it has 'calligraphic' moments as well.

It is evident that Ozu worked with the piecemeal style – partly because of its generic predispositions, partly because of Kido's policy, and partly because of the possibilities it holds for mixing playfulness and rigor. In Chapter 5, I shall discuss how Ozu recast the piecemeal approach into his own distinctive stylistic system. But we should note at this point that Ozu's films are far purer instances of the piecemeal approach than we find in other directors, and this points to a more general line of reflection.

Crudely speaking, poetic theory affords two principal conceptions of the relation between the major artist and the norms of his or her period. There is the 'consummate expression' model, whereby the artist perfectly embodies the tradition. Burch writes that 'there is no break in continuity between [the work of Ozu and Mizoguchi] and that of a large body of directors working in similar genres.'[14] This ignores, however, Ozu's major differences from Japanese norms. The rigor of his style resembles neither the narrative linearity nor the decorative eclecticism present in the work of ordinary filmmakers. Ozu's work is, for better or worse, eccentric. (His peers thought so too.)

Are we then justified in introducing a second model, one of conflict between the artist and the reigning norms? Such a view often assumes that transgression is necessary for broader aesthetic change. Yet Ozu does not fit this role easily either. He was not at war with norms; he simply sought a greater concentration, consistency, and individuality of style than his milieu required. In effect, he sought to purify and deepen the piecemeal approach to découpage. Our study will reveal him to be far more stylistically rigorous (even in his earliest films) than were his contemporaries; far more stringent in his choice of elements; far more bold in his patterned expansion of such canonized elements as interruptive cutaways and deep space; and far more systematic, concentrating upon tactics by which stylistic organization, springing from the need to transmit and decorate narrative, becomes a vehicle of self-conscious narration and at times the dominant element of the film's structure.

Ozu and the norms of his early period cannot, of course, be starkly separated, since he also shaped them. Many Shochiku directors of the 1930s, such as Yasushi Sasaki, Kenkichi Hara, and Minoru Shibuya, started as his pupils, and his influence is easy to spot in their films. Hara's *Kofuku no kazoku* (*A Happy Family*, 1940) uses the 360-degree space which Ozu pioneered. Sasaki's *Shimpi no otoku* (*Mysterious Man*, 1937) contains a pensive passage in which two men leave the 'Arc-en-ciel' bar and three shots linger on bar signs being switched off; the scene is reminiscent of *The Only Son* (1936). *Apart from You*, *Nightly Dreams*, *Kagainaki hodo* (*Street without End*, 1934), and *Tsuma yo bara no yo ni* (*Wife, Be Like a Rose* 1935) suggest that Naruse sought to make the florid track-in and -out his personal signature, the equivalent of Ozu's low camera position. (Perhaps this was why Kido upbraided him: 'Naruse, we don't need two Ozus.'[15]) Shimazu, dean of the *shoshimin-geki*, was not above extensive borrowings from *I Was Born, But . . .* in *Miss Yae*. Jiro Kawate, who worked at Shinko studio, was also impressed by *I Was Born, But . . .*, and his *Tsuruganeso* (*Lily of the Valley*, 1935), with its facetious transitions, is reminiscent of Ozu's early work. Ozu's friend Sadao Yamanaka was so taken by *Dragnet Girl* that he memorized the script. His lost *Furyu katsu-jin ken* (*Sword of the Elegant Swordsman*, 1934) is said to have been an imitation of Ozu, and his *Ninjo kami fusen* (*Humanity and Paper Balloons*, 1936) relies so consistently upon the low-height camera position that one can only take it as a homage. The many Ozu touches in Shochiku home dramas of the late 1930s make it likely that he contributed to the studio 'look' by innovating a highly noticeable stylistic system which other directors drew upon as eclectically as they had drawn upon Hollywood. Yet we must not forget that Ozu remained firmly within the 1930s Shochiku context, taking from it as well as giving. Shibuya's *Atarashiki kazoku* (*A New Family*, 1939) and Shimazu's *Ani to sono imoto* (*A Brother and His Younger Sister*, 1939) may offer pastiches of Ozu, but their use of Shin Saburi's star image and their stories of family crises among the professional class paved the way for *Brothers and Sisters of the Toda Family*.

For the most part, Ozu's career after the war reinforced the stability of his position in the industry and the consistency of his style. The decades after 1939 saw the industry decline (1939–1945), revive (1946–59), and decline again (after 1959). During the war, output dropped dramatically, as did attendance. The domestic drama became the home-front drama, and after the war it reappeared, eventually to emerge as a television staple comparable to American soap operas. Stylistically, Japanese cinema became far more sober and conformist after 1939. Apart from a tendency toward monumental *jidai-geki* (of which Mizoguchi's *Genroku Chushingura* [*The Loyal Forty-Seven Ronin*, 1941–2] is most famous), most directors' works came to resemble Hollywood or European cinema of the period. This trend continued under the Occupation. Shochiku emerged intact from the war and quickly renewed the 'Ofuna flavor' in such sentimental fare as *Kimi no na wa* (*What Is Your Name?*, 1953) and *Nijushi no hitomi* (*Twenty-Four Eyes*, 1954). In 1956, Kido became president of the entire Shochiku company.

Ozu remained the loyal employee, continuing to win critical praise, making movies for other studios only after he had met his firm's requirement of one film per year. More often than is recognized, he sought to keep abreast of industry trends. For example, his 'estranged-wife' films of the early 1950s (*The Munekata Sisters, The Flavor of Green Tea over Rice*) can be seen as parallel to Mizoguchi's more sensual *Yuki fujin ezu* (*A Picture of Madam Yuki*, 1950), which stars Michiyo Kogura (of *Green Tea*) and Ken Uehara (who plays a comparable role in *The Munekata Sisters*). Similarly, the years 1956–58 saw increasing criticism of Kido's Ofuna-flavor films.[16] This, along with the success of teenage romance movies and *taiyozoku* ('sun-tribe') films depicting licentious youth, doubtless had some effect on Ozu's brief turn toward tales of adultery (*Early Spring*) and teenage sex and abortion (*Tokyo Twilight, Floating Weeds*). He also began using popular, clean-cut young stars like Ryo Ikebe, Keiko Kishi, Ineko Arima, Yoko Tsukasa, Mariko Okada, and Keiji Sada. None the less, he adhered to the style he forged in the 1930s, developing his reputation as a colorful conservative and enraging younger talents such as Shohei Imamura, who as his assistant chafed under his old-fashioned ways.[17] For postwar audiences, Ozu's version of Shochiku's piecemeal découpage may have created a purely aesthetic nostalgia, recalling the life of early Showa by evoking the style of prewar movies. Perhaps it was an awareness of this nostalgia and an ironic recollection of the lachrymose bedside scene which climaxed the typical Kamata/Ofuna film that led Ozu, dying in the hospital, to murmur to Kido: 'Well, Mr. President, after all – the home drama.'[18]

A Traditional Practice?

One more set of norms needs to be considered. Most Western critics have found Ozu's films to embody traditional Japanese aesthetic principles and, more deeply, to present a fundamental attitude reminiscent of Zen Buddhism. Marvin Zeman takes Zen to be the basis of all Japanese art and looks in Ozu for nine characteristics of *haiku*, flower arrangement, and the tea ceremony.[19] For Schrader, Ozu counterposes Zen unity to the disunity of cultural conflict and then surpasses the opposition by achieving a 'transcendental' stasis.[20] Richie agrees with Schrader, identifying Ozu's philosophy of resignation with the Buddhist concept of *mono no aware*, which Richie glosses as 'sympathetic sadness, serene acceptance'.[21] Such views might seem admirably suited to a culturally specific explanation of Ozu's work, yet I believe that they are insufficiently historical and miss the real significance of 'Japanese tradition' and 'Zen aesthetics' in his career. The chapters to come will develop this point in detail, but it is convenient to lay out my case in summary form here.

We can start by asking how such features might contribute to a causal explanation. We might say that Japanese aesthetic traditions and Zen precepts simply pervade the culture, and as a Japanese Ozu is naturally drawing on them. But this dispositional explanation is inadequate. Not all Japanese directors fit the 'Zen aesthetics' case, so Ozu's living in Japanese society is not enough to cause its presence in his work. A causal explanation must specify why Ozu's work embodies these qualities more than other directors' works do. The logical step would be to posit an urge in Ozu to present these qualities in his films. This urge might be spontaneous and unreflective, or calculating and strategic. To prove either case, we would have to adduce biographical data. Zeman might try to show that Ozu's early life gave him an unusual interest in the traditional arts, Schrader and Richie that he was a devout Buddhist or that he had a keen interest in Zen. Unfortunately, these critics adduce no such evidence. Indeed, I can find virtually nothing that would support an explanation of this type. As we have seen, Ozu's youth was consumed by a passion for Western culture. Apart from one remark about Japanese verse, which needs to be interpreted carefully (see p.159), he typically refrained from comparing his work to traditional forms. The widescreen frame reminds him not of *emaki-mono*, or scroll painting, but of toilet paper. And he once remarked of foreign critics: 'They don't understand – that's why they say it is Zen or something like that.'[22]

The exasperated reader may protest that surely Japanese aesthetic traditions and Buddhist philosophy must have something to do with Ozu's work. In certain ways, they do. But I can spell out those ways only by showing that the very concepts 'Zen Buddhism' and 'Japanese aesthetics' need to be understood within particular historical contexts.

Japanese Buddhism is not a unitary phenomenon. The variety of sects, the shifting relations between Buddhism and Confucianism, and Buddhism's mixture of otherworldly and purely pragmatic concerns have made it subject to periodic revision, often for immediate social ends. (During the late 1920s, for example, some ideologues combatted Westernization by exalting Budd-hism as an expression of pan-Asian culture.) The Zen sect enjoyed particularly fluctuating fortunes. Founded in China around 1200 and taken up by the Japanese samurai class, it is less important as a religious doctrine than as an aesthetic attitude. With the rise of Confucianism, Zen became predominantly an artistic practice.[23] Austerity, asymmetry, small details; subdued colors, empty space as a positive element, splashes of ink representing flashes of enlightenment; an emphasis on natural landscapes and pure contemplation – all were Chinese aesthetic principles transferred to Japanese art, forming a broad stylistic trend opposed to the tendency toward flamboyant decoration and vivid drama to be found in other Japanese traditions (themselves also Buddhist-influenced).

Like Buddhism generally, Zen also took assumed concrete social func-tions. Whatever religious meaning the tea ceremony once had, by 1400 it had become a purely aesthetic experience, and by 1900 it was wholly commer-cialized. Before World War I, it was a hobby for rich women, and afterward it became popular with the masses, with firms offering low-cost courses to women employees. In 1911, Kitaro Nishida's spectacularly successful book *Zen no kenkyu* (*Studies in Goodness*) proposed a revival of Zen practices and a search for individual enlightenment. This new doctrine owed a good deal to such Western sources as Hegel and T. H. Greene and influenced many Japanese intellectuals' retreat from political action.[24] In contrary fashion, during the war, military authorities invoked the spartan qualities of Zen in order to inculcate obedience and self-discipline. In sum, Zen is not the only source of Japanese aesthetics, nor does it exemplify a pure essence uncontaminated by historical reinterpretations.

Indeed, to speak of 'Japanese aesthetics' itself is to suggest that the tradition is more homogeneous than it is. Japanese art has always subscribed to a variety of doctrines – mimetic, object-centered, expressionist, craft-centered, didactic, cathartic, and connoisseur-centered.[25] Theories of dispassionate virtuosity vie with theories emphasizing sheer emotional expression. The Zen idea of *sabi* – solitary serenity attained by immersion in nature – differs significantly from *iki*, an urbane flair and sensuousness. *Shibui*, the beauty of reduction and astringency, contrasts with *hade*, the beauty of brilliancy and exuberance. Moreover, such traditional concepts were constantly being revised and reinterpreted. In medieval aesthetics, *yugen* referred to an impersonal, elegant beauty; but the noh playwright Zeami recast it to include a feeling of sadness at the mutability of life. There is no single or monolithic Japanese aesthetic tradition. It is a highly variable construct to which artists and polemicists of different periods appeal even as they redefine it for contemporary purposes.

What, then, of Ozu? There are obvious citations of Buddhism in his work. In *Days of Youth*, a rude college student jams chewing gum on a statuette of Saigyo, the wandering Buddhist poet. *There Was a Father* makes extensive use of Buddhist imagery. (See pp. 290–1.) These references can be traced to the changing fortunes of Buddhism in Ozu's social milieu: skepticism among 1920s youth, 1942 mobilization of Buddhism for the war effort. At the thematic level, Ozu's world seems quite un-Buddhist: no attribution of life's sorrows to sins during previous existence, no trust that after numerous rebirths the spirit will attain Nirvana. Stylistic features present a more difficult case. Schrader has argued that certain features of Ozu's compositions, cutting and acting exemplify Zen religious principles, such as ritual, unity, and *mu* (emptiness as presence).[26] It is worth noting that at least one Japanese scholar has recently disputed the relevance of Zen to Ozu.[27] I shall be arguing later that we can find more integrative and complex functional explanations for formal features. For now, I simply propose that any such use of Zen in Ozu is not direct, let alone directly religious, but will be mediated by proximate historical practices.

The concept of *mono no aware*, so central to Western discussions of Ozu, perfectly illustrates this process. *Aware* suggests an emotional quality present in all things; *mono no aware*, perhaps best translated as 'the pathos of things', connects beauty and sadness. *Aware* emerges as an aesthetic concept during the Heian period (eighth to eleventh centuries). Issuing from an aristocratic élite that cultivated an exquisite sensitivity to beauty, *aware* had a firm class basis: no commoner could have it. It quickly became a literary convention. In the eighteenth century, the literary theorist Norinaga Motoori used the term *mono no aware* as part of a reinterpretation of Heian aesthetics. Motoori claimed that modern man had lost natural human feelings by virtue of conflicting moral codes – *bushido*, Confucianism, Buddhism. *Mono no aware*, a phrase which seldom occurs in Heian literature, was thereby made into what Raymond Williams calls a 'selective tradition'.[28] By cultivating a sensitivity to the pathos of things, one can transcend modern moral confusion. (Note that *mono no aware* is here *opposed* to Buddhism.) By virtue of Motoori's longing for Heian purity, *mono no aware* becomes a nostalgic concept, shot through with a sense of loss. But then this was turned into an aesthetic device. Shoyo Tsubouchi's treatise *Shosetsu shinzui* (*The Essence of the Novel*, 1885-86) finds *mono no aware* present in a variety of works, including Scott's *Bride of Lammermoor*. During the nationalistic 1930s, however, a new selective tradition emerged. Writers were summoned to 'return to' *mono no aware*, now characterized as a distinctive quality of Japanese literature and the 'core' of Heian writing.[29] While certain features like a general notion of 'acceptance' continue to be part of *mono no aware*, the concept is not immutable, and it can be mobilized within historically different projects.

Particularly important in this process is the post-1868 encounter with the West. In different ways, both Tsubouchi's *Essence of the Novel* and the 1930s urgings to return to tradition exemplify the recasting of literary ideology in order to define Japan in relation to Europe, Russia, Britain, and the United States. 'Japaneseness' becomes a critical issue once the nation has encountered a foreign Other. This is not simply to say that Japanese artists were forced to choose between Japanese and alien traditions. Rather, the very definition of Japanese traditions became subject to dispute. For example, by 1900 Japanese fiction writers had grown used to many foreign genres and styles, and this acquaintance 'defamiliarized' Japanese traditions as such. Rimer puts it well in discussing the great novelist Yasunari Kawabata: 'Kawabata's very distance from his tradition gave him a self-conscious awareness of the workings of the tradition necessary to permit him to adapt them for his own particular purposes.'[30] The debates that tore through the literary world of the twentieth century – the arguments over the 'I-novel' (*shishosetsu*) versus the 'mental-attitude' novel (*shinkyo shosetsu*), Soseki Natsume's invention of the '*haiku*-novel', the quarrel between practitioners of the art novel and proponents of 'popular literature', the Tanizaki-Akutagawa plot controversy which I shall consider in Chapter 7 – all these show how the revelation of foreign art compelled artists to forge their own versions of 'Japaneseness', either as ideal or as anathema. In the Taisho period especially, as Miriam Silverberg has shown, a 'Japanese tradition' was being produced and packaged for domestic as well as foreign consumption.[31] Later, during the 1930s, when nationalistic political pressures intensified, many writers were said to 'discover Japan', but this Japan was no less a construct out of contemporary exigencies than was the 'Japaneseness' synthesized out of the initial encounter with the West. A similar process took place in the postwar period, when artists could treat the war era as a 'dark valley' and find true Japaneseness in some new selective tradition (*haiku* but not *bushido*; liberal democracy of the 1920s interrupted by 'militarists'). In the chapters that follow, we shall see how Ozu's career traces its own fluctuations in relation to shifting notions of Japanese art, as well as of Japaneseness itself.

Granting these qualifications, we can see that Japanese filmmaking of Ozu's formative period did assimilate certain features of aesthetic traditions. In the 1920s, some directors self-consciously set out to study such literary techniques as the *kodan*, the device of abbreviated statement, curt dialogue exchanges, and rapid shifts of scenes.[32] One convention of Japanese classical cinema thus became the crisp, economical cut to synecdochic details of action. Some filmmakers turned to *haiku*'s atmospheric brevity as a model for cutaway shots of nature or objects (although such images can also be found in American films of the 1910s and 20s as well).[33] The meaningless images of *renga* linked verse, distributed through the poem in rule-governed asymmetries, find their counterparts in shots which are subordinated to a geometrical play of similarity and difference, as in the repetitive editing pattern of *Town of Love*. More generally, as literature, calligraphy, music and the graphic arts prized the ornamental flourish, so virtuoso stagings in depth or perfectly-timed camera movements testify to the director's decorative control. Because of foreign influences, Japanese films had a more 'Western' dramaturgy and style than prior traditions would have allowed, but filmmakers also borrowed eclectically from native sources in order to display an 'indigenously Japanese' quality. Cinema disrupted native traditions by reinforcing a pull toward Western models of narrative and representation that was already being felt in Meiji literature and theatre. But filmmakers could embellish American-based plot structure and style with asides, elaborations, and fine points that harked back to 'traditional' arts.

In this context, Ozu's mixture of classical Hollywood principles and studied citations of Japanese elements makes sense. His films draw not on some amorphous entity called 'Japanese tradition' but upon mass culture of his moment. His 1930s films in particular are closely indebted to trends in popular novels and to urban fads. During the postwar period, Ozu's plot construction recalls the work of such twentieth-century writers as Toson, Tanizaki, and Ton Satomi (the author of novels that would become *Equinox Flower* and *Late Autumn*). In his early days, Ozu's 'modernity' was modern, and in later years so was his 'traditionalism'. The next chapter will show how he recast not a pure 'Japaneseness' or traditional art but specific post-Meiji materials, themselves shaped by the encounter with the West. That recasting was centrally mediated by such cinematic factors as Hollywood norms, Japanese cinema's 'decorative classicism', and the practices of a commercial film industry.

3
Materials

When such a person as I walks the streets of a city in the Kansai, he is overcome with nostalgia for his own childhood. Today the plebeian flatlands [*shitamachi*] of Tokyo have lost the last vestiges of their former appearance, but sometimes, in an old part of Kyoto or Osaka, you come upon rows of the same heavy-roofed houses, the same latticed fronts. . . . You say to yourself, as if remembering your long-forgotten home, 'Ah, Tokyo was once like this'.

Junichiro Tanizaki, 1933[1]

The historical poetics that I am proposing here is not one that 'elevates form over content'. The Russian Formalist tradition rejects the form/content dichotomy. The Formalists have bequeathed us two analytical schemas devoted to this problem: Shklovsky's distinction between form and material, and Tynianov's between material and the 'constructive principle' (the two constituting 'form').[2] Each schema has its advantages, but I shall not discuss either one in detail here. The crucial point is that the art work's form is not an external shape, an ornamental appendage, or a mere vehicle for something ineffable. The work's material is what it is made out of; the form is the process and system of the making.

But what can an art work be made out of? Shklovsky distinguishes three sorts of material. There is physical stuff, such as paint and canvas in painting, sounds in music, or language in literature. (The physical material need not itself be raw or unshaped, as musical tonality or verbal syntax shows.) Secondly, there is referential material, what we usually call subject matter. For the painter, the external world functions as material in the sense that the painting may portray recognizable objects or states of affairs. Finally, the art work is made of what we might call 'conceptual' or thematic material. 'Even meanings,' Shklovsky notes, 'are used as material for artistic construction.'[3] What a character believes, what an event implies, what a sentence states or a character advocates or an icon symbolizes – all these furnish thematic material for formal development.

In excessive moments Shklovsky denigrated referential and conceptual material as 'non-artistic'. But as his 1923 essay and other writings of Formalist theorists make clear, all these sorts of material must be considered important to the making of the art work. It will not do to privilege only one type, such as thematic material. We can best see the work's materials as diverse and heterogeneous, neither pristine nor necessarily compatible, with the art work's form relying upon their interaction. Instead of content, we find context and contest.

The physical material of Ozu's cinema – images and sounds – will become pertinent to our inquiry at a later point. We can here address the referential and thematic dimensions of his work. Ozu's material is, at one level, a body of well-worn referents; his subject matter is concrete and often directly citational. At a more abstract level, Ozu's thematic material can be thought of as consisting of clichés or commonplaces – in the sense that all artists build works out of inherited meanings and *idées reçues*. The two most usual notions of the 'content' of Ozu's work – his quotidian realism and his transcendental values – can be seen as issuing from the films' use of particular referents and thematic commonplaces. Detailed analysis of these materials is reserved for the film-by-film discussion of Part Two; some general tendencies will be traced out here.

Ozu's referents and commonplaces come to him already 'processed'. In the broadest sense, these materials are circumscribed by the ideological horizon of post-Meiji Japan: the landscape of emergent industrial capitalism, urbanization, growing state bureaucracy and struggle for political power that constitutes Taisho and early Showa history. As we shall see, Ozu's films are firmly fixed in the social field. More specifically, between the overall social formation and Ozu's films lie crucial mediations, some of which I have already mentioned. For instance, Ozu's materials bear the traces of the continuous revision of 'innately Japanese' aesthetic traditions in the light of changing social demands. We shall have occasion to pause on ways in which Ozu's subject matter and themes are self-consciously linked to contemporary reinterpretations of aesthetic precepts. Another crucial mediation is Ozu's working milieu at Shochiku, where Kido's genre policies dictated domestic subjects and humanistic themes.

Still another mediating factor, seldom discussed but absolutely central to Ozu's work, is that of the burgeoning urban culture of Taisho and early Showa. As Tokyo was rebuilt after the 1923 earthquake, there arose a teeming, flamboyant mass culture. Movie theatres, revues, dance halls, cafés, bars, and mah-jongg parlors sprang up, replacing the variety theatres and Japanese-style restaurants of a decade earlier. The rebuilding of Tokyo accelerated popular culture trends of the 1910s. By 1920, consumer goods had begun to enjoy nationwide distribution; after the Kanto quake, advertising in the European mode expanded hugely. Newspaper circulation soared into the millions, and popular magazines began to cater to a huge readership. The expansion of publishing required a new popular literature, known broadly as *taishu bungaku*, which, like the cinema, owed much to Western models. Critics and highbrow novelists tended to disdain mass literature, but whereas an 'art' novelist's work might sell only a thousand copies, a novel serialized in *Shufu no tomo* (*Ladies' Companion*) would reach a hundred thousand avid readers. After the quake, radio and phonograph records began to disseminate both Western popular music and Japanese hit songs. One historian credits Taisho music with giving the Japanese a consciousness of their own mass culture.[4] We know that Ozu was at home in this robust milieu; again and again, in a variety of ways, we shall find his films drawing upon subjects and ideas already elaborated in popular culture. We shall even discover that he uses iconography also developed by contemporary cartoonists, novelists, journalists, sociologists, and photographers. The director so often identified with ascetic otherworldliness turns out to be constantly referring to contemporary concerns, alluding to passing fashions, and developing political ideas.

Everyday Modernity

Early and late, Ozu's films are highly referential. As *gendai-geki*, they concentrate on contemporary life; as Kido/Shochiku products, they seek direct relevance to their lower middle-class, predominantly female audiences. His master referent is thus a cliché: the modernized, urbanized life of the contemporary Japanese.

Like most of his peers, Ozu situates each film in a definable economic setting. Several of the pre-1945 films present a strongly working-class milieu consisting of cramped alleys, shabby apartments, and laundry billowing on washlines. These surroundings form a tangible reminder that the 1930s was the major period in the development of an urban proletariat. Most salient here is Ozu's 'Kihachi' series (*Passing Fancy*, *Story of Floating Weeds*, *An Innocent Maid*, and *Inn in Tokyo*). These films refer to the plight of the seasonal or short-term worker – uneducated, poorly paid, toiling in unregulated industries. In the postwar period, Ozu's proletarian has become a small tradesman: *Record of a Tenement Gentleman* presents Kihachi as a dyer, while the estranged mother in *Tokyo Twilight* runs a seedy mahjongg parlor, and Hirayama's war buddy in *An Autumn Afternoon* has his own garage.

Another milieu of interest to Ozu is that of the college student. Between 1928 and 1936, he made college films on the American model, and these too were filled with references that would have appealed to contemporary viewers. During the 1920s, Japanese colleges and universities were being established at a rapid rate, and by 1928 they held over 60,000 students. Although competition for university places was severe, once a student was accepted he was virtually guaranteed a diploma. University life was highly Westernized, boasting European-style curricula and sports such as tennis and skiing. Given two principal stereotypes of the student – the passionate radical and the apolitical, unruly nonconformist – Ozu's college comedies draw upon the second. He updates the popular 1920s literary tradition of the *gakusei-mono*, the story of such ups and downs of campus life as love affairs and 'exam hell'. Even the film's title may be a cliché; his 1929 *Days of Youth* recalls a Nikkatsu student film of 1924, *Days of Our Youth* (*Warera no wakaki hi*). He centers his tales at Waseda University, less prestigious than its imperial competitors and more hospitable to students from impoverished families. In Ozu's earliest films, college is a place of irresponsibility, of drinking, sports, and romance. The only problem is exams; then one must cram and cheat. By 1936, in *College Is a Nice Place*, the university has become an utter dead end, and the students idle their days away, too dispirited even to make mischief. A year later, all is nostalgia: in *What Did the Lady Forget?* Setsuko promises to return to Tokyo to see a Waseda baseball game.

In the popular imagination of the 1930s, the student was something of a vagabond. So too were other marginal figures of Ozu's work of that period. He made two films set among Tokyo street gangs, *Walk Cheerfully* and *Dragnet Girl*. Owing something to popular fiction that romanticized hoodlums, instantly recognizable as rewritings of American gangster films, they are nonetheless grounded in the contemporary life of the *yotamono*, petty thieves and swindlers. Their bars and hideouts are at once reminiscent of Hollywood and specific to Tokyo: *Dragnet Girl* is partly set in the Florida Cabaret, an actual Tokyo nightspot. At the same period Ozu turned his hand to another *déclassé* milieu, that of the traveling entertainer. *Story of Floating Weeds* uses this very old *topos* to take Kihachi on the road as manager and star of a tattered Kabuki troupe. Its image of itinerant players recalls Kawabata's novella *The Dancing Girl of Izu* (adapted by Gosho into a Shochiku film the year before Ozu's). Ozu remade *Story of Floating Weeds* in 1959 for Toho, and both versions seem curiously anachronistic. Once Ozu leaves the city, he loses many of his reference points.

If the urban proletarian, the college student, and the drifter fade out of Ozu's work, the salaryman is a constant from start to finish. During the first two decades of the century, Japan's modernization led to the creation of a 'new middle class' of white-collar workers and bureaucrats. During the 1920s the ranks of salarymen swelled: by 1930, one out of five non-agricultural male workers was a clerical employee in a firm or government bureau. After the Kanto quake, much of Tokyo's urban culture was addressed to the salaryman and his family. Magazines, cafés, bars, and cinema were bent on amusing these white-collar aristocrats, creating a milieu somewhat akin to the *Angestellten-kultur* analyzed by Kracauer at the same period.[5] Just as Ozu began directing films, Hajime Maeda scored a popular literary success with his *Sarariiman monogatari* (*Tales of the Salaryman*, 1928). Such Ozu films as *The Life of an Office Worker*, *The Luck Which Touched the Leg*, *The Lady and the Beard*, *Tokyo Chorus*, *I Was Born, But . . .* , and *Where Now Are the Dreams of Youth?* portray a lifestyle that dominated the popular media of the time. The correlation becomes evident if we compare a 1928 cartoon satirizing the conformity of the salaryman's lifestyle (fig. 1) with any shot of Tatsuo Saito, Ozu's perennial salaryman (fig. 2). The humor is complex, since the magazine, like Ozu's films, addresses itself to the very workers and wives who were being satirized.

There is a female equivalent of the salaryman, the stenographer-typist who works for the firm. *Walk Cheerfully*, *Dragnet Girl*, and many postwar films also present this figure's milieu – one that referred to a genuine reality, since women have long formed the 'invisible proletariat' of Japan. Again, popular culture aimed its wares at such relatively independent women, so that Ozu's films, especially of the pre-war period, would have contributed to the perpetuation of the ideological construct of the *moga*, or 'modern girl'.

In the pre-1937 Ozu film, most characters are haunted by the fear of unemployment, a very tangible referent for contemporary audiences. The depression which began in 1927 and continued into the 1930s made the ranks of the jobless increase steadily. Bank failures triggered massive dismissals of white-collar employees. By 1932, one out of five unemployed workers was a salaryman. Ozu's *Life of an Office Worker*, about a salaryman who is fired on the day he gets his seasonal bonus, must have struck a chord in 1928. For students the jobless rate was even higher: by 1931, only a third of university graduates were finding work. Ozu borrowed a rueful catchphrase of the period for the title of *I Graduated, But . . .* , a film about a graduate who

1. Salarymen ride a train to work in this cartoon from 1928

2. A shot from the home movie in *I Was Born, But . . .*

must pretend to be employed. *I Flunked, But . . .* celebrates the student who fails his exam and is spared the futile effort of looking for work. In *Tokyo Chorus*, Ozu portrays Tokyo as 'the city of unemployment', in which a graduate, fired for defending an older colleague, must take a menial job – again, a refraction of the class anxieties of a white-collar audience. Most of these films solve the unemployment problem by fiat: a job appears miraculously. Even in *Inn in Tokyo*, a sombre portrayal of the unemployed proletarian, Kihachi does find work. In the more grim *That Night's Wife*, the penniless sign painter must rob an office to get medicine for his child, and his fate is capture and imprisonment. By *The Only Son*, there is little hope for the advancement that Ryosuke had come to Tokyo to find. The employee can forget launching a career; he is lucky to have a job. And his aged mother must return to the country, where she can look forward only to a life in the silk mill – still the most common form of female work in the 1930s.

Things have changed in the postwar films. Now unemployment is no threat. The office girl is a short-term employee, working to help out the family until she marries. With the expansion of Japanese industry, the salaryman became the new role model for contemporary Japanese workers. Enjoying regular hours, lifetime employment, and guaranteed advancement, the salaryman represented the 'bright new life' of booming Japan. As Ezra Vogel puts it: 'For the rest of society the salary man mediates the direct impact of Westernization and industrialization by offering a model of life which is modest enough to be within the range of realistic hopes and modern enough to be worthy of their highest aspirations.'[6] As in the 1930s, popular culture catered to this audience. Workers took up golf, flower arranging, and pachinko. A Sumitomo salaryman assumed the name Genji Kita and chronicled his class's aspirations and foibles in such successful stories as 'The Guardian God of Golf.'[7] While salarymen appear in most of Ozu's post-war films, their lifestyle is most closely dissected in *Early Spring* and *Ohayo*. The former is an astringent critique of the way that young clerks become trapped in the toils of the impersonal company. Ozu's image of crowds of white-shirted workers pouring out of the train station echoes a cliché of popular culture seen in a contemporary cartoon (fig. 3). Throughout his postwar work recur the sights of the new Japan: office buildings, construction sites, and the company-owned apartment block.

3. 'Morning Depression' by Wataru Hasumi (1960)

Despite the ideological salience of the salaryman, Ozu's films refer to other middle-class prototypes. There is the independent entrepreneur who keeps a small bar, restaurant, or *sake* shop, or who runs a family-centered business such as the Kohayagawas' brewery in *End of Summer*. There is also the highly-educated professional, typically a teacher (*There Was a Father*, *Late Spring*, *Late Autumn*) or a doctor (*An Introduction to Marriage*, *What Did the Lady Forget?*, *Early Summer*, *Early Spring*, *Tokyo Story*). There is the super-salaryman, the highly-placed manager who comes to prominence in *The Flavor of Green Tea over Rice* and subsequent films. Above this rank there is the bourgeois as such, the successful owner of a large-scale business – sometimes as a secondary character, as in *The Lady and the Beard* or *I Was Born, But . . .*, more rarely as a central figure, as in *Where Now Are the Dreams of Youth?* (It is significant that, contrary to common critical opinion, Ozu's

35

wealthiest families all appear in his prewar films.) All these class milieux were commonly seen in Japanese popular culture throughout Ozu's life. Shochiku is an important influence here; during the late 1930s Kido seems to have encouraged films to be set among richer circles.

This survey of economic strata ought not to imply that Ozu's films afford a comprehensive view of Japanese life 1927–62. They ignore certain *topoi* of popular culture, such as the impoverished widow who raises children while slaving at subcontracted piecework, or the geisha who suffers for love of an unattainable youth. This selectivity doubtless owes something to Shochiku's artistic division of labor, which encouraged directors to specialize in certain material. Such partiality ought also to be kept in mind when we turn to the subject that critics have taken as Ozu's most typical: the family.

Not all of Ozu's films center on families. In the college comedies and gangster films, families play no significant role. It would be fairer to say that Ozu's pre-1941 films use family relationships as one, usually privileged, arena of social conflict; and that after 1941, more often than not, character relationships (at work, in the neighborhood) are usually plotted with reference to family relationships. In any event, his handling of the subject makes reference to many cultural constants.

The family is an absolutely central ideological construct for Japanese society. The *ie*, or stem-family system, stretched back to Japan's feudal era, and it was strengthened by the Meiji Civil Code. The *ie* was the family line, transmitted through the eldest son and dominating all branch families that might be set up by his brothers. This patriarchal concept of the family had been much stronger among the samurai class than among the rural and urban masses, but the emerging industrialists of the early 1900s promoted it as a pervasive and inherently Japanese cultural value. The patriarchal family became the model for several social institutions: the industrial workplace, overseen by a paternalistic manager or employer; the government office; the economic marketplace, run under the watchful eye of the ruling class; and finally the nation-state, with the citizens owing filial loyalty to the emperor. This master analogy played a strategic role in building a stable, modern work force. Family worship was promulgated by education, by state Shinto, and by appeal to Confucian precept. Explicit appeal to this ideology intensified during the 1930s, when the most popular word for 'citizen' had become *harakara*, literally 'same placenta', and immense emphasis was placed on the Japanese *kokka*, the 'country-family'.

Yet there were also contradictions between ideology and lived experience. Even in late Meiji, while the family was being canonized, the *ie* was itself breaking down, especially in the impoverished countryside and in urban areas influenced by Western individualism.[8] Throughout the pre-war decades, domestic patriarchy was being undermined by unemployment, the growing importance of urban nuclear-family units, and the economic power of younger sons who, by emigrating to the city, had surpassed their older brothers who had stayed on the farm.

During the 1950s other tendencies became evident. Central among Occupation reforms was an attack on the patriarchal family, principally through granting women the vote and ending the legal authority of the main family over the branches. Economic changes also created smaller households on the Anglo-American model: generations split off, family occupations waned, married women began working outside the home.[9] Urban growth promoted a more atomistic family life in typical company apartment blocks, in the '2DK unit' (two rooms with dinette-kitchen). The company began to take over the role of the family in providing security, welfare, and a sense of tradition. As a result of these and other factors, there grew up the ideology of *maihomushugi*, or 'my-home-ism' – a redefinition of the family as parents plus children plus their domestic possessions. The modern family was united by a new degree of affection, individual privacy, and consumer obligations.

The new situation was most evident in the change in marriage customs. Before the war, a central means of keeping *ie* spirit alive was the arranged marriage, or *miai-kekkon*. The Occupation discouraged such practices, and there appeared a rise in the 'love marriage', often growing out of acquaintances made in school, clubs or the workplace. The sense of a transcendent unity of families across generations was increasingly replaced by the integrity of the married couple, often under the benevolent auspices of the company. Again, however, social change was not a simple replacement of one norm by another. The *ie* lingered as an abstract ideal, and the *miai* was still favored among many families. Parents seemed especially reluctant to let daughters marry for love.

These changes in the family leave their traces on Ozu's work, but not in any simple one-for-one way. The popular culture of the pre-war era bears marks of the tensions which capitalist and imperialist expansion put on the *ie* system. While the government used the press to reiterate that the family was the bulwark of tradition and that *katei bunka* (family culture) crossed all class lines, films and popular culture presented broken families. Instead of fearsome patriarchs and dutiful wives, urban culture was filled with images of absent or debilitated fathers, weak husbands, rebellious sons, and strong women and children. Ozu's films are no exception. The feeble husband of *Body Beautiful*, tyrannized by a successful wife; the ineffectual husband who says he lets his wife think she's boss (*What Did the Lady Forget?*); the wry salaryman of *I Was Born, But . . .* , reconciled to his subjection; the cowardly suitor in *Where Now Are the Dreams of Youth?* who dares not compete with his boss for a girl; the pugnacious Kihachi of *Story of Floating Weeds* confronting the failure of his Kabuki troupe; the despondent teachers of *The Only Son*, defeated by Tokyo – throughout Ozu's films of this period trudge men who attest to the failure of paternal authority. Even ostensibly strong males, like the hirsute protagonist of *The Lady and the Beard* or the gang leaders of *Walk Cheerfully* and *Dragnet Girl*, get tamed: the Beard becomes a shaven salaryman, the tough hoodlums end up weeping, chastened, and in prison.

Usually the real vigor comes from the marginal family members. Wives rescue their husbands at gunpoint (*That Night's Wife*) and teach them manners (*What Did the Lady Forget?*). Sisters sacrifice for brothers and upbraid them for stupidity (*Woman of Tokyo, Dragnet Girl*). Mothers spur their sons to achievement (*I Was Born, But . . .* , *The Only Son*). Sons criticize their fathers (*I Was Born, But . . .* , *Passing Fancy, Story of Floating Weeds*) and neglect their mothers (*A Mother Should Be Loved, The Only Son*). One could argue that as a narrative form, cinema needs transgression of social norms in order to create conflict; but what is remarkable about Ozu's work of the 1920s and 1930s is how seldom the patriarchal norm is reestablished at the close. Like other Shochiku directors, Ozu – addressing a predominantly female audience – had no compunction about leaving his family melodramas suspended on a point of uncertainty or equivocal resolution. It is only with the more explicitly optimistic wartime products, *Brothers and Sisters of the Toda Family* and *There Was a Father*, that the *ie* ideal is redefined in terms of duty, hierarchy, and proper place – just as it was treated in other Shochiku films of the period.

The postwar era likewise leaves its marks on Ozu's representation of the family. After *Record of a Tenement Gentleman*, a work that harks back to the *shitamachi* setting of *Passing Fancy* and *An Innocent Maid*, Ozu takes up the problem of the postwar family in the Mizoguchian *Hen in the Wind*. According to Sato, Ozu was thereafter told by friends that he had reached the limits of his formal powers. He set out to find a stable subject through which he could refine his technique, and the life of the middle-class family was his choice.[10] After *Late Spring*, his films would concentrate on the bond of parent and child or husband and wife. Dramatic crises would no longer revolve around unemployment or failures in job advancement, but rather the death of a parent, the conflict of generations, or the marriage of a daughter. Ozu's films still addressed a female viewer, with *maihomushugi* furnishing the occasion to dramatize and satirize the new urban Japan. The salaryman coming home late to a dutiful wife, the child studying, the daughter cooking or commuting to work, the separate worlds of the husband's cronies and the wife's school friends – these stereotyped social images, instantly recognizable to Ozu's audience, became the basis of his patient exploration of domestic conflict and social change.

Economic strata and representations of the family are geographically localized in these films. Despite an occasional use of rural settings, Ozu's films are overwhelmingly urban. Our survey of Ozu's referential materials would not be complete without a consideration of how he taps his audience's assumptions about the nature of city life.

Japan entered the twentieth century as a rural society, but the city exercised an influence on national culture out of all proportion to its population. After World War I there began a massive movement of penniless farmers and ambitious younger men to the city, where they formed an urban proletariat. It was in the city that Western elements first took firm hold, that new industrial techniques transformed the work day, that the press and mass-market book publishing built a base of support. By the 1920s, thanks to the mass media, Japanese culture was becoming redefined as *urban* culture. This process was not without its tensions, as when a sentimental song or novel contrasted the gay life of the city with the truer morality of the countryside.[11] During the war period, the formation of neighborhood groups (*tonari-gumi*) recalled the units of village life, 'the three houses opposite and the one on either side'.[12] Still, these were atavistic remains of rural life, quickly swept away after the war. Between 1953 and 1965, the rural population plummeted from about forty per cent of the total to twenty-five per cent; by 1980, over ninety per cent of people lived in cities or towns. Despite Ozu's occasional forays into rural areas, he remained a director of city life, which represented everything that was dynamic, dramatic, and modern.

Central to the urban life of Ozu's period was Tokyo, which by the 1880s began to dominate Japanese society. The city was to be the showcase for innovation, the symbol of how Meiji Japan could succeed with Westernized learning.[13] The government, the economy, education, and the mass media were all controlled from Tokyo.[14] Between 1920 and 1930, the city grew from two million people to five million. Tokyo became the mecca for ambitious youth and the center of cosmopolitan culture. Once the quake had leveled much of the city, Junichiro Tanizaki could look forward to living in the capital of the modern world:

> I imagined the grandeur of the new metropolis, and all the changes that would come in customs and manners as well. An orderly pattern of streets, their bright new pavements gleaming. A flood of automobiles. The geometric beauty of block towering upon block, and elevated lines and subways and trolleys weaving among them, and the stir of a nightless city, and pleasure facilities to rival those of Paris and New York.... Fragments of the new Tokyo passed before my eyes, numberless, like flashes in a movie. Soirées, evening dresses and swallowtails and dinner jackets moving in and out, and champagne glasses floating up like the moon upon the ocean. The confusion of late night outside a theatre, headlights crossing one another on darkly shining streets. The flood of gauze and satin and legs and illumination that is vaudeville. The seductive laughter of streetwalkers beneath the lights of Ginza and Asakusa and Marunouchi and Hibiya Park. The secret pleasures of Turkish baths, massage parlors, beauty parlors. Weird crimes....[15]

As Tanizaki had hoped, recovery from the Kanto quake spurred the growth of mass entertainments. Taxis, subways, private cars, and express trains were all in use by the end of the 1920s. Houses had one room decorated in Western fashion, while *mogas* and *mobos* adopted flapper and sheik hairstyles. Foreign words poured in, and urban sophisticates prided themselves on knowing some English. A perceptive foreign traveler noted in 1930 that movies, radio, and dancing catered to the two hundred thousand white-collar workers with ready spending money. She also noted how post-quake culture had created new roles for Japanese women – the café hostess, the flirtatious waitress, the permed typist, even girl billiard markers.[16]

Of Ozu's fifty-four films, forty-nine take place in Tokyo, and five of those mention the city in their title. His work is saturated with references to the teeming mass culture of the metropolis. The films celebrate the city's streets, alleys, cafés, bars and wharves. His characters indulge in *gimbura* – strolling through Ginza – and use local landmarks, such as the Hattori clock tower, as compass points. He pays homage to the city of lanterns when Otsune in *The Only Son* visits the giant lantern at Kaminari Gate, or when in *Tokyo Story* three carousing old men are filmed over the top of a huge lantern. His characters relax in Ueno Park or on the rooftop of an office building; long-shots show narrow alleys, apartment houses sprinkled with quilts

4. Young women participate in the 1933 yoyo craze

5. *Dragnet Girl*

hanging on balconies, deep perspectival views of skyscrapers, or the RCA Victor building. The city's fleeting fads are recorded immediately. Yoyos appear in the Yokohama-based *Dragnet Girl*, produced the very year that they became a craze (figs. 4–5); the boys in *I Was Born, But . . .* make reference to Lion toothpaste, a popular brand of the period. Several postwar works feature pachinko, the pinball game derived from America. The 1950s passion for bicycle racing is shown in *End of Summer*, and hula hoops, a still-vivid icon of the 60s, are prominent in *Ohayo*. Tanizaki's references to secret passions and weird crimes reminds us that the city culture also promised the naughty and bizarre. Ozu's prewar films sometimes tantalize with their glimpses of the sordid or worldly side of the capital. How scandalous *Dragnet Girl* must have looked in 1933, with its gangster hero living openly with a typist who leads him into armed robbery. The movie posters dotting the early films must have seemed the limit in up-to-date decor. As one example of these early films' willingness to play upon 'sophisticated' associations, consider the icon of the woman with a fedora. In Gosho's *Burden of Life* (1935), the bar hostess has donned a customer's hat, yielding its conventional Western association of casual, faintly sexy merrymaking (fig. 6). But five years before this, Ozu had used it for a dramatic gag in *That Night's Wife*, when the detective flourishes it as mocking proof that the husband is hiding (fig. 7). In 1941 Ozu could use the same motif to create a breathtaking shift in tone. When the younger Toda son returns to find his father dead, he casually claps his hat on his weeping sister's head, undercutting her sorrow with a *nansensu* gag (fig. 8). Ozu's deepening of the motif would not have been possible were he not attuned to its clichéd cuteness.

Class, family, and urban life do not, of course, exhaust the range of reference at work in Ozu's films. There is, on a few occasions, religion – Shinto in *Story of Floating Weeds*, Buddhism in *There Was a Father*. The latter film and *Brothers and Sisters of the Toda Family* also deploy highly-charged iconography of the war period to reinforce their arguments about the need for a spiritual purification and renewal of Japan. The early post-war works bear the stamp of the Occupation not only in their explicitly liberal themes but also in their references to Coca-Cola, American movie stars, and Western appliances. Even if the action centers on Tokyo, the later films range freely across the new Japan, citing many famous views – Lake Biwa, Kiyomizudera Temple in Kyoto, the Horyuji Temple in Nara, the seafront at Atami, the sand garden at Ryoanji. *Late Spring* and subsequent films increasingly insist upon icons associated with a pure 'Japaneseness'. But such icons already push us beyond the concrete references that the notion of 'subject matter' includes. We are moving into the more abstract realm of theme.

The Broken Promises of Meiji

Ozu's films draw upon a variety of thematic materials, but two sorts seem to me central. The first involves a reflection on the past, the second a recognition of the impermanence of the present. Neither is of course unique to his work, but they furnish a body of materials appropriate to his use of narrative structure and style.

Ozu was born into nostalgia, for his childhood neighborhood of

Fukugawa exuded the atmosphere of old Edo. Kafu Nagai wrote of it in 1909: 'Even then, before the streetcar tracks were laid, the beauty of the city was being destroyed, and that sad, lonely vista beyond the river still let one taste of decline and decay and an indescribably pure and harmonious beauty.'[17] The passage is symptomatically significant. It implies that loss has become a thematic commonplace available to any Japanese artist of this century. Moreover, loss is at once personal and deeply social and historical. Loss becomes not only a rhetorical resource but a genuine expression of such social forces as technological change (the streetcar tracks). And so it turns out to be in Ozu. In his films, loss, while felt at the individual level, has its sources in a reaction to the vicissitudes of Japanese history.

6. *Burden of Life*

The promise of the Meiji era was that Japan could modernize without suffering a dislocation of what were defined as its central traditions. Cities would grow, but the village could remain the symbol of meaningful community. The family would flourish despite the pressure to send its members off to serve the state and private enterprise. Young men of ability, whatever their origins, could compete in the marketplace without tearing the cooperative fabric of society. The notion of *risshin shusse*, or 'getting ahead in the world', promised that education and hard work would assure the young man of material success in harmony with public service.[18] For most Japanese, however, the promises of Meiji were not kept. As we have seen, the city became the center of culture; the traditional family system strained and snapped; the fragile economy could not support the vast numbers of college graduates looking for work. During the 1920s, there was a growing discrepancy between the dominant ideology of Meiji prosperity and the real conditions under which people lived. By the 1930s, the official line became both more coercive and more contradictory.[19] This is the essential backdrop for the thematic dynamics of Ozu's pre-1947 films.

7. *That Night's Wife*

His extant 1920s and 30s works constitute a sustained critique of the failures of Meiji. His college boys display a degenerate parody of *risshin shusse*. In school only to have fun, lacking all prospects of employment, they while away their time in trivial pranks. His tales of unemployment, such as *Tokyo Chorus* and *Inn in Tokyo*, constitute poignant answers to the question of how modernization has advanced the Japanese nation. *The Only Son* is a detailed examination of how believing in advancement through education leads to self-sacrifice, dead-end jobs, and the futile recycling of desperate boys through a monotonous educational system. The salaryman, a central figure in the Meiji ideology of improvement, stands in Ozu's films as a bitter, frustrated man who will never get ahead and may be fired at any moment. The films are full of fractured families: mothers raising fatherless children, boys with only a father. At one moment in *Inn in Tokyo*, a boy claims that 'it's asking too much' to have both a father and a mother. Some films cut still deeper, as when *I Was Born, But...* interrogates a prime component of Meiji ideology, the naturalness of hierarchy; or when *Until the Day We Meet Again* traces the grim effects of the 'China Incident'. The social criticism that seems evident in 1930s Ozu is thus expressed through the theme of loss – the disparity between Meiji promises and contemporary reality.

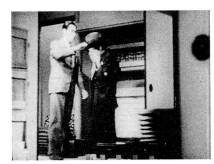

8. *Brothers and Sisters of the Toda Family*

Not that this is a radical critique. It takes for granted that if modernization had brought all that it had promised and had not caused social upheavals, there would be no reason to question class hierarchy, military imperialism, or industrial exploitation. Ozu's films, so often labeled reactionary, become in this historical context liberal protests against the failure of the state's social responsibility.

Within a slightly different context, Ozu's two wartime films offer a delicately negotiated optimism. In both, loss is represented as the death of the father; but these deeply didactic works explicitly respond to the earlier critique of Meiji promises. *Toda Family* shows how the energy of *risshin shusse* can be harnessed to imperial aims abroad and a reconstitution of Japanese society at home, through the efforts of the country's loyal youth. *There Was a Father* demonstrates how the individual can contribute to the purity of the nation by accepting his or her proper place in the hierarchy. Such revisions show that the films' ideological terrain remains mapped within late Meiji co-ordinates.

Loss, represented in the prewar works as the gap between political promise and reality, takes a different form after 1947. One could argue that by 1960 the Meiji promises had, however belatedly, been kept. High employment, college education, and material prosperity were the hallmarks of burgeoning Japan. Now the businessman had achieved the Meiji ideal of serving as a public leader, no longer the despised merchant of the feudal era but the *jitsugyoka*, the 'man who undertakes a real task'.[20] Nevertheless, Ozu's 1950s films continue to project the theme of loss. Now, though, nostalgia gains a new historical dimension. Although the 1930s films had portrayed the decade as a time of misery and dashed hopes, the postwar films look back to that as an era of innocent happiness. To take only one example: in *The Flavor of Green Tea over Rice*, the businessman Satake recalls his friendship with Noburo's brother, killed in the war; Satake's wife and her friends reminisce about high-school days; Satake meets an old war buddy, and together they recall the beauty of the Southern Cross over the Pacific. Often in these films the past is recalled through verbal memory and popular songs – the latter another cue to the culturally mediated nature of this nostalgia. In *Green Tea*, the reminiscing women sing a tune from Girls' Opera ('I first met you in violet-blossom time'), while Satake's friend sings a battle song:

> I enter the town of Singapore with his ash-box in my arms.
> My friend, who rushed in to be the first to enter and died there.
> My friend, see the Ocean and the Southern Cross – that is a star that we saw together
> On our hard-marching route.

Even the smug *jitsugyoka* of the late films continue to dream of their student and soldiering days, while the more plebeian characters, such as the heroines of *Record of a Tenement Gentleman* and *A Hen in the Wind*, frankly look back to a time before the war had spoiled their happiness. Ozu here may have captured an important aspect of popular memory: a mid-1950s survey revealed that forty-five per cent of the Japanese preferred the 1930s to the postwar era.[21] Indeed, he doubtless felt some of the same nostalgia: *Green Tea*'s violet-blossom tune was his favorite drinking song.[22]

Recognizing this socially specific sense of loss permits us to render in historical terms the personalized themes that critics have usually identified in Ozu. For example, the claim that Ozu 'had but one major subject, the Japanese family, and but one major theme, its dissolution'[23] is both inaccurate and incomplete. The family aptly embodies the disparity between Meiji ideals and actuality, or the nostalgia for a purer time. In Japanese film of the 1930s and 1940s, the incomplete family was a convention, which Ozu turned to his advantage in presenting the aftermath of Meiji promises. In his postwar work, the shrinking Japanese family finds its representation in families lacking a parent or in vast extended families that break up. It is likely that Ozu was aware of this side of his work. Of *Tokyo Story* he remarked: 'Through the growth of parents and children, I described how the Japanese family system began to disintegrate.'[24] But the ideal of community can be expressed outside the family as well, as in the college students' gang, the salaryman's *batsu*, or the close-knit neighborhood, and these too can become objects of nostalgia in the late films.

Ozu's characters often register this nostalgia in another, equally socially significant way. Yann Tobin has pointed out that Ozu seems to search for a lost world of childhood, an age of innocence that revolts against authority, refuses the workaday world, and finds family ties arbitrary and stupid.[25] In the post-Meiji context, childhood is a period when all seems possible, before one realizes the futility of individual effort and the hollowness of official promises. The adult can escape by a return to childhood. Hence the infantile behavior of Ozu's dejected college youths and salarymen. Most explicit are the many occasions on which grown-ups recall their own pasts. In *Inn in Tokyo*, while their children play, the homeless Kihachi and Otaka sink into a reverie: 'Let's go back to our childhood.' *Record of a Tenement Gentleman* consists largely of the discussion of childhood; at one point the heroine reminisces with her sister about how they wiped their noses when they were schoolgirls. The return to childhood becomes the individual's last resort.

As I have already suggested, the strong woman and the weak man were conventional figures of Shochiku *shoshimin-geki*, and these put in their appearance in Ozu's work as well. What makes them germane to the theme of loss is the extent to which their qualities embody the critique of Meiji promises that undergirds the films. A prime component of Meiji ideology was the valorization of the father as center of the family: he was the mediator of all social authority and the link to the ancestral tradition. 'Earthquake, thunder, fire, and father' were considered the four chief terrors of life. But the fragmentation of the *ie* led post-Meiji Japan to become what Takeko Doi calls 'a fatherless society'.[26] The plots of Ozu's early films concentrate on fathers and sons, mothers and sons, gangs of young men, students, and salarymen. Nearly all of these men are despondent, demoralized, and defeated. The humiliation of the male, especially in front of his family, is an almost ritualistic feature of these films, and vividly dramatizes another disparity between social conditions and Meiji ideals.

In the postwar works, as Tadao Sato points out, the loss of paternal authority is no less evident.[27] The father who cannot master his children, the elder brother who cannot lead the family, the young married man unable to create a stable home, the drunken husband or pensioner – these are the men of the new Japan. Exceptions like Somiya of *Late Spring* (a film much marked by Occupation reforms) exercise authority in a most untraditional way: he gently urges his daughter to marry instead of sacrificing her youth to hold their family unit together. Nothing could be less accurate than the claim that Ozu's family is an 'authoritarian state in miniature', ruled by 'a strong, benevolent patriarch'.[28] Instead we find images of impotence, ineffectuality, and loss; the heroic ideal of masculine achievement is activated only in ironic evocations of samurai spirit or of prowess in war.

As these last examples imply, the woman's role is defined in relation to the failure of masculine identity. In many of Ozu's earliest films, romantic rivalry plays a central part. Two friends are in love with the same woman, or a young man sets out to win a girl, or an ineffectual husband tries to retain a wife. In Ozu's social comedies, the woman is at once a target of satire and a figure of authority, often curbing a meek husband. The dramas have recourse to the figure of the self-sacrificing woman, as in *That Night's Wife* or *Until the Day We Meet Again*. In extreme cases, male frustration erupts into violence against women, as in *Story of Floating Weeds* or *Dragnet Girl*. In *Woman of Tokyo*, the sources of this sadism are made explicit when Ryosuke slaps his sister and she cries: 'Do you feel good if you slap me? Have all my hardships turned into your slapping me?' Like Taki no Shiraito or O-sen in Mizoguchi's films of the period, Ozu's heroine may suffer for the male's impotence, but here the men are pathetic in their weakness, displaying little of the swaggering brutality of some of Mizoguchi's males. The first half of *A Hen in the Wind*, Ozu's second postwar film, is harshly Mizoguchian, showing how a well-meaning mother is driven to prostitution; but the second half shifts point of view to concentrate on the returning husband's violent response to her infidelity. The final scene didactically stresses the need for him to change his values.

Subsequent films turn more explicitly upon woman as an object of exchange in a declining patriarchy. The central issue of most films after *Late Spring* is the role of woman in maintaining the family, with the issue couched in referential terms we have already considered: arranged marriage versus love marriage, family choice versus individual choice, and so on. In now concentrating on relations between parents and daughters, Ozu again emerges as a liberal, suggesting that by and large women should be allowed to choose whether they want a *miai-kekkon* or a love match. In *Late Spring*, Noriko marries the man picked by her aunt, but in *Early Summer*, *The Flavor of Green Tea over Rice*, and *End of Summer* young women resist their families' choices. *Tokyo Twilight* depicts an ineffectual father who has forced his elder daughter into marrying a cruel and drunken man. In *Equinox Flower*, the father is tricked into letting his daughter marry the man of her choice. In most cases, the daughter's marriage is less important for its effects on the couple than for its effects on the masculine context in which it occurs – changing the overall dynamics of the family (*Early Summer*), abandoning the father (*Late Spring*, *An Autumn Afternoon*), or, as in *Late Autumn*, fulfilling the explicit fantasies of three older, interfering male friends of the family. The plot of *Tokyo Twilight* concentrates on the two sisters, but it is not surprising that Ozu claimed that the film is really about the father, about 'how a man who has been deserted by his wife continues to live.'[29]

The theme of loss is represented iconographically as well. The offscreen hammering in so many of Ozu's 1930s poor neighborhoods signals the ceaseless labor of the artisan, an urban echo of the village barrel-maker or smith. Sato goes so far as to suggest that every natural landscape in the films taps a specifically Japanese nostalgia for the countryside and one's family's hometown.[30] Postwar films may ironically evoke the vanished military tradition, as in the statue of Saigo at the end of *Record of a Tenement Gentleman*, the poem and song about Masashige in *Equinox Flower*, or the 'Warship March' in *An Autumn Afternoon*. More generally, the many icons of 'Japaneseness' that crowd these late films – noh, kabuki, the famous shrines, temples, and views – function less as specific symbols than as general place-holders for 'the past'. Ozu's approach to these icons of tradition is not always reverential: he will preface a tea ceremony with discussions of torn trousers (*Late Spring*), or will let men attending a death anniversary argue about the best places for steaks (*Late Autumn*). His reliance on standardized images and his flexible treatment of them are well illustrated in the recurring figure of Daibutsu, the Great Buddha of Kamakura. In *Walk Cheerfully* (1930), our petty-crook hero takes his girlfriend and her sister to the Buddha, and their mimicking of its expression is typical of Ozu's satiric treatment of tradition in his early films. The superiority of modern life to Japanese tradition is underscored by ending the scene with a close-up of the car racing away, leaving behind a paper balloon, yet another stereotyped image of 'Japaneseness'. The Buddha lives in a world sealed off from the dynamic present. In the wartime *There Was a Father* (1942), the Buddha is treated reverently, as one station in students' field trip through the glories of the Japanese past. In *Early Summer* (1951), Daibutsu becomes at once a historical relic (like the aged uncle, a reminder of the past) and a matter-of-fact neighborhood setting for Sunday chat and family comedy. Such imagery of the past is common in Ozu's work, but the tone taken with respect to the loss it evokes will vary strikingly.

If the past becomes the object of so much reflection, the films' sense of the present cannot go unchanged. Here Ozu introduces another thematic commonplace of Japanese culture, the idea that the present is evanescent. Because of the country's precarious natural conditions – earthquakes, fires, typhoons, and the like – and the instability of Japan's wooden dwellings, historians have long attributed to the Japanese an awareness of life's ephemerality. Many traditional arts concentrate on rendering the fugitive moment, as in the haiku's snapshot or the energetic 'action painting' of calligraphy. Whether or not the Japanese are unusually sensitive to impermanence, the notion has functioned as a cliché or 'ideologeme', a conceptual construct available to self-conscious artists in this century. Thus Ozu on *Early Summer*: 'I wished to portray the cycle of life or mutability rather than the action itself.'[31]

Often enough the topic is directly stated in Ozu's dialogue, or in songs like that which closes *Tokyo Chorus*:

UNIVERSITY OF WINCHESTER
LIBRARY

> Time flies, and so did our three years at school.
> Friends, we shall miss your youthful faces.
> After this, when will we see them again?
> Sometime, somewhere, on our journey of life.
> Will we ever meet again under an olive tree?
> Will we ever talk again about our schooldays?

The theme also emerges from recurrent iconography. Smoke, wind, and steam are poetic clichés for evanescence, seen in almost every Ozu film. Some works of the 1930s make use of a dramatic burst of fireworks that fades to nothingness. In the early works Ozu often has recourse to shots of spinning ventilators atop buildings; *Late Spring* and the films that follow would use ocean waves, or grasses tousled by the breeze. Some works, like *Walk Cheerfully*, *Story of Floating Weeds* and *End of Summer*, will treat fluttering, descending shreds of paper in a similar fashion. The chirruping of cicadas is a comparable poetic device, used extensively in *Tokyo Story*, *Floating Weeds*, and *End of Summer*. An insect flicking against a lamp or lantern is a poetic convention that will reappear at moments of dramatic tension. Still another icon of evanescence is the *kinen-shashin*, the commemorative photograph that plays such an important role in modern Japanese culture. Significantly, of all the class and family portraits that are taken in Ozu's work, none functions to symbolize the act of memory. Whereas a Hollywood film would use the photograph as a prop in a later scene to recall the earlier period, we never see Ozu's commemorative photos after they have been taken. The *kinen-shashin* marks a moment as fleeting.

It would be easy to connect these images of mutability to Japanese aesthetic traditions. Smoke and wind have a long history in Japanese poetry, as in this lyric by Saigyo:

> Trailing on the wind,
> The smoke from Mount Fuji
> Melts into the sky.
> So too my thoughts –
> Unknown their resting place.

Fluttering shreds might metaphorically recall the drifting of snow or cherry blossoms. On the whole, however, it is remarkable that such obviously 'poetic' films as Ozu's fastidiously avoid most of the iconography of Japanese verse. There is no use of such clichés as the moon, snow, cherry blossoms, the cuckoo, plum blossoms, mist, and autumn leaves; and almost no use of clouds, flowers, or rain. In this respect, Mizoguchi is far more conventionally 'lyrical'. Again, Ozu's icons of evanescence are most proximately connected to his concrete historical milieu. Some of the images are simply commonplaces of mass culture. For example, Hiroyuki Araki has shown the prevalence of images of wind and the sea in popular songs after 1912.[32] Other motifs, such as the twirling ventilators and the *kinen-shashin*, were commonplaces of Shochiku films generally. But more fundamentally these themes of transience bring us back to urban culture and the way it was regarded in Ozu's day.

As Tanizaki's bustling fantasy of modernized Tokyo has already sug-

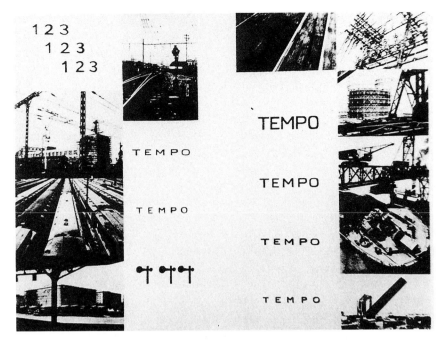

9. 'The Characters of Great Tokyo' by Masao Horino (1931)

10. *An Inn in Tokyo*

gested, the city's reconstruction after the Kanto quake came to embody an idea of 'modern life' (*kindai seikatsu*, or simply the Anglicized *modan raifu*). The thriving dance halls, movie theatres, department stores, cafés, and neon-lit arcades were, however, interpreted in different ways. In a superb discussion of 'Tokyo as an idea', Henry DeWitt Smith II has isolated three main attitudes emerging in the late 1920s. The city's pleasures could be seen as a nihilistic escape from everyday life; or as a revival of Edo's exotic realm of confidence tricksters; or as the arena of a new 'ordinary life', an everyday round of commuting, work, shopping, and diversion.[33] While all these attitudes seep into films of the period, Ozu's work is firmly attached to the third interpretation – modern life as the new ordinary world, the contemporary equivalent of life in the village or town.

This attitude is most clearly seen in the contemporary impulse toward documentation. If Tokyo had become the new arena of everyday life, then one could try to capture its minutiae. There emerged a 'modernist' literature in the late 1920s called 'Club of Rising Art', linked with journalism and concentrating on the factual depiction of the Westernized life of the city. At around the same time appeared the school of *shinko-shashin* photography, which sought to record the mechanistic metropolis in an impersonal fashion.[34] Masao Horino's 1931 photo series called 'The Character of Great Tokyo', with its massive water tanks and slantwise tracks and power lines, has obvious affinities with Ozu's imagery of the time (figs. 9–10). In the same period Kon Wajiro launched an odd amateur sociology somewhat akin to the Mass Observation movement in Britain. Kon's 'modernology' (*kogengaku*) consisted of microscopic documentation of what Tokyo people wore, how they furnished their homes, what routes they took through the city, and so on. His

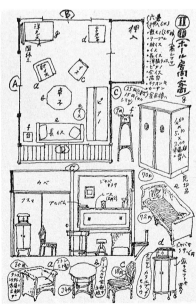

11. Household objects, with dimensions and prices noted; from Kon Wajiro's *Modernologio-Kogengaku* (1930)

47

painstaking sketches of homes, garments, and household objects (fig. 11) recall Ozu's concentration upon such details of contemporary life. We also ought not to overlook the flourishing of caricature and cartoon art in the press, which took as their targets the most ephemeral fashions of the day. Whatever direct influence these trends had upon Ozu, his work shares with them the goal of recording the texture of what had come to be the everyday life of modern Japan.

If *modan raifu* requires this sort of intensive documentation, that is because it is impermanent. In the great earthquake Tokyo lost most of the buildings that linked it to its distant past. Now it was rebuilt, and in the late 1920s massive urban renewal created major thoroughfares and modern apartment buildings.[35] Landmarks vanished. The new Tokyo was a monument to mutability. *Gimbura*, idly strolling past the ever-changing Ginza window displays, became the most obvious symbol of Tokyo's celebration of transience. This new 'floating world' exuded a self-conscious melancholy which many writers attributed to the psychological effects of the quake. The writer Haruo Sato remarked: 'Well, it is not bad after all to enjoy momentary life on such a dangerous, horrible earth as this.'[36] Yet in the work of Ozu and other artists, the ephemerality of the city was not a matter of furtive pleasure, from which one returned to a mundane everyday life. Ordinary life itself was permeated with ephemerality, consisting of constant changes wrought by modernization, social strife, and natural disasters.

12. In this 1926 cartoon, the salaryman is depicted as supporting wife, child, and mother while living on tofu, sake, and cheap cigarettes; his salary passes over his head, straight from his company to the grocer

Such, for example, may be the social point of Ozu's emphasis on commodities. The postwar notion of 'my-home-ism' simply articulates a consumerist ideology that was present in urban culture since at least the 1920s. The Westernization of everyday life then began in earnest. Lured to modern department stores by mass-market advertising, the citizen of the new Japanese city was pledged to consumption. People began to buy radios, phonographs, electric fans, cheap eyeglasses, and American toys and appliances. Interestingly, such objects could be acknowledged as counters in an ephemeral round of getting and spending, as in a 1926 cartoon depicting the salaryman's life as a cycle of transient objects (fig. 12). The war in China and the Pacific checked public acquisitiveness by force, but once urban Japanese recovered from the war, they embarked upon a new phase of commodity worship that seems still far from ending. Postwar affluence allowed some families to own a car and many to acquire the 'electric treasures' – televisions, washing machines, refrigerators, rice cookers and vacuum cleaners. An American observer in 1951 noted that a family's status in the neighborhood rested largely on the consumer goods they owned.[37] A Japanese sociologist has claimed that *maihomushugi* had the effect of squeezing women out of the labor market in order to protect the domestic front but then, because of the ideology of consumption, forced them to earn extra money through low-paying part-time work.[38] Many passages of Ozu's films come immediately to mind in this connection. In the college comedies, the students are surrounded by Western trinkets. The children in the 1930s films forever pester their parents to buy them a cap, candy, or a baseball glove. A character's dandyism is quickly conveyed by a commodity: a white aluminum coffeepot, a fur wrap, a *jinsang* breath mint. In the postwar films, characters yearn for washers or refrigerators. *Ohayo* is built around two brothers' intrigue to acquire a television. Ozu concentrates on his commodities with the intentness of the photographer Horino or the sociologist Kon, using techniques we shall examine later to create still-life compositions out of vacuum cleaners, radios, and low-slung chairs. Such humble objects constitute the ever-changing surface of modern urban life, and the desire to possess them becomes at once a source of humor and a substitute for unresolved social conflicts. The student who has no job at least has his Western suit (*I Flunked, But . . .*). The cashiered salaryman buys his son a bike (*Tokyo Chorus*). The impoverished mother placates her son by buying him a baseball mitt (*The Only Son*). The self-centered brother ignores his sister but gets his MacGregor golf clubs (*An Autumn Afternoon*). The meddling managers force a breach between a mother and her daughter, but treasure the English pipes she has given them (*Late Autumn*). Commodity fetishism is part of the texture of everyday life in the new Japan.

In representing urban ephemerality Ozu goes on to 'naturalize' it. Consider one of his most common icons: the switching on of the city's lights as dusk falls. In the 1920s and 1930s, Tokyo's power utility turned on all domestic lighting at evening and turned it off at dawn. As households had no switches of their own, urban Japanese slept with the lights on all night.[39] Yet Ozu's prewar films often link this custom with the coming of sunrise or sunset. In *Passing Fancy*, for instance, he cuts from gloves and work clothes hanging on a wall at dusk to the same clothes illuminated by a hanging lightbulb. In postwar films, Ozu's camera crouches waiting for streetlights to switch on at twilight. The city's rhythm is synchronized with that of nature. More generally, the filming of the city throughout Ozu's career makes it a discrete set of landscapes and still lifes, a gallery of pictorial constructions that often evoke Hiroshige's late woodcut series, *100 Famous Views of Edo* (figs. 13–14). The postwar films only exacerbate this tendency by moving the action outside Tokyo for a scene or two, pushing the cityscape to the same functional and visual level as a famous view at Kyoto or Nara or Onomichi.

Naturalization is also evident in the postwar films' use of metaphorical titles. Phrases like 'floating weeds' or 'twilight in Tokyo' furnish self-consciously poetic images of fleeting sensation. Most obvious are stock seasonal associations, at once literal and figurative. The title may be metonymic, as when *Samma no aji*, 'the taste of *samma*' (translated into English as *An Autumn Afternoon*), suggests the late summer when this mackerel-like fish is at its freshest. Most seasonal titles are, however, metaphorical, connoting a phase of the protagonists' lives. *Early Spring* takes place in midsummer but is about young people starting out on married life. *Late Spring* (set during the summer) is about a daughter getting too old to marry, while *End of Summer for the Kohayagawa Family*, *Equinox Flower* (a reference to the September-blooming amaryllis), and *Late Autumn* (better translated as 'Bright Autumn Weather') concentrate on late middle age. The traditional nature of these seasonal commonplaces is not in dispute; Ozu's originality consists in applying them to modern urban life. Even the film industry's schedule co-operates: Ozu's 1950s films, released every fall, enfolded the audience into a seasonal rhythm: the film offers itself as a record

13. *Ushimachi, Takanawa* (1857), from Ando Hiroshige's *One Hundred Famous Views of Edo*

14. *Walk Cheerfully*

of Tokyo life in spring or summer, seasons that the audience 'lived through' with the characters. This practice directly evokes an acute sense of evanescence. Thus Ozu builds his image of the city out of pictorial and poetic commonplaces, taking it for granted that the impermanence valorized by aesthetic traditions has found its contemporary shape in the new Tokyo.

A lost past and a fleeting present often intermingle in the films. As we shall see in the next chapter, most Ozu films contain a scene of idyllic contemplation in which some characters sit or stroll in more or less natural surroundings and reflect upon their lives. Such a scene typically blends a sense of loss with an awareness of the transitory moment. In *The Only Son*, while mother and son sit on an industrial prairie by a garbage dump, they discuss the fact that he has failed in his ambition to make good. They look up to watch larks; Ozu cuts to an empty sky, with no larks visible. Cut to the two of them, already risen and walking away. The moment has passed. In *Equinox Flower*, the family is on an outing at Hakone. While the daughters row on the lake, Kyoko recalls that the family were closest together during the war. The entire scene takes place under the aegis of her earlier remark: 'This may be our last outing together.' As the line suggests, part of the poignancy of the passing instant comes from the *premonition of* the nostalgia that one will later feel. This sort of 'anticipated nostalgia' is central to many Ozu scenes, as when Professor Somiya in *Late Spring* tells his daughter that he will always remember this trip; or when the brazen *moga* of *What Did the Lady Forget?* becomes, for once, subdued as she looks out the café window at the city and realizes that tomorrow she will be in Osaka, remembering her adventures in Tokyo. Part of the pathos of the *kinen-shashin* portrait stems from the implication that each participant will for years to come ruminate over this record of ceremonial tranquility.

A good many of these qualities are conveniently crystallized in the recurrent image of the railroad train.[40] The train was a key factor in industrializing Japan during the Meiji era. Since the country lacked a modern highway system until the 1960s, the railroad became an emblem of contemporaneity. The electric commuter train, an Ozu favorite, evokes the transitory, mechanized daily life of the modern commuter and pleasure-seeker. His long-shots of a train snaking through an urban landscape, perhaps bearing a couple on a honeymoon while friends watch from an office building, epitomize the transience of the modern city and the changes in friendships that it inevitably brings. Longer train rides recall the past, as when in *There Was a Father* the son's final journey with his father's ashes recalls their earlier trip together. Like other Ozu icons, the train, taken within urban Japanese culture, is at once concretely referential and thematically evocative. The materials that Ozu employs in his poeticization of everyday life are fully and deeply historical.

4
Structures, Strictures, and Stratagems

I don't think the film has a grammar. I don't think film has but one form. If a good film results, then that film has created its own grammar.

Yasujiro Ozu[1]

The materials upon which Ozu draws are further organized by particular constructive principles. No other cities or families in cinema are like his, and this uniqueness proceeds from a series of formal processes which will occupy me for the next three chapters.

A poetics – derived from *poiesis*, or 'active making' – puts at the center of its concerns the problem of how art works are constructed to have certain effects and uses. The artist's craft, including both abstract principles and particular practices, takes on major importance. In narrative cinema, this requires understanding how materials are deployed in *structural* patterns – progression, repetition, equivalence, and so forth – as well as how the spectator is prompted to dynamize those patterns in time through the process of what I call *narration*. If you notice that a film's ending echoes its beginning, you have spotted a structural feature; if you go on to observe how the knowledge implicit in this ending modifies your impression of the beginning, you are tracing the process of narration. In this connection, let me roll out a few pieces of analytical machinery that will help the inquiry along.

In the process of narration, various aspects of the film become cues for spectatorial activity. Of these cues, the most salient here are those proffered by the *syuzhet*, the substance and sequence of narrative events explicitly presented in the film. For example, *Tokyo Story* begins with the elderly father and mother packing to visit their children in the city; in the next scene, the couple arrive in their son's Tokyo household. These scenes constitute distinct syuzhet components. The syuzhet prompts the spectator to build the *fabula*, or total system of story events, explicit as well as implicit. In the *Tokyo Story* example, the spectator must not only construct the narrative units of packing for the trip and arriving at the son's home; the spectator must also infer the trip itself, which is not dramatized in the syuzhet. Later we learn that the old couple also stopped en route to Tokyo and visited another son. Overall, the action complex of leaving home/travel/visit to son/travel/arriving in Tokyo constitutes, in gross outline, the fabula. As the example suggests, the syuzhet invariably contains some gaps in presenting the fabula, and the choice and control of these gaps contribute mightily to the overall effect of the film.[2] (I have borrowed the Russian Formalists' terms for these processes because no English words unambiguously capture the distinctions that they make.) In accordance with contemporary usage, I shall also employ the term 'diegesis' to refer to the total world of the fabula – its spatiotemporal frame of reference, its 'furnishings', and the characters that dwell and act within it. Thus in constructing the fabula, the spectator is simultaneously building the diegesis. Narration is thus the process whereby syuzhet/fabula relations and features of the film medium (what I shall call *style*) interact to elicit story-constructing activities from the spectator. In this chapter I shall be concerned mainly with the principles of syuzhet/fabula organization in Ozu's films. Chapters 5 and 6 will be devoted to problems of style.

Narration is a formal process that we can characterize along four dimensions. A narration may be more or less *knowledgeable* in both the range and subjective depth of knowledge to which it lays claim. It may be more or less *communicative*, telling the spectator all s/he needs to know at any point or withholding crucial information to some degree. It may be more or less *self-conscious*, directly addressing the audience or concealing itself 'behind the scenes'. And it may take up *judgmental* attitudes, ranging from mockery to compassion. The degree to which a narration is 'overt' or 'unreliable' will depend on several of these factors, the syuzhet context, and larger transtextual norms.

The theory emphasizes the activity of the spectator as well. The viewer is constantly holding assumptions, building and testing hypotheses, drawing inferences, and arriving at conclusions. The spectator seeks to distinguish pertinent events and states of affairs, posit causal and temporal connections among them, and unify the material that the syuzhet presents. All the formal features mentioned so far cue the spectator to perform these activities in specific ways. Since a film, like a novel or play, unfolds in time, the spectator's construction is subject to constant revision and recasting. A poetics of cinema must recognize that narrative films are so made as to exploit the time-bound nature of viewing in order to achieve particular effects. Especially important is the tendency of the film to establish, in its early portions, an 'intrinsic norm' of narrational method that serves as a stable base for spectatorial assumptions and hypotheses. Of course, if later stretches of the syuzhet do not adhere to this norm, the viewer will be confronted with the need to revise the initial schema. A film might begin by restricting us to what one character knows and then abruptly widen our range of knowledge in a fashion that asks us to discard certain inferences about that character's actions. Finally, because all strategies and tactics of narration vary across periods and places, this account needs to be no less historically grounded than was the discussion of pertinent contexts in Chapter 2 and of referential and thematic materials in Chapter 3. Like all formal processes, narration is firmly rooted in the history of cinema and other representational media.

Forces for Unity

It is common to treat the unity of an Ozu film as a matter of constraint. While we shall shortly find that in fact many unifying strategies introduce some positive principles, we can conveniently note some obvious ways in which Ozu consistently refuses orthodox narrational options.

An external indication of Ozu's commitment to a highly unified plot construction is the relatively strict durational boundaries he sets on the action's unfolding. *That Night's Wife*, which extends over the period from dark to dawn, is only an extreme instance of Ozu's temporal concentration. Most of his films take place over a few days or weeks. This concentration is all the more remarkable in that normal filmmaking practice of his period had frequent recourse to long time periods for the unfolding action. Ozu's early work does, however, display some exceptions to the rule of a short syuzhet time span. The most unusual case is *There Was a Father*, which follows a son from childhood to adulthood. *A Mother Should Be Loved* offers a less gradual, more splintered time scale: the early scenes of the family are set in the boys' childhood; the bulk of the film focuses on the sons as young men; the plot closes with an epilogue set three years after the main action. In other cases, the handling is more rigorous: Ozu breaks the film into two parts, separated by a fairly long time gap. *Tokyo Chorus* and *The Only Son* each offers a prologue, then skips over some years to present the action. In *Where Now Are the Dreams of Youth?*, the first half concerns Horino's student life, and the second half, set a year later, follows up his work as company president. These films remain the only deviations from Ozu's self-imposed rule: for the last twenty years of his career, he adhered to a far more circumscribed temporal unity.

Along with this durational concentration go limits on the depth and range of knowledge to which the narration lays claim. Ozu never presents such subjective states as dreams, memories, fantasies or hallucinations. We know the human agents only 'behaviorally', through their words, gestures, expressions, routines, and decisions. The closest Ozu will come to interiority is an occasional representation of optical point of view, and as we shall see later, his point-of-view tactics usually do not offer unequivocal cues for character vision. Normally, the narration presents itself as external and, in this sense, 'objective'.

At first glance, the range of Ozu's narration seems virtually omniscient. The syuzhet will not restrict the flow of story information to what one character knows or experiences, as, say, *The Big Sleep* confines us to the ken of Philip Marlowe. One critic has pointed out that an Ozu film has no single 'subjective center'.[3] This is nicely mirrored in the titles of an early series, which start by claiming a first-person protagonist (*I Graduated, But . . .*) but quickly equivocate about whom the 'I' would designate in *I Flunked, But . . .* and *I Was Born, But . . . .* The film's narration will thus move freely among characters and situations – or at least, somewhat freely. For Ozu surrenders certain options. Even his early silent films almost never avail themselves of crosscutting, a commonplace of American and Japanese filmmaking. When Ozu wants to give the spectator a broad range of knowledge, he will move from one knot of characters to another on a scene-by-scene basis. His late films have recourse to a sort of 'character-contiguity' principle, whereby a secondary character in one scene becomes a major character in the next, and a minor character in that scene goes on to dominate the next one. Whatever the local cohesion principle Ozu uses, he will very seldom base a sequence upon alternating shots of disparate actions. Ozu also avoids building the syuzhet around past events that must come to light in the course of the film. When an Ozu melodrama does turn upon the revelation of such a secret, the prior event will be recounted, not dramatized. No surviving Ozu film contains a single flashback – an important omission in the context of a national cinema that pioneered complex flashbacks in such works as Kinugasa's *Page of Madness*, Mizoguchi's *Orizuru Osen* (*Downfall of Osen*, 1934) and Kurosawa's *Rashomon* (1950). Even ordinary movies of the 1930s and 1940s routinely used brief expository flashbacks or long segments to supply background on character motivation.

More generally and more daringly, Ozu just declines to tell much about his characters' lives before the movie started. Some specific events are never recounted or explained. Why is Tomio sporting an eyepatch early in *Passing Fancy*? What has led to the estrangement of the tinker and his daughter in *Record of a Tenement Gentleman*? How and when did the wives of all those Ozu widowers die? This narrational tactic contributes to some of the most commonly felt effects of the Ozu film: its 'realism' (as in real life, characters don't explain all) and its intimacy (we come to 'know' these characters because their existence is almost completely circumscribed by the span of the film). As usual, even fleeting effects are anchored in particular formal choices and cues.

Ozu's narration submits to so many reductions of choice that it might seem a fairly obvious approach to filmmaking. But theorists of narrative have shown that every 'simple' choice harbors rich, often unremarked possibilities.[4] Ozu's restricted options function within a complex dynamic consisting, on the one hand, of broader factors that give the films great narrative coherence, and on the other hand, of tendencies toward the opening-up and revision of the narration's self-imposed strictures. The basic aesthetic duality of unity and variety here becomes a dialectic of structural rigor and narrational playfulness.

Central to any narrative is a series of incidents related by cause and effect, and Ozu's plots adhere to this condition. The 1930s films, with their roots in genres like *nansensu*, the salaryman film, and the hooligan film, all pivot around strong actions and rapid shifts of situation. They employ strongly motivating circumstances, such as a desperate need for money or medicine, the obligation to pay a bill, the desire to find a job or conceal a secret. The very earliest films often hinge upon romantic rivalries, while after *Tokyo Chorus* the family may also furnish a source of conflict. Even family dramas like *Passing Fancy* and *The Only Son* use the stock device of the child suddenly taken ill in order to precipitate a new series of actions and reactions. In fact, one can argue that Ozu goes out of his way to increase the causal intricacy of these early works. After working in different genres, he starts to mix them, so that a domestic or college comedy also becomes a salaryman drama (e.g. *Tokyo Chorus*). Or scenes belonging to one genre will alternate with scenes typical of another, as when in *Where Now Are the Dreams of Youth?* school pranks alternate with home drama, or salaryman comedy switches to melodrama. A critic might object that the causal machinery is no longer prominent in Ozu's wartime and postwar works, with their greater emphasis on 'everydayness'; but such claims will not bear scrutiny. The cliché that 'nothing happens' in an Ozu film rings fairly hollow when one looks at the intensity of story events depicted. In *Brothers and Sisters of the Toda Family*, the father's death leads to a string of family crises. *There Was a Father*, by contrast, ends with the father's death, but what could have been a simple chronology of a man's life is set in motion by a traumatic accident during a school outing. The other films are no less dependent upon conflicts, intrigues, crises, misunderstandings, and traditional dramatic choices. In *Late Spring*, the father and his sister deliberately mislead the daughter into thinking he will remarry; in *Floating Weeds*, a father returns to his wife but hides his identity from his son; in *Tokyo Twilight*, a daughter rediscovers her long-lost mother and later has an abortion. Conspiracies to manipulate people emerge in *Ohayo* and *Late Autumn*, while in *Early Spring* the protagonist tries to conceal his extramarital affair. Several of the late films revolve around the conflicts engendered by a daughter's marriage. Even *Tokyo Story*, the prototype for many critics' notion of the 'plotless' Ozu, is full of conflicts triggered by the grandparents' visit to Tokyo. Ozu will often force the dramatic issue by means of staple devices like job transfers and the old favorite, a sudden illness or death. In effect, critics who praise the 'non-causal' Ozu have confused three things: the degree of 'ordinariness' of the events; the register, or level of dramatic excitement they create; and the causal concatenation of them. In Ozu's *shoshimin-geki* and home dramas, certainly the events are more 'ordinary' than those depicted in, say, the street-gang films; but this is partly dictated by genre. The action's dramatic register is often low, although one cannot ignore how frequently Ozu's people weep, burst out in anger, and slap one another's faces. In all cases, however, a causal structure of considerable unifying power provides the basis for the film's syuzhet.

Another fairly conventional source of structural unity in the Ozu film is the use of narrative motifs. Like his Hollywood peers, Ozu would employ recurring sounds, gestures, props, settings, or lines of dialogue to accentuate the causal development of the film. The earliest works rely on such visual motifs as gestures or objects (e.g. gloves, socks), a practice which recalls the 'running gags' of American silent comedy. As in Hollywood, the motif may also serve to characterize individuals or to measure the development of the drama. In *Record of a Tenement Gentleman*, there is a motif of noses. The lost boy constantly sniffles; Otane recalls with her sister how they used to blow their noses as kids; in a photographer's studio, she orders the boy to wipe his nose, and this not only invokes a parallel to her childhood but expresses the new solicitude she feels toward him. A film's motifs are not, however, always linked to characterization. Often a clock or coffeepot or vacuum cleaner will recur as a motif of setting, presented as part of an 'omniscient' pattern of repetition. Moreover, as commonplace objects or landscapes, these motifs also 'poeticize' everyday life in the manner discussed in the previous chapter.

A later film such as *Tokyo Story* illustrates the structural rigor and richness of Ozu's use of motifs. Three recurring sounds define the acoustic texture: chugging boats, a train, and cicadas. All three are established in the first scene when the grandparents prepare to leave Onomichi. Their stay in Tokyo is punctuated by train whistles, as at the end of a scene between Noriko and the grandparents in her apartment, and at the moment Shige is awakened by the policeman hauling her drunken father home. Back in Onomichi, as the grandmother lies ill, the scene begins with a train whistle and closes as the chugging of harbor boats seeps into the house. In the next scene, as the family is gathered by the dying woman, the train whistle is heard. At the funeral, the tardy son Koichi can't stand the sound of chanting and so goes to sit outside the temple, where the rhythm of cicadas battles against that of the chant. The final scenes take place against the motors of harbor boats. Noriko leaves Onomichi on the train, and as she looks at her grandmother's watch, a piercing train whistle underscores the action. Cut abruptly to the sound of chugging boats in the harbor. After the grandfather has talked with his neighbor, the film ends with shots of the chugging boats; one emits a low whistle. No simple associations – say of the grandmother with whistles – will do justice to this complex recombining of motifs. The final new sound of the boat horn climaxes an abstract rhythm of repetition and development that can punctuate or accompany narrative action and recall prior scenes without being reducible to exact meanings.

The Garden of Forking Paths

The *Tokyo Story* example suggests how conventional narrative unity can pass over into a purely formal rigor. Ozu stands apart from other directors, Japanese and foreign, in the way in which he superimposes more abstract patterns upon the causal base. Three kinds of large-scale narrative structure are especially prominent: macrostructural symmetries, parallels, and cycles.

From his earliest surviving film onward, Ozu segments the syuzhet into symmetrical chunks. In the 1930s films, this is achieved through a range of tactics. He will use a day/night alternation or a recurrent pattern of locales to divide the film into equivalent parts. He will end the film on a variant of its opening, or use a recurrent gag to balance beginning and ending. Most idiosyncratic is Ozu's habit of dividing the film into two large parts according to tone. In the earliest films, the first part tends to be lively, often comic, and fairly tight causally, while the second part tends to modulate into greater melancholy and toward somewhat more episodic structure. *Days of Youth* moves from comedy on the campus and ski slopes to a more sombre treatment of the boys' rejection by the young woman they desire. *The Lady and the Beard* shifts from a lengthy series of gags involving the hero's beard to a serious crime-and-reformation situation. *I Was Born, But . . .* offers a perfect example of split structure, with the first part devoted to the comedy of the children's games and the second part concentrating on a grim lesson about power. Both *Tokyo Chorus* and *Where Now Are the Dreams of Youth?* exhibit the same division, here reinforced by a long temporal gap of the sort already mentioned. *Brothers and Sisters of the Toda Family* offers a slightly different model of split structure that will become important in the postwar films. Here the first part consists of a quite leisurely exposition, a series of scenes in which chronology is more important than causality. The second part forms the bulk of the film, creating strongly defined causal lines. *Toda Family* opens with the family gathering for a commemoration photo, and several subsequent scenes lay out the relationships among the characters, with only hints of ensuing problems. After the Toda father collapses and dies, however, sharp conflicts emerge. This is essentially the model that Ozu's films will follow from *Late Spring* onwards. Sometimes the expository scenes take up little time, but in other films they stretch on quite a bit (in *Early Summer*, for about half an hour). Such prolonged exposition is probably another source of the feeling, both among critics and audiences, that 'nothing happens' in Ozu, or that the film takes too long getting started.

Symmetries are macrostructural, independent of what is represented, and a matter of abstract formal geometry. Parallels, by contrast, emerge from concrete details of the film's action. Donald Richie was the first critic to point out the importance of parallels in Ozu, and my analysis takes his careful discussion as a point of departure.[5] From the standpoint of narrative poetics, parallelism consists of marking one syuzhet element as similar to another one. A character, object, or setting may be tagged as like another by virtue of any sort of auditory or visual cue – intrinsic identifying features, placement in the plot, sharing of a recurrent motif, or whatever. Now there is no doubt that Ozu was aware of parallelism as a key principle of his construction. Richie quotes this extract from his diary: 'March 23, 1963. Work. The fight between Saburi and Ryu; the small edition of that, the fight between Oda and Kita; on top of that, the fight between the children.'[6] The very manner in which Ozu and Noda constructed the scripts after *Late Spring* demonstrates their concern for parallels. Each scene would be summarized on a card, and the cards would be arranged in columns and rows on a table, as if the scenario's design anticipated a Lévi-Straussian structural analysis.[7]

In Ozu, parallels create equivalences among characters, actions, situations, scenes, locales, props – virtually any distinct entity one could identify in the text. In *Days of Youth*, the scene of a boy caught cheating after an exam finds its distant echo in the encounter between our two heroes and the same professor at the end of the film. In *Equinox Flower*, each of three daughters is involved in quarreling with her parents about marriage. Sometimes a character will call our attention to a parallel, as when in *The Only Son* Ryosuke looks at his sleeping child and vows to make sacrifices so that the boy will be able to succeed. These parallels might be said to be 'in the script' in that syuzhet construction is central to creating them. But the film's narration can make parallels manifest by means of repeated and varied stylistic figures, as when in *Passing Fancy* backward camera movements become associated with Otome's café and are recalled in the boat bearing Kihachi to Hokkaido. One measure of Ozu's stylistic uniqueness is the degree to which a fairly small range of film techniques is used to mark minute similarities among situations and locales.

While likeness provides the basis for any parallel in any text, the device inevitably involves a degree of difference. Once some cues establish an equivalence, other cues can mark contrasts or oppositions. In *Equinox Flower*, for instance, the three daughters are contrasted in character, attitudes, and action: one has left home to live with her lover, one stays at home dutifully with her mother, and a third tricks her father into letting her marry the man of her choice.

In any narrative, parallels can function in diverse ways. At the least, they can support the causal development that is the narrative's 'dominant' structure. This is particularly apparent in a time-bound art like the cinema. For instance, parallels may retard and block the causal line, stretching out the plot and creating suspense. In addition, the differences emerging from the comparison of parallel units may tend to register as measures of *change*. If a film's first two scenes show the hero getting up and going to work on time, and the third scene shows him oversleeping, we may infer that he has become lazy, or that some carousing is taking its toll. Ozu masterfully varies routine actions so as to suggest a plot development. A clear example occurs in *I Was Born, But . . .*, where small changes in the family's morning regimen become an exact measure of domestic upheavals. Ozu will also use the minute deflections of routines to surprise us, making them the apparently trivial vehicle of new causal information.

Critics usually seize upon another function of parallels, their ability to carry thematic meaning. In Ozu's most didactic works, this function comes to the foreground. Many of the stylistically underlined parallels in *I Was Born, But . . .* explicitly liken schoolboys to salarymen. In *The Only Son*, Ryosuke's insight is that he must now sacrifice for his child as his mother sacrificed for him, and this enhances the theme of parent/child relations that is central to the film. If parallels become numerous, the result may be a rich thematic comprehensiveness. *Toda Family* and later 'extended-family' films create so many parallels among generations, situations, and locales that there emerges a sense of surveying a spectrum of the human condition.

But not all parallels, in Ozu or in other filmmakers' works, can be pinned down by a thematic point. Ozu will often multiply parallels for the sake of gags, either obvious or quirky. In *I Flunked, But . . .*, the hero has four roommates and four pals in his gang. There is no causal or thematic need for so many characters, but Ozu is thus able to wring humor out of contrasts between two largish groups. In *Ohayo*, a parallel between the boys eating pumice and the zoo seals dying from such a diet simply yields a comic motif that culminates in an aborted gag when one mother contemplates dabbing her dwindling pumice stone with poison. The 'stacked' structure of Noda and Ozu's scripts suggests that Ozu often expects his viewer to enjoy parallelism for its own sake, as a contributor to formal unity. During early scenes of *Inn in Tokyo*, Kihachi and his sons repeatedly glimpse the woman and daughter who will later be integral to the plot. A Hollywood script would either have made the families meet on the first occasion, or have used the repetition for suspense, but Ozu employs the repeated sightings as units in an intricate structure of parallels that dominates the first half of the film. (See pp. 264–5 for a detailed discussion.)

It is the number and the varying functions of parallels in Ozu that set his work apart from that of other masters of this mode of construction. In Griffith's *Intolerance*, parallels are brought to our attention by self-conscious intertitles and crosscutting (two tactics that Ozu almost never employs), and these parallels are heavily thematic. In Renoir's *Rules of the Game*, the parallels involve characters and situations, deploying master/servant and love-triangle patterns as Ozu uses teacher/pupil and kinship relations. Unlike Renoir, however, Ozu also draws parallels by strongly marked stylistic devices. In *Tokyo Chorus*, for instance, he parallels a character's situation at two points by means of barely varied point-of-view shots, and goes on to parallel this character to others by means of comparable images. Moreover, Ozu pursues parallels as a source of sheer structural complexity. André Tournès compares

Ozu's films to Borges' story 'The Garden of Forking Paths', in which each turning point in the plot conjures up a range of possibilities that are represented elsewhere. 'The daughter's marriage is free or arranged, the father will marry or remain alone, or the daughter stays with the father and grows old along with him.'[8] Renoir's parallels are always at the service of a tight dramatic-thematic structure, whereas Ozu's often exist as sheerly nuanced pattern-making (the *Inn in Tokyo* case) or suggest an indefinitely large paradigm of 'virtual' similarities and differences.

Aside from symmetries and parallels, Ozu creates narrative structure by means of a broad 'semantic rhythm' that undergirds many of the films, a kind of metaphysics of eternal return. Call this a *cycle*. The fabulas of most of Ozu's films presuppose a particular cycle of life, a movement of growth, decay, and separation of partners and generations. We can envision it schematically, using one column to indicate a pattern of narrative continuity and another to set off actions which abruptly terminate a phase:

Generation 1:	1. Family life: parent(s) raise child.	
	2a. Parent sacrifices for child.	2b. Separation of family members.
Generation 2:	3. Youth grows up.	
	4. Youth gets education.	
	5a. Youth gets/holds job.	5b. Separation of family members.
	6a. Youth marries.	6b. Separation of family members.
	7. Family life: couple faces domestic crises.	
Generation 3:	8. Family life: couple raise children.	
	9a. Grandparents, parents, and children share household.	9b. Separation of family members through departure or death.
	10. Family continues.	

In a sense this is Ozu's fundamental myth, but only if we take the term in an Aristotelian sense of *mythos*, or plot structure. Some films concentrate on only a small portion of this process; a few sweep across many stages. Many films assume that most of these phases have already occurred 'offstage' in prior fabula events; the syuzhet thus devotes itself to presenting only portions of this overall rhythm. Here, as a quick list, is how Ozu's syuzhets present the pattern:

> *I Was Born, But . . ., Ohayo*: 1–2a
> *Inn in Tokyo, Passing Fancy*: 1–2a,2b
> *A Mother Should Be Loved*: 1–4
> *There Was a Father*: 1–6b
> *The Only Son*: 1–9b
> *Days of Youth, I Flunked, But . . .*: 4
> *The Lady and the Beard*: 4–5a

Story of Floating Weeds, Floating Weeds: 4–5b
Where Now Are the Dreams of Youth?: 4–6a
Tokyo Chorus: 4–8
Late Spring, Equinox Flower, Late Autumn, An Autumn Afternoon: 6a–6b
End of Summer: 6a–10
The Munekata Sisters: 6b–7
What Did the Lady Forget?, The Flavor of Green Tea over Rice, Early Spring: 7
Tokyo Twilight: 7–9b
A Hen in the Wind: 8
Early Summer: 8–9b
Brothers and Sisters of the Toda Family, Tokyo Story: 9a–10

Disclosing this overarching semantic rhythm lets us periodize Ozu's career along new lines. Generally speaking, his earliest films concentrate on early phases of the cycle, and deliberate throwbacks like *Ohayo* and *Floating Weeds* retrace these. With respect to narrative structure, the three pivotal films in his career are *The Only Son* (1936), *What Did the Lady Forget?* (1937), and *Toda Family* (1941). The first lays down a model of virtually the entire cycle of events. It summarizes much of the 1930s work, though leaving offscreen the education and unemployment actions that occupy the student comedies and the salaryman films. It also lays the basis for the handling of the grandparents' generation as narrative factors in the postwar work. *What Did the Lady Forget?* is the prototype of the childless-couple film, concentrating on phase 7 and prefiguring two later works. And the fabula of *Toda Family* serves as the rough cast for the extended-family structure that Ozu will use in some postwar works. We thus cannot distinguish formal features by means of a split between prewar and postwar 'periods', since key principles of Ozu's semantic rhythm are already laid out in pre-1942 works.

Not surprisingly, *There Was a Father* and *The Only Son* emerge as the most explicitly synoptic of the films, chiefly because they exhibit the most extended syuzhet duration in Ozu's work. But what the mere list cannot indicate is the way that extended-family films like *Brothers and Sisters of the Toda Family*, *Tokyo Story*, and *End of Summer* allow the syuzhet to catch different characters at different phases of the cycle or to let characters reminisce about actions in earlier stages. These films thus achieve a kind of 'squeezed' temporal perspective whereby, despite the concentration on a short syuzhet duration, the film surveys different points in the cycle. What *The Only Son* and *There Was a Father* accomplish by taking a few characters across a lengthy period, some of the late films achieve through presenting several characters across a short time span. Thus the late films often lead the viewer through at least three overriding structures: the structure of a family tree, the symmetries and parallels of plot action, and the structure of Ozu's cyclical myth.

Evidently Ozu 'naturalizes' his overall rhythm in several ways. Here is a crucial function of the seasonal titles, which, as we saw in Chapter 3, do not set the time of the film's action but rather connote different stages of life. Endings are also important in this naturalization, since they often appeal to an ongoing existence independent of, and indifferent to, the characters' petty problems. Ozu is a master of what Shklovsky calls the 'false close', a key feature of open-ended narratives. Here a concluding description of the setting, the weather, or some other noncausal feature constitutes, by convention, a substitute for causal resolution.[9] Ozu absorbs such conventional endings into the overarching rhythm of life, often by introducing at the opening the motif that will close the film, but there making it more causally functional as an establishment of the drama's locale. Hence the factory settings that open and close *The Only Son*, the landscapes that open and close *Late Spring*, the train station in *Equinox Flower*, the harbor shots in *Tokyo Story*, and so on. Such a device offers a good example of how material – the subject of the family – gets transformed by constructive principles like metaphor and narrative closure. This formal process will in turn prove essential to an ideological analysis of Ozu's work in Chapter 8.

Symmetries, parallels, and cycles superimpose an abstract logic upon the causal patterning of Ozu's films. They lend a diagrammatic shape to the plot, lodging each incident within a purer system of relations. When a single event finds a spot within all these structures, it gains an enormous narrative richness. Consider, as just one instance, the end of *Early Summer*. The grandparents have moved in with the uncle, and they sit in his house, looking out at the countryside. In terms of purely local causality, the scene is a consequence of Noriko's decision to marry Yabe. It also participates in two symmetries: it is the end of the film's second, heavily-plotted major part and the coda to its third 'act'. In addition, the scene constitutes a rigorous parallel to the film's opening, in which the family gathered for breakfast. (These points are discussed in detail on pp. 320–1.) The sequence also participates in the overall cycle of the parting of generations, constituting phase 9b in my schematic list. Three levels of pattern endow the scene with a rigorous density that owes only a part of its force to immediate cause and effect.

As if all these abstract patterns were not enough to 'overdetermine' the film's shape, Ozu has recourse to intertextual factors as well. I am not here thinking of genre, which certainly does contribute to the causal and motivic structure of the films. Ozu is unusual in that he self-consciously exploits his entire output as one vast 'text' of which each film can be seen as a chapter.

An obvious case in point is his reliance on remakes and series. Not only did his earliest films tend to be based on American films or stories, but Ozu remade two of the 1930s works – *I Was Born, But . . .* and *Story of Floating Weeds* – as *Ohayo* and *Floating Weeds*. A popular catchphrase led Ozu to create the 'I . . . but . . .' series. More unusual is his 'Kihachi' series of the 1930s. *Passing Fancy*, *Story of Floating Weeds*, *An Innocent Maid*, and *Inn in Tokyo* all center on an itinerant character played by Takeshi Sakamoto, who has a son, usually played by Tokkan Kozo. In each, Kihachi has a friendly or amorous relation with an older woman played by Choko Iida. Each film involves Kihachi with another woman before he is (usually) separated from his son. Nevertheless, the causal details of the films vary drastically. In some, Kihachi has somehow lost his wife, but in one the Iida character is his wife; in one, he has two sons. As Ozu pointed out, these films do not constitute a true series in that they are not really about the same character.[10] Kihachi even has a rather different personality from film to film: thick-headed but good-natured in *Passing Fancy*, more clever and surly in *Story of Floating Weeds*, and so on. The films are best considered a set of variant plots built out of the same actors and roughly equivalent *actants*, or functional character roles. In this spirit, one critic has suggested that in the postwar period Ozu launched a comparable 'series', his 'Shukichi' films, which center on a character seeking to marry off his daughter.[11] Such intertextual repetitions and variations add another layer to the set of abstract configurations at work in the individual Ozu film.

At a local level, it is apparent that far more than most directors Ozu also repeats motifs from film to film. Clocks, steaming teakettles, hands, and feet recur not only within each work but intertextually. Ozu unhesitatingly recycles gags, gestures, locales, and specific images across his career. Anyone who is sewing will use the needle to scratch his or her head; any 1950s apartment-dweller is likely to hear a neighbor singing scales. All Ozu children cry in the same way – knuckles to the eyes, elbows high up, arms horizontal. By contrast, when Ozu women cry they raise their arms vertically and blot out their faces with their palms. In *I Was Born, But . . .*, one boy plucks the leaves off a plant as the son in *Passing Fancy* will. In *That Night's Wife*, a cop removes his false teeth; the same actor performs the same gesture in *The Lady and the Beard* and *I Was Born, But . . . .* Characters rub their noses reflectively, complacently (*Late Autumn*), or as a code (*End of Summer*). They incessantly lose or find their gloves, slip on or take off socks, and call their schoolteachers 'Badger'. The 'Calorie' restaurant appears in both *Tokyo Chorus* and *The Flavor of Green Tea over Rice*. The piano music near an apartment in *Ohayo* has already been heard in *Equinox Flower*. The sewing machine in *Where Now Are the Dreams of Youth?* comes to the foreground seventeen years later in *Late Spring*. Through the early scenes of *Passing Fancy*, Kihachi's son inexplicably wears an eyepatch; in *Early Spring*, an office girl comes to a farewell party wearing one. Nipper, the 'His Master's Voice' dog, squats patiently in a record shop or bar. Throughout his career, Ozu liked to have rows of fedora hats stand as a synecdoche for the presence of a group of men. A fedora tossed on the floor and rolling in close-up is established in *A Mother Should Be Loved* for re-use in *There Was a Father*.

1. *Dragnet Girl*

Sometimes an image will recur exactly, as if Ozu had lifted a shot out of one movie and spliced it into another. In *Where Now Are the Dreams of Youth?*, *Passing Fancy*, and *Inn in Tokyo*, the same shot of bursting fireworks abruptly punctuates the action. The last shot of *Story of Floating Weeds*, a train rocketing down the tracks, has a close affinity with the last shot of *Equinox Flower*. Between 1933 and 1937, Ozu often attached his camera to an automobile fender and from this zany angle filmed the passing city and its reflection in a shiny headlight (fig. 1). Shots of trees, filmed from comparable setups, are inserted into *Tokyo Chorus*, *Where Now Are the Dreams of Youth?*, and *Passing Fancy*. The shot of Saigo's statue that is shown in the boss's home movie in *I Was Born, But . . .* appears in the final scene of *Record of a Tenement Gentleman* fifteen years later.

Not only particular motifs but more general plot components recur across films. Ozu's scenes constitute what Barthes would call 'action sequences' and what cognitive psychologists call 'scripts' or 'event schemas'[12] – stereotyped series of actions that add up to a familiar behavior, such as taking a train trip or visiting the doctor. Since all narratives require such proairetic sequences, what distinguishes Ozu's use of them? Richie has pointed out their 'modular' nature, implying that they are to some extent 'pre-measured' and part of a narrow stock of alternatives. In other words, Ozu's scenes can be imagined as detached units, members of a small paradigmatic class available for re-use in later combinations. A cheating scene in one student comedy might do duty for that in another. The modular concept is most readily applicable to the home dramas, which can be seen as built out of a fairly restricted range of action schemas. There is the family conference, the ceremony (a funeral or death anniversary, never a wedding), the class reunion, the scene of the old man reflecting on how his life has been wasted, the communal song, and the visit to the theatre or the hospital. There are the scenes of dining, either in a café or at home – so many such scenes that Ozu's home dramas became known as 'eating films'.[13] There is the scene of placating a child's tantrum, and its corollaries – giving the child money to buy candy and later discovering that the child is sick from overindulgence. There is the scene of taking the commemorative photograph, and there is the guest's tardy arrival (often at a funeral). In almost every film there is the 'idyll', a scene in natural surroundings during which characters sit quietly and contemplate their lives. In the sound films, these idylls have nondiegetic music playing throughout, and some films contain more than one, featuring different characters. While symmetries and cycles offer 'hollow forms', modules provide concrete actions familiar from social life and other Ozu films. It is as if one could list all the prototypical scenes, pick out several, shuffle them, and build a new Ozu film.

Intertextual repetition of motifs and modules cooperates with the films' reliance upon symmetries, parallels, and cycles to make each work vastly overdetermined. The most proximate 'genre' for any one film may thus, as Richie says, be all Ozu's other work.[14] Throughout his career, his tendency to repeat – to create a pseudo-series, to reiterate situations or gags, to mine a genre convention – invites us to treat each film as an explicit variant of others. Events omitted from one film will be dramatized in another: wedding preparations in *Late Spring* and *An Autumn Afternoon*, a wedding reception in *Equinox Flower*, preparations for a funeral in *End of Summer*, the funeral in several works. There is no need to show Akiko back in her apartment at the close of *End of Summer*, since we've already seen 'her' there in the conclusion of *Late Autumn*. The films may even string themselves together, as when *I Flunked, But...* ends with a cheerleading scene, and *Where Now Are the Dreams of Youth?* opens with an almost identical episode.

'In all fictional works,' explains the savant in 'The Garden of Forking Paths', 'each time a man is confronted with several alternatives, he chooses one and eliminates the others; but in the fiction of Ts'ui Pen, he chooses – simultaneously – all of them. *He creates*, in this way, diverse futures, diverse times which themselves also proliferate and fork.'[15] Like this imaginary novelist, Ozu makes each turning-point in any one film conjure up eventualities that will materialize in other works. In one film a boy will flunk his exam, in another he will pass. This film's salaryman will be fired, that one's will be transferred. One daughter will be forced to marry, another will pick her husband, a third will remain unmarried. A widowed father will remarry, or not. One grandparent will die suddenly, another will pull through. The films may even engage in dialogue. In *Tokyo Chorus*, you may be fired, but your pals can help you. But, asks *I Was Born, But . . .*, what if you have no pals and you face the boss alone? You must knuckle under. Then, replies *Where Now Are the Dreams of Youth?*, what if the boss *is* your pal and exercises his authority? Can you accede to his will without destroying friendship? It is as if, having chosen his founding 'myth', Ozu sought to present all its possible implications, to trace out each permutation, every possible consequence and reaction – but cumulatively, across dozens of films, leaving the spectator to assemble the paradigm out of all these minute differences. The rigor of Ozu's unifying strategies finds its proper culmination in the way that each event derives not only from local causal necessity but from a grand combinatorial logic that uses the individual film as only a partial fulfillment of its design.

Unserious Business

The unity of syuzhet construction in Ozu's films encourages the spectator to form a stable set of expectations. Across the film, durational concentration, the linear time scheme, the narration's objectivity and self-imposed constraints on information, and the macrostructural symmetries, parallels, and large-scale semantic rhythms provide a firm base for anticipations. Transtextually, the viewer familiar with other Ozu films is likely to have quickly-confirmed assumptions about what particular motifs and modules will appear. So 'overdetermined' is the films' structural unity that they run the risk of becoming not rigorous but rigid. The need is for dispersion, deviation, deflection. Ozu's extraordinary principles of unity are dynamically countered by a tendency toward playful unpredictability. The issue is crystallized in those early titles *I Graduated, But . . .* , *I Flunked, But . . .* , *I Was Born, But . . .*: there is always a but, something to disturb the stability assumed from the outset. The most obvious device here is the tendency toward sharp disruptions of tone. Ozu is fond of undercutting sombre scenes with comic bits. As Tomio lies sick in *Passing Fancy*, Kihachi explains what made him ill, and the catalogue of fruit and candy runs to a hilarious length. The dying grandfather in *End of Summer* abruptly revives and trots to the toilet. In *I Graduated, But . . .* , at the pitch of Minoru's contrition before his wife, he suddenly slaps her forehead. She's startled, but he shows her that he has slain a mosquito. Both versions of *Story of Floating Weeds* alternate comic and serious scenes. Sometimes the shifts of tone can be rapid and breathtaking, as in the case of the fedora at the funeral in *Brothers and Sisters of the Toda Family* (p. 40); or when Tomio, back to health in *Passing Fancy*, resumes his pestering ways and Kihachi remarks that he should have died; Tomio replies that his father just wanted to eat funeral cakes. Such switches of tone bring the narration forward as an active, unbalancing force. Perhaps it was Ozu's tendency to play down scenes of high emotion that impelled him to comment that every director has a register or 'octave', and that while Kurosawa and Mizoguchi worked at a high octave, his and Naruse's octave was 'low'.[16]

In broader terms as well, certain aspects of syuzhet construction loosen up the appearance of stringent rigor. As many critics have suggested, Ozu's opening scenes, especially in the postwar films, often seem to dawdle in setting up the film's central conflicts. Richie remarks of the dialogue in these initial portions that 'it is never, apparently, *about* anything.'[17] We are half an hour into *Early Summer* before the main causal line emerges. Richie takes this tactic as a way of heightening realism, a reflection of the demands of 'the daily world'. Surely this is one basis of its appeal, but realism is only part of a range of compositional effects provided by this oblique exposition. The delay in presenting the central conflict permits the establishment of a leisurely rhythm of narration. It also permits Ozu to lock in many intrinsic norms, setting up symmetries and his mythical cycle of life. The tactic involves some playfulness as well. It typically fills the opening stretches with parallels that will turn out to be secondary but which because of their initial highlighting seem to constitute the film's main issues. *End of Summer* starts with Akiko meeting a salaryman whom her brother wants her to marry. There follows a scene in which she talks with her sister Noriko about the latter's own marriage plans. The third scene introduces the family at their brewery; then we return to Noriko and follow her to a farewell party for the young man she admires. It seems certain that the film will center on her romance. But in the seventh scene, the focus shifts back to the family business, which occupies most of the rest of the film. The Akiko and Noriko lines of action are parallels, brought up at intervals but subordinated to the causal thrust of the family's decline, Manbei's amorous liaison, and his eventual death. Parallels thus become not only delaying devices but narrational decoys, luring our anticipation into tangled paths.

As if perversely to complement the oblique and dilatory opening, the narration will take us by surprise by introducing an important issue or motif very late in the syuzhet. Sometimes this puts the causal development of the plot in a new light, as when the discovery of a knitted baby shoe at the close of *Dragnet Girl* raises the possibility that the heroine is pregnant. In other cases, as with the sea in *Toda Family* or the reunion song in *Equinox Flower*, the motif furnishes a factor that can be used to close the film. Either way, the long-delayed motif – often one that could have been announced much earlier, had the narration so chosen – works to jar expectation, dislodge the tidy equivalences of plot construction, and reveal the narration as playfully suppressive.

Still more overt are blatantly self-conscious asides. Ozu will use every film technique to signal a comically overt narrational manipulation. In *Late Spring* he cuts from a discussion of the marriage of a character named Hattori to a shot of the Hattori building, a prominent Ginza landmark. When in *The Munekata Sisters* Mariko sings and plays an imaginary violin, Ozu inserts nondiegetic harp music. At a photography session in *Record of a Tenement Gentleman*, Ozu presents us with the still camera's inverted view of the action, then represents the snapping of the shutter by a brusque and prolonged black frame. (See pp. 300-1.)

Such explicit intrusions are not confined to camerawork, editing, and sound – the techniques that film criticism has most readily recognized as 'narrational', seeming to come from 'outside' the diegesis. Ozu makes it clear that the profilmic event is no less a product of narration than those techniques which appear to capture it from without.[18] A simple case is the use of English in the films. Ozu knew English fairly well,[19] and during the 1930s the study of

English was compulsory in all Japanese high schools. In the 1930s films, English-language pennants, signs, posters, poems, and graffiti clutter the shot and create narrational asides that issue from within the diegetic world. In *Late Spring* and *Ohayo*, characters lapse into English and, in the latter film especially, become vehicles for the narration's polyglot humor. But Ozu's self-consciousness can also be purely visual. In one stunning shot in *I Was Born, But . . .* , the camera tracks down a row of salarymen working at their desks, and each one yawns on cue as the camera passes. Then the camera glides past one who does *not* yawn. The camera backtracks to him, and then he yawns. It is not that the camera catches some independently existing action; rather, the narration acknowledges its power to *create* the profilmic event and to synchronize it with a camera movement for the sake of a gag.

Taken in isolation, some of these particular devices can be found in other Japanese films, particularly from the 1930s. Many films occasionally make the narration overt. Shimazu's *A Brother and His Younger Sister* (1939) creates an Ozu-like gag around a mountain that seems to rest on a character's palm. A scene in *Nihonjin* (*The Japanese*, 1938) prefigures the gag in *Tenement Gentleman* by starting with an upside-down image of the family gathered for a portrait, as seen through the lens of a still camera. But Ozu was no mere copyist. His films were so influential that his ludic narration was imitated by many directors. Furthermore, his approach differs from that found in the work of his peers. In most other directors, such intrusions are intermittent, fleeting, and ungoverned by any larger purpose; they help create that cinema of rhetorical flourishes that we have already considered in Chapter 2. In Ozu, the principle of a ludic narration pervades the entire film. His narrational asides are only the most evident outcroppings of a systematic narrational playfulness. A clear example is provided by the way his silent films use intertitles. By the time that Ozu began directing, the Western silent cinema had normalized the device along fairly strict and simple lines. An expository title or two might preface the film and open early scenes, but most titles would convey dialogue. These would be inserted into the flow of shots according to one of two schemas:

> shot of speaker/dialogue title/shot of speaker
> shot of speaker/dialogue title/shot of listener

Despite the presence of the *benshi*, Japanese films of the late 1920s used many titles,[20] mostly in obedience to the norms of Hollywood. But in the early 1930s directors began to experiment with alternative arrangements of images and titles. For instance, the Western schemas prompt us to expect dialogue by first presenting a shot of a speaking character. But in Gosho's *Dancing Girl of Izu* (1933), we get this arrangement:

> shot of speaker looking/shot of object speaker sees/
> dialogue title/ shot of speaker

The director could go further and eliminate the speaker's shot altogether, as in these common Japanese schemas:

> shot of listener/dialogue title/shot of listener
> shot of object A/dialogue title/shot of object B

Such 'offscreen' dialogue titles can be found as early as 1931, though they seem to have become a fashion in 1933 and a major narrational alternative in

2. *Dragnet Girl*

3. *Dragnet Girl*

4. *Dragnet Girl*

the years that followed. Evidently the freedom to eliminate Hollywood's redundant cueing of titles was encouraged by several factors. First, the Japanese language possesses many features that can carry information about the pragmatic relations of speaker and listener. Pronouns, for instance, distinguish not only person and number but the gender of the speaker, the social status of the referent and the addressee, and the degree of the speaker's intimacy with the object of discourse. Secondly, the *benshi*'s accompaniment would distinguish among the characters' voices and help the audience 'place' the source of an utterance. Finally, it is likely that the arrival of American and European talking pictures encouraged Japanese directors, still working in a silent cinema, to free up their approach to dialogue – ironically, exploiting the *benshi* in new ways just as he was about to disappear.

Ozu was sharply aware of the narrational overtness of intertitles, once commenting that in a silent film the lines belong not to the character but to the director.[21] In his 1932–33 films the number of titles increases dramatically, from twelve per cent of the shots to twenty-seven per cent of them. (See Appendix.) In 1933, like other filmmakers, he begins to tinker with the placement of titles. He will start a scene with a dialogue title and then cut to a character's reaction to the line before identifying the speaker; or he will sandwich the title between two shots of an object or a listener. He remarked of *Passing Fancy*: 'Given the tendency of the times, I couldn't do too much with silent films. I couldn't avoid adopting talkie techniques to this silent. For example, I dared to insert the subtitle of A's dialogue into a close-up of B who is listening to A.'[22] But while other filmmakers use this tactic sporadically to create a momentary flourish, Ozu organizes it to create playfully suppressive patterns. He often increases a title's ambivalence by omitting linguistic features that might specify the speaker, and he organizes the titles in relation to recurrent visual motifs. In *Dragnet Girl*, for instance, the scenes in the record shop are predicated on two strings of gags, one involving Nipper, the RCA Victor trademark dog, and the other involving sound. Ozu develops the first line by means of a visual play with the numerous dog statuettes scattered around the shop (fig. 2). At one point, we see a shot of a dog in the foreground (fig. 3). When Hiroshi comes forward to scratch it, the dog is revealed to be enormous (fig. 4). The sound gags (in a silent film) revolve around the use of the shop's listening booths: characters conduct conversation through the glass door. The two motivic lines merge in a pair of striking moments that make Nipper anthropomorphic. When Misako discovers Jyoji in the booth, she taunts him. He replies: 'Shut up. Even a dog is listening.' Cut to a shot from outside the booth that presents Nipper as actively attending to their conversation (fig. 5). Misako leaves the shop to phone Tokiko, but Ozu links the scenes elliptically:

1. (*ms*) Nipper statuette (fig. 6).
2. *DT*: 'Do you understand?'
3. (*ms*) Tokiko on the phone (fig. 7).

The immediate effect is comic surprise, but in retrospect the gag emerges as a logical climax of Nipper's ongoing role as witness to the drama. Through the integration of images and dialogue titles, Nipper looks, listens, and speaks.

The thoroughgoing playfulness of the intertitles has its analogues in the

5. *Dragnet Girl*

6. *Dragnet Girl*

7. *Dragnet Girl*

use of nondiegetic music in the sound films. In many ways, as we might expect, Ozu's deployment of this resource obeys his principles of 'overdetermined' rigor. There are musical motifs, often associated with locales or characters and often heightening visual parallels. And there is the usual intertextual migration of motifs: the same jaunty tune turns up in *Early Spring*, *Tokyo Twilight*, and *Equinox Flower*. But Ozu's music can function ludically as well. The Hawaiian guitar was a staple of Japanese soundtracks of the mid- to late 1930s, and in *What Did the Lady Forget?* Ozu uses languid guitar tunes to provide plangently mocking comments on the films' characters. The rhythms and textures of *Ohayo*'s score create musical equivalents of its characters' flatulence. More pervasively, Ozu freely blurs several distinctions that normally shape our auditory expectations – that between music that links scenes and music that does not, that between 'expressive' and 'indifferent' music, and that between diegetic and nondiegetic sound.

In any film, music may operate as continuous accompaniment to a piece of scenic action or as a transitional factor. Ozu has recourse to both options. In each case, however, he will weave expectations only to unravel them. Within the scene, he will often run cheerfully banal music at the same level throughout – in a home, perhaps the incessant tinkle of a music box; in a bar or café, a brittle tune or some anodyne Muzak. At first hearing, these are simply 'appropriate' accompaniments. But they are neither clearly diegetic nor nondiegetic. We never see the source of the 'Home, Sweet Home' that runs through the domestic scenes of *Early Summer*, and when we hear a jukebox in *An Autumn Afternoon*, it is acoustically quite different from the 'background' music that prevails at other points in the scene. That such music is in fact nondiegetic is suggested by the fact that in *The Flavor of Green Tea over Rice*, when Noboru sings 'Gaudeamus igitur', the endless rumba on the soundtrack cuts abruptly off. Yet if the wallpaper music of such scenes is nondiegetic, it becomes in itself a disconcerting factor. This effect is exacerbated when obviously poignant visual action is occurring: refusing to empathize with a character, the music rolls happily, mindlessly on. Ozu insisted that such music should be detached from the drama: 'Even if the character is sad, make the music a shower of sunshine.'[23] It seems likely that the music's indifference to character pathos not only sets that emotion in relief but carries a measure of urban *anomie*. During a salaryman's funeral in *Early Spring*, 'bar' music creeps faintly in, neither clearly diegetic nor nondiegetic. *Nansensu* survives in this mechanical music: its pitiless lyricism crystallizes both the cheap beauty and the indifference of the modern city. This is the music of everyday life in the new Japan.

Transitional music reveals the same sorts of equivocation. After *Tenement Gentleman*, Ozu will often signal the end of a scene by music that swells up in the last shot of a scene, with a harp or string glissando accentuating the cut to a new locale. Music will rise across whatever transitional shots there may be, and then fade out, to be replaced by diegetic sound – noise, dialogue, or simply offscreen laughter. At least, this is the intrinsic norm that the film will set up. But Ozu's narration will playfully vary this. When an episode has banal accompaniment throughout, the music may run end to end across a scene, as if measured and cut from an endless roll. One consequence of this is to prevent the viewer from anticipating a shift to the next scene. Alternatively, Ozu may borrow early sound devices used by Clair, Lang, and Hitchcock and bleed the diegetic sound of the next scene over the end of this one. (Funeral drumming and chanting are especially common for this purpose.) Thus as the film goes on it may deflect the norm and the expectations set in place at the outset.

Equinox Flower offers a fair specimen. Of the first six transitions, five use nondiegetic music as a link, while one uses diegetic sound to 'bleed over' scenes. The spectator thus gets strongly accustomed to some sort of aural cue signalling a scene's end and smoothing over the cut's disruption. But the seventh transition has no sonic linkage at all, abruptly cutting from a medium shot of one character to a long shot of a new locale. The next transition is even more harsh: there is nondiegetic music, but it starts abruptly at the beginning of the ensuing scene. The narration has now questioned the centrality of music as an assured continuity factor, and as the film goes on, it will reinstate the use of music for linkage while challenging it with purely visual transitions or abrupt cuts. The film's last transition cuts abruptly to nondiegetic music in the new scene — the least favored option during the film's early portions. Of course such manipulation of the music cannot be divorced from its more immediate contextual functions; the point is that tacit expectations about this narrational factor are no less subject to the schema-and-correction process than are any other sort.

The overtness of Ozu's narration becomes pervasive in yet other ways, such as in its blatant refusal to communicate certain pieces of story information. Any narration may be more or less communicative. Although in its unfolding course it will never tell or show all, a narration may aim at full disclosure of all information that is relevant at any given point. But like Hitchcock, Lang, Preminger and other masters of suppressive narration, Ozu is far from offering his viewer such free access to story data. The fact that expository portions often do not explain prior events affords one example of this tendency. Within the syuzhet, Ozu also works to create gaps in our ongoing story construction. The usual tactic is to move from one scene to another, letting the conventional cues for a temporal ellipsis cover the omission of some more or less important piece of information. Because the viewer normally assumes that skipped-over stretches of time contain no events of consequence, the delayed revelation of significant data brings the narration's maneuver to our notice. A simple instance: At the end of one scene in *Passing Fancy*, the boy Tomio lies severely ill, and all indications point to his imminent death. The next scene opens with his father picking through his possessions, hoping to pawn enough to pay the hospital bill. Ozu daringly prolongs this scene before finally informing us that Tomio is cured and has returned home.

In *Early Spring*, the office clerk Shoji is having an extramarital affair with his co-worker 'Goldfish'. After their initial lovemaking, we never see them alone together, and the focus shifts to their gang of fellow workers, who begin to guess their secret. But the narration never shows the actual events that precipitate the gang's suspicions. It presents only their recounting of incidents — an embarrassing episode on a train, a glimpse of the two walking together. The narration thus skips over both the affair itself and the 'public' events that trigger suspicions; we must infer what has happened across long intervals, with the concomitant uncertainty about the validity of our judgments. Ozu goes on to equivocate still further when the co-workers hold a noodle party to interrogate the couple. First Goldfish arrives and undergoes pointed questioning. Before the party ends, the narration moves to the home of the dying worker Miura, whom Shoji visits. The next scene presents Shoji arriving home; he tells his wife he's had noodles. The gaps force us to juggle hypotheses: since we did not see him go to the party, perhaps he ate noodles elsewhere; but since he has been lying to his wife and since he refers to noodles, perhaps he went to the party and was grilled in his turn. Once gaps are introduced between scenes, temporal ellipses become 'elliptical' in the sense that they leave much to the imagination.

Such passages suggest that typically Ozu will 'flaunt' the gap he creates, letting us notice it and puzzle over it when it occurs. The alternative, pursued by Lang and Preminger, is to hide the gap, using vivid cues for temporal and causal continuity to suggest that nothing has been concealed and later surprising the spectator with the revelation that a major event has been skipped over.[24] This is the operation of a *retrospectively* overt narration. But Ozu usually seeks to maintain our constant awareness of the narration's selection and combination of what we learn. One particularly playful manifestation of this occurs in what we might call the Case of the Disappearing Suitor. In *Late Spring*, *Early Summer*, and *An Autumn Afternoon*, a woman protagonist is pledged, engaged, or even married to a man whom we never see. In *Early Summer*, the narration flagrantly avoids every opportunity to show us Noriko's marriage prospect, declining even to cut in to a picture of him that she is examining. The narration's lack of communicativeness is underscored by its 'wilful' withholding of such crucial information.

Admittedly, such ellipses are not wholly deviant, for they can also cooperate with larger structural patterns. An ellipsis can be created for the sake of a parallel, as when the return to a familiar setting becomes more valuable to the syuzhet than the presentation of a more important event elsewhere. Sometimes the slot created by an early ellipsis will be filled by a comparable action later. In *Flavor of Green Tea*, Noboru and Setsuko go out for noodles – a sign of a possible romance – but the narration skips over their date. Much later, after Setsuko has run out on her *o-miai*, a scene shows her eating noodles with Noburo, thus providing us with the 'meal' module we lacked before. And here we can find another function of the 'cycle of life' macrostructure. Ozu's late films assume that it is known to the spectator and can form the basis of judicious ellipses, oblique references, substitutions, and so on. We can omit the wedding near the end of *Equinox Flower* because we have heard about one at the beginning. As often in Ozu, the dynamic interaction between rigor and playfulness constantly modifies each principle's concrete application. The portrayal of character is perhaps most visibly affected by the process. Both the films' overarching structural rigor and their overtly playful narration work to minimize character psychology as a textual feature. Donald Richie's claim that all motifs and actions work to reveal character seems finally untenable.[25] Motifs often circulate independent of character, as larger systems issuing from the relatively unrestricted narration.

There is also a great range of character construction in the films: the 'flat' figures of the comedies or secondary plotlines, the 'rich' but unmysterious characters like Kihachi (*Passing Fancy*) and Otane (*Tenement Gentleman*), and the highly opaque heroines of Ozu's late works. His films invariably had their inception in typecasting: the characters would be created to fit the stars available to play them. In 1949 he went on record as approving of the star system because famous performers guaranteed a film's success.[26] In one sense, Ozu uses stars exactly as his Hollywood counterparts would, as a repository of associations from other roles. Moreover, the presence of a type allows Ozu to make the character as nuanced as he likes.

But finally characterization must be seen as a function of narrative structure and the narrational process. The film's narration often gives the characters no pasts or childhoods, little expository fleshing-out, and still less psychological motivation. The unrestricted range of knowledge, the refusal to penetrate subjective states, and the gap-ridden presentation of the action all make it difficult to ascertain mental states, let alone determine how a decision has been arrived at. The strongest cue to character psychology is, as Richie indicates, dialogue; but, given the prevalence of both politeness and embarrassment in Ozu's world, we cannot use speech as an infallible clue to feelings. Another critic suggests that Ozu's characters choose to look and act as if they were content because they don't want to disturb the people around them.[27] The point is not that, as a third writer puts it, all Ozu's characterization is 'superficial'[28] – we shall see later (pp. 249, 330) that some films hinge on the revelation of character – but rather that in all cases it proceeds from large-scale formal strategies; and insofar as these make the narration external, restricted, or suppressive, characterization will tend to be cryptic, and often secondary to the larger dynamic of information-transmission.

8. The opening credit of *Days of Youth*

Camera movements that double back to catch a figure who 'fails' to yawn on cue, dialogue titles that mislead us about who is speaking, an ellipsis that emphasizes that a significant action has been omitted – these and all the rest of our evidence point to a narration that is not only pervasive and suppressive but highly self-conscious. It signals its awareness of presenting material for our eyes only. Early in his career, Ozu used the expository title, a common vehicle of such address to the viewer. According to reports, *Beauty's Sorrows* opens with a superimposed epigraph: 'Neither the snow in the sky nor the beauty of woman is long-lasting.' At the film's climax, as the heroine is dying, her husband combs her hair and spills perfume across her mirror. The narration heightens the image of evanescence by inserting the epigraph again.[29] Other Ozu films of the early 1930s end with an external narrational 'voice', often for comic effect, and as late as *The Only Son* Ozu was starting the film with a didactic title of this sort. Another conventional device of extradiegetic address is the credit sequence, which Ozu turned to his benefit. In the early films, the credits announce a ludic narration by means of cartoon sketches that evoke contemporary *manga*, or comics: pennants and buttons in the college comedies (fig. 8), dice in *Walk Cheerfully*, a fish picked clean in *That Night's Wife*, and so on. In 1935, with *An Inn in Tokyo*, we find the earliest instance of the burlap-backed titles that (despite its use in other Shochiku films) became identified with his unique brand of narrational self-consciousness. His last film, *An Autumn Afternoon*, returns to illustrated credits, sporting graceful multi-colored stalks of grass.

This narration's self-consciousness emerges in a more unorthodox guise. From his earliest *gendai-geki* onward, Ozu was fond of explicitly citing other films in his own. A common form of visual reference is the movie poster tacked to a wall. While realistically motivated (college apartments and cafés are likely spots for such items), the posters, always from American or European films, also introduce inside jokes. As college students prepare to cheat in *I Flunked, But . . .* , a poster from *Charming Sinners* looks down on them. The boys who intend to go on a silence strike in *Ohayo* are framed against *The Defiant Ones*. The boxing milieu of *The Champ* makes it an appropriate mention in *Dragnet Girl*, while a harbor brothel in *A Mother Should Be Loved* is an ironically apt site for a poster from *Rain*. In *Days of Youth* the web of reference becomes quite intricate. Two college students study under a poster for *Seventh Heaven*. When they need money, Watanabe boasts that he'll get them some. 'I'm a very remarkable fellow,' he tells his pal, and adds, 'Look up.' Both lines are motifs in Chico's dialogue in Borzage's film. Watanabe goes on to claim that he will get the money *from* Seventh Heaven, and an expository title stresses it: 'The Seventh Heaven he mentions . . .' It turns out to be a pawnshop. Here Ozu makes a multilingual pun: in Japanese *shichi-ya*, or 'pawnshop', contains *shichi*, which means both 'pawn' and 'seven'.[30] Perhaps the reflexive limit of such citation is reached in the lost *Spring Comes from the Ladies*, when one character recommends seeing an Ozu film.

In other works, the intertextual self-consciousness embraces films projected within Ozu's film. The lost *Young Miss* appears to have included a scene from Paramount's *The Shopworn Angel* (1929). *Woman of Tokyo* contains an extended excerpt from *If I Had a Million* (1932). Elsewhere, footage *en abîme* is often used for parody. In *The Only Son*, Ryosuke takes his mother to Willi Forst's *Leise flehen meine Lieder* (1933). He explains, 'This is the talkie.' She looks apprehensive, then falls asleep. The coy performances and aggressive close-ups and tracking shots in Forst's effort make the muted rigor of Ozu's style stand out in greater relief. *I Was Born, But . . .* goes even further, parodying not only the home-movie genre but Ozu's own style. The boss's amateur film bores and scandalizes its audience by turns, and certain stylistic features, such as the camera height and the tracking shots, resemble those of Ozu's surrounding film. Perhaps too the bizarre japes of Tatsuo Saito in the home movie can be taken as a farewell to the coarse humor of *nansensu*.

Ozu's narration is thus not only consistently overt; it has a certain tone, or judgmental attitude. This tone is best described as playful. Ranging from comic disruptions of serious scenes to the extremes of suppressiveness, from displacement of expectations to self-reference and parody, this narration teases, equivocates, and deflates. By appealing to unity, the narration sets up a rigorous, self-contained system and then undermines that through withheld information, flaunted gaps, and self-conscious asides. The Garden of Forking Paths turns into a maze. As Ozu himself suggests, art is not after all such a serious business: 'I follow the general fashion in ordinary matters and moral laws in serious matters, but in art I follow myself. Therefore I won't do anything I don't want to do. Even if something is unnatural and I like it, I'll do it.'[31]

5

Towards Intrinsic Norms

It is actually in the passage from the *rule* to the *constraint* that the stumbling block appears: people accept the rule, they tolerate technique, but they refuse constraint. Precisely because it seems like an unnecessary rule, a superfluous redoubling of the exigencies of technique, and consequently no longer belongs – so the argument goes – to the admitted norm but rather to the process, and thus is exaggerated and excessive. It is as if there were a hermetic boundary between two domains: the one wherein the observance of rules is a natural fact, and the one wherein the excess of rules is perceived as shameful artifice. . . . To the extent that constraint goes beyond rules which seem natural only to those people who have barely questioned language, it forces the system out of its routine functioning, thereby compelling it to reveal its hidden resources.

Marcel Benabou[1]

A film begins. Quickly or slowly, the viewer starts to understand it: the story it 'tells', the way it represents space and time, what is likely to come next. The film ends. The spectator has understood – perhaps not everything, but something, and in most cases something that is shared by other viewers. How, though, did this process occur?

The question is central for a historical poetics of cinema. Intuitively, we can sketch an answer. The viewer needs basic physical and perceptual equipment, as well as some familiarity with broad conventions of visual and auditory representation. The viewer needs some acquaintance with materials such as those referents and themes discussed in Chapter 3. The viewer also needs skills of narrative comprehension, for in fact the film does not tell the story; it prompts the spectator to *construct* the story on the basis of the syuzhet, the style and many schemata which the spectator has acquired. The viewer thus needs at least some knowledge of *extrinsic* norms of film narration – those bodies of conventions, developed across the history of cinema, that mobilize syuzhet and style into patterns that guide spectators in understanding the stories they help make.

Viewers are also guided by a film's *intrinsic* norms, the premises 'locked in' the moment the film starts. These norms involve all aspects of materials and form, but they operate most subtly in the domain of narration. Everything we have considered in the previous chapter illustrates Ozu's attempt to create unique intrinsic norms. The same purpose governs Ozu's use of the film medium, which will occupy us in this and the next chapter.

Casually considered, as they were in the West for some time, Ozu's films seem stylistically simple but 'normal'. When looked at more closely, as they were in the mid-1970s, they emerge as very odd indeed. Yet if something looks odd only under scrutiny, is it really odd? Put another way, Ozu's style is undeniably unusual, yet his films pose no drastic problems of narrative comprehension, so their use of style does not fit that current concept of 'transgressiveness' that is supposed to oppose the classical film's 'transparency'.

We will not have a full solution to this problem until the next chapter, but let me start here. Ozu's films certainly make visual style more prominent than in classical cinema: his narration constantly emphasizes the organization of the image and the sequence. In this respect he exemplifies what I have called 'parametric' narration, a concept to be explored in the next chapter.[2] At the same time, his stylistic organization derives from extrinsic norms, and in two ways. First, he adheres to the broad, canonized *structures* and *functions* established by classical film narration. Secondly, he excludes many particular compositional devices, selecting only those for which he can find 'his own' equivalents. At the levels of the image and of editing, Ozu makes a few initial decisions, some of which can seem quite arbitrary by the logic of the classical extrinsic norm, and he then carefully articulates all the implications of these decisions. We have here a director who creates an intrinsic norm by narrowing his choices, 'homogenizing' various elements, and integrating them into a system that is *more* internally coherent than the extrinsic set is. He thus has it both ways: a 'legible' style which, in being more rigorous than it needs to be for normal syuzhet purposes, thus emerges as a salient pattern in its own right.

Unreasonable Images

Whereas other studios emphasized the sequence as the film's basic unit,[3] the 'piecemeal' approach to découpage was preferred in Kido's Shochiku. Even so, Ozu's production methods display a unique, near-obsessive concern with controlling every aspect of the image. For him, as for his Hollywood or Soviet counterparts, the shot was the basic unit of construction. For each shot he would draw a sketch in a notebook or the margins of the script.[4] Like Hitchcock, Ozu came to identify the film with those images he had notated. 'He told me,' Chishu Ryu recalled, 'that he was happiest when a scenario was completed. He also told me in jest that he had often been disappointed to find these images broken as he cast the parts and went on the set.'[5] He would lead his crew on long treks searching for locations that best fit his drawings.[6] Unlike Hitchcock, however, he insisted on sizing up each shot through the viewfinder. He stalked through the set lining up every camera position. (Compare Naruse, who would constantly ask his assistant director about the best spot for the camera.[7]) During rehearsals, Ozu watched through the camera and assigned actors their positions. He spent a very long time arranging objects within the frame.[8] When working with Mohara, Ozu employed only 50mm and 75mm lenses, but when Atsuta became his cameraman Ozu limited himself almost completely to the 50mm lens, the internationally standardized 'normal' focal length during the silent era. Although most filmmakers of the 1940s and 1950s moved toward 40mm or 35mm lenses, Ozu claimed that such lenses invariably distorted movement into depth.[9] Once Atsuta persuaded Ozu to look through a wide-angle lens. 'Just as I thought,' Ozu replied. 'Not as good as the fifty.'[10]

When a shot was finally prepared, the camera was locked into place, and the nervous assistants avoided bumping it. 'Once it was set, no one was allowed to touch the camera,' recalls Atsuta. 'This was an ironclad rule.'[11] Atsuta ruefully reflected that since Ozu took over so many of his duties that he became not cameraman but *camera-ban*, 'the guardian of the camera.'[12]

Control did not relax once the action was staged. During the filming, Ozu recorded the shot's duration with a specially made stopwatch that measured both seconds and frames. To assure absolute accuracy, the scriptgirl would also measure the shot with her own stopwatch. Later, during the screening of rushes, Ozu would time the shot once more.[13] In the editing phase, Ozu dictated absolute shot lengths, often independent of what was on screen.[14] He gave strict instructions to his editor Yoshiyasu Hamamura about the length of each speaking shot and he insisted on a 6–8 frame interval after every line of dialogue.[15] Ozu would time his 'empty shots' of scenery by abstract metrical patterns. This explains why he praised one shot of the clock in *High Noon* – not for its content but for its length.[16]

Thus for Ozu the individual shot was as 'modular' as were those event-schemas and local motifs that could be shifted from film to film. His concern for the shot as a material piece is apparent on the screen as well as in production. The clearest case is that of metric editing, the pattern of shot duration. Here is the opening of a scene from *The Only Son* (footage is given for the 16mm format):

1. (*mls*) Dyed fabric on poles: 5 feet
2. (*mls*) Clotheslines: 5 feet
3. (*mls*) Ryosuke, Otsune's knee in *fg*: 2 feet
4. (*ms*) Otsune looking right: 2 feet
5. (*ms*) Sugiko and the baby: 3 feet
6. (*mls*) Clotheslines, variant of 2: 5 feet

Ozu's metric editing avoids the complex patterning of, say, Jean Epstein's silent films,[17] favoring simple repetition (shot B is the same length as A) or additive intervals (shot C equals the total of A plus B). Many other examples of this practice could be adduced. Here is a more metrically elaborate transition from *End of Summer*:

1. (*mls*) Phone rings at clinic: 3.0 feet
2. (*ls*) Clock ticking: 3.5 feet
3. (*ls*) Corridor of house: 3.0 feet
4. (*ls*) Empty room: 3.5 feet
5. (*ls*) Corridor of house: 3.5 feet
6. (*ls*) Family gathered by father: 7.0 feet

For the spectator, such repetitive meter creates a subliminal norm. There will be no sudden accelerations, no flurry of rapid shots; the calm pace of the cutting will match the unfolding syuzhet events. Ozu's exact measurement of

1. *Walk Cheerfully*

2. *Story of Floating Weeds*

3. *An Inn in Tokyo*

4. *Equinox Flower*

time on the set and of footage in editing reveals the craftsman's concern not only to control the most minute aspects of his material but also to instil a set of tacit expectations in the perceiver.

But these metric patterns, as the examples show, are intimately governed by what the shots show. Ozu gives us time to see everything. And by making images durationally equivalent he strengthens their identity as distinct *pictorial* units. Indeed, his attention to the image made him subordinate everything to the shot as a composition. He claimed to avoid dissolves and heavy filters because they spoiled the clarity of the image.[18] 'I like to have each 4 x 5 frame contain one simple picture. If a scene has sixty-five shots, there should be sixty-five pictures.'[19] He also insisted that the spectator should be conscious of the frame edges.[20] This promotion of the image is a crucial step in fulfilling the strategy of homogenization, of selecting only certain technical options and purifying them.

Every viewer would agree that Ozu succeeded in creating a distinctive approach to visual design: upright shapes and parallel lines arranged for balance across the frame; a tendency toward bilateral symmetry on the vertical axis; static elements near the edges of the frame which introduce graphic equivalences or tensions. But the distinctiveness of the Ozu shot owes most to a single, highly controversial framing choice. The urge to make every image sharp, stable, and striking is the 'dominant' of each shot, and as always in art the dominant deforms all the techniques under its sway. The most remarkable and puzzling deformation takes place in the choice of camera position.

Recall some critical commonplaces. Ozu is said to employ a low camera angle, setting the camera two to three feet off the ground. This is said to be a constant, unvarying position. Most critics assert that this represents the eye-level view of a person seated on the floor, the 'traditional' vantage point of the Japanese kneeling on a *tatami* mat. Some writers identify it as the viewpoint of a child, or a god, or a dog, or even the seated movie audience.[21] It is also sometimes said that Ozu's camera position is a convention of the home-drama genre, or part of a wider stylistic trend to which several directors belonged.

In all respects these claims are questionable. Most often, it is true, the shot is in some sense 'low', though Ozu will occasionally employ high angles of landscapes. But he does not shoot from a low camera *angle*. Almost always the camera is level, or tipped only a few degrees up from a horizontal axis. (Compare fig. 1, a genuine low angle from *Walk Cheerfully*, with virtually any other frame in this book.) What makes Ozu's camera seem 'low' is not its angle but its *height*. And that height is not fixed at two feet, three feet, or any particular distance. Ozu's rule is to set the lens axis between halfway and two-thirds of the way down the object to be filmed. When shooting a human figure, this position puts the head quite high in the shot (fig. 2). In filming something close to the ground – a baby, a table, a slumped-over person – the camera gets lowered correspondingly (fig. 3). If the filmed object is at a considerable height, say a building or a lamp hanging from the ceiling, the camera position is elevated (fig. 4). Atsuta recalls how Ozu and his crew would move up through a building floor by floor, trying out camera positions at different windows, in order to find the ideal horizontal level for shooting the

76

building opposite.[22] Thus Ozu's camera position is not absolute but proportional, always lower than what it films but varying in relation to the subject's height.

This fact makes it untenable to identify the camera position with an 'invisible observer' seated on the *tatami*. I have elsewhere criticized the idea of an invisible observer as an explanation for narrational and stylistic effects in Western cinema.[23] The idea serves to 'naturalize' what are purely aesthetic choices and to locate the film's 'narrator' in the camera, which becomes an anthropomorphic witness. To apply this idea to Ozu's framing propels us rapidly toward absurdity. First, the camera is almost never at the literal height of a seated observer, as Atsuta demonstrates in Wenders' film *Tokyo-Ga*. Fig. 5, from that film, shows that the camera is in fact viewing the scene from a very low crouch. Ozu also used an even lower tripod (fig. 6), which forced the operator to stretch out on the ground. Secondly, what sort of observing entity is almost always lower than anything it sees, even in streets, train aisles, and office corridors? Third, if the frame represented an invisible, squatting witness, it should remain constant. It does not. As we have seen, the camera height changes in proportion to the filmed object. An adult figure is filmed from a higher position than is a child (figs. 7, 8), and a building is filmed from a much higher vantage point. Fourth, Ozu changes the camera's height even when filming the same object. Note how the height varies according to whether a figure is seated or standing (figs. 9, 10) or according to the distance of the compositional elements from one another (figs. 11, 12). If we want to keep the notion of an invisible observer, we will have to stretch him (her? it?)

5. Atsuta demonstrates a typical camera

6. *Tokyo-ga*

7. *I Was Born, But . . .*

8. *I Was Born, But . . .*

9. *Early Summer*

10. *Early Summer*

11. *Tokyo Twilight*

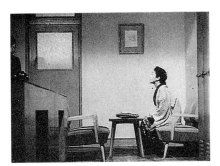

12. *Tokyo Twilight*

13. *Mysterious Man*

14. *The Family Has Three Sons and Two Daughters*

15. *The Family Has Three Sons and Two Daughters*

out prone on a hovering magic carpet that rises or drops a few inches or feet every time the shot changes. Probably this is too great a price to pay for retaining a concept that has outlived its usefulness anyhow.

Late one night, at the home of Daisuke Ito, Ozu drifted out into the garden and set a *sake* bottle on a rock. He crouched down and exclaimed, 'This low position is great! The *sake* bottle is precisely the position of the lens and the position one meter behind it is mine. This is exactly it. Absolutely mine. I'd never let anyone sit in this position, the position I've created. You understand.' When his taxi came for him, he was still repeating, 'That stone – that is *my* position, Ito, and you know it!'[24] While we cannot hold directors to all they say under the influence of drink, Ozu was not idly boasting. His camera position cannot be explained as simply a Japanese film convention. Of course in Japanese cinema characters often sit on the floor, and this has certainly encouraged many directors to lower their framing accordingly. (In this respect, Mizoguchi's fondness for steep high angles sets him somewhat apart.) But I can find no films that use Ozu's low height before he adopted his characteristic approach sometime during 1931–32. His camera position is clearly lower than is usual, and he uses it consistently throughout a film. Other directors might include such shots sporadically, and all the evidence I can find suggests that when they do, they are usually imitating Ozu. For example, Gosho's *Dancing Girl of Izu* utilizes such framings occasionally, as does *Mysterious Man* (fig. 13), made by Ozu's pupil Sasaki. In *Ie ni sannan niji ari* (*The Family Has Three Sons and Two Daughters*, 1943), an Ozu-like shot of children is followed by an utterly atypical framing of an adult (figs.14, 15). Yamanaka uses the low height consistently throughout *Humanity and Paper Balloons* (1936), but not in his *Tange Sazen yowa: Hyaku-man ryo no tubo* (*Pot Worth a Million Ryo*, 1935). There is every reason to think that the later film's framing derives from his detailed knowledge of the work of his close friend. Finally, we must not forget that Ozu's crew and fellow directors were as baffled by his stylistic choice as critics are today. Again and again, directors, cinematographers, and journalists asked him why he chose this camera height, and they seem never to have gotten a straight answer. The evidence clearly indicates that Ozu's low camera position is unique, both in Western and Japanese cinema.

We cannot be sure where this camera position came from, but Ozu, an amateur photographer, may have sought to create a filmic analogy for the view through a twin-lens reflex camera. No matter what is filmed, the photographer holds such a camera down at waist or chest level, and the filmed object looms correspondingly higher in the image.[25] If this is the source, it would add an extra dimension to Ozu's stylistic appropriation of Western 'ways of seeing'. In any event, the question of the *purpose* of the low camera setup remains. Instead of asking 'who' the camera represents, we ought to ask how this framing *functions* and what *effects* it has. And we ought not to expect that its functions necessarily create explicable *meanings*. Meaning is only one effect of form and style, and not always the most important.

One major consequence of Ozu's decision is its sheer novelty, a factor not to be despised in the history of art. More than in most countries, the Japanese director was encouraged to develop an idiosyncratic visual style. Kazuo

Miyagawa, cameraman on *Floating Weeds*, points out that Ozu introduced the device at a time when directors were seeking to renew their national cinema's style.[26] Shiro Kido agrees, suggesting that Ozu's training as a cameraman encouraged him to distinguish his work through its unusual framings.[27] At the same time, as we have seen, most directors were far more eclectic in the range of stylistic devices they chose to flaunt. 'Following a single principle to its extreme in this way is something I don't believe is a very Japanese trait,' commented Masahiro Shinoda. 'So for me, Ozu is in a certain sense a very un-Japanese director.'[28]

Idiosyncratic innovation is certainly part of the answer, but it is not very specific. Let me suggest some more precise functions of the low camera height; I will then trace some of its effects on other film techniques.

Most obviously, the restricted camera height becomes the emblem of all Ozu's refusals. Given the infinite number of points that his camera may occupy, he voluntarily limits his choice to a range that orthodox directors would find intolerably narrow. But like a painter deliberately restricting his palette or even the writer who creates an entire novel without the letter *e*, Ozu picks a narrow range not only to purify his style but to show that this range is in fact capable of a discrimination, depth, and nuance that ordinary practice has overlooked. For instance, the framing enhances the verticality of shot design and permits low-lying objects to stand out sharply. It also subtly discriminates among various aspects of setting and figures. In short, instead of looking for someone 'behind' the camera, we could profitably look at what's in front of it, and how the framing affects the total composition. We shall see shortly how the choice of a low height has enormous effects on setting, acting, and depth.

The camera position also functions to create, by a means at once simple yet unique in the history of cinema, a *constantly overt* narration. By restricting the camera position in this way, Ozu can *for every shot* 'distance' the characters' drama, interposing a narration that will not wholly subordinate itself to their deeds and desires. This is why I have insisted on the *non*-anthropocentric qualities of the camera's placement. Exactly because the camera cannot be presenting the viewpoint of an intelligent agent, either a character or a person-like invisible witness, it can serve as the basis of an *impersonal* narrational system. Shinoda points this out astutely: 'The reason he placed the camera so low was to prevent it from having a human viewpoint.'[29]

Ozu's camera position is an ideal choice for this narrational purpose, since it is at once simple, flexible, and compelling. It is simple because it can be controlled by the director during filming and is not subject to elimination at later phases of production (as, say, printing or editing devices would be). It is flexible because more than other eccentric framings it retains a tie to the normal cues of dramatic filmmaking. To take an extreme counterexample, Ozu could have decided to film every scene from a bird's-eye view, looking straight down at the characters, but that would have posed insuperable problems in production and would have eliminated most of the cues of gesture and facial expression that narrative cinema relies upon. And Ozu's camera position is compelling because it is both self-conscious and enigmatic, calling attention to itself while resisting conventional thematic readings. A consistently high-angle position would invite the spectator to take it as a 'godlike, detached' point of view. True, the low *angle* position has been similarly codified, as representing an object or person as 'powerful'; but apart from the fact that Ozu's camera does not adopt a low angle anyhow, if *every* character is filmed in this way, the code loses its pertinent differences and becomes irrelevant.

Of course, Ozu was not successful in avoiding critics' 'recuperation' of his decision, as we have seen; but, given the unlimited capacity of critics to domesticate even the most peculiar works of art, no artist can really stop them. Jonathan Culler's description of the writer's task is relevant here:

> What the writer must do is to create a text which continually makes us aware of the cost at which we naturalize, which flaunts the difference between verbal surface and naturalizing interpretation so that we see how much richer and less banal the former is than the latter. . . . The poet or novelist succeeds in challenging naturalization not by going beyond the bounds of sense but by creating a verbal surface whose fascination is greater than that of any possible naturalization and which thereby challenges the models by which we attempt to comprehend and circumscribe it.[30]

Ozu's visual 'surface' offers a comparable fascination, one that will not yield easily to interpretation. But he forces us to press even further, since in his search for open structures he does take us beyond 'the bounds of sense'. He achieves this partly through the sheer and systematic *arbitrariness* of the choice of the low camera position. What Kristin Thompson has called Ozu's 'unreasonable' style finds its most telling expression in this simple but far-reaching aesthetic decision.[31]

The effects of this can be seen on a small scale in Ozu's treatment of camera mobility. Again, received opinion misleads: Ozu did not eliminate camera movements from his style. He narrowed their range by absolutely refusing certain sorts, such as the pans that were fundamental to the 'calligraphic' style. Such movements would make the composition too unstable.[32] Ozu subordinated camera movements to visual design by favoring tracking shots that kept the composition constant – such as traveling back to follow walking or bicycling characters, or tracking forward down a corridor, or gliding laterally left or right to create an orderly procession of planes. Like other directors, he could use camera movements independent of character movement to suggest an overt narration; but the camera's height prevents the shot from being understood as the view of a moving invisible witness. Sometimes his early films made the camera slide through upper regions of space, coasting along a washline (*That Night's Wife*) or a ceiling (*Passing Fancy*). He could use camera movements to draw parallels or to 'frame' scenes, as in the tracking shots that punctuate *I Was Born, But* . . . . In *Walk Cheerfully*, *Early Summer*, and *Flavor of Green Tea over Rice*, Ozu 'geometricizes' camera movements, making them create distinct semi-autonomous patterns laid over the syuzhet. But we must not also overlook the 'unreasonableness' that this technique also entails. For instance, Ozu ceased to use *any* camera movements when he made color films, as if he divined a secret incompatibility between the two techniques. The logic may finally be Carrollian. Asked in 1958 why he didn't move the camera, he replied, 'My camera angle is very low, and we don't have a camera which can move at such a low angle.'[33] Of course, for thirty years up till then Ozu had been perfectly capable of moving his low-slung camera, but his reply reveals a characteristic attitude. To justify one exclusion by an equally arbitrary one is the mark of an artist pursuing an integral aesthetic system.

16. *Late Autumn*

The purification of the image affects the settings too. In filming a Japanese home, Ozu wanted to minimize the dark edges of *tatami* mats running horizontally across the shot. These would striate the frame and unduly weight the lower half of the composition. 'Because the Japanese room has a lot of sliding doors,' he explained, 'when you look down from too high a position, the horizon is lowered. If you frame a scene that way, the top part of the frame seems light and the balance looks wrong.'[34] The camera position again dictates a restructuring of the image. The low height plays down the *tatami* (fig. 16). To achieve depth, Ozu's set designer Shimogawara sometimes had to build large or uneven walls.[35] The minimization of the ground plane might also affect the ceiling. Kido recalled that in the 1930s Ozu was the only Shochiku director who needed ceilings on sets.[36] Sometimes Ozu's studio shots of the period do show ceilings, but usually the sets just have very high walls, like those in Lubitsch's silent American comedies (figs. 17, 18). The fact that the camera does not adopt a true low angle often allows Ozu to avoid showing upper regions. Just as recessional vertical uprights define the depth in the ground plane, Ozu often lets lighting fixtures hanging into the frame imply a ceiling (fig. 18). (Atsuta has confirmed that only occasionally did the later films need partial ceilings; normally Ozu's ceilings were much higher than those in real interiors.[37]) Ozu is thus able to avoid recessional horizontal planes at both ground and ceiling levels.

17. *Lady Windermere's Fan* (Lubitsch, 1925)

In order for the image to 'process' settings still more thoroughly, after 1931–33 Ozu adopted a strategy of filming each *type* of locale in a certain fixed way. These 'templates' of setting could then be recycled through the films, much as the scene-types furnished modules of plot construction. In a very early film like *I Flunked, But . . .* , a teacher in the classroom might be filmed fairly 'normally' (fig. 19), but by the time of *A Mother Should Be Loved*, he would be framed in the aisle between desks (fig. 20). The latter became the preferred template (fig. 21). The boss's private office underwent a similar

18. *Where Now Are the Dreams of Youth?*

19. *I Flunked, But . . .*

20. *A Mother Should Be Loved*

21. *There Was a Father*

22. *Tokyo Chorus*

23. *Dragnet Girl*

24. *An Autumn Afternoon*

25. *Equinox Flower*

transformation between *Tokyo Chorus* and *Dragnet Girl* (figs. 22, 23); subsequent films followed suit (fig. 24). Stretches of desks in a large office would change into the rank-and-file work areas of the later films. (See pp. 219, 336.) Village streets or tenements would, after 1934, be filmed through doorways of adjacent houses. (See pp. 298, 357.) The apartment-house hallway of *The Lady and the Beard* needs only the low camera position to become that of *An Autumn Afternoon*. The earliest films avoided shots of corridors within a family's home, but *What Did the Lady Forget?* initiates that deep perspectival framing that would become one of Ozu's preferred formats for filming domestic space. (See pp. 277, 369.) Cafés, bars, railroad platforms, and train cars each had their settled Ozuian template. Again we encounter that overt, self-conscious narration that makes every technical choice follow from an arbitrary decision. Each setting, no matter how idiosyncratic, becomes only a variant of a prior conception of composition and camera placement. At the same time, certain aspects of a locale, such as lobbies or elevators in office buildings, are almost never shown. Although Ozu's domestic sets always had stairways built in for the sake of timing actors' movements, these were seldom presented on screen, so that it comes as a shock when *A Hen in the Wind* and *An Autumn Afternoon* make dramatic use of their staircases.

Objects within the set cooperated with the tendencies we have already examined. Ozu seldom called on the prop department at Shochiku, preferring instead to let actors and friends bring to the set the objects he wanted in the shot.[38] He spread cushions around the floor to break up the low horizontals of the tatami mats.[39] Looking through the viewfinder, he would dictate the exact position of cups, bottles, and other small props, asking his crew to move a glass three centimeters 'toward Tokyo'.[40] Even more remarkably, he would in the 1950s films vary the size of a prop according to camera distance. If he were filming a table in long shot, a large beer bottle would be visible at that shot scale. Then, in shooting a closer framing, Ozu would replace the bottle with a smaller one that would command a proportional amount of attention in that shot.[41] Such objects also introduce minute compositional variety within Ozu's locale-templates, which otherwise could seem oppressively uniform. One bar advertises Johnny Walker whisky, another features White Horse brand. One office includes a hat rack, while another contains a white ashtray (see figs. 25, 26). Where one home puts a sewing machine, another puts a chest of drawers.

As Atsuta became Ozu's *camera-ban*, his chief task involved overseeing lighting. Ozu insisted on a bright, hard-edged look to evoke the crisply defined images he had visualized in his notebooks. Even a film noir like *Dragnet Girl*, which is shot in a lower key than most of his works, remains generally committed to a high-key tonal scale. Occasional early films such as *Walk Cheerfully* employ Hollywood edge lighting to outline planes (fig. 27). More often, though, Ozu did not adopt the insistent edge lighting which puts an extra stress on the actor, pulling him or her forward from a vague background (fig. 28); Ozu integrates the actor into the overall shot design, as one plane among many (fig. 29). Similarly, where most American directors and many Japanese directors would dim the background light levels to throw still more emphasis on the performer, Ozu steps them up, lighting the background and foreground uniformly. This allows the setting and objects to claim a visual importance comparable to that assigned to the actor. For the same reason, actor-oriented enhancements like filters and diffusion devices were of little use to Ozu. Even after 1932, when Japanese studios changed from arc lamps and orthochromatic film to tungsten lamps and panchromatic stock, his images did not become particularly soft. After the war, with *A Hen in the Wind*, Ozu resumes the use of arc lighting, and the brilliant blacks and whites of subsequent films exploit the range of effects which this (and perhaps faster film stocks) could achieve.

26. *An Autumn Afternoon*

The constraints operating in camera position, set design, and lighting can be seen in the realm of color as well. For his color films, Ozu insisted on controlling the hue of every object in the shot.[42] He could design shots involving many color schemes, but he favored neutral or pastel shades for floors and walls and bright, saturated colors for objects. In this way, a prop would stand out vividly. He was especially fond of red ('People who like red are either geniuses or madmen,' he told Atsuta[43]) and Shimogawara kept a special reserve of red matchboxes, cups, teakettles, and other props.[44] In these films, Ozu will occasionally edge-light not the human figures but the colored objects, making them still more prominent. Color is for him a purely pictorial factor, a compositional resource to be explored through careful observation. 'There are about ten different shades of red,' he told an interviewer. 'When you look at this beer bottle [where did this interview take place?], you can see the different shades and hues of color in its various parts.'[45] Lighting would have to bring these out. Eventually, Ozu claimed, he hoped to use all ten varieties of red as distinct colors.[46] Ozu once quoted a sutra, 'Form is nothing but emptiness and emptiness is nothing but form,' and pointed out that the Sanskrit word for 'form' is the same as the Chinese character for 'color'. In a typically deflating move, he added punningly that the priest who devised the sutra may have 'taken color' – that is, gotten sexually aroused.[47] Like narration generally, color could be the object of rigorous inquiry conducted in a playful frame of mind.

27. *Walk Cheerfully*

Since at least the second decade of the century, a central convention of narrative cinema has been that the film's fabula, or story action, will highlight the human being as a causal agent. In watching a narrative film, we watch people, or at least people-like entities, and our expectations are geared to their behavior and its changes. Ozu's problem of 'homogenizing' the image, of elevating it to a level of intrinsic interest, is thus posed most acutely with respect to actors. Directors who want pictorial qualities to dominate the drama face the need to define a distinctive performance style. Like Tati and Bresson, Ozu cultivated a 'behaviorist' acting that confirmed the director's conception of the image. As a studio director, Ozu could imagine his shots peopled by stars under contract. Roles were written with particular players in mind. During filming, Ozu would deploy the actors within all the technical coordinates that the shot's visual design required. First the shot would be set up, with doubles used to arrange composition and lighting. Then actors would replace the doubles, and Ozu would look through the camera to decide the exact framing. The lighting would be established exactly; once it was set, it would not change, and the actor's position would be adjusted in relation to it. Then Ozu would turn the lights off so that he could rehearse the actors in

28. *Rosita* (Lubitsch, 1923)

29. *End of Summer*

comfort. When he was satisfied with the performance, the lights were switched back on and the shot was taken.[48] Ryu puts it well: the director 'fixed each actor into each shot.'[49]

The performer was thus subordinated to all the factors of composition already considered, most obviously framing. The actor is never seen in extreme close-up; hands or feet may be visible in close-up, chiefly in the silent films; but most actions are observed in medium shot, medium long shot, or long shot. When the camera tracks to follow an actor, that movement will retain the stable balance of a static composition. During the 1930s, Ozu drove Atsuta to tears by compelling the actors and technicians to count their steps during a tracking shot, forcing them to move at exactly the pace set by the camera.[50]

30. *Late Spring*

Ozu locks the actor into the compositional design in another important way. The widespread convention of reframing – that is, slightly panning the camera to keep a moving figure in the frame – implicitly acknowledges the saliency of the human agent: the composition will acquiesce to the actor. In all of his refusals, Ozu is most absolute in this. After 1929, none of his surviving films contains a single reframing – an extraordinary insistence on the shot as rigid picture. Yet as Sato indicates, this poses new problems. If the camera does not reframe figures, they will soon move out of the central strip of screen space. Ozu overcomes this difficulty in several ways. If a character stands up or starts to leave the frame in the course of a scene, Ozu will cut to another shot that includes the actor in a wider composition. He will sometimes move his actors along diagonals, or will track to keep them centered. In the late films, as Sato notes, he will use walls, screens, or doors to block off the sides of the frame so that people walk into a central depth or, if they move laterally to the camera, their action remains enclosed within a central slot (fig. 30).[51] Ozu's 'neighborhood' films *Record of a Tenement Gentleman* and *Ohayo* furnish many examples of framing left-right movement from a distance down a street, through a doorway, or within the slits of eaves or clotheslines. Ozu thus restricts the actors' movements and concentrates the audience's attention upon a fairly predictable zone of screen space.

31. *The Only Son*

There are still more unusual ways that the actor is tamed by the frame. Ozu was well-known for his *sojikei*, or 'similar-figure', compositions. He arranges two actors so that in posture, placement, or orientation they became compositionally analogous. Sato finds the earliest perfecting of the *sojekei* technique near the end of *The Only Son*, when Ryosuke and his wife slump down in comparable poses (fig. 31).[52] Clearly, however, this technique has its roots in earlier comedies. The sandal-fight in *I Was Born, But . . .* extracts visual humor from the way that the framing brings out the perfect coincidence of two actions (fig. 32). This climaxes when the sons, now reconciled to their father, eat in unison with him (fig. 58, p.227). All the earliest films betray the former soldier's interest in orchestrated movement – students drilling, gangsters strutting or dancing – that constitutes a kind of *sojikei* in time. This 'acting in unison' is a unique feature of Ozu's performance style and still further subordinates the individual to the frame's overall spatial or temporal rhythm. The effect can be poignant, as in a shot from *Early Summer*, which is typical of the late films in showing two characters, backs three-quarters to us; here hoops

32. *I Was Born, But . . .*

84

echo their bodies' shapes (fig. 33). An exquisite moment in *End of Summer* presents two sisters slowly squatting by the river, moving in perfect synchronization. They talk, and when they are done, they effortlessly unfold themselves to full length again, still moving in identical ways. Or acting in unison may retain its comic effects. A very funny *sojikei* composition in *Floating Weeds* presents a lascivious actor put in his place by the doughty barberwoman. In *Late Autumn*, the men who have gotten pipes from their dream woman mock the one who lost out by scratching their noses (fig. 34).

33. *Early Summer*

Even this degree of subordination was not enough for Ozu. Dialogue had to be recited exactly as written, and Ozu would insist on many repetitions to remove excess emotion. He saw as part of his task the restraining of feeling. 'Get rid of all the dramatics and show a sad character; without using drama, make the audience feel the emotion.'[53] He praised Bette Davis' impassive scene with her dying husband in *The Little Foxes*: 'No facial expression or anything – just making tea without any emotion. The only thing you can hear is the click of the cup and the saucer.'[54] Another scene roused him to exclaim: 'Look at Henry Fonda [leaning propped up in his chair] in *My Darling Clementine*: motionless and expressionless – there is the greatness of John Ford.'[55] Ozu's directing thus ruled out empathetic interpretation: the actor became a repository of pictorial behaviors. 'You are not supposed to feel, you are supposed to do.'[56] Ozu strove to make the images fulfill the film he had envisioned. 'He had made up the complete picture in his head before he went on the set, so that all we actors had to do was follow his directions, from the way we lifted and dropped our arms to the way we blinked our eyes.'[57] The same rigor lies behind his control of movement. Ozu instructed his actors in exact gaits and gestures. He liked to measure out the precise number of steps a character would take in passing from room to room, even if the movement itself would be offscreen.[58] Actors' movements could thus become motifs across the film. *Record of a Tenement Gentleman* depends on two specific behaviors: the boy's lice-induced wriggling of his shoulders, and Otane's wiping of his nose – both of which become linked to her growing concern for him. *Passing Fancy* makes complex use of a carefully narrowed range of hand gestures (pp. 250–1). The late films restrict such movements so much that the ones that remain have a striking purity – a man slowly raising a glass, a wife tapping her fingers as she listens to kabuki over the radio, or a young woman covering her face as she bursts into tears.

34. *Late Autumn*

Imamura quit as Ozu's assistant director because he believed that the master made his actors into puppets,[59] but there are other ways to regard the style. Sato feels that the lack of naturalness in Ozu's acting creates a ceremonial quality.[60] Ryu has gone on record that Ozu's behaviorist approach taught him to become 'an empty page' – which then allowed him to develop into the actor he now is.[61] In my opinion, Ozu was no less an 'actor's director' than Cukor or Bergman. Who would dare ask for better performances than we get in *Tokyo Story* or *I Was Born, But . . .* or *Passing Fancy*? Ozu made his actors subordinate themselves to a larger, predetermined aesthetic system, but within that system they could achieve nuances which a less rigorous context could not sustain.

In taking the material shot as his building block, organizing all techniques

35. *Marching On*

36. *Marching On*

37. *Marching On*

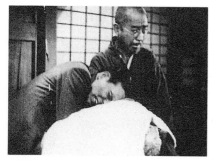

38. *Marching On*

around a camera position that conferred an external, non-human vantage point on the action, and subordinating actual locales and bodies to severe principles of balance, symmetry, line, and tonality, Ozu creates a pictorial cinema. But is it, we can now ask, a *flat* cinema? Do all these design factors rob the image of depth, making it seem all the more an abstraction? It is tempting to think so. Noël Burch has suggested that Japanese cinema of the 1930s sought to achieve the 'flatness' of traditional pictorial art, and that Ozu is particularly successful in this: 'Ozu uses every technique at his disposal *to produce the filmic image as picture plane.*'[62] But the issue is more complex.

Pictorial depth is not a single property but an emergent quality that may be present in different ways and degrees. A sense of depth is created by depth *cues* – figure/ground relations, placement of elements in the picture format, tonality and color, linear perspective, overlapping contours, atmospheric perspective, lighting effects, texture differences, assumptions of familiar size, and other factors. A very 'flat' image will still contain at least some depth cues, minimally the figure/ground difference. A very 'deep' image will utilize several cues. So we have to consider not only 'how deep' the image is but what cues are employed to suggest depth. The problem can be more precisely situated in relation to the 'rhetorical flourishes' canonized by the filmmaking norms of 1930s cinema.

To achieve greater expressivity or ornamentation, the ordinary Japanese filmmaker was expected to find technical devices which would momentarily intensify or interrupt syuzhet continuity. *Contra* Burch, one means of achieving this was to stage scenes in much greater depth than would the director's Western counterpart. Architecture would be used to create distinct layers of space, with significant material tucked in various planes. The eye is thus led on a zigzag path, on that 'wanton kind of chase' which Hogarth identified with pleasure in decorative art.[63] Compositions could be quite densely packed, permitting the eye to roam and rummage. Depth was also evoked through a play with focus, either by leaving significant elements in foreground or background out of focus or by racking focus from one element to another. Depth could be articulated through figure movement, and the Japanese were masterful in using small shifts of figure position to create arresting compositions. By the end of the 1920s, Japanese directors were also utilizing wide-angle lenses far more frequently than their Western peers, and for two chief purposes: to exaggerate depth and to distort geometrical shapes and the human body.

A handy summary of several typical tactics of the period occurs in Kiyohiko Ushihara's *Shingun* (*Marching On*, 1930). The son must go to war, and he and his mother start to weep; a wide-angle view vigorously distorts them (fig. 35). As they embrace, cut to a new angle that puts the father in sharp focus in the foreground (fig. 36). After another shot of mother and son, followed by a dialogue title, cut about 180 degrees to a shot that not only puts the father in the distance but reveals how the wide-angle lens can pack the frame quite tightly (fig. 37). Ushihara now exploits slight figure movement: the mother bends over, then the son does, and the father turns a little and raises his head (fig. 38). Fade out. This is hardly a cinema of 'flatness'. Depth is cued in many ways – probably more than in the American cinema of the time – and is used to enhance emotional qualities or to attract the eye as a self-consciously decorative value.

Put in this context, Ozu is revealed as once more refusing a great many options, picking a few that can be explored in rich detail, and organizing them homogeneously. Certainly many shots 'look flat' by virtue of some frontal positioning of figures or objects, the absence of perspectival recession, and a uniformity of tonalities in figure and background. The low camera height, when it minimizes both floor and ceiling, can cut objects free of their support, making them appear to be solids hanging in a vacuum. Still, there are always other depth cues present, such as overlap or familiar size. Tonalities also create depth, especially in the color films, where dark values advance against light backgrounds, and warm, concentrated accents stand out against cooler shades. On the whole, Ozu presents a space of considerable depth.

A major source of Ozu's depth is a reliance on perspective principles. Long shots of exteriors will emphasize the diagonals of streets, buildings, and tree lines (fig. 39). In large interiors, such as temples, Ozu will arrange pillars and persons so as to present strong recessional planes (figs. 40, 41). Corridors and aisles display sharp perspective (fig. 42). In Atsuta's shooting notes on *Late Autumn* we find: 'Attention was paid to creating a three-dimensional effect in the scenes in Japanese rooms.'[64] The set designer Shimogawara pointed out that Ozu's camera position is well-suited to bring depth into Japanese architecture.[65] He is fond of a 'picket-fence' effect which can reduce objects or people to a row of geometrically receding slats (fig. 43). In closer views of people, the low height creates vivid middle grounds, in which the

39. *Record of a Tenement Gentleman*

40. *Late Autumn*

41. *Brothers and Sisters of the Toda Family*

42. *The Munekata Sisters*

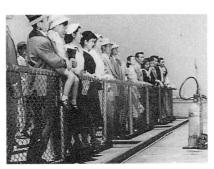

43. *The Flavor of Green Tea over Rice*

44. *A Hen in the Wind*

45. *What Did the Lady Forget?*

46. *I Flunked, But . . .*

47. *I Flunked, But . . .*

closer element tends to be higher in the format than is the more distant element (fig. 44). One must look very hard to find a shot in which Ozu frames a character against a perpendicular surface. It is thus not surprising that Ozu was very taken with *Citizen Kane* and admired the ability of 'deep focus' to make the audience notice objects.[66] Of course, his is a more balanced and spacious depth than that of Welles – or of his Japanese contemporaries, for that matter. Shots like figs. 43 and 44 decline the chance to create looming foregrounds like those in *Marching On*.

For closer views of people and objects, Ozu frequently employs cinema's equivalent of atmospheric perspective, selective focus. This was, as we have seen, a wider convention of the Japanese cinema of his day. Once more, though, Ozu's handling is selective and purifying. He will sometimes put foreground objects in focus while leaving distant characters blurred (fig. 45). He goes still further and uses *degrees* of focus as a depth cue. That is, the space of certain shots is presented as measurably deep insofar as objects gradually recede from a sharply focused foreground. An early and simple example occurs in *I Flunked, But . . .*, when the students see their buddies on the curb and run into the distance, getting steadily more diffuse (figs. 46, 47). This effect owes a good deal to Ozu's refusal to dim the lighting on background planes: slight differences in clarity are enhanced by even illumination. Thus in a sunny open space, such as the urban prairie of *Inn in Tokyo*, Ozu can control the precise degree to which each plane 'falls off' (fig. 48). This is a layered space not unlike the planes created by the receding shoji of domestic architecture. Ozu's use of 'gradual' depth continues throughout his career, as in the wedding banquet and bar signs of *Equinox Flower* (figs. 49, 50).

These are Ozu's major depth cues. What do they add up to? The prevalence of depth factors makes Ozu's shots not exclusively or particularly 'flat', but they do stand out as *self-conscious* images. If these shots seem to lack depth, that is simply because they *look like pictures* – landscape photographs, still-life paintings, and portraits. The shots are so intricately composed, so much the result of idiosyncratic, purely pictorial artifices like the low camera position or 'picket-fence' linearity or *sojikei* arrangements, that they achieve an autonomous splendor that becomes the culmination of Ozu's search for a cinema of the absolute image. The issue is not a matter of depth or flatness but rather a question of how both are used in a process that confines the pictorial system to certain elements and precise visual dynamics.

Decentered Circles

Ozu's visual strategies have two principal consequences. By and large they make for a high degree of 'legibility' within each shot. Arranged in simple metric patterns and based in such well-known pictorial principles as symmetry, balance, clarity, and perspectival depth, these images simplify the viewer's task. At the same time, the reduction of stylistic choices provides a ground for a freer pattern-making. Once these visual strategies are established as the film's intrinsic norms, they can either be minutely varied or can serve as neutral supports for more vivid devices. Before we consider how this happens, though, we need to extend our analysis of Ozu's style to the level of inter-shot relations.

As a Shochiku director, he worked firmly within the conventions of the 'piecemeal' approach to découpage. Early in his career, his *Life of an Office Worker* was praised for its opening montage of the hero's daily routine; brief shots of the family's morning exercises were apparently linked through flowing dissolves.[67] Several of Ozu's films, both silent and sound, contain over a thousand shots. Between 1935 and 1942, Mizoguchi's films range from an average shot length of sixteen seconds to ninety seconds, but Ozu's range from nine to fifteen seconds. (See Appendix.) Gosho is sometimes considered the fastest cutter in the classic Japanese cinema, but Ozu is often on par: compare *L'Amour* (1933: 5 seconds ASL) with *Passing Fancy* (1933: 4 seconds ASL), or *Entotsu no mieru basho* (*Where Chimneys Are Seen*, 1953: 10 seconds ASL) with *Tokyo Story* (1953: 10.2 seconds ASL). Although Ozu's shots grew somewhat longer when he converted to sound, he disliked long takes, complaining that Shochiku hurried him in making *Toda Family* so that 'I couldn't avoid shooting lengthy shots.'[68] After this film, his takes got steadily shorter; his last six films, despite their impression of tranquil immobility, change shots, on the average, every seven seconds. This director of the image was no less a director of the cut.

And, of course, of *controlled* cuts. Ozu approached editing as he approached the shot, using the conventions of Western cinema as a pool of elements that could be selected and recombined. Whereas most of his Japanese contemporaries cultivated a decorative, eclectic classicism, Ozu limited his editing alternatives to a few simple but profound choices. He accepted the need for the unified sequence, establishing and reestablishing shots, shot/reverse-shot cutting, matches on action, and other devices of continuity editing; but he found his own equivalents for them. He then took the crucial step of making these equivalents *more systematic* than the originals (and thus achieved an organization seldom found in his contemporaries). He then filtered these equivalents through his idiosyncratic rules of shot composition. Thus 'processed', Ozu's editing procedures are at once 'legible' (being functional equivalents for the procedures of ordinary cinema) and eccentric (being arbitrarily systematic in all manner of details). Ozu granted the validity of Western and Japanese editing conventions as macrostructural organizational principles, but he deflected them through particular 'unreasonable' devices. He revised classical découpage not by rejecting it but by decentering it.

Like any classical filmmaker, Ozu assumes that at the level of editing, a movie consists of sequences of shots, and that each sequence's internal organization conforms to the needs of the syuzhet. In classical filmmaking practice, there are, roughly speaking, three types of sequence: scenes, summaries (such as 'montage sequences'), and transitions. Already we can see Ozu's 'decentering': he uses scenes, does not use summaries, and puts extraordinary emphasis upon transitions. Let us look first at the editing strategies used in constructing dramatic scenes, and take up transitions in the next section.

Cast in simple functional outline, the Ozu scene as a syuzhet unit looks like this:

1. Identification of the locale of the action.

48. *An Inn in Tokyo*

49. *Equinox Flower*

50. *Equinox Flower*

2. Identification of the characters involved in the action.

3. Interaction of the characters, to some point of conclusion.

The functions of phase 1 may be fulfilled through many types of shots. Ozu may begin with 'placing' shots of signs or the exterior of a building, or he may start with a detail – a corner, a hallway, a set of objects – that indicates (more or less precisely) where we are. These are exactly the options open to a classical Hollywood director.[69] Once the locale has been even minimally identified, the sequence goes on, as in the Hollywood film, to identify what characters will participate in the scene. There may be an establishing shot of several persons, or a shot showing a character coming to interact with another. In any event, the second phase of the scene assembles the participants in a definite space. The scene proceeds to trace their interaction, usually through a series of shots isolating each individual speaking his or her lines. Typically, Ozu conveys a dialogue exchange by means of alternating shots of speakers, but in his 'longer take' films of the war period dialogue may be carried in a shot containing two or more characters. Again, these options conform wholly to mainstream principles. In the course of the action, the editing may provide a new establishing shot, or cut to another character entering the locus of action, or follow one character leaving the space, or cut away to objects adjacent to the action. The scene will characteristically conclude on a *portion* of the total space we have seen, a character or an object or a locale.[70] Here again Ozu is in conformity with classical practice.[71] Ozu's scene is comprehensible to viewers because at a basic level it is patterned to fulfill the same narrative functions as the scene of orthodox cinema. His initial revision of classical découpage now comes at the level of devices. Just as the choice of a low camera height was a simple stroke that implied very wide-ranging changes in the image, another 'unreasonable' decision governs staging and framing of the action for cutting.

The classical Hollywood cinema canonized the rule of the '180-degree line' or 'axis of action'. This assumed that characters could be arranged so as to face one another and that various shots of their interactions would be taken from camera positions on one side of that axis. A long shot might show Phil on the left and Mary Ann on the right. A closer view of Phil would show him looking right, at Mary Ann offscreen; the corresponding 'reverse shot' of her would show her looking off left. The camera's location is always determined by the 180-degree arc of possible positions it could assume on the 'correct' side of the line. The sources of the axis-of-action system run deep into Western traditions of theatre and visual art.

It is easy to see that Ozu typically does not obey these precepts. Here, from *Story of Floating Weeds*, is one example out of hundreds:

1. (ls) Kihachi and Otsune seated and talking (fig. 51).
2. Dialogue title.
3. (ms) Kihachi, looking right (fig. 52).
4. Dialogue title.
5. (ms) Otsune, looking right (fig. 53).
6. Dialogue title.
7. (ms) as 3. Kihachi, looking right (fig. 54).
8. (ls) The two of them. She rises to fetch more *sake* (fig. 55).

51. *Story of Floating Weeds*

52. *Story of Floating Weeds*

53. *Story of Floating Weeds*

54. *Story of Floating Weeds*

55. *Story of Floating Weeds*

After shot 3, each cut violates the 180-degree principle, putting the camera 'on the other side' of the axis. The cuts create 'false' eyeline matches, since the glances do not cross one another but suggest that both persons are looking off right at a common object. The final shot reestablishes the two, but views them from the side opposite to that from which shot 1 is taken. Japanese critics call these cuts *donden*, or 'sudden reverse' cuts.[72]

What are we to make of them? Noël Burch treats them as powerfully disruptive. He asserts that each 'bad' cut:

> produces a 'jolt' in the editing flow, a moment of confusion in the spectator's sense of orientation to diegetic space, requiring a moment's readjustment. The resulting effect of hiatus emphasizes the disjunctive nature of the shot-change, which the developed 'editing rules' had perceptually obliterated.[73]

But it is not self-evident that there is a jolt at each cut. Do empirical, 'naive' spectators perceive one? In my experience, they do not, unless it is pointed out. Furthermore, how many jolts will it take before the spectator ignores these violations on the assumption that this movie just does not obey the 180-degree rule? Moreover, comprehension of the scene's action is not thwarted: the establishing shot, the norm of alternating shots of characters, and the common-sense assumption that Kihachi and Otsune are looking at each other guide the spectator in constructing the space.

According to Burch, Ozu also challenges the notion of the viewer as

91

invisible observer, a 'transparent relay in the communion of two characters.'[74] 'Once the spectator is unconsciously obliged to rectify with each new shot change his mental position with respect to the players, the trap of participation no longer functions in the same way.'[75] Here Burch takes one of Hollywood's rationales for the 180-degree system as an adequate description of how the system actually works. But the invisible observer will not do as a theory of how a film seeks to 'involve' the spectator, not even if the concept is dressed up as 'suture' theory. Our construction of a film's space involves a great many perceptual and cognitive activities that cannot be reduced to the invisible-observer account.[76]

Finally, Burch claims that the violations of the 180-degree system cooperate with a 'flattening' of the image, since in normal cinema crossing eyelines are 'necessary complements of the receding and converging parallels of deep space'.[77] Since, as we have seen, Ozu's shots in fact contain many orthogonals of this sort, this explanation topples too.

Note that Burch's account is both atomistic and negative. It concentrates only on the moment of the cut, and it sees it purely as a violation, a 'challenge' to continuity. But if we look at how the series of shots constructs the total spatial context through the patterning of shot scale, angle, and staging of movement and figure position, we find that Ozu presents a *positive* system of his own, one with many stabilizing features. Ozu does not attack or criticize the continuity rules; he transforms them into something which becomes part of his film's intrinsic norm.

Ozu conceives each scene's site of narrative action as a 360-degree space, a set of circles, as opposed to Hollywood's single half-circle. In the simplest case, a character occupies the central point and the camera films from some point on the circumference. In order to constrain his choices, Ozu puts the camera only at certain positions on the circle. Once he has defined a camera orientation, say in long shot, he will film the next shot from the same angle *or* from an angle at some multiple of 45 degrees to the prior one. The abstract geometry of the system looks like this:

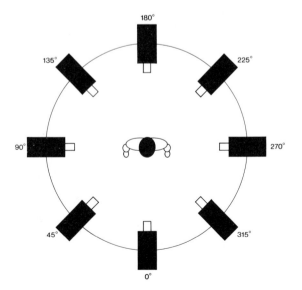

Diagram 1

Almost any scene would illustrate Ozu's tactics. Our example from *Story of Floating Weeds* presents a 180-degree shift between shot 7 and shot 8, with the camera facing exactly 180 degrees opposite to its previous view of Kihachi. A 90-degree shift can be seen in *Passing Fancy*: as Harue hands Kihachi a tray (fig. 56), Ozu cuts 'counterclockwise' to the two of them (fig. 57). In *End of Summer*, a cut shifts 135 degrees rightward (figs. 58, 59). It is significant that Ozu can use the 360-degree system when cutting into or out of the space: it can link long shots and closer views. This makes Ozu's space constitute a set of concentric rings around a character. Sometimes, however, Ozu will maintain the same camera distance across the shot, creating a marked 'flipover' of the composition (figs. 60, 61). Moreover, the most common shifts are cuts of zero or 180 degrees; 90- and 135-degree cuts are less frequent, whereas Ozu almost never cuts only 45 degrees in relation to the previous shot.

The rule of the circle gets extended when Ozu puts two or more characters together in the scene. Sometimes the characters are set side by side. Then Ozu treats them as if they constituted the center of a circle that he could flank according to his usual principles – head-on, 180-degree reverse, or multiples of 45 degrees. (See figs. 62, 63.) At other times, side-by-side figures are filmed from 'in between' them, as if each were the center of a single circle. Often this creates a flagrantly 'impossible' view, since the characters are more close to one another in the long view than the closer shots reveal them to be (figs. 64–66).

When characters are turned toward one another, Ozu creates a complex illusion. The impression is that they face one another, and that they are filmed

56. *Passing Fancy*

57. *Passing Fancy*

58. *End of Summer*

59. *End of Summer*

60. *Late Autumn*

61. *Late Autumn*

62. *The Flavor of Green Tea over Rice*

63. *The Flavor of Green Tea over Rice*

64. *Late Spring*

65. *Late Spring*

66. *Late Spring*

from points along a perpendicular axis that connects them (diagram 2). This would be the effect of filming 'on the line' of Hollywood's 180-degree system. In fact, however, Ozu has staged the action quite differently. He places the actors in an angular relation to one another, according to two options. Sometimes the figures are placed at right angles (diagram 3). More often, they face one another but *en décalage* (diagram 4). Although I am not aware that any Japanese critic has named this latter alternative, I shall call it the 'staggered' or *sujikai* ('diagonal') option, as a parallel to Ozu's *sojikei*, or 'similar-figures' staging. In either case, Ozu then films the arrangement in his customary way. That is, each figure is treated as the heart of a complete circle, capable of being filmed from angles that change in 45-degree multiples.

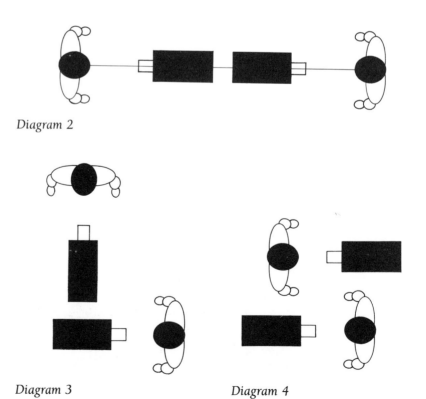

Diagram 2

Diagram 3   *Diagram 4*

94

When shooting a right-angled arrangement, Ozu can create 90-degree shifts, as indicated in diagram 3; when filming a *sujikai* arrangement, he can shift the camera position 180 degrees for reverse shots. In both cases, the shot-change also involves a *lateral* displacement, something that does not happen when a solitary character is the object of the découpage. In either situation, the 360-degree filming space transforms the actual arrangement of the actors: the shots on the screen usually give the impression of a direct confrontation of two characters who are not in fact *en face*. What makes the *sujikai* variant particularly cunning is that the establishing shot is often at an oblique angle and from a considerable distance, so that one cannot easily tell that the characters are not really opposite one another. A look back at the first shot from the *Story of Floating Weeds* passage will show that the staggered staging becomes apparent only if one is looking for it. Unusually clear instances are in figs. 67–68.

Ozu pursued these staging procedures from a very early point in his career. *Walk Cheerfully* contains several attempts at them, but they are imprecise. When Kenji is arrested, for instance, he faces the police. They look to their left in their own medium shot (fig. 69), but the next shot puts him squarely to their right (fig. 70). In addition, the exact camera positions have not been decided – probably because Ozu had not yet hit upon a fully 360-degree shooting space. In *I Flunked, But . . .* and *Tokyo Chorus*, he uses the *sujikai* variant more frequently, and begins to employ true 180-degree shifts. By 1932, staggered staging is in full force (figs. 71,72) and it becomes an Ozu commonplace. In later films, Ozu will use hallways, bars, and other architectu-

67. *The Munekata Sisters*

68. *A Hen in the Wind*

69. *Walk Cheerfully*

70. *Walk Cheerfully*

71. *Where Now Are the Dreams of Youth?*

72. *Where Now Are the Dreams of Youth?*

ral structures to displace characters laterally (figs. 73, 74). The displaced staging cooperates with the 360-degree principle by creating overlapping circles of scenographic space.

It also explains some peculiar qualities of Ozu shot/reverse-shots. Throughout his work Ozu mixes 'correct' with 'incorrect' eyeline matches, although after 1932 the latter, such as those in our original *Story of Floating Weeds* example, predominate (figs. 51–55). Again, however, we must see these not as simply random snipings at an oppressive Western découpage but rather as part of an internally coherent alternative system. As usual, Ozu was fully aware of his stylistic choices. When his editor Yoshiyasu Hamamura criticized Ozu's mismatched eyelines, Ozu would reply, 'But it's all the same, isn't it? It doesn't make any difference, does it?'[78] That is, I take it, the audience is not disoriented and always knows who is looking at whom. There *is*, however, a difference from Western practice. Ozu's staging options let him create not only violations of the 180-degree line but, more positively, a fresh approach to shot/reverse-shot cutting. To appreciate this we must separate out three distinct cues that most directors do not distinguish but which Ozu's nuanced range of choices lets him discriminate in fine detail: cues of *glance*, cues of *head position*, and cues of *bodily orientation*.

With respect to these, Ozu once more offers himself only two options. (1) He may stagger the staging and film a character's body and head almost exactly straight on (figs. 75, 76). (See also diagram 4.) The eyeline may then be straight on (but it will still not be directed at the viewer, since the low camera height assures that the glance passes over the top of the camera).

73. *Equinox Flower*

74. *Equinox Flower*

75. *Tokyo Twilight*

76. *Tokyo Twilight*

77. *I Was Born, But . . .*

78. *I Was Born, But . . .*

79. *The Lady and the Beard*

80. *The Lady and the Beard*

81. *The Lady and the Beard*

More often, the eyelines will fall at least slightly to the right or left of the lens axis (figs. 77, 78).[79]

(2) Ozu may instead use the staggered staging to justify an angled placement of the figure. In the silent films, the head and body may have the same off-centered orientation as the eyes, and the angle of the filming may bring this out, as in the *Story of Floating Weeds* specimen. This option can occasionally be found in later works. Almost from the start of his career, however, Ozu also exploits a slight *contrapposto* or 'torquing' of the figure that turns the eyes at one angle, the face at another, and the torso at yet another. A good early example is found in *The Lady and the Beard*. In the establishing shot, a typical staggered staging sets the mother's and daughter's bodies in opposite directions (fig. 79). But the heads are turned sharply up to each character's left (fig. 80). And yet the mother's eyeline goes off still farther to her left, while the daughter's is angled slightly to her right (fig. 81). This makes each character's glance far more sidelong than in Western cinema.

A brief passage from *Early Spring* conveniently pulls together all the aspects of 360-degree space I have been trying to bring out. Shoji 'confronts' his wife in a right-angled seating arrangement shown in establishing shot (fig. 82). Ozu cuts 180 degrees and in to him (fig. 83). His body points sharply to the left, his eyes are directed sharply to the right. Cut 180 degrees and laterally to Masako (fig. 84). Her body, face, and eyes are configured exactly as his are. Another *donden* cut brings us to a reestablishing shot (fig. 85) that is precisely 180 degrees to the previous setup and to the initial establishing shot. The logic is the same as that in *Story of Floating Weeds*,

82. *Early Spring*

83. *Early Spring*

84. *Passing Fancy*

85. *Early Spring*

made twenty years before, but the character position and cues of orientation are more nuanced.

So much, then, for Ozu's 'frontality'. Whenever we use this term we must distinguish among frontality of body, of face, and of eye position. Ozu's 'torqued' figures are present from the early 1930s, as are more straight-on framings of face and body. Both options continue through his career, with one more common in a film or phase than another; but neither is ever given up entirely. What is important is how Ozu's 360-degree space redefines and refines the problem of staging and filming character interaction.

One main purpose of these rigorous staging, shooting, and editing techniques is not scenographic but graphic. Ozu's shot/reverse-shot cuts create 'graphic matches' of figure position from shot to shot. Nearly all the examples we have considered illustrate how uncanny is the effect when the 360-degree space, the staggered staging, the straight-on or torqued figure, and the sidelong eyelines are continued across the cut: two different figures look startlingly similar. Shoulders and elbows in the foreground can add still other elements of graphic continuity. A brilliant instance is that in *Passing Fancy*, where the *sujikai* staging is confirmed by Jiro's grabbing Harue's left wrist with his left hand; Ozu then cuts 'across the line' so that the two figures match

86. *Passing Fancy*

perfectly (figs. 86, 87). Ozu instructed his cameraman to film medium shots of different-sized characters from different distances, so that the figures would be the same size in each shot.[80] 'Ozu's essential goal,' Atsuta recalls, 'was that successive shots showing two characters looking at one another should have an identical visual value: the same configuration of the body. The cut was based not on contrast but on similarity.'[81] Even the eyes had to be in exactly the same position from shot to shot, as most of my illustrations confirm. In Ozu's stylistic development, the desire for graphic matching came first. It is strongly present in his very first surviving film, *Days of Youth* (see pp. 190–191), and it persists in such shots as figs. 52–54, 71–72 and 79–85 on pp. 91, 95 and 97 above. It seems likely that *donden* cutting and off-center staging were devised to allow him opportunities to create an extraordinary graphic continuity from shot to shot. Once more we encounter the primacy of the pictorial and the urge to homogenize all shots, to make them equivalent visual units.

87. *Passing Fancy*

As if all these spatial constraints were not enough, Ozu also sets limits on the timing of the cut. To the metric editing that is most prominent in introducing a scene there corresponds a strict regulation of cuts during the scene. Again, he revises and transforms extrinsic norms by selecting only a particular option and exploiting its unexpected range.

For shot/reverse-shot dialogue exchanges, classical Hollywood cinema had standardized its own fairly narrow range of editing choices. One could cut before a character finished speaking a line or after it was spoken. The preferred 'dialogue cutting point' was to cut to the listener just before the last syllable or two of the speaker's line. This allowed the spectator to anticipate the listener's reaction to the line, while also supposedly distracting attention from the shot-change.[82] In a 1934 interview Ozu is sensitive to the fact that the timing of sound film editing had to vary from that of silent cinema. In the silent film, he claims, the actor had to display an emotion visually, which would then be interrupted by the title's specification of it: in a sense, the shot prepared for the information to be delivered in the title. But in the talkies, the actor delivers the line 'first', and the emotional effect of it emerges afterward. Time is required to absorb the full impact of the words.[83] Ozu had to break his actors of the habit of conversing too quickly; he forced them to pause for a measured interval between lines.[84] For the spectator, the dialogue pause becomes another cue for the rhythmic regularity of the découpage. If the speaker pauses and there is no cut, the speaker will continue. If there is a cut, another character is sure to reply or respond in some way. In either case, neither a character nor the narration will interrupt the speaker for the sake of 'picking up the pace'. The shot is an integral visual-verbal block.

88. *Early Spring*

But Ozu will interrupt character *movement*, especially if it threatens to disrupt the stability of the image. More often than even the Hollywood director, he continues physical action across a cut. His films contain perhaps the most consistently perfect matches on action the cinema has ever seen. He mastered the technique very early, as the skiing scenes of *Days of Youth* show. In the post-*Late Spring* films, when a person starts to stand up, the narration is almost sure to prompt a cut to a more distant view that continues the action. He will match not only principal gestures but subsidiary ones. He can match action in the center of the frame or on the edges of it. Significantly, Ozu's action cuts are smooth even if the shots constitute 180-degree reversals. In *Early Spring*, Masako flings out Shoji's shirt in an incredibly flashy match, a *donden* cut (figs. 88, 89) which keeps the framing scale almost identical from shot to shot. Indeed, so prevalent and powerful are these matches that they become a major source of the legibility of dramatic space. Contrary to Hollywood precept, which would discourage across-the-line action-matching, Ozu's movement cuts frequently tone down the radical shifts created by the 360-degree spatial system. At other times, as when characters seem to walk into themselves, the match on action can call attention to a flipped-over composition. This is especially the case if the character's screen position does not coincide in the two shots (figs. 90, 91). But even here, the cuts to an opposite view are not denotatively confusing, since they are likely instantiations of the film's intrinsic découpage norm.

89. *Early Spring*

The internal predictability of Ozu's découpage obviously makes the films highly 'legible', even if they are eccentric with respect to extrinsic norms. We can close our consideration of Ozu's scenes by looking at some other procedures that assure the stability of the represented space.

90. *The Munekata Sisters*

Most generally, there is the fact that most of Ozu's locales are prototypical – homes, inns, offices, classrooms, and so on. Because of the remarkable uniformity of Japanese building practices, the viewer is likely to have a fairly good 'cognitive map' of the space. In addition, Ozu's use of 'template' locales across his films allow the experienced viewer to hypothesize that the layout of space in this setting will be a variant upon that seen in another film. More specifically, Ozu took care to make his locales completely consistent. With his set designers he would draw a detailed map of an entire house, including areas that would never be filmed. Ozu would use this floorplan in plotting camera positions and working out the number of steps each actor would take during a scene.[85] He also took care to reorient the spectator to a locale by including

91. *The Munekata Sisters*

92. *Floating Weeds*

93. *Floating Weeds*

establishing and reestablishing shots and by repeating camera setups of a setting over the course of the film. Ozu understood that his spatial discontinuities could jar the viewer, and he took care to minimize the perceptual effort of 'mental rotation' required to comprehend them.[86]

Most particularly, Ozu's scenographic space is stabilized through principles of *contiguity*. He will often include in one shot at least a portion of space or an object seen in a previous shot. Although his rotational cutting often shifts backgrounds completely, the object or person at the center of the circle remains a point of reference. When Ozu gives us lateral shifts as well, some space usually overlaps on one edge of each shot.[87] He is fond of slicing up foreground elements in this way. A character's legs will often serve as pivots in a *donden* series (figs. 92, 93). Or objects on the table will overlap from shot to shot (figs. 94, 95). In the course of a scene from *An Autumn Afternoon*, various angles on Koichi use him as a fixed point to anchor a series of 90- and 135-degree shot changes (figs. 96–98). Such elements prevent the *donden* cuts from being too disruptive. Although the sudden switches of orientation might pose problems for the viewer's identification of the image, prominent landmarks probably minimize mental rotation time.[88] In the 1930s films, Ozu will use a background element, even if it is out of focus, to link spaces in a similar way (figs. 99, 100).

The centrality of contiguity indicates one more way in which Ozu creates stringent intrinsic norms. We can summarize his editing 'rules' in a simple outline:

94. *End of Summer*

95. *End of Summer*

96. *An Autumn Afternoon*

97. *An Autumn Afternoon*

98. *An Autumn Afternoon*

100

1. *When* is a cut permissible within the scene?
   When a character is about to leave the frame.
   When a character has completed an action (looking, speaking lines, etc.).
   When a shot has run a length that gives it an arithmetical relation to adjoining shots.

2. *How* to cut permissibly within the scene?
   Not by nondiegetic cutting.
   Least commonly by crosscutting between two locales.
   Most commonly by two principles:

   > *Pictorial similarity*: the graphic match.
   > Achieved through right-angled or staggered staging and frontal or 'torqued' figures; or through matches of setting.

   > *Spatial contiguity.*
   > Onscreen: part/whole spatial relations, presented through analytical cuts or 180-degree shifts. Comprehensible to the viewer by virtue of explicit enlargement/de-enlargement or angular shift with respect to the action.

   > Offscreen: part/part relations, linking space onscreen with space to the left, to the right, or 'behind the camera'. Comprehensible to the spectator by virtue of assumptions about this type of locale deriving from prior filmic or extrafilmic experience; assumptions about this specific locale as cued by earlier portions of the film; particular cues in this portion of the film (e.g. spatial 'anchors').

   > Contiguity will be presented as views that change angles either by 0 degrees or in multiples of 45 degrees:
   > Very seldom by a change of only 45 degrees from the prior shot.
   > More commonly by a change of 90 degrees or 135 degrees from the prior shot.
   > Most commonly by a change of 0 degrees or 180 degrees from the prior shot.

99. *Dragnet Girl*

100. *Dragnet Girl*

Rather than treating this scheme as an abstract, quasi-linguistic 'grammar' of options, we should see it as a functional 'default hierarchy', a tabulation of the tacit assumptions that come to govern the spectator's construction of space.[89]
It is now plain that all these staging and filming decisions exist not simply to 'violate' norms of story space but, more positively, to establish unique rules governing both scenographic and graphic space. In terms of the construction of story space, Ozu's system is as coherent as the classical Hollywood system but *more specified in detail*. He not only obeys certain principles but also enriches them through consistency and a deepening of small differences. But what of other Japanese directors of his formative period, the 1920s and 1930s? On the basis of studying almost a hundred pre-1940 Japanese films, I believe that both Hollywood's anatomy of a scene and its corresponding 180-degree system constituted extrinsic norms in Japanese film as well.[90] There are certainly more violations of the axis of action in Japanese cinema

than one finds in Hollywood (our *Marching On* example, figs. 35–38 above, contains two), but these are neither majority practice, nor pervasive, nor (with certain exceptions) systematic. Some directors will employ 'correct' shot/ reverse-shot but use a *donden* cut for a reestablishing shot. A few directors will employ an occasional graphic match during a shot/reverse-shot passage. Some directors will stage fairly frontally, with shot/reverse-shot over the camera. We must also remember that by 1932 Ozu was a very prominent director, and that he had considerable influence on other filmmakers. His pupils all applied his techniques sporadically in their own films, so that the Shochiku product of the period uses certain Ozuian devices in a diffuse, eclectic way. Certainly his innovations furnished resources for that local elaboration of the syuzhet that Chapter 2 has presented as typical of Japanese 'decorative classicism', but his rigorously patterned *system* was almost certainly unique.

Sidelong Spaces

Ozu's construction of a scene's space may be thought of as reinforcing certain overall features of his narrational process, particularly those involving the range and depth of knowledge and the degree of self-consciousness. That the camera can take up a position 'on the other side' of the axis of action pushes the narration toward omniscience, or rather what we may call 'omnipresence'.[91] The match on action often anticipates the filling of a space, as if the narration 'knew' when and how the character would move. The insistence upon flanking the action from the periphery of a circle is consistent with Ozu's overall emphasis on narrational objectivity and externality. The degree of frontality involved in bodily position, head angle, and eyeline puts the characters 'on display' for the audience to a greater degree than in the Hollywood system of modified frontality. What should be noted, though, is that Ozu's system remains more rigorously constrained than that promoted by the extrinsic norm. Although the camera can 'cover' 360 degrees, it will only take up a position defined as a multiple of 45 degrees. It will not supply extreme close-ups or steep low or high angles. The character will face only in certain directions. Ozu gives himself only two or three options and then refines them by distinguishing among component cues that normally go unnoticed.

A comparable attention to context, pattern, and narrational function reveals that Ozu's transitions between scenes also work toward rigorous and systematic intrinsic norms. In narrative cinema around the world, the distinction scene/transition is a fundamental protocol of construction and comprehension. A narrative film is presumed to consist of relatively self-contained dramatic episodes, or scenes, connected by transitional markers or passages. For the spectator, this premise operates as a 'default' value, resting in place unless explicitly countermanded. Upon this premise rests another one: scenes are more likely to be rendered using covert narration, while transitions are the privileged site of more overt narrational presence. The narration is expected to 'come forward' more explicitly when setting the scene and rounding it off; more often than not, the characters take charge of what happens in between. This is one reason that classical Hollywood films are not equally 'transparent' at all points.[92] Ozu's films, like those of other Japanese directors, recognize these normative assumptions, but once more he uses the canonized features of a strategy as a point of departure. On either side of each scene, he typically presents one or more shots that depict the scene's locale, or a locale that is in some proximity to the action. Up to a point such a schema helps unify the plot and guide the viewer. At a scene's close a 'still life' of an object can signal that the action is over or suggest that an object is significant causally, referentially, or thematically. The next shot may announce the new scene, establish the setting, or suggest the passage of time. As in Hollywood cinema, a sign may explicitly indicate the new locale. Any of the transitional shots may help create parallels or symmetries with previous scenes. Thus Ozu subscribes to the basic *format* of orthodox cinema. But this is only a base for his 'decentering' of the traditional device and its accepted functions.

Several particular tactics set Ozu's transitions apart. First, he uses an unusual number of transitional shots, sometimes six or more. This tends to give the transitional passages more weight than those in the works of his Western contemporaries. Even Japanese directors of the late 1920s and early 1930s, more disposed toward elaborate transitions than their American peers, seldom used more than one shot for this purpose. While increasing the number of shots, Ozu drastically reduces the number of purely photographic cues for a transition. Both Western and Japanese filmmakers codified 'punctuation' devices like dissolves and fades as extra cues for the ending or beginning of a scene. Ozu gave up dissolves some time between 1929 and 1930. 'The dissolve,' he cryptically remarked, 'is not an element of "film grammar" or whatever, but is simply an attribute of the camera.'[93] Elsewhere he called it 'camouflage', perhaps because it spoiled the clarity of the individual image.[94] He began to eliminate fades after 1930; *Tokyo Chorus* (1931) contains only two; the films from 1932 and 1933, none; *Story of Floating Weeds* (1934), two. In his first sound film, *The Only Son* (1936), half the scenes end with fades, but from *What Did the Lady Forget?* (1937) on, fades would be used only after the initial credit sequence and before the end title. With *Equinox Flower* (1958) even this 'bracketing' use of the fade ceases. The absence of such conventional punctuation thus makes the transitions still more individually striking.

In addition, Ozu's transitional shots are often not informative on causal or temporal grounds. Instead of showing us the building that houses the action, a shot may show a street corner nearby. Hence the term I shall use for these transitional images: 'intermediate spaces', those pieces of space that not only come between two scenes but also lie between two sites of dramatic activity. Furthermore, Ozu's transitions often seem 'inefficient' by both Japanese and Hollywood standards. For example, some shots may be superfluous with regard to the function of simply identifying the locale. Or a 'placing' shot may include not only a building but passers-by in the distance, often dressed in a bright red that makes us notice them. The shots' superfluity is especially evident when we return to a space. In an ordinary film, the most explicit establishment of a locale occurs when that locale is first shown. Subsequent scenes assume that the spectator no longer needs such overt 'placing'. Ozu, however, will sometimes increase the number of establishing transitional shots upon a setting's second or third appearance.

Such peculiarities have attracted critical attention. Some Western writers explain the transitions as reflecting such Zen precepts as *mu*, the void.[95] Richie sees them as motivated by the character's contemplation of *mono no aware*.[96] He interprets the intermediate spaces as being associated with characters' mental states, so that 'we experience only what the characters are experiencing.'[97] Other critics see the transitions as having thematic significance – either general, such as suggesting the transience of life,[98] or literal, such as when corridors are said to represent 'passages' from one stage of life to another.[99] Each of these is unsatisfactory because it is unresponsive to context – Ozu's overall narrational system, the immediate context of the particular film. Any transitional shot, composed any old way and stuck together with any other shots, could be said to convey *mu* or *mono no aware* or the transience of life. Moreover, if we are intent on making Ozu a heavy-handed director, nothing stops us from punning on his images of passageways; but then we run up against the problem that any shot of a corridor, in any film in which characters change, can be considered a symbol of what the 1970s American culture industry dubbed life's 'passages'. And the claim that transitions convey characters' experience is flatly inaccurate, as one of Richie's own examples shows: in *Ohayo* Ozu cuts from a boy talking about his father's farts to the father, far away, farting. Ozu's transitions are in fact so overt partly because they proceed from an omniscient narration that refuses to confine us to a single character's frame of reference.

Noël Burch has sought to contextualize Ozu's transitions more exactly. He defines them in relation to two frames of reference: the dramaturgy of Western cinema and the Japanese poetic tradition. He argues that Ozu's transitions (as well as cutaway shots in the course of the scene) 'never contribute to the narrative proper' and depict space that is 'invariably presented as outside the diegesis, as a pictorial space on another plane of "reality" as it were, even when the artefacts shown are, as is often the case, seen previously or subsequently in shots that belong wholly to the diegesis.'[100] Thus Ozu's transitions 'suspend' the progress of the narrative, negating the human drama at the center of orthodox Western cinema. According to Burch, the transitional passages achieve this goal by their stillness, their prolonged duration, and their lack of a compositional center. ('They demand to be scanned like paintings.'[101]) Burch draws his evidence from several films, tracing how a transition gradually moves from inanimate shots to the moving world of fictional action. Burch calls such transitional images 'pillow-shots'. This is an analogy to the *maku-rakotoba*, or 'pillow-word' of Heian poetry, the stock epithet modifying a word.[102] The pillow-shot becomes poetically evocative, freeing itself from narrative denotation to the point where, in *Woman of Tokyo*, 'the suspension of meaning itself acquires the weight of pathos and, thereby, a second meaning, a connotation.'[103] Burch thus argues for a continuity between Ozu's narration and a particular literary tradition, just as he will call Mizoguchi's camera movements 'scroll shots' on the analogy of *e-makimono* painting.

Burch's argument draws attention to some important features of these transitions, but it is fundamentally untenable. Many intermediate spaces do not fit his descriptions, since they often depict movement. Further, his tendency to favor opening sequences and Ozu's early work does not adequately cover the range of Ozu's transitional tactics. As for his theoretical premises, he tacitly holds two definitions of 'diegesis': the diegesis as the spatiotemporal framework (setting, objects, etc.) of character action, and the diegesis as the character action itself, conceived as physical movement. At one point Burch claims: 'The essence of the pillow-shot, its extra-diegetic character lay precisely in its stillness,'[104] but this makes such a transition extra-diegetic only with respect to the moving world of character action. Even if unmoving, such a shot remains firmly within the spatio-temporal world of the fiction. Yet Burch also claims that the pillow-shot is spatially and temporally removed from the scene, on another 'plane of reality'. He asserts that the pillow-shot is 'unsituated . . . in diegetic space-time.'[105] When he must deal with actual examples, Burch becomes entangled in these incompatible assumptions and must distinguish between 'pure' pillow-shots and 'impure' ones which participate in the diegetic world a little bit: 'the shot of the socks, in its second appearance, is diegetically superfluous and is thus partly expelled from the diegesis.'[106] Burch may actually be smuggling in a third definition of 'diegesis' here – that of 'story information', according to which any shot that does not carry a specifiable weight of information somehow gets catapulted outside the fictional world altogether. All this will still not prepare the reader for Burch's most curious claim, that Ozu's pillow-shot is empty because 'the shot is outside the film.'[107]

From the perspective of a historical poetics, Burch's struggles result from an inadequate theory of narration. He analyzes material units (a certain 'kind of shot'), not strategies, systems, and functions. His conception of narrative remains undefined, referring indifferently to causal, temporal, and spatial principles of organization and to parallels and thematic connections. His account does not recognize the distinctions among narrational knowledge, communicativeness, or self-consciousness, or the degrees to which each one can be present. He extracts a string of shots from its context in the film as a whole and then ignores how that series is internally organized. (On pp. 237–9, all these points are discussed further with respect to his most elaborate example, *Woman of Tokyo*.) As for his borrowing of the literary term 'pillow-word', suffice it to say at this point that Burch does not argue for the analogy. In many respects, Ozu's intermediate spaces also resemble the *jo* (the extended pillow word) and the *kakekotoba*, the 'pivot-word' that constitutes a transition between two different clauses. Burch's book proposes a broad argument that Japanese cinema of the 1920s and 1930s represents a direct continuation of Heian aesthetic principles, and the 'pillow-shot' becomes simply a fluffy metaphor to bolster, so to speak, such claims.

Not until the next chapter will I be able to give an account of the full functional complexity of Ozu's transitions. But I can make a start by pointing out the degree to which they are 'legible' expansions of two Hollywood devices: 'placing' shots and cutaways. The former consists of one or a few shots that lead in to the locale that will be shown in establishing shots. For instance, before we see an establishing long-shot of a police chief's office, we might be shown an exterior shot of police headquarters, then a shot of a door labeled 'Chief of Police'. Although such 'placing' shots are considered time-wasting in contemporary cinema, they were Hollywood staples of the 1920s and 1930s. Cutaways are inserted shots that interrupt the main action by enlarging a detail not present in the prior shot; they do not represent any character's optical viewpoint. For instance, shot 1 may present a character looking out the window; shot 2 could be a cutaway to a close-up of the doorknob that was offscreen in shot 1. Both placing shots and cutaways are comparatively overt. This highly knowledgeable narration can 'go anywhere' independently of the characters and can become very self-conscious, mounting these shots explicitly to enhance the viewer's construction of the action. The Hollywood film has domesticated these devices by reserving them for certain portions of the scene – the lead-in at the scene's opening, the cutaway for a moment of tension or surprise. (Consider, by contrast, how puzzling it would be if the narration interrupted an action in the police chief's office by a cut to an exterior shot of headquarters and then returned to the action inside.)

What attracted Ozu about these devices, I think, was exactly their degree of narrational overtness. They offered a way for transitions to become as self-conscious as the non-anthropocentric camera position or the 360-degree space. He thus expanded the 'placing' shot and the cutaway, making them the basis of his transitional sequences. The underlying premise was his recognition that both devices relied upon a loose notion of *contiguity*. The spectator assumes that the chief's office is inside the police station and that the door with its sign is attached to the office; the spectator infers that the turning doorknob is in the same locale as the person looking out the window. As usual, Ozu made these rough assumptions precise by teasing out various cues that could create prolonged and carefully organized transitions.

To some extent Ozu could assume that his viewer's prior knowledge would unify his transitions. Our familiarity with a landscape or a building's architectural features could help situate these intermediate spaces. But more often Ozu provides explicit details of setting to assist us in following transitions. He will literalize the concept of contiguity by showing overlapping objects or areas in successive shots. In *Toda Family*, the mother and youngest daughter are associated with the mockingbird and potted plants that they carry with them from household to household. Ozu sidles us into one scene as follows:

    1. (*ms*) Bird in cage.
    2. (*ls*) Mother tending plants, birdcage in foreground.

This is a minimal case, but Ozu can multiply such 'hypersituated' objects, thus prolonging or complicating transitional stretches. At the start of *An Autumn Afternoon*, five shots are used to carry us into Hirayama's office:

    1. (*els*) Factory (fig. 101).
    2. (*ls*) Smokestacks and buildings (fig. 102).
    3. (*ms*) Smokestacks, seen through a window (fig. 103).
    4. (*ls*) Corridor, with windows' shadows (fig. 104).
    5. (*ms*) Hirayama in his office (fig. 105).

Shot 2 enlarges a portion of shot 1, but shot 3 uses the smokestacks as a pivot to bring us inside the factory. Shot 4 is retrospectively linked to shot 3 by a subtle cue: the shadows of the windows and of the smoke seen on the left wall. Only after this does Ozu give us a more orthodox cutaway to Hirayama at his

101. *An Autumn Afternoon*

102. *An Autumn Afternoon*

103. *An Autumn Afternoon*

104. *An Autumn Afternoon*

105. *An Autumn Afternoon*

desk, but even here the window and smoke visible behind him provide a retrospective orientation with respect to shot 4: because of that window we assume his office is on the right-hand side of the corridor shown earlier. We are very far here from the loose contiguity assumed in 'placing' the shot of the police chief's office within police headquarters generally. Note too that in these cases Ozu's use of 'hypersituated' contiguity cues helps specify exactly how the camera position shifts in multiples of 45 degrees.

Ozu's hypersituated objects create adjacent spaces from the very start of his career, as we shall see in examining the early films in Part Two. A famous early case occurs in *The Only Son*, allied with a self-conscious play on focus and depth. A scene in Ryosuke's home starts with a shot of a hanging kimono, with a pillow visible out of focus in the background (fig. 106). Ozu cuts 135 degrees to a shot of the pillow in the foreground, with Ryosuke and his wife out of focus in the distance (fig. 107). As in the *Toda Family* example, the object is causally significant, since the topic of discussion is whether the mother is sleeping well. Ozu then moves to the shot/reverse-shot phase of the scene. At the dialogue's end he cuts back to a different version of the second framing, with the pillow now out of focus and the couple in focus (fig. 108). Here Ozu's 'sidelong' passage through space is constantly reorganizing the principle of the cutaway, employing it for the sake of a distinct punctuation in the action.

Ozu is not only revising and decentering Hollywood classicism in these transitions; he is once more going beyond his Japanese contemporaries. A

106. *The Only Son*

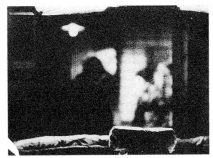

107. *The Only Son*

108. *The Only Son*

salient device of Japanese 'decorative' classicism is the atmospheric cutaway. The narration will occasionally interrupt the action to insert a shot of natural phenomena (trees, flowers, weather, clouds) or of significant props. Even fast-moving swordfight films can spare a shot of the moon or rain thrumming on a roof. But typically these are laconic, unorganized visual accents. In Ozu the 'poetic' cutaways are rigorously orchestrated and thus get raised to a new level of functional significance. They both accord with a basic function defined by classical cinema – that of stressing a spatial component independent of character attention – and create powerful intrinsic norms peculiar to Ozu's work. They also reflect his interest in a spatial organization that embodies an overt, self-conscious narration. We shall later see, however, that the principle of spatial contiguity is by no means unequivocal, and that Ozu will exploit it for other, less firmly orientational ends.

His emphasis on the visual is thus controlled by the same sort of rigor we have seen in the construction of the syuzhet. By his 'unreasonable' exclusion of certain choices and his concentration on only a few technical parameters, Ozu is able to develop a unique and fine-grained system of intrinsic norms – derived from extrinsic ones, but 'decentered' as a result of his adherence to rules of his own devising. His intrinsic norms of composition, staging, and cutting are at once singular at the level of devices and still legible in the broad, functional terms laid down by classical practice. We can follow these films because they respond to the general schemata we know from extrinsic norms of classical film and because the repetition of the few devices Ozu has selected 'automatizes' them for us. We accept them without conscious awareness. But Ozu's devices are so 'arbitrary' and his narrational system possesses such richness and nuance that the grosser functions are subtly modified. His images are informative, but the information is filtered through unique compositional principles. His scenes are dramatic, but they are shot and cut according to his own rules. His transitions still shift us from place to place, but they also answer to an inner logic. Ozu's 'overdetermined' syuzhet finds its parallel in an 'overdetermined' spatial representation that gives visual style an unusual saliency.

Needless to say, this entails that film style has now another task – that of violating its own intrinsic norm, of 'decentering' its own order, of injecting into the very texture of spatial representation that ludic quality which constantly challenges the stability of coherent representation. Just how the playful side of Ozu's narration emerges in the most minute twists of visual style is the concern of the next chapter.

6
Freedom and Order

Although I may seem the same to other people, to me each thing I produce is a new expression, and I always make each work from a new interest. It's like a painter who always paints the same rose.

Yasujiro Ozu[1]

Ozu's sparse intrinsic norms create an 'overunified' formal system, one in which even framing or gestures or cuts that are initially motivated by causality come to bear a stylistic surplus. But 'parametric' narration, in Ozu as in other directors, does not simply set stylistic manipulation alongside syuzhet patterns. The dynamic of the two is far more energetic. Ozu's specific form of this dynamic first takes the shape of a wry wrenching of his carefully established intrinsic norms. Just as rigorous syuzhet patterns find a counterpart in ascetic stylistic choices, the ludic side of narration gets manifested in stylistic terms as well. But Ozu goes further. Like Bresson, Dreyer, and other parametric directors, he proceeds to organize the very violations of his own norms. But before we consider the dizzying possibilities of this step, let us look at how narrational playfulness gets manifested in Ozu's 'unreasonable' style.

Walnut Circus

For Ozu, any film technique, once 'homogenized' by his stylistic rigor, can become the basis of playful deviation. The obsessive top/bottom balance of his framing is challenged by shots that shear off a character's head and chest (fig. 1). Elliptical editing can be disruptive, as when a dialogue title covers a change in characters' positions in *Passing Fancy* or when cutaways mislead us about characters' positions offscreen. Acting in unison always has comic potential, especially in the early films when students or gangsters execute their dance steps, but Ozu can press this a little further. In *Early Summer*, when the parents shoo their son away, he walks in a circle and returns to listen in; the father then rises to chase him off and walks in a circle that inadvertently mimes his son's. A very odd gag on perspective occupies one shot of *What Did the Lady Forget?*: coiffeured women are lined up watching a kabuki performance (fig. 2), but nestled in a gap between them is the tiny head of a man slumped down (in boredom?). Even Ozu's camera movements, eccentric as they normally are, can be further 'decentered' – as in the car-headlight shots already mentioned (p. 62) or in a tracking shot through a hospital (*Inn in Tokyo*) that for once presents a genuine, and absurdly steep, low-angle view, of the ceiling.

Ozu's concentration on the design of each image calls forth a playfulness at the purely graphic level as well. We have seen (p. 86) that one decorative

1. *An Autumn Afternoon*

2. *What Did the Lady Forget?*

3. *Late Autumn*

4. *I Was Born, But . . .*

5. *Tokyo Twilight*

6. *Dragnet Girl*

7. *An Autumn Afternoon*

8. *An Autumn Afternoon*

device of Japanese cinema is the intricately zigzag composition that leads the eye on Hogarth's 'wanton kind of chase'. Ozu has occasional recourse to such images, but not simply as an embellishment. In the context of his overall narrational and stylistic system, such shots deflect the 'legibility' that dominates most of his images. He sometimes creates a 'montage' of signs within the frame, refusing to lead in clearly to where the action will take place (p. 89, fig. 50). He is also fond of opaque long shots that will not unequivocally establish the space of the action. When in *Late Autumn* Akiko goes to talk with the supervisor of her sewing school, the first shot hardly gives us much to go on (fig. 3). As these shots suggest, the opacity often stems from the way that Ozu's low camera position and oblique perspective make furnishings dismember or blot out characters. The introductory shot of the parlor in *I Was Born, But . . .* (fig. 4), of the teahouse in *Late Spring*, of the restaurant in *Tokyo Twilight* (fig. 5) and of the inn room in *The Flavor of Green Tea*, all suppress important spatial information: the eye bumps against surfaces that conceal character placement. Ozu is especially likely to film temple interiors in this fashion (p. 87, fig. 40). In the supremely packed spaces of 1933 films like *Passing Fancy* (p. 93, fig. 56) selective focus increases the opaque long shot's 'illegibility'. Even in this phase, though, Ozu's opaque space remains fairly 'open': compare fig. 6, from *Dragnet Girl*, with the shots from *Marching On* (p. 86).

Subtler than the opaque framing is a quietly playful attitude toward the design of even the 'legible' shots. A bright red accent, borne by a trivial object and pushed to the periphery of the frame, deflects the viewer's eye. The purely graphic interplay across shots gets carried down to levels anticipated only in the films and writings of Sergei Eisenstein.[2] As we have seen, the cut will often make characters' positions, bodies, faces, and eyes coincide. Ozu will carry one character's movement across a cut by perfectly matching it to another character's (figs. 7–8). A transition may connect objects by their graphic qualities and their position in the frame, as in *Ohayo*, when a hanging light and clock in one shot coincide with a different light and clock in another locale. Alternatively, Ozu explores bold graphic displacements, as in the series of compositions that introduces a scene in *Late Autumn* (figs. 9–11). With such graphic matches and discontinuities, we arrive at a paradox that will reemerge later: the possibility that extreme rigor, in its arbitrary founding gestures and its passion for precision, is itself intrinsically ludic. Sato writes eloquently of how

110

9. *Late Autumn*　　　10. *Late Autumn*　　　11. *Late Autumn*

Ozu's style has achieved 'freedom in order': 'Deliberately imposing a severe order upon itself, it transforms the order itself into one form of recreation.'[3]

How far can graphic play go? To a literal 'decentering' of the image, an unprecedented scrutiny of elements which other filmmakers have considered minor or marginal. Shinoda recalls:

> He busied himself with positioning things like teacups in front of the camera. . . . Looking through the viewfinder, he'd tell the assistant director, 'Move that teacup three more centimeters toward Universal Studios,' and then, 'No, no, no. Back six centimeters toward Santa Monica.' Saying things like that, he gradually arranged everything in its own space. Then finally he'd say, 'Call the produce market' [Ozu's term for the cast, derived from 'radishes' as a slang term for bad actors].[4]

12. *Where Now Are the Dreams of Youth?*

The mixture of meticulous attention to composition and a light attitude toward that rigor is profoundly characteristic of Ozu. But the joke goes still further. Ozu also rearranged the objects between otherwise identical setups. Sometimes this was motivated by the development of the scene's action, so that the changed position of a cup or jug became an index of temporal progression. But sometimes he would shift the objects without dramatic motivation.[5] Edward Branigan notes: 'A viewer's mind can become quite unwired in an attempt to fix the geography of an Ozu dinner table.'[6]

13. *Where Now Are the Dreams of Youth?*

The point of the joke is for the viewer to create, on the fringe of the action, a zone of purely pictorial play. Within each shot Ozu calls attention to these tabletop objects by lighting them strongly, using them to weight the bottom half of the frame, and giving them vibrant hues or patterns. His cuts in shot/reverse-shot often create varying degrees of playful transformations of objects. At one extreme we can watch objects jump around the frame. In *Where Now Are the Days of Youth?* three beer bottles hop from frame edge to frame edge, serving not only as spatial anchors but also as a source of compositional interest (figs. 12, 13). Ozu will end the scene on a foreground composition of the bottles while the characters, out of focus in the background, leave (fig. 14). A bright white ashtray executes similar acrobatics in *An Autumn Afternoon*. At the other extreme Ozu will keep the size and position of the tabletop objects constant across the cut, even when the shots show different characters. Although the prewar films occasionally explore such

14. *Where Now Are the Dreams of Youth?*

15. *A Hen in the Wind*

16. *A Hen in the Wind*

17. *Late Autumn*

minute graphic matching, it becomes an important factor with *A Hen in the Wind*, in which a mah-jongg game is the occasion for precise, low-lying continuity in each player's tiles (figs. 15, 16). Chopsticks can provide the same diversions (figs. 17, 18). As the table fills up, the possible carryovers multiply. A full table in *Equinox Flower* presents a fruitbowl that skitters across the frame, a glass of orange soda that stays in the same area of the screen across shots, and a good-natured yellow can labeled 'Walnut Circus' that vanishes and reappears unexpectedly.

Ozu will also destabilize his norm of 360-degree space. Although it is hard to find a scene which is completely classical in maintaining a 180-degree axis of action – chiefly because Ozu adopted his characteristic staging patterns very early in his career – he will sometimes present 'correct' shot/reverse-shot cutting. In *End of Summer*, a three-way conversation is handled in orthodox shot/reverse-shot, but this is in fact partly due to the demands of a *sujikai* figure arrangement. More typical is *Tokyo Story*'s scene in the train terminal's waiting room, which mixes 'correct' and 'incorrect' shot/reverse-shot within the same scene. Such switches change the rules under which the style operates, 'defamiliarizing' the orthodox approach. The ludic effect of juggling eyelines can be seen when we get 'correct' shot/reverse-shot only when the characters, though both present, are *not* looking at each other (*The Munekata Sisters*) or indeed when the characters are in different locales (figs. 19, 20, from *Green Tea*). Similarly, once the 'torqued' figure and the sidelong glance become the norm, Ozu can push these cues to absurd lengths. In *Late Autumn*, two women leaning *leftward* on the same rail look off *right* at each other (figs. 21–22); there is no way that the eyelines can be accurate.

Even Ozu's transitions are not sacrosanct. In general, bridging passages, as decentered revisions of Hollywood's 'placing' and 'establishing' shots, create their own intrinsic norms, which will form the basis of the viewer's expectations across the film. But this norm can be violated too. Our first visit to the Luna Bar in *Equinox Flower* opens with a shot of a street and the bar sign. On our second visit the transition starts on a more general placing shot of the neighborhood, but this does not really orient us until we see the second shot – the Luna sign. It would have been easy to splice the neighborhood shot in before the first Luna Bar shot, but Ozu wanted to dislodge our expectations later. What, incidentally, does the neighborhood shot show? Another condensation of whimsical gags: a huge outdoor advertisement, a moving V of light

18. *Late Autumn*

19. *The Flavor of Green Tea over Rice*

20. *The Flavor of Green Tea over Rice*

21. *Late Autumn*

22. *Late Autumn*

23. *Equinox Flower*

that drives our eye from Nipper the RCA Victor dog to Leo the MGM lion (fig. 23). At every turn we find Ozu's ludic narration sliding into an off-center comedy.

Within both scenes and transitions, we have seen that spatial continuity depends upon specific cues for contiguity. If a sequence uses a person's legs or a prop as a spatial anchor from shot to shot, we are invited to take the narration as sidling and rotating through space, using a bit of setting as a 'hinge' from shot to shot. Ozu can indicate how comically slim the hinge-space can be, as when a bun sticks slightly into the frame in a shot/reverse-shot (fig. 24). Much more elaborate is the opening of *Passing Fancy*. In

24. *I Was Born, But . . .*

fifty-eight shots, Ozu creates a dazzling number of gags on the idea of adjacent spaces. At the scene's outset, a lateral tracking shot establishes the audience for a *naniwa-bushi* performance, sitting on the floor. Then Ozu cuts into the middle of the audience, using foreground and background relations and focus to pivot from one spectator to another, establishing contiguity within each frame. After this 'static' establishment of characters' zones Ozu introduces an object. A coin purse is discovered in the aisle, and one by one various spectators surreptitiously grab it, open it, find it empty, and toss it aside. Ozu's editing follows the purse as it is passed to the back of the audience, undergoing various changes. (At one point Kihachi takes the original purse and replaces it with his own, so that people now find a different one to pique their curiosity.) Ozu then exploits the idea of adjacency using still more slender means: a flea. Near the end of the purse episode, in the background of one shot, the barber starts to scratch. Later he leaps up, scratching himself wildly. He jumps down one row to Kihachi, who then begins to scratch himself. The flea is passed through the audience as the purse was, until finally the chanter on stage becomes the victim. This hilarious sequence depends on the rigorous application of the contiguity idea (four trips through the audience), handled through stylistic variation (the first trip emphasizing camera movement; the second depth within the frame; the third contiguity cutting; the fourth a single long shot at ninety degrees to earlier orientations). But the scene also debases the notion of contiguity by means of the ridiculously narrow margin between zones of space. Branigan has remarked that the overlapping spaces between Ozu's shots might be no more than the breadth of a playing card; in this scene, the gap between areas is narrow enough for a flea to vault.

Games with staging, framing, continuity, and contiguity come vividly into focus around the problem of point of view. As we found in Chapter 4, Ozu does not systematically restrict us to a character's range of knowledge, nor does he plunge to the extremes of mental subjectivity. Yet he appeals to the unifying conventions of optical editing: shot of a character looking/shot of what a character sees. There can be no doubt that, especially in his early work, Ozu often uses this schema correctly. He seems also to have briefly experimented with markedly subjective moving shots, such as the handheld images in the ski scenes of *Days of Youth*. Yet on the whole, Ozu deviates from the conventional handling of point of view, both in Western and in Japanese film. His films constitute an encyclopedic survey of virtually all the ways in which subjective point of view may be undermined by a playful narration. Branigan's remarkable analysis of this narrational problem remains the most subtle and detailed account, so he will be my guide here.

The conventional schema for optical point-of-view (POV) consists of six primary cues:

1. Point
2. Glance
3. Transition
4. Camera position from point
5. Object
6. Character presence or awareness.

These are normally distributed across two shots as follows. In shot A, a point in space (1) is portrayed and a character is shown glancing (2). The transition (3) relies on temporal continuity and is typically a cut. Shot B presents an object (5) from a position (4) that purports to be point 1. The entire scheme is held together by a presumption that the character is a sentient and continuing presence. Many secondary cues may derive from the specific nature of the space or objects or character depicted, but these six parameters form the essential features of the POV structure.

Branigan demonstrates that the film's narration can make every one of these equivocal, and he illustrates the process by drawing from a number of Ozu films. For instance, he shows how both *Tokyo Story* and *Floating Weeds* undermine the point/glance cues by presenting a shot that initially appears to be seen by a character and later presents the same shot when the character is *not* looking at the object: 'We then realize that our first view may not, in fact, have been a POV shot; that the men may not have been looking at the objects.'[7] Branigan's analysis helps us pick out a comparable undermining of the glance factor in *A Hen in the Wind*, which presents Tokiko on a picnic, lying back and facing the sky, but with her eyes closed. Cut to a low angle of the clouds, as if seen from her POV; cut back to her, eyes still closed. Branigan shows that a celebrated camera movement in *Early Summer* misleads us about factor 4, the place of view (see p. 320), while certain shots in *An Autumn Afternoon* and *Equinox Flower* make factor 5, the object of vision, quite uncertain.[8] In the latter film, one transition presents a shot of Yukiko and Hirayama looking up, her to one side. (The shot thus equivocates about which character is the 'point' and whose glance will shape the structure.) Ozu then cuts to a low angle of the hospital. This turns out to be a 'false' POV, since

25. *Late Autumn*   26. *Late Autumn*   27. *Late Autumn*

Yukiko is not looking at it, and the transition does not present temporal continuity. Then, after a brief scene in the hospital, Ozu presents an exterior view of the building, followed by a shot of Yukiko and Setsuko as the former says, 'Mother's room is around there.' This suggests, as Branigan remarks, 'that they may or may not be able to see the window from their vantage point. This ambiguity raises a second question: did we as viewers see the mother's hospital room, or was it just around a corner?'[9]

Branigan goes on to show how the normal large-scale patterning of POV can also be deflected. The orthodox structure, which operates as the viewer's most salient assumption, is both 'prospective' (cues 1-5 are presented in order) and 'closed' (the shots take an ABA shape, with the third shot confirming the POV structure). Again Ozu furnishes many examples of violations. *An Autumn Afternoon* ends with a 'discovered' POV structure, which presents an object and then, after some delay, the looker, but through an ordering of shots that attenuates the character's mastery of the space.[10] (See pp. 375-6.) One could add other instances. Branigan speaks of 'multiple', or 'interlocking' POV as well, whereby the same object of vision is shared by different characters seen in different shots (e.g. ABCBD, etc.). We can find a possible case in *Late Autumn*. When the daughter looks out a window (fig. 25), the mother does the same (fig. 26), and we get a scenic view (fig. 27). But the camera position equivocates by not assuming an identifiable angle 'from point' (cue 4); the framing is located *between* the women and thus suggests either a sharing of vision or a narrational source independent of either.

Branigan's analysis is so suggestive, and Ozu's range of POV experimentation is so broad, that one can press still further to find fresh and peculiar cases. For instance, in *Dragnet Girl* a rapid tracking shot past a time clock does not initially imply a character POV, since comparable shots open the film and are not claimed by character vision. But then Ozu cuts to Jyoji and Tokiko striding purposefully down the hall, captured by a tracking movement at the same rate. The first shot now holds the possibility of being a sort of 'hypothetical' POV – what they would see *if* they were walking through the office. Similarly, if Branigan's 'open' POV consists in never showing the object at which the character looks, there must also be a structure which marks a shot as subjective without ever showing a looker. Ozu often presents such an incomplete POV structure, by means of a compositional device which he has made his own: the 'establishing shot' taken from inside a window. A shot like

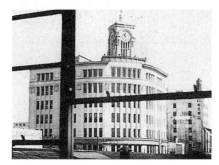

28. *Late Spring*

29. *The Flavor of Green Tea over Rice*

30. *The Flavor of Green Tea over Rice*

31. *The Flavor of Green Tea over Rice*

32. *Passing Fancy*

33. *Passing Fancy*

fig. 28, from *Late Spring*, suggests that someone may be seeing this view. In an Ozu film, this is seldom the case. The window shot typically introduces a locale, raising but suspending the question of who is seeing this view. Such a rich device serves many purposes: it denotes both an interior and an exterior space; it revises the cliché 'placing' shot by putting it on an intimate scale appropriate to Ozu's human drama; and, most pertinently here, it sets up ambivalent anticipations, since the next shot can logically present either another part of the room or another view of the outdoors. Ozu will sometimes pursue one option, sometimes the other. As a result, the narration can take us on some unexpected detours. In *Green Tea*, a window shot (fig. 29) is followed by a long shot of the spa (fig. 30) – including a window that might be the source of the previous shot. Then the narration takes us to an external view of a private room (fig. 31). The narration will never reveal the room from which shot 1 is viewed.

In its broadest compass, Ozu's play with optical POV brings us back to one of his founding 'arbitrary' choices, the proportionately low camera position. Even if all the other cues are 'right', this choice consistently challenges factor 4 in Branigan's scheme: the shot of the thing looked at is clearly *not* from the character's proper angle or distance. In *Passing Fancy*, even when Otane looks up, scratching (Kihachi still has fleas), and there follows a shot of the washlines (figs. 32–33), that fire hydrant squats there to make sure we cannot assume this to be her POV. It would be easy to take *Late Spring*'s tracking shot of Noriko as the view of Somiya, were it not for the grotesquely low position of the moving camera. When fathers and mothers in *I Was Born, But . . .* survey

116

their sons in an interlocked POV, the change of angle is optically plausible, but the camera height is consistently not (figs. 54–57, pp. 226–7). Some critics have wanted to make every dialogue exchange in Ozu subjective, since they interpret the 'frontality' of staging to impel the viewer to identify with each character in turn.[11] As we have seen, Ozu characters do not look at the camera but rather just over the top of it, or to one side. But even if they did look at the camera, the framing is resolutely lower than human eye level, so it does not present a correct cue for their interlocutor's line of vision. Again, it is not plausible to take the camera placement as the POV of a human agent, be it the invisible observer of classical narration or the tangible character inhabiting the fiction. This was probably one reason Ozu chose the framing in the first place.

34. *Late Spring*

Ozu's disruption of orthodox optical POV sheds light on one important crux in his work. In *Late Spring*, Noriko and her father Somiya retire for the night in a Kyoto inn. As the two lie on the floor, she apologizes for saying that their widowed friend Onodera was 'unclean' for remarrying, but Somiya has already gone to sleep. She looks off left and upward, smiling (fig. 34). The narration cuts to a wall, revealing a vase and a pattern of leafy shadows (fig. 35). Cut back to Noriko, the smile now gone (fig. 36). She turns her head. Cut back to the wall (fig. 37), and the scene is over. Schrader interprets the scene as conveying Noriko's sorrow at the necessity of parting from her father; the vase becomes a representation of her emotion in purified form.[12] Richie claims that Noriko knows she must marry, and the vase holds our emotion as well as hers, a fact which creates an identification with her.[13] Although neither critic's argument is as clear as it might be, both seem to assume that Noriko *sees* the vase and this causes the change in her reaction. She comes to a realization, Richie says, 'precisely during the time that *both we and she* have been shown the vase.'[14]

35. *Late Spring*

Yet both internal and external evidence suggests that these interpretations rest on shaky premises. Ozu's resolutely 'behavioral' narration makes it very hard to know what beliefs or insights cause Noriko's change of expression. (In plot terms, she has *not* yet fully accepted their separation, since she will later ask Somiya if they cannot stay as they are.) Moreover, as usual the camera angle does not tally with the character's angle of view. Worse, in earlier shots the shoji wall is established as *behind* Noriko, so that neither the first nor the third shot can show her looking at the vase. It is not even clear that the vase is the object at issue in the cutaways, since the overall pattern of shadows is just as salient compositionally. Finally, the first draft of the original script made no mention of the vase and simply had Noriko looking at the ceiling; the second version describes not the vase but the 'bamboo silhouettes' on the wall and still has her looking at the ceiling.[15] I am not saying that POV expectations do not come into play here, since some cues are undeniably present. But once more Ozu has undermined them. The scene may constitute another variant of 'false' POV, like that of Tokiko's closed-eye 'vision' of the sky in *A Hen in the Wind*. Moreover, the POV structure remains open: there is no fifth shot to confirm or deny the direction of Noriko's new glance. Ozu's fraying of POV cues makes the scene fairly unstable, and any interpretation of it must take such equivocations into account.[16]

36. *Late Spring*

37. *Late Spring*

Ozu's use of optical POV vividly exemplifies his overall narrational approach. The manipulation of POV becomes more overt in its deviation from codified norms. By refusing to accord with the canonical representation of character subjectivity, Ozu also establishes the enveloping narration as the principal source of knowledge. The 'decentering' of classical subjectivity creates a more unrestricted range of access to the fabula world. The narration gains a measure of playfulness in its ability to make spatial and temporal relations ambiguous and thus undermine our expectations.

Art works that rely upon idiosyncratic intrinsic norms often call attention to them by means of the process Russian Formalist critics identified as 'baring the device'. This usually takes place through imbedded representations, like pictures or performances, or through actions not easily motivated by causality or other principles of coherence. Unlike, say, Dreyer, who lays bare the device by means of an embedded work of high art or a portentous citation, Ozu nearly always invokes comedy. He mocks his own *sojikei* technique in *The Lady and the Beard*, where a framing compares the freshly shaven Okajima with Karl Marx (fig. 38). The memorial photograph of Mr Toda captures him in a typical torqued posture. In *Early Summer*, a photographer not only films the family from Ozu's preferred position (fig. 39) but instructs them to look over the top of the lens. Ozu's intermediate spaces are laid bare during the projection of the home movie in *I Was Born, But . . .*. (See p. 229.) Ozu will go on to flaunt his 360-degree space as well. Two fathers arguing in *Late Spring* point off in different directions, each at a 90- or 180-degree angle. In *There Was a Father*, Horikawa asks his son about the radius of a circle, and later a diagram on the blackboard demonstrates how to segment a circle in 45-degree multiples (fig. 40). This baring of the device had been seen already in *The Only Son*, when Ryosuke explained that two angles inscribed within the circle are equal because they add up to a right angle (fig. 41). Then there is the Kohayakawas' beautiful family crest in *End of Summer*: a circle *made out of* circles, each satellite occupying one of Ozu's permissible camera positions (fig. 42; see also fig. 302, p. 369). In the light of such playful barings of various devices, we ought not to be surprised that Ozu's production stills deviate so peculiarly from the films. Actors are caught not in a dramatic moment from the narrative but in startled or smiling or politely calm poses, photographed from Ozu's low position but now for once looking directly at the viewer (fig. 43) – as if these studio-produced images were Ozu's own family *kinen-shashin*, records of the fleeting instant of filmmaking and invitations for the viewer to recognize the relaxed artifice that pervades the films.

38. *The Lady and the Beard*

39. *Early Summer*

40. *There Was a Father*

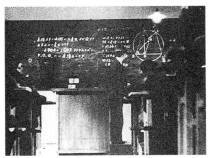

41. *The Only Son*

42. *End of the Summer*

43. *End of the Summer* (production still)

44. *Where Now Are the Dreams of Youth?*

45. *Where Now Are the Dreams of Youth?*

46. *Where Now Are the Dreams of Youth?*

47. *Where Now Are the Dreams of Youth?*

Rules for the Unruly

Once you start to notice the films' deviations from their own rigorous intrinsic norms, you also wonder – such is the critic's compulsive push toward pattern – whether these disunities are not in themselves taken up within a larger system. Consider, for instance, the opening of *Where Now Are the Dreams of Youth?* Shot 1 tracks leftward down rows of clapping students to end on four of our heroes leading an intricate cheer (fig. 44). Ozu uses the contiguity principle to sidle up and down the cheerleaders as, facing in different directions, they rotate in synchronization:

2. (*pa*) The fat boy turns clockwise to face the crowd and the two behind him turn away (fig. 45). Cut on action as:

3. (*pa*) Horino turns and looks off left (fig. 46).

4. (*pa*) Fat boy, others in the *bg* (fig. 47). He turns clockwise to face the crowd. He looks off left.

5. (*pa*) Another boy turns counterclockwise as the others in the *bg* turn (fig. 48). Cut on action to:

6. (*pa*) Horino turns counterclockwise (fig. 49) and the others complete their turn (fig. 50). Track leftward back to the audience (fig. 51).

The sequence is undeniably playful in flaunting the way that contiguity premises pivot us through space, linking shots by foreground and background overlaps in an overt 'baring' of the principle of circular space. But the scene's high degree of patterning is also apparent. Similarly, there are so many opaque long shots in *Brothers and Sisters of the Toda Family* that one is tempted to take a shot like fig. 52, from the death anniversary, as a climax of a visual pattern initiated at the funeral (fig. 53). (Part Two, pp. 294-5, discusses a comparable use of opaque staging in *There Was a Father*.)

Is it possible that Ozu's rigor/playfulness dialectic is absorbed by a still larger unifying logic? We have seen that local ellipses can cooperate with broader structural patterns, such as the creation of parallels. Is this ludic narration itself rule-governed, just another manifestation of the overdetermined unity that occupied us at the outset?

Well, there are rules and rules, unities and unities. They differ in terms of *what* gets ruled or unified, and what their underlying principles involve, and how relatively 'closed' they are.

The fabula, or story, has a firm teleology, grounded in principles of causality, temporal duration and order, and spatial adjacency. The syuzhet, the totality of narrative cues which the film lays before us, can commit itself wholly to the task of prompting us to construct the fabula (albeit always in a specific way, for specific effects). But causality and the principles of temporality and spatiality that pertain to the comprehension of story events are not the only systems that a film need display. We may find other patterns claiming our attention as well. In narrative poetry, rhythm and rhyme need not completely subordinate themselves to the demand of telling the story; in art song or opera, 'autonomous' musical structures may require that the story grind to a halt while particular harmonic or melodic patterns work themselves out. Similarly, in some films, temporal or spatial qualities can lure us with a patterning that is not wholly dependent on representing fabula information. These independent patterns are no less narrational than any other, but they

48. *Where Now Are the Dreams of Youth?*

49. *Where Now Are the Dreams of Youth?*

50. *Where Now Are the Dreams of Youth?*

create unusual spectatorial demands. As I have tried to show elsewhere, as non-teleological principles they cannot establish clear-cut hypotheses about their recurrence. Yet they do 'move' across the film, shaping our expectations, coaxing us to form hypotheses or, retroactively, to fit them into a whole. These additive, open-ended patterns can prod the spectator to seek a logic not only behind story events but also behind the narration's presentation of them. They may also, as we shall see, encourage the spectator to contemplate the abstract possibilities of the medium in its own right, when it is not used for fabula-constructing ends.[17]

51. *Where Now Are the Dreams of Youth?*

All this sounds very abstract, but the issues are central to the narrational processes that we have been tracing in Ozu's work. Causality, macrostructural symmetry, parallelism, 360-degree space, and so on constitute quite closed formal strategies. By contrast, the ludic principle creates a comparatively open stylistic system, built additively out of unpredictable elements. The rigors of unity lay down the premises without which the narrative cannot be understood; they guide our comprehension. The ludic principle invites the spectator, at another level, to participate in an open-ended, self-conscious game of formal construction. In holding out the possibility of a 'hidden' and less teleological unity, the film's style triggers a search for a new, less explicit and self-contained logic of narration. The narration thus reveals the viewer's inferential operations and makes those continually reshaped expectations as explicitly central to the experience of the film as the act of story-making normally is. Ozu is usually not reflexive in any ordinary sense, but his films build into themselves an awareness of our gradual engagement with the explicit rules, the violations, and the more elusive rules *behind* the violations that each film offers. Thus we cannot predict the sidelong cuts that swing down the line of cheerleaders, nor say how long the shot-string could last: predicated solely on contiguity and successivity, on 180-degree rotations and matches on action, the passage could go on as long as the boys had enough wind. We cannot predict an opaque shot nor say exactly what it means, since the exact design of its opacity is not a cause/effect matter. Additive form implies infinite form. Not the least accomplishment of Ozu's playfulness is to tease us with the *possibility* of a still broader unity that might enclose the entire dialectic; but it is a unity without closure, one that can never be confidently foreseen, one which we can only glimpse.

52. *Brothers and Sisters of the Toda Family*

53. *Brothers and Sisters of the Toda Family*

Ozu's narration, like that of other parametric filmmakers, proceeds in two major steps. First, the narration must mark certain technical parameters as targets of manipulation. This is initially facilitated by the film's unique intrinsic norm, which in Ozu's ascetic approach already offers a sharply limited bundle of possibilities. Against this ground, the narration will highlight certain 'stylistic events', which may involve any technique at its disposal. In *Green Tea*, Ozu will foreground forward or reverse tracking shots, usually by continuing to move the camera after a character has left the frame. Ozu may highlight a framing by emphasizing blockage and revelation, or presence and absence, as when the opaque views in *Toda Family* and *There Was a Father* vary from the very legible shots that make up most of each film. In other cases, intrinsically normalized stylistic configurations will be marked by virtue of their recurrent relation to a concrete locale, as in Ozu's use of 'placing' shots at transitions or his views of landscapes seen through windows. Most perceptible as a marked stylistic event are those devices which get foregrounded by virtue of a cessation in the cause-effect chain. Story-making recedes to the background, and the narration dwells upon isolated parameters, such as the rotational cutting in *Where Now Are the Dreams of Youth?* Once the narration has marked certain stylistic events for exploitation, the next step becomes the organization of these events into ongoing variational patterns. In the course of the film, for instance, an opaque view comes to constitute a strong *secondary* option for an establishing shot, or rotational cutting among the protagonists may form the basis for future stylistic choices. In both stages, the spectator's task is to form assumptions and project hypotheses not only about the story but about the style. The viewer is to notice nuances of parametric repetition and variation, not for the sake of thematic meaning but as a way of searching for an abstract, non-narrative logic controlling the surface of the film.

The marked stylistic events will enter into larger-scale patterns. In Ozu's work, these are governed by an implacable logic consisting of four non-causal and non-chronological principles. They operate at both the level of the shot and the series of shots, but editing, as the chief means of creating local patterns in Ozu's cinema, displays them most clearly. The principles are:

1. **Adjacency** A shot or a series of shots can be understood as denoting certain spaces as perceptually contiguous. Within the shot, this is most vividly stressed when Ozu uses his depth-marking tactics (linear perspective, size variation, or gradual falling-off of focus). Across shots, adjacency is most visible in Ozu's contiguity cuts, of the sort we have considered earlier. Now contiguity is of course an important assumption in all of Ozu's scenes. A dialogue passage or movement from room to room requires us to see the spaces as adjacent. But when the fabula's cause-effect chain is no longer governing a shot or a shot-change, adjacency can come forward as the next most salient strategy for creating coherence.

2. **Categorical inclusion** A shot or string of shots can also be made to cohere if we assume that there is some *conceptual* link between elements of denoted space – specifically in Ozu, a category or class to which those elements belong. Examples of this principle are fairly uncommon within

the shot, but one tactic from the early films exemplifies it. The movie posters in the 1930s films often suggest (ironically) that the characters in the film share semantic features with Hollywood films – a brothel in *A Mother Should Be Loved* recalling that of *Rain*, or the boys in *Days of Youth* compared to the vigorous Chico of *Seventh Heaven*. To take a different sort of category, the opening shot of *Woman of Tokyo* links a stove and a rice cooker as tokens of 'household cookware'. At the level of the shot, though, such conceptual affinities tend to be overridden by perceptual adjacency cues. The categorical-inclusion strategy can become much more salient at the shot-to-shot level. Ozu will cut from one sign or street to another, or from one person eating to another person eating. As we shall see, these conceptual links come forward strikingly in transitional passages.

3. **Graphic resemblance** We can unify a shot or series of shots according to 'non-semantic' features as well. One such is the abstract *similarity* among items. Within the shot, this 'rule' gives us Ozu's *sojikei* and acting-in-unison techniques. He will also use color to suggest resemblances; in *Floating Weeds* a pattern of red flowers at the bottom of the frame is compositionally parallel to a stretched awning. Across shots, the resemblance principle yields graphically matched editing, involving the same component or ones that look similar. We have already seen how Ozu's filming of the human body yields many cues for graphic continuity, but again when the story action ceases, such editing may become the dominant means of linking shots. In *Ohayo*, Ozu cuts from a washline to a living room; we cannot link the shots by inclusion and their spaces are only 'adjacent' in a loose sense; what links them are the red shirt in the upper right corner of shot 1 and the red lampshade in the same spot of shot 2.[18]

54. *Late Autumn*

4. **Symmetry** This bears upon the *total arrangement* of non-semantic elements – the overall composition of the shot, or the abstract pattern of shots in a series (e.g. ABA). Again, if the causal line is suspended we can examine the shot simply as a design, or anticipate that the editing will repeat or vary images we have just seen. The graphic 'flip-overs' we have already considered (p. 99) can be subsumed under the principle of symmetry, as can a scene's découpage, which, as Branigan has shown, alternates shots or arranges them in simple palindromic patterns.[19]

55. *Late Autumn*

All four of Ozu's principles may get combined with one another. We can then no longer be sure that contiguity is the primary principle for linking spaces. Consider what appears to be a simple case from *Late Autumn*:
1. (*els*) Golf course (fig. 54).
2. (*ls*) Golf course, seen through doorway (fig. 55).
3. (*ls*) Three men at the bar, seen through doorway (fig. 56).
The foreground tree in shots 1 and 2 and the doorframe in shots 2 and 3 seem to suggest that the shots denote precisely adjacent areas. But because Ozu may also use the categorical principle to connect shots, there may be two different trees, or two different doorframes. Furthermore, the doorframe in

56. *Late Autumn*

123

57. *Passing Fancy*

58. *Passing Fancy*

59. *Passing Fancy*

60. *Passing Fancy*

shots 2 and 3 may be there because it allows Ozu to create a vivid graphic match of the vertical line along the left frame edge (not to mention the match created by the tree in 2 and the right edge of the doorframe in 3). The categorical-inclusion rule becomes at once 'logically' unifying and perceptually open – especially when Ozu uses it to mobilize objects that look identical: not only doorframes but building facades (recall the hospital from *Equinox Flower*, p. 114), bottles, cubical signs, and other artifacts of uniform surface or shape. Look back to the opening of *An Autumn Afternoon* (pp. 106–7, figs. 101–5) and the same uncertainty will emerge: one can ask whether the smokestacks that link the shots are necessarily the same ones on each appearance. Playfulness is lurking behind the pattern.

We also find a pattern behind overt playfulness. The crabwise circuit of the boys in *Where Now Are the Dreams of Youth?* is now revealed as a bold mixture of adjacency, resemblance, and symmetry, with perhaps a hint of categorical inclusion (all the boys are cheerleaders). A similarly striking portion of *Passing Fancy* illustrates how several of these principles combine to create an arc of surprise and retrospective, if somewhat tentative, unity.

1. (*cu*) Tomio's hand sketches an alarm clock, copying the one at his side. It reads 7.15 (fig. 57).
2. (*ms*) Shelf (fig. 58).
3. (*ls*) Lane (fig. 59).
4. (*ls*) Laundry hanging against oil tanks (fig. 60).
5. (*cu*) As 1: Hand drawing alarm clock. The real one now reads 7.21 (fig. 61).
6. (*pa*) Tomio turns from his drawing.

Here is a classic Ozu digression. The sequence's basic narrative gag hinges on the inability of Tomio's drawing to capture passing time. Expectation is dislodged, though, by the odd ordering of shots: a moving hand (no 'extra-diegetic pillow shot', this), a shelf, a street, and a landscape. The orthodox sequence would run exactly the opposite way, moving from the static shot of the tanks outside to the lane, then inside to the shelf and finally to the boy drawing. (Recall our imaginary but canonical example of the 'placing' shot of police headquarters.) Instead, Ozu's narration uses the ordering of shots to mislead us about where the scene will take place and who will be involved. Shot 5 (fig. 61) hints that the three previous ones were in some sense byplay, and shot 6 finally seems to stabilize the action. In other words, by delaying our construction of a cause-effect chain, the narration takes the opportunity to be at once overt and unreliable.

But of course shots 2-4 are not 'pure' digressions. We make the sequence cohere by applying some of the rules already outlined. Shot 1 depends upon adjacency, upon a resemblance between the drawn clock and the real one, and upon inclusion (the category of clocks). Shot 2 calls upon a tacit assumption of contiguity – that the shelf is somewhere in the same interior space as shot 1 is, perhaps near the door. (Are we 'moving out of the room'?) Adjacency is again called on by shot 3, which seems to put the street in an unspecified proximity to the room implied in 1 and 2. The links to shot 4 are equally tenuous: either contiguity (the pole, clotheslines, and rooftops so prominent in shot 3) or inclusion (perhaps only poles and clotheslines and rooftops of the same *sort* as in shot 3), or both. Now too a rough graphic continuity emerges, when the vertical mass of shot 4 fills the space defined by the house-edge in shot 3, and the diagonal clotheslines carry the rooflines of the earlier composition to the other side of the street. Finally we are back to the first image, six minutes further along in story duration. We are asked to create a symmetry between shots 1 and 6, bracketing the intervening shots as an interpolated descriptive passage that evokes 'morning' in this neighborhood.

61. *Passing Fancy*

A proponent of a semiotic approach to film analysis would go on to talk of Ozu's 'figurative' narration. But an approach from within a constructive poetics lets us be more precise and accurate. Cinematic 'metonymy' has typically been theorized as only a matter of contiguity, whereas Ozu's rules include other principles as well.[20] Nor would 'synecdoche', the trope of part for whole, correspond to Ozu's categorical-inclusion principle; synecdoche is either broader than Ozu's use or his is a special case of synecdoche. 'Metaphor', whose classic cinematic instantiation is *Strike*'s cut from a slaughtered bull to slaughtered workers, would not do justice to the purely compositional features operating according to similarity and symmetry. Ozu's parametric narration here is not figurative in the sense proposed by a linguistically-grounded semiotics; it is perceptual and conceptual, guiding us in the construction of the *literal* space and time of the fabula or leading us into the channels of *purely stylistic* variation. For all four principles have this in common: like an aria in an opera, they could go on and on, developing their own formal processes and suspending causal progress indefinitely.

In such ways, the rules of adjacency, categorical inclusion, graphic resemblance, and symmetry are capable of organizing local stylistic play. Ozu adds to this the possibility of non-causal parametric organization over the film as a whole. This consists in taking a marked stylistic event and repeating or varying it. The results form an open set, created through addition and recombination of initially marked elements. The recurrences and variations push the spectator to the very limits of what can be perceived in watching a film.

Let us start with an early, quite perceptible set of variations. In *Days of Youth*, the two heroes are contemplating going on a skiing trip. They look out their apartment window to check the weather.

1. (*mls*) Yamamoto and Watanabe look up right.
2. (*ls*) Tall chimney, with wind blowing smoke.
3. (*ls*) Top of another chimney.
4. (*mls*) As 1. Yamamoto and Watanabe look down right.
5. (*ls*) Another chimney.
6. (*mls*) As 1. The two boys look to the left.
7. (*ls*) Whirling ventilators.
8. (*ls*) Windmill.
9. (*ls*) As 7. Whirling ventilators.
10. (*mls*) As 1. The boys react. Fade out.

This interpolated passage contains curious ambivalences. One could imagine these landscapes appearing in a later work, but divorced from characters' glances. Even here, though, Ozu marks the set for noticeable reworking. At the local level, all four principles of adjacency, categorical inclusion, resemblance, and symmetry apply. (A graphic match connects shots 2 and 3.) The sequence presents itself as an optical POV structure, but it includes not only one image (the single chimney) sandwiched between point/glance shots (4 and 6), but also two variations: *two* images representing the boys' (differing?) POV (shots 2 and 3 enclosed within 1 and 4), and *three* images, even more tenuously representing the objects (?) of their look (shots 7–9 within and 10). An insistence on repetition is also evident in metric editing. Shots 2 and 3 are almost exactly the same length (24 and 25 frames respectively) as are shots 7-9 (23, 22, 22 frames). Within itself, the sequence becomes a brief permutational cadenza, exploring how an additive order can open up POV structures.

A later scene marks these elements still more strongly. When the boys believe that they are not going skiing after all, they look out the window again and the same series of ten shots shows them eyeing the same chimneys, windmill, and ventilators. Ozu now varies his treatment along a more imperceptible dimension. He arbitrarily changes the duration of some inserted shots (shot 2 is now 43 frames, while shot 3 remains constant at 25 frames; shots 7–9 now run to 38 frames each), while maintaining shot 5 at 49 frames exactly.

At the film's close, Ozu creates a condensed variation:

1. *ET*: 'In the capital, the wind was blowing from the West again that morning.'
2. Fade in: (*els*) Chimney, with wind blowing smoke. [As shot 2 above.]
3. (*mls*) Yamamoto, looking right, shivers and looks up right. [Parallel to shot 4 above.]
4. (*els*) Chimney, wind blowing. [As shot 5 above.]
5. (*mls*) As 3. Yamamoto looks left. [Parallel to shot 6 above.]
6. (*els*) Whirling ventilators. [As shot 7 above.]
7. (*ls*) Windmill. [As shot 8 above.]
8. (*ls*) Ventilators. [As shot 9 above.]
9. (*mls*) As 3. Yamamoto turns from the window. [Parallel to shot 10 above.]

With this variation Ozu moves toward a more overt narration, not only in the expository title but in the use of shot 2 of the chimney as a more self-conscious 'placing' image, initially unmediated by character vision. Certain variations stand out. He has eliminated one character. He has eliminated the first shot, that of the lookers, and the third shot, that of the second chimney. He has also, less obviously, once more varied duration: the chimney shot (2) is now 132 frames long, while the ventilator/windmill series in shots 6–8 run 23 frames, 51 frames, and 24 frames respectively. Nothing in the causal line justifies such permutations of POV patterns and shot duration; the thrice-presented sequence punctuates the narrative as an abstract 'cine-poem' reminiscent of a pair of verses by Ozu's contemporary Mantaro Kubota:

The ventilators	They spin
On all sides	On all sides –
Spin.	The ventilators.[21]

62. *An Autumn Afternoon*

63. *An Autumn Afternoon*

64. *An Autumn Afternoon*

65. *An Autumn Afternoon*

66. *An Autumn Afternoon*

From Ozu's first (extant) film to his last: *An Autumn Afternoon* shows how Ozu could develop intratextual permutations into a formal game with viewer expectation. When Hirayama is first taken to a bar, Ozu begins the scene with these shots:

1. (*mls*) Down row of bar signs (fig. 62).
2. (*ls*) Down street, lined with bars (fig. 63).
3. (*mls*) Sign for Torys Bar (fig. 64).

The narration plays a trick from the start. The first shot would seem to 'place' the scene in one of the bars whose signs we see. Instead, by the principle of adjacency we move to the second shot, which includes the signs in a broader view of the street (fig. 63). Only then do we get the traditional placing shot that sets up the real site of the action, Torys Bar. (Note that the other bar signs are still visible in the distance.) This passage is somewhat analogous to the digression that slides us away from Tomio's drawing in the clock scene of *Passing Fancy*. The action then moves into the bar, and at the scene's close, the narration shows lamps on the ceiling (fig. 65) and returns to the Torys sign (fig. 66).

67. *An Autumn Afternoon*

In the next scene at the bar, the narration accords with conventional economy. A single shot of the Torys sign suffices to place the action, and at the scene's close no cutaway to the ceiling or the sign occurs. But it later becomes apparent that this economical version is used simply as a variant in a three-part *combinatoire*. For the last scene at the bar starts with the now completely superfluous shot of the row of *other* signs (fig. 67) before cutting to a long shot of the street as Hirayama staggers into Torys (fig. 68). (A permutation: in

68. *An Autumn Afternoon*

127

69. *An Autumn Afternoon*

70. *An Autumn Afternoon*

71. *An Autumn Afternoon*

the first scene we did not see him arrive.) And now there is no cut to the Torys sign as in the first scene. In the course of the sequence in the bar, Ozu cuts away from Hirayama to a shot of the ceiling lamps (fig. 69). In the earliest scene, this was a cue that the scene was ending, but now Ozu defeats this hypothesis by cutting back to Hirayama (fig. 70). Will the scene continue? No: Ozu cuts back outside to the Torys sign (fig. 71) and the scene is over. The process is of schema and correction at the level of marked stylistic parameters – a few notable shots reshuffled in scene after scene, varied in unreasonably logical ways:

First bar scene	*Second scene*	*Third scene*
1. Bar signs		1. Bar signs
2. Street with bars		2. Street with bars
3. Torys Bar sign	1. Torys Bar sign	
. . .		. . .
4. Ceiling lamps		3. Ceiling lamps
		4. Hirayama
5. Torys Bar sign		5. Torys Bar sign

The sign we see at the end of the last scene is not only that 'missing' from the opening shots but an echo of that ending the first scene, and the sign-shot of the second bar scene can now be regarded as a 'premature' expenditure of the sign-shot that 'should have' been saved for the last scene. But then would there have been room for the extra shot of Hirayama?

Ozu can impose his additive, permutational logic upon any canonized découpage structure. In *Walk Cheerfully*, he borrows the 'City Symphony' genre's marking of landscapes and urban routines in order to build a pattern whose symmetry is deflected by systematic variation. The first scene shows the start of a day:

1. Shutters rise on shop windows.
2. Another set of shutters rises.
3. Shutters rise, seen from inside.
4. On the sidewalk, people's legs pass.
5. People's feet enter office doorways.
6. Hands hang hats on hooks.
7. Steps: people stride into a building.
8. Hands hang hats on hooks.
9. A row of secretaries yank the covers off their ranks of typewriters.

The second scene, at the day's close, starts by showing shutters descending, but in an order reversing that shown earlier (variants of 3, 2, 1). The sequence then permutes the earlier actions by showing people finishing work (9, 8) and leaving the building (5, 4, 6, 7). The narration adds an extra shot of shutters and concludes with a sidewalk shot (4) showing people walking in the opposite direction. My discussion of *Walk Cheerfully* (pp. 200-2) will explore how this somewhat mechanistic shuffling forms the basis of a more dynamic pattern of expectation.

128

Permutational form can also emerge from the variations in framing that Ozu employs when returning to the same figure or locale. Ozu's reestablishing shots will not necessarily repeat the framing employed in the establishing shot's setup.[22] In *Early Summer*'s restaurant scene, a noticeable variety of shots establish and reestablish the characters' situation in space. Such shifts in framing may also be spread across the entire film. *Record of a Tenement Gentleman* uses 'just-noticeable differences' in camera setups to return to Otane's apartment, marking the difference by degrees of obliqueness (figs. 72, 73). More strikingly, *Ohayo* works comic variations on framings of a distant electric tower. The narration presents a variety of camera setups framing a stretch of street and hillside. In each setup a distant tower varies in its position. Sometimes it is not visible at all (pp. 352-3, fig. 259), sometimes it is, but at different points in the gap between the rooftops (figs. 258, 262). At one moment the device is bared: an old woman seems to be praying to the tower (fig. 264). Ozu uses this tower as if it were the needle on a gauge, measuring precise displacements of camera position. As Branigan has suggested, such shifts in framing can have a variety of functions: marking a switch in a conversation, facilitating graphic matches, introducing new graphic elements, and more generally, subtly affecting our apprehension of time.[23] Roland Barthes describes Robbe-Grillet's use of objects in his novels in terms that capture the effects of Ozu's shifting framings:

72. *Record of a Tenement Gentleman*

73. *Record of a Tenement Gentleman*

> It is a mutability whose process is invisible: an object, first described at a moment of novelistic continuity, reappears later on, endowed with a scarcely perceptible difference. This difference is of a spatial, situational order (for instance, what was on the right is now on the left). Time dislocates space and constitutes the object as a series of slices which almost completely overlap each other: in that spatial 'almost' lies the object's temporal dimension. . . . Space can tolerate only *completed* variations: man never participates visually in the internal process of decay: however parceled out it may be, he sees only its effects. . . . Robbe-Grillet's entire endeavor is therefore to invent for the object a space endowed in advance with its points of mutation, so that the object is dislocated rather than decayed. . . . Robbe-Grillet's objects never decay, they mystify or disappear: their time is never degradation or cataclysm: it is only change of place or concealment of elements.[24]

74. *Equinox Flower*

The relation of Ozu to Robbe-Grillet is not as culturally far-fetched as it may seem, since the latter pioneered a parametric approach to novelistic narration that has many affinities with Ozu's film practice.[25]

All of these large-scale variations are more or less noticeable, chiefly because they occur at moments when causality is slackened and the rules of additive form can come to the foreground. But we must face the fact that Ozu will bury some barely visible parametric differences within more causally dominant passages too. Who can notice the shift between two shots of Kyoko in *Equinox Flower* (figs. 74–75)? How many viewers will spot the change in the reestablishing shot at the end of the hospital scene in *A Hen in the Wind*

75. *Equinox Flower*

129

76. *A Hen in the Wind*

77. *A Hen in the Wind*

(figs. 76–77)? (Only the bottle in the right foreground indicates the minute shift of the camera.) The playful circulation of objects from shot to shot becomes far less noticeable when they are shifted from scene to scene. The viewer's memory can accommodate only so much spatial detail. Still more 'unstorable' are the combinations of découpage patterns in conversation scenes. As Thompson shows, Ozu will make every dialogue scene symmetrically differentiate the order of establishing shots, medium-shots of participants, and reestablishing shots, creating 'almost mathematically precise variations.'[26] Yet perhaps only a memory expert could seize and retain these while still constructing the ongoing fabula action. The critic comes to feel like Saussure unearthing (or hallucinating?) the anagrams concealed in Virgil's phonological patterns.[27] Fortunately our evidence of 'subliminal' patterning is far stronger than Saussure's was, not least because we are working within the framework of a poetics that assumes the filmmaker to be choosing among alternative formal options. Still, we will need, a little further along, to consider the overall effects of Ozu's decision, like that of the composer of 'total serialism', to build into his work an order that is not fully perceptible under normal conditions of reception – in other words, the decision to adopt yet another unreasonable approach to narration.

Dominants and Overtones

The playfulness and open-ended patterning of Ozu's parametric strategy are most clearly illustrated in his transitions. As highly self-conscious and often suppressive passages, they overtly cue the spectator to recast assumptions and expectations about the narration's own procedures. At the same time, we shall see that the transitions become privileged sites for the emergence of non-causal patterns – localized ones relying on adjacency, categorical inclusion, resemblance, and symmetry; or permutational ones involving additive variations across the film. The transitions usually manifest the most perceptible stylistic play and the most tantalizing hints of the rules behind the variations.

Most minimally, we could point to the straightforwardly humorous transition that marks itself clearly as commentative digression. The clock-drawing sequence of *Passing Fancy* is one example. Ozu's early films, with their inserted details of hands or other body parts, offer other instances. Usually, however, even these gags are not 'throwaways', participating as they do in motivic patterns. *The Lady and the Beard*, for instance, ends one scene with a close-up of Okajima scratching himself and tugging at his socks. Cut to a close-up of the spoiled young woman walking her fingers along a chair arm (a cut on categorical inclusion – 'finger gestures'). But the scene ends with a close-up of the posterior of the young woman's suitor, who rubs the spot where his mother has pinched him. Cut to Okajima's socks, as his hands try to conceal their holes. The gag arises from the four parallel gestures, but upon this Ozu has imposed a simple structure: socks/fingers//fingers/socks. Somewhat more attenuated is a link between scenes in *A Mother Should Be Loved*. The narration cuts to a poster for *Poil de carotte* on the wall (itself an ironic comment). The next shot shows a closer view of the feet of the boy in the poster. Cut to a close-up of shoes in another locale, and we are into the next scene.

130

Ozu will also exploit transitions for parodic purposes. One of his favorite targets is the assumption that the viewer ought to be oriented to the time of the next scene's action. As we have seen, he will replace clichés of sunrise and sunset with urban routines like the central switching-on of Tokyo's lights. These not only serve as a diegetically specified equivalent of the fade-out or -in, but they also permit Ozu to maintain graphic continuity across the cut. He will go on to parody the conventional emblem of such ellipses, the shot of the clock. In his 1933 films, Ozu's transitions delight in making clocks disagree. In *Woman of Tokyo*, Harue is summoned to a nearby phone, leaving Chikako looking at a clock reading 8.17. Cut to Harue coming to a phone in a store full of clocks, all of which read 8.29. Ten shots later, after Harue has gotten the message, the clocks all still read 8.29. Cut to the clock at home, now reading 8.32. Harue comes in three shots later. Given the implausibility of the intervals of story duration (twelve minutes for Harue to get to a neighborhood phone versus three minutes to return home), we can only assume that either her clock at home is slow, or all those in the store are fast. *Dragnet Girl* extracts comparable humor from the disparities between an office clock and employee time clocks. *Passing Fancy*'s 'morning' sequence offers a sprightly baring of this transitional maneuver: while using the real clock to measure the time taken by the cutaways, Ozu also uses Tomio's drawing to mock the movie cliché whereby an alarm clock indicates a morning scene.

The clock examples suggest that Ozu will often employ transitions to mislead the audience about the situation at the start of a scene. Both *Passing Fancy* and *Record of a Tenement Gentleman* begin with scenes in which the apparent narrative action turns out to be a story recited by a character within the diegesis. In *A Hen in the Wind*, a scene parodies the conventional 'dialogue hook': Tokiko's friend suggests a picnic; cut to another day and an empty road; cut to shots of Tokiko at home. Eight scenes later, the two women have their picnic. In *I Was Born, But . . .* , a boys' gang eat sparrow eggs to boost their virility. A scene starts with an expository title: 'The sparrow's egg begins to take effect.' Cut to the heroes' mother looking worried. Cut to her hand holding a doctor's stethoscope. Cut to a shot of her and one son sprawled out on the porch. The clear inference is that one boy is sick. But then Ozu reveals that the doctor is tending the boys' dog, to whom they have fed a sparrow's egg. (This gag also parodies the staple Kamata child-illness scene.) Forty years after *I Was Born, But . . .* , Ozu was still appealing to the unreliable transition. In *An Autumn Afternoon*, Hirayama invites his friend Kawai to go out drinking with him and Horie, but Kawai insists that he's going to the baseball game. The scene ends with the two still discussing it. After a cut to the window, the narration moves to the baseball stadium, and three prolonged shots dwell on the lights while we hear the announcer's commentary on the game. We expect to see Kawai, possibly accompanied by Hirayama, in the stands. But Ozu cuts to a television set over which the game is broadcast. The next shot reveals several men at a bar watching the TV. Cut to a long shot of the corridor adjacent to the men, and then to a private room, where Hirayama, Horie, and Kawai sit eating. The narration even has the nerve to let Kawai ask the waitress what the game's score is.

Through interpolated gags, parodies, and misleading cues, a transition may deviate from that intrinsic norm of scene/ transition/scene which forms a part of the viewer's assumptions in watching an Ozu film. There may be even sharper deviations when the transition challenges the spectator's ability to plot the scene's overall shape, or even to recognize the scene as distinct from the transitional passage.

This effect becomes most apparent when we examine the range of transitional patterns at work. The canonical schema is the 'full' transition:

last shots of scene A action	shot(s) of object or locale A	shot(s) of object or locale B	first shots of scene B action

While this is indeed common in Ozu, especially in his silent films, it by no means prevails. In the sound films, most scene shifts employ only 'half' transitions:

last shots of scene A action	shot(s) of object or locale A	first shots of scene B action

last shots of scene A action	shot(s) of object or locale B	first shots of scene B action

The 'zero' or null transition is comparatively rare and looks like this:

last shots of scene A action	first shots of scene B action

As we might expect, Ozu tends to establish the full transitions early in the film, then introduce partial or null ones – not only to recast our expectations about the boundaries of the scene but also to throw any later 'full' ones into sharper relief. Ozu is able to use the breadth of transitional structures to control the most minute aspects of the film's rhythm, while maintaining a game of hypothesis and revision. In this, as in so many ludic aspects of his transitions, the refusal of the instantaneous cueing provided by dissolves or fades is central to the play of expectation.

Once the intrinsic norm for full transitions is part of the viewer's assumptive set, the narration can undercut it in various ways. Ozu may cue us for a transition but then return to the action and continue the scene, as in the last Torys Bar sequence of *An Autumn Afternoon*. The spa sequence of *Green Tea* opens with two landscape shots (already discussed on p. 116), then shows us an exterior view of the pond and room in which the women sit drinking (fig. 78). They gossip and sing. As their song goes on, Ozu cuts back to a variant of the pond shot, now darker (fig. 79), with insect noises rising to compete with the song. The editing and sound suggest a bracketing of the scene by this pair of shots. Yet then Ozu cuts back to the women inside, singing full volume (fig.

78. *The Flavor of Green Tea over Rice*

79. *The Flavor of Green Tea over Rice*

80. *The Flavor of Green Tea over Rice*

80). The scene lasts only five more shots, but then is joined to the next one by a 'zero' transition.

A more intricate play with expectation occurs in the park scene of *Early Summer*, when the narration continually interrupts the dialogue with long shots of the characters, constantly suggesting that the scene is about to end. The presence of half or zero transitions can also create a new source of spatial ambiguity when we cannot tell which scene an object 'belongs to'. In *Early Summer*, the grandparents look up at the end of a scene and Ozu cuts to a shot of carp-kites flying. The visual logic is that of an eyeline-match, so the kite shot links with the previous scene, but according to the narrative context the kite-shot may be in a much later time, on 'Boys' Day'. (Lest this be thought a failure of cultural knowledge, sophisticated Japanese viewers have confessed some uncertainty about how to take this transition.[28]) Diegetic sound can contribute powerfully to such momentary equivocations, as a scene from *Brothers and Sisters of the Toda Family* illustrates. The Toda daughter looks up at the photograph of her father. Cut to a close view of the photo, not from her POV. Over this shot ceremonial music begins. Cut to a temple, at which friends and family are gathered to celebrate the father's death anniversary. The music makes the transitional shot a more flexible pivot than it would otherwise have been. And if an 'empty' transitional shot may belong to either scene, withholding human action from it may weaken our ability to spot the transition. During the school outing of *There Was a Father*, the narration cuts from the boys having their photo taken to a shot of stone monuments in a grassy plot, with the boys' singing heard offscreen. Cut to a shot of an empty road, the voices still audible; but the hikers never enter the shot. Yet if we think that the sequence is over, Ozu cuts to a shot of the boys' legs marching past the camera. The empty road oscillates between being the last shot of one scene and the first shot of the next.

Several of these examples have already indicated how Ozu's principles of additive unity inform playful transitional passages. Categorical inclusion may become important, as in the clock/shop transitions in *Woman of Tokyo*; more often, contiguity is posited, even if it is challenged, as in the baseball/TV transitions of *An Autumn Afternoon* and the false eyeline match involving *Early Summer*'s kites. Ozu will also use the resemblance principle to create graphic matches between shots in different spaces, as we saw in *Ohayo*'s cut from the red shirt to the red lampshade. In *Early Summer*, the narration creates an odd 'match on action' by cutting from two women drinking (fig. 81) to the grandparents eating in a park (fig. 82). As usual, though, Ozu is not content with unsystematic organization. He devises a specific tactic for transitions that combines additive indeterminacy with the four principles of non-causal unity. I shall call this the 'dominant/overtone' procedure.[29]

Ozu's stressing of the image's depth and his desire to discriminate objects through lighting and color allow him to give each transitional shot two or three distinct visual components. In the dominant/overtone tactic, Shot 1 of the transition will contain at least two elements, one more compositionally salient than the other. Shot 2 will present us with an image in which the 'overtone' has become salient and the other element, or a third one, becomes the overtone. Subsequent shots may continue the process indefinitely, by

81. *Early Summer*

82. *Early Summer*

83. *Equinox Flower*

84. *Equinox Flower*

85. *Equinox Flower*

86. *Equinox Flower*

87. *Equinox Flower*

88. *End of Summer*

89. *End of Summer*

adding more components or by weighting the existing ones differently. A clear example occurs at the start of *Equinox Flower*:

1. (*ls*) Tokyo Central train station (fig. 83).
2. (*els*) Roof of the train station; trains below (fig. 84).
3. (*mls*) Train clock: 15.21 (fig. 85).
4. (*ls*) Wedding party on platform (fig. 86).
5. (*pa*) Cleaning men in foreground, wedding party in background (fig. 87).

The façade of the building dominates shot 1, while the roof moves into prominence in shot 2. The train platforms, subordinate in shot 2, become more prominent in shot 3, while the station roof now dwindles to unimportance. In shot 4, the platform girders and roof now frame the dominant compositional element, the bowing families. Cut to shot 5 of the two men, with the wedding party now small in the distance. Dominant/overtone cutting, being purely pictorial, creates a non-causal means of guiding viewer expectations through intermediate spaces.

A glance back through previous pages will show that most of the transitions already examined exemplify this tactic: the birdcage cut in *Toda Family* (p. 106), the smokestack transitions in *An Autumn Afternoon* (p. 106), the conversation of Ryosuke and his wife in *The Only Son* (p. 107), the golf-course scene in *Equinox Flower* (p. 123), the alarm-clock scene in *Passing Fancy* (with the laundry serving as an overtone between shots 3 and 4 (p. 124)), the Torys Bar lead-in in *An Autumn Afternoon* (p. 127), the scene of the sick dog in *I Was*

90. *Floating Weeds*

91. *Floating Weeds*

92. *Floating Weeds*

Born, But . . .(p. 131). The dominant/overtone procedure embodies assumptions about contiguity within and between shots, about symmetries of visual design, and especially about categorical inclusion.

The narration can use such assumptions to take us on a detour whose topography shifts between the perceptual clarity of landmarks and conceptual links from shot to shot. In *A Mother Should Be Loved*, all that story causality requires is to show that Kosaku is driving a truck to his mother's suburban house. And indeed the narration starts by establishing this, with a shot of a signpost (the dominant) and the truck in the distance (the overtone). Ozu cuts to a closer view of the truck, now dominant, as it passes a second signpost. But then the narration moves on a categorical basis – to yet another post, as a train passes in the rear. The truck is nowhere to be found. The train provides the link to the next shot, which foregrounds the housing settlement that was a minor overtone of the previous shot. The shoji frame of this image is echoed categorically as a 180-degree cut shows Kosaku's truck, now arriving out of focus in the background. The signpost and the train have led us on a tangential route to an unexpected rendezvous with Kosaku, and the process has relied upon dominant/overtone patterns grounded in contiguity and categorical inclusion.

93. *Floating Weeds*

Things are not of course always so simple. A shot containing more than two significant elements may cause some hesitation about which will serve as dominant or overtone in the next shot. In *End of Summer*, a shot of an office counter offers several possibilities about what will overlap into the next shot: in retrospect the clock and its pillar would seem to be the dominant (fig. 88), since they become an overtone of the next shot (fig. 89). But surely we are meant also to enjoy the sheer leap in physical orientation that reveals the family crest on the left, slices off the hatrack and the hanging bag, and – most delightfully – skitters the bottle rightward to a spot exactly under the clock. Or the narration may keep an overtone constant while changing the dominant. This occurs in the spectacular opening of *Floating Weeds*:

94. *Floating Weeds*

    1. (*els*) Lighthouse, with bottle (fig. 90).
    2. (*ls*) Lighthouse, with ships' prows in the *fg* (fig. 91).
    3. (*ls*) Lighthouse, with waterfront in the *fg* (fig. 92).
    4. (*ls*) Lighthouse, with post office box in the *fg* (fig. 93).
    5. (*ls*) Interior of post office, with post box in the *bg* (fig. 94).
After shot 1 (a superb case of 'similar figures'), the next four shots use the

95. *I Was Born, But . . .*

96. *I Was Born, But . . .*

97. *I Was Born, But . . .*

98. *I Was Born, But . . .*

contiguity principle to move us backward and laterally through space. But instead of making, say, the ships' prows of shot 2 an overtone of shot 3, the narration treats the lighthouse as our constant (overtonal) reference point. We do not have a cut 'on the dominant' until shot 5, in which the red post-office box of shot 4 becomes an overtone, visible through the window. The dominant/overtone tactic thus remains flexible, capable of its own variation in the course of a transition.

Like most of Ozu's techniques, this leads us back to a ludic disruption of expectation. The dominant/overtone tactic can evidently work to enhance the ambivalence of scenic boundaries. The continuing element in shot 2 may not be strictly identical with its counterpart in shot 1; they may simply belong to the same category. Thus a transition in *An Autumn Afternoon* becomes uncertain because we initially are not sure whether a corner of a room belongs to one house or another. Moreover, Ozu's transitional details are often objects of a standardized or uniform appearance, like bottles or trees or telephone poles, so that we may be uncertain whether we are seeing the same object again or a similar object elsewhere. An early case, being somewhat impure, helps us see how this might work. The passage is from *I Was Born, But . . .* :

1. (*ls*) Yoshii and his sons walk past a telegraph pole (fig. 95).
2. (*ls*) Top of a telegraph pole (fig. 96).
3. *ET*: 'Morning.'
4. (*mls*) Back yard: shirts in the *fg*, Yoshii in the *bg* exercising (fig. 97).
5. (*ms*) Yoshii exercises (fig. 98).

The telegraph pole that dominates shot 2 may or may not be that whose base is presented in shot 1. (Although the expository title seems to mark the end of the scene, there *are* other poles in that locale.) All that is needed for the transition is for shot 2 to show some member of the class of poles. Shot 4 presents a densely packed image, with several components offering various possibilities for dominant/overtone development. The shirts dominate here, but there are several overtones that might structure the next shot. That image highlights Yoshii, brings forward the gate, eliminates the shirts, and retains the picket fence and another telephone pole, making one pole or another a constant overtone for the entire transition. We should also note that a bit of Tati-like playfulness in shot 4 makes Yoshii's exercising posture echo the shapes of the shirts. Significantly, this 1932 film uses a title to interrupt the play of dominants and overtones. Without the title, the transition would be more 'open', since we could not assume so readily that the pole of shot 2 is not one depicted in the background of the next scene.

Four years later Ozu adopts a far more equivocal approach in the famous opening of *The Only Son*:[30]

1. (*ms*) Hanging lantern (fig. 99).
2. (*ms*) Lantern in *fg*, women walk down street in *bg* (fig. 100).
3. (*ms*) Sign: 'Women workers wanted' in *fg*, women walking in *bg* (fig. 101).
4. (*ls*) Women at steam bins (fig. 102).

The lantern in shot 2 may not be the one shown in the prior shot, just as the women or the building in shot 3 may not be present in shot 2. There is no guarantee that the dominant/overtone pattern is supplying concrete spatial contiguity. In such ways, Ozu's transitions may work to break down the very distinction between a scene and a transition: the narration hesitates, slowing the flow of causal information enough to permit the spectator to send out tentative probes about potential sites of action. As with all the elements we have considered, the violation of extrinsic and intrinsic transitional norms is not simply disunifying. It tantalizes us with the possibility of rules yet to be revealed, encouraging us to suspend our conclusions, readjust our assumptions and expectations, and explore inferential byways. This new unity remains additive, highly unpredictable, open-ended, and resolutely playful.

99. *The Only Son*

Acts of Attention

The last three chapters' survey of Ozu's parametric form may have left the reader with many questions about the sort of criticism that this brand of poetics produces. It is not, evidently, a sort that is very common in film studies today. I can conclude this analysis by showing how my explanatory scheme compares with alternative analyses of Ozu, which themselves exemplify broader schools of thought within film criticism.

There is initially the dominant trend in film criticism: what I shall call 'thematization'. When applied to Ozu, this approach has usually played down film style, especially stylistic patterns and contexts. When style is noticed, it is 'read' in a manner at once atomistic and vague. The critic treats narrative denotation as merely the base for what films are really concerned with – conveying general themes, principally through momentary asides that, if read symbolically, carry the director's thematic point. In Ozu, corridors can be taken as 'obvious symbols of passage', bridges as representing movement from one phase of life to another.[31] The shifting découpage of *Late Spring* parallels the need of the characters to change their moral world, while the asymmetrical compositions in the teahouse symbolize the disharmony of the drama to come.[32] The inconsistent eyelines may be taken to show characters in agreement.[33] As roomy as they are inaccurate (the films often present major conflicts by means of 'agreeing' eyelines), these interpretations refuse the art work its full range of stylistic novelty and power. Had earlier chapters adopted such a conception of criticism, they could not have disclosed the dynamics of Ozu's narrative structures, nor his unique manipulation of story information, nor his parametric approach to style – for none of these activities has any apparent bearing on symbolic interpretation. Themes are important as material for the art work, but thematization tends toward 'recuperation', toward pulling the work back into our most anodyne habits of thought. To treat interpretation as the highest goal of criticism is to foreclose the possibility that a work may challenge us not through new meanings (what new meanings *are* there?) but through new *patterns*, *processes*, and *effects*.

The comparative success of semiotic theory, or at least of semiotic terminology, within mainstream academic criticism suggests that despite important theoretical differences, a search for symbols is easily recast as a search for signifieds. The principal step which late structuralist theory took beyond thematization was to offer an explicit account of how the text bears traces of the author or the viewer – through 'enunciation', either in the register of *histoire* or *discours*. But these concepts never received careful definition, let

100. *The Only Son*

101. *The Only Son*

102. *The Only Son*

alone substantial argumentative backing.[34] They were thus easy prey for raids conducted by practical critics who, after all, simply want some help in producing interpretations. The remarkable distortions and extrapolations of the 'enunciation' concept suggest that in many cases its value is less theoretical than rhetorical, as a new *topos* to justify the move to meaning.

In the study of Ozu, only one critic has to date employed the enunciation model, and the resulting confusions are wholly typical of the approach. Ozu's films, Alain Bergala declares, present themselves 'as if the enunciation preceded the enounced.'[35] In the linguistic theory that founds this theory, the 'enounced' is the stretch of text that is produced; the 'enunciation' is the total process that produces it.[36] Bergala has appropriated these terms in a disarmingly straightforward fashion, taking editing and camera position to constitute enunciation and assuming that the action staged for the camera constitutes the enounced.[37] Shorn of semiotic trappings, Bergala's point is that Ozu's framing and cutting are so systematic that they seem to precede (logically? temporally?) the action they portray. Although this ignores all the systematic aspects of the staging of the action, let us go on to ask what Bergala takes this system to be. By 'abandoning' camera movement that follows moving figures, marking as 'arbitrary' any camera movement independent of the characters, refusing to rack focus or reframe on moving characters, avoiding the 'suturing' effects of shot/reverse-shot cutting, and dwelling on shots of empty space, Ozu constructs an enunciation that will not adhere to the fiction. Bergala then takes a further step. He claims that the arbitrariness of Ozu's enunciation posits no author, no point of origin. The spectator can identify neither with the characters nor with the enunciator: hence there is only 'an empty mirror.'[38] This assumes that normal cinematic narration does create a human-like agent, a narrator or enunciator with whom we identify. Of course we need not assume this, and as I have argued elsewhere, there is no good reason to do so.[39] Cinematic narration does not necessarily require us to construct a narrator with whom we 'identify'. Bergala not only fails to describe the *positive* system that drives Ozu's style, but he reinstates a personalized agent as a source of meaning in orthodox cinema, very much along the lines of the 'invisible witness' of mainstream theory.

The work of Noël Burch presents a more complex case. In his *Praxis du cinéma* (translated as *Theory of Film Practice*), in my view the most important piece of film theory published in the 1960s, Burch sketched a case for a poetics of cinema – specifically of a sort that I have been calling 'parametric', the very term deriving from Burch's borrowing from serial music.[40] *Praxis du cinéma* reconnoitered the terrain of orthodox theory with a view toward a serialization of all available techniques. It was inevitable that, out of both polemical intent and the absence of relevant work in narratology, Burch's seminal work lacked an adequate account of the relation between stylistic structures and narrative or other large-scale organizational principles. Burch subsequently deepened the book's discussion with some rich particular analyses, especially of *M* and *Dr Mabuse*.[41] Soon, however, he began to incorporate his serial aesthetic into a semiotic model drawn ultimately from *Tel Quel*. The results, in his book *To the Distant Observer*, are a continual reaffirmation of the importance of signification (the book is subtitled 'Form and Meaning in the

Japanese Cinema') and a remarkable faith in the liberating power of the signifier. But Burch's couplet 'full sign' (= realism, transparency, ideological mystification)/'empty sign' (= transgression, critique, ideological subversion) is questionable, committed as it is to a static, acontextual notion of meaning (an affair of discrete entities called signifieds, ruled by signs and codes). In other hands, this couplet licenses a new thematization (the viewer 'produces' meanings or readings, usually merely fresh readings of a Lacanian or Derridean variety). In Burch's case, it underwrites a criticism that mutely points at how the empty sign, with monotonous regularity, sends this or that ideologically complicit code crashing to earth. From a poetics of cinema Burch has moved to a celebration of 'deconstruction'.

True, in his discussion of Ozu, he concedes that this director will not stop at simple deconstruction of codes. 'He organizes the resulting gaps and ambiguities with a refinement attained by none of his contemporaries.'[42] But Burch never in fact dissects Ozu's organization, in gross outline or in fine detail. He does not consider any of the principles of rigor that we have examined already, nor any of the stylistic deviations from that, nor the non-causal principles that govern the films' parametric play. He does not trace Ozu's 'systemics' across a single film, or consider them in relation to narrative structure. He is content to catalogue some devices, attribute them to distant Japanese aesthetic traditions, and praise Ozu's 'radical' departures from Western découpage. Burch's evolution from poetician to semiotician shows how difficult it is to resist the lure of defining film aesthetics wholly in terms of meaning, constructed on either a thematic or semiotic model. Nevertheless, the historical poetics that I am testing in this book owes Burch's early writings a very substantial debt.

It owes even more to Russian Formalist poetics of literature and cinema. These scholars pioneered the theorization and analysis of both large-scale organizational principles and fine-grained stylistic procedures. They initiated, in the constructs of syuzhet and fabula and in the study of *skaz* or pseudo-oral literature, a rigorous approach to understanding narration. They also sought to ground their theory and analysis in an 'anthropological' account of how social convention and psychic activity cooperated to produce a range of aesthetic effects. Poised between the empirical study of literary form in history and a theoretical account of what makes 'literature' possible, the Formalists initiated a rich research program. Too rich, as it turned out. The psychology, sociology, and art history of their time offered little to help them define their vague intuitions about 'defamiliarization' or the role of norm and deviation in art. And the research program was quickly cut short by official Soviet aestheticians who combined invincible obtuseness with servility and opportunism. Today, however, some of the Formalists' promissory notes can be paid off. The development of Constructivist perceptual and cognitive psychology, the theory of intrinsic and extrinsic norms developed in literary stylistics, the rational-agent model of social and anthropological explanation – these and other emerging trends support, in general outline and considerable detail, the Formalist project.

Since this book as a whole embodies this approach, I need only sum up how a historical poetics can lead to a richer, more comprehensive account of

Ozu's stylistic dynamics than we find in other approaches.[43] Here a film is taken not as a 'text' to be 'read' but an artifact to be *used* by the spectator to produce certain *effects*, of which 'meaning' in its most elevated sense (themes, implicit messages) is only one. The work prompts a range of perceptual, emotional, and cognitive effects – guidance of attention, establishment of expectations, thwarting of hypotheses, retroactive reconsideration of information – which are essential to the work's uniqueness. This is not a plea for 'reader-response' criticism, which soon enough takes us back to a theme (usually the claim that the text is 'about' the very difficulty of deciphering texts). Rather the critic can treat the film as cueing the spectator to perform certain constrained but not wholly determined *activities*. At the base of these are quite complex information-processing mechanisms (for vision, language, and so on) and higher-level processes involving cross-media skills and conventions of narrative comprehension. Here lie the filmmaker's primary materials – not images and sounds as such, but the habitual ways in which spectators create coherent patterns of space, time, analogy, and causality.

From this perspective, Ozu's parametric approach to narration looks more interesting than from the perspective of thematization or semiotics. All the strategies I have considered – the playful violations of the rigorous stylistic norm; the non-causal rules of adjacency, categorical inclusion, resemblance, and symmetry; the use of dominant/overtone procedures to unify transitional passages – address perceptual-cognitive skills. These strategies need not mean anything beyond their function of prompting certain open lines of hypothesis-testing and inference. Rather than being interpolations in the story for the sake of thematic commentary, or 'deconstructions' of the Western norm of linearity, these stylistic strategies invite the viewer to engage in precise acts of attention: scrutiny, discrimination, comparison, recollection, revision. Ozu's parametric play valorizes nuance, not by appeal to the hedonism of pure sensation – as if such a thing existed anyhow – but by posing problems, by asking that we search for principles that order such finesse.

For those who cannot or will not play the game, such richness registers as a vague aura of evocation,[44] and perhaps the basis of mystical thematizing readings. Exceptional rigor and additive form create an elusiveness of connotation. Such powerful order, the critic thinks, must *mean*. But Ozu's art, like that of Bresson and Dreyer, evokes the ineffable as a by-product of remarkably constrained and exact choices. The point is not what it means but what it *does*: train us in nuance, suggest new possibilities for ordering experience, and – not least – invite us to contemplate the possibilities of the film medium when it is no longer subordinated to story construction. In this way a historical poetics can describe and explain the formal mechanics that produce the felt need for thematizing readings.

It is here that the most minute effects of Ozu's rule-governed play become significant. We have seen that some of his parametric variation is not only apparent but stressed; some is visible if you know where to look; and some is probably measurable only on the printed page. I have argued elsewhere that a parametric approach tends to fight the time-bound nature of film viewing and to superimpose more abstract 'spatialized' patterns. The approach thus raises the question of what, finally, is possible in this medium. Although there are psychophysical limits, viewers could certainly see more in any film than they normally do, and parametric cinema is important to film theory partly because it explores how this retraining of the spectator might be conducted. The cognitive base of much cinematic perception is demonstrated in the fact that one can *learn* – partly through the poetician's analytical enterprise –to notice the range of Ozu's stylistic processes. His spectrum of effects carries his dialectic of rigor and playfulness to the threshold of perceptibility, inviting the spectator to probe the subtleties of the film medium. Like the poet who reveals new possibilities in language or the composer who restructures our apprehension of sound, Ozu opens a theoretical dimension as well. He shows us new things that cinema can do.

The traditional critic will cry at this point that I have forgotten 'content'. Not at all. Ozu's materials, his themes and subjects, enter into the overall formal system as both the occasion for the dynamics of rigor and playfulness and the basis of significant effects. Shindo has suggested that Ozu's style seeks 'to capture the subtle beauty in the common man's everyday habits and experiences.'[45] 'Captures' is perhaps too strong, since it implies that Ozu discovers rather than produces; but in any event, one can argue that his formal system 'processes' his materials in a way that poeticizes everyday life. Shochiku's policies and the *shoshimin-geki* genre gave him 'everyday life' (conceived under a specific ideological description) as his material; he arrived, through influences we will chart in the next chapter, at his constructive principle of constraint and choice, arbitrariness and freedom. In their interrelation, materials and form yield a body of work that turns the mundane into the lyrical. He makes the average household into the sort of museum Mondrian might design. He treats the ordinary human body as a compact set of symmetrical surfaces and gently shifting shapes. His transitions domesticate the city by inviting us to subject it to a patient scrutiny that reveals purely perceptual connections among transient phenomena. In 1938, a Japanese writer complained that Tokyo had suffered under urbanization:

> Where does the heart of a civilized city lie? It lies, it is said, in the spaces which serve to purify, physically and spiritually, the city atmosphere befouled by the unnaturalness of urban living. The Japanese are utterly unaware of how to provide such a heart – in other words, how to 'naturalize' the space of their cities. . . . The inhabitants have to take their pleasure in districts such as the Ginza or Shinjuku, in an atmosphere polluted in every sense of the word. Nor are these amusement areas in any sense a product of typically Japanese cultural models, but are 'colonial' amusement districts, transplantations of all that is most vulgar in the third-rate quarters of Western cities.[46]

The resting spaces and parks which Hasegawa calls for are provided by Ozu, but at one remove, in film form and style. He turns even the 'vulgar' amusements into landscapes of elusive splendor. I suggested in Chapter 3 that Ozu's style 'naturalizes' the city and 'sophisticates' nature, but it might be more accurate to say that in his films, nature is transformed into artifice and artifice becomes hyperartificial.

All of which might imply an arid aestheticism. Not the least of Ozu's accomplishments, though, is the way he infuses the serious business of 'artistic form' with an attitude that is deeply comic. One could never call the dialectic of parametric norms in Dreyer or Bresson 'playful' in the same sense that Ozu's is. Unlike these directors, he discovered that if at a certain point play becomes rigorous, from the very start an overweening discipline is inherently comic. His unreasonable choices of camera position, 360-degree space, and graphic matching are as absurd as dancing walnut cans, nearly imperceptible shifts in composition, camera movements that glide through an empty room, or editing that lets Nipper take part in a conversation. For Ozu, all pure art has something silly about it.

7
Pillows and Curtains

> Tradition, the basic concept of the established history of literature, has proved to be an unjustifiable abstraction of one or more of the literary elements of a given system within which they occupy the same plane and play the same role. They are equated with the like elements of another system in which they are on a different plane, thus they are brought into a seemingly unified, fictitiously integrated system.
>
> The main concept for literary evolution is the *mutation* of systems, and thus the problem of 'traditions' is transferred onto another plane.
>
> Yuri Tynianov, 1927[1]

A *historical* poetics cannot rest content with the analysis of syuzhet and style in Ozu's work, even if we have sought always to retain a sense of the pertinent backgrounds provided by contemporary practices. We want more. We want to explain, in a historically plausible way, how these strategies came to be as they are. Our intrinsic analysis thus becomes an indispensable methodological step, since it reveals an overall system of narration that must be explained in its concrete and dynamic totality, not through vague evocations (*mono no aware*, *mu*) or excessively local analogies (transitions as *haiku* or 'pillow words'). Our systematic analysis, if coupled with a study of historical factors both proximate and pertinent to Ozu, can yield a richer sense of the narration's sources.

Poetry and Poetics
A dialectic of rule-governed unity and variety can be found throughout Japanese poetic traditions. Pre-Meiji verse relied on elaborately codified forms. Rules dictated metrical structure, line formats, imagery, time of year, and many other features. Court poetry of the Heian period most commonly utilized *tanka*, a five-line stanza of thirty-one syllables (arranged 5, 7, 5, 7, 7). Auditory techniques and fixed epithets, such as the 'pillow word', were rigidly stipulated. Between 1300 and 1900, *renga*, or 'linked' verse composed orally by three people in turn, became a display of virtuoso rule-following. Each stanza existed as both a free-standing *tanka* and as a link from the stanza before to the one that followed. The poem was expected to display continuity in scene, mood, and season, while recondite conventions dictated that it use specific images and words in particular stanzas. The most sophisticated Western explicator of *renga* confesses that he cannot set down a complete list of rules because no one seems to know them all![2] The *haiku* tradition also had its own strict canons of composition, often revisions of the conventions of

court verse.[3] By Basho's day, the three-line *haiku* was expected to split into two components, juxtaposed to create a tension between the evanescent and the eternal. Even the nature descriptions were dictated to a great degree.[4]

The stringency of Japanese poetic conventions itself points to a gamelike conception of art. As we might expect, the poet's skill lay not only in obeying the rule but in the unexpected twists which he could provide. The extraordinary ambiguity of conversational Japanese already biased the language toward suggestion and equivocation. Court poetry created startling compression by exploiting the language's ellipticality, which permits the speaker to delete pronouns, noun phrases, and main verbals. A poem might drop topic, subject, and particles, leaving only an object phrase and an inflected verb.[5] The convention of the 'pivot-word' (*kakekotoba*) allowed single units to participate in two clauses by virtue of creating two different meanings; thus the vast number of homonyms in Japanese was exploited to create 'serious puns'. *Renga* and *haikai* verse were themselves popular, even frivolous, developments out of court poetry. In the linked form, the circumstances of collective composition and the sparkling shifts in the stanzas' reference, diction, and tone all reflect a light-hearted attitude toward verse. Earl Miner stresses the elusive dynamic that results:

> Each renga stanza is . . . subject to constant reinterpretation by its successor, and the same 'text' may yield quite different results. . . . [Linked poetry] gives us, on the one hand, a sense of the almost giddy possibility that exists in any language and that is taken over for resource by literary versions of a particular language. Selection and emphasis imply wide ranges of ambiguity and of non-sense out of which order and sense and clarity can be made to emerge.[6]

Although the more crystalline *haiku* lyric lacks the dazzling overlapping of the *renga* sequences, it was developed out of them and uses a caesura at the end of the first or second line to create a surprising shift that makes the poem's two components 'echo', as Basho put it. The mind 'goes and then returns.'[7]

All this sounds so much like Ozu that we might be tempted to halt right here and start to list borrowings. His self-imposed constraints could be seen as like those rigid codes of the poetic tradition. His ellipticality and suggestiveness would thus become modeled upon that of the language as a whole and upon the explicit suppression of subject and action in verse. Even his overt but elusive narration has an analogue in linguistic resources which Japanese poetry exploits – the implied presence of a speaker or witness, as in this *haiku* by Basho:

> The water birds
> Must be asleep, too,
> On Lake Yogo.[8]

It is no harder to find cultural analogies to Ozu's visual style. The 'giddy possibilities' of language in *renga* seem not far removed from the perceptual nuances opened up by dominant/overtone cutting and graphic matching, especially as these cinematic tactics depend strongly on a notion of arbitrary linkage comparable to that in *renga*. Moving outside literature, we find in the Japanese painting tradition non-anthropocentric strategies that seem to be echoed in Ozu: 'In order to learn to paint, one must invariably learn to paint rocks. . . . If one has mastered the painting of rocks, he has acquired the ability to paint all other subjects equally well.'[9] The Japanese landscape garden is designed so that the axis of the bridge and that of the southern steps must be slightly out of true, in a *sujikai* relationship.[10] One could march a long way in this direction: Ozu's 360-degree cutting pattern resembles the 'fifth circle' in a fifteenth-century noh master's theory of Zen performance.[11]

We could ascend to an even broader cultural level. Only recently has the West discovered the complex ways in which Japanese culture defines perceptual and social space. The native term, *ma*, bristles with meanings (ranging from 'a room in a house' to 'attention to circumstances'), but essentially space is defined negatively. Whereas the Westerner often thinks of space as a hollow container for objects, *ma* signifies the *interval* necessarily existing between two entities – space as spacing. The concept of *ma* governs both space and time (since both can be conceived in terms of intervals). It privileges sheer empty spots, so that *ma* is not opposed to 'void' as 'space' may be in the West. It emphasizes each locale's unique identity and puts the burden upon the individual to respond to an unrepeatable situation. It suggests that between concrete places there exists a fundamental discontinuity, especially of point of view. It favors attention to transitions, margins, and thresholds – the *en*, or 'border', which is neither of one place nor of another. It encourages the recognition of 'mis-timed' elements in speech or music, as in the samisen accompaniment that never coincides perfectly with the voice's contours. Most broadly, it conjures up a sense of existence as perpetual flux, a contingent movement between stable points.[12] *Ma* is at once an empty space, a blank or pause, and a displacement or disjunction that allows the perceiver to charge the gap with a range of potential meanings.[13] All of these implications can be seen in Japanese aesthetic practices: in the 'cellular' discontinuity of the *e-maki mono* picture scroll, in the empty spaces of architecture and painting, in the conception of the house as a set of fluid boundaries between vacant modules, in the pillow word as creating *ma* within the verse line, in the fusion of separation and linkage found in *renga* verse. And all offer tempting analogies with aspects of Ozu's work.

Illuminating though they might be, however, all such cultural analogies are premature, for both substantive and methodological reasons. Take, for example, the parallels between poetry and Ozu's strategies of narration. Japanese court and popular poetry never posited quite the sort of rigor and playfulness we find in Ozu's work. Classical Japanese verse, like the Zen arts of flower arranging and painting, avoids the sort of formal symmetry upon which Ozu dotes. Moreover, the rules of verse promoted stringent control of small-scale textural features, not broader unities. A sequence of court poems might be based upon a seasonal principle, or on the vague progress of a love affair. The *renga* verse had no overall representational unity, with beginning, middle, and end, or development and climax.[14] Its requirement that each stanza serve as both unit and transition promoted local cohesion at the expense of overarching unity of story or topic. This tendency toward fragmentary construction reaches its apogee in the autonomous *haiku* of the Meiji era. The history of Japanese poetry is thus to a large extent the turning away from macrostructural unity and 'long forms'. Furthermore, the power of poetic convention ruled out *violations* of the rules. The poet had to obey the dictates of the form without ever challenging it. Ozu's playful disruptions of expectation obviously go much farther in this direction than classical verse would allow. We need to exercise methodological caution as well. There is no doubt that at a very basic level, certain artistic practices and broad cultural assumptions about space and time affected Ozu's work. Yet exactly because the level is so basic, it must also have affected every Japanese filmmaker, every artist, indeed every individual in the culture. But no other filmmaker's style resembles Ozu's. A precise historical explanation cannot simply assert a continuity between centuries of Japanese poetry and the work of a film director born in 1903. And if all Japanese participate in the perceptual and linguistic construct known as *ma*, what makes it more pertinent to Ozu than to any other Japanese artist? Is he somehow 'more Japanese' than his contemporaries? Furthermore, an appeal to 'tradition' often conceals a loose, untheorized, and imperialistic approach to 'Japaneseness'. The danger is the sort of ahistoricity that Tynianov warned against and which is very common in studies of Japanese culture. 'Everything,' writes one critic acerbically, 'can be compared with everything in the hands of a skilful and well-versed scholar who draws our attention to parallels in works which are centuries apart.'[15] We are back to the problem posed in Chapter 2, where I argued that a causal explanation (rather than a dispositional one) requires us to spell out Ozu's concrete historical circumstances, and to consider the ways in which they may transform many long-range cultural influences. We must start from the assumption that historically specific mediations impinge upon the individual filmmaker. Chapter 3 has shown that Ozu's films draw upon a range of post-Meiji materials. Now we must situate his narrational and stylistic choices within the most proximate and detailed modern contexts we can construct.

For Ozu's approach to narrative and style, the most pertinent factors involve certain developments in prose narrative and graphic styles during late Meiji, Taisho, and early Showa. These realms, as we might expect, are closely tied to the emergent mass culture of the period. They were already mediated by Ozu's position in a commercial film industry. And they embody various syntheses of Japanese and Western traditions. But even this way of putting the problem is too simple. The 'purely Japanese' traditions are not always so pure; and the synthesis, no matter how dependent on foreign models, may be taken as somehow intrinsically Japanese. (We have already seen this happen with *mono no aware* back in Chapter 2.) The task of the Meiji artist was to modernize and remain Japanese; but what is it to be Japanese? To retain some mysterious, uncontaminated essence, or to create a distinct synthesis out of many, often disparate sources?

We can conveniently start by considering some vicissitudes of Japanese narrative forms. Although poetry has dominated all Japanese literary forms to a degree uncommon in the West, there remain important native traditions of narrative. Poem sequences, as we have seen, might vaguely suggest a story. Intermediate forms also arose: the poem with a prose headnote describing the circumstances of composition; the *uta monogatari*, a prose narrative dotted with lyrics; the literary diary, chronicling events and pausing for a *tanka* outburst.[16] In theatrical forms such as noh and kabuki, poetry became harnessed to the necessity for overall dramatic progression. There were also important streams of pure prose narrative – the tale of love, adventure, dreams, and ghosts; the *monogatari*, or long tale; the first-person essay describing witnessed events; and the stories of such Tokugawa writers as Saikaku.[17] Between 1770 and 1867, the colorful mercantile culture of Edo produced a vigorous popular fiction known as *gesaku*, or 'playful compositions'. *Gesaku* writers offered their public melodramatic romances, fairy tales, stories of vendettas and lost loves – usually flamboyantly illustrated with woodblock prints and dwelling upon the bawdy and the comic.[18] Still further from the elevated heights of court verse lay powerful oral narrative forms. Variety halls hosted performances of comic yarns (*rakugo*), historical and contemporary stories (*kodan*), and ballads sung to samisen accompaniment (*rokyoku*, or *Naniwa-bushi*). The Edo period constituted an immense explosion in popular narrative art, which in turn became a major source of twentieth-century mass-market fiction.

Ozu was born during a period of great turbulence in Japanese fiction and drama. The central impetus was the Meiji-era influx of translations of Western literature. Japanese writing was soon exposed to all European literary movements.[19] Most major writers traveled abroad, and many taught or translated foreign works.[20] By the end of the century, Japanese writers had to confront the novelty of the novel, and many a theorist, like Shoyo Tsubouchi in *The Essence of the Novel* (1885), urged his fellows to adopt Western practices. Similarly, there emerged *shimpa*, or 'New School' drama, whose adaptation of foreign models included the notorious production in which Hamlet entered pedaling a bicycle.[21] It was at this period that mass audiences finally lost touch with the conventions of court poetry and noh, and the more plebeian conventions of *renga* and kabuki.[22]

The task of creating a modern Japanese literature and drama led to a range of synthetic narrative forms. The dominant trend of the period 1890-1920 was Naturalism. Quite different from its source in Maupassant and Zola, Naturalism lay closer to European Romanticism in emphasizing the author's identification with an alienated, drifting hero. Naturalists also retained the episodic construction of pre-Meiji fiction and perpetuated the self-expressive aspect of Japanese traditions. The 'mental-attitude' novel (*shinkyo shosetsu*) offered a purified autobiographical meditation, as in Katai Tayama's *Futon* (*The Quilt*, 1907). Shortly there emerged the 'I-novel' (*watakushi shosetsu*, or simply *shishosetsu*). During its heyday (1915–1920s), the *shishosetsu* became a purely confessional genre, often reveling in the most sordid details of the author's life. Other syntheses included Soseki Natsume's recasting of the traditions of travel diaries into the genre of 'haiku-novel' and the 'White Birch' school's attempt to combine Flaubertian aestheticism with Tolstoyan humanism. Some writers discovered similarities between native traditions and European modernism. The neo-Perceptionist school of the 1920s replaced *haiku* precepts with a grab-bag of notions scavenged from Dada, German Expressionism, and other movements. Yasunari Kawabata compared the associational style of traditional Japanese literature to the 'stream of consciousness' of Joyce and Woolf.[23] All such responses signal that a wedge has been driven, a difference created. Henceforth one can be 'traditional' and Japanese, or modern and Western; or traditional *and* modern *and* Japanese *and* Western. In any case, the writer now confronts his tradition from the outside, with an awareness of other possibilities and an obligation to choose.

These experiments took place primarily in the higher reaches of the literary community. At the same period, modernization brought in its wake a mass literature, often with explicit ties to the *gesaku* fiction and oral recitation of old Edo. Soseki Natsume's *Wagahai wa neko de aru* (*I Am a Cat*, 1905–6) stands as a fair sample of the satiric popular novel derived from colloquial forms. After World War I, the boom in large-circulation magazines and cheap books served to isolate coterie literature and create the *taishu shosetsu*, the 'novel of mass appeal'. This was also the period of the greatest success of Western-style *shimpa* drama.

Whether aiming at the populace or the elite, writers faced the pressure to choose among traditions or to synthesize several. This made them confront specific narrational problems that are familiar from our survey of Ozu's work. There was, first, the matter of overarching plot unity. Most major Japanese novels were written for open-ended serialization, with episodes often being published in different journals, so that any one reader may never have seen the 'whole' text.[24] This practice could only exaggerate the episodic tendencies of Japanese fiction generally. During the 1920s, some writers struggled against the loose autobiographical forms of Naturalism and sought a tighter fictional framework. The exemplary episode here is the 1927 polemic between Junichiro Tanizaki and Ryunosuke Akutagawa. Tanizaki declared an interest in Poe-like stories of fantasy dependent on complicated plot geometry, while Akutagawa insisted that novels should depend upon ordinary, unsensational incidents.[25] What is important here is not each man's solution but the fact that both were reacting against the I-novel and seeking a modern, urbanized Japanese literature.

A second difficulty of the writer's craft involved the construction of the narrative unit. Many writers opted for a laconic, neutral sketch of characters' thought, behavior, and dialogue, punctuated by brief and detached descriptions of surroundings. Here is the end of Tayama's *The Quilt*:

All at once he was stricken with desire, with sadness, with despair. He spread out the mattress, lay the quilt out on it, and wept as he buried his face against the cold, stained, velvet edging.
The room was gloomy, and outside the wind was raging.[26]

In Toson's *Ie* (*The Family*, 1908), a scene concludes:

Finally, the mother and child began to cry together.
In the adjoining house, the preparations of rice cakes began and the pounding noise sounded loudly through the thin walls.[27]

148

These Shklovskian 'false endings' may be regarded as the last gasp of the poetic insert; the lyrical instant no more stands out from the prose fabric than would a weather description in Maupassant.

Such 'flat' passages also suggest a third problem for the writer, that of narrational voice. Masao Miyoshi argues that the modern writer has become an 'accomplice' of silence because the vagueness and ellipticality of the Japanese language create an unstable, shifting rendition of verbal point of view. The common practice of omitting the subject of a sentence allows the novel to glide unexpectedly from first- to third-person narration. The result is a narrating voice that lacks a distinct identity, a 'communal storytelling persona that can slip into any story and take on the voice of an undifferentiated narrative self. *Who* tells the story doesn't seem to matter much . . .'[28]

All these issues – plot versus incident, unity versus diversity, drama versus lyricism, sensational versus mundane action, stable versus unstable narration – come to tangle in Ozu's work as well. Like his peers in literary circles or the popular press, he had to resolve them; but he worked in a mass medium open to a very wide range of influences. Indeed, that medium was itself one source of change in the Japanese narrative tradition.

The cinema arrived in Japan in 1896 and quickly became a central means of Westernizing the country.[29] As a modern foreign invention, it had the air of exotic sophistication later associated with the streetcar and the radio. As a popular entertainment, it dealt a severe blow to kabuki and eventually vanquished *shimpa*.[30] As a vehicle of communication, it became a conduit for portraying European and American life. As the public's most vivid access to customs and ideas from abroad, it was clamped under the censorship designed for the press. The increasing presence of American films after World War I introduced filmmakers to the emergent consolidation of the 'classical' Hollywood style.[31] Thus it is only partially true to suggest that cinema recorded and perpetuated Japanese aesthetic traditions, even granting the benshi's precedents in popular theatre.[32] Like Western novels and plays, Western cinema to a large extent challenged domestic traditions.

It also harbored partial solutions to the writer's problems of craft. Hollywood's plot constructions, derived from the well-made play, the novel, and the short story, accustomed audiences to far more compressed and linear forms than were in common circulation. Cohesion devices like dialogue hooks, appointments, and deadlines offered new constructional resources. Viewers grew to accept the motivated ending, not to mention the *hapii endo*. Interpolated descriptions of objects and surroundings could be motivated as cutaways or establishing shots, as in the opening tour of the dining room in William de Mille's *Miss Lulu Bett* (1921) or the atmospheric transition from country to city in *Mantrap* (1926). The result for Japanese cinema was, as I suggested in Chapter 2, a mixed dramaturgy, a fairly conventional Hollywood framework studded with digressions and decorations. Finally, as a visual medium, cinema posed no difficulty of narrational voice. A movie had no pronouns to omit. It may thus be symptomatic that in 1917 Tanizaki expressed faith in the artistic development of film and shortly wrote his first scenario, the influential Western-style *Amachua Kurabu* (*Amateur Club*, 1920).[33]

Visual artists of Ozu's day faced no less acute problems than did writers. Like *mono no aware* or the attentuated poetic insert, the concept of *ma* underwent profound changes in the crucible of Meiji. In architecture, the introduction of Western theories, materials, and methods marked, in the words of one historian, 'the end of the intuitive understanding and acceptance of *ma*.'[34] A difference has once again emerged: there will be Japanese architecture, Western architecture, or, somehow, both. Designers returned from European educations in the 1920s and created buildings modeled on the German Secession or the work of Le Corbusier. In the graphic arts, factional splits emerged between 'Western-style' painting (*Yoga*) and 'Japanese-style' painting (*Nihonga*), between European-influenced schools of printmaking and 'pure' Japanese ones. But again traditions were selective: painting and prints in the 'Japanese' style were infused with Western styles and techniques, just as the 'Western-style' works often owed much to native compositional practices. Since the eighteenth century, Japanese woodblock print artists had borrowed extensively from Western techniques of perspective, and by the 1880s they had achieved European standards in the portrayal of movement, anatomy, and light and shadow.[35] French *plein-air* techniques took strong hold in academic painting and became canonized in a variety of schools and societies.[36] Graphic artists, like their contemporaries in the literary world, had to make their peace with a different sort of spatial representation, even if that meant rejecting or redefining *ma*. Painters like Takeji Fujishima and Misei Kosugi created unique syntheses of two traditions, such as volumetric, Western-style figures set against a flat, decorative 'oriental' ground.[37]

1. An advertisement for Sapporo beer, 1923

Also like their contemporaries in literature, many of these artists worked in relation to the emerging cosmopolitan lifestyle. Popular woodblock prints reemerged in the 1890s as a kind of pictorial journalism before being definitively eclipsed by Western printing methods brought in for mass publication. Both painters and printmakers began to earn their living as commercial illustrators. One of the most important artists of Taisho, Yumeji Takehisa, started as a caricaturist before devising satiric and self-consciously 'urban' portraits of *moga* and bohemians. The artists' problem became that of defining a 'Japaneseness' that could also accommodate the changes brought about by modernization. A common solution was *citation*: the paralleling of New Tokyo with Old Edo. Thus the *Shin Hanga*, or 'New Prints', movement was begun by a shrewd publisher who urged his artists to create works obviously 'Japanese' enough to sell in numbered editions on the foreign market. As a result, Goyo Hashiguchi, who trained as a Western-style painter, sought to reinvoke the spirit of Utamaro in his portraits of women, while Shinsui Ito revived Hiroshige's approach to landscape but treated it in Western fashion.[38] Just as the interpolated lyrical digression becomes a laconic aside when wedged into a modern novel, so the *ukiyo-e* style looks quaint when rendering automobile traffic under Ginza neon.

But even this account keeps too much to the level of high art. The visual experience of Ozu's Tokyo was defined less by the work of painters and printmakers, no matter how celebrated, than by advertising and the popular press, which flooded the city dweller with images derived from European and American design. The three decades that saw the decline of noh, kabuki, *renga*, and the popular woodblock print saw the birth of promotional design, trademarks, poster art, popular photography, and comic strips. These media inserted 'intrinsically Japanese' components into a Western format designed to sell consumer goods. Like the mass novelist drawing on oral forms, the commercial artist cited clichés of 'Japaneseness'. In an ad for a department store, a woman portrayed according to Meiji Western standards browses through a volume of *ukiyo-e* prints. A Japanese girl against vaguely Art Nouveau cherry branches offers you a glass of Sapporo beer (fig. 1). By the time that Tokyo rebuilt from the 1923 quake, the canons of Western representation had sunk deeply into the texture of daily life. During the Taisho era, the very term *ma* became differentiated from a new one, *kukan* – space as a positive entity on the Western model, space as an infinite volume populated by solid bodies. Even something as linguistically and perceptually specific to Japanese culture as this sense of space became framed as merely one alternative mode of thought after the Meiji era's 'dawn to the West'.

Graphic and literary traditions merged in many metropolitan trends, one of the most striking being that known as *ero-guro-nansensu*, or 'erotic-grotesque-nonsense'. As hard to define as it is easy to recognize, *ero-guro-nansensu* drew inspiration from everything that was vaguely Western, up-to-date, and salacious. The eroticism might flaunt art deco pin-ups or sado-masochistic motifs; the grotesquerie recalls both Grosz and comic strips; the nonsense ranges from the inane to the incomprehensible (figs. 2, 3). Such imagery may have fueled Tanizaki's fantasy of post-quake Tokyo, boiling with 'secret pleasures' and 'weird crimes'. The correlative literary trend included such works as Yu Ryutanji's *Horo jidai* (*Years of Wandering*, 1928), about two young men who live in a garage with a young woman. One boy dresses shop windows and the other sells passers-by a chance to look at the moon through his telescope, while the girl, described as 'nonsensical and cheerful', goes to high school.[39]

As a worker in the film industry, Ozu was in a position to take advantage of current trends in graphic design and mass literature. Most ready to hand, though, was the cinema itself, especially that imported from America. As we have seen, Hollywood not only embodied the modernity of the West but offered an accessible model of narrative unity that was seldom seen in Japanese literary traditions. Moreover, Hollywood inspired Ozu with an awareness of overt narration and stylistic playfulness. Still less, then, can we posit a direct transmission of 'inherently Japanese' traits to Ozu. His most pertinent frame of reference was always that of the cinema. We are now in a position to see in more detail how the process of mediation worked.

Three American Mentors

Ozu's tendency toward 'overdetermined' unity must be seen in the light of the powerful influence which the American cinema had over him. From very early, he took up the Hollywood canons of construction with unusual fervor. His 1930s scripts are more severe and tightly plotted than other films that survive from the period. A comparatively relaxed film like *Days of Youth* nonetheless exhibits a structure of careful symmetries, repetitions, and climaxes quite unlike that of, say, *Marching On* (1930) or Gosho's *Madam and Wife* (1931).

2. An *ero-guro-nansensu* cover from *Tokyo Puck*, 1929

3. A Berlin-flavored *ero-guro-nansensu* illustration from 1929

Around a pencil and pad the opening scene of *Tokyo Chorus* builds a theme-and-variations gag worthy of Keaton. A more mature film like *I Was Born, But . . .* is a masterpiece of syuzhet construction in the American vein; I know of no equivalent in Japanese cinema of its period. While some of Ozu's *gendai-geki* peers moved toward slice-of-life constructs, he sought from his scriptwriters plots highly unified around causality, interwoven motifs, and parallels. To take only one example, *Brothers and Sisters of the Toda Family* is single-minded in its minute exploration of the effects which the father's death has on the family, and it springs as many complications as a soap opera. (In fact, it strongly resembles McCarey's 1937 *Make Way for Tomorrow*.)

More specifically, Ozu learned from three American filmmakers who had raised narrative unity to heights of finesse. With *A Woman of Paris* (1923), Charles Chaplin won critical praise not only for the 'realism' of his story material but for its rigorous handling. Building his plot around a single initiating incident in the characters' past, Chaplin cleverly developed motifs of props and dialogue and exploited a range of parallel structures in order to compare characters. Like other Japanese filmmakers, Ozu was immensely impressed by *A Woman of Paris* and throughout his career cited it as a model of the well-constructed film. Ernst Lubitsch was also taken with Chaplin's achievement, and *The Marriage Circle* (1924) pushed further along several lines. Here Lubitsch declares an interest in abstract plot geometry. While *A Woman of Paris* centers on a love triangle, the five major characters of Lubitsch's film enter into a roundelay of romantic misunderstandings that keeps spinning to the very last shot. By the mid-1920s, Lubitsch's films constituted the epitome of streamlined plot construction, and Ozu was not the only Japanese director to be influenced.

Ozu acknowledged Chaplin and Lubitsch as mentors, but he seems to have made no mention of a third source, Harold Lloyd. Of course no Japanese director could have been unaware of this peppy star, since not only his films but his trademark, the eyeglasses with perfectly circular lenses, were basic *mobo* equipment and were known simply as *roydo*. Ozu paid homage to Lloyd through frequent citations. *The Freshman* (1925) became the prototype of Ozu's college comedies, and its film-poster-within-a-film probably inspired the cinephiliac Ozu to try such a device in many later movies (fig. 4). A poster for *Speedy* (1928) (Lloyd's nickname in *The Freshman*) adorns one wall in *I Graduated, But . . . .* Lloyd's influences on Ozu are various, but here what is most salient is the American director's commitment to tight script unity. Lloyd prided himself on plotting comedies as carefully as other producers planned dramas, and his works abound in recurrent motifs and explicit parallels, such as the sewing-motif in *The Freshman*, which both initiates Harold's courtship and becomes the basis for a string of gags at the big college party.

Upon the base provided by Chaplin, Lubitsch, and Lloyd, Ozu was able to build still other structures derived from post-Meiji absorptions of Western literary conventions. He grew up reading Taisho fiction and declared his admiration for Tanizaki, Akutagawa, Naoya Shiga, and Ton Satomi.[40] From such sources he took certain aspects of dramaturgy and style. His interpolated views of settings echo the literary convention of the locale description we have

4. *The Freshman*

already considered, while his scenes of silent meditation recall many such in Meiji and Taisho Westernized fiction. Ozu accepts the Western cinema's narrative structure and narrational principles while expanding them at codified moments: a description of setting or quiet meditation at a scene's beginning or end, the very points of narrational overtness privileged by classical filmmaking.[41]

A similar synthesis is visible in Ozu's 'cycle-of-life' rhythm. Writers affiliated with the Naturalist school cultivated one sort of novel chronicling the fortunes of a single large family. Katai Tayama's trilogy *Sei* (*Life*, 1908), *Tsuma* (*The Wife*, 1908–9), and *En* (*The Bond*, 1910) describes the life of a small-town family as older generations decay and decline. Toson Shimazaki's autobiographical novel *Haru* (*Spring*, 1908) uses the season as a metaphor for the youth of his characters, as Ozu would later. Most important was *Family* (1908), a chronicle of two fading rural families. Ozu obviously owes much to this tradition's handling of narrative structure. These works concentrate on the conventional theme of a decline from prosperity and treat it by shifting point of view among households. Both Tayama and Toson 'de-dramatize' the novel by minimizing melodramatic conflicts and concentrating on ordinary routines. Even particular motifs like the commemoration picture are employed by these authors. But Ozu's prior commitment to Hollywood's concentrated unity transforms such conventions. His abstract cycle of life is more sharply delineated and his symmetry and parallels are far more rigorous. His films mix a more focused, 'Western' dramaturgical structure with motifs and temporal patterns drawn from late Meiji fiction.

Closer to Ozu's later films is Tanizaki's masterful novel *Sasame Yuki* (*The Makioka Sisters*, 1943–8). Here we find detailed treatment of family routines, a tracing of the family's decline, and a portrayal of the opaque heroine. One line of action involves marrying off the daughter Yukiko, while another revolves around a daughter with a scandalous past. The action is even haunted by a dead father. Moreover, it has a strong sense of repetition and parallelism among events, usually motivated by seasonal changes. Although Tanizaki's work generally lacks particulars of Ozu's underlying cyclical myth, *The Makioka Sisters* is in many respects an Ozu film in print. Yet one may also wonder whether films like *Toda Family* did not in fact influence the cinema-conscious Tanizaki.

In any event, the growing 'literariness' of Ozu's work is evident in the extent to which the postwar films draw upon prestigious sources. *A Hen in the Wind* comes from a story by Shiga, *Late Spring* from a story by Kazuo Hirotsu; *The Munekata Sisters* is based on a novel by the famous Jiro Osaragi; *Equinox Flower* and *Late Autumn* are taken from novels by Ton Satomi, a pillar of Taisho literary culture. Like Mizoguchi at the same time, Ozu turned to safe literary sources, partly as a refuge during the Occupation, but also because his work was growing more similar to that of older-generation writers. It was at this period that he began to pay visits to such venerable figures as Satomi and Shiga.[42] By this point, however, such literary sources have also become reconstituted by Ozu's idiosyncratic narrational strategies.

So much for the proximate sources of his rigorous approach to plot. The contemporary sources of his playfulness are no less heterogeneous, and again they arrive filtered through his situation in the film industry. Ozu's apprenticeship to Tadamoto Okubo in the *nansensu* genre doubtless contributed most here. *Nansensu* comedies, while trying to suggest some of the naughtiness of their literary and graphic counterparts, were prevented by censorship from plunging into truly bizarre regions. Okubo's *nansensu* are often remembered as vulgar and stupid, but in the absence of any surviving instances, it is likely that *Days of Youth* is a late example – in which case the genre would be far from despicable. When Ozu started directing, comedy was becoming the favored mode of sophisticated 'modern' filmmaking. Yutaka Abe, a director who had worked in Hollywood, came to Japan and made *Ashi ni sawatta onna* (*The Woman who Touched the Leg*, 1925). Based on *The Marriage Circle*, it won the first *Kinema Jumpo* award and quickly became a model comic film for young directors.

Ozu's most obvious debt to his *nansensu* origins is his constant interest in jokes on bodily functions. Almost none of his films is too solemn to avoid vulgar treatments of urination, flatulence, or itches that one must scratch. True, such coarseness is characteristic of certain Japanese artistic traditions. A renga stanza by Sokan reads:

> Even at the time
> When my father lay dying
> I still kept farting.[43]

But again these native traditions reach Ozu mediated by the popular mass culture of his moment; *ero-guro-nansensu* relied heavily on scatological humor. For Ozu, bodily functions become another way to shake the geometrical expectations of narrative structure. Children and old men interrupt scenes to rush to the toilet. Little boys scratch their genitals and men test their sweat by sniffing their fingertips. In *Tokyo Chorus*, employees sneak off into the men's washroom to peep into their bonus envelopes, but one clerk drops his money into the pissoir. *Ohayo* does interesting work with boys and men breaking wind. Usually such comedy constitutes another jab at masculine dignity, but in *Record of a Tenement Gentleman*, the heroine and her sister's recollection of how they blew their noses in childhood becomes a moment of shared nostalgia.

Even when the humor is not so earthy, an abrupt or far-fetched gag may deflect our expectations. Ozu's earliest films tend to be thoroughgoing comedies or to shift, as we have seen, into a lyrical or dramatic tone from a comic base. Certain cues lead us to expect the film to have a tightly unified shape, but individual scenes are often given surprising comic twists. In *The Lady and the Beard*, Teruo is trying to convince his sister that she should find his bearded friend Okajima attractive. He points to portraits of great men with beards and reminds her of the sages depicted on Japanese currency. But then Okajima enters, fresh from the barbershop and carrying his beard wrapped in paper. He strokes the beards in the photographs before trying vainly to reattach his own beard to his face. The gags stem from the basic premise, but they develop in nonsensical directions. This sort of unpredictable comedy persists, though in more muted form, throughout Ozu's career: the comparison of husbands and carp in *The Flavor of Green Tea over Rice*, the gag of the broken breadloaf in *Early Summer*, and the scene in *Tokyo Story* when, after the grandfather excuses a child's tantrum by saying, 'A boy should be lively,' a bag is flung clattering into the frame.

Nansensu, however, leads us back to the American silent cinema, for Hollywood comedy contributed to the emergence of that genre. Chaplin and Lubitsch often created satiric social commentary through overt narration. In *A Woman of Paris*, a gentleman's intimacy with the unmarried heroine is conveyed by his breezy extraction of a handkerchief from a dresser in her boudoir. At a party a woman swathed in a sheet is slowly unwrapped as the camera concentrates on avid watchers. In *The Marriage Circle*, Lubitsch made the narration still more overt by means of cynically mocking intertitles and close-ups of objects divorced from character attention. Through such means, and a penetrating insight into the resources offered by glances and doorways, Lubitsch implied that intricate desires and counterplans lurked beneath banal social exchanges.

Ozu's satiric bent emerges in his earliest films and survives throughout his career. *An Introduction to Marriage* reads like a pastiche of Lubitsch: a faintly smutty title, satire of a bourgeois milieu, and interlocked plot lines involving two couples. *What Did the Lady Forget?* mocks the married couple's hypocrisy while also teasing the young for their frivolity. *Equinox Flower* makes scathing fun of the executive yes-man. Even a non-comic film like *Early Summer* shows characters using sociable chat to conceal real feelings – a device that is promoted to dominance in *Ohayo*. At some point in almost every Ozu film, performers like Saito, Ryu, or Hara must mask feelings by politeness. All this is rendered through a consistently overt narration that often echoes its American sources: a frayed sock that deflates the father's tirade in *I Was Born, But...* recalls *The Marriage Circle*'s first shot, a close-up of a sock with a hole in it.

A somewhat different sort of comic device and tone emerges from the influence of Harold Lloyd. Ozu fancied Lloyd's zanier gags: he borrowed the glad-handing jig from *The Freshman* for use not only in the college films but also in his gangster movies, thus creating unexpectedly sprightly thugs. More pervasively, both filmmakers were drawn to situations of acute public humiliation. A 1920s Lloyd film alternates between the 'thrill comedy' for which he is justly famous and prolonged scenes of painful embarrassment. Harold is shamed as a weakling in *The Kid Brother* (1927), exposed as a coward in *Grandma's Boy* (1922), and mocked as a stammering fraud in *Girl Shy* (1924). *The Freshman* presents a relentless succession of scenes of public ridicule, climaxing in a school party at which Harold's new suit comes to pieces at the seams.

Similar scenes occur throughout Ozu's early work. In *Body Beautiful*, an unemployed husband must pose for his wife's paintings until he is thrown over for a man with a better physique. *Tokyo Chorus*'s lavatory gag pays off with the clerk drying his damp money on his blotter, displaying not only his humiliation but the amount of his bonus. Later films use less physical comedy but still center on embarrassing situations – a father mocked for his opposition to his daughter's marriage (*Equinox Flower*), a daughter blamed for acting impetuously (*Early Summer*), an office worker exposed as a seductress

5. *Days of Youth*

6. *Days of Youth*

7. *Days of Youth*

8. *Girl Shy*

(*Early Spring*), a father revealed as a buffoon (*I Was Born, But . . .*), a woman shamed for descending to prostitution (*Woman of Tokyo, A Hen in the Wind*), an aunt left to entertain a marriage prospect when her niece skips the *o-miai* (*The Flavor of Green Tea over Rice*), a man who fails to get a pipe from a woman who has given pipes to his friends (*Late Autumn*), or a widow whose brother tries to marry her off to a leering salaryman (*End of Summer*). Certain cultural constants, such as the role of 'shame' as a sanction in Japanese society, may have sensitized Ozu to Lloyd's brand of comic masochism;[44] but the American's comedy of embarrassment also supplied, as we shall see shortly, concrete narrative strategies.

Traces of Ozu's three American mentors mingle fruitfully in his silent work. He pays homage to Chaplin's film in the very title of *Woman of Tokyo*, a tale of another oversensitive young man who commits suicide and leaves two women grieving over his corpse. The same film also pays tribute to Lubitsch by including a lengthy excerpt from his episode of *If I Had a Million* (1932). (For a discussion, see p. 241.) More detailed are the cross-references in an extended gag in *Days of Youth*. The student Yamamoto leans his hand on a pole marked 'Wet paint' while his foot scuffs at a glove on the ground. When he pulls his palm away (fig. 5), he finds it covered with paint. His girlfriend Chieko arrives, and he quickly conceals it from her. In the next scene he sits with her in a coffee shop, and still trying to conceal the damp smear, he leaves fingerprints on his cup (fig. 6). Yamamoto's humiliation comes when he absently rests his cheek on his hand and leaves a perfect palm-print on his face (fig. 7). The gag's premises clearly derive from American sources. In *Girl Shy*, Lloyd leans on a tree sticky with pitch (fig. 8) and winds up attached to it, then to his trouser pocket, and finally to the young woman he courts. In *A Sailor-Made Man* (1921), Harold rests his hand on a freshly painted cable before blowing a kiss to his girl (figs. 9–10). The close-up of the coffee cup comes evidently from *The Marriage Circle* (fig. 11). In addition, both Lubitsch and Lloyd employ analytical editing that cuts in to a detail so that we cannot miss its significance. Ozu's piecemeal découpage does the same thing, breaking the gag into distinct close-ups.

Of course, other Japanese directors learned from the same models. Naruse's *Apart from You* (1933) lifts the hole-in-the-sock gag from *The Marriage Circle*, while his *Kagirinaki hodo* (*Street without End*, 1934) includes a scene from *The Smiling Lieutenant* (1931). But the three Hollywood direc-

9. *A Sailor-Made Man*

10. *A Sailor-Made Man*

tors' influence on Ozu extends not only to comic devices and motifs. He learned from them how narration could become pervasively playful. When, in *A Woman of Paris*, former lovers greet each other after a year, one says: 'Well,' and the other replies: 'Well.' The crisp dialogue titles convey exactly their hesitant, exploratory reconciliation; but they also reveal a narration that has chosen to reveal and stress just these, potentially superfluous, monosyllables while in other scenes entire sentences are never transcribed. When *The Marriage Circle* opens with a title proclaiming that 'The day starts late, but gloriously, in the home of Professor Josef Stock,' and proceeds to present a slam-bang quarrel between husband and wife, we are in the presence of a sarcastic, mildly unreliable narration that aims to undercut expectations. And such overtness need not emerge solely from intertitles. In Lloyd's *For Heaven's Sake* (1926), a romantic scene under the stars is jolted into absurdity when the moon is revealed to be a neon sign for the Crescent Laundry. A quarrel in Lubitsch's *Lady Windermere's Fan* (1925) is ironically underscored by a cutaway to birthday flowers gone unnoticed on a table. American comedy thus revealed to Ozu the resources of overt narration. In conspiracy with the audience behind the backs of the characters, it could achieve an encompassing distance on the action. In league with the characters against the audience, it could suppress information, deflect or shatter expectations, and compel the viewer to recast assumptions. It could become frankly artificial, unpredictable, and gamelike – that is, playful even at 'serious' dramatic moments.

11. *The Marriage Circle*

It is here too that we find the most proximate source of Ozu's parametric use of style. All these directors relied on centered, symmetrical framing, and they were undoubtedly influential in establishing the general popularity of the piecemeal approach to découpage. Lubitsch took particular interest in graphic interplay among shots. Ozu normally disliked dissolves, but he recalled in 1933 that Lubitsch had used them well in *The Marriage Circle*, in order to show two old friends chatting rapidly with one another.[45] Here Lubitsch creates a flow of graphic qualities by dissolving back and forth between mirror-image compositions (figs. 12–13). Ozu also adopted Lubitsch's exact timing of frame entrances and exits and his use of slight vacancies in the frame to prime the viewer for the next bit of action.[46] As Sato indicates, in *The Marriage Circle* Lubitsch often has actors move in the same posture or at the same rate (Ozu will extend this to *sojikei* staging and acting in unison),

12. *The Marriage Circle*

13. *The Marriage Circle*

UNIVERSITY OF WINCHESTER
LIBRARY

14. *Grandma's Boy*

15. *Grandma's Boy*

and he relies on the unmoving camera to foreground the actors' smallest gestures and expressions.[47] Even Ozu's deviations from the extrinsic norm can be found, undeveloped, in his American sources. While Lubitsch and Lloyd had mastered classical staging and editing, Chaplin was prone to make exact 180-degree cuts, as in the first bar scene of *The Gold Rush* (1925), which looks very much like an instance of Ozu's *donden* cutting. In Lloyd's *Grandma's Boy*, an 'incorrect' shot/reverse-shot at a piano presents striking graphic matching (figs. 14–15). On the whole, Ozu's sensitivity to technique put him on the lookout for what he could sharpen, extend, and turn to minute effects. '*A Woman of Paris* and *The Marriage Circle*,' he recalled, 'had very sophisticated styles which could express even the smallest nuances of emotion.'[48] American comedy revealed to Ozu that classical film style, even in its momentary inconsistencies, harbored the possibility of a subtle and systematic play of coherence and deviation. Thus his 1929–31 films are fully 'Hollywood', containing virtually all the stylistic options upon which he would later rely, as well as more orthodox choices.[49] With *Tokyo Chorus* and *I Was Born, But . . .*, Ozu began to winnow out what he could no longer exploit, and he continued to sift and weigh choices well into the 1950s. In his stylistic development, film by film, Ozu built his norms out of a revising and decentering of the American cinema.

By radicalizing his teachers' narrational overtness, Ozu made it offset an overdetermined rigor of narrative structure and create a rich aesthetic tension. Comedy could not only disturb textual order; it hinted at other patterns hovering in the background. Take *Days of Youth*'s paint-gag again. For all that it owes to Hollywood, it contains some off-center qualities. Yamamoto leans on the pole because he is looking at a cast-off glove lying on the ground. When paint covers his hand, he conceals it from Chieko, but a passer-by sees the stray glove and then spots Yamamoto's smeared hand, which looks as if it is encased in a glove. Therefore, the gentleman concludes, the stray glove belongs on the other hand. When Yamamoto declines it, the man tosses the glove back into the street. The digressive gag will later be made a part of a larger motif of hands and feet that passes through the film. (See pp. 189–90.) This motif does not generate gags in the Hollywood sense, but its repetitions point to a quirkily teasing narration. In subsequent films, the principle of free system-building would be extended beyond motifs to every domain of narration, from delaying the main line of action to creating additive variations in framing. This ludic, open-ended narration is the legacy of Ozu's understanding that overt play with expectation is central to comedy, and it exemplifies Shklovsky's dictum:

> One of the reasons that the poet blurs the boundary between the serious and the humorous is that humor remains the least codified form, yet it most vividly creates a sense of the disparities of meaning. Humor prepares new forms for serious art.[50]

Ozu's narration, then, springs from a rich matrix of sources, current and of great age, domestic and foreign. If a 'traditional' analogue must be found, we might look to the great woodblock-print artist Hiroshige Ando, who trained

158

in schools of Chinese and Japanese art, adopted Western techniques of perspective and coloring, and retained close ties to the popular urban culture of his day. For Ozu, Japanese poetry and visual art provided general models of rigor and play; urban mass culture and American cinema, inflected by twentieth-century Japanese fiction and graphic art, yielded the most concrete and powerful impulse behind his unique approach to film form. Like writers and graphic artists and other filmmakers, he could self-consciously cite the norms, both native and foreign, that he drew upon; but unlike most other filmmakers, he absorbed them into a larger, dynamic system. Far from being 'purely Japanese', Ozu's films constitute no less a modern synthesis than do the works of his peers in other arts.

In all this, Ozu displays a devotion to the particular problems of his medium that finally makes all talk of sources secondary to his accomplishments. In a 1947 interview he recalled composing renga verse while in a PoW camp. 'Since *renga* is similar to film editing, I found it a good learning experience.'[51] He comes to linked poetry as a man of the cinema, using verse as a chance to practice skills he cannot exercise any other way. The historian's search for sources, if carried out in the hope of finding simple correspondences, will lead to such aporias as that in the critical literature surrounding, again, the 'empty' images in his transitions. For one Western critic, these are 'pillow shots', like the pillow words of classical verse. But Japanese critics have called the same images 'curtain shots', analogous to the break between acts in Western proscenium theatre.[52] Both 'Japanese' and 'Western', Ozu exploits his sources in order to reveal the richness of specifically cinematic form.

8
Uses and Effects

I have devoted myself to the minor arts.
Yasujiro Ozu[1]

Ozu's accomplishment, I have tried to show, consists of taking a limited set of familiar materials and transforming them by means of a unique formal system. This system consists of a narration at once rigorous and playful, one that displays specific strategies of syuzhet organization and stylistic development. In particular, Ozu creates an alternative to classical Hollywood narration that remains indirectly grounded in it; and he develops stylistic features to an unprecedented level of saliency and nuance. The general effect is, I believe, twofold. Through the work of his formal system, certain referents and commonplaces become deepened and enriched. He 'poeticizes' the post-Meiji modernity depicted in urban culture and the mass media. The city, the economic milieux of his characters, their family situations – all fairly stock materials – are revivified. Like the rhetor who amplifies and intensifies set topics, Ozu uses plot and style to make well-worn things fresh.

A second effect is more traditionally 'aesthetic'. Here the familiar materials become the starting point for an exploration of the resources of cinema – its large-scale narrative structures, its narrational options, its stylistic possibilities. From this standpoint Ozu becomes an experimental filmmaker, testing the results of formal decisions and making new demands upon the audience. Here too we are invited to perceive afresh, but what we notice is not a novel reworking of subjects and themes but new possibilities of filmmaking and film viewing. The first general effect emphasizes meaning; the second, pattern. We can switch between these two options as we like; but we always know that the other possibility is there. To feel the force of the poeticizing of everyday life, one must sense, however vaguely, the fine grain of the poetic organization itself. To follow the labyrinth of form and style one must take, even tacitly, concrete human problems as a point of departure. In sum, Ozu has achieved what many filmmakers have dreamed of: he made commercial films of wide human appeal, but at the same time he probed the deepest possibilities of the medium.

My discussion has stressed function and context; but there remains one more set of problems around these notions that a historical poetics must confront. What can it say about the *social* functions and contexts of a film? The previous chapter has already shown that within the social sphere of Japanese art and popular culture, Ozu created his own synthesis of native and alien forms, a synthesis which illustrates the shifting and equivocal nature of the notion of 'Japaneseness'. What of the broadest social implications of his films? A poetics cannot offer a full-blown theory of society, but it does presuppose some concepts of social action and relations. The poetics which I propose does imply certain things about how a film functions within the social formation, and I will sketch them briefly.

First, and very generally: My insistence throughout this book on mediations should suggest that the institution and the medium of cinema transform, to various degrees, the material on which they draw; that the specific context of film production and reception establishes its own mediated relationship between the film and its maker or audience; and that the history of culture, especially popular culture, impinges at every point on the film. Secondly, and centrally: Any adequate account of the social uses and effects of cinema cannot rest content with a description of theme and subject matter. The formal and stylistic norms of cinema, themselves social and historical, constitute an indispensable frame of reference for the study of a film's social functions; and the particular use that the given film makes of those norms is crucial to assessing its social role. Thirdly, and most controversially: This poetics starts from a 'rational-choice' model of filmmaking and film viewing. This point requires a bit more explanation.

The language of rational action – strategies, tactics, choice, selection, decision, problem, solution – has permeated my account of Ozu's art. That is because a conception of the filmmaker and the film viewer as deliberating agents is central to the historical poetics I propose. My assumption can be spelled out with the help of Jon Elster's model of rational social action. He proposes a two-stage 'filter'. First, out of an abstract set of possible choices, the structural constraints of a situation narrow the options to a feasible subset. Then from this subset an agent makes an intentional choice based on beliefs, desires and rational goals.[2] Ozu offers a perfect example. As we have seen, he faced structural constraints: what Shochiku policy and budget established as a feasible subset of story materials and dramaturgical and technical options. He took as his goal the making of films at once rigorous and playful, accessible and experimental in the ways I have already analyzed. From the options available to him he selected those materials and forms that would help him achieve this goal. (This is not to say that the goal arrived fully-formed; doubtless immersion in the materials and forms had some reciprocal effect on the very formation of the goal. The process had a trial-and-error aspect. What is being reconstructed here is not the empirical psychological process but the underlying logic of the situation.[3]) What makes Ozu unusual is the degree to which he voluntarily limited his choices; he added more rule-governed constraints than most other directors would. A remark of Elster's confirms from a theoretical angle Chapter 6's point about freedom in order: 'If we regard an action very generally as the outcome of a *choice within constraints*, then typically the choice will represent an element of freedom and the constraints an element of necessity. If, however, the constraints are themselves freely chosen, the element of necessity is to some extent mastered and harnessed to a purpose.'[4]

In arguing for a social explanation of such activity, the analyst must reconstruct the choice situation by spelling out the circumstantial constraints and showing how they narrow options down to a feasible subset; explicate the basis of the agent's choice; and explain the social effects of the action. The analytical task will thus involve a causal explanation of mental states, an intentional explanation of individual action, and a causal explanation of aggregate social phenomena.[5] For example, to show that Ozu intended to use everyday life as a source of effects, we can cite evidence not only from the films and the cultural context (Chapter 3, Chapter 7) but also from his own testimony. 'Some day in the future my movies will appeal to foreigners. . . . My films are describing what Japanese life is like.'[6] Yet he also claimed that film must transform this 'uncinematic' material. A man sits in the entrance way of a house untying his shoes. 'There, no matter what you do, the drama stagnates. Therefore in Japanese film you must "cinematize" that life which so easily becomes flat. More than anything else, actual Japanese life must be made more filmic.'[7] At the same time, Ozu's aesthetic decisions spring from an intention to explore the medium, as when he notes his preferences for stable compositions or the color red.

This model does not, incidentally, involve the so-called intentional fallacy, since Wimsatt and Beardsley's notorious essay did not argue that an intention was irrelevant to explaining the historical constitution of an art work, only that it was irrelevant to judging or interpreting the work's aesthetic effects.[8] Nor is this model committed to what contemporary jargon calls a 'voluntarist subject'. As a Marxist, Elster emphasizes that intended acts necessarily have unintended consequences, and that causal explanations operate 'behind the back' of the social agent.[9] He is also careful to underscore that the model is a *regulative* one in that it is most fruitful to assume that social action is the result of goal-directed choice unless there is evidence to the contrary. 'Not all human behavior is rational or intentional, but there is a well-grounded *presumption* that this will be the case.'[10]

The rational-agent model might be seen as automatically subscribing to a communication theory of art, whereby a 'sender' deliberately inserts some message into the film for the 'receiver' to take out. The sender can be the individual artist who wishes to communicate a vision of the world, or a social group that transmits a message by means of the work. The clearest case is propaganda, which conceives the film as a vehicle for a doctrine.

The individualistic conception of communication is familiar to us from much Ozu criticism. He is typically portrayed as having a particular vision of Japanese life, chiefly involving the dissolution of the family, which he sought to convey to his audience. The personal-communication model gets extended to style when the critic treats Ozu as deliberately evoking a respect for traditional values by use of *mu, mono no aware,* and other Zen concepts. After the war, as an older-generation director he tended to make public pronouncements that revolved around national identity, as when he remarked in 1947 that directors needed to make 'inherently Japanese' films.[11] One writer sees the asceticism of his style as revealing his tragic awareness of a decaying world: it 'betrays the desperate obstinacy of the last representative of a tradition.'[12] Yet everything that I have argued so far suggests that Ozu used materials that were clichéd and already to hand, rather than personally derived; and that he pursued formal innovation on its own historical terms, not as a vehicle for a set of private meanings. This is not to say that Ozu did not in some sense believe in the 'messages' one can attribute to his films; he probably did, as do many viewers. But to reduce the film to its message beggars the range and richness of his accomplishment as a filmmaker. Nor is this to assume that no film can take a communicative purpose as its 'dominant'; plainly many films do. (Recall the wartime American film *Four Methods of Flush Riveting*.) The point is simply that a personal-communication account will have to produce as 'thick' a description *in communicative terms* of materials, narrative, and style as have the foregoing pages, showing that each feature functions somehow to convey a message. (And not a banal or redundant one, for our inquiry presupposes that Ozu is not a banal or redundant filmmaker.) If we take poetics to presume that the artist produces a work which has effects and uses, we need not limit ourselves to assuming that communication is the only or most important of them. The film-as-communication theory holds rational-agent assumptions, but the rational-agent model does not commit us to that theory.

Seeing Ozu's work as a means by which a social group furthers an ideological project – the second 'communication' alternative I have sketched – is much more promising, since it is plain that such a rational goal is commonly held by institutions. Thus, for instance, it is plausible to argue that in the 1930s Shochiku's emphasis upon the *shoshimin-geki* genre was a deliberate attempt to woo a middle-class feminine audience and perhaps as well to use a mildly critical humanism to attract a liberal intelligentsia. As the decade wore on, the studio seemed definitely to shift toward upper-class milieux and protagonists, often using working- or middle-class characters for subplots and counterpoint. To a considerable degree, Ozu's subjects, themes, and many dramaturgical and stylistic options make sense as a shifting 'feasible subset' furnished by studio policy. Similar constraints, predictably, operated on Ozu's war-related filmmaking. Japan was at war for most of the first forty years of Ozu's life, and once he had achieved some notoriety he was recruited to assist in propaganda efforts. It was common for writers and graphic artists to be sent to observe the war in China and publish memoirs or thinly fictionalized treatments.[13] As a result of the success of his wartime films, Ozu was sent with Atsuta to Singapore to make *Haruka nari fubo no kuni* (*Far-Away Motherland*). It was to be about friendship among a troop of soldiers in battle. Although Sato calls the script 'a home-drama at the front', in summary it sounds very much like a typical battle film of the pre-Pearl Harbor period, such as *Tsuchi to heitai* (*Mud and Soldiers*, 1939) and *Go-nin no sekkohei* (*Five Scouts*, 1939).[14] In any event, Ozu was unable to go to Burma to shoot *Far-Away Motherland*, and so began work on a semi-documentary about the Indian independence movement in Singapore. When the British recaptured Singapore, Ozu burned the footage before being taken prisoner.[15]

Yet Ozu's wartime work also illustrates how the rational agent can complicate the communication process, deflecting or decentering a straightforward ideological project. There is much evidence that Ozu vacillated about pursuing a pure government-policy line. His films of the early 1930s do not on the whole address Japan's imperial ambitions, but the lost *Until the Day We Meet Again*, originally called, 'The Soldier and the Prostitute', was regarded by some critics as questioning the 1931 Manchurian invasion.[16] In 1937 Ozu was drafted and sent to China. He dropped a jaunty postcard to a friend: 'I'll just go and see the war a little bit.'[17] He served in the army's poison-gas unit, participated in mainland fighting, and was present during the rape of Nanking, the worst Japanese atrocity of the war. In 1938, he encountered his friend Yamanaka, who asked him if he intended to make war films. 'I answered that I didn't know.'[18] When he was demobilized in 1939, he proposed to make *The Flavor of Green Tea over Rice*, a home-front film with a clear national-policy message; but censors refused to pass the script. (See pp. 280–1.) With Ryosuke Saito Ozu started a script based on war diaries, but the army wanted a stronger military emphasis and so this too was abandoned.[19]

While abroad, Ozu sent war letters to the *Asahi Shinbun*, one of which runs: 'I do not want to make any more films that are skeptical about society. If it's there, it's good.'[20] Yet once he was home, Ozu's public comments display a notable reluctance to make a full-blown patriotic effort. He remarked in 1939 that war is difficult to dramatize, not least because of propaganda aims: 'When the war reporting is done by one's allies, then it's simply the assertion of one's own merit.' Nothing impressive comes from the celebration of victories; the best war literature is about the tragedy of loss.[21] In 1941, when asked if going to war had been a good experience, he replied evasively: 'Well, I got what I could out of it. Making a movie is in some respects more difficult than fighting in a war, though it's a bad comparison to make.'[22] In *Brothers and Sisters of the Toda Family* and *There Was a Father*, the war is not explicitly presented; they concern themselves with the spiritual rejuvenation of the home front. Even the vaunted *Far-Away Motherland* seems to have been only half-heartedly pursued, since Ozu spent most of his time in Singapore relaxing at poolside and watching captured American films. Atsuta had only a silent camera and shot soldiers drilling. In sum, Ozu's wartime career exhibits the mixture of institutional constraints and individual decision that a rational-choice model would lead us to expect, and no simple notion of filmmaking as communication is likely to account for all the historical forces at work.

The rational-agent model is perhaps most usefully applied in problem-solution terms. Assigned to make a film on a certain subject and theme, Ozu could take these as materials to be elaborated by the formal system he had devised. For example, the cult of the family, important to both *Toda Family* and *There Was a Father*, was an explicit feature of wartime ideology, as eloquently set forth in the 1937 document, *Cardinal Principles of the National Entity of Japan*:

> The basis of the nation's livelihood is . . . neither the individual nor husband and wife. It is the home. The domestic life does not consist in a lateral relationship, such as between husband and wife or elder brother and younger brother; but that which forms its root is a dimensional relationship between parent and child. . . . Consequently, a family is not a body of people established for profit, nor is it anything founded on such a thing as individual or correlative love. Founded on a natural relationship of begetting and being begotten, it has reverence and affection as its kernel; and is a place where everybody, from the very moment of his birth, is entrusted with his destiny.[23]

In *Toda Family*, the youngest family members must remind their brothers and sisters of what they all owe their parents. *There Was a Father* takes the step from filial piety to national loyalty. At the same period Zen was deliberately exploited as an 'intrinsically Japanese' religion, a point that *There Was a Father* develops explicitly. But Ozu is able to treat these materials in an almost wholly characteristic way: his system 'processes' them. Part Two of this book will consider how narrative construction and cinematic style mute and lyricize the didactic messages of these and other films. This is the work not of a filmmaker blinded by ideology but of an intentional agent aware of structural constraints, adjusting means to ends, and in the process modifying the ends. Such modification, of course, depends upon film form, and an adequate account of film as 'institutional communication' will presume the sort of analysis of narration and style that a historical poetics provides.

Expressions, Reflections, Symptoms

For all its power, the rational-agent model needs supplementing, since as a regulative principle it falls short of explaining more 'involuntary' aspects of the filmmaker's actions. However intentional a social practice may be, it will also have unintended causes and consequences. Within film studies three approaches to identifying involuntary social meaning have emerged: the 'expression' approach, the 'reflection' approach, and the 'symptomatic' approach. In Part Two I shall use them to throw light on particular features of this or that film. Here I want only to introduce them, show how they can enrich the rational-agent approach, and suggest in turn that a historical poetics of cinema can make each one more exact and exacting.

The first option constitutes what might roughly be called an 'expression' theory. We can see the work as spontaneously expressing some aspect of the artist's life or temperament. Expression theories are very common in the history of Japanese aesthetics; art has often been identified as the realm of the artist's emotional fulfillment.[24] Ozu invoked this commonplace when he remarked in 1946: 'I hope to make films which clearly show my own self.'[25] According to many observers, he had already done that. Mizoguchi remarked of *Toda Family*: 'This is "The Brothers and Sisters of the Ozu Family".'[26] Sato has sought biographical parallels, claiming that Ozu grew up strongly attached to his mother, a fact which made him shy, reluctant to marry, and abnormally sensitive to the break-up of the family.[27] Sato thus finds some films to be strongly autobiographical. *There Was a Father* reflects Ozu's separation from his father while in middle school; *Floating Weeds* suggests that Ozu saw himself as the aging head of an acting troupe.[28] Another critic finds that Ozu's late films mirror his own immediate existence, as he grew old living with his mother.[29]

An expression account confronts classic problems – a drift toward atomism or vagueness, the need for grounding in some theory of psychological development, the tendency to play down form and style in favor of subject and theme. But we cannot dismiss biographical material as irrelevant to a historical poetics. For one thing, it may supply the basis for the artist's 'biographical legend', a construct that is eminently social and that has an important effect on how audiences use films. In the present context, biographical material can also furnish some insight into the basis of the artist's preferences within the choice-making situation. For instance, Shochiku transferred Ozu to the 'modern-life' unit after he had made one *jidai-geki* film, so here institutional constraints affected his action. But once there, Ozu explored a variety of genres before settling into the home drama, and personal causes, running back into his past, may have been one factor in his choice. We cannot reduce the work to the biography, as Chapter 1 has already indicated; but neither can we ignore the biography as a source of some causal factors.

In a similarly partial way, certain aspects of Ozu's filmmaking can be related to his personality. Kido speaks of his stubbornness and recalls that Ozu thought that the Kamata flavor was too cheap and easy on its audience.[30] His teasing humor, his scrupulous personal neatness, and his air of casual indifference obviously shaped his films. But again, the analyst must be alert to mediations, to the fact that biographical material does not arrive innocent and that documents around the films are also shaped by formal presuppositions. The biographical legend is one example. So is the 1927 letter, written *en route* to joining the army, that offers a bravura mixture of 'Japanese' and 'American' motifs:

> The light railway train was running on a couple of lines sweeping the equinox flowers outside the window from left to right – my equinox flowers, see you again! Elinor Glyn's *Three Weeks* deals with the development of erotic intrigues surrounding a man. The three weeks of my call-in are the waste of weariness and fatigue.[31]

There is likewise Ozu's description, in an article for *Kinema Jumpo*, of how he bade farewell to Yamanaka, called to the front. On a hot August day, Yamanaka visits Ozu with some friends. A script sits on the desk. The men open some beers. They talk of what must be taken to the front (notebook, knife, mentholatum). Yamanaka looks out at the garden and compliments Ozu on a blooming tree. 'It was so quiet that no one could believe there was a war going on.'[32] The parting is written as a scene from an Ozu film.

A second approach to contextualizing Ozu's work is less individualistic than the expression-centered account. I call this the 'reflectionist' approach. On this account, any of the themes and referents surveyed in Chapter 3 could be taken not as materials Ozu has selected but as signs bearing collective meanings of which he was not aware. Thus the failure of Meiji promises can be interpreted more broadly as the consequence of the development of Japanese capitalism, which exploited the aspirations of several classes. The centrality of woman to the declining patriarchy can be related to the 1930s emergence of woman as the 'custodian of Japanese culture', which became identified either with home and mother or with the romanticized tradition of the geisha.[33] Ozu's spontaneous shift from a 'downtown' milieu to a wealthier one, while itself a deliberate choice on his part, has a symbolic status in a culture that has long identified the 'low city' with old Edo and the 'high city' with bourgeois refinement.[34] The late films' salaryman drama often reflects the linkage of the postwar firm to the army: not only were management and staff bound by shared wartime memories, but factory units competed as they had in battalions.[35] Consumerism, while a target of satire or a source of pathos in Ozu's films, can be seen as reflecting a larger dynamic within twentieth century Japanese capitalism: in the 1930s, Japan's growing involvement in a world economy; in the 1950s, the nation's take-off. Operating from a broad social perspective, reflection theory treats referents and commonplaces as escaping the control of social agents.

The reflection approach could examine isolated motifs too: the globe-spinning game in *What Did the Lady Forget?* as an enactment of imperial Japan's discovery of the world (the boys 'hit' India, Canada, and Formosa); the resignation at the end of so many films reflecting the cliché phrase *Shikata ga nai* ('There's no help for it'); the literalization of the phrase *madogiwa-zoku* ('workers who sit by windows') in shots such as fig. 241, p. 336. But of even more consequence are the general cultural patterns that a reflection account would seek to disclose. From one perspective, Ozu's films perpetuate the values of the Shirakaba ('White Birch') school of literature so popular in his youth; his aestheticism, 'apolitical' humanism, tolerant liberalism, and prizing of feeling and sensitivity probably owe much to such writers as Shiga. Seen from another angle, his biography itself enacts a familiar pattern. Many men who grew up in the Taisho era went through typical phases: a youthful infatuation with the West during the 1920s and early 1930s followed by a phase of *Nihon kaiki*, a 'return to Japan'.[36] The writer Junichiro Tanizaki is an often-cited case. The man who, as we saw earlier, fantasized a rebuilt Tokyo as a modern metropolis and who argued that Japanese writers must learn plotting from Poe became in the early 1930s an ardent spokesman for an 'intrinsically Japanese' culture: traditional architecture, lacquerware, noh, bunraku, and well-behaved women.[37] Soon Tanizaki would undertake his modern translation of *The Tale of Genji*, to be followed by *The Makioka Sisters*. One could argue that a similar change took place in Ozu's career, when he moved from his early Hollywood-style comedies and dramas to more 'Japanese' works like *Story of Floating Weeds*, *Kagamijishi*, *The Only Son*, *Toda Family*, and *There Was a Father*. (As in the case of Tanizaki, however, the situation is not simple, for there is evidence that both men clung to their Western interests even in their 'Japanist' phase.[38]) After the war, the *Nihon kaiki* stage was often replaced by a new Westernism born of the Occupation: embracing of women's rights, alliance with the Western powers against Communism, and pride in economic growth. Again, Ozu's 1950s work can be taken as a reflection of this new shift in the attitude of many men of his generation.

The social-reflection account can advance to still broader terrain by suggesting that Ozu's works bear traces of a characteristically Japanese definition of the individual. Because of contemporary film theory's insistence that language is the determining force in the construction of the subject in society, there has been a tentative effort to treat Japanese cinema as reflecting certain features of the nation's language,[39] but these are probably so elusive and pervasive that one cannot specify Ozu's difference by means of them. A richer region of inquiry has been that surrounding the concept of *amae*, or the mutual solicitude and forgiveness that binds a group together against outsiders. Takeo Doi has argued that the *amae* relationship, originating in the mother's indulgence of her infant, is peculiar to Japan and that it explains many aspects of the social formation.[40] The resourceful Sato takes this as a point of departure, suggesting that Ozu's films reflect the *amae* relationship. Most basically, Ozu faithfully describes the psychic basis of *amae*, as in his depiction of the rebelliousness of pampered children who know they will be forgiven. Unlike other directors, however, Ozu stresses the need to *control* one's dependence on the group. His films show how people can avoid falling into excessive *amae*. The son must learn to live apart from his father (*There Was a Father*), the daughter must leave her parent (*Late Spring*, *An Autumn Afternoon*, *Late Autumn*). Older men, such as the father in *Equinox Flower* and the grandfather in *End of Summer*, must also learn to control *amae*. The self-aware Ozu character understands the propensity to be overattached to a group and seeks to restrain it. This, Sato argues, keeps the films from falling into the sentimental self-pity of other Japanese works that deal with the family. Sato links this theme to biographical information as well, suggesting that Ozu's attachment to his mother made him an *amaebo*, an 'amae-boy' who knew the joys and drawbacks of dependence.[41]

But even the concept of *amae* is not historically very specific. Such an account might be supplemented by an investigation of the controversy around individualism in the early twentieth century. Before 1868, the concept of the individual was wholly negative; even the first-person pronouns *shi* and *watakushi* were treated as reflecting attitudes that failed to fulfill public ideals. With governmental and industrial expansion in the Meiji period, intellectuals promoted what Sarah Hamilton Nolte has called a *statist* concept whereby the individual was defined in terms of national service. Later, in Naturalist literature there emerged a *privatist* notion whereby the self was permitted free expression and development, but not in the public sphere. After the Russo-Japanese War of 1904–6, a *liberal* version promoted individual identity as the basis of state and society.[42] In Taisho thought all possibilities were present; the privatist version proved especially unstable, shifting toward one of the other concepts.

The concepts seem easily applicable to Ozu, yet here again particular formal principles qualify the reflectionist point. Ozu's narrative construction often enacts the struggle between the liberal trend and the privatist one. Initially, his characters refuse to be defined completely by their duty to the state or the family. The recalcitrant childen, reluctant salarymen, prankish students, and headstrong daughters all behave as if they were working out their own futures. In the course of the plot, the character may be pulled back toward a willingness to define individuality as it is sanctioned by the private sphere – friendship and family. Ozu's films still register the cost of such absorption, especially when the parents' sacrifice for their children registers as a precious loss of personal happiness. *I Was Born, But . . .* goes so far as to criticize the subordination of identity to both familial and public hierarchies. The wartime films are, predictably, the exception in that individuality is harnessed to state ends – implicitly in *Toda Family*, explicitly in *There Was a Father*. More broadly, the films' narrative structure assimilates individual identity to their cycle of natural progression, an alternative not central to Taisho debates. Here again *a priori* generalizations (about, for instance, the power of the Japanese language to construct subjectivity) can be replaced by a more historically precise investigation of social mediations.

The different paths pursued by the reflection approach lead us back to the fluctuating nature of 'Japaneseness' – in early Showa, a cosmopolitan synthesis of East and West; in the war years, a notion of pure national essence; in the 1950s a tradition combining aesthetic sensitivity, adaptability, and team spirit. In this light, Ozu can be made to reflect a variety of attitudes. For Burch, his 1930s and early 1940s films:

> extolled, implicitly or explicitly, those traditional values which constituted the ideological basis for the new totalitarianism. . . . His entire effort, from the mid-1930s onward, constitutes a single anguished query as to the possible disappearance of that pillar of Japanese society, the traditional family system. And it is no accident that his most important film made during the Pacific War [*There Was a Father*] is almost the only film in which he seems to see hope for the system, in the lifelong camaraderie of father and son.[43]

Yet Sato makes the same film more equivocal, suggesting that certain aspects criticize 'the system'. By showing how wartime conditions impose hardships on the *amae* relationship, *There Was a Father* demonstrates that militarists are near to obliterating the traditional Japanese family.[44] Any reflection theory will need to stipulate what is being reflected in the film, and to establish that external reality as both solid and pertinent; if the external social process can be interpreted in different ways, the interpretations of the film will vary accordingly.

To the expression theory and the reflection theory can be added a third that has come into increasing prominence in film studies of the last decade. The symptomatic-reading approach, inaugurated in the literary theory of Pierre Macherey, rests upon an extended analogy with Freudian psychoanalysis. Ideology becomes parallel to consciousness, the unified and complete expression of knowledge. But just as consciousness cannot be wholly unified, ideology is necessarily torn by tensions and contradictions. In writing a book, the author accepts an ideological project: to utter some truth which ideology sanctions. But in mobilizing ideological meanings, the writer (necessarily?) reveals the inadequacies of the ideology: they slip out unawares, like the symptoms that fracture the discourse of the psychoanalytic patient. Thus the critic must play psychoanalyst, looking in the work for the breakdown in unity, the disparities and silences that betray ideology wracked by internal conflict.[45] The critic's task is to perform a 'symptomatic reading' that explains how the work's silences (what it cannot say, on pain of betraying an ideological contradiction) and its inconsistencies (meanings drawn from conflicting ideological sources) create 'determinate disorder'. Macherey will draw on such Freudian concepts as displacement to describe this disorder. His method, worked out in close collaboration with Louis Althusser, was applied to film by the editors of *Cahiers du cinéma*. In a celebrated essay on *Young Mr. Lincoln*, they sought to make such films 'say what they have to say *within* what they leave unsaid, to reveal their constituent lacks', their 'structuring absences'.[46]

In Ozu there are absences aplenty: virtually no representations of manual labor (except for Otsune at her steam table in *The Only Son* and Kihachi at the brewery in *Passing Fancy*); few hints as to what these salarymen's companies actually produce; no representation of the *burakumin*, or outcasts associated with 'polluted' occupations; no murder, little theft, no incest (all in a day's work in an Oshima or Imamura movie). But any film necessarily omits a lot more than it shows. A structuring absence must be a pertinent absence. Hence the crucial importance of the 'ideological project', which commits the film to a message. Pertinent absences are revealed when the ideology censors its own project or when something swerves the film off its ideological trajectory: for Macherey, this deflection can be achieved by the historical state of literary forms; for the *Cahiers* editors, by the 'authorial writing' that is characteristic of the director. The resulting displacement in the film's handling of ideological material is as symptomatic of underlying tensions as is displacement in the Freudian analysis of dreams or slips of the tongue. But this ideological maneuver has its own relation to the social totality: it enacts the real contradictions of the ideology which gave birth to it.[47] In this way, the symptomatic-reading approach absorbs aspects of the two prior models: the intentional agent's communication of a message (the 'ideological project') and the unwitting reflection of larger social processes (the involuntary traces of ideological contradiction).

The mechanism of displacement is particularly apparent in Ozu's treatment of referential material in the early films. The college comedies, for instance, systematically suppress the political dimension of actual campus life. During the 1920s students often became social activists, striking for the removal of unpopular teachers and of military training. In March of 1928, when the police rounded up massive numbers of suspected communists, the public was shocked to learn that many university students were charged with leftist activities. The very site of Ozu's films, Waseda University, was recognized as a fairly liberal school and was the scene of much student unrest during the 1920s. Yet the films are almost without reference to Waseda as a political arena. (A copy of *Revolutionary Theatre* can be glimpsed in one shot of *Days of Youth*.) To some extent, the antics of Ozu's troublesome students may be a displacement of the political turmoil associated with Waseda. Many years later, his memory took the films as a faithful reflection: 'Back then, students didn't fight with the police. They were good material for comedy.'[48] More generally, the happy endings of most of his salaryman films require displacements of social problems – unemployment, arbitrary authority – onto familial ones that can be solved by face-to-face understanding. And Sato has suggested that Ozu's mimicking of American movies is a symptom of a longing for freedom that was unattainable in a period of repression; the citations became an intellectual's fantasy substitute for the liberal revolution that never occurred.[49]

As for the wartime projects, a symptomatic reading would point out how *Toda Family* keeps Shojiro's trip to Tianjin offscreen, as if showing this occupied city would undercut the film's claim that it simply represents a new business frontier; or how *There Was a Father*'s unrelenting insistence on the father's pursuit of duty produces a troubling 'excess' not unlike that 'monstrousness' the *Cahiers* critics find in the unwavering righteousness of Lincoln.

This approach's 'hermeneutics of suspicion' would doubtless also add a sexual layer to the repressed material in the film's 'unconscious'. The emphasis on malé bonding in all Ozu's work would appear especially important, as perhaps the displaced vestige of a lost, gender-defined warrior caste. In the postwar work, the expulsion of the daughter from the household could be read as the displacement of incestuous desire, the Oedipal trajectory treated from the standpoint of father and daughter. The unseen suitor may be the consequence of textual repression, as if presenting the rival for paternal affection would be too traumatic. For the communication-centered critic, the moment in *Tokyo Story* when the old father gives Noriko his dead wife's watch creates a bond between the two women; but for the symptomatic-reading approach, the *real* bond would be incestuous, wedding father to daughter-in-law.

At a broader level, the very 'everyday life' upon which Ozu's work concentrates can be revealed as an ideological construct bearing symptomatic significance. The social category of everyday life is only now beginning to receive intensive scholarly analysis, from anthropological, phenomenological, and post-structuralist standpoints.[50] One of the most ambitious hypotheses has been the idea that in appearing to 'reflect' everyday life, mass culture taps genuine social aspirations. Fredric Jameson proposes that this 'utopian' or 'transcendental' potential makes any artifact of mass culture 'implicitly, and no matter how faintly, negative and critical of the social order from which, as a product and a commodity, it springs.'[51] While this hypothesis may turn out to be too optimistic (where is the subversive moment in Mantovani or mass advertising?), it does offer a more nuanced vision of mass culture than has been common. A 'utopian' reading of Ozu along these lines has been sketched by Stanley Aronowitz, who suggests that Ozu has made ordinary gestures and actions meet the intrinsic demand of the film medium for movement. In doing so, Ozu has sought to capture, even if incompletely, an everyday totality – a 'social time' of homely activities, and a perception 'that grants the spectator a chance to reflect.'[52] Ozu's characteristic nostalgia thus becomes highly critical of the present, suggesting a wholeness that is now lost; his utopian vision is that 'of a future in which the present is eternal except in the vivid remembrance of those things he offers us as the legacy of the past.'[53]

All three approaches can thus situate Ozu's choices within pertinent social frames of reference. Yet none, at least as currently practiced, can do without the constructive principles and procedures supplied by a historical poetics. It is no exaggeration to say that up to the present, critics employing these theories have used only the most rudimentary concepts of materials, form, and style. Expression-centered accounts have traditionally favored the revelatory personal detail at the expense of overall formal context. Reflectionist studies traditionally concentrate on subjects and themes, seldom seeking to explain matters of narrative structure or narration. As for the symptomatic-reading model, practitioners often claim to deal with form and style, but this is often not carried through. Macherey claims that he will concentrate on a history of 'forms of expression', but he immediately recasts this as a 'history of themes'.[54] The ideological project is also seen in wholly thematic terms.[55] The *Cahiers* reading of *Young Mr. Lincoln*, dependent upon

Marxist and Lacanian concepts, yields heavily thematic results. One can argue that neither Macherey nor the *Cahiers* writers even have an adequate theory of literary or cinematic form. As for the 'utopian' model, it is explicitly thematic and, at least in its current state of development, displays little concern for film history or close analysis.[56] Furthermore, the symptomatic approach sets no constraints on how it will interpret formal features. Any formal strategy or tactic can be considered, on some ground or another, a displacement of material from the two master-regimes, sex and politics. Anything in the film can be assigned an 'emancipatory' potential if the critic links it to some value that would be desirable in a more just human society. The roominess typical of any 'finalist' hermeneutic mode is here increased by psychoanalytic interpretation's unique mixture of reduction and equivocation.[57]

A historical poetics of Ozu's work can grant the usefulness of all these approaches without committing the analyst to a single or simple explanation. Consider, for example, Ozu's use of eyelines. In Japanese culture, it is considered rude to stare at the person to whom you are speaking; the preferred mode is to lower one's eyes or glance tactfully to the side.[58] More generally, the 'look of the other' constitutes a basic constraint on Japanese behavior; in a culture based on 'shame', *mirareru koto* ('to be looked at') is a source of anxiety. Japanese neurotic patients accordingly display a fear of eye-to-eye contact.[59] Yet Ozu's films, so often considered realistic, are completely unfaithful to this central convention of social interaction. We have seen that his displaced staging and 'torqued' figures make characters gaze fixedly at one another.[60] 'People, and especially we Japanese,' Hasumi notes, 'seldom stare into each other's eyes as frequently and consistently as Ozu's characters do.'[61] The most pertinent explanation for this staging option would treat it as neither a reflection of social processes nor an involuntary expression of Ozu's personality, but rather an intentional transformation of a convention of Hollywood cinema. Ozu, that is, selected these eyelines because they best met the goals he conceived for his formal system, not because they reflected a prior reality outside the film. Furthermore, to read this choice symptomatically – as, say, presenting a reversal of the male-dominated system of looks purportedly at work in Western cinema – would be excessively reductive. This interpretation would not address the choice as a deliberate solution to the problem of conveying contiguity, as a part of a larger system of spatial construction, and as a means of creating graphically similar shots. The symptomatic approach, pledged like the others to disclosing hidden meaning, subsumes analysis to an overriding interpretive aim; a historical poetics makes interpretation, of all three sorts, part of an overall formal analysis. It is in this heuristic spirit that I shall employ the three models in Part Two of this book.

What Do Viewers Want?

The rational-agent model can assist a historical poetics in a different way. The three general approaches already outlined concentrate on the forces that produce the film. By contrast, the 'conjunctural-appropriations' approach locates the film's social force in the ways that perceivers use it. The central assumption is that the text cannot dictate how it will be understood. There may be 'preferred readings', but spectators are always able to interpret a text in accord with their own aims and interests. In different 'conjunctures', a film will have different effects. Evidently a rational agent is required by this model, but now that agent is the spectator – capable of extracting what is salient for personal or group-derived goals and, on the account offered by John Fiske and others, even able to resist the text's ideological project.[62] In Ozu's case we can distinguish several appropriations by audiences and other filmmakers.

Back in Chapter 1, I suggested that Ozu the man could be appropriated in at least two ways: as an example of the conservative Japanese craftsman; and as one prototypical Japanese, who lived a life congruent with that of millions of others. His films, dependably if moderately successful at the box office, made reference to contemporary preoccupations and to wider cultural features. Kido recalls that after *Body Beautiful*, Ozu's early films steered a course between Shochiku's humane optimism and the 'tendency film' of social protest; he thus appealed simultaneously to middle-class viewers and left-wing moderates.[63] *I Was Born, But . . .* exemplifies this 'polysemous' appropriation, since according to a reviewer of the period, some viewers took it as a melancholy film, while others found it cheerful.[64] With their Western citations and strong ties to mass culture, Ozu's early works epitomized sophisticated modernity, but one emerging out of an 'intrinsically Japanese' context. The later wartime works were considered both popular and ideologically correct; stills from *There Was a Father* form the front matter of a 1942 history of world cinema, as if the film were the culmination of the medium's progress.[65]

After the war, about the time of *Late Spring*, Ozu's works began to be labeled old-fashioned. They were admired by older critics and audiences for their aesthetic perfection and perhaps as well for their echo of the prewar cinema: in continuing the Ofuna flavor, they created a kind of stylistic nostalgia. 'These days,' Ozu remarked, 'Noda and I don't rate story very highly. Content, social relevance, and story logic aren't what we're after. . . . What we seek to leave is a good aftertaste.'[66] To the younger generation, this could only make the films seem increasingly conservative, both in morality and form.[67] Although, as we have seen, Ozu sought to adapt his materials to the new liberality of the 1950s and although his work did remain referential to a great degree, the manner of his adaptation and the reference points he used did not on the whole satisfy younger audiences. His aesthetic strategy had a double-edged consequence: it could seem progressive or old-fashioned, Western (his early subjects and motifs, his insistence on pursuing his unique style) or 'Japanese' (his biographical legend, his later subjects, his 'formalistic' approach). To some extent, the changing conjunctural appropriations are due not simply to changes in his work but to changing definitions of 'Japaneseness'.

The conjunctural-appropriations model would claim that spectators take from films what their desires and beliefs, shaped by their class position and social experience, find rewarding. Thus one could argue that Japanese spectators seeking a reconciliation to their lot would find much in Ozu to comfort them: a definition of 'Japaneseness' that fluctuated over different periods but which was at any one point relatively stable and sanctioned by at least some contemporary trends; a proof that raffish Western sophistication could be part of the modern city; a display of the inherent 'Japaneseness' of certain artistic traditions; a reflection on family obligations and rewards. In a less acquiescent spirit, the films could be appropriated as illustrations of the effects of unemployment, criticisms of Meiji ideological formations, or, at a more self-conscious level, exemplifications of the power of bourgeois ideology to turn the contingent and cultural into the absolute and natural. Nor have Western critics, looking for their own versions of Japaneseness, been disappointed. They find Zen, or the family, or (in my case) everyday life.

Filmmakers have appropriated Ozu in distinct ways as well. Oshima's *Gishiki* (*The Ceremony*, 1971) can be taken as a critique of Ozu's family ethos, while the explicit references in Peter Handke's *Left-Handed Woman* (1977), Jim Jarmusch's *Stranger than Paradise* (1984), and Wayne Wang's *Dim Sum* (1985) can only seem homages. Most explicit of all, of course, is Wim Wenders, who has said of Ozu's families: 'I feel so close to them that if I had to choose, I'd rather sleep on the floor, and sit my whole life on the floor, and get drunk every day, than pass a single day as the son of Henry Fonda.'[68] His *Tokyo-Ga* of 1985 begins with the assertion that Ozu's work constitutes 'a sacred treasure of the cinema.' Most cinephiles mourn the lost classicism of Hollywood, but *Tokyo-Ga* is suffused with the despairing recognition that Japanese cinema is no longer a living presence either. Wenders' film conveys the nostalgic anxiety of a filmmaker who fears that no one can ever make films like Ozu's, or as good as Ozu's, again.

The Russian Formalists, the first 'reception critics', pioneered the conjunctural-appropriations approach, and it is indispensable to any comprehensive historical poetics. It allows us to balance the problem/solution model of rational-agent theory with a sensitivity to the shifting perception of audiences. To take Ozu as an example: Born in the same year as the first permanent film theatre opened, he grew up with his nation's cinema. The first generation of Japanese studio filmmakers, working in the 1910s and early 20s, were chiefly concerned with recording drama on film. At the start of the 1920s, Western-style filmmaking was only an emergent tendency, still overshadowed by adaptations of kabuki or *shimpa*. In the mid-1920s, Western-style filmmaking began to dominate, in no small part through the efforts of Kido at Shochiku. The new generation of directors – Shimazu, Shimizu, Naruse, Gosho, and Ozu – faced the problem of making 'modern' films that would also be 'Japanese'. Whereas most of his colleagues tackled the problem through the decorative approach I have mentioned so often, Ozu solved it through adopting a rigorous formal system derived, as we have seen, from both American cinema and contemporary currents in Japanese culture. It is this context that partly explains why he was able to evoke responses from disparate sectors of the audience: he synthesized a variety of appeals, both of materials and form.

But his 'formalism' also prepared the way for a reaction. In the late 1950s, a new generation of filmmakers identified him with an outdated concept of Japanese film. The problem they defined for themselves was not that of establishing a distinctive national cinema but that of self-expression through social engagement. Hence there appeared the Japanese 'New Wave', with its rough and technically flamboyant films that seemed to have more ties to contemporary conditions. Ozu thus paved the way for Oshima, Imamura, and

175

Yamada in that he represented what they reacted against. To a still younger generation abroad, however, Ozu came to represent a stable compromise between narrative accessibility and formal control – a significant tension for such directors as Wenders, Wang, and Jarmusch. 'Ozu was the one,' declares Wenders, 'who helped me, and who showed me that it was possible to be colonized, or imperialized, in such a way that you really accepted the language [of Hollywood cinema].'[69] Because of its emphasis on the 'choice situation' confronting the artist, a poetics can illuminate how filmmakers appropriate earlier films according to the options they perceive as offered by the medium at certain points in its history.

Yet as currently practiced, conjunctural-appropriations criticism lacks a solid account of film form and spectatorial activity. If in Macherey's work 'forms' and 'structures' become identified with themes, so in this method the 'discourses' that audiences mobilize are found to consist of thematic meanings. According to Fiske, children who watched an Australian television series set in a prison appropriated it as a metaphor for their life in school.[70] I have found no account in this tradition that goes beyond picking out themes and starts to analyze how different audiences' social frames of reference shape their skills in perceiving narrative structure or narration.[71] Moreover, the method has developed no sense of what aesthetic boundaries there are on any audience's capacity to 'read' the text. The tendency has been to assume that the text sets down no constraints and that the limits on appropriation are wholly those determined by the audience's social position. Yet this will not explain why at a *denotative* level, there are widespread agreements about the text across audiences and conjunctures. Even the children who treat the prison as a metaphor for school must at a more basic level be able to construct an intelligible narrative world, one comparable to that constructed by viewers who draw different connotations from the show. If the conjunctural-appropriations method is to identify and explain the formal specificity of films and the mechanics of spectators' construction of meaning, it needs to draw upon concepts provided by a historical poetics.

Such a poetics can press the 'conjunctures' model beyond thematic concerns and a gross text/audience opposition by means of the mediating concept of *extrinsic norms of comprehension*. Extrinsic norms govern such narrational matters as syuzhet/fabula relations and stylistic patterning. These norms are neither 'in the text' (since they precede, as hypotheses, apprehension of the film) nor 'in the viewer' (since they have an intersubjective sanctioning force). It is only through application of some norm of comprehension that the viewer can go on to 'read' the film in accord with her or his broader social agenda. And *which* norm is applied will doubtless affect the 'reading' available to spectators. I have proposed elsewhere that as far as narrative cinema is concerned, there have been four principal modes, or systems of norms.[72] Three of these are relevant in exploring how viewers and filmmakers have appropriated Ozu.

1. The **classical** norm, seen at its most elaborate in the Hollywood studio cinema, encourages the spectator to build the film around a strong cause-effect chain proceeding from clear-cut character psychology and working

itself out to a definite resolution. The narration is assumed to be reliable, at least most of the time and in most genres.

Certainly Ozu's films repay comprehension according to this mode. I have said enough about his unified plot structure, the legibility of his style, and his sources in Hollywood filmmaking to show that Ozu could be construed as a 'classical' filmmaker by popular audiences and the filmmakers of Japan's New Wave. He is still probably appropriated from that perspective by many Japanese and Western viewers today.[73]

2. The '**art-cinema**' norm encourages the viewer to build the film around psychologically ambiguous characters and a notion of an elusive external reality. The viewer is also expected to be alert for an overt and unreliable narration that evokes a range of tentatively applicable connotations. The film is assumed to be a vehicle for the director's vision of life, conveyed chiefly through symbolic actions and objects. Ozu's films, because of their ellipses, occasionally opaque characters, and overt narrational gestures, are also assimilable to this norm. It has been the mode favored by critics such as Richie, Zeman, Schrader, and others.[74] The 'thematization' approach discussed in Chapter 6 (p. 137) exemplifies this approach as well.

This norm is perhaps even more visible in the work of those filmmakers who have 'read' Ozu. Jarmusch's citation in *Stranger than Paradise* (a racing card includes horses named *Tokyo Story*, *Late Spring*, and *Passing Fancy*) is less typical than are the more thoroughgoing pastiches one finds in *The Left-Handed Woman* and *Dim Sum*, where cutaways and 'still-life' shots absorb Ozu through the grid of art-cinema expectations. The tendency is particularly evident in Handke's film, in which landscape shots and domestic objects imply a character's state of mind or the ambiguous borderline between authorial commentary and a character's mental state. This appropriation is echoed in critical writing on the film, which teases symbolic meanings out of shots of flowers, trains, and sewing machines.[75] The transformation of Ozu's strategies is also apparent in Handke's inability to use the devices with Ozu's rigor; one need only compare the handling of the train at the film's opening with the train scenes in *A Mother Should be Loved* (p. 135) and *The Flavor of Green Tea over Rice* (pp. 322–7). In general, it is as a model of 'art cinema' that Ozu is largely absorbed by filmmakers and academic audiences in the West.

3. The **parametric** norm takes the patterning of film style as being at least intermittently as important as narrative systems. The spectator is to attend to how the film establishes an intrinsic stylistic norm and then varies that through additive and variational processes, not only as a way of narrating the syuzhet but also as a distinctive effort at abstract, 'spatialized' form. Noël Burch pioneered this as an explicit appropriation in 1967, in his discussion of *The Only Son* in *Praxis du cinéma*.[76] It was developed further by Kristin Thompson, Edward Branigan, and myself in subsequent essays. Obviously, much that I have said in analyzing Ozu's stylistics and his playfully overt narration would exemplify this angle of approach.

The theoretical implications are clear. With some such concept of extrinsic norms of comprehension the 'conjunctural' approach could begin to take into account the formal specifics of a film. Because of differences in education and economic opportunity, spectators have varying access to norms; the classical norm is the most widely accessible one, the parametric the most 'academic'. Norms thus constitute concrete historical limits on the audience's options. Moreover, each mode constrains how the text will be appropriated. The concept of 'realism', for instance, is very different in the classical and the art-cinema modes, and those differences will affect how the spectator applies the film to problems of actual social life. Furthermore, if we can whittle the vast range of possible readings down to a few sets of formal options, the task of studying conjunctural appropriations becomes more manageable. One is no longer choosing between *the* 'reading' and an infinite variety of unique possibilities; there may be an indefinitely large number of particular 'readings', but all will be produced by applications of the same limited bodies of norms. Finally, the notion of an extrinsic norm retains a concern for the specificity of poetic processes. One risk of the conjunctural-appropriations method is that every use of an art work tends to get reduced to an *a priori* political strategy held by a group. Norms of comprehension form an important mediation, a realm in and through which political agendas are fought out. In such ways, a poetics can make explicit the underlying systems which enable audiences to experience and use the text differently.

The importance of Ozu for us today – our own most significant 'conjunctural appropriation' – lies exactly in the fact that his work may be taken up from so many angles. Critics' ordinary concepts of 'richness' and 'complexity' do not do justice to the great number of points of entry that Ozu's work offers. Taken as a classicist, Ozu becomes a great storyteller. Taken as an 'art-cinema' director, he becomes a profound moralist, sensitive to the ambivalence of a changing world. Taken as a 'parametric' director, he is one of the great experimental filmmakers. His work is legible on all these grounds, but he always offers more: more rigorous narrative structure than is needed to achieve classical coherence, more humor in his narrational overtness than is needed for art-cinema subtlety, more finesse and self-restriction than most parametric filmmakers attempt. His is a cinema of virtuosity (an attribute long valued in Japanese artists), one which aims to create an absolutely saturated form, the most dense film possible. In one sense Ozu is rightly considered a minimalist, but in another sense he creates uniquely 'replete' films, engaging us on more levels than does a Hawks or an Antonioni or a Bresson. He claims several domains and conquers each one. For a complete understanding of this virtuosity, the viewer of today must cultivate something that is seldom asked in cinema, a range and depth of viewing skills.

This is, finally, why I believe his parametric aspect to be so important: it involves the most extensive retraining of the spectator. Inevitably, we are more sensitive to Ozu's subjects, themes, and narrative structures than we are to his stylistics. Classical and art-cinema norms have inclined us to take style as a vehicle for syuzhet/fabula relations. With Ozu, we must adopt new viewing strategies, recognizing that film style can claim our attention in its own right, even if detailed awareness of its working eludes our grasp. We must also exercise those strategies at a level of nuance required by no other director I know.

For one last time, I should insist that what is at stake is no narcissistic aestheticism. The skills that Ozu would have us cultivate are exactly those which we need in order to lead finely-textured and responsible social lives. This modest virtuoso, who devotes himself only to the minor arts, demands that we exercise cognitive flexibility, perceptual discrimination, and visual and auditory acuity. He asks that we see the humor in rigor and the logic behind play. He coaxes us toward a cinema in which both grand structures and minute particulars become equally the object of reflection. What viewers want – 'want' in the sense of *lack* – is a cinema that, in its materials and forms, suggests fresh and subtle ways of understanding the social forces that constitute 'ordinary life' – constitute it even as a construct to be deployed by conflicting interests. This cinema should also lead spectators to reflect on the limits and possibilities of film itself. It is toward this cinema that Ozu points us. He offers both a poetry of everyday life and a vision of the poetics of cinema. All he asks is our attention.

Part 2

Introduction

What follows is a series of essays on each of Ozu's films. Each discussion highlights only one or two issues around the film – a stylistic strategy, a narrational approach, an important treatment of a subject or theme, a pattern of ideological tensions. Whatever this approach lacks, I hope that it lets me deepen and specify the general arguments made in the first part of the book.

The plot synopses and critical commentary for Ozu's lost films are based upon information in two sources:

Tadao Sato. *Ozu Yasujiro no geijutsu* (The Art of Yasujiro Ozu). Tokyo: Asahi Shimbunsha, 1978-1979. Two volumes.

Ozu Yasujiro wo yomu (Reading Yasujiro Ozu). Tokyo: Firuma Atosha, 1982.

The filmographic information is selective, listing major crew and cast members. Credit records are incomplete for films that do not survive. I have derived most of the credit information from *Ozu Yasujiro wo yomu*, and have included the length of each film, in reels and meters, as listed there. For the films that survive, I have indicated the running time in minutes.

Because Japanese syllabic writing can often be transliterated in several distinct ways, proper names can pose a problem. For example, Ozu's principal cinematographers have generally been known in the West as Hideo Shigehara and Yushun Atsuta. According to Hisashi Okajima at the National Film Center in Tokyo, however, these craftsmen's names are more properly rendered as Hideo Mohara and Yuharu Atsuta. The latter are the forms followed in this filmography. I am grateful to Tony Rayns for his help in clarifying this matter.

The Films

1927

Zange no yaiba
Sword of Penitence

Shochiku Kamata studio. Story: Yasujiro Ozu. Script: Kogo Noda. Cinematography: Isamu Aoki. Cast: Saburo Azuma (*Sakichi*), Kunimatsu Ogawa (*Ishimatsu*), Kanji Kawahara (*Tojuro Manabe*), Shoichi Nodera (*Shozaemon Yamashiroya*), Eiko Atsumi (*Oyae*), Miyako Hanayagi (*Oshin*). 7 reels, 1,919 meters. Released 14 October 1927. No script, negative, or prints known to exist.

As in most *jidai-geki*, the plot is complicated. Sakichi, a thief, visits his brother Ishimatsu, who has recently been released from prison. Ishimatsu wants to reform, but Shozaemon, his old partner, won't let him. Sakichi steals a hairpin and leaves it with Ishimatsu, who is jailed. The woman victim gets the innocent Isimatsu freed, but he loses his job and starts drinking. Eventually he returns to crime. The brothers are pursued, and despite another woman's attempt to save Sakichi, he is killed in a fight with Shozaemon.

In August of 1927, Kido promoted Ozu to director and assigned him to the period-film unit – a low-level job at Shochiku's Kamata studio. Noda supplied the script, which was based on George Fitzmaurice's film *Kick-In* (1922), released in Japan in 1926. Ozu directed all but the first scene before he was called to army service; the scene was filmed by Torajiro Saito. Sato reports that a contemporary review praised the film's style, especially its handling of romantic scenes in flashbacks.[1] When Ozu returned, the Kamata *jidai-geki* unit had been dissolved, so he turned to the Kido specialties: modern comedies and melodramas.

1928

Wakodo no yume
Dreams of Youth

Shochiku Kamata studio. Story and script: Yasujiro Ozu. Cinematography: Hideo Mohara. Cast: Tatsuo Saito (*Chokichi Okada*), Nobuko Wakaba (*Miyoko, his girlfriend*), Hisao Yoshitani (*Heiichi Kato*), Junko Matsui (*Yuriko*), Takeshi Sakamoto (*Okada's father*), Kenji Oyama (*tailor*). 5 reels, 1,534 meters. Released 28 April 1928. No script, negative, or prints known to exist.

Two students, Okoda and Kato, live in a boarding house. Comic complications revolve around Kato's tailor bill, which he evades and then pays with Okada's clothes. When Okada's father visits from the country, the youth has nothing to wear, so he borrows Kato's clothes – which don't fit. Through this intrigue are woven the young men's romances with two young women. The film ends happily with the two couples spending a pleasant day.

Even in summary, Ozu's first *gendai-geki* reveals motifs that will recur later: the friendly rivals, the penury of student life, the ill-timed visit from rural kin. The title will be echoed ironically in *Where Now Are the Dreams of Youth?* and in *Equinox Flower*. Critics at the time saw Ozu as 'progressive' (that is, both Americanized and cosmopolitan), and they singled out a moment of deflating comedy that looks forward to many gags on bodily functions. When Okada and his girlfriend are together in the park, he writes with a biscuit on his book: 'I love you.' Miyoko takes the biscuit and writes in reply: 'W.C.' before running off to the toilet.

Nyobo funshitsu
Wife Lost

Shochiku Kamata studio. Story: Ononosuke Takano. Script: Momosuke Yoshida. Cinematography: Hideo Mohara. Cast: Tatsuo Saito (*Jyoji*), Ayako Okamura (*Yumiko*), Shoichi Okajima (*detective*), Shuchiro Sugano (*thief*), Takeshi Sakamoto (*uncle*), Junko Matsui (*Yoko, Jyoji's wife*). 5 reels, 1,502 meters. Released 15 June 1928. No script, negative, or prints known to exist.

Although a husband has a gorgeous wife, he becomes infatuated with a dancer. The wife's uncle hires a detective to spy on the errant husband. Through a series of comic mishaps, the dancer winds up in a hotel with the husband, trailed by the detective and the wife. The film ends with a chase involving a motorcycle policeman.

In synopsis this sounds like a real Kamata *nansensu*-comedy, replete with *moga*, bored businessmen, car accidents, and chases through the streets of Tokyo. Billed as a 'Kamata Special Five-Reeler', this was evidently an example of Kido's using the short comedy as a testing ground for a fledgling director. According to Sato, critics complained that Ozu 'paid too much attention to details'.[2] This probably does not refer to the sort of intermediate spaces we find in later works but rather to the Lloyd- and Lubitsch-style inserted close-ups (hands, feet, props) which are common in the earliest surviving Ozu films. Perhaps he had not yet smoothly integrated such material.

Kabocha
Pumpkin

Shochiku Kamata studio. Story: Yasujiro Ozu. Script: Komatsu Kitamura. Cinematography: Hideo Mohara. Cast: Tatsuo Saito (*Tosuke Yamada*), Yurie Hinatsu (*Kanako*), Hidemaru Handa (*Kazuo*), Yoko Kozakuro (*Chieko*), Takeshi Sakamoto (*President*). 5 reels, 1,175 meters. Released 31 August 1928. No script, negative, or prints known to exist.

No synopsis available.

Another five-reel *nansensu* comedy. Tatsuo Saito, who appeared in Ozu's two previous films, stars as a young man with several girlfriends. *Kinema Jumpo*'s reviewer singled out Ozu's diligent framing and compositional effects, and Ozu has said that he was starting to learn continuity at about this time.[3]

Hikkoshi fufu
A Couple on the Move

Shochiku Kamata studio. Story: Ippei Kikuchi. Script: Akira Fushimi. Cinematography: Hideo Mohara. Cast: Atsushi Watanabe (*Eikichi Fujioka*), Mitsuko Yoshikawa (*Chiyoko, his wife*), Ichiro Oguchi (*landlord*), Kazuzo Nakahama (*Seiichi, his son*), Tomoko Naniwa (*pharmacist's daughter*), Kenji Oyama (*bill collector*). 3 reels, 1,116 meters. Released 28 September 1928. No script, negative, or prints known to exist.

A furniture man pays a call on a couple, only to find that they've moved out. He tracks them to their new house, but the wife pays him only part of the bill. In the meantime, at the local drugstore, the husband tries to help the shopgirl open the strongbox. When the wife comes by, she infers that the husband is flirting with the shopgirl and she goes home in a rage. Their landlord visits the couple's home, and the wife flirts with him to arouse her husband's jealousy. After a fight, they resolve to move again. But when they learn that the shopgirl and their landlord are to be married that night, they relax and decide to stay.

From the start of his career, Ozu shifts freely from the world of student life to that of married couples, concentrating again on financial hardships and resignation to shared problems. In its emphasis on the domestic milieu and integration into neighborhood life, the plot suggests that, as Richie indicates, Ozu was moving toward Kido's prized *shoshimin-geki*.[4] Based on a story by Gosho, Noda, Okubo, and Enjiro Saito (all writing under a pseudonym), the film won praise for its comic effect, but Ozu claimed to have lost interest when it was cut by other hands.

Nikutaibi
Body Beautiful

Shochiku Kamata studio. Story and script: Akira Fushimi. Cinematography: Hideo Mohara. Cast: Tatsuo Saito (*Ichiro Takai*), Choko Iida (*Ritsuko*), Kenji Kimura (*Zenuemon Okura*), Kenji Oyama (*student*). 5 reels, 1,505 meters. Released 1 December 1928. No script, negative, or prints known to exist.

The unemployed, henpecked Ichiro becomes not only his wife's house-keeper and errand boy but, despite his scrawny physique, the model for her paintings. When a rich patron comes to investigate her progress, he flirts with her under Ichiro's nose. Later, the patron humiliates Ichiro in a bar. Burning for revenge, Ichiro takes up painting himself while his wife invites a shot-putter to be her new Adonis. Ichiro's and his wife's paintings are both exhibited, and his wins a prize. She throws away her brushes and becomes a compliant wife – and his model.

One has only to imagine Saito in the husband's role in this comedy of masculine authority recaptured to wish that this film survived. There are other reasons as well. *Body Beautiful* is said to be the first film for which Ozu won recognition within Shochiku, and it was a popular success. The *Kinema Jumpo* review praised it for escaping the crudeness of *nansensu* and moving toward tragicomedy: 'We laugh precisely because it is sad.'[5] Sato considers this Ozu's first work within the home-drama genre.[6]

Takara no yama
Treasure Mountain

Shochiku Kamata studio. Story: Yasujiro Ozu. Script: Akira Fushimi. Cinematography: Hideo Mohara. Cast: Tokuji Kobayashi (*Tanjiro*), Yurie Hinatsu (*Somekichi*), Mariko Aoyama (*Bakuhachi*), Ayako Okamura (*Choko, the 'moga'*), Choko Iida (*geisha-house proprietor*). 6 reels, 1,824 meters. Released 22 February 1929. No script, negative, or prints known to exist.

A young man who lives in a geisha house falls in love with one of the women. His father refuses to give him money until he becomes respectable, and his *moga* girlfriend urges him to move out. Eventually he decides to leave the geisha house and goes to the modern girl in hope of romance. She has already become engaged, however. At a party he finds the geisha performing. The two are reconciled, he moves back to the geisha house, and the next morning he is seen eating green tea over rice.

Originally to be called *A Modern Spring Calendar*, this is an updating of an Edo-period vaudeville work. Its plot anticipates the love triangle of *The Lady and the Beard*. Contemporary reviews criticized the film for its slow tempo and lack of pictorial qualities.

Wakaki hi
Days of Youth

Shochiku Kamata studio. Story and script: Akira Fushimi, with revisions by Yasujiro Ozu. Cinematography and editing: Hideo Mohara. Cinematography assistants: Yuharu Atsuta *et al.* Lighting: Toshimitsu Nakajima. Set design: Yoneichi Wakita. Props: Kotaro Kawasaki, Matsunosuke Matsubara. Cast: Ichiro Yuki (*Bin Watanabe*), Tatsuo Saito (*Shuichi Yamamoto*), Junko Matsui (*Chieko*), Choko Iida (*her aunt*), Takeshi Sakamoto (*professor*), Ichiro Okuni (*Professor Anayama*), Shinichi Himori (*Hatamoto*), Chishu Ryu (*student*). 10 reels, 2,854 meters. Surviving prints: 103 min. Released 13 April 1929. Script, negative, and prints in existence.

The students Watanabe and Yamamoto are both attracted to Chieko, and they court her while studying. Once they have finished their exams, they join a college ski club on holiday in the mountains, where they unexpectedly encounter Chieko. They compete for her, but discover that she is there for a marriage-arrangement meeting, or *o-miai*, with Hatamoto, the ski-club leader. Disconsolate, they ride back on the train together and resolve to forget her. They encounter one of their professors, who sternly reports their failing grades. Back in Tokyo, Watanabe promises Yamamoto that he will find him a girlfriend through the ploy he used to meet Chieko.

Ozu's earliest surviving film cannot be called apprentice work. By his eighth effort, Ozu had mastered Western classical filmmaking. At the same time, we cannot help scanning the film for problems sighted, partial attempts, passages that point ahead to issues that Ozu would tackle later. This is no sketchbook – the script is too well-wrought for that – but *Days of Youth* does let us watch Ozu demonstrating his proficiency in certain conventions while displaying an urge to explore his own paths.

Days of Youth is clearly indebted to Japanese genres. As a student film, it refers constantly to Waseda University (the first expository title is a line from the college song) and flaunts the Westernized iconography of student life (pennants, skis, ukeleles, and so on). The credit drawings set the stage for a student movie, presenting bells, dice, alphabet letters, cocktails, musical notes, and a bit of English of which Ozu was fond: 'Two is company.' The film also constitutes a good instance of *ero-guro-nansensu* filmmaking, with the *ero* supplied by Watanabe's patting of Chieko's rear end, the *guro* by his scratching a doll's hindquarters and jamming gum in a statuette's eye, and the *nansensu* by the outrageous gag of the runaway ski and by such lines as a student admitting after an exam: 'I didn't memorize anything because I hate to forget things.' But in many respects *Days of Youth* is not a typical Japanese film. Its immediate debts are clearly to Lloyd and Lubitsch, and the structural rigor of the plot and style put it far closer to the Hollywood comedy of the mid-1920s than to the somewhat undisciplined Japanese film of its period. Already Ozu is a considerably more fastidious and rigorous a filmmaker than most of his contemporaries.

The plot is woven of two lines: Watanabe and Yamamoto's romantic competition for Chieko and their attempt to pass their exams. The first line of action is introduced in a series of gags. In the first scene Watanabe uses an 'apartment for rent' ploy to meet Chieko and then she encounters Yamamoto (leading to gags with wet paint, a glove, and hot chocolate). Once Watanabe moves in with Yamamoto, the romantic triangle is plotted and the 'exam hell' line of action commences. The script alternates vignettes of college life with scenes of Watanabe visiting Chieko. The second half of the film is devoted to a four-day skiing trip. After the massive retardation furnished by many skiing stunts and gags, both lines of action are resolved. In an epilogue back in the boys' apartment, Watanabe puts out a 'room for rent' sign so Yamamoto can find a girlfriend, and this buckles the film shut.

But the film's tidiness only begins there. The plot has a thoroughgoing macrostructural symmetry, with the opening carefully echoing the ending and many scenes calculated to rhyme with one another. Large-scale parallel structure is especially important in the skiing scenes, which could degenerate into simple repetitions of the two rivals' competition for Chieko. The script situates the skiing scenes within several frames, as can be seen schematically:

Train ride to the ski country
   Trek to the slopes
      First day's skiing
         Night: the students talk
      Second day's skiing
         Night: students dance and sing
      Third day: *o-miai* on snow
         Night: heroes pack, Chieko brings persimmons
      Fourth day: heroes leave
   Trek to the train
Train ride back to Tokyo

These parallels are not empty formulas. They permit us, for instance, to gauge the change in Watanabe's attitude when he helps Yamamoto during their trek back to the train. Still, the abstractly neat architecture illustrates Ozu's lack of interest in the more rambling construction of most Japanese films of the period and his quite untypical passion for pattern. This will have consequences at the stylistic level as well.

The 'room for rent' gag typifies the sort of motifs that thread through the whole film, tightening its abstract structure. Yamamoto is introduced asking Chieko about the socks she is to knit for him. Watanabe discovers the socks in Chieko's apartment and appropriates them, and he later taunts Yamamoto with them. One of the film's best dialogue gags comes when, having met Chieko on the ski run, Yamamoto sits down beside her, gazes at the sky, and oracularly reflects: 'All men are beggars, seeking something,' then adds: 'I seek socks.' He makes her a present of gloves, which recalls the early glove gag (see p. 156) and looks forward to the many gloves that will decorate the rest of the skiing scenes. Motifs also reinforce the symmetrical macrostructure. The parallel treks are foregrounded by symmetrical pans across telephone poles. In both train scenes, the boys discuss the socks and compute their exam grades on the steamed windows. And in this very early film we already find Ozu introducing a significant motif quite late in the plot. After the *o-miai*, Chieko visits all the boys at the lodge and tosses persimmons among them. These become objects for Yamamoto and Watanabe to brood over, intensifying their melancholy about the loss of Chieko. On the train, though, as Yamamoto mournfully starts to eat one, Watanabe shoves the persimmons into the prized socks and pitches them out the train window. An old motif and a fresh one merge in a climax that reinforces two characters' different reactions to their situation and dramatizes the thematic point that their shared life as friends is more important to them than any woman.

The structure of the plot is respected, even heightened, by the narration's transmission of information. Overall, we have a considerably greater range of knowledge than Yamamoto and Watanabe. We know, long before they do, that they are both courting the same young woman. We know, shortly before they do, that she is in fact engaged to Hatamoto, one of their ski-club friends. And isolated scenes allow us to share both boys' optical point-of-view. All this is Hollywood's 'limited omniscience'. The film's stylistic texture is also indebted to Western cinema, using techniques suited to the Kamata 'piecemeal' approach. Ozu utilizes correct shot/reverse-shot and eyeline-matching, superb matches on action, some rapid cutting, and shots which reestablish space when characters move around in it. There is a great variety in camera position, and he uses a wide range of camera movements – reframings, pans, tilts, tracking shots, and handheld shots. He places his characters either side by side, face to face, or (Hollywood's favorite) in slightly angled frontal postures; there is none of the staggered staging we will see later. He will indulge in some Western artifice, such as beginning scenes with shots of hands or feet, or even playing a whole scene with shots of hands.

Most overtly, Ozu uses style to call our attention to the patterning of his scenes, highlighting the motifs and symmetries we have been considering. The film's opening consists of five leftward pan shots across the Waseda campus to an apartment block, ending on the 'room for rent' sign. At the film's end, five rightward pan shots exactly retrace the geography of the opening. 'Dissolves in place' or close-ups of objects also stress a scene's abstract shape. Such tactics can be found in American cinema of the 1920s, especially at those moments which prize stylistic self-consciousness – openings and closings of scenes and the film as a whole.

Teleologies are suspect, but art works are, at least partially, intentional objects, and we can examine an artist's early work for trials and explorations, first attempts to define his or her difference. In Ozu's case, *Days of Youth* contains devices that Ozu would take up again later but which would be assigned different, more daring functions.

Amidst the generic requirements, the demands of the 'Kamata flavor', the eclectic camera movements and angles, and the Americanized rigor of construction, we can easily see what Ozu would later hold to. The movie references, here to *Seventh Heaven*, will recur in many later works (though seldom with characters explicitly imitating another fictional figure the way Watanabe mimics Chico in *Seventh Heaven*). Ozu already displays some interest in off-center compositional elements and in 90- and 180-degree cutting. One dialogue title appears between close-up shots of Watanabe's shoes. There are, in addition, some remarkable graphic matches. When Yamamoto confronts the streetcar conductor, Ozu's *donden* cuts across the axis of action match the figures and the row of rings behind each (figs. 1–2). He uses the skiers' poles as an occasion to liken vertical shapes in swinging movement. In addition, his persistent interest in composition in depth emerges during the scenes in the ski lodge. By the standards of later films, the geography is crude: two rooms, one in the foreground where Watanabe and Yamamoto sit, one in the background where their chums fraternize. The two rooms also present contrasting moods and actions, with the foreground always the realm of sedentary, often solitary brooding. On the first night, the boys in the background chatter while our heroes muse by the heater. On the second night, a moping Yamamoto reluctantly joins the dance in the next room. On the third morning, the boys grab Hatamoto's portrait of Chieko and eventually toss it into Yamamoto and Watanabe's space. Finally, when Chieko brings persimmons on the last night, she tosses them out to the melancholy pair in the foreground. The simple but strong depth (in a very cheap set) is an early attempt at the complexity of adjacent spaces in the postwar films, while

1.

2.

the bold match-on-action cut from Chieko in focus (fig. 3) to her out of focus in the background (fig. 4) looks forward to the use of focus in the major works of 1933.

With the possible exception of the graphic matches, these technical devices remain much more motivated by story causality than they would be in the later work. Similarly, the opening and closing pan shots literalize the contiguity of the spaces in a way that would later be conveyed more ambiguously by cuts employing visual dominants and overtones. A burst of acting in unison, as Watanabe and Yamamoto flop back simultaneously in the final scene, is not at all as marked as it would be in *I Was Born, But . . . .* Here beginning or ending a scene with isolated objects retains a tie to more orthodox Western usage, in that fades signal ellipses, the objects are significant as props or gags, and there is no prolonged shot-by-shot sidling from object to object. We have already seen (pp. 125–6) how the permuted windmill and smokestack shots weakly justify intermediate spaces as pseudo-point-of-view shots. Later Ozu would not use character eyelines as a pretext for such parametric variation. A comparable interest in abstract montage patterning can be found in the shot-refrain during the students' drunken dance, in which three images – the chanting boy, the drummer, and the chanting boy again – are given permutational and metrical treatment. Apart from the smokestack episodes, the most vivid anticipation of the later Ozu is a brief scene in a ski lodge, the 'Hütte Arlberg', and this is worth a momentary scrutiny.

3.

4.

Watanabe has just discovered that Chieko is about to be engaged to Hatamoto, and he and two pals have retired to the Hütte. In plot terms the scene offers fresh information: for once we see the swaggering Watanabe fall into the funk that is Yamamoto's chief characteristic. The scene adds nothing to the causal chain of the story, being included simply to dwell on Watanabe's reaction. Thematically, the episode dramatizes the motif of the weak male. It also becomes an occasion for Ozu to display his skill at Western filmmaking, to expose the hypersymmetry of his style, and to experiment briefly with the sorts of spatial construction that he will later exploit more thoroughly.

The scene starts with a massive piece of contiguity cutting. The camera tilts down a chimney seen from outside the lodge, then down a stovepipe, past a pair of gloves, to a stove and teakettle. In the left background a hand reaches for something; in the right foreground a hand thrusts wood into the stove. Cut to a shot of a box of Sunkist raisins and a cup of coffee; a hand scoops up raisins. Cut to Chishu Ryu bringing raisins into the shot, then extending them to the left. New shot: a student with a ukelele takes them from the hand that sticks into the right of the shot. The stove is in the left foreground. Cut back to Ryu, looking right. Cut to Watanabe, facing them obliquely, smoking his pipe dourly; the stove stands in the right foreground. Now an eighth shot establishes the boys' positions, confirming our inferences and adhering to the 180-degree system.

In what follows, Ozu relies on this layout to present consistent shot/reverse-shot patterns and to reestablish the boys' positions as they look outside. Seeing that the *o-miai* is over, Ryu and the ukelele player go outside. Watanabe follows them, but declines to go on to the main lodge and returns to

5.

6.

sit pensively by the stove. Ozu renders this in repetitive framings (about half of these shots are from previous setups) and creates imbedded editing patterns (ABCBA, etc.). To foreground the symmetry of the scene, Ozu ends with two shots tilting up, from the stove and the teakettle to the flue, and then up the chimney: a mirror reverse of the first two shots, and a microcosm of the bracketing pan shots at each end of the film as a whole. Camera movements and intermediate, contiguous spaces impose an abstract pattern on the scene, and most of the shots are from a low position and a slightly low angle. In all these respects; in the quiet recurrence of the glove motif; in the fact that such a rigorous narration is devoted to a scene emphasizing solitary meditation; and, not least, in the fact that as Watanabe returns to his chair the steaming teakettle (a favorite Ozu citation of transience) swivels ninety degrees with the change of shot (figs. 5–6) – in all these aspects, the scene is a pivot between what Ozu has mastered, and what lay before him. One can devote one's life to filming teakettles.

Wasei kenka tomodachi
Fighting Friends — Japanese Style

Shochiku Kamata studio. Story and script: Kogo Noda. Cinematography: Hideo Mohara. Cast: Atsushi Watanabe (*Ryukichi*), Hisao Yoshitani (*Yoshizo*), Eiko Takamatsu (*Ogen*), Ichiro Yuki (*Okamura*). 7 reels, 2,114 meters. Released 5 July 1929. No script, negative, or prints known to exist.

Two truck drivers invite a homeless girl to stay with them, and both fall in love with her. Despite their intense rivalry, she falls in love with Okamura, a young man in the neighborhood. The truckers wish her happiness and repair their friendship. After they glimpse Okamura with a bar hostess, they forbid the young woman to see him, but they learn that the hostess was only his sister. In the final scene, Okamura and his bride ride the train to a resort, while our smiling heroes drive their truck alongside.

The buddy-rivalry motif, which goes back to *Dreams of Youth* and *Days of Youth*, is here self-consciously linked to American films of male camaraderie, such as those of Wallace Beery and Raymond Hatton. The relationship of the two workers looks forward to the turbulent friendship of Kihachi and Jiro in *Passing Fancy*, while the final scene seems to be the earliest instance of one of Ozu's favorite synecdoches: a marriage represented by the honeymoon couple's train trip. (See *Where Now Are the Dreams of Youth?*, *An Innocent Maid*, *There Was a Father*, and *Late Autumn*.)

Daigaku wa detakeredo
I Graduated, But . . .

Shochiku Kamata studio. Story: Hiroshi Shimizu. Script: Yoshio Aramaki. Cinematography: Hideo Mohara. Cast: Minoru Takada (*Tetsuo Nomoto*), Kinuyo Tanaka (*Machiko*), Utako Suzuki (*mother*), Kenji Oyama (*Sugimura*), Takeshi Sakamoto (*secretary*). 7 reels, 1,916 meters. Released 6 September 1929. Script in existence; prints of 10 minutes in existence.

At his first job interview, Minoru Takada, a recent college graduate, is offered a post as receptionist. Protesting that this is beneath him, he leaves. When he returns to his apartment, he finds that his mother has come from the country and has, moreover, brought his fiancée Machiko. He cannot tell them of his destitute state, so he pretends to have a job. The couple marry. After his mother leaves, Minoru confesses to Machiko that he's unemployed. They quarrel over money, and she is distraught. With his friend Sugimura, he visits a bar and finds Machiko working there. That night, he berates her, but soon he realizes her sacrifice and, weeping, he confesses that he's been lazy and irresponsible. He returns to the firm he had spurned and gratefully accepts a job as receptionist. Instead, the boss tells him it was a test of character and offers him a salaried position.

Synopses of *I Graduated, But . . .* suggest a socially-conscious revision of *Dreams of Youth*. In the late 1920s, over two-thirds of university graduates could not find work. The title quotes a popular saying of the period, a rueful joke on the false promise of higher education. The juxtaposition of Minoru's failure and his visiting mother's belief that he has succeeded anticipates the dramatic crux of *The Only Son*, while the revelation of Machiko's job looks forward to the more melodramatic *Woman of Tokyo*. The now obligatory citation of Hollywood cinema, a poster for Lloyd's *Speedy* in Minoru's apartment, suggests a bitter comparison of American and Japanese conditions.

Yet the film's lightness of touch is also evident. We have already noticed one instance, the mosquito-slapping incident. Minoru informs Machiko that he's jobless by pointing to the banner of the *Sunday Mainichi* (i.e. 'Sunday Daily') and saying: 'For me, every day is like this.' The plot's construction appears to be symmetrical in the manner of *Days of Youth* and American comedy. The film begins and ends with a session with the tailor; and Minoru's two visits to the company are marked by encounters with a giggling secretary. Minoru deceives Machiko by pretending to have a job; then she deceives him by pretending not to have one. He sees her light a man's cigarette at the bar, and when she starts to light his own at home, he announces that he knows her secret. Yet the *Kinema Jumpo* critic found such playfulness jarring. The happy ending divorced the film from social reality, he claimed.[7] It was not a complaint which would be made about Ozu's next effort.

I Graduated, But . . . (production still)

Kaishain seikatsu
The Life of an Office Worker

Shochiku Kamata studio. Story: Yasujiro Ozu. Script: Kogo Noda. Cinematography: Hideo Mohara. Cast: Tatsuo Saito (*Shintaro Tsukamoto*), Mitsuko Yoshikawa (*Fukuko, his wife*), Tomio Aoki (*third son*), Takeshi Sakamoto (*Okamura*). 5 reels, 1,552 meters. Released 25 October 1929. No script, negative, or prints known to exist.

Sakamoto's wife is so delighted with his semi-annual bonus that he dares not tell her that he's also been fired. Sakamoto's friend Okamura offers him a job with his company, but his wife declines for him. In the meantime, Sakamoto investigates shady businesses and encounters swindlers who prey on the unemployed. When a friend from Sakamoto's old firm visits to tell him that his pals are trying to get his job back, his wife learns the truth and flies into a rage. Okamura returns to restate his offer, and the family's problems are solved.

The film's plot, revolving around a secret like that of *I Graduated, But . . .* , seems slight, but the film evidently had a richness of retardatory incident and textural detail. Critics praised its depiction of the salaryman's lifestyle, especially one scene of Sakamoto's family exercising to the radio, and Ozu's comic depiction of the hero's four (!) nearsighted sons. Even the happy ending seemed more smoothly motivated than that of the previous film. A *Kinema Jumpo* review compared Ozu's film favorably with a work of the veteran Minoru Murata, a remarkable compliment to one who had been directing for only two years.[8] It may well have been such praise for his first salaryman film that steered Ozu toward the *shoshimin-geki* for the rest of his career.

Tokkan kozo
A Straightforward Boy

Shochiku Kamata studio. Story: 'Chuji Nozu'. Script: Tadao Ikeda. Cinemato-graphy: Ko Nomura. Cast: Tatsuo Saito (*Bunkichi*), Tomio Aoki (*Senbo*), Takeshi Sakamoto (*boss*). 4 reels, 1,031 meters. Released 23 November 1929. No script, negative, or prints known to exist.

Playing hide and seek, a boy is abducted. To keep him quiet, the kidnapper buys him candy and toys. The kidnapper becomes so frustrated with the boy's mischievous ways that he takes him home, but his father demands that the abductor keep the boy. Baffled, the kidnapper returns the boy to his play-mates. The boy tells them: 'This man will buy you anything you want,' and the kidnapper runs off in fright.

This short, sketch-like work, obviously derived from O. Henry's 'Ransom of Red Chief', made the child actor Tomio Aoki so famous that he changed his name to Tokkan Kozo (literally, 'a boy who charges into you'). One of the four sons in *Life of an Office Worker*, he was to have major roles in several Ozu films of the 1930s. The film was shot in only three days and was Ozu's sixth film to be released in 1929. The author's name, 'Chuji Nozu', is a portmanteau word: *Chuji* or 'two Chu's' (the Chinese character *chu* appears in the names of Tadao Ikeda and Tadamoto Okubo), and then *No*(da), and (O)*zu*.

1930

Kekkongaku nyumon
An Introduction to Marriage

Shochiku Kamata studio. Story: Toshio Okuma. Script: Kogo Noda. Cinematography: Hideo Mohara. Cast: Tatsuo Saito (*Mitsuo Kitamiya*), Sumiko Kurishima (*Toshiko, his wife*), Shinyo Nara (*his brother*), Minoru Takada (*Shinichiro Takebayashi*), Shizue Tatsuta (*Mineko, his wife*), Mitsuko Yoshikawa (*bar hostess*). 7 reels, 1,943 meters. Released 5 January 1930. No script, negative, or prints known to exist.

Takebayashi, a dentist, and his wife are trapped in a boring marriage. Their trip to a spa to rekindle romance has been a failure. In the dining car of the train, Takebayashi flirts with a young woman, but she ignores his advances. He pockets the gloves she has left behind. In Tokyo, the woman's husband Professor Kitamiya is indifferent to her return. She complains of a toothache, and he urges her to visit the Takebayashi dental clinic. When she does, she recognizes her train companion. He gives her one glove back, but his flirtation is interrupted by his wife. That night, Kitamiya meets Takebayashi in a bar and invites him home. Frightened by recognizing his new friend's wife, Takebayashi flees. The next day, Kitamiya's wife calls on the dentist to get an explanation, but Takebayashi's wife sees them and calls Kitamiya to report the incident of the gloves. Searching the house, Kitamiya can find only one glove and confronts his wife with it. She tells him she wants to leave him. Kitamiya goes to Takebayashi's wife, who assures him that his wife is faithful and supplies the other glove. Meanwhile, Kitamiya's wife entrains to visit her father in Kyoto. She goes to the dining car, and there sits Kitamiya, who pursues her from table to table before offering her both gloves. Laughing, the couple are reunited.

What touches must have graced this Lubitschian tale! The symmetry of beginning and ending, the roundelay of bored couple and devoted couple, the motifs used to build comic tension (the gloves from *Days of Youth* here put to a more tightly motivated use), and even the faintly smutty title that suggests more *ero* than *nansensu* – all indicate a film made in homage to *The Marriage Circle*. For the first time, Ozu sets a plot firmly in the urban upper-middle class, a milieu he would exploit in his other Lubitschian exercises *What Did the Lady Forget?* and *The Flavor of Green Tea over Rice*. Now too he uses Sumiko Kurishima, a big star whom he would again pair with Tatsuo Saito in *What Did the Lady Forget?*. Although the film was considered a minor work, critics praised its continuity and its achievement of comedy through situation as well as through sight gags.[9] One can only imagine how Ozu filmed a scene in which Takimiya's wife feels the remaining glove in her husband's pocket.

Hogaraka ni ayume
Walk Cheerfully

Shochiku Kamata studio. Story: Hiroshi Shimizu. Script: Tadao Ikeda. Cinematography and editing: Hideo Mohara. Assistants: Yuharu Atsuta *et al.* Lighting: Tatsumi Yoshimura. Set design: Hiroshi Mizutani. Props: Kojiro Kawasaki, Tsunetaro Inoue. Cast: Minoru Takada (*Kenji Koyama*), Hiroko Kawasaki (*Yasue Sugimoto*), Nobuko Matsuzono (*her little sister*), Utako Suzuki (*her mother*), Hisao Yoshitani (*Senko*), Teruo Mori (*Gunpei*), Satoko Date (*Chieko*), Takeshi Sakamoto (*Ono*). 8 reels, 2,704 meters. Released 1 March 1930. Surviving prints: 96 min. Script, negative and prints in existence.

Kenji Koyama, a petty thief and swindler, begins to take an interest in the modest Yasue. Kenji's girlfriend Chieko helps their boss Ono lure Yasue into a hotel, but Kenji rescues her. He and his brother Senko decide to go straight. Senko becomes a hotel chauffeur and gets Kenji a job washing windows. When Chieko and Ken's and Senko's old pal Gunpei approach Ken to help them in a new crime, he refuses. Yasue overhears and discovers that Ken has truly reformed. Chieko and Gunpei are caught and inform the police of Ken's past crimes. After a stint in prison, the brothers return to Yasue and her family.

Evidently the Japan of 1930 did not have true gangsters. *Yakuza* gangs operated as secret societies steeped in mythical traditions of *bushido*. Nonetheless, there emerged in the late 1920s an image of the *yotomono*, the petty street hoodlum in American clothes, a product of the modernizing city. Crucial in establishing this type in popular culture was Yasunari Kawabata's book, *Asakusa kurenaidan* (*Asakusa Crimson Gang*). The quasi-reportage account depicts the gang as innocent and good-humored, indulging in movies, dancing, and jazz. Shochiku was quick to capitalize on such trends, and soon after the serialization of Kawabata's novel in 1929–30, the Kamata studio initiated their own series of 'hooligan' romances, to which Ozu contributed *Walk Cheerfully*. It remains a fascinatingly heterogeneous film. If *Days of Youth* displays proficiency, *Walk Cheerfully* is downright slick in its assimilation of Western conventions. As in *Dragnet Girl*, the exotic and formulaic genre allows Ozu to experiment stylistically, moving toward that highly overt narration that was to become his trademark.

Ozu's borrowings are evident. The basic story – the racketeer who reforms through the love of the good woman, while the bad girl and his old companions try to lure him back – derives from the late 1920s rash of American gangster films. The saloon scene is an elaboration of the scene in the Dreamland Café in Sternberg's *Underworld* (1927). The boss's nickname, Ken the Knife, echoes *The Threepenny Opera*. The film's climax, when Kenji is arrested, is capped by Yasue's farewell line: 'I'll always be waiting for you. Walk cheerfully.' (An epilogue supplies a happy ending when he and Senko come home from prison.) Stylistically, the film is even more 'Western' than *Days of Youth*, especially in its painstaking edge lighting (fig. 27, p. 83). One *film-noir* shot of Kenji and the cops on the stairway (fig. 7) echoes *Underworld*

7.

8.

9.

10.

11.

and is as sophisticated as the best Hollywood cinematography of the late 1920s. In most scenes the film's editing obeys continuity rules and makes heavy use of optical point-of-view cutting. Most striking is the great number of camera movements, far smoother and more daring than those in *Days of Youth* and typical of Ozu's work between 1930 and 1934.

Yet some of these stylistic devices are made oddly off-center by Ozu's usage. Instead of a single scene played out in hand gestures (as in *Days of Youth*'s pawnshop scene), we have several scenes with abruptly edited inserts of hands and feet, often independent of character vision. The camera movements become dissonant when, registered from a low height, they must also cue the point-of-view of an erect moving character; or when Ozu tracks in on an office door, with the word 'Private' reversed, for no discernible reason (unless it is an homage to a similar shot in *Girl Shy*); or when the repetition of a track-back from objects in Kenji's apartment not only informs us of the locale but marks the movements as parallel to one another. The increased number of 'unclaimed' shots and patterned framings suggests an increasingly overt narration.

Whereas the glove motif in *Days of Youth* was still tied to characterization, Ozu now presses toward the use of circulating motifs. As Senko is frisked, a close-up frames one tapping foot. In the elevator, Chieko is trying to win the boss over and she starts to tap her foot; then he does too. Instead of revealing character, these close-ups draw a whimsical, purely physical parallel. In the latter scene as well, Chieko says she will lure Yasue to the Luna Hotel. One scene later, Ken is staring out his window at the hotels in his neighborhood. Since he is unaware of Yasue's danger in another part of town, it is an impersonal narration that reinforces the motif.

A more complex example is the opening, which exploits the most prolonged independent camera movement in Ozu's surviving films. The camera starts on the grille of an automobile parked by a dock (fig. 8). The camera tracks back and back, revealing a long diagonal row of cars, with their drivers lounging alongside them (fig. 9). The camera stops, framing the scene in extreme long-shot (fig. 10). Pause. A man runs into the frame from the foreground (fig. 11). Another pause, and a crowd of men pursue him into depth and around the corner (fig. 12). The initial camera movement might seem a magnificent irrelevancy, but the peculiar logic of Ozu's narration justifies the shot on three grounds. First, cars become an important motif in the film. Second, and more specifically, the little man who runs past is Senko, who will eventually get a job as a limousine driver like the men in the shot. I shall discuss the third and most peculiar justification later, but the first two should indicate that the filmmaker now introduces his motifs in a highly oblique fashion.

He will develop the motifs in the same way. His trademark steaming teakettle, associated with Yasue's mother and their home, will be recast as the characters' steaming breath when Ken is arrested and then as a steaming white coffeepot in the epilogue. Mirrors recur as instruments of character vision, but in a scene we shall examine later, a mirror and its ricocheting reflection audaciously link locales.

Of course the opening camera movement can also be taken as a parody of the normal establishing shot (especially in the early talking film, with its bravura opening traveling shot seeking to deny the 'static' qualities of the talking picture to come). *Walk Cheerfully*'s narration becomes overt partly because it is so patently comic. The citations of American cinema (posters for *Our Dancing Daughters* (1928) and *Rough House Rosie* (1927)) within what is itself a pastiche only increase the sense of light-hearted artificiality. The gang boss played by Tatsuo Saito is an outrageous send-up, complete with white pomeranian, a long cigarette holder, and a beauty mark. The mob's high signs consist of jazz-baby dance steps, as if these thugs had seen too many early musicals. Ozu's favorite asides in English also make the narrational process fairly overt. Ken's apartment walls, plastered with American prizefight posters, sport such graffiti as:

12.

> Seeking a fair Senorita
> Fair and not too much meat
> Woo her a while in my Argentine style
> Carry her of off [sic] her feet.

As the police file upstairs to arrest Ken, Ozu dwells on another scrawl, the chalk silhouette of a gangster with the caption, 'Me and My Shadow'. Whereas the students of *Days of Youth* represent recognizably Japanese youths smitten with Western customs, the gangsters of *Walk Cheerfully* move through a fantasy landscape that is at once Japan and an America not far from Brecht's Mahagonny.

A 'progressivist' account of Ozu's early work would stress how *Walk Cheerfully* takes a step toward the 'mature' Ozu style: the greater reliance on low-height setups, the changes in objects used to convey the passage of time, the seating of characters at right angles to one another. We could point to occasionally staggered figure placement, as in the scene of Yasue and her mother at home; but in *Walk Cheerfully* the device often remains uncertain and imprecise, as demonstrated by the shots of Ken confronting the police (see p. 95). Fades still connect scenes, but the two parts of the first sequence are joined by the sort of atmospheric inserts (rickshas, a ship draining bilge) that would in later films link scenes through a play of dominants and overtones. The opening chase presents such picturesque long-shots that one could imagine the later Ozu simply eradicating the human figures and using the compositions as intermediate spaces. The progressivist version would also notice that although cutaways are still motivated by character interaction, especially by optical point-of-view, some of them are ambivalent. When Senko is frisked, he looks up; cut to a shot of flags on a mast; cut back to Senko, but now seen from the rear so that no cue for his glance can clinch the previous shot as representing his vision.

13.

What the progressivist account might overlook, however, is that certain devices of 'late' Ozu are here already given flagrant definition. Acting in unison is not simply present, it is foregrounded to a degree surpassed only in *I Flunked, But . . . .* Two hoodlums enter as if in a chorus line (fig. 13). During a pool game, a bevy of seated thugs kick their feet and flip their hands in synchronization. The device of 'similar figures' is bared when, watching Ken taken by the police, Yasue 'matches' the woman's profile drawn on the wall

14.

199

(fig. 14). The tactic of moving through contiguous sites and tracing a detour around the characters is made explicit by arrows chalked on the objects that interrupt Ken and Senko's walk. Thus Ozu experiments not only with certain tactics but also with ways they might function to mark an overt, self-conscious narration.

At its boldest, this narration invites us to participate in those games with expectation which characterize the Ozu film. There is a purely stylistic joke when a shot of the riders in a car darkens as if in a fade-out, and the next shot reveals that they are in a tunnel. But then *this* shot genuinely fades out. There is also the use of parallels to create a retrospective awareness of pattern. During Ken's outing with Yasue and her sister, the car drives off and a shot shows the tires pulling away from discarded paper balloons. First variant, confirmatory: later in the scene, the little sister tosses her mashed doll out of the car, and a shot shows the car pulling away from it. Second variant, based on Hollywood's 'rule of three': When the gang spot Ken, Yasue, and her sister on their outing, Chieko knocks Senko's bowler hat to the ground and he leaves the car to fetch it. Once he gets back in, the car pulls off, and his hat flies out of a window again. The car stops and he trots back to get it. He goes back to the car and gets in. But the car does not move and the shot holds, as if waiting for the hat to be tossed out again. The shot fades out of the poised car in the distance. The gag's outcome will not be known. Here is a Lubitsch gag 'decentered', looking forward to Tati in its invitation to imagine alternative payoffs. Given what this whimsical narration finds amusing, a third function for the opening tracking shot (figs. 8–12) can now be suggested. By concentrating our attention on the perspectival space in the distance, the shot leads us to assume that the salient action will emerge from around the corner; the eruption of the pursuit from the foreground into depth puts us at the 'wrong' point to see the action but traces, in reverse, the camera's own trajectory. I suggest, in seriousness, that we ought to find this funny.

The self-conscious rigor and playfulness of the narration is most vividly seen in two parallel scenes depicting the beginning and the ending of the working day. I have already remarked that these sequences recall the European 'city symphony' (p. 128). In the morning sequence, the first nine shots show shutters and blinds lifted, office workers' legs hurrying along the sidewalk, hats put on hooks, and ranks of secretaries unsheathing their typewriters. Then Ozu introduces his first twist. A secretary at the window

15.

16.

17.

18.

19.

20.

(fig. 15) leaves her compact there (fig. 16). These shots of a somewhat particularized interior lead us to assume that a scene will start, especially since Yasue has announced in the previous scene that she has a new office job. But the compact shot turns out to be a pivot back outside. Cut to a shot of the sidewalk outside, with a dot of light on it (fig. 17). According to the contiguity principle, this should be the reflection of the mirror; Ozu has made a transition on a beam of light. (He will do it again in *That Night's Wife*.) Yasue's feet come into the shot from off left, pause, and take a step back to stand exactly on the spot (fig. 18). What she is looking at is not the window with the compact but Kenji, high above, washing another window (figs. 19–20). So perhaps the reflection is not that of the compact but of Ken's window. The transition is thus rendered fundamentally ambiguous, but its importance for us here is its outrageously roundabout structure. One could go directly from the morning rush hour (shots 1–9) to the shot of Yasue stopping in the street; one does not need the detour via the secretary, her compact, the reflection, and an office which may or may not be that at which Yasue works.

In the sequence portraying the end of the working day, Ozu constructs a variant of the earlier scene. Windows close, typewriters are covered, hats are taken from their pegs, feet troop down steps and hurry across the sidewalk. The shots are reordered and Ozu omits the secretary and the light motif; but the number of shots remains identical to that of the first episode and creates a marked parallel. (See p. 128.) With the twelfth shot, the rhyme becomes exact, shot for shot. Yasue's feet now move leftward before stopping on the pavement (fig. 21). She looks up (fig. 22). Ken is not at a window (fig. 23).

21.

22.

23.

Now the narration asks us to toy with the reasons that there is no spot on the sidewalk – the compact is gone, the sun has moved, Ken is gone. That is, to the city symphony's clichéd, abstract representation of urban time Ozu adds references to the behavior of light and to the rhythm of human presence and absence, creating concrete, poetically ambivalent indications of a day's passage. This treatment is reinforced by that moment in the course of the same day when Yasue tears up her note to Ken and tosses the shreds away. The narration dwells on the pieces fluttering down from the rooftop and settling on the sidewalk: a poignant image of evanescence in the modern city. By citing the city symphony, by insisting on parallel patterning, and by detouring us by means of an ambiguous contiguity that is in any case later 'erased', Ozu insists on a narration at once arbitrary and obedient to a self-imposed discipline. Like the Western sets and costumes that are subordinated to rigorous framings, like Ken's American graffiti that become smeared and eroded after he goes straight, Ozu's borrowings from Western cinema are revised by the workings of an autonomous aesthetic system.

Rakudai wa shitakeredo
I Flunked, But . . .

Shochiku Kamata studio. Story: Yasujiro Ozu. Script: Akira Fushimi. Cinematography and editing: Hideo Mohara. Cinematography assistants: Yuharu Atsuta *et al.* Set design: Yoneichi Wakita. Props: Kojiro Kawasaki, Shotaro Hashimoto. Lighting: Toshimitsu Nakajima. Cast: Tatsuo Saito (*Takahashi*), Kaoru Futaba (*landlady*), Tomio Aoki (*her son*), Kinuyo Tanaka (*café girl*), Hiroo Wakabayashi, Ichiro Okuni (*professors*), Dekao Yokoo, Tokio Seki, Hiroshi Mikura, Goro Yokoyama (*flunking students*), Ichiro Tsukita, Chishu Ryu, Fusao Yamada, Kenji Satomi (*passing students*). 6 reels, 1,765 meters. Surviving prints: 64 min. Released 11 April 1930. Script, negative, and prints in existence.

Takahashi, his four roommates, and his four pals are all facing 'exam hell'. On the first day, his cronies try to cheat from crib notes written on one boy's shirt. That night Takahashi prepares new notes on his shirt, but his landlady sends it to the laundry. He and his pals flunk, while his roommates all graduate. But the roommates can't find jobs and spend their days idly wishing they were back in school. In the meantime, Takahashi's pals go back for the next term, and become cheerleaders.

I Flunked, But . . . is a slighter film than others that survive from 1930, and a *Kinema Jumpo* critic was quick to point out that it lacks the social bite of earlier works.[10] As the obverse of *I Graduated, But . . .* , told from the standpoint of one who escapes unemployment, it deflects attention from economic conditions and romanticizes student life in the manner of *Days of Youth*. Stylistically, the film does show clear instances of the staggered staging which Ozu would later refine. In other respects, however, it is a less audacious work than *Walk Cheerfully*. (For example, its lighting and matches on action are unexpectedly crude.) Still, the *Kinema Jumpo* reviewer singled out the work's basic virtue: it is very funny. Comedy is its 'dominant', the Russian Formalist term for the aspect of the work's system that subordinates other factors. This short film, shot in a week, offers a convenient occasion to analyze Ozu's characteristic comic techniques.

For once, the American sources of Ozu's comedy are not cited via movie posters. (The only one, for *Charming Sinners* of 1929, is used solely for its commentative title.) Still, the film's inspiration is clearly drawn from Ozu's two mentors. As in a Lubitsch film, the audience enjoys superior knowledge. From Lloyd's *The Freshman* comes the collegiate milieu and the remarkable jigs that the students dance. Both directors built their scenes out of many brief shots of isolated details and relied on objects, eyelines, and reaction shots. The two directors tutored Ozu in comic structure as well. They taught him how to establish and sustain running gags, how to build up extended comic scenes, and how to create gags out of overt narrational comments.

Days of Youth had already displayed Ozu's proficiency at handling running gags of socks, gloves, and room-for-rent signs. Here too most of the motifs are objects (as in American films): sugar cubes, the tie that Takahashi's girlfriend is knitting for him, the bread the cramming students order and later can't afford to buy. And, like the earlier film's motif of apartment-hunting, other running gags involve locales, such as the empty college courtyard. In *I Flunked, But . . .* , though, one motif gets developed in a 'conceptual' way not seen in the earlier film. During the first cheating scene, one of Takahashi's gang tries to read the answers off the fat student's shirttail, but the boy spills ink on it. The gag is inverted when, after Takahashi has prepared his own shirt as a crib sheet, his landlady sends it to the laundry: from blotting out the answers with ink to erasing them with bleach. Still later, after Takahashi has flunked, his girlfriend tries to praise him. 'I know you worked hard at it,' she says innocently. Cut to a close-up of the shirt, the crib notes still faintly visible. As she knots his tie, he quickly slides the shirt out of sight.

The most elaborate running gag involves acting in unison, here developed to a still higher pitch than in *Walk Cheerfully*. Ozu gives Takahashi two sets of four pals each so as to multiply the possibilities of movement *en masse*. Our introduction to Takahashi's gang consists of a lingering shot of the courtyard into which all five loafers shamble in synchronization. During the first exam, the boys break out in a rash of identical gestures. The gang has its own cross-legged march, as well as its fraternal jig. Variants appear. Sleeping in a row, the four roommates roll over one by one and start studying. As they awake all wield toothbrushes at the same time. The faculty seem to have caught the disorder from the students: when one student visits the office, the two principals thrum their fingers in the same tempo. The motif comes to a fine climax. In the last scene, in a repetition of Takahashi's gesture after he had flunked, the four unemployed graduates flop back one by one and then simultaneously swing their feet up onto the table and start to pound out a rhythm. Ozu cuts to a student audience applauding in exactly that rhythm, a powerful expression of the graduates' kinesthetic nostalgia for school days. Ozu then reveals Takahashi's gang as cheerleaders, executing a wigwagging

24.

25.

26.

27.

number – the ideal application of their choreographic abilities.

So comic motifs interweave. Ozu is no less concerned to build up to fully-developed comic scenes. His handling of ignorance and misunderstanding is skilful. Takahashi lounges in the confidence that his shirt will pull him through, but we have already seen it taken by the laundryman. When the landlady's son is told that flunking is 'something great', he tells Takahashi that he will grow up to be great: 'I'll flunk like you did.' The most prolonged case of the comedy of ignorance depends upon crosscutting, which Ozu even this early in his career usually avoids. While the bespectacled boy pleads with the faculty to pass Takahashi, we see one of Takahashi's pals check his own grade, learn of his failure, and notice that the posted grade list flops down at the end point. Cut back to the boy pleading. Cut back to Takahashi sidling through the crowd to the grade list, then lifting the flap to discover his name at the bottom of the class. Since we know that he has flunked, Ozu introduces the flopped-paper gag to create a minor comic delay.

The most extensive stretches of comic development are the two examination scenes, and here Ozu shows that he had nothing further to learn from his Hollywood masters. Each episode is constructed out of several shots (45 and 21 respectively), linked by eyelines and relying on contiguity. Sato points out that the details of action in these scenes are described in the scripts and that the perfect continuity of the resulting sequences suggests that Ozu was already sketching each shot beforehand.[11]

The first scene gives its gags a clear ABA pattern. One boy reads the answers off the back of the fat boy's shirt, then copies them onto a slip of paper. There follows byplay with the paper, which the boy pins to the rear of the professor's frock coat (a parallel to the fat boy's answer-on-the-back ploy). Takahashi tries in vain to retrieve the note. Cut to the fat boy's shirt, which gets spattered with ink. The gags, all based on spatial proximity, lay the groundwork for the second scene, in which much less happens but which displays more boldly the idea of contiguity. The fat boy acts as pivot. He looks first diagonally right to Takahashi, then diagonally left to another confederate in another row (fig. 24). He sees the boy idly toying with his watch (fig. 25). Cut to the boy, with the fat student now out of focus in the background (fig. 26). Then this boy looks diagonally left to another boy, who is boredly chewing gum (fig. 27). Cut back to the boy with the watch; behind him an innocent student rises (again out of focus) and walks forward (fig. 28). Ozu seizes this opportunity for an establishing shot (fig. 29) before cutting back to Takahashi, initially revealed to the right of the fat boy. Now he looks to his diagonal right and reveals the assiduous, bespectacled boy. The characters are thus laid out in staggered fashion across five areas:

Fat boy

Boy with watch   Takahashi

Boy with gum   Bespectacled boy

The tactic of arranging shots so as to move diagonally 'down the line', anchoring figures though out-of-focus backgrounds, will be brought to perfection in the *joruri* scenes of *Passing Fancy* (see p. 113), and it sketches out the principle of dominant/overtone patterning that will be important in the late films.

Both Lubitsch's and Lloyd's films are characterized by a degree of overt narrational presence. Both deceive the audience by encouraging untenable expectations. Lloyd was fond of satiric intertitles, and Lubitsch emphasized them along with highly judgmental cutaways, such as that in *Lady Winder-mere's Fan* which ironically points up the couple's quarrel by cutting to the birthday presents that the husband has bought. Like these filmmakers, Ozu will self-consciously mislead the audience. The lengthy opening shows us two boys quarreling, but they are of no consequence to the film's intrigue. After Takahashi has flunked, he gravely takes out scissors and tests their sharpness by pricking at his neck. He ceremoniously turns from the camera. *Seppuku?* A close-up reveals a *tabi* flung off, and a reverse-angle shot shows him starting to trim his toenails.

28.

More typical of Ozu are the more subtly humorous juxtapositions: the unemployed roommates' legs and the marching legs of Takahashi's pals, the newspaper read by the boys at school and that read by the unemployed boys, the five cheerleaders' megaphones on the playing field and the four pairs of feet in the apartment. When we think that a scene is over because the camera lingers on empty space, Takahashi's gang lopes in. Later, when we get a similar setup of an empty locale, we wait, but no one enters: the scene *is* over. A narration that creates such diversions, parallels, and permutations, while clearly derived from Hollywood practice, pushes cinematic humor in a more conceptual, whimsical, and self-conscious direction.

29.

As usual, though, the film's comedy is tempered with melancholy. The scenes after Takahashi's failure slow the film's rhythm in the manner of Yamamoto and Watanabe's brooding in *Days of Youth*. Takahashi's room-mates hold a dinner to celebrate their graduation, but the running gag of uniform movement turns sour here as they mimic his dejected gestures, slowing when he does, eating when he does. And when Takahashi asks the little boy what he wants to be, the boy says he will flunk as Takahashi has. The scene points ahead to one played by the same two actors in *I Was Born, But . . .*, when the answer will also be a gag but will reflect the film's theme of the futility of challenging power. This film moves through melancholy to a placid acceptance of the resources one still has. 'Even if you didn't graduate,' says the shopgirl, 'nobody can stop your wearing a suit.' And what one still has includes, principally, male friendship. At the end, the gang is back together, performing for a crowd of appreciative boys. *I Flunked, But . . .* traces, in a comic tint, the basic emotional trajectory of many early Ozu films.

UNIVERSITY OF WINCHESTER LIBRARY

Sono yo no tsuma
That Night's Wife

Shochiku Kamata studio. Story: Oscar Shisgall, 'From Nine to Nine'. Adaptation and script: Kogo Noda. Cinematography and editing: Hideo Mohara. Cinematography assistants: Yuharu Atsuta *et al*. Lighting: Shige Yamamoto, Tashimitsu Nakajima. Set design: Yoneichi Wakita. Cast: Tokihiko Okada (*Shuji Hashizume*), Emiko Yagumo (*Mayumi*), Mitsuko Ichimura (*Michiko*), Togo Yamamoto (*Detective Kagawa*), Tatsuo Saito (*doctor*), Chishu Ryu (*policeman*). 7 reels, 1,809 meters. Surviving prints: 65 min. Released 6 July 1930. Script, negative, and prints in existence.

To save his critically ill daughter Michiko, Shuji Hashizume, a commercial artist, robs an office. While the police pursue him, the doctor tells the mother Mayumi that if Michiko can get through tonight she will recover. Shuji hails a cab and comes home. He vows to give himself up tomorrow if Michiko pulls through. The cabdriver enters, now revealed as detective Kagawa, and tries to arrest Shuji, but Mayumi uses Shuji's pistol to get the drop on him. She keeps Kagawa covered through the night while Shuji ministers to the child. However, the couple fall asleep and Kagawa gains the upper hand. He agrees to wait until morning to arrest Shuji. Moved by the family's plight and Michiko's return to health, Kagawa lets Shuji escape, but the father returns, unable to face a life of flight. Kagawa leads Shuji off to jail.

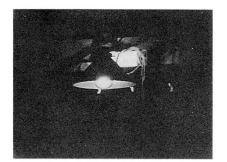

30.

31.

In his sixteenth film, Ozu continues to treat alien subject matter as the occasion for experiments in stylistic patterning. The immediate source is a short story, 'From Nine to Nine', published in the March 1930 issue of *New Youth* (*Shinseinen*), a magazine that specialized in Western-style mystery fiction. Behind this source stand two Hollywood genres, the crime thriller and the family melodrama. As in the college comedies and *Walk Cheerfully*, Ozu tests his skill by taking many genre conventions seriously. He shoots a robbery scene with suspense and he wrings emotion by prolonging the moment of tearing Shuji from Michiko's bedside. He creates uncertainty about the cabdriver by dividing knowledge: a moving shot from the cab introduces Shuji; we get the driver's mirror point-of-view on Shuji lighting a cigarette; after Shuji pays him off, the shot lingers on the cab, not driving away. At the same time, Ozu puts the genres at arm's length by such self-conscious citations as posters for *Broadway Babies* (1929) and *Gentleman of the Press* (1929) and English tags like 'Two is company, three is a crowd.' Togo Yamamoto, who portrays the detective Kagawa, had played villains and gangsters in Hollywood films of the 1920s, and the other actors were identified as Western-style players. By making Shuji a commercial artist who paints signs and posters Ozu motivates the complete absence of Japanese decor. Were it not for Mayumi's kimono, the film's *mise-en-scène* would not be recognizably Japanese.

The opening offers, in miniature, the characteristic formal strategies of *That Night's Wife*. The robbery scene, with its cutting between the police and the building guard and its abrupt close-ups of a phone receiver and a pistol, echoes the terse style of *Underworld* (1927) and Lang's *Spione* (1928). Yet this conventional scene is marked exactly *as* conventional by the way Ozu dwells on thriller iconography for its own sake. The camera tracks in to a handprint on the door, but this will be no clue, it will come to nothing. After Shuji calls the doctor to check on his daughter's progress, Ozu frames the dangling phone receiver in a sparkling close-up worthy of Paramount; but then there is no cut back to the doctor puzzling over the interrupted conversation. Sometimes these icons yield motifs which Ozu will pattern in abstract fashion. Hands will recur throughout the film, and the dangling receiver echoes the snapped-off phone receiver during Shuji's break-in.

32.

Ozu also uses the robbery as a pretext for moving through contiguous spaces and creating unexpected patterns. When Shuji shoves the guard into the office, the camera tracks left past the guard to show two men lying on the floor, bound and gagged, with the legs of a third man dangling into the frame from the desk. Ozu's principal contiguity rule would favor cutting to a medium-shot of the third man. Instead Ozu cuts back to the initial point of the 'line', the downed guard. Then he cuts to the medium-shot of the third man. In such ways, as well as through the now frequent across-the-line shot/reverse-shots, Ozu 'rewrites' Lang and Sternberg, announcing the subordination of thriller material to his playful stylistic strategies.

33.

Indeed, as the film develops, the opening comes to seem purely a pretext. Shuji steals the money for medicine for Michiko, but he never buys any. Once he gets home, the fact that tonight is the crucial night for her illness takes precedence, so that he can offer to go with Kagawa if the policeman will wait until morning. Dramaturgically, the robbery is but an alibi to get Shuji and Kagawa together in their apartment for a suspenseful night with Mayumi. This function of the opening is announced in the very first scene, which is as oblique and misleading as that of *I Flunked, But....* A policeman finds a tramp sleeping behind the column of a building and chases him off. Although the episode serves as a long-range counterpoint to the merciful action of Kagawa at the climax, in narrational terms it signals the skewed function of the entire opening portion.

34.

Ozu's characteristic style is also evident in his handling of another convention of the thriller. Crosscutting is rare in any Ozu film, but here Ozu uses it to alternate Shuji's flight with Mayumi's patient nursing of Michiko. But instead of the crisp, swiftly advancing cuts offered by Lang, this filmmaker employs crosscutting as a basis for prolonged transitions. He fades out from the assembled patrolmen and fades in a series of shots tracking down various areas of Hashizume's home, all delaying the introduction of the doctor. The next transition uses noncausal principles to create nuanced dominant/overtone relations. Instead of cutting directly from Mayumi at home to Shuji hiding from the police, Ozu cuts from a shot of her to a shot of a hanging lamp (fig. 30). This tacit contiguity cut is followed by another one, a cut to a shot of a potted plant (fig. 31). Now the contiguity link is reinforced not only by background knowledge but by the shadows (presumably) cast by the bulb. Ozu's next image compresses the two previous ones: a street light (the dominant) shining down on foliage (the overtone) (fig. 32). The cut relies on categorical inclusion, assuring the analogy between two lights and two plants. Ozu makes foliage the dominant of the next shot by presenting the shadows of leaves on a low wall (fig. 33). The logic of the cut resembles that linking the mirror to the reflected light in *Walk Cheerfully*. And the wall, or one like it, furnishes the link to Shuji, crouching in the darkness (fig. 34). This is crosscutting, but of a kind that is uneconomical by classical standards. Later, Shuji is in the cab and restlessly ties his shoelaces. Instead of cutting directly and simply to his wife, Ozu inserts a shot of the child's toy swing, whose cords resemble shoestrings, followed by a shot of adjacent magazines and then a shot that tracks along the floor to frame Mayumi's feet. As in *Walk Cheerfully* and *I Flunked, But . . .* , Ozu is more and more concerned to dwell on what is normally only connective tissue, to take us on detours through contiguous space before getting back to the causal line.

That both transitions to the family's apartment linger on details of space is not fortuitous. After Shuji comes home, Ozu uses the rest of the film to set himself a technical problem: how to present forty-five minutes of action within a single set? 'I really wracked my brains about the continuity of this one.'[12] Like Dreyer in *Thou Shalt Honor Thy Wife* (1925), and unlike Hitchcock in *Rope* (1948), Ozu will avoid establishing shots and rely instead on eyeline matches, frame entrances and exits, spatial landmarks, and medium shots of details.

Like Dreyer as well, Ozu will use these devices to show all walls and regions of the central area of the flat, so that we view the action from more sides than traditional continuity would allow.[13] Thus the early portion presents the action from an orientation favoring the child's bed and the dining table. When the detective enters and Mayumi keeps him at bay, the action develops a second zone, in the area near Shuji's paint table. The camera shifts its orientation accordingly, shooting from exactly the opposite direction. (Ozu had tried this strategy out in one scene of *Walk Cheerfully*, which makes a 360-degree survey of Kenji's apartment.) Although the space can be mapped, it requires close attention. The few long shots are cunningly designed to exclude crucial regions and to prompt the spectator to rely on such gross landmarks as the bed, the toy swing, the table, and even a straw boater hanging from a rafter. In addition, the viewer may be confused by Ozu's propensity to 'cheat' the position of the landmarks and to refuse right-angled corners. One need only compare two almost successive shots to see how the perspective shifts fairly drastically (figs. 35–36). The spectator's 'cognitive map' is much sharper at a shot-to-shot level, since most of the film's cues for contiguous regions rely on eyelines and frame entrances, and these (as Kuleshov knew) do not permit us to measure out a total space. Like Dreyer, or Pudovkin in *Storm over Asia*, Ozu lets the spectator build a space consisting of clear dramatic nodes within a vague overall area.

Unlike Dreyer, however, Ozu has no use for a spare decor that makes isolated objects and figures stand out. The apartment of *That Night's Wife* engulfs the spectator in a sea of signs, tools, trinkets, and bric-a-brac. The clutter provides continuous interest, as Ozu reveals ever-new aspects of the room, and it also keeps the apartment's geography somewhat uncertain. We are introduced to the set through a series of laterally tracking close-ups that eventually slide away a wall of posters to reveal the doctor at the child's

35.

36.

bedside. Like the poster shop in Godard's *Made in USA* (1966), this apartment is a collage of flat planes that simply provide a ground for the figures, a space free of normal cues for scale and distance. Multilingual advertising, maps, and graffiti make this flat a cubistic assemblage out of the detritus of Western culture.

The confinement to the apartment also lets Ozu create variations on strategies and elements displayed earlier. The rapid track-in and -out movements of the the robbery episode get abruptly juxtaposed. There is a knock on the door; track straight in to the door; dissolve to the other side to show a man's back, the shot tracking at the same rate, straight backwards. Still more startling is the quick track back from the gun in Kagawa's hands; cut to Mayumi's hands clutching her apron, and track back at the same pace; cut to a long shot that tracks, just as fast, in to Kagawa. The jarring quality of these passages is increased by Ozu's refusal to halt the camera movement before the dissolve or cut, so that two diametrically opposed optical effects are simply slammed together. Yet they are not isolated devices like those rhetorical flourishes of Ozu's contemporaries. The outré techniques are exploited as elements of a perceptual design, serving a narrative end (to create surprise or suspense) but organized to a degree that stresses the symmetries of pattern.

Pattern-making is no less emphasized in the two transitions that emerge during the apartment scenes. If the crosscutting portions stressed spatial disparities and simultaneity, the narrative purpose of later transitions is to emphasize ellipses. Mayumi keeps Kagawa covered with the two pistols, and Ozu must skip over long stretches of time. The first transition is straightforward, at least for Ozu. Kagawa winds his watch, which shows the time as 1.30. Fade out. Fade in on a clock which shows the time as 3.07. After a lateral track to a lamp and a pan down, and a cut to the doll on the swing, we get a shot of Shuji filling the icepack as a drowsy Mayumi continues to watch over Kagawa.

The second transition is more intricate, being a kind of displaced reprise of the lamp/plant transition in the film's early portion.

1. (*ms*) Mayumi.

2. (*mcu*) Track diagonally leftward across the floor to bottles and a dark stain.

3. (*cu*) Hanging laundry. Track leftward to the window. Light brightens outside as dawn arrives.

4. (*ms*) A street lamp by a sink goes out.

5. (*ls*) Street. A milkman arrives and opens his cart.

6. (*ms*) A fence top. His hands replace three empties with three fresh bottles.

7. (*ls*) Street, as 5. The milkman puts the empties in his cart and goes off.

8. As end of 3. Track rightward from the window to the hanging laundry.

9. (*ms*) Track rightward past the curtain to a shelf with a swinging paint can.

10. (*mcu*) Track diagonally rightward, down the floor past bottles and cans.

11. (*ms*) Track rightward to Mayumi, asleep. She suddenly awakes.

The overall symmetry of this transition, along with its minor nuances and surprises, should require only a little commentary. The sequence pivots around shot 6, with shots 5 and 7 and shots 3 and 8 serving as immediate parallels and shots 1 and 11 bookending the whole passage. There remain asymmetries as well. Shot 2 is paralleled by shots 9 and 10, while shot 4 (the culmination of the street-lamp motif) has no exact partner in the second half. The ambiguity of the cut from 2 to 3 is created by the question of whether the stain in 2 comes from the overturned bottle above it or from the hanging laundry revealed in shot 3. Similarly, the 'extra' tracking shot, number 9, creates its own enigma (what makes the can swing? Kagawa grabbing the gun?). To propose 'readings' here (the light of hope, nourishment blocked) would miss the force of the scene. Apart from recalcitrant data (there is that laundry and that paint can), such flat-footed interpretations neglect Ozu's transformations of the clichés of the city symphony, the way the sequence climaxes his usages of intermediate spaces earlier, and above all the play of expectation and correction, rule and revision, rigor and open-ended formal invention – a play that reveals a pattern in process. That pattern is completed only with the final shot, a diagonal perspective down a sunny street that in its composition echoes the darkened street that opened the film.

Erogami no onryo
The Revengeful Spirit of Eros

Shochiku Kamata studio. Story: Seizaburo Ishihara. Script: Kogo Noda. Cinematography: Hideo Mohara. Cast: Tatsuo Saito (*Kentaro Yumaji*), Hikaru Hoshi (*Daikuro Ishikawa*), Satoko Date (*Yumeko, a dancer*), Ichiro Tsukida (*her boyfriend*). 3 reels, 750 meters. Released 27 July 1930. No script, negative, or prints known to exist.

Kentaro and Yumeko commit a lovers' suicide by throwing themselves into the sea. Kentaro's friend Ishikawa finds him washed ashore, still alive. Although fearful of Yumeko's ghost, Kentaro returns to town. He learns that she too has survived and is now working in a dance hall. To get revenge Kentaro sneaks into the dance hall and tries to frighten her with rubber snakes, but she sees through his ploy and tricks him into fighting with Ishikawa. The next day, a boyfriend on each arm, she passes Kentaro on the street.

With the reputation of being the slightest film that Ozu ever made, *The Revengeful Spirit of Eros* may well typify the *ero-guro-nansensu* film of the early 1930s. It is said to have been fairly sexy in its original form, but censors cut out offensive parts, creating a mediocre comedy. Ozu said that he filmed it at a spa during a vacation he took at Kido's orders.[14]

Ashi ni sawatta koun
The Luck Which Touched the Leg (aka *Lost Luck*)

Shochiku Kamata studio. Story and script: Kogo Noda. Cinematography: Hideo Mohara. Cast: Tatsuo Saito (*Kotaro Furukawa*), Mitsuko Yoshikawa (*Toshiko, his wife*), Tomio Aoki (*son*), Mitsuko Ichimura (*daughter*), Takeshi Sakamoto (*section chief*). 7 reels, 2,032 meters. Released 3 October 1930. No script, negative, or prints known to exist.

Furugawa, a salaryman, finds a lost Y4000 and is rewarded with Y500 by the owner. Immediately his colleagues descend on him, selling him bonds, borrowing money, and sponging. By next morning, to his wife's dismay, he has only Y180 left. At work, his boss offers him chickens, roosters, and equipment for a poultry farm, all for only Y100. Furugawa is enthusiastic, but when he returns home, he finds that his wife has spent the money on a sewing machine and kimono material. They quarrel. Next morning, Furugawa again happens onto something wrapped in newspapers – a ball of rice. He gloomily continues on his way to work.

In description, the film sounds like a comedy – a fact also signalled by its ironic citation of Yutaka Abe's prize-winning *Woman Who Touched the Leg* (1925). Yet contemporary reviewers found it not particularly funny. The *Kinema Jumpo* critic called it a mixture of melancholy and humor, 'the first Japanese tragicomedy.'[15] Once more Saito and Yoshikawa form the couple, as they will in *I Was Born, But . . . .*

Ojosan
Young Miss

Shochiku Kamata studio. Story: Komatsu Kitamura. Gags by: Akira Fushimi, 'James Maki', and Tadao Ikeda. Cinematography: Hideo Mohara. Cast: Sumiko Kurishima (*Young Miss*), Tokihiko Okada (*Tokio Okamoto*), Tatsuo Saito (*Tatsugi Saita*), Kinuyo Tanaka (*Kinuko*), Ichiro Okuni (*journalist*), Togo Yamamoto (*principal of acting school*). 12 reels, 3,705 meters. Released 12 December 1930. Script exists; no negative or prints known to exist.

In a plot whose screwy vicissitudes defy synopsis, two reporters, Okamoto and Saita, are beaten out of scoops by the infamous girl reporter, 'Young Miss'. They strike up an acquaintance with her and together they investigate a secret club for wealthy men of voyeuristic tastes. Okamoto's article exposes the club. While Sumida, now the paper's film critic, goes off to a screening with his girlfriend, Okamoto is left loitering by a shop window with Young Miss.

'Young Miss,' one ad proclaimed, 'brings you the nonsense of modern life.'[16] Shochiku gave this New Year's release big production values, an unusually long running time, three of its major scriptwriters, and four of its biggest stars. The secret aristocratic club recalls the more odd *ero-guro-nansensu* publications that poured from the presses, while the plethora of silly gags in the script suggests an episodic, self-consciously 'modern' work. *Kinema Jumpo* reviewed it along with a Daisuke Ito film, claiming that the two represent the best of the current industry's output. The reviewer predicted that it would be loved by both city and country audiences, and claimed that it could successfully be shown in a theatre specializing in Western films.[17] This was a big hit and won Ozu his first *Kinema Jumpo* prize, a tie for second place in the contemporary-life division.

Young Miss (production still)

1931

Shukujo to hige
The Lady and the Beard

Shochiku Kamata studio. Story and script: Komatsu Kitamura. Gags: 'James Maki'. Cinematography and editing: Hideo Mohara, Minoru Kuribayashi. Cinematography assistant: Yuharu Atsuta. Lighting: Tashimitsu Nakajima. Set design: Yoneichi Wakita. Props: Kojiro Kawasaki, Takeshi Hoshino. Cast: Tokihiko Okada (*Kiichi Okajima*), Hiroko Kawasaki (*Hiroko*), Choko Iida (*her mother*), Satoko Date (*Satoko*), Ichiro Tsukida (*Teruo Yukimoto*), Toshiko Iizuka (*Ikuko, his sister*), Mitsuko Yoshikawa (*Mrs Tsukida*), Takeshi Sakamoto (*butler*). 8 reels, 2,051 meters. Surviving prints: 75 min. Released 7 February 1931. Script, negative, and prints in existence.

The bearded and conservative Okajima is invited by his friend Teruo Yukimoto to his sister's birthday party. On the way, he rescues Hiroko from a robbery at the hands of the tough girl Satoko. At the party, Okajima scandalizes and bores Ikuko's friends, and she vows to avoid him. When Okajima cannot find a job, Hiroko suggests that he shave off his beard. He does, and lands a job working in a hotel travel agency. Now Ikuko shows some interest in him, and she spurns a rich suitor. Meanwhile, Satoko tries to use Okajima as a confederate in stealing a brooch, but he traps her and takes her to his room. As she falls in love with him, she agrees to reform. In the morning, Ikuko and her family find the two together and are scandalized. Hiroko, however, retains her faith in Okajima. As she and he watch, Satoko departs for her new life.

A chronological review of Ozu's earliest available works casts doubt on the notion of a steady progress toward the 'Ozu film'. Of the fifteen films released in 1929–31, the surviving six display not a systematic evolution but rather a diffuse exploration of various regions of material, structure, and style. Like *I Flunked, But . . .*, *The Lady and the Beard* is a brief, unpretentious comedy shot in a few days. It shares traits with the other surviving films, but it lacks some features that Ozu had arrived at in those works. We should not be surprised that Ozu tried something, dropped it briefly, and tried something else before returning to the first option. It was probably a sound strategy for a director making so many films so quickly.

Of course *The Lady and the Beard* is recognizably an Ozu film from the start. The geometrical tracking shots into the kendo match, the mixture of 'correct' and across-the-line reverse cuts, the graphic matches on the players, and the gags based on identical movements would suffice to identify his style. The scene depends on a brief theme-and-variation structure, presenting one opponent who lacks teeth and a second who has too many. The references to American cinema include a poster for *The Rogue Song* (1930) and the Dietrich

213

37.

posture of a girl at Ikuko's party (fig. 37). The gags in the first part flow quite swiftly, and most involve Okajima's beard. In a job interview, he nervously plucks stuffing from a chair, but his interviewer thinks he's yanked it off his face. When Teruo tries to convince Ikuko that beards are respectable, he cites not only magazine pictures but paper money. Ozu also uses the beard motif for a bold transition. Okajima points to Lincoln, and there is a shot of a Lincoln portrait on his wall. Fade out. A title intervenes: 'Lincoln, 1931'. Fade in on an automobile hood: a Lincoln. There are Lloyd-like gags of embarrassment, as when Okajima visits Hiroko and her mother and must tug down his long underwear to create false *tabi*. There is also the characteristic Ozu mixture of vulgarity and deflation when Okajima comes out of the toilet before his interview, turns away, and elaborately refastens his fly. Moments later, in the office, he turns away and again wrestles with his midriff. After we have jumped to the properly improper conclusion, Ozu cuts to reveal that he is simply checking his lucky amulet. Finally, there are screwy *nansensu* gags like this exchange between Ikuko and a suitor:

'I won't marry a man who doesn't know kendo.'
'Why?'
'So he can protect me.'
'The police can protect you. They have the law.'
'Then I'll marry the police, or the law.'

The plot displays a somewhat looser construction than other early Ozu comedies. The drama is initially based on counterposing Okajima's conservatism to Ikuko's and Satoko's self-consciously Westernized ways. Ikuko thinks him coarse, and Satoko thinks him dangerous. When Ikuko complains, her brother Teruo responds: 'Then make him a modern man.' Modernizing Okajima becomes the goal of the first part of the film, and it is actually the modest, traditional Hiroko who convinces him that only with a shave and a haircut will he get a job. Once he does, Ikuko sees him as a potential suitor and Satoko sees him as an easy mark. Both are wrong, and it becomes the task of the film's second part to show it, by means of Satoko's curiously inexplicit robbery scheme and an inadequately motivated visit by Ikuko and her family.

As causality ebbs, the plot is taken over by a parallelism that contrasts Ikuko, Satoko, and Hiroko. (To which lady does the title refer?) Ozu frankly crosscuts Okajima's visit to Hiroko (who already has a marriage offer) with a rich man's wooing of Ikuko; both women spurn the suitors and fix their interest on Okajima. Similarly, a simple motif contrasts Hiroko and Satoko. One day Hiroko visits Okajima and suggests he get a shave; both look out the window at a barber pole. At night, he brings Satoko home, and she stares anxiously out at the pole as it blinks in the darkness. Predictably, when day breaks, Satoko departs to leave Hiroko with Okajima; and the couple look off at the barber pole.

The foregoing suggests how the film splits into a lighter part and a sombre one. The first section is dominated by Okajima's beard and the effect it has on Teruo, Ikuko, and her snobbish friends; this is also the section delineating Okajima's search for a job. This is the realm of comedy, and of most of the gags. In part two, the comedy wanes, Ikuko becomes secondary, and Satoko becomes more prominent. Once Okajima announces his love for Hiroko, the tone turns menacing. Satoko sets him up to receive the brooch she's stolen. He returns it to its owner, but meets her disguised in his beard and takes her to his home. She acknowledges her love, and though he spurns her, she stays the night. This puts off Ikuku and her mother, but Hiroko trusts him, and her trust gives Satoko the strength to reform. As in *Days of Youth*, *Walk Cheerfully*, and *I Flunked, But...*, the plot moves from comedy to some degree of pathos. This movement will be far more intensely exploited in *Tokyo Chorus* and the two surviving films from 1932.

38.

So much for constancies. Does Ozu break new ground in the film? We lack too many intervening films to say much on the matter, but we can note that the camera position is, sporadically, somewhat lower than is common in the earliest efforts. In the Japanese-style locales, the camera's height sometimes resembles that of the 1933 works, and in the Western settings, because characters and setting are more prominent in the foreground, the camera seems notably lower (fig. 38). There is a great deal of staggered staging (see the scene between Hiroko and her mother, p. 97) and out-of-focus background elements to which Ozu will cut, though not yet matching on action. Some cuts are organized as changes by multiples of forty-five degrees. During Ikuku's party, for instance, Okajima wishes her a happy birthday and Ozu cuts ninety degrees around him. Later, as he departs, Ozu cuts forty-five degrees. In the same scene, Ozu toys with a device that would become standard for him after World War II. As Okajima enters, a 180-degree reverse cut employs the champagne glasses in the foreground as a borderline between two halves of the room (figs. 39–40). Later in the scene, coffee cups on the table function to the same end (fig. 41). The fact that Ozu dropped this device for almost two decades and then used it obsessively thereafter should suffice to suggest the inadequacy of a purely progressive account of stylistic change in his work. One can also point out that *The Lady and the Beard* works relatively little on transitions (certainly not as much as *Walk Cheerfully* and *That Night's Wife*) and lacks the oblique opening and the late-entering motif that the other works have.

39.

40.

Perhaps, finally, the film's strongest novelty lies in the subject matter and thematic material it employs. For one thing, it is Ozu's most erotic surviving film. In the second half, Satoko is treated as a temptress, with her stockinged legs filmed in close-ups and foreground compositions. The climactic situation, involving her overnight stay with Okajima, has a sexual audacity we do not find again until *Dragnet Girl*.

The film's political implications are still more striking. To say that it 'contains' a critique of Westernization is to be literal, in that it holds it at bay. Okajima's transmogrification into a matinee idol involves giving up his beard, his kimono, and his kabuki dancing, and apparently his kendo. If one wanted a comic allegory of the price of modernization, it would not be hard to find here. Yet this can also be seen as a liberal's cautionary tale. In his contempt for Satoko's 'ugly Western clothes', his refusal to dance with women, his watered-down *bushido*, Okajima stands as a composite of many Japanese nationalists who, in 1930–31, urged a return to tradition. Since the early

41.

1920s Ikki Kita had called for a right-wing revolution, led by a military clique who would restore the 'national essence'. As the depression strengthened and party democracy waned, more and more young men were prepared to reject the decadence of modern Japan. Now *The Lady and the Beard* deflects this issue, chiefly through the miraculous device of Okajima's finding a job. Okajima's conservatism is treated satirically, and by the end, with his post as a clerk for Cook's Tours and his traditional fiancée, he has adapted himself to contemporary Japan, steering a middle course between chauvinist conservatism and corrupt modern sexuality. But the film resolves problems which the political formation could not. One month after *The Lady and the Beard* was released, it was revealed that Ikki Kita and certain military staff had plotted to overthrow the government and place it in the hands of the army. In September of the same year, Japanese troops started to occupy Manchuria.

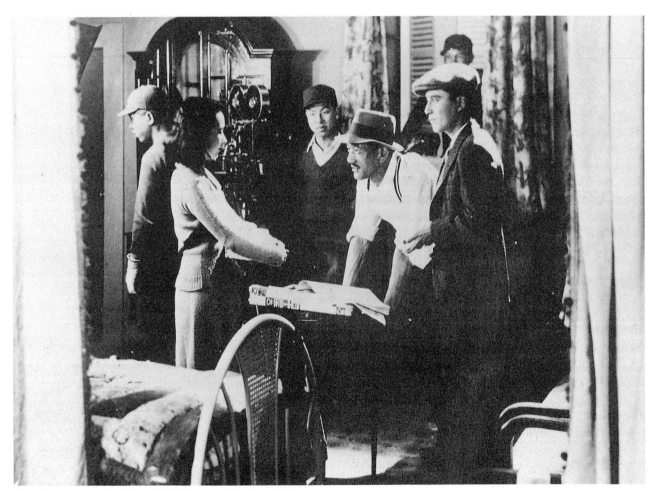

Ozu directs Kinuyo Tanaka and Tokihiko Okada in *Beauty's Sorrows*.

Bijin aishu
Beauty's Sorrows

Shochiku Kamata studio. Story: Henri de Regnier. Adaptation: 'James Maki'. Script: Tadao Ikeda. Cinematography: Hideo Mohara. Cast: Tokihiko Okada (*Okamoto*), Tatsuo Saito (*Sano*), Yukiko Inoue (*Yoshie*), Sotaro Okada (*Yoshida*), Mitsuko Yoshikawa (*Mitsuko*), Teruko Wakamizu (*Haruko*). 15 reels, 4,327 meters. Released 29 May 1931. Script exists; no negative or prints known to exist.

Okamoto and Sano become captivated by the new sculpture by their older friend Yoshida. Sano wheedles it away from Yoshida, but Okamoto marries the model, the artist's daughter Yoshie. The jobless Okamoto lives on money borrowed from Sano, who consoles himself with drink. During Yoshida's visit to Tokyo, Yoshie falls ill and dies. Grief-stricken, Okamoto demands that Sano give him the statue. When Sano refuses, Okamoto smashes the sculpture. The two men hurl themselves into a furious fight. Yoshida finds the two men's bodies, gathers up the fragments of the statue, and returns to the country. He buries the pieces beneath a tree.

Early on, Ozu was testing his skills with different material and various genres. This film, based on a Henri de Regnier story, was an attempt at a straightforward romantic melodrama. In the script, as the wife dies, a close-up shows spilled perfume trickling across a mirror, followed by a title: 'Neither the snow in winter nor the beauty of a woman lasts long.'[18] A Stroheimian detail early in the marriage makes a comparably heavy-handed point: a bar hostess's wedding present to the couple is a phonograph record with the Wedding March on one side and the Funeral March on the other. *Beauty's Sorrows* was harshly received by the critics, who charged Ozu with being infatuated with Yukiko Inoue, a beauty of German-Japanese origin.[19] Although it is hard to imagine an Ozu film of this period being uninteresting, the critical failure of the film probably steered Ozu away from such material for the rest of his career. Perhaps he sensed quite soon that he had failed: he later recalled that after he had finished this very long movie, he told Kido to take a pillow to the preview.[20]

Tokyo no gassho
Tokyo Chorus

Shochiku Kamata studio. Script: Kogo Noda. Cinematography and editing: Hideo Mohara. Cinematography assistants: Yuharu Atsuta *et al*. Sets: Yoneichi Wakita. Props: Mijiro Tanaka, Tamizo Kadota. Lighting: Toshimitsu Nakajima. Cast: Tokihiko Okada (*Shinji Okajima*), Emiko Yagumo (*Sugako*), Hideo Sugawara (*son*), Hideko Takamine (*daughter*), Tatsuo Saito (*Omura*), Choko Iida (*Mrs Omura*), Takeshi Sakamoto (*Yamada*), Reiko Tani (*company president*), Kenichi Miyajima (*his secretary*), Isamu Yamaguchi (*an employee*).

10 reels, 2,487 meters. Surviving prints: 90 min. Released 15 August 1931. Script, negative, and prints in existence.

42.

After a prologue portraying Shinji Okajima as an impudent middle-school student, the film skips several years. Today he and his family await the bonus he will get from his firm. But an elderly colleague has been unjustly fired; Shinji protests and loses his job as well. Soon his daughter falls ill and he must sell his wife's wardrobe to pay bills. By chance he encounters his old teacher Omura, who invites him to help promote his restaurant until he finds something better. Both Shinji and his wife resist the idea that a college graduate should descend to distributing handbills, but they reconcile themselves to it. While Omura hosts a class reunion in the restaurant, Shinji receives notice of a job in the provinces, and his classmates wish the family well with a sentimental school song.

43.

Usually the critic who runs through the film's plot in chronological order is just being lazy. Here it seems to me justified, if only because of the symmetry in the plot's movement from comedy to sobriety, the intricacy of the motivic development, the film's synthesis of earlier genre work, and some niceties of stylistic organization which quite surpass anything in earlier Ozu films.

The film starts with a piece of pure school comedy. Omura tries to line up a batch of unruly students, ticking off in his book every infraction of discipline. Sato has commented on the neatness of gag structure here, with many jokes coming in tripartite form and creating incremental variation.[21] Ozu claims that after *The Lady and the Beard* he stopped constructing continuity in advance, by which he seems to mean that he did not block out every move and gag in detail.[22] Nonetheless, the scene's sixty-four shots and three titles reveal an absolute mastery of découpage à la Lloyd. Although a fine bit of staggered staging permits across-the-line cutting (figs. 42–43), many of the shot-changes are rendered imperceptible. (One-quarter of the cuts are matches on action.)

44.

In addition, the prologue also constitutes a rich matrix of thematic material and narrational strategies. It introduces Shinji's pals and the teacher Omura, and it establishes Shinji as a cheerfully independent fellow. It prepares for the disparity between carefree school days and workaday adult reponsibility, which will become an explicit tension at the film's end. The scene lays out an important gestural motif when Omura tells Shinji to square his shoulders. The scene also initiates major narrational strategies. At the scene's close, Shinji looks up, and Ozu cuts to a low-angle shot of trees. In later works, he would not typically motivate his cutaways as point-of-view shots. Here, however, the point-of-view device forms a crucial aspect of Shinji's characterization and in fact becomes the basis of a later scene.

45.

More daringly, Ozu will now use his cutaways to 'cover' offscreen action, creating an ambiguous duration. Late in the prologue, the students march off, leaving Shinji standing alone. Cut to a long shot of the boys marching off, the rack in the foreground. Cut to a medium-shot of Shinji, now leaning against the rack. Since the portion of the rack in shot three is not included in shot two, we cannot be sure whether Shinji has moved during the early part of shot two, or if the cut is elliptical and the third shot presents Shinji at a later moment. Ozu's playfulness now extends to creating a marked uncertainty about characters' location and durational continuity.

Years later, salaryman Shinji is dressing to go to work. As he ties his tie, he looks out the window at a smokestack and telephone pole. By contrast with the placid outdoors, his surroundings are riotous: his children scamper around him, begging for toys. The bicycle that his son demands becomes an important unifying motif in the early part of the film, establishing Shinji's desire to be a generous father. Gags involving his record collection present a typical Ozuian mockery of paternal authority. The very low camera height is motivated partly by the prominence of his children, but Ozu has developed a new approach to filming domestic space, as is shown when the parents come to the foreground, chopped off at the waist (fig. 44), then leave the shot and children come in (fig. 45), making the shot in effect change scale as we watch. In general, the scenes in the household present the stylistic 'template' that Ozu will employ for the next dozen years or so.

46.

The third sequence, at Shinji's office, is the most famous one in the film and divides neatly into two parts. First the salarymen are lined up to get their bonus envelopes. Here Ozu's Lubitschian comedy is at its most corrosive. The boss remains offscreen, an anonymous benefactor. One by one each man tries to peek into his envelope, then because of prying eyes he retreats to the corridor or to the washroom. Once in the toilet, Shinji strides to the pissoir as a pretext for counting his money. But even here he is not safe; a brilliant gag on framing (fig. 46) presents another clerk's entry and recalls the last shot of the previous sequence (fig. 44). The next employee to take refuge in the toilet is so jittery that he drops his bills into the pissoir. This phase of the scene ends with the hapless clerk fretfully fishing out his soaking bonus while – the final insult – another employee watches through the keyhole. One could not ask for a more savage satire of petty-bourgeois job envy, of the fetishization of money and commodities (the sequence begins with close-ups of white shoes and a fancy sundae), and of the degradation of the white-collar employee.

47.

That degradation is immediately reaffirmed as the plot reaches its first point of crisis. The elderly Yamada has been abruptly fired. The scene moves from Shinji's learning of the dismissal to the gradual involvement of the whole staff, and Ozu sketches this through a series of dominant/overtone shots that pass from the newspaper rack, Yamada, and the staff (fig. 47), to Yamada, with the rack in the background (fig. 48), to the men, with Yamada in the foreground (fig. 49). A braggart challenges Shinji to complain, and he does. His fearlessness in bucking authority, established in the prologue, precipitates a confrontation.

48.

Now the boss is shown onscreen. When Shinji demands justice for Yamada, Ozu employs his acting-in-unison technique to convey escalating conflict, as each man's reaction comically imitates the other's action. The boss's assistant intervenes, but – again Ozu's comedy of class-based embarrassment – he loses the heel of his shoe and Shinji casually tosses it over to him. Shinji is fired and he leaves to join old Yamada in packing up. And here Ozu introduces the first of two transitions that are significantly unlike anything in previous work. As Shinji packs his briefcase, Ozu cuts to an

49.

219

outside wall of an office building or warehouse, and then cuts to a shot of Shinji's son gnawing a watermelon in a vacant lot. We cannot say whether the wall-shot belongs with Shinji's office (the building looks too shabby to house the firm) or functions as a contiguous locale in relation to the field in which his son stands. Unlike the highly structured transitions in *Walk Cheerfully* and *That Night's Wife*, this is fundamentally indeterminate and provides a contrast to earlier, highly motivated point-of-view cutaways. The two shots require two acts of retroactive reflection.

With the plot at a turning point, Ozu creates a drama of divided knowledge. In the fifth scene, instead of returning home with a bicycle, Shinji brings a lowly scooter. His son throws a tantrum. In the next sequence, the boy fusses and Shinji, frustrated, spanks him fiercely, as if working off his rage at being fired. His wife chastises him until he shows her his dismissal notice. Ozu here exploits our superior knowledge, playing our understanding of Shinji's conduct off against his children's ignorance and his wife's misunderstanding. Again, Ozu employs great spatial depth, often with bold use of focus and cuts from out-of-focus to in-focus shots. The scene ends with Shinji offering to buy a bike and his kids making a paper airplane out of his notice.

'Tokyo: Town of Unemployment', declares the film's most didactic title in introducing the next scene. The scene informs us that Yamada has found a lowly job distributing leaflets for Health and Hygiene Week and that Shinji is still jobless – because, he tells Yamada, of his superior education. We will later learn that Shinji is too proud to seek manual work. The scene also develops two parallels. First and most obvious is that between Shinji and the unemployed men sitting on the curb, who look up at smokestacks just as he had earlier. At greater length Ozu dwells on one of his favorite early themes – the parallels between children and salarymen. *The Life of an Office Worker* had ended with the hero, now employed, sitting on a child's merry-go-round. Here Yamada and Shinji sit idly in a zoo and playground and watch a spoiled child (a parallel to Shinji's son) scream and toss her shoes away. 'I envy children who express their feelings,' says Yamada. In popular salaryman culture generally, the worker is depicted as oppressed and repressed; Ozu exploits nostalgia to introduce the contrast between the child's forthright selfishness and the man's meek compromise, a disparity that will emerge again in *I Was Born, But . . . .*

After this idyll, complications pile up swiftly. Segments seven through ten are devoted to the sudden illness of Miyoko, Shinji's daughter (an illness caused, as so often in Ozu, by overindulgence in sweets). Shiro Kido's 'Kamata flavor' emerges full strength from a hospital scene that contrasts the parents' anxiety with mild gags involving the son, and a scene in which Shinji's wife discovers that her kimono wardrobe has been sold to pay the hospital. The latter ends with her joining in a family clapping game, holding back tears, missing a beat, but then resolutely smiling. Certain touches, however, would have occurred to no other Kamata director. The hospital scene is introduced by another ambivalent shot, a close-up of a flower against power lines. The shot could link to Shinji's neighborhood or to that of the hospital. In the hospital, Ozu employs another ambiguously elliptical cutaway, in which a shot of a fan covers Shinji's offscreen change of position. Even the clapping game, with its many symmetrical across-the-line cuts, becomes a variant of the acting-in-unison introduced in the prologue's marching drill.

Scenes eleven and twelve initiate a countermovement toward solving Shinji's financial problems, but they also present a new psychic obstacle. Encountering his old drillmaster Omura, Shinji is offered a job, but he hesitates. 'Though I'm hard up, I'm still rather fussy.' Omura takes him along to his restaurant, the 'Calorie', where he gives him curry rice and tells him they need customers. Shinji brightly suggests inviting his college chums in to publicize the place. Omura agrees but insists that Shinji must pass out handbills as well. Shinji glumly accepts, but plainly his pride has taken a blow. The parallel to Yamada, washed up just before retirement and passing out handbills, is too strong. Here Ozu presents the intellectual proletarian's moment of truth: If hard times drive your teacher to run a greasy spoon, why are you too proud to blister your hands?

Whereas we were shown Shinji's dismissal so that we could measure his family's reaction, now his new job is initially rendered through the eyes of his children. They look out of a streetcar and glimpse him trudging the streets with Omura, carrying banners and distributing handbills. His wife denies it: 'Your father will never do that.' This 'plants' the factor that will precipitate the climax that evening. Ozu then alternates vignettes of the mother and children at home with an episode of the two men's canvassing. The latter echoes the prologue in that Omura sets the pace and orders Shinji to carry two banners. ('If you had trained properly as a student, it would be easy.') Staggered staging and across-the-line cutting clinch the parallel (figs. 50–51; compare figs. 42–43). And now, as passers-by toss away the handbills and Omura rushes to scoop them up for re-use, we understand why scene six had introduced Yamada by tracking across a sidewalk strewn with handbills.

50.

That evening – we have reached the fifteenth and crucial scene – Shinji returns home. The immediate parallel is scene five, when he brought the scooter and the bad news, but now as he wearily undresses, the parallel reaches back to the second scene, when he dressed in the morning. He pounds his shoulder, chafed from bearing the banner. His undressing is punctuated by Sugako's gradual revelation that she knows of his new job. Suddenly, reflexively, he touches his shoulder, and the gesture recalls not only his work of the day but also the first scene, when Omura made him straighten up. Now Sugako tells him of her shame. He drops his fan (an echo of the boss's fan in scene three) and turns away. He gingerly peels off his suspenders. 'I don't want you to degrade yourself,' she says. He responds that Omura was his teacher and will help him find better work. 'Can you trust him?' she demands. 'At bottom,' he says, 'you trust people.' This is, finally, all one has – one's family, one's *batsu*, the circle of kin and school friends that can see one through adversity.

51.

Shinji turns and looks outside, and Ozu repeats the point-of-view shot of the smokestack from scene 2. But he introduces a variant as well. Shinji shifts his glance, and Ozu cuts to a shot of children's clothes on the washline. Shinji looks; again the clothesline shot. The image, admirably unspecific (whose clothes? whose children?), crystallizes many elements – his son's demands, Shinji's family obligations, his mundane suburban surroundings, the parallel

221

52.

of salaryman and child. He smiles. 'These days I'm losing all my youthful enthusiasm.' Now Sugako looks out, sees the clothes, and is chastened. 'I'm going to work for your teacher tomorrow.' As so often in Ozu, the characters' epiphany remains somewhat mysterious, but it plainly marks the typical moment of cheerful resignation to whatever life brings. As Sugako gathers up his clothes, he smilingly shows her the callouses on his hands, the traces of his fall from mental to manual labor. And he stands up, yielding a cut-off framing (fig. 52) that echoes that at the close of scene two (fig. 44).

If this film is, as Sato claims, a 'cheerful tragedy', the last scene not only supplies a happy ending but casts the whole plot in a new, more sombre light.[23] The middle-school class reunites in Omura's restaurant. The parallel with the prologue is strengthened by the tardy arrival of the fellow who came late to drill in scene 1. Omura makes a speech advising them to show school spirit and to be self-reliant; then, alarmed at the amount of food doled out, adds that he will have to charge them. Here the film might end. But a telegram arrives. Omura has arranged for Shinji to teach English in a girl's school, but it will mean moving to rural Honshu. In the kitchen, Shinji and Sugako agree, regretfully, to do it. 'We can come back to Tokyo someday,' Sugako says. Shinji returns to the dining room to join his classmates, who congratulate him. As this Tokyo chorus sings, Ozu's superbly timed cutting of reverse-angle close-ups gives a final insight into the prologue by dwelling on the sadness of teacher and pupil. The shots of the melancholy Shinji and the quietly tearful Omura, coupled with the song ('Will we ever talk again about our school-days?'), intensify the motif of male nostalgia in Ozu's work, the romantic longing for student life encapsulated in the later title, *Where Now Are the Dreams of Youth?*. Perhaps too the scene hints that in their new enterprise Omura and Shinji have achieved something of the master-pupil relation that the early scene mocked. The film's title also makes the song the celebration of Tokyo itself, not only a city of unemployment but also a city of small, interlocked groups that can take in the individual and absorb some of the shocks of everyday life in the new Japan. To leave Tokyo is to face the world naked. The film closes on the long shot of men singing (with women and children tidily set off to one side): 'After this, when will we see them again?'

In mixing the college comedy, the salaryman film, and the domestic drama, and in using each to modify and nuance the others, *Tokyo Chorus* represents a new peak in Ozu's work. It ranked third in *Kinema Jumpo*'s poll of the best films of 1931. From this point on, Ozu is a major director.

1932

Haru wa gofujin kara
Spring Comes from the Ladies

Shochiku Kamata studio. Story: 'James Maki'. Script: Tadao Ikeda, Takao Yanai. Cinematography: Hideo Mohara. Cast: Jiro Shirota (*Yoshida*), Tatsuo Saito (*Kato*), Setsuko Inoue (*Miyoko*), Hiroko Izumi (*Masako*), Takeshi Sakamoto (*Sakaguchi*), Reiko Tani (*company president*). 7 reels, 2,021 meters. Released 29 January 1932. Script exists; no negative or prints known to exist.

In avoiding the tailor Sakaguchi, who demands payment for bills, the student Kato leaves his girlfriend Masako at the café where she works. When Sakaguchi catches up with him, Kato says he'll pay his bills if the tailor will take his place in the exam. Sakaguchi fails utterly. Kato, after a brief spell of gloom, cheers up at the prospect of spending another year in the student coffeeshop with Masako. Meanwhile, Kato's friend Yoshida, who also owes the tailor, meets the tailor's sister Miyoko. Hoping to get the newly graduated Yoshida to pay his bill, Sakaguchi helps him get a job, but still Yoshida escapes responsibility. Yoshida's boss arranges his marriage to Miyoko while the frustrated Sakaguchi frantically starts giving out bills willy-nilly to passing students. 'Spring comes from the ladies, but debts must be postponed.'

Like many early Ozu films, this seems a recombination of familiar modules and motifs: the tailor pursuing deadbeat students (*Dreams of Youth*), the cramming and exam scenes (*Days of Youth, I Flunked, But . . .*), and the search for work (*I Graduated, But . . . , The Lady and the Beard, Tokyo Chorus*). In tone as well, the film seems to have been a lighter effort than *Beauty's Sorrows* or *Tokyo Chorus*, reaching back to the casual comedy of *The Lady and the Beard*. Indeed, the original title was to have been 'The Gentleman and the Skirt'. But the most staggering evidence of Ozu's self-conscious citation of prior work comes during a scene in which Kato consoles the tailor for failing the exam. Failing is not so bad, he assures him: 'Have you seen Urada's movie *I Flunked, But . . . ?*'

Umarete wa mita keredo
I Was Born, But . . .

Shochiku Kamata studio. Story: 'James Maki'. Script: Akira Fushimi. Cinematography and editing: Hideo Mohara. Cinematography assistants: Yuharu Atsuta, Masao Irie. Sets: Takejiro Kadota, Yoshiro Kimura. Set furnishings: Shintaro Mimura, Tsunetaro Inoue. Lighting: Toshimitsu Nakajima. Cast: Tatsuo Saito (*Yoshii*), Mitsuko Yoshikawa (*his wife*), Hideo Sugawara (*elder son*), Tokkan Kozo (*younger son*), Takeshi Sakamoto (*Iwasaki*), Teruyo Hayami (*Mrs Iwasaki*), Seiichi Kato (*Taro*). 9 reels, 2,507 meters. Surviving prints: 90 min. Released 3 June 1932. Script, negative, and prints in existence.

The Yoshii family moves to a Tokyo suburb, putting the father near his boss Iwasaki. The two Yoshii sons have an initial skirmish with the local bully and Iwasaki's son Taro. Fearing the bully, the boys skip school and forge an assignment. The teacher tells their father and he orders them to school. Once in school, the brothers vanquish the bully with the aid of a *sake*-shop delivery boy. After the boys have taken over the gang, they insist that their father is the best. At a screening of Iwasaki's amateur movies, however, they see their father playing the fool. At home, disillusioned, they insult him. A clumsy tussle makes them decide on a hunger strike. Next morning, the brothers and their father reach a reconciliation. In an epilogue on the way to school and work, they urge Yoshii to greet the boss and they tell Taro that he has the best father.

Subtitled 'A Picture-Book for Adults', this is a *film à thèse*, an unusually explicit demonstration of a lesson. Most Ozu films of whatever period have an elusiveness of connotation that *I Was Born, But . . .* almost wholly lacks. By means of its organizational unity and stylistic control, the film achieves great didactic rigor.

The film is built around the social use of power. As the boys rise in the neighborhood gang, their father reveals more of his subordination at work. In the world of the boys, power comes from age, brains, and brawn. If the big bully beats up the brothers, they must coax the still bigger delivery boy into punishing him. In one scene, after a tiny gang member picks up a dropped bun, another boy, only slightly bigger, wrests it from him. Ozu often lines the boys up by height, diagramming their pecking order. The sons, both tyrants, know that power need not be exercised fairly, but they cannot grasp that not everyone has an equal chance to acquire it in the first place. To the boys' belief that ability comes from mythical sources (raw pigeon eggs), the film juxtaposes the fact that in the world of the grownups power is implacably social, derived from money and position. Iwasaki is neither strong nor smart; he is just the boss. The brothers' illusion is that all power can be won through straightforward abilities, as they are able to take over the gang by outfighting the others. The *sake*-shop boy has already given them one lesson: he beats up the bully for them because their parents buy beer, but he won't beat up Taro because his father buys *sake*. In the climactic scene, when Yoshii is asked why he must bow to his boss, he explains that they depend upon Iwasaki. Ryoichi replies: 'I'm stronger than Taro and I get better grades.' After their fight, and during their reconciliation the next morning, the younger brother clings to the old premise: he will grow up to be only a lieutenant general because the older brother is to be general. Yet the hunger strike ends, as if the boys' recognition of the need for survival has reconciled them to the need to obey. 'If he didn't pay me,' the father had said, 'then you couldn't go to school – you couldn't eat.' The film preserves the protest against the established order while dramatizing the necessity of submission.

The script, Sato tells us, began as a social comedy, and a satiric tone is preserved in the various rituals of power that are compared.[24] From the start, with his mud-trapped truck tire and futile, drooping posture, Yoshii is presented as a loser. His first act upon arrival at the new home is to call on the boss. The motif of submission is made explicit by two subordinates: 'That's the way to get ahead.' Yoshii bows to the boss and his friends, as he will later humbly enter the boss's office. When he sees Taro sprawled on the ground in the boys' game, he rushes to lift him up and brush him off. The Yoshii boys, however, resist the gang through cunning and strength. Eventually they take over the ceremony of 'killing' any gang member who disobeys. (The process utilizes the evil eye and a mock graveyard ceremony.) This hilarious rite parodies both Christianity and the adults' arbitrary exercise of power. Thus *I Was Born But . . .* does for the behavioral gestures of social exchange what *Ohayo* will do for language. What shocks the Yoshii boys is learning how deeply their father will submit. In Iwasaki's home movies, they see him clowning for the boss's benefit, and the social satire turns bitter. Ozu represents both the pain and the pleasure of submission. In his onscreen performance and in his reaction during projection, Yoshii is at once discomfited by his lack of dignity and mildly proud of his comic skills. For the boys, there is only shame at seeing to what lengths the rituals of power will go. Ozu's comedy of embarrassment – the film's credit title shows a boy guarding his genitals (fig. 53) – ends in the revelation of abasement.

To the worlds of school, playground, and office, Ozu counterposes that of the home. Sato notes that in the film social compromise is inevitable, but 'the important thing for Ozu is that these unfortunate conditions do present an opportunity for lonely, separated members of a family to reunite. Ozu affirms that only in the solidarity of the family unit can one find the necessary resolve to silently bear the burden of these conditions.'[25] The family is also the site of the recognition that paternal authority, so prized in Meiji ideology, is a sham. Halfway through the film, the issue of power has become entwined with that of the greatness of one's father. With the revelation of Yoshii's shame, the film shows that paternal dignity also answers to the cash nexus. The reconciliation of father and sons over rice balls signifies a return to honest relationships, free of illusion and social artifice. (Another simple meal will have a comparable effect in *The Flavor of Green Tea over Rice*.)

Once the familial healing has started, external social relations can be readjusted. The epilogue, which consists of boys and fathers marching off to school and work together, presents a veritable orgy of images of resignation. Yoshii's boys encourage him to greet the boss, Ryoichi admits that Taro's father is the best, the boys salute the teacher, and the bully rushes ahead to make sure that the teacher sees him doff his cap. True, even in these excessive

53.

moments of submission, the film reasserts the Yoshii boys' authority: they 'kill' Taro and leave him in the road, and Ryoichi solves the ring-puzzle that baffles the bully. Now, however, these have become only games, played in a moment of life when rituals of power exact no cost.

The didactic unity of the film is supported by its narrative organization. The cause-effect linkage is quite episodic – the main thread is the boys' adjustment to their new neighborhood – and the five-day plot pattern encourages a condensed accumulation of events characteristic of a short story. Crisscrossing these structural principles are parallel events: two visits to the boss's house, two trips to school (one aborted, one completed), two pauses at the railroad crossing, two eatings of pigeon eggs, two scenes in the schoolroom, two trips in the boss's car, two breakfasts, three encounters with the delivery boy, three fights among the boys. After the curtain-raiser establishes the family's arrival, virtually every scene forms a parallel to another. The scenario anticipates *Inn in Tokyo* in being constructed around routines that can be replayed, reordered, and varied so as to create a dense web of similarities and contrasts.

It is of course the narration that brings such parallels to our attention, often through such obvious devices as the lateral camera movements that link school and office, likening drilling boys to bored salarymen. More subtle is the way that Ozu's narration plays off the grownups' view against the boys' range of knowledge. The bulk of the film is restricted to the boys, following them in their encounters with the gang, local vendors, and their parents. When they plan to skip school a second day, they – and we – are surprised to see Yoshii sternly watching to make sure they go in. Ozu nonetheless embeds the boys' experiences within a larger view that includes the adult world. At the start, Yoshii's visit to the boss is presented as an obligatory courtesy. The later crosscutting of school and office is not merely a thematic analogy: it introduces the father at work and reinforces his subservience to the boss. But once Yoshii is inside the boss's office and Iwasaki picks up his camera, Ozu cuts outside to the door ('Private') and then tracks back to the employees speculating on how Yoshii is currying favor. (This echoes the parallel scene early in the film when subordinates comment on Yoshii's visit to the boss's home.) Later, however, the narration will reveal that the cutaway was timed so as to conceal from us Yoshii's capers for Iwasaki's movie. By suppressing this event, the narration makes us share his sons' surprise.

After the fight between father and sons, the narration shifts openly to the adults' frame of reference. As the boys sleep, the father fetches out his whiskey bottle and muses on his failure. For the first time, we see the parents alone and discussing their lives. Yoshii moves from self-assured pragmatism ('They'll have to live with it all their lives') to self-justifying shame ('I'm not trying to please the director because I like to – Oh, it's silly'). He and his wife look in on the brothers and ask, 'Will they lead the same kind of sorry lives we have?' After so severe a restriction to the boys' ken, this gradual unfolding of Yoshii's attitudes and doubts puts the home-movie scene in a more encompassing perspective. Yoshii grovels because he can do nothing else. He retains a slender hope in *risshin shusse*: 'Just so they don't become an employee like me.'

The next morning, the narration's frame of reference remains with the

54.

55.

56.

57.

parents. The scene opens with them at breakfast and reveals the boys obstinately sitting in the yard. Much of the film has been structured through the boys' optical point of view but now, for the first time, they are caught in a crossfire of parental glances: Yoshii looks at them from one window, his wife from another (figs. 54–57). (Note, however, Ozu's characteristically uncomfortable point-of-view structure: the low camera height is inconsistent with the posture of the lookers.) Each parent goes out to cajole the boys into eating, and each echoes their dialogue of the night before. The wife urges them to be greater than their father, and Yoshii asks what they want to grow up to be. The reconciliation that now takes place marks not only a narrative resolution but a narrational one, the coincidence of children's and parents' perspectives on the action.

This scene also demonstrates Ozu's absolute stylistic assurance. He has used his acting-in-unison technique throughout, most notably in a brilliant fight scene (p. 84, fig. 32), possibly based on an idea in Naruse's *Koshiben ganbare* (*Little Man, Do Your Best*, 1931). The mimicry of gestures is usually motivated as the younger brother's imitation of Ryoichi. In the breakfast reconciliation, the two brothers' munching of the rice balls is taken up by the father, so we have a visual climax as well as a dramatic one (fig. 58).

58.

Compared to the seven preceding films we have available, *I Was Born, But . . .* is somewhat reticent in style. Its transitions have little of the intricacy of those in *Walk Cheerfully*, *That Night's Wife*, or *Tokyo Chorus*. (The most interesting intermediate spaces are analyzed on p. 136.) But the film does show a definite commitment to depth compositions, especially in 'opaque' establishing shots (e.g. fig. 59, a shot of the removal van arriving at the Yoshii household). The 360-degree cutting is now virtuosic, with one outrageous cut during Iwasaki's screening displaying how physically wrong but perceptually right Ozu's editing can be. In the first shot, Chishu Ryu is threading the projector (fig. 60). In the second shot, a 180-degree reverse, the boss and his wife are in the center, and the floor lamp is where it should be, but Ryu has now vanished, shifted completely out of the way (fig. 61). (I suspect that the graphic continuity involving the angle of Ryu's reach, coupled with the extreme shift in direction, lets the cut pass unnoticed.)

Most remarkable is Ozu's adoption of a consistently lower height than he had used previously. This is not, as some critics have suggested, due to an attempt to represent a 'child's point of view.'[26] Figures 7 and 8 (p. 77) show

59.

60.   61.

that the camera is stationed lower than the children. In *I Was Born, But . . .* we get the first of many 'picket-fence' perspectives upon objects and human agents, both indoors and out. By cutting off the ground on which people stand and relying on considerable depth, the low-height framing makes objects and figures hover in various zones of foreground and background.

The opening, for instance, is unlike anything we have seen in Ozu before.

1. (*ms*) A truck wheel spins in the mud (fig. 62).
2. (*mls*) The driver looks down, and Yoshii comes around to the front of the van (fig. 63).
3. (*ms*) Yoshii looks (fig. 64).
4. (*ms*) As 1. The tire spins (fig. 65).
5. (*ms*) As 3. Yoshii looks up (fig. 66).
6. (*mls*) The two boys look down (fig. 67).

In its piecemeal découpage, the scene exemplifies the one-shot-per-point method of American comedy à la Lloyd or Lubitsch. The situation is gradually revealed, the characters are introduced singly, and the father is emphasized by closer views and repeated shots. But Ozu's camera does something here too. The low camera position fills all but two shots with sharp diagonals, and these (thanks to Ozu's constant crossing of the axis of action) lend not only greater depth to the space but also greater graphic play to the compositions. Each shot is a neat, almost fussy composition, locking each character into a separate space. The truck is chopped in half just ahead of the spot where the boys stand (shot 2/shot 6), and nearly all elements – father, driver, boys, and truckbed – float free of the earth. Only the wheel is grounded. Ozu's compositional rigor, certainly present as early as *Days of Youth*, has achieved a new, self-conscious pictorialism.

I Was Born, But . . . is dominated by its didactic point, but certain things escape thematic control. There are many gags, especially in the father-comparison contest, that owe a lot to the *nansensu*. After the quarrel, the younger brother sneaks into the kitchen to get a cleaver, a hair-raising subterfuge that becomes a gag. The Clair-like comparison of school and office is qualified by a self-conscious aside that mocks the obviousness of the device (see p. 66). A symptomatic interpretation would dwell on the film's characterization of social class. The bully and other gang members come from

62.

63.

64.

65.

66.

67.

proletarian families, and the fearsomeness of their fathers (one yanks his false teeth out) contrasts bluntly with the rich Iwasaki and the ineffectual Yoshii. Not until *Passing Fancy* will the waning of paternal authority be depicted in a working-class household.

Finally, there is Iwasaki's remarkable home movie. Itself full of good gags, the movie constitutes Ozu's first surviving 'excerpted' citation of cinema. Iwasaki's 'Sunday Snapshots' and his second, untitled, opus offer the Ozuphile several points of entry. There are so many random shots of streets and boats in Iwasaki's footage that one speculates that these do duty for all the intermediate spaces that do not appear in *I Was Born But . . .* itself. (Significantly, these shots make Iwasaki's audience yawn.) There is also the classic home-movie joke whereby the filmmaker is shown in his own movie, filmed by some unknown hand. Yoshii's clowning may also constitute a mockery of the *nansensu* slapstick of Ozu's mentor Okubo. And the camera position in reel two's footage is worth a moment's notice. Too low to represent the vantage point of an adult, too high to match that of *I Was Born, But . . .* generally, it recalls nothing so much as the camera height in Ozu's preceding films. In later works he will compare his style with those of Lubitsch and Willy Foerst, but here, in 1932, he compares his new stylistic device with one he has discarded.

Seishun no yume imaizuko
Where Now Are the Dreams of Youth?

Shochiku Kamata studio. Story and script: Kogo Noda. Cinematography and editing: Hideo Mohara. Cinematography assistants: Yuharu Atsuta *et al.* Lighting: Toshimitsu Nakajima. Cast: Ureo Egawa (*Tetsuo Horino*), Kinuyo Tanaka (*Oshige*), Tatsuo Saito (*Taichiro Saiki*), Haruo Takeda (*Kenzo Horino*), Ryotaro Mizushima (*Kanzo, the uncle*), Chishu Ryu (*Shimazaki*), Takeshi Sakamoto (*college janitor*), Choko Iida (*Saiki's mother*), Ayako Katsuragi (*Mrs Yamamura*), Satoko Date (*Miss Yamamura*). 9 reels, 2,523 meters. Surviving prints: 86 min. Released 13 October 1932. Script, negative, and prints in existence.

The rich Horino enjoys student life with his three friends and the soda-fountain girl Oshige. With the aid of his reprobate father, he skilfully turns aside prospective brides. In the midst of cheating on final exams, Horino learns that his father is dying. Horino inherits the firm. His pals come to him for work and he helps them pass the company entrance exam. Horino now meets Oshige again and hopes to marry her. Saiki, the least talented of Horino's school chums, is engaged to her but steps aside in order to keep his job. When Horino learns of the couple's engagement, he berates Saiki for his cowardice and thrashes him. The friends are reconciled and Horino and his pals see Saiki and Oshige off on their honeymoon.

It is easy to see any Ozu film of the 1930s as looking both forward and back, but *Where Now Are the Dreams of Youth?* seems especially pivotal, summing up much of Ozu's earlier work while looking forward to what was to come. It is his last student comedy and his last salaryman film for a long time. Stylistically, it echoes many devices and functions canonized in previous work, but it also presses into new regions. Moreover, the film contains startling, even shocking disparities. There is some hilarious comedy, but also considerable cruelty. There is pathos but also pain: with this film, a violence going far beyond the spankings in *Tokyo Chorus* and *I Was Born, But* . . . enters Ozu's world. The emotional intensity of certain parts looks ahead to the melodrama of *Until the Day We Meet Again*, *Woman of Tokyo*, and *Story of Floating Weeds*. The treatment of class relations is now less satiric, more perplexing and ambivalent. To call the film a 'contradictory text' might go too far, but many of these disparities crystallize around the film's structure and style and its treatment of the two central male characters.

The title credits present the film's structure schematically. A cartoon showing a bakery-café alongside an office building diagrams the film's two parts: student days and then, a year later, the salaryman's life. Other generic factors crisscross both halves. The student comedy is mixed with home-drama episodes of Horino and his father, and the first part culminates in a sombre death scene. Similarly, the salaryman section moves from comedy to romantic drama to a very grim confrontation.

At first, the film seems to have started up where *I Flunked, But* . . . left off, with its pep rally and gang of cheerleaders. It is fully a student comedy, with a fusillade of American posters (*Hell's Angels, Billy the Kid, The Miracle Woman, Million Dollar Legs*). The café scene is reminiscent of that in *Days of Youth* (though it benefits from Kamata's new, slicker sets). Gags in the early classroom scenes, in which the school porter tries to sneak out, recall the end of *I Flunked But . . .* , while the cheating scene uses a sling and cast to work a variant on the shirt-as-crib-sheet in the earlier film.

The film also exploits some social comedy in its characterization of Miss Yamamura, the smoking, hard-drinking, thrill-crazed *moga*. But a new complexity of tone enters these early scenes. While his pals are cheerleading, the diligent Saiki tells Oshige that he has no time to play because he is poor. (No references are made to the class background of Yamamoto in *Days of Youth* or the bespectacled boy in *I Flunked, But . . .*.) Later, when Horino goes home and starts drinking with his father, he confronts Miss Yamamura, whom his uncle has brought as a marriage prospect. In a lengthy scene, Horino feigns drunkenness, spins her around, throws her lighter away, taps cigarette ash into her purse, and calls her bracelet a fake. All this seems less comic than brutal, a quality underlined by the incessant guffaws of Horino's father. (Ozu's comic passages are usually played absolutely straight, with no underlining of their humor, though a character might laugh at the very end.) Ozu comes close to presenting his students not as charming sinners nor as living in Seventh Heaven, but as spoiled sadists. Another deflation occurs near the end of the first half, when the exam-cheating gags are interrupted by a messenger announcing that Horino's father is dying. Such severe wrenches in tone are new to Ozu's work.

Stylistically, the first half also consolidates prior expectations. The opening, analyzed on p. 120, is a stunning piece of contiguity cutting, with striking dominant/overtone work and virtuoso matches on action. In many sequences, staggered staging with across-the-line cutting is in full force. The classroom cheating scenes are handled through a diagonal deployment of students that echoes *I Flunked, But . . .*. As in many previous films, hands and objects create transitions. After the father lights Horino's cigarette with a match, Ozu cuts to Mrs Yamamura taking her lighter out of a bag. Apart from Takeshi Sakamoto's scratchy portrayal of the porter and a purse gag (both of which anticipate *Passing Fancy*) and some false optical point-of-view work as Horino drives home, the innovations in the first part come principally at the climax, the father's death. The earliest deathbed scene in Ozu's surviving work, this sequence obeys the precepts of Kidoism while also displaying that patterned use of hypersituated objects, planes of depth, 360-degree space, and minute variations of framing which was to become uniquely his.

The scene delays an establishing shot for eleven shots and one title, starting instead with a medium-shot of an electric fan (glimpsed earlier in the Miss Yamamura scene). People are vaguely visible off left (fig. 68). As a nurse crosses the shot, Ozu cuts in and around 180 degrees to reveal the housekeeper (fig. 69). Two shots present the father lying ill and, with another 180-degree cut, the uncle bending over him (fig. 70). The nurse is in the background and will continue to serve as a continuity factor. Cut back to the housekeeper, in a slight variant of fig. 69. Another 180-degree cut presents her hands and the father's blanket in the background (fig. 71). Woman, uncle,

68.

'69

70.

71.

moving nurse, blanket – all these overlapping spatial cues suggest but do not stipulate the spatial arrangement. In a new setup, the housekeeper turns and looks up (fig. 72). Horino comes into an adjacent room, which is identified as contiguous by the fan of shot 1 (fig. 73). In a minute variant of fig. 72, the housekeeper rises. 'Master Tetsuo . . .' In a variant of fig. 73, Horino comes back out and strides right (fig. 74). Still another variant of fig. 72 reveals more of the father's body as the housekeeper looks up (fig. 75). Horino stares (fig. 76) and drops his books. In a match-on-action, the books fall and he starts forward in the scene's first establishing shot (fig. 77). This framing clarifies the position of all the elements in the dominant/overtone play so far. After this, there will be no comprehensive establishing shot, only more cueing of contiguity through body parts.

The next shot, number 15, creates a 180-degree shift and shows Horino joining the uncle, in a variant that puts the nurse and the housekeeper in the background. This framing will itself be varied no fewer than five times! In a dialogue title, the uncle explains the stroke. In the next shot, a variant of 15, the nurse in the background rises. After another dialogue title, another variant of the last framing includes the housekeeper. Horino asks: 'You were all right this morning. So why this?' The framings steadily bring the father's face more and more into the composition, as the next shot illustrates (fig. 78; cf. fig. 70). In a staggered 180-degree cut, the doctors pronounce him dead. Another variant (fig. 79) as Horino, weeping, clasps his father's hand. In shot 24, the housekeeper weeps and bends over (fig. 80). A new long-shot presents the nurses kneeling in the foreground (fig. 81); but this is no establishing shot, since the fan is now excluded. A 180-degree cut takes us to a new framing on Horino and the uncle, with the nurses now out of focus in the background (fig. 82). The scene ends with a variant of shot 24, of the weeping housekeeper (fig. 83). In a scene of twenty-three images and four titles, there is not a single repeated framing – instead, a core of setups that are subtly permuted. We shall see this tactic again in *A Mother Should Be Loved*. Space is constructed obliquely, through minute overlaps and recurrences and through an interplay of foreground and background, objects and depth.

When *Where Now Are the Dreams of Youth?* opens, the camera shifts from the cheerleaders to Saiki, wandering in a studious fog. During his talk with Oshige we might expect that he will be the protagonist (especially if we have seen *Days of Youth*, *I Flunked But . . .* , and *I Was Born, But . . .*). Instead, the narration moves us to Horino, whom we follow home. Ozu's typically oblique opening is put to organic use by signalling Saiki's later significance. Horino becomes the central character, the hinge between the student comedy/home drama of the first part and the salaryman comedy/romantic drama of the second. His characterization encapsulates many of the film's heterogeneities. As a student, he is prankish; as his father's son he is coarse. He refuses to grow up. After his father's death, he declines to give a long-winded speech to the firm's staff and he introduces himself casually. 'A year later,' the title informs us, 'the president still has a studentlike air about him.' He embodies a conflict between temperament and role; in a reinforcement of the lesson of *I Was Born, But . . .*, he will learn that when you hold power you cannot retain the equality of friendship.

72.

73.

74.

75.

76.

77.

78.

79.

80.

81.

82.

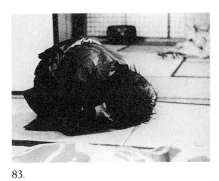

83.

In the film's second part, Ozu injects some stylistic features that would be exploited in later works. He uses dialogue titles in ways that look forward to the boldness of the 1933 films: he will cut from the end of one scene to a dialogue title before showing the new scene's speaker, or he will insert a title between shots that do not show the speaker at all. He starts to make foreground objects into anchors for 90-degree and 180-degree cuts, as when Saiki's bouquet of flowers links Horino and Oshige deep in the scene in her apartment. More and more, adjacent objects are simply presented as cutaways, without motivation by character glance. In the scene at Saiki's home, beer bottles and fruit are used as borderline objects to depict contiguous space, a function that is recalled at the scene's close when the three school friends leave in an out-of-focus background (p. 111, figs. 12–14). Finally, motifs have acquired the sort of flexible 'typing' that they will later have. The fan near the father's deathbed is recalled by the overhead fan in the bar, which stops when Saiki agrees to let Horino pursue Oshige, and by the paper fan which Saiki fretfully picks apart in his home. Of course, most stylistic and narrative features persist. The company exam scene parallels the school cheating scene, while the close-ups of hands that introduce the uncle's new marriage prospect echo the introduction of Miss Yamamura in the first part. As usual, Ozu seizes opportunities to cut from an out-of-focus object to the same object in sharp focus, preferably linked by a match on action. And by now the camera has definitely assumed the position it will have for many years.

The film's second part interweaves two lines of action, employment and romance, into a complicated skein. The three schoolmates call on Horino to get a job, and immediately Saiki, the man of least prospects, flatters him. 'You have the dignity of a president.' Ozu's staging and cutting tactfully keep Saiki offscreen during this speech, emphasizing Horino's response: 'Don't be a bootlicker.' Thanks to Horino's patronage, and his help in cheating on the company exam, the old friends win places. Horino then encounters Oshige, now on hard times. After he helps her move, he becomes oblivious to the romantic implications of Saiki's visit, simply teasing him about loafing on the job. Horino's thoughtlessness is underscored when in the bar he asks his three pals if anyone objects to his pursuing Oshige. Kumada and Shimazaki glance at Saiki, who slumps over and grins crookedly: 'No objection.' Horino is doubly ignorant. He does not know that Oshige and Saiki are engaged; but more seriously, he does not realize that his friends, now his employees, cannot speak their minds. Here Ozu balances both psychological and social commentary: the youth who takes his privileges for granted, and the way that class relations distort human feeling.

The film's climax is thus double. Horino discovers that Oshige is betrothed to Saiki. She thought Horino was lost to her, and she decided to brighten the poor employee's life. Horino is not angry, and he leaves her with the injunction to love Saiki forever. But when he encounters his three friends on the road, his wrath falls upon Saiki. In one of the most savage scenes in all of Ozu, he berates Saiki for ignoring friendship, for not being frank, for giving up Oshige. He begins to beat him. 'I'm hitting you out of friendship!' Ozu's style registers the violence of Horino's action and the ineffectual numbness of the friends in shots that are, for once, at steep and stark low angles (fig. 84).

84.

Psychologically, the scene constitutes Horino's discovery that he has lost both his woman and his friends. 'You've treated me like the boss!' On the social level, Horino punishes Saiki for being too servile, making this the culmination of his 'Don't be a bootlicker' line.

The scene is fascinating in its tensions. Ozu criticizes the petty bourgeois for his servility, echoing the satire on obsequiousness in *I Was Born, But . . .* and the valorization of Shinji's rebellion in *Tokyo Chorus*; but he puts the criticism in the mouth of the boss himself. The social dilemma is evidenced by the validity of Saiki's defense – 'My mom and I live off you. Bucking you would ruin my life' – and the friends' reluctance to intervene. In a sense, the film presents the obverse of *Tokyo Chorus*, which demonstrated the value of the school *batsu*. Here, using the *batsu* to get you work may destroy whatever friendship lay at its base. The immemorial *giri-ninjo* duality is here revised, in the light of hard economic fact, into a choice between financial dependency and fidelity to individual desires.

The dilemma is not so much resolved as canceled through narrational intervention. Early in the film Saiki as a student had looked off, and a cut to a clock tower had represented his optical point of view. Now, however, Ozu cuts repeatedly from Horino or the friends to shots of trees around them, quivering in the wind. The insistence of these cutaways – four tree shots interrupt the action – does not make them any more comprehensible. Once Horino's rage has passed, he and Saiki shake hands, but the tree shots have deflected us from a concrete resolution of the problem. Horino is still the boss, Saiki the timorous employee; Horino can give up Oshige, but has either man changed? A final (offscreen) embrace among all four suggests how tried the male bond has been and how fragile it is. Here Ozu uses his cutaways not to elide time but to transcend social disparities by means of a reference to nature. All that remains is a happy ending of Horino and his chums on the office rooftop, waving to the train that bears Saiki and Oshige to their honeymoon. Seldom before in Ozu's work has the woman's role been so evidently that of an object of exchange that maintains masculine identity. Oshige, who seems to prefer Horino, is surrendered to Saiki in order to preserve the *batsu*. No wonder, perhaps, that Ozu's next three films will emphasize woman's attempt to break out of this position.

Mata au hi made
Until the Day We Meet Again

Shochiku Kamata studio. Script: Kogo Noda. Cinematography: Hideo Mohara. Cast: Yoshiko Okada (*woman*), Joji Oka (*man*), Shinyo Nara (*father*), Hiroko Kawasaki (*sister*), Choko Iida (*maid*), Satoko Date (*girlfriend*), Mitsuko Yoshikawa (*another girl*). 10 reels, 2,127 meters. Released 24 November 1932. Script exists; no negative or prints in existence.

A young man has been disowned by his prosperous family because he loves a prostitute. Drafted, the son prepares to go off to war without telling his father, but the girl informs the family. They hurry to the train station as his train is pulling out. That night finds the prostitute back on the streets.

The loss of this film is particularly regrettable. Contemporary critics commented upon Ozu's explicit treatment of the 'Manchurian Incident' of 1931, when Japanese troops used a railway explosion as a pretext to push into China. Sato reports that some critics saw the film as supporting a militarist ideology because the son seeks to leave for war without reconciling with his father. It is more filial, the son argues, to go off to war without having been forgiven, since if he dies, his father's grief will be less.[27] Another critic suggested that the sombre treatment of Japan in wartime and the penultimate scene in which the prostitute sits motionless on a bench give the film an anti-military cast.[28] Perhaps, like many Japanese films of the period, *Until the Day We Meet Again* was constitutively ambiguous, made to be interpretable from different political standpoints.

The film would also be of interest as the first of three works in which Ozu centers on 'fallen women', but unlike the protagonists of *Woman of Tokyo* and *Dragnet Girl*, the heroine of the film does not seek to lead a double life. In addition, the film would doubtless contribute to a stronger sense of Ozu's visual style. The opening scene, a lengthy presentation of the prostitute's nightly rounds, prompted one critic to praise Ozu's use of parts of a street lamp in different shots, with prostitutes visible out of focus in the backgrounds.[29] This testifies to at least some Japanese viewers' awareness of Ozu's stylistic manipulations, and it suggests that such critical responses may have encouraged Ozu to repeat and refine certain stylistic devices.

1933

Tokyo no onna
Woman of Tokyo

Shochiku Kamata studio. Story: Ernest Schwartz, 'Twenty-Six Hours'. Script: Kogo Noda, Tadao Ikeda. Cinematography: Hideo Mohara. Editing: Kazuo Ishikawa. Cinematography assistants: Yuharu Atsuta et al. Lighting: Toshimitsu Nakajima. Cast: Yoshiko Okada (*Chikako*), Ureo Egawa (*Ryoichi*), Kinuyo Tanaka (*Harue*), Shinyo Nara (*Kinoshita*), Chishu Ryu (*reporter*). 4 reels, 1,275 meters. Surviving prints: 47 min. Released 9 February 1933. Script, negative, and prints in existence.

The student Ryoichi believes that his sister moonlights from her office job to work as a translator. His girlfriend Harue learns from her brother, Officer Kinoshita, that the police suspect Chikako of illicit prostitution. Harue tells Ryoichi, and he is devastated. When Chikako returns that night, he slaps her furiously, ignoring her defense that she is sacrificing herself for his education. He dashes out into the night. Next morning, Chikako calls on Harue; neither has seen Ryoichi. Harue is summoned to a phone and told by Kinoshita that Ryoichi has killed himself. The two women weep over his body. Newspaper reporters who have investigated cynically dismiss the story.

With its *shimpa* overtones and its echoes of Mizoguchi's *Taki no Shiraito* (1934), this film invites a political analysis. The sadism of the humiliated Ozu male has seldom been so explicitly criticized by a woman as when, after Ryoichi has slapped her, Chikako asks: 'Do you feel good if you slap me? . . . Have all my hardships turned into you slapping me?' Bending over his body, she reproaches him. 'You innocent boy, to die for such a small thing! . . . You cowardly boy!' Apparently Chikako is investigated because an unlicensed prostitute would have avoided the government tax of 7–10 per cent on her earnings. In the original script, Chikako's prostitution served not simply to support Ryoichi but also to contribute to the Communist Party.[30] In October 1932, during a campaign to wipe out the Party, the government initiated a mass arrest, and in early 1933 the police arrested key Party leaders. A more intensive study of the script might reveal important political displacements and ellipses in the resulting film. Here, however, I want simply to use the film as a test case of Noël Burch's arguments about Ozu's work, since *Woman of Tokyo* is the film which Burch discusses most thoroughly and which furnishes the main evidence for his conclusions.[31]

Burch's remarks about *Woman of Tokyo* rest almost entirely upon four specimen passages from the film. His case is weakened, however, by a significant number of omissions and inaccuracies.

The first scene portrays Ryoichi dressing after breakfast while Chikako tidies up. Burch neglects to mention that the sock tree hanging outside is

85.

visible some shots before Ozu cuts away to it. He insists that in the rear of the second shot Ryoichi is 'perfectly motionless', but he is moving. More significantly, Burch's account entirely omits the scene's third shot, which shows Ryoichi dressing in the foreground and Chikako (and the sock tree) in the background (fig. 85). This is an important establishing shot and provides a dominant/overtone link by contiguity from the second shot. Contrary to Burch, there is no delay of Chikako's entry into shot 17 (Burch's no. 16), and her action is perfectly comprehensible because the previous shot of the sock tree showed the window being slid open. In describing the following shot as 'trees silhouetted against sky with rooftops', Burch overlooks the most important motif, the smokestacks and wind that will recur later.

Burch's description of the scene's ending is no less misleading. He has reversed two phases of the scene (1b and 1c), mistimed Chikako's actions (she sits at the mirror no more than six seconds, not nine; after she leaves the shot, the mirror is empty less than three seconds, not as much as five), and he has misdescribed her as being immobile (she is continually in motion).[32]

Later, in the sequence showing Chikako waiting for Harue to return, Burch again misses crucial cues. In the shot of the hanging kimono, it is the water in the tub that provides the contiguity link: its reflection (like that of the compact in *Walk Cheerfully*, p. 201) falls on the clock. This supplies a categorical-inclusion transition to the clocks in the shop. Apart from minor errors in describing action and screen direction, Burch also ignores the lapse in time that the sequence traces, from 8.17 to 8.29 on the shop clocks to 8.32 on Harue's clock. (See p. 131.)

Finally, Burch says that in the film's epilogue, the reporters go out of the shot before the cut, and they do not. Perhaps he made this error because, once again, he has omitted a shot from his description.

Now my corrections would be pedantic fussiness if Burch did not use these inaccuracies as crucial evidence for claims about Ozu's style. If Ozu is to be treated as a filmmaker of startling 'nondiegetic' intrusions, then shots which clearly establish zones of space and cuts which link contiguous areas would be recalcitrant data. If Ozu's 'pillow shots' are necessarily static 'still lifes', then one will be disposed to overlook the fact that they often contain a movement – smoke, feet, gestures. And if Ozu's work exemplifies Zen, as Burch claims the last sequence does, then one can use this gaseous generalization to avoid analyzing what, earlier in the film, structurally motivates the conclusion.

This is to say that Burch's descriptive errors issue from an inadequate conception of Ozu's style. As far as *Woman of Tokyo* is concerned, he characterizes that style by two features: 'incorrect' eyeline matches and 'pillow shots'. Since I have discussed both issues in previous pages, my comments here can be brief. Burch's characterization of eyeline-matching is wholly negative and localized. Relying on a simplified version of suture theory – itself a simplistic theory[33] – Burch asserts that these cuts create a momentary confusion in the spectator's comprehension of the space. Empirically this does not happen, and theoretically there is no reason why it should. If there are two people facing one another and Ozu carefully supplies establishing shots, we will understand across-the-line shot/reverse shots by virtue of understanding the spatial givens of the situation. Moreover, Ozu uses so many across-the-line cuts that they form part of the film's intrinsic norm, come to be expected, and are in no way surprising. Burch does not consider the larger, positive functions which the *donden* cutting accomplishes – construction of a 360-degree space, geometricization of space into 45-degree chunks, creation of graphic matches. Nor does he recognize that Ozu's découpage helps make 'incorrect' eyeline matches (and 'incorrect' screen direction, which Burch does not discuss) legible through a macrostructure derived from classical Hollywood style: the use of establishing and reestablishing shots, eyeline matches, shot/reverse shots, and especially matches on action. (Forty per cent of the image/image cuts in the first scene are matches on action.) And Burch simply ignores the fact that in many cases, as in earlier films, Ozu's cutting is perfectly 'correct'.

As for 'pillow shots', I have criticized the term earlier (see p. 104), chiefly on the grounds of its narrow notion of 'diegetic information'. In his account of *Woman of Tokyo*, Burch gets entangled in claiming that the first shot of the sock tree is an 'impure' pillow shot, because Chikako is looking at it; but the second shot is 'diegetically superfluous and thus partly expelled from the diegesis'.[34] I offer no argument on the first point except to point out that a poetics of narration will recognize the cut to the first shot as more self-conscious than the optical point-of-view structure that retroactively 'claims' the shot. On the second point, Burch never explains how something can be partly in the fiction and partly not. Furthermore, if every shot that is diegetically 'superfluous' becomes partly expelled from the diegetic world, a great many interpolated musical numbers and comic bits in Hollywood B-movies will become prime instances of alternative signifying practice. In any case, the second shot is not superfluous, since by showing the window sliding open, it implies that Chikako goes out onto the balcony. Again I would argue that Ozu's revision of classical découpage devices (cutaways, point-of-view shots) lays over their traditional functions an oblique or 'decentered' function within a continuously overt narration.

Burch's failure to contextualize the devices he picks out could be avoided by assuming a broader theory of filmic construction and comprehension. Within this one can see how *Woman of Tokyo*, like all of Ozu's films, revises classical dramaturgy by virtue of making particular stylistic patterns prominent. And if one analyzes the whole film, not just sequences pulled out of context, one can see that the narration manipulates knowledge, creates parallels, and foregrounds stylistic permutations even within the confined compass of forty-seven minutes. For our purposes, *Woman of Tokyo* is a privileged example because it is 1933 Ozu in miniature.

The syuzhet as a whole covers two days. On the first, Chikako is investigated, Harue learns of it from her brother and tells Ryoichi, and Ryoichi confronts Chikako and leaves, angry. On the second day, Chikako calls on Harue, Harue learns that Ryoichi has killed himself, and reporters come to pester the two women. Upon this simple scheme is superimposed an unusual amount of mystery for an Ozu film. Segments 2–6 build up uncertainty about Chikako. We are not told why she is being investigated, nor – once Kinoshita informs Harue of the police's suspicions – whether she is in fact a prostitute. She is observed wholly by others. Only after Harue tells Ryoichi does the narration confirm her account by cutting to a dance hall and showing Chikako washing up with other women. After a brief passage depicting Ryoichi's anxiety, Ozu shows Chikako phoning him before getting into a car with a customer. The plot reaches its first climax in scene 8 when Ryoichi confronts her and leaves. Sequence 9, showing Ryoichi wandering the streets, constitutes a pivot into the second enigma, posed the next morning. What has become of Ryoichi? The question is answered by the phone call, and the second climax comes with the two women's vigil over Ryoichi's body. The epilogue of the callous reporters follows. In the use of a narrational ploy characteristic of melodrama – using conversation to transmit information about offscreen action and letting characters react accordingly – the film looks forward to the suppressive and ellipitical narration of Ozu's postwar works, though they will typically not revolve around such scandalous secrets.

If this strategy of concealment were all there were to *Woman of Tokyo*, we would hardly consider it very important. As usual, the power of the film lies in Ozu's use of narration to establish and vary expectations, to cite adjacent traditions, and to create parallels. Employing only four sets, two of them quite sketchy, Ozu presents a fragmentary space, introduced through details and adjacent objects. While *I Was Born, But . . .* and *Where Now Are the Days of Youth?* had sporadically used shots of foreground objects and out-of-focus human figures in the distance, such images come into their own in *Woman of Tokyo*, creating uncertain gulfs of space between foreground and background. At the end of scene 4, for instance, there comes a shot of a brazier, with Harue in the background; the next shot, starting the fifth scene, shows the sewing machine in the foreground and Ryoichi out of focus in the rear.

The film also marks an advance in that detail shots do not serve only as transitions. Across the whole film we come to expect them to participate in Ozu's construction of space, and they form an intrinsic norm – which he can then undermine. The narration will insert a detail shot and then reveal that it has in fact 'covered' an offscreen action. We have already seen a mild example when Chikako goes out to the balcony, conveyed in a shot of the sock tree and the sliding door. Any cutaway or dialogue title may serve the same purpose, as when a shot of Chikako typing and an 'offscreen' title ('Is there something wrong?') yield to a shot of the manager and the policeman, who have – *during* the last two shots – left the office area. Ozu's suppressive narration is especially overt in the scene after Ryoichi's death, which begins on details of the room, takes us to Chikako at the door with the reporters, and, only after a reporter peeps in, reveals that Harue is present.

The best example of such undermining occurs when Harue gets the phone call from her brother. As Chikako waits, her glance follows a light beam from a tub of water to the ceiling clock. Cut to the clocks on display in a shop. Harue gets the news and starts to put the receiver back. Cut to the clocks. Here, in the name of symmetry, we expect this shot to end the scene. But it is only an interruption. Cut back to Harue, hanging up. Cut back to the clocks. Another interruption, before we see Harue again? Or a fully-fledged transition? We have no way of knowing, so our expectations must be suspended. The next shot returns us to Harue's room, supplying a variant of the earlier clock shot, with the light beam still present. Symmetry would dictate that we cut back to Chikako, looking up, but again Ozu thwarts us: we get a shot of her hands and knees beside the brazier and teapot. Only then do we return to Chikako, who is now looking *down*. Like the wind scenes in *Days of Youth*, the transition to the milk bottles in *That Night's Wife*, and the use of the compact mirror in *Walk Cheerfully*, this clock scene erects expectations based wholly on stylistic patterning and then asks us to notice how the narration equivocates about fulfilling them.

Ozu also cites the norm he dislodges, but for the first time in a surviving work, he uses not movie posters and photographs but actual footage – here, from *If I Had a Million* (1932). The material is principally from the Lubitsch episode, though some credits are included. The sequence can be linked thematically to what precedes it (Chikako's office is echoed by Laughton's office) and what follows (Laughton goes in to confront authority; cut to Kinoshita's police gloves and sword). The rags-to-riches theme of the film ironically echoes Chikako's sacrifice in sending her brother to school. There is also some humor in the shift from Chikako typing in English to an English credit list, as if this were her text. In any event, a dialogue hook prepares for the next scene when Harue says that she will tell her brother about the film. Stylistically, Ozu takes liberties with *If I Had a Million* by skipping fifty minutes from the credits to the Laughton scene. The ellipsis is outrageously 'covered' by a four-second shot of Harue and Ryoichi watching. But Ozu respects the internal duration of the Lubitsch sequence: the shots of Harue and Ryoichi talking almost exactly correspond to the duration of the offscreen action in the Laughton clip. Here also Ozu masters his master, subordinating Lubitsch's long-take shots to a more detailed découpage. But the two styles are reequalized when, as Laughton passes through door after door on his way to see the President, Lubitsch supplies a series of graphic matches on various doors. Ozu's playfulness reemerges when he refuses to show Laughton's delivery of a raspberry to his boss. We must be cinephiles enough to fill in the gag's payoff.

The narration also foregrounds stylistic patterning by means of parallels. The comparison of the two households, each consisting of a brother and sister, is strengthened by motifs and by patterns of staging and cutting. For instance, the Chikako/Ryoichi household is associated with socks. He asks for his socks in the first scene; later, when he stalks through the city, the camera will concentrate on his feet. The Harue/Kinoshita household, however, is linked to gloves. The home is twice introduced through a close-up of Kinoshita's gloves, and in the scene of the policeman's visit to the office, gloves are made a synecdoche for the police. The opposition becomes very explicit when Chikako's sock tree is paralleled by the glove tree hanging outside Harue's door. In effect, Ozu has here used two of his favorite motifs, which stretch back to *Days of Youth* and will return in *Passing Fancy*, in a tightly organized way.

But this is not all. The first scene, which shows Ryoichi dressing and putting on socks after breakfast, is paralleled twice in Kinoshita's flat. At night, Kinoshita is shown *undressing* and putting on clean socks. The next morning, in a scene which initiates the second enigma of the film, Kinoshita is shown dressing. In the course of the scene, Kinoshita takes his purse (cf.

241

Ryoichi taking his allowance from Chikako), and Harue goes to her dresser (as Chikako had gone to her mirror.) And Ozu's découpage works to permute his handling of the film's first scene.

Scene 1	Scene 2
1. (*mcu*) Track back from stove to rice cooker.	
2. (*ms*) Table with strewn dishes and Ryoichi's leg in background.	1. (*ms*) Table with dishes and teakettle, Kinoshita's leg in background.
3. (*mls*) Ryoichi dresses and looks back; Chikako out of focus in background.	3. (*mls*) Kinoshita dresses in foreground, Harue in background.
4. (*pa*) Chikako.	5. (*pa*) Harue.
5. (*pa*) Ryoichi dresses and talks to her.	2. (*pa*) Kinoshita dresses and looks at Harue.
6. Dialogue title.	
7. (*pa*) Chikako.	
8. (*pa*) As 5. Ryoichi sits down.	4. (*ms*) As 2. Kinoshita.
9. (*ls*) Ryoichi in foreground, Chikako in background.	6. (*ls*) Kinoshita in foreground, Harue in background.

The first shot of the later scene, so closely resembling the second shot of the first, raises the expectation of parallels that are varied in the actual working out. The stylistic echoes go beyond the thematic parallels, which have long since been established. Once more we are in the realm of abstract pattern-making. Much the same holds for the brief sequence of Chikako at her mirror after the fight (paralleling the end of the first sequence) and the shots of her waiting for Ryoichi (paralleled to the earlier shots of him waiting for her).

A complete analysis of Burch's specimen sequences should thus reckon in Ozu's interplay of rigorous pattern with unpredictable deviation, as well as his use of motifs and parallels to make concrete actions and objects parts of a larger equation. Only such an approach can explain one of the puzzling portions of the film. In the last major scene, Harue and Chikako are alone with Ryoichi's body. A medium shot of Harue (fig. 86) shows the teakettle out of focus in the background, steaming. Cut 180 degrees to a long shot of the two as Harue slumps down; the teakettle is in the upper foreground, *not* steaming (fig. 87). This disparity has drawn considerable critical attention.[35] Cut 180 degrees to the kettle in medium close-up, steaming again (fig. 88). Then cut outside to a low-angle shot of the trees and smokestacks in the wind (fig. 89). Finally, there is a cut back to Chikako (fig. 90), and the sequence ends. What is going on here?

Most generally, it is a typical case of how Ozu's interplay of dominants and overtones sidle us unpredictably through space. More specifically, in the course of the film, the teakettle has been both a spatial anchor for Ryoichi's apartment and a significant contiguous object. While Ryoichi listens to Harue's tale, his anger rises and the kettle steams over. Cut to the faucet in the

86.

87.

88.

89.

90.

brothel, and Chikako comes to wash her hands. Soon there is a cut back to the teakettle, now cold. I suggest that the later scene's series of three teakettle shots parallels and recapitulates this earlier passage. This possibility is lent credibility by the fact that in the Ryoichi-Harue quarrel, Ozu also, if more subtly, mismatches the teapot. (It is boiling in one long shot, then not boiling in the next shot, then boiling again.) In addition, the scene recalls, yet again, the first sequence. The shot of Harue (fig. 86) reveals the ventilator outside in the background. The shot of the teakettle (fig. 88) presents both the ventilator and the sock tree. The cutaway to the landscape (fig. 89) recalls Chikako's initial point-of-view shot, and in a thick clustering of motifs, the final shot of Chikako (fig. 90) includes in its background Harue, the kettle, the sock tree, and the ventilator. Ozu's foreground/background interactions, his threading of motifs, and his evocation of parallels have created a purely stylistic climax, with his typical images of poetic evanescence – wind and vapor – present throughout.

No need, then, to explain the final shots by appeal to *satori*, as Burch does. Awareness of the context of the overall film shows, as usual, a pervasive system at work. When Ryoichi went out at night, the action was conveyed by tracking down along the empty sidewalk and gradually catching up with him. In a later shot, the camera 'lost sight' of him still more, tracking down a litter of broken pipes and jugs and *not* framing his feet. Now, after the reporters start down the street, the narration cuts into the space that they have vacated: once to enlarge a light pole in the foreground, again to the base of a more distant pole, and finally to a curb, along which the camera starts to track, in the same direction in which the reporters have gone; but this shot will never catch up with its human subjects. After a climax linking objects associated with Ryoichi (teakettle, sock tree), Ozu closes on an evocative but rigorous – that is, evocative *because* rigorous – echo of his absence.

Hijosen no onna
Dragnet Girl

Shochiku Kamata studio. Story: 'James Maki'. Script: Tadao Ikeda. Cinematography: Hideo Mohara. Art director: Yoneichi Wakita. Editing: Kazuo Ishikawa, Minoru Kuribayashi. Cinematography assistants: Yuharu Atsuta *et al.* Lighting: Toshimichi Nakashima. Cast: Kinuyo Tanaka (*Tokiko*), Joji Oka (*Jyoji*), Sumiko Mizukubo (*Kazuko*), Hideo Mitsui (*Hiroshi*), Yumeko Oushi (*Misako*), Yoshio Takayama (*Senko*), Koji Kaga (*Misawa*), Yasuo Nanjo (*Okazaki, the president's son*), Chishu Ryu (*policeman*). 10 reels, 2,730 meters. Surviving prints: 100 min. Released 27 April 1933. Script, negative, and prints in existence.

By day Tokiko works as a typist, but she lives with Jyoji, the leader of a small-time gang. Hiroshi, a student, joins the gang, and Jyoji becomes attracted to Hiroshi's sister Kazuko. Tokiko finds out and sets out to scare Kazuko off, but she takes a liking to her and resolves to reform herself and Jyoji. Jyoji throws her out. Tokiko is approached by her boss, who has been pursuing her, but she decides to return to Jyoji. He agrees to quit crime and get a respectable job. Hiroshi, however, has stolen money from the shop where Kazuko works, and Jyoji must pull one last job in order to cover Hiroshi's theft. Tokiko and Jyoji rob her boss and give the money to Hiroshi, saving him from a life of crime. Fleeing from the police, Tokiko begs Jyoji to surrender; when he refuses, she shoots him. Wounded, he agrees to be arrested and the two are captured, locked in an embrace.

Sadao Yamanaka was so fond of *Dragnet Girl* that he would recite lines from the script on a moment's notice.[36] It is indeed one of Ozu's most appealing films, chiefly because of its use of gangster-film conventions. In the three years since *Walk Cheerfully*, the public's interest in 'hooligans' had not waned. 1933 would see police embark upon roundups of *yotomoto* ruffians. Yoichi Nakagawa's book *Rotaki hana* (*Elegant Flower*) enjoyed huge popularity for treating street hoodlums as good-hearted delinquents. Ozu's film unashamedly lifts specific incidents and lines from *Walk Cheerfully* and reycles its basic story of reforming crook, good girl, and bad girl. (Unlike the earlier film, this one lets the bad girl keep the crook.) Yet *Dragnet Girl* is murkier than its predecessor, less a fantasy of the American underworld. One reason may be that Ozu's own work was turning more sombre. Moreover, Ozu now takes the conventions more seriously. Between 1930 and 1933, *Little Caesar*, *The Public Enemy*, and *Scarface* all appeared in Tokyo, and the genre's canonical forms were more evident than they had been at the time of *Walk Cheerfully*. Moreover, Ozu's recent stylistic explorations could use aspects of the American *policiers* to create virtuosic effects. Sternberg, a vital influence on the Japanese cinema generally, is the reference point, and Yokohama, the most Westernized area of the country, is the site of Ozu's homage to and transformation of the brooding pictorialism of *Underworld* and *Blonde Venus*. He will use both stylized sets and real locales – the Aoiya RCA Victor shop and the famous Cabaret Florida, where Brooklyn blacks played jazz – to create an

American genre picture revised and corrected by the force of style.

That style's uniqueness is, by mid-1933, clearly visible. Ozu is now using synecdoches to establish every locale: typewriters for an office, rings for a gym, saxophones for a nightclub. He employs his acting-in-unison technique systematically, both to make his gangsters look as childish as the boys in *I Was Born, But . . .* and to create a motif whereby the mechanical synchronization of two thugs in the beginning rhymes with the pace of two marching policemen at the close. He is now invariably staging character confrontations in a staggered *sujikai* fashion, even through a glass door. All dialogue scenes use 90-degree and 180-degree cuts, with reestablishing shots either repeating the original establishing shot or placed at 180 degrees to the original framing. The first scene in the Florida Cabaret exemplifies Ozu's dependence upon character eyelines to define offscreen areas at right angles and his use of jutting foreground elements to anchor characters with respect to one another. The matches on action are perfect, usually smoothing over cuts into or out from a portion of space; but in order to accentuate moments of violence, as when Jyoji punches Hiroshi against the alley wall or when he flings Tokiko's suitcase down, Ozu can employ brutally elliptical editing reminiscent of Soviet filmmaking. The long climactic scene in which Jyoji and Tokiko decide to go straight repays close study in all these respects. Here the confrontation of two characters and the successive intrusions of two others are handled in 170 shots and 56 titles, orchestrated into rigorous patterns of 90- and 180-degree space and relying upon our cognitive mapping to sustain long passages of shot/reverse-shot cutting.

91.

92.

In such ways, Ozu's unique style 'processes' his gangster tale. He also uses stylistic conventions of American film as pretexts to push his style to new heights of abstraction. His camera height is a litle lower than in the 1932 films, as if to exaggerate the way that these Americanized characters perch on tables or loll in deck chairs. The stylized dialogue is integrated into his découpage with boldly minimal cues. Sometimes lines come from 'offscreen' sources (listener/title/listener); a dialogue title may open a scene very abruptly, or create a gag, as when Nipper, the RCA Victor dog, seems to be talking on the telephone. (See p. 67.)

93.

The *mise-en-scène* is Ozu's most densely packed since *That Night's Wife*, making the long shots more opaque than usual. Now the settings are crammed with decor, objects, and figures. Ozu exploits this Sternbergian clutter to create abstract shot designs, such as the use of Nipper as a pictorial element in several scenes (p. 67) or the line of ten cocktail glasses at the bottom frameline (fig. 91). Now too Ozu's selective focus and bright backlighting not only pick out the foreground elements but 'layer' more distant planes in precise degrees of clarity. In the Florida Cabaret, Tokiko is in the foreground of a very cluttered shot, and her prominence is measured against the steady dissolution of shape of the figures behind (fig. 92). Ozu often calls attention to this by cutting from a long shot in which a moving figure is a speck in an unfocused background to a closer view of that figure. Figure 93 shows Tokiko's boss sitting down in the lower right background, while the next shot (fig. 94) magnifies him. (See also figs. 99–100, p. 101.) That such cuts don't disorient us suggests that Ozu organizes his composi-

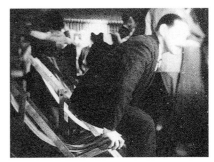

94.

245

tions so that we subliminally register such marginal movement and will accept a shot that centers and identifies it.

The packed settings and gradually diffused planes are enhanced by Ozu's use of two more gangster-movie icons, glass surfaces and geometrical patterns of light. The first scene introduces both: the window blinds cast striated shadows on the office walls and floors, while the boss's son is introduced behind the massive glass doors of his office. No Ozu film shoots through so many shop windows and doorpanes. The Toa Boxing Club is one large fishbowl, with the gym separated from the locker room by plate-glass doors. And of course the RCA Victor listening booth offers many occasions for the decorative use of glass. By the end of the film, however, pulsations of light have become more important. Here the early evening switching on of Tokyo's power prefigures the rhythmic light bursts of the flashing Club Toothpaste sign that illuminates the couple's getaway. Ozu's use of this cliché respects its generic functions of evoking a nocturnal atmosphere, but he also treats it as a purely visual pattern. He twice cuts to the sign itself, making it a contiguous object in its own right, and he tracks in to the window after Jyoji and Tokiko have gone through it, fastening our attention on the rhythmic fading of light on the sill. Moreover, the decision to stage the action under the blinking sign offers Ozu a chance to display his virtuosic timing of cuts, whereby the key phase of action is revealed at the brightest point of the burst. In the context of the rhythmic use of light, the film's last shot – the gradual brightening of daylight on the plant at the apartment window – takes on a consummatory visual significance.

If a single setting could be taken to epitomize Ozu's transformation of received conventions, that might well be Jyoji's apartment. Five of the film's twenty-seven scenes take place there, and most are lengthy and intense confrontations. The setting has its own synecdochic object, the white coffeepot, which is used permutationally. In the first scene in the flat, the camera arcs around the coffeepot before racking focus to the door in the background; in the fourth scene, the camera again arcs around the pot, now festooned with yarn from Jyoji's and Tokiko's fight. In the second scene, a victrola has replaced the coffeepot as the initiating object. In the third, the shadow of the ventilator has. In the final scene in the flat, the camera arcs around what now sits in place of the pot – Jyoji's suitcase, awaiting his getaway. And the apartment furnishes new objects to the very end. The potted plant on which the narration dwells at the end is introduced only in the last scene, as a casual detail.

In all, Ozu's style systematically absorbs and recasts conventions of the American gangster film. We might be inclined to see the result as florid, even mannered, but compared to a vigorous exploitation of Hollywood crime-film conventions like Uchida's *Police* (1933), Ozu's handling can only seem austere. Uchida freights his film with Langian superimpositions, rapidly-paced flashbacks, handheld camera movements, and a series of racing tracking shots of a frantic chase across a bridge. Ozu rejects such flourishes and prefers a narrow range of devices, patiently varied in nuanced ways. And compared to an obviously Sternbergian film like Yasujiro Shimazu's *First Steps Ashore* (1932), with its misty waterfront and chiaroscuro-laden taverns, Ozu's crisp lighting and framing seem plain. As with *Woman of Tokyo*, *Dragnet Girl* appears flamboyant only by the standards of later Ozu. Compared to the ornamental expressivity of his contemporaries, *Dragnet Girl* is sober film-making.

As the film progresses and the viewer becomes more habituated to its intrinsic norms, the stylization becomes less striking. This is perhaps one reason Ozu introduces new aspects of Jyoji's flat and new locales, such as the bar to which Jyoji retreats and the room to which the boss takes Tokiko. Many motifs that start out as predominantly visual become more 'psychologized', more absorbed into the causal movement of the story. The coffeepot, initially an echo of *Walk Cheerfully* and a generic icon used as a synecdochic anchor, becomes an emblem when Tokiko glimpses a similar pot in the window across from the boss's flat and decides to return to Jyoji. The imagery of hats, a descriptive detail in the first scene, gets causally motivated when Hiroshi switches between his student cap and his gangster cap, and when Jyoji, just before deciding to reform, takes off his hat for almost the only time in the film. Yet by introducing elements in isolated cutaway shots, Ozu tinges later appearances with a degree of overtness. The 'manly art of self-defense' sign is not exhausted by the immediate comment it seems to make on the story action, since we have seen it 'on its own' earlier. During Tokiko's and Jyoji's robbery of the office, cutaways to various clocks would fulfill only canonized suspense functions did we not recall how the opening scene established the clocks as independent visual elements and the source of a joke which may still be in force (are the clocks, labeled 'Synchron', indeed synchronized?). The self-consciousness of Ozu's narration, established and reinforced throughout the film, is not completely erased when motifs are motivated in realistic or compositional ways.

The sense of overt narration is reaffirmed at the end, when Ozu introduces fresh, often puzzling information and picks up old points. The flashing sign and the potted plant, as we have seen, furnish new motifs for the style to exploit. After Jyoji and Tokiko are taken away, one policeman finds a knitted baby shoe and hangs it on a railing. Ozu's narration now becomes ambiguous. Is this simply a stray object on the street, or has Tokiko dropped it? If the latter, is she pregnant with Jyoji's child, or has she simply been anticipating the day she and Jyoji will go straight? The narration leaves the gap open. Finally, after the police have signalled to one another and the officer in Jyoji's apartment has left, Ozu dwells on the detritus on the floor, remnants of the couple's fight and flight. As so often in Ozu, and as the permutations in the settings have suggested, we are asked to recall story events and measure their progression by virtue of the changes in objects and surroundings. Our perception and cognition are trained, tested, and stretched. An exercise in style has become an exercise of viewing skills.

Degigokoro
Passing Fancy

Shochiku Kamata studio. Story: 'James Maki'. Script: Tadao Ikeda. Cinematography: Shojiro Sugimoto. Art director: Yoneichi Wakita. Editing: Kazuo Ishikawa. Cinematography assistants: Hiroyuki Nagaoka, Hideo Hoshii. Lighting: Toshimitsu Nakajima. Cast: Takeshi Sakamoto (*Kihachi*), Nobuko Fushimi (*Harue*), Den Ohikata (*Jiro*), Choko Iida (*Otome*), Tokkan Kozo (*Tomio*), Reiko Tani (*barber*), Chishu Ryu (*man on boat*). 10 reels, 2,759 meters. Surviving prints: 103 min. Released 7 September 1933. Script, negative (duplicate), and prints in existence.

The day laborer Kihachi Kimura, with the help of his pal Jiro, is raising his son Tomio. Kihachi becomes infatuated with the young girl Harue, but she is attracted to Jiro, who rebuffs her savagely. Kihachi's longing for Harue leads him into dissipation and a brutal quarrel with his son. Once their differences are patched up, Kihachi resolves to help Harue win Jiro. Through Kihachi's overindulgence, Tomio gets catarrh. He survives, but Kihachi must pay the hospital bill. Harue volunteers to help, but Jiro confesses his love for her and, after getting a temporary loan from the neighborhood barber, sets off to work in Hokkaido. Kihachi refuses to let him depart and, leaving Tomio with the café-keeper Otome, makes off to take the job. En route to Hokkaido, he becomes lonesome for his son and leaps off the boat.

Passing Fancy is the last of Ozu's three masterworks of 1933. It won him his second *Kinema Jumpo* first prize, and it remains one of his most accessible films. As the synopsis indicates, the plotlines are intertwined, one involving the two men and Harue, the other involving Kihachi's relation to Tomio. The second is far more important, with consequences for characterization which I shall consider below. Remarkably little happens overall, certainly far less than in *Dragnet Girl*. Moreover, the plot stutters, starting over twice. In the first and longest phase of the action, Kihachi pines for Harue and falls into slovenly, drunken habits. The climax of this portion comes when Tomio, taunted by his schoolmates, destroys his father's *bonsai* plant and then, in a late-night tussle with Kihachi, calls him a fool. There begins a new portion revolving around Kihachi's giving Tomio fifty sen. This phase consumes a much shorter time span than the first one, including many sudden crises. Tomio gets sick, and within a few days recovers; Jiro confesses his love for Harue and prepares to pay off Tomio's hospital bill. All that would seem needed to round off the action is a brief epilogue showing Kihachi, his son, Otome, Harue, and the barber all seeing Jiro on his way. But, daringly, Ikeda's script starts over. We are back to Kihachi and Tomio, with Kihachi impulsively deciding to take Jiro's place in Hokkaido. On the boat, however, Kihachi changes his mind again and returns to Tokyo.

This loose, additive structure may cite the tradition of *Naniwa-bushi*, the sort of rambling tale told in the first scene in the variety hall. Altogether foreign to that tradition, however, is the intricate web of details and motifs that unify the film's texture. No previous Ozu film depicts a milieu with such

248

exactitude. Cutaways to tall grass, water towers, laundry, fire hydrants (see p. 116) and crowded streets evoke the neighborhood to a degree nowhere seen in *I Was Born, But...* or *Woman of Tokyo*. In *Dragnet Girl*, the RCA Victor shop is exploited to disorienting spatial effect, but in Otome's café, the hanging lamp, poster, keg and tables become reference points that 'realistically' frame the action. As in *Dragnet Girl*'s use of the potted plant, the set can expose new objects up to the very end. Kihachi's domestic god-altar, his *butsudan*, is revealed in a slow diagonal tracking shot at the start of the third phase of the action, reinforcing the sense of a new beginning; the last scene on the ship picks up the motif by tracking back from a *butsudan* to reveal men jammed in the hold, an ironic contrast to Kihachi's real home. The specificity of the season (summer 1933, culminating in the fireworks of the August Sumida River festival) also furnishes motifs: people are constantly wiping off sweat and fanning themselves. These culminate in a final cooling off when Kihachi hurls himself into the river. The last shot shows a breeze stirring trees.

Some Ozu films minimize characterization, but here it is the film's 'dominant', the component that structures and defines others. The two plotlines issue from aspects of Kihachi's personality, his idealistic romanticism and his shallow sense of duty to his son. Kihachi is indeed one of the richest characters in all of Ozu's work. His pursuit of Harue is motivated by his claim that she reminds him of a woman he once loved (perhaps Tomio's mother). Genially slow-witted, he nonetheless acts impetuously. (The film's title would be better translated *Impulse* or *Caprice*.) After telling Tomio that you can't put leaves back on a tree, Kihachi tries to do so. Many of the gags are motivated by cultural assumptions about the rough, happy-go-lucky *shitamachi*, or 'downtown' type which Kihachi incarnates. As Tomio lies sick, Kihachi thoughtlessly takes off his son's cold compress in order to wipe his own brow. He seizes on the chance to go to Hokkaido, even though there is no need to repay the barber immediately, and he gladly leaves Tomio behind, saying he doesn't need much care – this shortly after the boy has nearly killed himself. Early in the film, he overdresses to visit Harue, and his neighbors suggest he looks like he's going to a funeral. Later, as his son lies sick in the hospital, he remarks thoughtfully: 'We may have to have a funeral for him. I'm glad I have formal summer wear.' Kihachi is a blend of American borrowings (Sato points out that the film is a reworking of *The Champ*, *One Night in a Downpour*, and *Kick-In*) and a Japanese character type (Ozu based the character on his father and other men encountered during his boyhood in Fukugawa).[37]

The other elaborate characterization is that of Tomio. Played by the diabolical Tokkan Kozo, the younger brother in *I Was Born, But...*, Tomio is that rare son who is genuinely smarter and more mature than his father. Apart from a welter of concrete behavioral details, Tomio well illustrates the principle that the more mysterious and elliptical a motif, the greater the 'effect of reality' that is produced. What has become of his mother? Why is he wearing an eye patch early in the film, and why does it vanish later on?

Only a little less enigmatic is his riddling, which forms a running gag. Early in the film, he asks Kihachi why a hand has five fingers. The answer: if it had only four, it wouldn't fit in a glove. 'Very funny,' says Kihachi. This motif threads through the film's first two parts (Kihachi's gloves are made prominent) and culminates in the hospital scene. At the beginning of the third part, Tomio poses Kihachi another puzzle. Why is sea water salty? Because salted salmon live there. The new riddle strengthens the sense of the third part as the plot's fresh start, but it soon pays off. In the final scene on the boat to Hokkaido, Kihachi tries to tell the glove riddle to the other laborers, but one beats him to the punchline. And after he jumps into the river, Kihachi repeats the riddle about sea water before remarking, 'Very funny,' and paddling to shore. Sadao Yamanaka was so taken with this gag that he used a variant of it in his *Pot Worth a Million Ryo* (1935), and Alain Bergala has found it a parody of the Zen *koan*.[38] Tomio's riddles confuse causal explanation with functional explanation; as such, they are admirably suited to measure Tomio's cleverness and Kihachi's obtuseness. We shall see, though, that their logic is at least as much narrational as psychological.

The relation between Kihachi and Tomio seems to form the main plotline partly because in the other line of action characterization is much more rudimentary. Harue is the dutiful, innocent girl sold to the spinning factory, a type made familiar by Shimpa drama and *gendai-geki* films. Jiro is more mysterious but no less schematic. Cynical and harsh, he stubbornly resists Harue's friendship until, for virtually no reason, he suddenly reveals his love in a line from a thousand Hollywood films: 'Don't you know how I feel?' *Days of Youth, Fighting Friends — Japanese Style*, and *Young Miss* show that Ozu was influenced by the American roistering buddy-rival films of the late silent era, and Jiro seems derived from such characters. At the level of dramaturgy, then, we are left with a film that confirms both Richie's claim that character depth is central to Ozu's work and Burch's suggestion that 'Ozu's "psychology" is systematically *superficial*.'[39] This can be taken, I think, as a symptom of Ozu's great freedom in combining disparate conventions within an overall architecture.

The extent to which characterization determines macrostructure can be seen in the way that idiosyncratic gestures become motifs. The barber applauds in a stropping motion; he is reintroduced later stropping his razor. Jiro refuses to touch anyone except Tomio, but when he declares his love for Harue he grabs her arm (in a forceful graphic match we have already considered on p. 98). Kihachi and Tomio communicate through pokes and slaps, gestures which culminate in their furious, flailing struggle. A similar parallel is drawn through repeated close-ups of their feet. Close-ups of hands, used in *Days of Youth* as synecdoches for entire scenes, now economically become transitions that link gestures: Tomio rubbing a hole in his coat/ Otome sewing it up; Kihachi shaking out his coat on the street/ Kihachi hanging it up at home. Kihachi is himself an endless source of characterizing gestures, forever spitting, wiping his nose, swabbing his ear, tugging his *hachimaki*, scouring away sweat. At the beginning of the film, in the *yose* hall, he wears his neckerchief folded squarely on the top of his head, and at the end, floating in the river, he sets it neatly there again. He is introduced rapping with his fan on Tomio's hip, a prefiguration of all the swipes that he will take at him later.

The film's most developed, and amusing, gestural motifs involve scratching and stroking. In the *yose* hall, the rampant flea sets Kihachi scratching (see p. 113), and he will not stop for the rest of the film. In Otome's café, he tweaks Harue's chin, scratches his neck, and ambles outside past Otome – who, once he has passed, starts to scratch *her* neck (see p. 116). During the fight, every time Kihachi swats Tomio's head, the boy scratches his face instead of crying out. It is in the same scene that the slapping between father and son ends. After Kihachi tearfully apologizes, Tomio reaches out and strokes his cheek. This gesture of tenderness becomes central to the rest of the film, most specifically the hospital scene, which condenses several motifs. Kihachi slaps a flea off Tomio and scratches the spot. Then, bending over the boy, he grasps Tomio's hand and presses it up to his cheek, asking: 'Why are there five fingers on the human hand?' Just as the sea-water riddle prefigures Kihachi's act of jumping ship, the fingers motif is revealed as foreshadowing this string of gestures. Finally, in the boat to Hokkaido, he recalls Tomio through concrete behavior: he tugs his kerchief and then kneads his cheek on the spot Tomio had touched. Character is made manifest through gestures at once expressive and scrupulously patterned.

Episodic plot, atmospheric details, rich characterization reinforced by a network of physical and verbal associations – all this might lead us to take *Passing Fancy* as a milestone of Ozuian realism. The story is indeed realistically *motivated*, but the narration absorbs it within a game of expectations, foiled and fulfilled. The most obvious large-scale trick is the suppression of Tomio's fate. He lies near death, and the scene shifts to Kihachi's home, where he worries about how to pay the hospital bill. Tomio is nowhere in sight. It is not until well into the scene that we learn that Tomio is still alive. The importance of ellipsis in the film has been announced earlier, when Tomio sketched an alarm clock and the narration overtly marked the duration that its cutaways skipped over. (See p. 124.) At a more local level, there is a play with offscreen dialogue that goes beyond even that of *Dragnet Girl*. With *Passing Fancy*, Ozu's use of titles increases dramatically, now composing over a fourth of all shots in the film. (See Appendix.) These brief and fragmentary titles offer excellent opportunities to mislead us. The film starts by giving us what looks like an expository title but which turns out to be a passage from a chanter's tale. Thereafter, dialogue titles will come from nowhere, presenting speech before we can know the speaker. Titles from the next scene will interrupt this one, and the cutting will often omit the very act of speaking. Ozu plays on every permutation – speaker/ title/ listener, listener/ title/ speaker, listener/ title/ listener, object/ title/ object, and so on. The effect is jarring and often comic, as when a shot of Kihachi petulantly clapping for more *sake* is followed by the title: 'I've got news! This boy's dad is stupid.' An overt, self-conscious, unreliable narration interposes itself between us and the 'realistically' represented diegetic world.

The same sort of mediation is evident through Ozu's spatial strategies. The opening has already been discussed (p. 113) as an outstanding example of Ozu's metonymic space and his Lubitsch/Lloyd gag structure. The scene is typical of the film as a whole. There is considerable depth in staging, but lens focus drops off sharply. As a result, characters in the background are at once flattened (being out of focus) and suggested as lying on different planes (being out of focus to different degrees). An 'opaque' establishing shot in

251

95.

96.

97.

98.

99.

Otome's café affords one instance of this device (p. 93, fig. 56), but a more dramatically charged one occurs in the hospital scene, where Kihachi sits in the foreground in focus, Jiro sits further back somewhat out of focus, and Harue, sitting farthest away, is still more blurry (fig. 95). Ozu's composition and use of focus impose a design upon the action that invites the viewer to strain to see, to imagine what is diffusely or incompletely shown.

Expectation and imagination are also required to grasp the permutational transitions, which here mark a move beyond what we see in *Woman of Tokyo* or *Dragnet Girl. Passing Fancy* is most like Ozu's postwar films in its varying repetition of a set of locale shots. During Tomio's sketching of the clock (p. 124), we stray outside to a street (fig. 59) and wash hanging before water tanks (fig. 60). At the start of two later scenes, we get a new view of grass and tanks, then the wash and the tanks (fig. 96). Then, after Tomio flees his schoolmates, a shot presents the tanks, but he runs into the frame (fig. 97). Against all our expectations, the intermediate space has become part of the drama. We expect the next shot to continue his itinerary, but we get instead – again – the laundry and the tubs, without Tomio (fig. 98). Only then does Ozu give us a shot of Tomio coming home (fig. 99). It is as if the logic of dominants and overtones required that a shot of tanks and a shot of laundry could be linked only by a shot of tanks plus laundry. This is a narration that plays by its own rules, even if it changes them at will.

1934

Haha o kowazuya
A Mother Should Be Loved

Shochiku Kamata studio. Story: Syutaro Komiya, adapted by Kogo Noda. Script: Tadao Ikeda. Cinematography: Isamu Aoki. Cast: Iwata Yukichi (*Mr Kajiwara*), Mitsuko Yoshikawa (*Chieko*), Den Ohikata (*Sadao*), Seiichi Kato (*Sadao as child*), Hideo Mitsui (*Kosaku*), Shusei Nomura (*Kosaku as child*), Okazaki (*Shinyo Nara*), Kyoko Mitsukawa (*Kazuko*), Chishu Ryu (*Hattori*), Yumeko Aizome (*Mitsuko*), Choko Iida (*a maid*). 9 reels, 2,559 meters. Surviving prints: 71 min. Released 11 May 1934. Script in existence; no negative known to exist; surviving prints lack reels 1 and 9.

At breakfast the Kajiwara family plans an outing, but while the two boys are in school, the father collapses and dies at his office. Eight years later, the college student Sadao learns that he is actually the son of his father's first wife. He refuses to be consoled by his stepmother Chieko's assurance that she has kept him ignorant of his origins in order to make him feel a part of the family. Chieko is reluctant to discipline Sadao as severely as she does her natural son Kosaku, which causes Kosaku to feel resentful and Sadao to feel privileged. Sadao takes refuge in a Yokohama brothel with Mitsuko, but he quarrels with her. He returns home and provokes a fight in order to bring Chieko and Kosaku closer together. Chieko reveals the secret of Sadao's parentage to Kosaku, who now feels guilty for having misunderstood his brother. Chieko goes to the brothel and he rebuffs her, but the maid reproaches Sadao for his callousness: 'A mother should be loved.' Sadao returns home and asks his mother's forgiveness. All are reconciled. Three years later the family moves to a small suburban house.

The loss of the first and last reels of *A Mother Should Be Loved* damages it in several ways. For the sake of causal continuity we need to see the Kajiwara family whole, presided over by the kindly father, so as to sense his loss more acutely. We also require a stronger sense of the functions of Sadao's rowing pal Hattori and the fate of the prostitute Mitsuko. It would be good to understand why the plot, uniquely in Ozu's work, inserts a three-year time gap before its epilogue. At the level of motifs, the boys' playing in the family car after the father's death would take on full meaning only if we recognized that they did the same thing before he drove to his office and his death. Similarly, the film is said to have concluded on the mother unpacking in her new house, discovering the father's picture; this would have climaxed the photograph motif that runs through the cental section. Still, even with the additional reels, this would probably not have been one of Ozu's most accomplished works. Despite interesting attempts to give Sadao complex and conflicting impulses, the film becomes somewhat monotonous in its lachrymose scenes. (It thereby anticipates some of the excesses of *Tokyo Twilight*.) As Ozu put it:

> The script should've been polished more. The main plot is the fall of a great house. This could be a good theme today, but at that time it wasn't enough. So I added on the story about the brothers who have different mothers – their relationship becomes a disaster. But because I added this story, the film turned out to be rather dull.[40]

Once again the drama hinges upon the decline of masculine authority: paternal, filial, fraternal. (Biographical critics note: Ozu's father died during the shooting, but *after* the script was written.) As in *Until the Day We Meet Again*, the straying son turns for solace to a prostitute, but here the film seems to come down more squarely for the virtues of family devotion.

For the most part, the film shows Ozu's technique to be constant from the 1933 pictures. Orthodox shot/reverse-shot cutting is outweighed slightly by *donden* cutting and the graphic matching of postures and compositions. Short, isolated camera movements are still present. Landscape views through windows are used to define locales and establish, tacitly, a human-scale space 'behind us'. Dialogue titles will bracket a shot of a listener or of an object, or will open a scene. The use of movie posters for wry comment has become almost a tic: apart from posters for *Don Quixote* (1933), *Poil de carotte* (1932), and *Daughter of the Regiment* (1933), the waterfront brothel also boasts a poster of Joan Crawford in *Rain* (1932). There are, however, some areas of style in which *A Mother Should Be Loved* elaborates Ozu's previous tendencies. We have already seen an example of a misleading, 'detoured' transition in the scene of the truck and the railroad train (p. 135). Another example occurs early in the footage that remains. After the boys have run out of the schoolyard, Ozu gives us this passage:

1. (*mls*) The family's grandfather clock reads 8.15.
2. (*ls*) The clock: 8.15.
3. (*ls*) The upper floor of the house, seen from outside.
4. (*ls*) The dining room: mother and sons sit brooding.

100. *Three Beauties*

As in the scene in which Tomio draws his alarm clock in *Passing Fancy* (p. 124), the shots could be reordered into a much more normal progression – say, 3–2–1–4. Ozu's narration takes us from an interior detail (the clock, presumably on the ground floor, though perhaps reel 1 would have established it more exactly) to the exterior, and then again to the interior (the dining room, probably not on the upper floor we have seen in shot 3). We cannot guess how the pattern will fulfil itself until the fourth shot, which forces a retroactive understanding of the space traversed.

Other scenes display a greater emphasis on permutational composition than is common in the 1933 films. One series of shots plays a set of variants upon three compositional elements. In shot 1, we have a house, with a mountain behind. In shot 2, a mill wheel is in the foreground and the house now stands in the background. Shot 3 puts the mill wheel in the foreground again, with the mountain behind. All three shots are essentially irrelevant to

101. *Street Without End*

102.

103.

104.

105.

106.

the action of the scene, but they create a small-scale lyrical passage that prefigures the rich play of visual dominants and overtones in *Ohayo*.

The parametric handling of another scene is especially interesting because it illustrates how Ozu's construction of interpersonal space differs from that of his contemporaries. Most Japanese filmmakers, I pointed out in Chapter 5, often staged action in considerable depth and filled the frame quite densely. (See the example from *Marching On*, p. 86.) Often these tactics led to a use of selective focus that, contrary to usual Hollywood practice of the period, placed significant dramatic elements out of focus. Different options were thus open to the director. A common solution, taken by Gosho and other directors, was to use rack-focus to control what the viewer concentrated on at various moments. In *L'Amour* (1933), Gosho rack-focuses from a doctor's hands mixing medicine in a close foreground to the patient in the background. Another, though rarer, alternative was to use a very short focal-length lens to articulate foreground planes relatively sharply and to center the various elements in perspectival fashion. (See fig. 100, from Shigeo Miyuta's *San ren ka* (*Three Beauties*, c. 1934). Or the director could control our attention by darkening the background plane and having distant figures turn from us, as Naruse does in *Street Without End* (1934). Naruse is also noteworthy for constantly moving his characters between foreground and background in order to vary the main point of interest. A shot like fig. 101, which puts several figures out of focus in depth, constitutes a fleeting moment in a continuously mobile staging pattern.

The pertinent comparison in Ozu's film is the scene in which the family friend Okazaki visits their home. During the string of medium-shots of Okazaki talking with Sadao, the mother Chieko sits in the background. As the scene goes on, Okazaki explains why the family has deceived the boy, and both son and mother begin to weep. An orthodox Japanese director would have either kept our attention on Okazaki by darkening the background or turning Chieko away from us, or made our attention ricochet between foreground and background by keeping Chieko in focus and more or less centered. Ozu takes none of these options.

In the course of the dialogue, the framing of Okazaki passes through no fewer than five slight variants (figs. 102–106). In each one, different background elements (always out of focus) are visible: the lamp, the hanging kimono, the right *shoji* wall. The one constant element is Chieko herself, out of focus but not quite out of sight – although by the last two variants she is sinking past the lower left corner (figs. 105–106). In *Street Without End*, Naruse skilfully varies each image by making his characters stalk and circle one another. Ozu, relying on a restricted version of the foreground/ background interplay he had exploited in *Where Now Are the Dreams of Youth?*, plants his characters in one spot and uses just-noticeably-different setups to create a nuanced interplay of foreground and background, distinctness and diffusion. Chieko's reaction is still (barely) graspable, but she is dominated by a patterned circulation of frame events that offers not only narrative development but an autonomous perceptual shape.

Ukigusa monogatari
Story of Floating Weeds

Shochiku Kamata studio. Story: 'James Maki'. Script: Tadao Ikeda. Cinematography and editing: Hideo Mohara. Art direction: Toshio Hamada. Cinematography assistants: Yuharu Atsuta, Masao Irie. Lighting: Toshimichi Nakagima. Cast: Takeshi Sakamoto (*Kihachi*), Choko Iida (*Otsune*), Hideo Mitsui (*Shinkichi*), Rieko Yagumo (*Otaka*), Yoshiko Tsubouchi (*Otoki*), Tokkan Kozo (*Tomibo*), Reiko Tani (*his father*). 10 reels, 2,438 meters. Surviving prints: 86 min. Released 23 November 1934. Script, negative, and prints in existence.

The acting troupe of Kihachi Ichikawa comes to town. His mistress and lead actress Otaka discovers that long ago Kihachi fathered a child by the café-keeper Otsune and that he lingers in town in order to be with his son Shinkichi. Shinkichi, however, believes that his father is dead and that Kihachi is his uncle. Otaka bribes the young actress Otoki to seduce Shinkichi. Otoki succeeds, but they fall in love. Kihachi, furious, berates Otoki and beats Otaka. Meanwhile, days of rain and lackluster attendance have driven the troupe into bankruptcy. After Kihachi sells his props and pays off his actors, he returns to Otsune's café. Shinkichi returns with Otoki. In a tense confrontation, he declares that he wants no father. Kihachi leaves, asking Otsune to take care of Otoki. He meets Otaka at the station. They team up again and take the train to start afresh.

The artist, Pierre Macherey points out, never starts from scratch:

> The writer, as the producer of a text, does not manufacture the materials with which he works. . . . They are not neutral transparent components which have the grace to vanish, to disappear into the totality they contribute to, giving it substance and adopting its forms. The causes that determine the existence of the work are not free implements, useful to elaborate any meaning. . . . They have a sort of specific weight, a particular power, which means that even when they are used and blended into a totality they retain a certain autonomy: and may, in some cases, resume their particular life.[41]

This insight is not new. The Russian Formalists tirelessly pointed out that although the material of the art work is shaped by its formal construction, there is in fact a dialectical relation between the two forces. Material is never raw. Themes, subjects, elements of everyday life all have their own social weight, and they can resist, more or less strongly, the process of formal assimilation. The 'dominant', or primary principle of construction, enters into tense relation with other factors. Here is one point at which ideology enters the art work: in its encounter with constructive principles, the material can tone down overt formal devices. *Story of Floating Weeds* offers a good example.

The film's overall shape is familiar from Ozu's previous works. The plot is built out of Kihachi's return to his former wife Otsune and the effects this has on his mistress Otaka, his son Shinkichi, the actress Otoki, and his theatre troupe. Sato has shown that the film is based rather closely on George Fitzmaurice's *The Barker* (1928), which won seventh place in *Kinema Jumpo*'s 1928 ranking of foreign films.[42] Ozu adds a mother to the cast of characters, permitting her a *shimpa*-like revelation of Kihachi's identity. There emerges an emphasis on the father's loneliness that prefigures some of Ozu's postwar work. Parallels not only retard the dénouement but establish thematic comparisons: the three women with similar names, the likening of Kihachi's deception of his son to the uneasy mistrust between the old actor and his son Tomibo. The circular structure of the syuzhet, whereby the troupe arrives on the train and Kihachi and Otaka leave on it, is filled in by the alternation of a few locales. The running gag of Tomibo's lucky cat-bank makes troupe life more concrete (and perhaps provided Ozu's friend Yamanaka with yet another prop for his *Pot Worth a Million Ryo* of the following year). Kihachi himself, played by Takeshi Sakamoto, is an echo of the protagonist of *Passing Fancy*, though he is neither as stupid nor as carefree as his predecessor.

The muting of Kihachi's character derives, like other subdued factors, from the surrounding material which Ozu has included. The film is played in a remote rural village, a realistic locale for the traveling troupe but an unusual setting for Ozu at this point in his career. The cinéaste of urban Tokyo, of *nansensu* and *moga*, must now impose his narrational system on a different Japanese iconography: the village street, the landscape, the forlorn café, the decaying theatre. He must film a traditional, if ineptly staged, performance. He can no longer cut away to Lincolns or spinning ventilators or Nipper the RCA dog. Ozu now experiments with treating centuries-old material in his own, recently matured manner.

His attempt is thoroughgoing. Instead of puckish cartoons behind the credits, he uses burlap, as if to assert the rustic purity of his tale. The characters wear kimono and play Japanese chess. The very title is a change for Ozu: instead of the vernacular catch-phrase, the joke, or the apothegm, we have a self-conscious metaphor comparing itinerant players to duckweeds that drift with the tides.

Most strikingly, Ozu draws upon the iconography of Japanese religious traditions. Religious motifs are justified by the rural milieu, but Ozu absorbs them into characteristic cutaways. The scene of the troupe's unpacking is prefaced by a close-up of one *kamidana*, or Shinto 'god shelf'. Later Ozu cuts from a second *kamidana* to a third, fully laid out with cut paper, rope, and salt.

107.

108.

109.

110.

Here the two *kamidana* are employed as an ambiguous transition moving from a rehearsal to a premiere. Later this traditional sign of good fortune is employed ironically. When the performance is interrupted by rain, Ozu cuts back to the third *kamidana*. Another religious image, derived more from folk traditions than from shrine Shinto, is the 'god' tree near which Otoki waits to seduce Shinkichi. Ozu treats it in his characteristic dominant/overtone manner. A shot of the hanging lantern (fig. 107) is followed by a shot of the fluttering banners (fig. 108), with the mountain as a contiguity link. Then the banners, reversed 180 degrees, become the link to the next shot (fig. 109), which shows Otoki waiting. Once she catches Shinkichi's attention, the narration integrates all the cutaway elements into one depth composition (fig. 110). Otoki's casual intrusion into a sacred space underlines the extent to which the actress is an outsider to the village, and again the religious motif is introduced ironically: a holy spot used to make a date.

Significantly, Ozu's characteristically late introduction of a motif is here reserved for the *daruma* at which Otsune looks twice in the film. The *daruma*, the roly-poly doll that always rights itself, is Japan's popular image of Bodhidarma, the founder of Zen Buddhism who is said to have have meditated so long that his legs dropped off. As a customary image of good fortune and successful achievement, the *daruma* forms a Buddhist equivalent for the Shinto *kamidana*, and its employment is no less ironic. Otsune first glances up at the *daruma* after Shinichi goes out on a secret visit to Otoki. In the climactic scene, she consoles Kihachi for the loss of his troupe ('Even a doll is pitiful if you let it alone for a long time') and Ozu cuts to the *daruma*. Finally, after Kihachi has left for good and his family stands weeping, the narration cuts back to the *daruma* and then to the upstairs room where he had played *shogi* with his son. In the context created by the *daruma*, the steaming teapot in the rear (a motif associated with Otsune's household) cites the poetic cliché of life's evanescence. (Similarly, the earlier fishing scene insists so much on the way that father and son stand in the river that it evokes Shinto's doctrine of purification by water.) An interpretative critic might go on to see the film as enacting a 'battle' of Japanese religions, with official Shinto and folk religion 'defeated' by a final emergence of Zen Buddhism. But this would miss the obvious and clichéd nature of the imagery which Ozu uses opportunistically, as pretext for asides (are these not the picturesque cutaways of an urban outsider?) and as realistically motivated material for formal patterning.

Yet this material, unlike the yoyos and victrolas of *Dragnet Girl*, resists complete assimilation. The toning down of Kihachi's character and the replacement of decentering gaps by a subdued irony are only two symptoms of a general muting of formal work. It is as if the rural subject and the religious iconography could not, at the risk of transgressing one currently powerful definition of Japanese tradition, become completely obedient to Ozu's aesthetic system. The *daruma* cannot be made the butt of visual jokes as Nipper is, and village life cannot be satirized as severely as can the student or salaryman culture. The resistance of Ozu's material manifests itself in the way that his narration continues the process of tempering we find in *A Mother Should Be Loved*. Tactics are repeated, even moderated. The finely broken-down découpage makes marked use of spatial anchors, as in the scene of the troupe unpacking, where the boy Tomibo links the actors to Kihachi's female companions. In this film, acting in unison serves to express not comic conformity but psychological and spiritual harmony (fig. 111). Here locales are identified through brief synecdochic motifs – Shinkichi's bike, the theatre windows – with no significant prolongation or variation. Camera movements are sparse. Ozu even includes 'motivated' fade-outs (lights are switched off) and one genuine fade-in. In such a conservative context, blatantly correct shot/reverse-shot becomes typical. An omniscient, communicative narration allows us no surprises comparable to the death of Ryoichi in *Woman of Tokyo* or the revival of Tomio in *Passing Fancy*. (The most vivid shock is the lingering on the café after Kihachi has chased Otaka out, followed by a cut to her holding her cheek: Kihachi's slap is elided.) During one scene, the narration anticipates Shinkichi's view of a clock, but this moment of overt intervention pales beside the flashy use of clocks in the 1933 films. Sometimes a cutaway will lead us falsely to expect that a scene's end is coming, but this undermining of expectation is mild in comparison to Ozu's previous work. The ideological gravity of Ozu's material weighs down those qualities of self-conscious playfulness that contrast so fruitfully with stylistic rigor. In the experiment of *Story of Floating Weeds*, despite passages of undeniable beauty, Ozu's system risks acceding to one limited conception of 'Japaneseness'.

111.

1935

Hakoiri musume

An Innocent Maid

Shochiku Kamata studio. Story: Sanu Shikitei. Script: Kogo Noda, Tadao Ikeda. Cinematography: Hideo Mohara. Cast: Choko Iida (*Otsune*), Kinuyo Tanaka (*Oshige*), Takeshi Sakamoto (*Kihachi*), Tokkan Kozo (*Tomibo*), Ryoichi Takeuchi (*Arata*), Kiyoshi Seino (*Murata*), Mitsuko Yoshikawa (*Otaka*), Shusuke Ken (*the old master*), Kenji Oyama (*the young master*). 8 reels, 1,847 meters. Released 12 January 1935. Script exists; negative and prints not known to exist.

Constantly scolded by his son, Kihachi lives in a back alley making rice cakes. Around him boils a complicated romantic situation. Oshige is courted by a cotton-shop owner, but she loves Arata, a young man boarding at a neighbor's. Oshige's mother Otsune plans to marry her to the merchant. On the wedding day, Kihachi interrupts the ceremony and in a cold sweat asks that they all consider everyone's opinions. In the last scene Arata and Oshige take their honeymoon in a northbound train.

After *Story of Floating Weeds*, Ozu returns to the *shitamachi* neighborhood. The subtitle, 'A Story Heard at the Public Baths', signals the plot's debt to Shikitei Sanba, author of Edo *gesaku* fiction. Synopses make Kihachi almost a bystander to a romantic drama involving three families and several misunderstandings, but doubtless there were scenes exploiting the interplay of Sakamoto and Tokkan Kozo. Shochiku had planned an entire 'Innocent Maid' series and pushed Ozu to finish the film quickly,[43] but portions were cut by censors and the series was abandoned.

Kagamijishi
Kagamijishi

Kokusai Bunka Shinkokai. Shochiku production. Cinematography: Hideo Mohara. 2 reels, 530 meters. Surviving prints: approx. 25 min. Produced 1935, but no official release date. Prints in existence.

112.

A documentary about the Kabuki theatre and one actor, the celebrated Onoye Kikugoro VI, who performs the lion dance *kagamijishi*.

In the mid-1930s, the government began heavily promoting 'cultural films' (*bunka eiga*). Initially, these were short educational and propaganda documentaries celebrating indigenous Japanese traditions and circulated to schools and clubs. Such a project, sponsored by the Japan Cultural Association, occasioned Ozu's making his first sound film.

The first half is shot in Ozu's usual fashion: low camera position, static shots, contiguous fragments of space. In the first four shots, the lantern's position is permuted according to dominant/overtone logic (figs. 112–115). We are taken into Kikugoro's dressing room, where he reads a play; the cutting displays Ozu's 90-degree shifts. As Kikugoro makes up, the voice-over commentator explains the plot of the play and Ozu cuts away to views of the actor's costume.

113.

Once the dance begins, the style changes drastically. The performance is filmed from various angles around the auditorium, some conforming to Ozu's norm, but others much more orthodox. The stylistic freedom of the first part derives from its being shot silent, whereas the need for synchronized sound during the dance (apparently before an audience) considerably inhibits the choice of camera position. (It is possible that the act was filmed with several cameras at once.) The stiffness of the synchronized portions may have been one reason that Ozu resisted sound: given Shochiku's still fairly inferior sound reproduction, his style would be harder to preserve in talkies. Not until the noh scene in *Late Spring* would Ozu find a satisfactory way to film theatrical performance, but even after that he preferred to show only the audience and not reveal the stage.

114.

115.

Tokyo no yado
An Inn in Tokyo

Shochiku Kamata studio. Story: Winthat Monnet (Ozu, Ikeda, and Masao Arata). Script: Tadao Ikeda and Masao Arata. Cinematography and editing: Hideo Mohara. Cinematography assistants: Yuharu Atsuta *et al.* Music: Keizo Horiuchi. Lighting: Toshimitsu Nakajima. Cast: Takeshi Sakamoto (*Kihachi*), Tokkan Kozo (*Zenko*), Takayuki Suematsu (*Masako*), Yoshiko Okada (*Otaka*), Kazuko Ojima (*Kimiko*), Choko Iida (*Otsune*), Chishu Ryu. 10 reels, 2,191 meters. Surviving prints: 80 min. Released 21 November 1935. Script, negative, and prints in existence.

Over three days Kihachi and his sons Zenko and Shoto roam through industrial Tokyo's flatlands looking for work and encounter Otaka and her daughter Kimiko. One evening Kihachi runs into an old friend, Otsune, who runs a café. She finds him a job. After a brief time of peace and friendship with Otaka and Kimiko, Kihachi discovers Otaka working as a *sake*-house waitress. She explains that her daughter has dysentery and she must pay the hospital bills. Failing to borrow money to help her, Kihachi resorts to theft. He sends his sons to take the money to Otaka. He asks Otsune to look after his boys and then sets out for the police station to give himself up.

With its sobered and smarter Kihachi wandering with his sons in a desolate industrial landscape, *An Inn in Tokyo* resembles works of Italian neo-realism. Sato has compared it to *Bicycle Thieves*, and in 1958 Oshima looked back to Ozu's 'prewar naturalism' as one of the few alternatives to traditional ideology.[44] Yet as usual, Ozu balances referentiality (exact mentions of the districts in which the action takes place) with formal patterning. *An Inn in Tokyo* is at once more episodic and more rigorously organized than a neo-realist effort like De Sica's. As Kristin Thompson shows, *Bicycle Thieves* has a goal-oriented plot, several deadlines, and a careful motivation of many events.[45] Ozu's plot material and linkage of incidents is considerably closer to a 'slice of life' than De Sica's. At the narrational level, *Bicycle Thieves* relies wholly on that normalized technique of classical Hollywood cinema, and style does not achieve salience. By contrast, *An Inn in Tokyo* brings style into prominence through repetitive patterning and parametric variation. Ozu's narration remains both referential and 'poetically' organized.

Structurally, *An Inn in Tokyo* is Ozu's most schematic film to survive from the 1930s. For two-thirds of its length, every scene or motif creates parallels. By means of a rigorous additive patterning, Ozu produces a 'tabular' theme-and-variations structure. One indication is the film's temporal scheme. The syuzhet duration spans six or seven days selected from roughly a two-week stretch. Every day is shown in two sections, each taking place in similar or identical locales – the daytime scenes outdoors in the weed-choked fields around the factories, the night scenes in an inn, a café, or a geisha house. Most important, the 'action-modules' established in scenes 1 and 2 are repeated, varied, and added to in subsequent sequences, and the style constitutes itself as a system by mobilizing these parallels in the service of minute variations.

Consider the first few sequences. On the first day, Kihachi and his sons tramp down the road, he asks a factory gateman for work, they watch children marching off to school, Shoko complains that he's hungry, and they spy a dog and give chase before Ozu cuts to a poster advertising a reward for stray dogs on 'rabies prevention day'. The third scene shows a comparable portion of the following day. Now Zenko complains about an unsympathetic gateman (the narration has elided Kihachi's job search), Kihachi watches men trooping off to work, the family discusses its hunger, and the boys pursue another dog – but this time we see the capture. On the following day, shown in scenes 5 and 6, Zenko again comments on a gateman's rudeness, the boys mime eating a good meal, and Kihachi sees a job poster and sets off down the road. Moreover, the virtually identical landscapes make the scenes remarkably repetitious. In the same way, scenes two and four, each set at night, present obvious echoes. Both are set in the same area of the inn of the title, a *kichinyado* or cheap lodging for the poor. In both scenes, the sons try to cheer Kihachi up, and Zenko flips a coin to determine their fate, each time saying, 'We'll make it tomorrow.' By the end of scene 5, after three daytime scenes and two nighttime ones, the mundane routines that neo-realism would depict in a more scattered, random fashion have been represented through a rigorous system of parallels.

What keeps the action going, creating causal connections amidst all the parallels, are the elements which creep in additively and only later get pulled into parallel structures. In the first inn scene (scene 2), Zenko and Shoko see a boy with an officer's cap. The next day (scene 3) Zenko uses the dog's bounty to buy one for himself – a waste of money for which Kihachi gloomily upbraids him. That night, in the inn (scene 4), Zenko regrets buying the cap. On the third day (scene 5), after Kihachi has dashed off in hope of a job, Zenko and Shoko quarrel and they lose the family's bundle – a much more serious mistake than buying the cap. Because of this, Kihachi gives them a choice of sleeping in the inn or eating, so a nighttime scene of them in the café (number 7) substitutes for the inn scene. This new factor, the café encounter with Otsune, leads to Kihachi's finding a job and breaking the cycle established so far. Most significant for narrative causality is the unbalancing of symmetry created by the encounters with Otaka and Kimiko. Kihachi and his boys see them in the inn (scene 2), glimpse them in the fields (scene 3), spot them again in the inn (scene 4), and meet and talk briefly in the fields (scene 5). From a formal perspective, the various incidents on the road serve as retardation devices to postpone the moment when Kihachi meets Otaka, but Ozu *organizes* these retardations to a degree that makes them not only 'realistic' in their depiction of a cycle of homelessness and poverty but also abstract in their precisely aligned symmetry.

As in earlier films, the equivalences and variations in action-modules are 'excessively' marked by stylistic permutations. Scenes 2 and 4 in the inn are more orthodox in that the second offers a condensed variant on the first, omitting two 'detour' shots of other customers. The start of each daytime

116.
117.
118.

scene, however, offers significant play with our expectations. They constitute tabular alternatives:

Day 1 (Scene 1)	Day 2 (Scene 3)	Day 3 (Scene 5)	Day 3 (Scene 6)
1. (*ls*) Weeds, cable spool and field (fig. 116).	1. (*ls*) Weeds and tanks: in *bg*, Kihachi and sons walk in field (fig. 118).	1. (*ls*) Weeds and tanks (fig. 119).	1. (*ls*) Weeds and tanks: in *bg*, Kihachi and sons sit on spools (fig. 121).
2. (*ls*) Kihachi and sons walk down road (fig. 117).		2. (*ls*) Kihachi and sons walk into field (fig. 120).	

In fact, these elements – weeds, spools, tanks, road, distant factories – will be permuted throughout the film, serving not only to define the locale but to create a pattern of expectation and revision for the spectator. This degree of stylistic prominence and unity is of course unknown in neo-realism.

After the café scene (number 7) in which Kihachi runs into his old friend Otsune, there is a time gap of about a week, and a new cycle of action-modules, based on the old ones, begins. It is introduced by two shots, the first showing laundry on a line (Ozu's recurrent synecdoche for domesticity, which we will never see again in this film), the second showing tanks, weeds, spools, and the distant factory – itself a replay of such shots as fig. 116. The logic of contiguity – from clothesline to field – leads us to expect the sort of daylight roaming that initiated the first three days, but we retrospectively realize that the shot is there to show us that Kihachi and his boys did not have to sleep outside, for Ozu then cuts to Zenko and Shoko asleep indoors, in the quarters that Kihachi has rented from Otsune. The family's hopes have been realized: Zenko goes to school and Kihachi goes to work (another variant shows him striding to the factory across the field; fig. 122).

The film launches a new rhythm of day and night. Kihachi sees Otaka and Kimiko on his way to work and makes them his guests at Otsune's café (scenes 8–9). That night he asks his sons if Otaka mentioned him when they played together (scene 10). In scene 11, the next day, we see Otaka, Kimiko,

119.

120.

121.

and the boys playing. The locale and action echo scenes 1, 3, and 5, but with a twist: Kihachi, now employed, brings snacks for the children. From this point on, the scenes become briefer, the time scheme more fragmented. That night, while Kihachi drinks in a tea house (scene 12), Otaka and Kimiko are sitting in the inn at the spot where Kihachi and his boys had sat (scene 13). Kimiko is ill. Cut to daytime, perhaps the next day, with the boys waiting for their playmates (scene 14). An ambiguously placed dialogue title – 'I wonder what happened to her' – links their vigil to their telling Kihachi about it that night (scene 15). Once more, the symmetry of locale and incident is reinforced by découpage, as when Ozu plays a suite of variants on the spools and tanks that echo scene 6, a brief exchange between Kihachi and his sons (fig. 123; cf. figs. 116, 119, 121).

122.

The film's last phase, scenes 15–21, takes place on a single evening. Now causality becomes more important than parallels. After meeting Otaka and learning of her plight, Kihachi fails to borrow money from Otsune, goes to a bar, steals money which he takes to his sons, and confesses to Otsune before leaving to give himself up. But Ozu does not neglect parallels and permutations entirely. Kihachi's second visit to the *sake* house echoes his first but varies the opening by adding a shot. During his first visit he shows the waitress the scarf he has brought for Otaka, and during the second visit he scornfully offers the scarf to the waitress. When just before the robbery Kihachi fills a glass to overflowing with *sake*, the gesture echoes the poignant imaginary feast in the field, when Zenko had mimed pouring *sake* for his father and had been warned not to spill any. Now, on the verge of robbery, Kihachi becomes desperate and reckless, indulging profligacy as a kind of farewell to his few days of prosperity. The last few scenes employ the same fireworks shots which Ozu had used in *Where Now Are the Dreams of Youth?* and *Passing Fancy*, again presumably to evoke the August Sumida River festival, as if to brake the intense narrative action and to rekindle a sense of abstract design. And the final shot of Kihachi trudging to the police (fig. 124) offers the only night view of the plot's principal landscape and thus provides a concluding variant on the film's major permutational set.

123.

In other ways, *An Inn in Tokyo* constitutes a summary of Ozu's silent work. His male ethic is clear from the way the narration restricts itself principally to Kihachi and the boys, only venturing into Otaka's ken when Kimiko falls ill (and thus supplying us with a significantly greater degree of knowledge than

124.

Kihachi has). Again the father fails, and two mother figures, Otaka and Otsune, must restore familial continuity. Still, every artistic achievement contains something new as well, and one can find here some stylistic and narrational ploys that would be more fully exploited later. In the geisha-house scenes, Ozu is starting to experiment with putting objects on the bottom frameline and jumping them from shot to shot. He uses telegraph poles as a graphic element that masks the left or right of the shot, as he will later use corridors and doorways. The pathos of *A Mother Should Be Loved*, *Story of Floating Weeds* and this film point ahead to the profound sadness of *The Only Son*. The quiet scene of Kihachi and Otaka wishing they were children again, sitting on the ground together as Ozu cuts to the sky, the weeds and tower, and the sky again – all this sketches the more prolonged and plaintive scene, in another blasted industrial desert, when a son and his mother will sit by a sewage plant, reflect on their disappointments, and listen to larks in an empty sky.

1936

Daigaku yoitoko
College Is a Nice Place

Shochiku Kamata studio. Story: 'James Maki'. Script: Masao Arata. Cinematography: Hideo Mohara. Cast: Toshiaki Konoe (*Fujiki*), Chishu Ryu (*Amano*), Tokuji Kobayashi (*Nishida*), Kenji Oyama (*Kawahara*), Tsuruhiko Ikebe (*Inoue*), Akira Hikabe (*Aoki*), Sanae Takasugi (*Chiyoko*), Tatsuo Saito (*a lecturer*), Kiyoshi Seino (*owner of a boarding house*), Choko Iida (*his wife*), Takeshi Sakamoto (*a teacher*). 13 reels(?), 2,352 meters. Released 19 March 1936. Script exists; no negative or prints known to exist.

In a boarding house, various students lie about and struggle through their studies while graduates seek jobs. Fujiki and Amano attend class and suffer through drill practice. Aoki, an injured baseball pitcher, lies in his room all day staring at the ceiling. Nishida, an older student, loafs and sponges off the others. Eventually Amano quits school to return to the country. Fujiki swipes money from his wife Chiyoko's household savings to hold a farewell party. After the party, when Amano has left weeping, Fujiki cries out in despair: 'Will we ever become anything?' Chiyoko reproaches him for his pessimism. The next day, the students return to their routines, with Fujiki marching in drill.

All accounts of the script agree: the melancholy that gradually creeps into Ozu's previous college comedies has turned bitter and now suffuses the whole film. From the title onward, *College Is a Nice Place* seems filled with harsh irony. What would have been rueful gags in earlier movies become evidence of the utter failure of Meiji promises, the futility of higher education, the inevitability of unemployment. When a boy quits school, the registrar tells him that he is the fourth to leave that day. Far from the fun-loving rascals of *Days of Youth* are the two heroes, whom the script describes as constantly scowling. An unusually didactic montage replaces Ozu's customary scenes of classroom mischief: as a professor lectures on a book called *The Poverty of Education*, Ozu tracks past empty classroom seats, then cuts to students peddling trinkets on the streets, going to the movies, lounging at Saigo's statue in Ueno Park, watching baseball practice, or just sleeping. Chiyoko's final urging not to give up has a desperate edge that anticipates the dogged encouragement offered by Otsune in *The Only Son*. One must keep trying or sink into utter despair. 'Not a cheerful look at college days,' Ozu recalled. 'A dark story.'[46]

Hitori musuko
The Only Son

Shochiku Ofuna studio. Story: 'James Maki'. Script: Tadao Ikeda, Masao Arata. Cinematography: Shojiro Sugimoto. Sound recording: Hideo Mohara, Eiichi Hesegawa. Art direction: Toshio Hamada. Music: Senji Ito. Cinematography assistants: Yuharu Atsuta *et al.* Lighting: Toshimitsu Nakajima. Cast: Choko Iida (*Otsune Nonomiya*), Shinichi Himori (*Ryosuke*), Masao Hayama (*Ryoichi as a child*), Yoshiko Tsubouchi (*Sugiko*), Mitsuko Yoshikawa (*Otaka*), Chishu Ryu (*Okubo*), Tomoko Naniwa (*his wife*), Bakudan Kozo (*his son*), Tokkan Kozo (*Tomibo*). 10 reels, 2,387 meters. Surviving prints: 83 min. Released 15 September 1936. Script, duplicate negative, and prints in existence.

1923: In Shinsu, Otsune raises her son Ryosuke alone. At his teacher Okubo's advice, he vows to go on to school. Otsune agrees to keep working in a silk mill to support his education. *1935*: Otsune tells her friend that she will soon visit her son in Tokyo. *1936*: When Otsune arrives, she learns that Ryosuke is now a husband and father; worse, he has a poor teaching post in a night school. Treating his mother as an honored guest, Ryosuke borrows money for gifts, snacks, and outings. They visit Okubo, now running a tiny pork-chop café. Eventually Ryosuke admits that he has failed, and in a tense late-night scene she accuses him of giving up. When the neighbor widow Otaka's son Tomio is kicked by a horse, however, Ryosuke gives her the money he was to spend on his mother. Otsune praises him: better a kind man than a rich one. After she has started home, Ryosuke vows to try to better his lot. Back in Shinsu, Otsune puts on a good face for her friend, but alone she falls into a posture of weary resignation.

'What chance is there today of getting back all the capital poured into school and university fees? All those parents down in the country who expect their son to walk into a provincial governorship or a directorship with Mitsui as soon as he leaves the university are going to be somewhat surprised when they at last get the letter announcing that he has got a job as a tram-conductor or a policeman.'[47]

Thus did the author of *Story of a Salaryman* (1928) express that disillusionment with Meiji promises which would inform many of Ozu's films of the 1920s and early 1930s. *The Only Son*, another film about the failure of *risshin shusse*, 'getting on', is also the most sweeping in its referential scope. Its thirteen-year time span includes a portrait of rural life more detailed than that in *Story of Floating Weeds*, a rare depiction of the silk-spinning industry, and a vision of Tokyo quite different from the nostalgic *shitamachi* or the jazzy metropolis seen in the earlier films. As we analyze the film's narrative structure and narrational strategies, we shall need to notice how Ozu's form molds such socially concrete material.

The syuzhet is intricate in its shifts of period and locale. Part one, set in the rural town of Shinsu, contains four scenes. In the manner of *An Inn in Tokyo*, two parallel segments in the spinning mill (1 and 3) are set off against two in Otsune's home (2 and 4). During scene 2, Otsune learns that Ryosuke has told his teacher he intends to go on to middle school, and she slaps him. In scene 4, she tells him she has changed her mind and is willing to keep working to support him through college. To some extent, this replays the stereotyped *shimpa* motif of the self-sacrificing woman supporting the young man (cf. Mizoguchi's *Taki no Shiraito* and *Downfall of Osen*). There is a special force to this situation, though. Normally the eldest son of a rural family would have been expected to make his life at home, serving as principal heir while younger sons migrated to the city. Hence the problem summarized in the film's title: the widowed Otsune is giving up a comparatively comfortable old age because she has only one child.

The alternating scenes in the factory function partly to show exactly what this sacrifice will entail. After the Meiji era, most textile industries relied heavily on female labor, bought or contracted at low rates and maintained in grim conditions. The film's first and third scenes emphasize female work – the sign reads, 'Women workers wanted', and we see only women staff – and both scenes stress the hot repetitive labor of boiling silk fabric in soap and water. The fifth scene will contrast the vat method of silk boiling (scenes 1 and 3) with a newer, more mechanical one that jams each woman into a narrow vertical cage (fig. 125). In all, these glimpses of the mill's interior are absolutely unique in my viewing of Japanese fiction films of the 1930s. Although Ozu does not present the harshest circumstances of most factory girls' lives, the sheer decision to depict such an important part of the rural economy was apparently breaking a tacit convention about what subject matter could be shown on the screen. Later, when Otsune confesses to Ryosuke that she has sold their home and is living in company housing, this announces to a 1936 audience that a steep decline in her fortunes has forced her into a dormitory on the grounds. This prepares us for the final scene, in which the factory courtyard comes to resemble a prison yard.

125.

After the five scenes in Shinsu, in which alternating ones are all paralleled and varied, a new phase of the plot starts in Tokyo, as Otsune arrives for her visit. After one of Ozu's running-board tours, the film settles down in a neighborhood in a bleak factory suburb. Motifs condense the difference between Otsune's village and Ryosuke's Tokyo: a city dyer's dangling strips of yarn echo the textile mill, while the kerosene lantern in Otsune's home contrasts with the hanging electric lights in Ryosuke's classroom. Yet this is a new, raw Tokyo. We are no longer in the coffeeshops of the college comedies, or the trim streets of *Walk Cheerfully* and *Dragnet Girl*, nor even in the downtown of *Passing Fancy*. The city of *The Only Son* is a cluster of ramshackle tenements pasted against a wasteland of factories and weedy plains straight out of *An Inn in Tokyo*. The early silent films had reveled in an urban landscape that is kept insistently offscreen here. No outside views show the streets around Ryosuke's school or the hospital where Tomio is taken. Okubo's pork-chop café sits in a dusty stretch of laundry lines, power poles, and vacant lots. Ryosuke and Otsune go sightseeing to Asakusa, Ueno Park, and the Kudan hill, which offers a fine view of the city; but we merely hear reports of this tour. The expedition that the syuzhet shows us consists of mother and son squatting before the city garbage-treatment plant. *The Only Son* originated as a silent film to be called *Tokyo Is a Nice Place*.

Ugly Tokyo is the correlative of the failure of Meiji aspirations. Otsune's 'Nowadays you have to have knowledge to get ahead' was already anachronistic in 1923. By the early 1930s, there was a huge oversupply of college graduates, and in 1936, 44 per cent of graduates could not get jobs. Typically the major companies recruited their staffs from only a few prestigious schools. No surprise, then, that Ryosuke and Okubo have not made good. And Ryosuke is still far from rock bottom, since the ten yen he borrows from two colleagues would have fed an average working-class family for three weeks. Still, Ozu refuses to tell us the source of Ryosuke's ill fortune. What university did he attend, and what subjects did he study? Why has he given up a municipal office job to teach night school? Earlier films would have answered such questions, but here Ozu's narration conceals prior story material in order to strengthen both the social criticism and the family drama. By omitting specific causes, the plot can elevate Ryosuke into a typical case and can concentrate on how his failure affects him and his mother.

Moreover, the early portion of the syuzhet is carefully confined to Otsune's range of knowledge, so that weight is thrown upon the surprise of learning of Ryosuke's wife, child, and poverty. By an inverse movement, at the film's end we are fairly clear about Ryosuke's attitude, but now Otsune becomes more psychologically opaque. She has told Ryosuke that she is disappointed and that he must not give up. She has later praised him for helping Otaka with the money: 'I'm glad you didn't become rich.' So nuanced is Ozu's distribution of story information that we can take her approval as sincere and yet still interpret her final, glum solitude in the mill yard as suggesting a piercing unhappiness. The point is complex: she finds him not a failure, but he is still disappointing.

This is to say that as usual Ozu has moved from concrete referential material to broader themes; but here one can argue that the themes generalize the social criticism. Even more didactic than *I Was Born, But . . .*, *The Only Son* frankly bases itself on three ideas. The first is stipulated at the outset: parents, in order for their child to have a happier life than they have had, will sacrifice nearly everything. This is Otsune's chief action, and it is seen in minor key in the way that Okubo bribes his boy, or Otaka promises her child a ball; by the end, Ryosuke himself is pledging to sacrifice all for his baby. A second theme gives the first a bitter twist. Once you have seen your children grow up, your hopes will inevitably be disappointed. Otsune cannot hide her chagrin at Ryosuke's failure, and even after she has praised his self-sacrifice in giving money to help out Otaka, the plot concludes with the scene of her facing a bleak life back at the factory. Both ideas are encapsulated in the opening epigraph from Ryunosuke Akutagawa: 'The first act of the tragedy of life begins with a parent and a child.'

Linked to these two themes is that of nostalgia. Otsune and Ryosuke tell Okubo of the changes in their village and he replies: 'When the milkweed flowers, I always think about going back.' This theme gets drawn into the parent/child structure. Ryosuke might yet succeed, but the tardily-introduced motif of the baby bottle, which he fingers thoughtfully after his mother has gone home, suggests not only his concern for his son's future but his own impulse to flee back to a childish life. ('I should have stayed with you,' he has told Otsune at the garbage plant.) Ryosuke's play with the bottle echoes the moment in *An Inn in Tokyo* when Kihachi and Otaka wish themselves back to their childhood, 'the best part of life'. Seldom has an Ozu film offered so little hope: the vanishing home town, the oppressive silk mill, the desolate city of poverty and broken ambitions, and a future that promises only disappointment. The family, where the child rules, cannot cushion the child, or the parent, from these social shocks. Optimistic Kidoism can gain little foothold here: without denouncing larger causes, the film depicts a world that guarantees that children and parents will always fall short of expectations (a remarkable thesis for a film addressed to Shochiku's female audience). Once grown to adulthood, the individual preserves integrity by small, rash acts of kindness (like Kihachi's in *Passing Fancy* and *An Inn in Tokyo*) that briefly relieve others' misery.

The plot has worked all this out in terms that complete the symmetries initiated earlier. The scenes in the mill (1,3,5) are matched by the last scene, with Otsune (now a cleaning woman) and her friend scrubbing the floor, and the first scene's movement 'into' the mill is balanced by our following Otsune outside at the very end. Her visit to Ryosuke's home and their first scene indoors rhyme with Ryosuke and his wife returning from taking leave of his mother and with their lengthy emotional climax inside. To proceed still further into the syuzhet's nested structure, Otsune's stay in Tokyo is itself crossed by a rhythm of day and night, family outing and evening talk. Early phases of her visit are marked by cheerfulness and a mocking satire of Germany. She and Ryosuke attend a screening of Forst's 1933 Schubert biopic, *Leise flehen meine Lieder*. When he informs her that it's a talkie, she nods apprehensively before dropping off to sleep. Later Tomio's serio-comic game identifies the horse with the German travel poster in Ryosuke's home. As Otsune's story goes on, the number of melancholy and pensive scenes increases. Ryosuke and Otsune sit listening to the larks at the garbage plant; then, that night, Ozu crosscuts Ryosuke musing in class with Otsune frowning at home. After Tomio's accident, the narration takes us into Ryosuke's home, showing the members of the family sitting quietly. Finally, a double climax completes the alternation of mother and son: Ryosuke's meditation at his baby's side prepares for Otsune's solitude at the close. That modulation of rhythm from insouciance to thoughtful solemnity, so characteristic of Ozu's silent work, is here crystallized in prolonged pensive moments that will reappear from *A Hen in the Wind* onward.

Ozu speaks of *The Only Son* as a continuation of his prior work. 'Because I couldn't get rid of the mood and style of the silent movies at all, I became quite bewildered. In spite of my understanding perfectly well that everything is different in a talkie, this movie had the style of a silent.'[48] The bold depth effects, such as in the scene of the train's arrival; the play with layers of focus in backgrounds; the use of staggered staging and *donden* cuts; the way cutaways break up conventional ABA point-of-view editing; even the several fades – all these refine earlier procedures.

The intermediate spaces, while adding nothing to what Ozu had already accomplished, serve brilliantly to refine parallels (such as the variants of Otsune's window at home) and to raise the stakes in the narration's ongoing

126.

127.

128.

129.

game with expectations. Early in the film, the intermediate spaces operate as transitions between discrete episodes, all with 'full' lead-ins and -outs. As the film goes on, however, these spaces start to function ambiguously. When Ryosuke and Otsune visit Okubo's café, a cutaway to the sign identifies the locale. They greet Okubo and he starts to wash up, asking Ryosuke for a towel (fig. 126). Cut to a view of clotheslines seen from a window (fig. 127). Cut, on dominant/overtone and contiguity principles, to a shot of a pump on a street (fig. 128). At this point we might expect a fade-out, since such shots have previously closed scenes. But Ozu returns to the sign (fig. 129) and then to a corner of the kitchen (fig. 130) before cutting back to the threesome (fig. 131). It is not just that Ozu has elided the brief action of Okubo's clean-up; he has misled us into thinking that the scene is over. Later in the conversation, brief shots of parts of the café seem to anticipate closure before we retrospectively 'place' them as cutaways plugging holes in the conversation. Ozu employs the same tactic after the hospital scene, when he uses intermediate spaces to lead us to the family sitting at home, then cuts outside again, as if the scene were going to consist only of pensive characters, before he cuts back again to Ryosuke lifting his head to speak (p. 75).

Yet another momentarily misleading effect occurs at the end of the café scene, when Ozu cuts from Okubo (holding up the talisman) to the restaurant sign. Another cutaway before resuming the dialogue? No. Cut to the talisman, now pinned to the wall of Ryosuke's home, and then to a shot of Sugiko sewing. So now we have a scene in Ryosuke's house? No again. Cut to a shot of the mother's bag in a corner by the pin-up of Carole Lombard. And cut to an appalling close-up of the female lead of Forst's film, linked by similarity to the Lombard photo: we are, as in *Woman of Tokyo*, suddenly at the movies. Although this recalls the roundabout window-and-compact transition in *Walk Cheerfully* (pp. 200–201), earlier films show no exact equivalent for this manner of representing a character's activity by taking us first to where the character is not. It will, of course, be exploited again in *Flavor of Green Tea over Rice* and *An Autumn Afternoon*.

In other respects, *The Only Son* continues Ozu's silent style. Permuted sequences will be used to stress parallels, as in the variants which introduce the spinning mill by re-identifying the locale and measuring the changes in factory machinery. Ozu also bids temporary farewell to his lateral tracking shots by using Forst's footage of hero and heroine galumphing through a wheatfield, and Forst's coy cut-in to a dropped scarf serves as an ironic citation of what Ozu's shots of objects do not do. Boldest of all, Ozu lays bare his scenographic principles in Ryosuke's lesson to his class (p. 119, fig. 41), which he explains in terms of circles and right angles.

Yet Ozu's remark about persisting in a silent style should not distract us from his accomplishments in the domain of sound. *The Only Son* introduces several of his characteristic sound techniques. The lyrical music, with one theme based on 'Old Black Joe', is not yet used to signal and smooth over transitions, but it runs throughout two scenes, the scene in 1923 when Otsune agrees to send Ryosuke on to school, and the idyll in 1936 when they sit by the garbage-plant and he confesses that he has failed. The second of these sequences, with the music punctuated by offscreen bird calls, initiates Ozu's handling of many similar outings. With respect to dialogue, Ozu is already practicing the restraint he would maintain for the next twenty-five years: he will not cut so as to break a character's line, not even by a syllable. *The Only Son* also initiates Ozu's rich use of offscreen noises – the steady gnashing of the factory in Ryosuke's neighborhood, the call of a Chinese-noodle vendor, the hammer of a barrel-maker. One of the film's most delicate transitions, which also involves some misleading narration, uses offscreen sound to evoke urban solitude and stasis.

130.

After a fade-out from the scene near the garbage plant, we fade in on hanging lamps. Honky-tonk café music drifts in. Across three more shots, we see Ryosuke's pupils writing and hear the faint scrape of pens on paper; then Ryosuke at the classroom window; then a medium-shot of him looking out. Cut to Ryosuke's home, evoked by the synecdoches of teakettle and talisman. A clock is ticking offscreen. Cut to Otsune sitting, thinking, the clock still ticking. Cut back to Ryosuke at the window, the honky-tonk music back again. Cut in to him. And now a bold deception. Cut to the window, revealing a flashing 'B' sign outside and suggesting at last the source of the music. Ozu holds this shot for fifteen seconds, keeping the sound volume constant. Abruptly the room lights are switched off. If we took this to be Ryosuke's optical point-of-view, we are fooled in just the way the garbage plant scene fools us (see p. 50). While our back is turned, as it were, the characters leave the scene. But here the deception is compounded by Ozu's suppression of offscreen noise, for he refuses to let us hear Ryosuke dismiss the class or hear the roomful of boys leave. In his first sound feature, Ozu lets offscreen sound surprise us with acts of uncommunicative, self-conscious narration.

131.

We could go on studying this masterful film for a very long time, but the opening and closing sequences aptly summarize how Ozu's narration mobilizes his fully-developed principles and yet retains the force of immediately referential material. Spatially the first shots move up to the factory on a dominant/overtone principle, as we have seen on pp. 136–7, figs. 99–102. Offscreen noise also plays a significant role, since Ozu now introduces into a sound film his pet joke about clocks telling different times: two clocks chime nine o'clock successively. With the cut to the sign, the mill noise begins. Now Ozu links the shots 'categorically', semantically, moving from a sign soliciting women workers to a shot of one woman, Otsune's friend. The next shot shows Otsune. Burch praises this opening for its development from stillness to movement.[49] Otsune is also at a boiling vat, with wheels in the background. Cut to wheels (an overtone of the prior shot). The last three shots are all virtually identical in length. What will be the next shot? Ozu cuts to a long-shot of the village – the 'establishing' shot that a Hollywood filmmaker would have put first – while, by way of a linkage, keeping the mill noise on the soundtrack. Using seven shots and no dialogue, Ozu has situated Otsune in her most significant surroundings, depicted the grimy routine of silk milling, introduced several motifs such as the lantern and the mill, and created a steady rhythm of image and sound to set the pace for the rest of the film.

132.

Ozu's manipulation of expectation at the film's end serves to delay closure

133.

273

134.

135.

136.

137.

138.

139.

140.

by making it difficult to predict the end of the action. After a cutaway to women spinning, Ozu shows Otsune trudging out into the yard with her pail (fig. 132). In an extreme long-shot, she pauses with her pail and goes to sit (fig. 133). After she is seated, in medium long-shot (fig. 134), the music starts, slow and mournful. Cut to a long-shot (fig. 135), different from the earlier setup and offering a conventional cue for closure. Instead, another cut in to yet a fourth variant framing (fig. 136) as Otsune hangs her head. Now, as Ozu cuts away to the yard with its baskets and gate (fig. 137), the music shifts to a lilting vibraphone version of 'Old Black Joe'. Then comes a shot of the gate, straight-on (fig. 138), followed by a very low, oblique framing of the gate and grass (fig. 139) as the music brings the film to an end. This ending has been prepared at the start of scene three by a 'hinge' shot that presents women in the factory yard (fig. 140): the flat hats pick up the costume of the women at the film's opening (p. 137, figs. 99–102), the kerchiefs look forward to Otsune at the close. The clear social referent – Otsune, unwilling to burden her son's family, shut in the mill for life – is presented by a narration that makes it no less legible but thoroughly organized, poetically enriched by prolongation and revision of expectation, daringly complicated by the cheerful music that clashes with the stock connotations of entrapment.

1937

Shujo wa nani o wasuretaka
What Did the Lady Forget?

Shochiku Ofuna studio. Script: Akira Fushimi, 'James Maki'. Cinematography: Hideo Mohara, Yuharu Atsuta. Editing: Kenkichi Hara. Music: Senji Ito. Lighting: Toshimitsu Nakajima. Cast: Sumiko Kurishima (*Tokiko*), Tatsuo Saito (*Komiya*), Kayoko Kuwano (*Setsuko*), Shuji Sano (*Okada*), Takeshi Sakamoto (*Sugiyama*), Choko Iida (*Chiyoko*), Ken Uehara (*himself*), Mitsuko Yoshikawa (*Mitsuko*), Masao Hayama (*her son Fujio*), Tokkan Kozo (*Tomio*). 8 reels, 2,051 meters. Surviving prints: 71 min. Released 3 March 1937. Script, duplicate negative, and prints in existence.

Professor Komiya and his wife Tokiko host their niece Setsuko on her visit to Tokyo. Tokiko browbeats Komiya into a golfing weekend but instead he sneaks off to a bar and to hide out at the apartment of his assistant Okada. Setsuko learns of his ploy and insists on being taken to a geisha house. When Okada brings her home drunk, Tokiko is furious. Komiya swears Setsuko to keep his secret. To satisfy Tokiko, Komiya must harangue Setsuko on proper behavior. This makes her urge him to stand up to Tokiko, using violence if necessary. That night, Komiya slaps Tokiko. Setsuko and Komiya soon apologize, however, and all are reconciled. Setsuko, now romantically involved with Okada, leaves Tokyo, and Komiya and Tokiko prepare for a night of marital pleasure.

What Did the Lady Forget? is usually regarded as marking Ozu's true acceptance of talkies. *The Only Son* was filmed using the sound system devised by his cinematographer Hideo Mohara and was shot in Shochiku's recently abandoned Kamata studio. (Most scenes were shot at night because of train noise during the day.[50]) With *What Did the Lady Forget?* Ozu used Shochiku's Dobashi system and began working in the Ofuna studio. The film is also traditionally seen as marking Ozu's shift to an interest in the moneyed classes, caused by his moving his own household to the prosperous suburb of Takanawa. This is something of an exaggeration, however. Ozu had made films about wealthy families before this, and he would make films about less well-off families afterward. Then, too, he hardly required a personal excuse for changing his subject matter. A shift to a bourgeois milieu was a general Shochiku trend around 1937; until the end of the war, for reasons that are at least partly political, the studio began concentrating on wealthy, professional, or middle-class life. This trend corresponded to a broader tendency in Japanese popular literature of the time. Kan Kikuchi's newspaper novel *San katei* (*Three Families*, 1934) was a literary soap opera about the problems of three middle-class women. Teppei Kataoka's *Hanayome gakko* (*A School for Brides*, 1934) satirized bourgeois life, concentrating on the marriage plans of spoiled daughters; it became so popular that he wrote many similar stories. Kido, always alert for a fad that would attract a female audience, probably sensed that public interest had drifted from *ero-guro-nansensu* to melodrama and satire involving the privileged classes.

Western critics have not paid much attention to *What Did the Lady Forget?*, yet it is one prototype for Ozu's post-1948 work. The social comedy of *The Flavor of Green Tea over Rice, Equinox Flower, Late Autumn*, and *An Autumn Afternoon* can be traced back to this film. While *The Only Son* foreshadows the pathetic tone of Ozu's postwar work, *What Did the Lady Forget?* sets the comic one; only the extended-family structure of *Brothers and Sisters of the Toda Family* remains to be added to the repertory.

Stylistically the film may seem somewhat muted after the self-conscious intricacy of *The Only Son*, but it uses tactics that Ozu will thereafter draw on frequently. Take the transitions. Most early scenes are not linked by intermediate spaces at all, so that Ozu will simply cut from a shot of characters in action to the first shot of the new scene, often with dialogue providing the link. As the film goes on, Ozu begins to insert some intermediate spaces, but most transitions are still only 'half' complete in that the narration shows intermediate space associated with only one locale. Usually both the 'zero' and the 'half' transitions create abrupt comic juxtapositions. Setsuko in medium shot says she wants to go to a geisha house; cut to her in medium shot in a geisha house. Tokiko's maid reports that Komiya and Setsuko have sneaked out through the garden; cut to their feet on the sidewalk.

Not that Ozu has eliminated permutational variants. Each return to Setsuko's room begins with the birdcage and plant by the window, in different configurations (as in *Toda Family* four years later). Every visit to Okada's lodging shows a different aspect of the room. And no Ozuphile can object to the first transition to the Cervantes Bar. The camera tracks down the sign ('I drink upon occasion and sometimes upon no occasion – Don Quichotte'), but before cutting to customers, the narration concentrates upon a bar cart in focus in the foreground (p. 87, fig. 45). This gives us time to listen to the thunking sound of the dice in the hostess's cup. Then we get a shot of Sugiyama and the hostess. Finally, as Komiya joins them, Ozu cuts back to a different view of the bar cart, now out of focus. This slim dosage of intermediate spaces is more characteristic of all Ozu's subsequent films, including *Toda Family* and *There Was a Father*, than it is of the silent work and *The Only Son*.

In other respects, Ozu's stylistic concerns persist. There are several camera movements, including the last usage of his camera-on-the-running-board setup. *Donden* cutting, 180-degree reestablishing shots, and staggered staging are present in full force. A play with focus during conversation scenes appears from the start, when Chiyo is trying to figure out Fujio's arithmetic problem and Tokiko sits out of focus in the rear; cut to Tokiko, in focus; cut back to show all three, now from a new angle. When Setsuko and Komiya stalk back into the house, their synchronized strides and turns create an acting-in-unison effect, but Ozu gives the shots great graphic force by making the couple form two black columns on a grey ground and by staging the scene so that Setsuko, the smaller, stands slightly forward and evens up their sizes.

The film also contains some of Ozu's boldest graphic matches, as when Fujio and Tomio play their 'hit the spot' game with the globe (figs. 141–2), or when Tokiko rises to follow her niece (fig. 143) and Ozu cuts to Setsuko continuing her aunt's movement at exactly the same spot on the screen (fig. 144). Finally, in one scene, a whiskey bottle jumps obligingly along the frame edge as so many items will in later works.

141.

What Did the Lady Forget? also deserves attention for its comic use of sound. David Owens points out that now Ozu incorporates dialogue more fully into his film, exploiting the characters' chatter and Setsuko's grating Osaka accent.[51] There are noise gags, such as Chiyo's cooing attempts to laugh without making wrinkles. But most of the humor involves music. Setsuko sings a pop song as she reads a magazine featuring Marlene Dietrich, while the boys sing a mocking song whenever they defeat an adult, which is fairly often. Most evidently, here is the funniest score for any Ozu film, a mixture of a lilting waltz for strings and flute and two lazy, insolent Hawaiian themes for electric guitar and banjo. The latter tunes are associated with the *moga* Setsuko, one entering over shots of her littered room and a second recurring during her strolls with Okada and Komiya. (In Japan banjos and electric guitars were associated with American jazz and were to be banned outright in 1944.[52]) The twang of the guitar also punctuates the scene when the wind blows Komiya's study door open and Setsuko takes the opportunity to punch him in the stomach. By the film's end, though, the second guitar tune has taken on a mournful quality as Setsuko looks out over the city she must leave. In this context, a Hawaiian-flavored melody effectively evokes the *moga*'s Tokyo nostalgia. Here *What Did the Lady Forget?* reveals Ozu, not for the only time, as akin to Tati. Although direct influence is unlikely, Ozu's sound gags look forward to the French director's, and the device of defamiliarizing clichéd music by moving it through satire to genuine emotional expressiveness will emerge very powerfully in *Play Time*.

142.

Structurally, the film sets the pattern for how Ozu will insert music into his subsequent films. When he wants an abrupt juxtaposition, he will cut directly to a new scene with the music starting exactly at the cut. Otherwise, music will sneak into the last shot of a scene, signalling that a transition is coming up. We have already seen (pp. 67–9) how this process shapes the viewer's hypotheses. We might now notice that, at this early a date, Ozu is already calculating editing, music, and speech to a rigorous rhythm. He cuts from Komiya's household to a shot of two topcoats on the wall at Okada's room (10 seconds long), and then to a shot of golf clubs beside the coats (also 10 seconds); music has accompanied both these. Cut to a shot of Komiya and Okada eating beside the window as rain pours down; the music gradually fades out; and ten seconds into the shot, Koniya raises his head to speak. No less than Eisenstein, Ozu realizes that music can be integrated very precisely with a film's overall visual rhythm.

143.

Most of the comic uses of technique, of course, serve the film's primary purpose, to satirize bourgeois manners in the fashion of *The Marriage Circle*. Ozu spares little. He mocks the bourgeoisie's obsession with cleanliness (Mitsuko wants a clean young tutor, Tokiko tells Setsuko to wash behind her ears); its eclectic bric-a-brac (Komiya's study houses samurai armor, a fencing

144.

foil, and a J & B mug); its acquisitive conception of tradition (Setsuko swaps her purse for a geisha's); its bluntness (Tokiko, assuming her guests are leaving, hurries them away with a thoroughly bored invitation to linger; Komiya coolly tells a patient, 'You'll never have children,' and hangs up). Sometimes Ozu mixes his satire with *nansensu* silliness. Visiting Tokiko, Chiyo grows hungry. Her hostess offers a biscuit, but Chiyo says that's not filling enough. She elaborately describes what she'd like, eel with rice, and when Tokiko agrees to fix it, Chiyo adds: 'And if that's not enough, I'll have a biscuit too.' On a later visit, when Tokiko has stepped out, Chiyo treats her hostess's house as a restaurant, whispering to Mitsuko: 'Ask for the eel. They do wonders with it.'

As in Lubitsch's films, no character is a paragon, and none escapes the director's irony. Ozu maintains comic detachment by an oblique opening (starting with Chiyo, a secondary character) and by an omniscient movement from one batch of characters to another – both strategies which will become important in later films. He relies on our knowledge of the topography of a well-to-do house. In addition, he uses the bourgeoisie's fascination with tradition to motivate the insertion of two passages of performance, an offscreen kabuki show and an onscreen geisha dance, which by virtue of their length and gravity counterpoint the superficial culture of the rich. In most previous films Ozu has satirized 'traditional Japanese' iconography; here it is handled respectfully, as it often will be from *Late Spring* onward.

The central issue is, as often in Ozu, the loss of masculine authority, but here it breeds a peculiar rebellion. From the start, these men are henpecked. Chiyo orders her husband to drive straight to his office, and Komiya sits passively by when Tokiko forbids Setsuko to smoke. Even Okada, Komiya's assistant, is diffident, short on brains, and no match for Tokiko or Setsuko. The plot revolves around a two-faced deception of Tokiko. Komiya pretends to go on a golfing trip but instead stays in Tokyo carousing. Much depends upon a fake postcard Komiya had his friend Sugiyama send from the golf course: the card says the weather is fine, but it has rained all weekend. Setsuko learns of the hoax and forces Komiya to take her out on the town. When she comes back drunk, Tokiko blames Okada and expects Komiya, upon his return, to discipline Setsuko. Such a comic contrivance, reminiscent of Lubitsch plot mechanics, gives Ozu the chance to make Setsuko, the *moga*, the tool for revealing bourgeois hypocrisy. When Komiya pretends to scold her, Setsuko is disgusted ('What a good liar!'). She upbraids him for his cowardice, telling him to hit Tokiko. 'I couldn't,' he says, and falls asleep at the bar.

Still, the seeds of male resistance are there too, when in the first scene Fujio tells his mother he doesn't want to come in to listen to a lot of women's chatter. Setsuko and Komiya come home to Tokiko and when Tokiko starts to cross-examine them, he slaps her. 'You're the insolent one. I treat you well and you walk all over me.' What makes this different from Thurberesque sexism? First, Tokiko is shaken but she does not capitulate. Second, Ozu's script introduces a quick series of ironic twists. As if stunned by what actual violence is like, Setsuko comes to Tokiko immediately, apologizes, tells her about the golf hoax, and admits that her uncle is in error. Then Komiya comes to his wife and apologizes as well: 'Hitting you was wrong.' She apologizes too and all is

almost well again. Delighted, Komiya scampers upstairs balancing a newspaper on his finger, only to be confronted by Setsuko, who criticizes him for
apologizing. 'The man should be stronger.' Like Noriko in *Late Spring*, this
moga turns out to be more old-fashioned than her elders. Komiya assures her
that men should not treat their wives badly, but then adds a pragmatic
evasion: 'They like to think they're in control.' Ozu grants the impossibility of
a patriarchal authority grounded in violence, but he will not spare the
husband who justifies his subjection by invoking the invisible hand, what
Komiya calls the 'opposite approach'.

The film's last three scenes trace out comically varied responses to
Komiya's slap. In a store, the three wives discuss the incident, expressing
respect for an assertive husband. Tokiko will buy Komiya a new tie, since he is,
after all, still 'a young man'. In a café, Setsuko and Okada discuss the 'opposite'
approach: will they use it when they marry? She warns him that if he does,
she'll use the 'opposite-opposite' approach. Finally, at home, Tokiko coyly
invites Komiya to an evening of romance. (An earlier scene has presented a
parallel instance of male potency regained when Chiyo confesses that she's
expecting a child.) Setsuko's visit and the reassertion of masculine authority
that it precipitates reunite the couple on a middle ground between patriarchy
and abasement. What did the lady forget? Sugiko forgot to appreciate her
husband, while Setsuko forgot that modern men cannot and should not
behave like samurai. What did the film forget? It forgot that previous films
placed the decline of masculine authority within a broader historical context –
the failure of Meiji, the impossibility of *risshin shusse*, the breakdown of the
family. In this social comedy, the problem can be solved by a little tolerance
between husband and wife. The dividends in humor and satire are great, but
even an irony that spares no character goes only so far.

1939

Ochazuke no aji
The Flavor of Green Tea over Rice

Reading of political efforts to control Japanese citizens' thinking, writing, and actions during the 1930s, one might think that no one escaped indoctrination.[53] Japan's 'dark valley', the fifteen-year war from 1931 to 1945, seems one long period of repression and censorship. Yet this image is not entirely accurate. Throughout the 1930s, there was much more passive resistance, covert evasion, sheer indifference, and outright defiance than is generally recognized.[54] In the realm of cinema, for example, during the period in which individualism was supposedly rejected and familial loyalty was promoted, there appeared films like *Composition Class* (1938), *Robo no ishi* (*A Pebble by the Wayside*, 1938), and *Hataraku ikka* (*The Whole Family Works,* 1939), all of which took as their theme the fulfillment of individual aspirations, often in the teeth of paternal or social directives. The film industry, like other older business enterprises, was not entirely sympathetic to the military cliques that had overruled party government, and filmmakers were not always or easily tamed. It was not really until 1939, with the passage of the Motion Picture Law, that scenarios were censored before shooting and a more rigid control came into place. Ozu was one casualty of the new system.

When he returned from China in 1939, he and Ikeda wrote a script, *He's Going to Nanking*, later to be called *The Flavor of Green Tea over Rice*. It would not be a battlefront film, which Ozu had no interest in making. ('I'm still young.') The script recalls the central situation of *Until the Day We Meet Again* and the marital comedy of *What Did the Lady Forget?* A snobbish wife dislikes the vulgarity of her husband, a down-to-earth businessman. The plot turns on his receipt of a draft notice. He takes the news calmly, but his wife is upset. On their last night together, the couple make rice and tea and share an intimate dinner. Annoyed by her husband's nonchalance, the wife demands to know if he's afraid of death. 'What difference does it make?' he replies. 'Your life is on the line whether you're in Tokyo or on the battlefield.' He explains that he puts his whole effort into working for the company. The wife bursts into tears and the husband abruptly slaps her. He criticizes her selfishness. Suddenly she feels happy, loving him wholly for the first time. The film concludes with a scene of her telling her friends about what happened; they agree that most men would behave the same way.

Although Ozu borrows the slapping scene and the admiring chorus of the wife's chums from the climax of *What Did the Lady Forget?*, the film is obviously no mere comedy. Even an autobiographical reading will not do justice to it. (Sato argues that it expresses Ozu's own egotistical devotion to his craft: 'Everything I do, I do to the utmost.'[55]) In summary, *The Flavor of Green Tea over Rice* would seem to be an ideal piece of home-front morale-boosting. Like other Shochiku films of the period, it would have shown the bourgeoisie as loyal Japanese, serving their country through their business transactions. To judge from the available synopses, the husband becomes a synthesis of all Japanese men: wealthy but with plebeian tastes, a businessman who will become a soldier. Slapping the wife is not a gesture to shock her into respecting him, as in *What Did the Lady Forget?*; it is a reminder of her patriotic duty.

It is all the more surprising, then, that the industry's censorship board refused to pass the script. The official reason was that the film portrayed the couple eating homely rice rather than the 'red rice' traditionally reserved for seeing off a war-bound husband. This objection would seem to miss the point of green tea and rice as a basic symbol uniting all Japanese. The film violated other directives of the 1937-1938 Home Ministry Code in that it was somewhat frivolous and contained many Occidental words and customs. More broadly, the script may not have seemed to fit any contemporary genre. The Ofuna comedy of manners was rare now, and the film's humorous aspects were out of keeping with the aims of war films and home-front 'women's pictures.' Ozu's cinematographer Atsuta has said that the refusal of Ozu's script marked the beginning of Shochiku's decision to cooperate with the military,[56] but certainly earlier Shochiku efforts like Shimazu's all-star *The Japanese* (1938) were already firmly in the national-policy mold. In any event, in 1952 Ozu made *The Flavor of Green Tea over Rice* from a revised version of the 1939 script.

1941

Todake no kyodai
Brothers and Sisters of the Toda Family

Shochiku Ofuna studio. Story: Tadao Ikeda, Yasujiro Ozu. Cinematography: Yuharu Atsuta. Art direction: Tatsuo Hamada. Music: Senji Ito. Lighting: Kazuni Naito. Cast: Hideo Fujino (*Shintaro Toda*), Ayako Katsuragi (*Mrs Toda*), Mitsuko Yoshikawa (*Chizuru*), Tatsuo Saito (*Shinichiro*), Kuniko Miyake (*Kazuko*), Shin Saburi (*Shojiro*), Yoshiko Tsubouchi (*Ayako*), Mieko Takamine (*Setsuko*), Kayoko Kuwano (*Tokiko*), Sokichi Kawamura (*Suzuki*), Choko Iida (*Kiyo*), Masao Hayama (*Ryokichi*), Mayuko Takagi (*Mitsuko*), Chishu Ryu (*friend*), Takeshi Sakamoto (*an antique dealer*), Reiko Tani (*a photographer*). 11 reels, 2,896 meters. Surviving prints: 105 min. Released 1 March 1941. Script, negative, and prints in existence.

After the unexpected death of their father, the Toda brothers and sisters discover that they must sell his home and care for their mother and youngest sister Setsuko. After the youngest brother Shojiro leaves to work in Tianjin (Tientsin), Mrs Toda and Setsuko are shunted from one household to another. The mother and daughter end up in the family's dilapidated seaside villa. On the first anniversary of Toda's death, Shojiro returns. He criticizes the selfishness of his brothers and sisters and proposes to take his mother and Setsuko back to China. In an epilogue, Setsuko offers to arrange his marriage to her working-class friend Tokiko.

To what extent can Ozu's 1941-1942 films be seen as propaganda for the war that Japan was waging in China and the Pacific? Joan Mellen has worked up a strong case for Ozu's ideological involvement, and her arguments about *Toda Family* can be reduced to three points. The father is a 'formidable patriarch', and his death threatens the family system, which is then restored by Shojiro, proving the power of male authority. Secondly, China is not treated as a war-ravaged country but rather as a spot where Shojiro has a good chance for business advancement. Finally, the film's references to German culture show the extent to which Japanese society had become 'Teutonized'.[1]

Mellen is certainly right to point to certain of the film's symptomatic absences. In Japan's attempt to subdue China, military forces seized Chinese factories for private firms, and by 1941 Tianjin was an occupied city. The 'Teutonic' elements, however, are treated as jokes, to some degree like the horse that is associated with Germany in *The Only Son*. Moreover, there is no evidence that Mr Toda is a strong patriarch. The film is much more centrally about the way in which Toda's death constitutes a test of the children's devotion to the family.

The test takes place within a society redefining itself. Since mid-1937, the government had mobilized all sectors of life to support the army's push into

China. Under the new order of wartime Japan, frivolity had to be put aside and the nation had to be 'disciplined spiritually'. Although city dwellers continued their fascination with Western fads, authorities were warning that English words and women with permanents could corrupt the authentic Japanese spirit. Price controls and shortages compelled citizens to practice thrift: 'Extravagance is the enemy'.[58] A new faith was placed in the young, with schools emphasizing martial calisthenics and community projects. A 1941 Education Ministry handbook for young people attacked 'individualism, liberalism, utilitarianism, and materialism.'[59]

Under such conditions, Ozu's film shows, Japanese tradition must be recast. To remain loyal to your nation you must criticize the conduct of your own family. According to the prewar family code, the main family – that of the eldest son – inherited the bulk of the property and was obliged to provide for needy and elderly members. Shinichiro Toda recognizes this when he asserts that as the older son he must take in Mother and Setsuko. But what is remarkable here is that the elder siblings – the most powerful, mature, and supposedly worthy of respect – fail in their responsibility, while the youngest, weakest, and supposedly most carefree, Shojiro and Setsuko, do not. Setsuko passes the test spontaneously, while Shojiro comes to a complex recognition of how he has neglected his duty to his parents. The film *is* patriarchal, and does bear the traces of wartime ideology; but in the sense that the new Japan will fulfill its parental obligations better than did the old.

Mellen also, I think, misses an important element of social criticism in the film: its attack on a decadent bourgeois lifestyle. Sato points out that the film shows a resistance to government policy by dealing with the lives of the rich, a suspect subject at the time.[60] Ozu depicts this world with some harshness. In the households of Shinichiro, Chizuo, and Ayako, disregard for their widowed mother goes hand in hand with frivolity and wastefulness. Again, the correct criticism comes from the mouths of the youngest. It is not simply that Shojiro becomes identified with Father; Setsuko and Tokiko, women of the New Japan, reject upper-class decadence and are thus linked to the mother. Thus the film is truly about the brothers and sisters of the family. As we shall see, the new Japanese order presented at the film's close includes both old and young, male and female.

In its effort to embody the new spirit of Japan, the film develops elements present in earlier Shochiku works. Shimazu's *The Japanese* (1938) told a story of how some young people criticize their jazz-crazed peers and continue the military tradition forged in the Russo-Japanese war. In Minoru Shibuya's *Atarashiki kazoku* (*A New Family*, 1939), the young reporter played by Shin Saburi struggles against a domineering father played by Tatsuo Saito. Kozaburo Yoshimura's *Danryu* (*Warm Current*, 1939) featured Saburi as a new hospital administrator who straightens out the tangled lives around him and who incidentally attracts the nurse played by Mieko Takamine. Shimazu's *A Brother and His Younger Sister* (1939) paired Saburi and Kuniko Miyake as husband and wife, with Takamine as his sister, in a tale of how a decent salaryman tries to keep clear of office politics, resigns in disgust, and moves his family to the new frontier of China. A contemporary critic singled out the last two works as members of an emerging genre of 'city films' from Shochiku

Ofuna, and he included *Toda Family* in the group.[61] It seems likely that after the censorship problems of *The Flavor of Green Tea over Rice* Ozu adapted himself to this trend, perhaps using it as a safety zone much as Mizoguchi used the *Meiji-mono* genre in the same period. Ozu attributed his film's commercial success to the cast, all of whom had appeared in one or more similar efforts. The film's critique of upper-class excesses, implicit in *What Did the Lady Forget?* and *Green Tea*, allowed the studio to present the spectacle of bourgeois life while explicitly condemning it. That Ikeda had written the script of *Warm Current* and that the Shibuya and Shimazu films borrowed heavily from Ozu's style probably also prepared the way for the success of *Toda Family*.

There is much in the film that Ozu will lock into place for later works. He has arrived at the characteristic way in which he will subsequently film the Japanese house: corridor shots through which characters pass, lengthily-held empty shots of rooms or hallways that allow the character time to arrive at a new locale before the narration cuts to that spot. The film's score is a model for the postwar efforts, with its surging, melancholy theme, its string runs and harp glissandi, and its use of the vibraphone to pick out the melody (as at the close of *The Only Son*). Now music will bridge scenes a little more often than in *What Did the Lady Forget?*, and the credits theme reappears at crucial points to underscore motifs associated with Mr Toda – his bird and plants, his photograph, and his villa. Specific motifs are anticipated as well: Shojiro teases an old waitress as other men will in *Equinox Flower* and *An Autumn Afternoon*, while Chizuko's telling her maid to pack mourning clothes anticipates Shige's behavior in *Tokyo Story*. Perhaps most important is the way in which *Toda Family* introduces the extended-family plot structure that would be so important in certain 1950s films. *The Only Son* had utilized a significant range of parallels in parent-child relations, but *Toda Family* goes far beyond this. There are sixteen different characters, including Shojiro's two friends, Setsuko's friend Noriko, the two family servants, and eleven Todas:

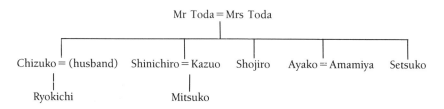

As in *The Only Son*, the breadth of age and experience is very great, and much mention is made of age differences, which run from tiny Mitsuko to sixty-nine-year-old Mr Toda. This vast range of interpersonal relations allows Ozu to compare the reactions of different characters and to trundle Mrs Toda and Setsuko 'down the line' as each branch family takes them in turn. Variants of this compositional strategy will govern *Early Summer*, *Tokyo Story*, *End of Summer*, and *An Autumn Afternoon*.

From a formal standpoint, the extended family has several functions and effects. First, it creates considerable retardation, building up a rhythm of expectation as one household after another finds Mrs Toda and Setsuko a nuisance. We could in fact divide the film into four broad sections on the basis of the mother and daughter's shifts of household: Mr Toda's death and its aftermath; the stay with Shinichiro and Kazuko; the stay with Chizuko; the stay at the villa. Second, the extended-family device creates neat parallels among the siblings and among their spouses. Ozu will occasionally stress a parallel by means of crosscutting, as in the sequence in which phone calls notify the various households of Mr Toda's collapse.

In addition, the disparity among branch families brings forth a fairly tight scenario construction. There are strong dialogue hooks (as in the references to the potted plants and the mockingbird), and considerable foreshadowing, as when Amamiya is reluctant to visit Mr Toda after his collapse, or when early in the film he mentions the decrepit villa. The retardatory effect of the branch families creates 'subplots of annoyance', scenes in which Setsuko and Mrs Toda get on the nerves of their hosts. These include isolated incidents, such as Mrs Toda cutting a dahlia from Kazuo's garden, and more prolonged arguments, such as that between Setsuko and Kazuo about the piano playing. In order to strengthen the unity of the central portion of the film, during which Shojiro is absent from Japan, the script braids some of these subplots together. Kazuo asks Mrs Toda and Setsuko to do some shopping for her; while out of the house, Mrs Toda visits Chizuko's son Ryokichi, who is playing hooky. This will become an issue only much later, when Chizuko finds out that Mrs Toda has kept Ryokichi's secret.

The extended-family plot also motivates a constant shifting from one knot of characters to another, and thus a highly unrestricted range of knowledge. This in turn permits surprising ellipses, as when at the outset the family outing is skipped over, or when Mrs Toda and Setsuko approach Ayako to tell her they've decided not to move in with them (an act which startles us as much as it surprises her and her husband). The arbitrary restriction upon knowledge permits suspense as well. Because we do not follow Shojiro to Tianjin, his accusation of his brother and sisters comes as a vivid indication of his new maturity.

Yet another effect of the extended-family plot structure is to split the functions of protagonist between two characters, Setsuko and Shojiro. Setsuko undergoes less of a character change, figuring throughout as a loyal daughter who seeks to take care of her mother, even if it means getting a job. Her devotion is contrasted to the selfishness and thoughtlessness of the other siblings; at one point Ozu's mise-en-scène nicely likens her to Kazuo's maid. Later, tidying up after Kazuko's party, Setsuko stares at the untouched fancy cake and comments: 'It would make Tokiko angry to see this!' Her criticism is ratified by Mrs Toda when she sees a barely-cut apple. 'How fastidious!' This critique, mild in the mouths of weak family members, will be amplified in Shojiro's denunciation at the film's climax.

The film's other protagonist undergoes more character change. In the first scene, Shojiro is established as happy-go-lucky. He is late for the family portrait and he has so often fouled up picture-taking that Mr Toda has hired a professional photographer. Relations between him and his father are strained. Ryokichi reports that Mr Toda is angry, and Shojiro replies calmly: 'Don't scare me.' He misses his father's death because of a fishing trip, and his behavior at

145.

146.

147.

148.

the funeral switches from outrageous casualness to matter-of-fact resignation ('*Sake* killed him') and then to outward shows of piety (he offers incense and prays). He later explains his reactions: 'He died so suddenly. I don't know if I'm sad or not.' In a later scene he admits to his friends that his father died just when he had ceased to scare him. What now saddens him is, as so often in Ozu, childhood nostalgia: his memory of Mr Toda in that very restaurant, dining while a fly lights on his hand. Shojiro has vowed to go to China and work hard – as a proof, the dialogue suggests, of his claim to his mother: 'I could have been better if he'd lived a little longer.' Shojiro's eventual alliance with Setsuko and Mrs Toda is also hinted at by the very untypical stratagem of optical point-of-view. As Shojiro packs to leave for China, a shot of Mrs Toda from the rear is motivated by a subsequent shot of Setsuko looking (figs. 145–6). Three shots later, after Mrs Toda has left, Shojiro comforts Setsuko, and now her back is to us, as if from his optical angle (figs. 147–8).

Near the end of the film Shojiro reappears. At the ceremony celebrating the first anniversary of Toda's death, he comes in late – a parallel to his tardiness for the photography session and his delayed arrival at Toda's funeral. He settles down unpretentiously beside the servants. Ozu privileges him by again letting his glance structure the découpage. Shots of him surveying the scene alternate with shots of various family members and friends. This visual centrality becomes verbal authority in the next scene, when the family eats its celebratory meal. Shojiro dismisses the maids. He criticizes his family for letting Setsuko and Mrs Toda move to the villa. He tells them they are insincere and reminds them that father would not have approved. Pair by pair he sends them packing, until only he and Setsuko and their mother remain. He eats calmly, talking as if his father knew of his action but musing that if the others mend their ways, 'then Father will forgive my behavior.' The prodigal son returns from China in his military tunic and becomes a tough spokesman for traditions that those at home have forgotten. Soon he will suggest Tianjin as a place free of the hypocrisy and selfishness of Japan. Patriarchal this film certainly is, but here a 'traditional' view of filial duty is injected with a new desire to break out of the stultifying false traditions of the contemporary bourgeoisie.

This narrative and didactic structure is filled out by characteristic Ozu motifs. The hats that synecdochically represent the mourners are echoed when Shojiro claps his hat on Setsuko's head – Ozu's breathtaking variant on the fedora-wearing woman icon. (See p. 41.) The plants and birdcage get varied parametrically, marking Setsuko's and her mother's itinerant household: at Shinichiro's (figs. 149–50), then at Chizuko's (figs. 151–2), and then at the villa (fig. 153). The mockingbird will also serve as a minor motif, as in the shot of Setsuko listening while Chizuko berates Mrs Toda (fig. 154). Yet just as characteristic is Ozu's refusal to show the commemorative photo that is taken in the first scene, or to establish the father's mockingbird early in the film. (The plant motif is announced in the film's second shot.) And the sea becomes a key motif only in the last few scenes.

Stylistically the film grows fairly directly out of *What Did the Lady Forget?* As in the earlier film, Ozu often employs dialogue hooks or action comparisons to link scenes. Mrs Toda and Ryokichi eat; cut to Setsuko and

149.

150.

151.

152.

153.

154.

Tokiko in a coffee shop. There are relatively few intermediate spaces between scenes, and most function to signal the locale straightforwardly. (For once Ozu abandons the use of signs to establish settings.) The most striking series of intermediate spaces remains denotatively functional, often indicating, by a shot of a clock, the passage of time. One scene brackets the phone calls among households by a shot of a grandfather clock at Shinichiro's (it is 9.20) and by a shot of an antique clock at Amamiya's (reading 9.47). Here the ticking anticipates the rhythm of the funeral drum in the next scene, and the emphasis on time echoes Amamiya's comments about aging. More prominent in *Toda Family* is Ozu's habit of creating the *effect* of intermediate spaces by lingering on shots after characters have left the frame. Because Shochiku hurried him, Ozu claims, he was forced to film lengthier takes.[62] (The film's average shot length, 13.3 seconds, represents a significant increase from *The Only Son*, ASL 9 seconds, and from *What Did the Lady Forget?*, ASL 11.5 seconds.) Thus Ozu frames figures in long-shot and holds establishing and reestablishing shots much longer than in his previous work. During a long passage when Shojiro is packing to leave, Setsuko walks about the frame and eventually winds up at the right edge – a tactic that would be very unlikely in the silent films, dominated as they were by a 'piecemeal' approach to staging movement within the set. The new tactic lets Ozu prey upon our expectations, as when, after Kazuko's party is over, Setsuko and Mrs Toda walk down a corridor and leave the shot. After a pause the lights go out. Then we see another shot of the room in which the party was held, and while we wait for a

155.

156.

157.

158.

character to enter, the lights go out. (The use of lighting to create a similarly 'naturalized' fade-out occurs at the end of *What Did the Lady Forget?* as well.)

As if to compensate for a reliance upon longer takes and more distant framings, Ozu complicates *Toda Family*'s style by the use of oblique compositions and blocked views. He will begin a scene showing only a beer bottle and an elbow in long shot (fig. 155) and will cut Shojiro's friends off by a wall (fig. 156). The temple anniversary ceremony is a permutational orgy of opaque compositions, while in the next scene the waitresses impede our view of Shojiro until he asks them to leave (figs. 157–8). This not only sharpens out attention but prepares for a humorous twist at the film's very end.

We are back in the villa, and the introductory shots permute the earlier lead-in. There we had a shot of the seashore, then a shot of the wall, then a long-shot of Setsuko hanging out washing. Now we have only the wall, then a corridor shot including the potted plant and the mockingbird. Ozu handles what follows with terrific lightness. After Setsuko, Mrs Toda, and Kiyo all agree to go to Tianjin, Shojiro asks the mockingbird too. The major motifs come to rest. Setsuko hangs up the hat that Shojiro had once plopped on her head. He will find her a husband, as he had promised at his departure – 'A sunburned, well-built type, not too handsome'. She in turn will arrange his marriage to Tokiko, which he halfheartedly resists: 'I'll marry if Hitler does.' Tokiko shows up, for the first time wearing kimono rather than a Western suit. Shojiro is too shy to meet her, comparing his weakness to Siegfried's. Setsuko has a sharp response to these Teutonic conceits: 'Stop that nonsense.' She goes out to meet Tokiko, receives a gift of dried fish eggs, and returns to the table where Shojiro was sitting. The norm of oblique framing leads us to expect that he is there, just off frame left, but as Setsuko enters, Ozu tracks back, revealing that Shojiro is gone. Kiyo reports that he left in a hurry. Cut to the seashore, the element 'missing' from the shots leading into the scene. Shojiro flees down the sand, but then he hesitates and strides pointlessly to and fro. On this image of comic indecision the film ends.

Propaganda, no doubt, but not of a simple sort. In a villa the new Japan is forged out of courageous old women, dutiful young women who see through bourgeois hypocrisy, and a young ne'er-do-well who learns to work hard and honor his family obligations. We are told that the other Toda siblings have apologized and will welcome Setsuko and their mother back home, but Ozu keeps their change of heart offscreen so as to stress the creation of a model, purified community outside the city. Masculine authority, so often lost in Ozu's films, is regained by a diffident, casual youth who likes fishing. Two years later, Tanizaki's serialized novel, *The Makioka Sisters* – which strongly resembles Ozu's extended-family film – would be suppressed because censors judged its mundane drama of family routine too unrelated to the war effort.[63] Ozu's film preserves itself from that charge. If, as Ozu has suggested, *A Mother Should Be Loved* was really about the fall of a family, *Brothers and Sisters of the Toda Family* is about a family's decline and rise, its reintegration under the leadership of the real guardians of tradition, the young.

1942

Chichi ariki
There Was a Father

Shochiku Ofuna studio. Script: Tadao Ikeda, Takao Yanai, Yasujiro Ozu. Cinematography: Yuharu Atsuta. Art director: Tatsuo Hamada. Editing: Yoshiyasu Hamamura. Lighting: Kazumi Naito. Music: Kyoichi Saiki. Cast: Chishu Ryu (*Shuhei Horikawa*), Shuji Sano (*Ryohei*), Haruhiko Tsugawa (*Ryohei as a child*), Shin Saburi (*Yasutaro Kurokawa*), Takeshi Sakamoto (*Makoto Hirata*), Mitsuko Mito (*Fumi*), Masayoshi Otsuka (*Seiichi*), Shinichi Himori (*Minoru Uchida*). 2,588 meters. Surviving prints: 87 min. Released 1 April 1942. Script, duplicate negative, and prints in existence.

The schoolteacher Horikawa leads his students on an outing, during which one boy drowns. Horikawa takes responsibility and resigns. He moves to Ueda with his son Ryohei. Insisting that duty and striving for excellence take precedence over living together, Horikawa puts Ryohei in a dormitory while he goes to work in Tokyo. Over the years the father and son see each other sporadically as Horikawa works to advance his son's education. Ryohei graduates from college and begins teaching in Akita. During Ryohei's twenty-fifth year, he meets his father at a spa and later comes to Tokyo for a visit while he takes his conscription exam. Soon after a reunion of his former students, Horikawa is stricken ill and dies, still advising Ryohei to stick to his duty. An epilogue shows Ryohei, now married to Fumiko, the daughter of a friend of his father's. The couple are riding a train back to Akita, bearing his father's ashes.

This is an earnest piece of work, with almost no humor and virtually none of the playful narration that is present to the very last shot of *Brothers and Sisters of the Toda Family*. *There Was a Father* is more didactic than *I Was Born, But . . .* , and at least as solemn about Japanese tradition as *Story of Floating Weeds*. One can sympathize with Mellen's criticism of the film,[64] for its ideological work mixes explicit appeals to patriarchy, Buddhism, and 'Japaneseness'. But it is able to make these appeals by virtue of particular patterns that have already emerged in early Ozu films.

In this movie full of males, father knows best. Horikawa decides his own life, his son's education, and each man's duty. Ryohei acquiesces because his father is, simply, right. Obedience to duty causes pain to both, and the film does not mitigate this; but the pair know that they must endure it. Ozu's parallels straightforwardly reiterate the father/son motif. In a rare piece of distantly-fetched exposition, Horikawa tells of how his father sold his house to send him to school. As the syuzhet unfolds, he will make comparable sacrifices for Ryohei. Teaching in Akita, the grown-up Ryohei grants a pupil permission to go home to visit his father, and a scene among the boys, who stare off at a distant train, demonstrates that they have the same longing for home as Ryohei still has. (The train motif links fathers and sons again and again.) The two fishing scenes parallel father and son at two stages of their lives, while within each scene the two characters are likened by a 'naturalization' of Ozu's acting-in-unison technique: they cast their lines in perfect synchronization. Horikawa's friend Hirata also has a son, Seiichi, and at the class reunion the two old fathers discover that all their pupils have married, that many have become fathers, and that one has to be absent because his wife just gave birth to . . . a boy. Even the film's running gag bears on the theme: at each school, Ryohei's classmates seem determined to call his father 'badger' and him 'son of a badger'. At the film's epilogue, riding a train with his bride Fumiko, Ryohei suggests that her father come to live with them. Ozu's later shot of the bundle of Horikawa's ashes on the luggage rack suggests that this is the last journey the son will take with his father.

Ozu's characteristic strategies of narration and style wring the maximum out of this simple relationship. He films the father's announcement of going to Tokyo so that smoke curls up in the background; this cliché of evanescence looks forward to the steam in the scenes of Horikawa and Ryohei meeting at the spa. Ozu also introduces and interrupts the spa episode with shots of rocks in a stream that both recall the fishing scene and momentarily mislead us about the site of the upcoming story action. More conventionally, he reserves his close-ups for dramatic impact. The first close view of Horikawa comes when at the boy's funeral he learns that the parents are coming. Later, Ryohei opens a book and a photograph of his father is revealed. Ozu will use his *sojikei* technique to liken the two fathers Horikawa and Hirata when, at the reunion, both lift their *sake* cups and drink in unison. The tardy entry of a motif is well exemplified when, near the end of the film, Horikawa remarks on the scar Ryohei got as a child. A Hollywood film would have shown or at least mentioned this event earlier. And in the epilogue on the train, Ozu cunningly cheats our expectations by apparently ending the film with a shot of the train speeding off before cutting back to the train carriage, prolonging and intensifying the final link of father and son: a shot of Ryohei turning gravely to the window; a shot of Horikawa's ashes among other luggage on the rack; and a final shot of the train vanishing in the distance.

In Chapter 2, I argued that Ozu's films were not all and not equally 'Buddhist'. There can be no doubt, however, that just as Shinto iconography permeates *Story of Floating Weeds*, this film frequently draws upon Buddhist imagery. Many intermediate spaces consist of still-life shots of Buddhist *stupas* (fig. 159), squat stone pillars consisting of stacked solids, each with a symbolic value: the cube (earth) surmounted by a sphere (water), a pyramid (fire), a crescent (air), and a sphere with a pointed tip (space). By cutting away to them when the boys hike on the road, when Yoshida drowns, and when the young Ryohei fishes with his father, Ozu connotes an overriding harmony and calm. On the boys' outing they visit the Great Buddha statue in Kamakura and have a commemorative photo taken. We see Buddhist funeral rites, complete with drum and chanting, and for a time Horikawa lives in a Buddhist temple with a priest. Upon visiting his father, Ryohei pays his respects to his dead mother at the family *butsudan*, and shortly Horikawa

159.

smilingly does the same. We must recall here not only Ozu's earlier, satiric use of such imagery but also the fact that by 1942 Buddhism had become a distinct political and ideological force. In March of 1941, only a year before *There Was a Father* was released, the Great Japan Buddhist Association (Dai Nihon Bukkyokai) was formed, with the purpose of supporting the government and the war effort. After Pearl Harbor, temples sent priests to war plants and embarked on fund drives to pay for aircraft.[65] In this film, Buddhism operates not as a vague transcendental atmosphere but as a historically specific construct and a citation for particular ideological purposes.

More broadly, *There Was a Father* participates in ideological production by virtue of its constant references to 'Japaneseness'. The school outing is a veritable itinerary of traditionally revered spots: the Imperial Palace, the shrine of the Emperor Meiji, the Yasukuni shrine dedicated to valiant soldiers, the Kamakura Buddha, and Lake Ashinoko, across which – as one postcard-view in the film shows – one can see majestic Mount Fuji. The Ashinoko area contains many stone Buddhist images, including the *stupas* which Ozu uses as intermediate spaces. The road down which the boys hike is the famous Tokaido highway, immortalized in poetry and woodblock prints and granted a remarkably empty shot by Ozu. Because Horikawa's father was a lecturer in Chinese classics to the castle dwellers, Horikawa becomes linked to the traditional past, as is Hirata, by virtue of his current job of editing a history of Tokyo. The film's very first image, two women passing on a bridge and framed by tree branches, introduces a picturesque, self-conscious 'Japaneseness' closer to Mizoguchi's late 1930s work than to Ozu's previous films. The cutaways to the river during the spa episode and the shots of the steaming tub there evoke the Shinto purification rite of *misogi*, or ablution; as we shall see, purity becomes a thematic issue in the film. The castle at Ueda, the *go* motif, shots of temple gardens, mention of a classic verse about primroses blooming by a river – all cite intrinsic Japanese traditions. No reference to Western life – not even the Germanic references of *Toda Family* – mars this placid, insular world. Go to the museum, Horikawa urges the grown-up Ryohei, and look at the paintings: 'Traditional Japanese art is profoundly beautiful.'

Tradition, however, is always selective, and this film's Japaneseness consists of self-sacrifice and acceptance of one's rank. Horikawa's doctrine of supreme effort leads him to quit his job – 'I didn't do my best' – even though no one blames him. The first words he speaks in the film reveal his austerity, when he insists that his old shoes will still last. This attitude had a particular significance in 1942, not only because of the increasing deprivations suffered on the home front but also because, as John Dower has shown, austerity became identified with the sanctified concept of purification. *Yase-gaman*, or 'emaciated endurance', came to be treated as a spiritual exercise which would prove the Japanese superior to other peoples.[66] Horikawa's insistence on separating himself from his son becomes a domestic analogue of the toughening of the soul that the war required of every citizen.

Along with purification went the notion of 'proper place', of commitment to one's allotted task, no matter how lowly it might be. 'Diminish the self, do public good' went one slogan. The family ideology was particularly apt for exploitation along these lines. One could trace the idea back to the principles of Confucianism, but the pertinent document is the *Kokutai no Hongi* (*Cardinal Principles of the National Entity of Japan*), published in 1937 as an official statement of government ideology. The *Cardinal Principles* put the family at the center of Japanese culture and emphasized the adage 'Be filial to your parents.'[67] Once one's proper place in the family is accepted, social peace will reign. 'In order to bring national harmony to fruition, there is no way but for every person in the nation to do his allotted duty and to exalt it.'[68] Horikawa's philosophy might have come straight from this document. 'We each have our jobs,' he tells Ryohei, and duty demands that they stick to them. He makes it clear that Ryohei's teaching is an atonement for his own failure: 'I couldn't do my duty, but you must.' Almost to the last apothegm, the father is a spokesman for 'tradition' as defined by post-1937 government policy. One slogan of the period ran, 'Every day is a work day'; during his collapse, Horikawa tries feebly to rise, saying, 'I never take a day off.' *There Was a Father* received a Bureau of Information award as an outstanding national-policy film.

What the foregoing discussion does not take into account is the way in which the unfolding of the film *modulates into* the wartime propaganda stance. Horikawa's initial motivation is psychological, since his failure to keep the boys off the lake makes him more severe in his dedication to duty. Moreover, his justification of the separation from Ryohei comes straight from *The Only Son*: he will work to earn the money to send his son to high school, and then college. The beginning of the plot identifies Horikawa's self-sacrifice with the stereotype of the late-Meiji parent who sees education as the only way to advance. 'Without schooling you can't become somebody.' But once Ryohei grows up and the story moves into the contemporary period, Horikawa appeals to a new principle, that of doing one's appointed job, no matter how lowly or grim. 'A man has to serve his country.' In this respect, *There Was a Father* is a reversal of *The Only Son*. Whereas Otsune pleads for her son to show ambition, Horikawa urges acceptance. According to Sato, the original script for *There Was a Father* was written in 1937, immediately after *The Only Son*, and he sees it as an implicit answer to the dilemma of the early film. Teaching in a backwater is not demeaning if one's job makes a contribution to society.[69] Thus the later film becomes a critique of the *risshin shusse* careerism depicted in Ozu's early 1930s work, but a positive critique, one whose point is all the more acceptable in that the national-policy message becomes a 'natural' outgrowth of Meiji assumptions about material advancement. Through appeal to character development and psychological motivation, film form unobtrusively links two 'ideologemes' drawn from distinct ideological formations.

To a greater extent than in *Story of Floating Weeds*, the ideological demands of the film deform Ozu's normal operating procedures. The fabula time span stretches over about fifteen years. Many scenes are clustered around two distinct phases – the period around the student's death and the last year of Horikawa's life, when he and Ryohei see each other twice. Most other scenes simply pluck one moment out of several years' time span. The central sequences are organized quite episodically, and they make no use of expository titles (such as in *The Only Son*), so each scene's dialogue must fill us in on what has happened in the interval since the previous scene. On occasion Ozu will take advantage of these 'suppressed' gaps between scenes to surprise us. One scene shows Ryohei studying for his high-school entrance examination and planning to go fishing tomorrow. The next scene shows father and son fishing, but several weeks later, after Ryohei has passed his exam. In general, the central portions of the film require a constant reinforcement of the passage of time, and since they do not make much use of intermediate spaces, each scene carries more of an expository burden than is usual for Ozu. Perhaps Ozu hinted at this quality when he remarked that his cutting sought to invigorate a somewhat muted story, and he was dissatisfied: 'If something is not dramatic . . ., you can't *cut* in a dramatic way.'[70]

At either end of the film, however, stand sequences that clearly issue from Ozu's previous work. Early on is a shot of telegraph poles that has all the ambiguity of certain images in the silent films: it could belong with either the scene before or the scene after. Burch justly praises the boating scene as an example of de-dramatization.[71] The boy's funeral is concluded with a piercing shot of a hanging lamp and flowers that recalls *That Night's Wife* (figs. 30–34, p. 206–7); here, however, a moth bats against the lampshade. It is difficult to discuss other transitions, since some beginnings and endings of reels do not seem to have survived, but the sparing use of intermediate spaces would be consistent with the 'half' transitions that came in with *What Did the Lady Forget?*. The parallel fishing scenes echo a comparable scene in *Story of Floating Weeds*. And Ozu's découpage is by now firmly committed to including reestablishing shots that are set at 180-degrees to the initial establishing shot. In particular, certain elements play off *Toda Family*. The 'opaque' long shot of the class reunion (fig. 160) is a recasting of the staging of the Toda anniversary dinner (p. 288, fig. 157). More playfully, the narration presents Horikawa returning from the dinner pleasantly drunk and asking Ryohei to fetch him a glass of water. Since the same situation precipitated the elder Toda's death, Ozu counts on our having seen the previous film and then cheats our expectations: Horikawa feels fine. (Another trip through the garden of forking paths: one father dies from asking for a glass of water, another does not.) On the next day, when Horikawa *does* collapse, he does so offscreen, and we are distracted by following Ryohei as he loafs about. In general, the film's theme of paternal authority constitutes the explicit 'answer' to all those films of the 1930s that had questioned the father's efficacy. In the films that follow, however, Ozu will return to questioning and mocking paternal power.

There Was a Father is very much a Kido film as well, and it shows how the Kamata/Ofuna flavor could be turned to muted but powerful didactic ends. The familiar cast is headed by Chishu Ryu and Shuji Sano, both of whom had become major stars by 1940. As late as 1937, in Shimizu's *Star Athlete*, the two had portrayed college students; now they play father and son. Ryu's early 1940s career seems to have built upon the ideological purity his character projects in *There Was a Father*; he plays a comparable role in *Rikugun* (*Army*, 1944). In addition, the hospital-bed scene – a staple ingredient of the Kido product – becomes the occasion for Hirokawa's last injunction: 'Work hard.

160.

Don't be sad. I did everything I could . . .' Still, trust Ozu to find an unexpected but utterly typical way to film this deathbed episode.

Many Japanese directors had experimented with fresh ways to stage, shoot, and cut the gathering of weeping relations around the hospital bed. *Haha wa tsuyoi* (*A Mother Is Strong*, 1939) is least fresh, though its spreading of six heads around the frame (fig. 161) is typical of the densely packed space of many Japanese frames. In *Haha no kao* (*A Mother's Profile*, 1939), the bed is shot from far off, and the son's hand rises up from the bedclothes as he expires (fig. 162). The flashy *Three Beauties* (c. 1934) takes an opposite approach, with jammed wide-angle close-ups that anticipate the Welles-Toland look of *Citizen Kane* (fig. 163). Naruse's prolonged sickbed scenes are characteristically eclectic. In *Apart from You* (1933), he places the boy's mother by the window in the foreground, then lets her brush the shade cord as she leaves, creating a filigree line that sweeps through the shot. The climax of the brilliant *Street Without End* (1934) mixes close-up depth shots (fig. 164) with more distant and decentered views (fig. 165). As in other cases, Ozu's handling of his hospital scene derives from this tradition of decorative elaboration of a stereotyped situation, but it becomes more refined and rigorously patterned.

The scene begins with an opaque establishing shot (fig. 166) in which the zigzagging planes lead the eye to Horikawa's head, tiny in the distance. The scene is then cut up into reverse-angle medium-shots as the father delivers his last advice. When Horikawa dies, Ozu cuts back to the long-shot, and the two students rise in the foreground, blocking out the distant characters at the bedside and leaving only Horikawa's head visible (fig. 167). (The act of rising also reveals a new element, of both motivic and compositional significance: the hat on the left, echoing the father's fallen hat at the moment of his attack, now balances the one on the right.) After more analytical cutting, a minutely different master setup centers Ryohei as he leaves (fig. 168). The deployment of a few compositional givens within a range of variations recalls another scene of a dying father, that in *Where Now Are the Dreams of Youth?* (pp. 231–3). This sequence, however, reveals a new austerity that is wholly in keeping with this film and with Ozu's sound style generally. Naruse shuttles his characters around the sets so constantly that a decentered composition like that of fig. 165 is only a fleeting phase; but Ozu's scene consists of just two physical movements, the rising of the men in the foreground and Ryohei's exit. For Ozu, the emotion is concentrated in showing a chair occupied, then showing it vacant. 'Things that were in the frame at the beginning had disappeared, or their position had been changed,' recalled Shinoda. 'He thought that was very dramatic.'[72]

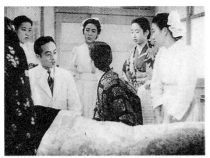

161. *A Mother Is Strong*

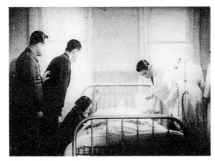

162. *A Mother's Profile*

163. *Three Beauties*

164. *Street Without End*

165. *Street Without End*

166.

167.

168.

1947

Nagaya Shinshiroku
Record of a Tenement Gentleman

Shochiku Ofuna studio. Script: Yasujiro Ozu, Tadao Ikeda. Cinematography: Yuharu Atsuta. Lighting: Haruo Isono. Art director: Tatsuo Hamada. Editing: Yoshi Sugihara. Music: Ichiro Saito. Cast: Choko Iida (*Otane*), Hohi Aoki (*Kohei*), Eitaro Ozawa (*father*), Mitsuko Yoshikawa (*Kikuko*), Sokichi Kawamura (*Tamekichi*), Hideko Mimura (*Ukiko*), Chishu Ryu (*Tashiro*), Takeshi Sakamoto (*Kihachi*), Eiko Takamatsu (*Tome*). 7 reels, 1,973 meters. Surviving prints: 72 min. Released 20 May 1947. Script, negative, and prints in existence.

Otane, a widow who runs a kitchenware shop, is forced to take care of Kohei, a homeless boy. At first she hates him and does all she can to evade responsibility, but he will not be put off. After he wets his bed one night, he runs off and she anxiously searches for him. He turns up, and she realizes that she has grown to love him. She takes him to the zoo and to a photography studio. That night his father appears, relieved to have found his son. Moved both by her concern for the boy and the evident love of father and son, she resolves to adopt a child.

Record of a Tenement Gentleman is both an echo of prewar cinema and a muted specimen of the 'Occupation film'. The very title – more accurately translated as *A Who's Who of the Tenements* – evokes the Kamata flavor of the early 1930s. The settings resemble those glimpsed at the start of Naruse's *Street without End* (1934). The characters, including Otane, Tamekichi the tinker, and Tashiro the freelance fortuneteller, all recall the *shitamachi* milieu of the classic Kido product. The cluttered depth of shots in and around Otane's home owes a great deal to the dense layering of space in 1920s and 1930s Japanese film generally. (See pp. 86–7.) Ozu's series is cited by having Sakamoto return as Kihachi the dyer, now with wife and kids. Here, however, Choko Iida, the mother-figure in the Kihachi films, has become the protagonist. In a sense, this is a sequel to *Passing Fancy*, told from Otane's point of view, as if Kihachi had really left Tomio with her. There are still other recollections of *Passing Fancy*. Tashiro's recitation at the party echoes the *naniwa-bushi* scene in the earlier film, and the opening scene's play with our expectations (initially Tamekichi seems to be demanding a divorce, but then we realize that he's alone) recalls the disruptive opening and equivocal titles of the 1933 film.

At the same time, the film emphasizes contemporary conditions. Tamekichi's daughter Yuki is the first 'postwar woman' to stride through Ozu's work. The characters live on rationing and barter; the boy Kohei scavenges nails and cigarette butts. The plot's central issue, that of finding Kohei's father, makes reference to the problem of war orphans (see also Shimizu's *Hachi no su no kodomo-tachi* (*Children of the Beehive*), 1948). Otane's final speech, in which she accuses people of becoming too selfish, can be taken as the film's moral lesson to a population struggling to survive during what were called the 'bamboo-shoot' days. If the tough Otane can take in a homeless child, so can many others, and the film's last scene in Ueno Park offers tangible evidence that 'we worry too much about our own lives.' The mixture of prewar genre conventions and postwar subject matter yields a new tone that will reappear in Ozu's subsequent films. As Otane and the geisha-house mistress Okiku discuss how hard postwar conditions are on children, they recall their own girlhoods. Yearning for childhood, common in Ozu generally, here gets linked to a nostalgia for prewar life.

The plot, one of Ozu's most linear, is based on the developing relationship of Otane to Kohei. The script makes her eventual acceptance of the boy psychologically plausible by a series of forced maneuvers and vacillations of attitude. Tashiro leaves him with her and runs off, while Tamekichi tricks her into making the search for the boy's father. On the search, she shares her lunch with Kohei, but then tries to leave him behind. She tells Okiku not to give him a pastry – 'It's too good for him' – and she scolds him for wetting his bed. She accuses him of eating her dried persimmons, but then finds him to be innocent, so gives him persimmons to make up for her hasty judgment. The pivot occurs when, after another bed-wetting, Kohei runs off and Otane searches fruitlessly for him. She now realizes he 'had a good heart,' and her sympathy is expressed – as often in Ozu –in gesture: she starts to wriggle her shoulders as he did. (Of course, this has a material cause: she has caught his lice.) Once he returns, she starts to spoil him. But then his father arrives to take him away.

Across this simple story of a change of heart, Ozu lays his characteristic structures. The plot spans five consecutive days, which allows Ozu to create a rhythm of day and night. Within this scheme, his typical parallels flesh out the action. The mornings of the second and fourth days are likened by the bed-wetting episodes, as well as by stylistic handling that I shall consider below. Kihachi's son wins Y2,000 in the lottery, but Kohei doesn't. Otane's attempts at losing Kohei are paralleled by her search for him after he has left. In scene 1, Tashiro brings Kohei to Otane; in scene 12, he brings him back again and the film recycles itself, giving Otane a chance to start fresh. On the way back from searching for the father, Otane buys potatoes; when the father appears, he brings her potatoes. Tamekichi's initial monologue and Tashiro's recited story form thematic parallels *en abîme*, since both involve separation. As usual, Ozu uses particular motifs to make almost every scene link 'paradigmatically' with others, enriching what could have been a simple sketch.

Scripted in twelve days and shot on what must have been a small budget, *Record of a Tenement Gentleman* turns its limitations into strengths by virtue of ingenious uses of setting. Ozu will shoot the same portion of a set from two oblique angles separated by 45 degrees; this gives us common reference points in the background but varies the foreground element. Another strategy also involves depth. On the whole, movement in the neighborhood is shown only from *inside* nearby houses. Typically, when a character crosses the street, a perpendicular shot from inside the house which he or she leaves shows the destination out of focus directly in the rear. Then Ozu cuts 180 degrees to reveal the character arriving at the other house, seen again from inside. This tactic is established as an intrinsic norm in the first scene, when Tashiro leaves Tamekichi's house and walks straight to Otane's home opposite. Cut to him arriving at Otane's, with Tamekichi's house still visible behind. Of course, Ozu goes on to vary this, once by racking focus from the background to the foreground plane. Most spectacularly, after Kihachi's party, Ozu uses the neighborhood homes to create intermediate spaces and then mislead us about where the next scene will take place. The party is interrupted by a cutaway to Otane's home, where a cat eats and a teakettle is visible in the distance (fig. 169). Ozu then cuts to Kihachi's parlor, with a cold teakettle; the room is empty (another echo of the opening scene of *Passing Fancy*), but we hear voices off (fig. 170). Cut to Tamekichi's home, a teakettle in the foreground steaming (fig. 171); rack focus to the middle plane as the two men enter and Otane goes into her home in the background (fig. 172). Cut back to her home as she enters (fig. 173). (This last framing is another example of the 45-degree variation on a space; compare other shots of Otane's home.) Ozu switches us from one empty home to another, suspending our sense of where the next scene will start. Such spatial restriction is itself violated at the film's denouement, when Otane goes outside to watch Kohei leave with his father. Here, for the first and last time, Ozu shows his characters on this street, opening the film up at the climax.

While the few interiors are subjected to such 'perpendicular' organization, a slightly different strategy is reserved for exteriors. Otane's and Kohei's walk to Chigasaki is presented in extreme long-shots, with bottles or tubs in the foreground and diagonal planes slanting into the distance. Lingering on such a composition after the pair have passed, Ozu manages to suggest intermediate spaces. A similar foreground/background interplay is at work during Otane's search for Kohei, although here Ozu also has recourse to cutaways. Closer to the rectilinear handling of the interiors' views of the street are the opening of the two parallel quilt scenes, with the neat stylistic variants recalling *Woman of Tokyo* and *Inn in Tokyo*:

First scene	*Later scene*
1. (els) Clotheslines, quilt in distance (fig. 174).	1. (els) Clothesline, quilt in distance (fig. 177).
2. (mls) 0 degrees to 1. Clothesline with quilt (fig. 175).	2. (ls) 0 degrees to 1. Clothesline with quilt (fig. 178).
	3. (ms) 225 degrees to 2. Quilt, with stain (fig. 179).
3. (ls) 45 degrees to 2. Quilt in foreground, Otane and Kohei in background (fig. 176).	4. (ls) 180 degrees to 3. Quilt in foreground, no one in background (fig. 180).

169.

170.

171.

172.

173.

174.

175.

176.

177.

178.

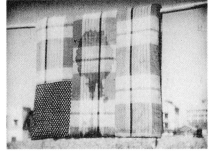

179.

180.

The extra shot in the second sequence tells us all we need to know, standing in for the lengthy dialogue that followed shot 3 in the earlier scene. Moreover, in the first episode, Otane orders Kohei to fan the quilt dry. After the fourth shot of the later scene, Otane is shown talking with Tamekichi, who asks: 'He's fanning again?' The omniscient narration has already shown us that he (probably) isn't, but Tamekichi's line – coming shortly before his judgment that this is a case of 'piss and run' – creates an amusing diegetic 'baring' of the narrative and stylistic parallels.

All of Ozu's 'intermediate spaces' exemplify a dialectic of presence and absence, but in *Record of a Tenement Gentleman* this becomes prominent throughout the film's stylistic organization. From the very start, the film's narration plays upon it: we think that Tamekichi is talking to his wife, but actually there is no one there, and the film never explains why he launches into this monologue. The oblique transition out of Kihachi's party (figs. 169–73) and the quilt scenes (figs. 174–80) tend to present empty space when we expect to see characters. The dialectic beomes especially apparent in two parallel sequences. At the beach, Otane tries to run away from Kohei, and Ozu presents her evasive maneuvers in ways that playfully undermine our sense of where she is. If she leaves the shot, Ozu holds on the empty frame for a time before cutting to a new space, also empty, which coaxes us to speculate about how and where she will enter. The scene's découpage thus anticipates the hide-and-seek game in *End of Summer*. In the last extreme long-shot of the scene, Otane walks to the far left edge of the frame, turns to watch Kohei enter from frame right, then runs to the right to chase him out before turning and walking, full of dignity, back toward the left edge again. Ozu here cuts to the next scene, leaving us in uncertainty about whether Kohei galloped back to her. Later, when Otane searches for the boy, a similar stylistic suspense about where and when she will enter the frame plays on the presence/absence dialectic. Moreover, Ozu uses foreground material to sharpen the sense of emptiness, as when Otane pauses near the timbers where Kohei had sat earlier. Out of the boy's absence the narration then constructs a bleak dominant/overtone passage: Otane looking; the empty planks with blowing papers as the overtone; then scudding papers with street lamps as the overtone; and finally street lamps as the dominant.

All of which might still be seen as mere repetition of the director's characteristic devices were it not for a flagrant scene without equal in any previous Ozu work. The sequence occurs at the photographer's studio, where Otane and Okiku take Kohei for a portrait. The resulting photo will not be shown or mentioned again. As usual as well, there is some fussing before the photographer actually takes the picture. Kohei's new cap is too big, and Otane must hold it from behind; she wipes her nose and so does he, while Okiku, sitting out of camera range, recalls how Otane used to wipe her nose on her sleeve. But then comes a series of outrageous shots. After the photographer presses the shutter, cut to darkness. Where are we? Cut to a shot of Kohei and Otane upside down, as if seen through the photographer's camera (fig. 181). Does the black stretch, then, represent the shutter before it opens? Sure enough, we cut to darkness again, as if the shutter had closed. But then we get no image of the studio, and we hear the dialogue continue over the black

181.

300

frame. The photographer thanks them, Otane asks Okiku how she looked, and so on. It is as if we are trapped inside the photographer's camera after the lens has been capped. Then the darkness wipes away from bottom to top, as if a curtain were lifted, to reveal the studio now empty (fig. 182). Not only have the characters vanished; not only do the empty chairs recall their presence; but the still camera itself has disappeared. Perhaps it has been moved to the very position 'we' now occupy. (But if the view is then made a diegetic POV, who 'lifts the curtain'? And why is this gradual opening of the shutter so different from the instantaneous change earlier?) Or perhaps the stretch of darkness has become a completely nondiegetic narrational gesture. In either event, this remarkable scene lays bare the way in which the film leads us to expect character presence and then supplies absence – not only empty settings but pure black blankness.

182.

Otane has seen Kohei go off with his father, has resolved to be less selfish, and has asked Tashiro the fortuneteller where she should look for a boy to adopt. Folk superstition coincides with contemporary economic conditions: he sends her to Saigo's statue in Ueno Park. Ozu ends the film with a sequence that at once pulls the film together and opens it onto a broader referentiality. In six shots, Ozu presents a crowd of homeless boys around the famous statue of Saigo. The scene parallels two earlier ones of orphans fishing, and by showing boys picking up cigarette butts it recalls how Kohei had scavenged butts for his father. In its spatial construction, the scene encapsulates Ozu's stylistic strategies by presenting the statue from all sides and cutting in multiples of 45 degrees, so that shot 2 is 135 degrees to shot 1, shot 3 is 45 degrees to shot 2, shot 4 is 90 degrees to shot 3, and so on. The music, now in quantity and quality exactly what Ozu would use for the rest of his career, is at its most soaring, as strings call up a broad, hymn-like tune. The scene also echoes a prewar Ozu film: in *I Was Born, But . . .* the boss's home movie contains a virtually identical shot of Saigo and his dog. Saigo Takamori was a samurai who helped create the Meiji imperial government and who, in 1877, led an unsuccessful rebellion against it. A popular figure of both conformity and protest, Saigo is also remembered for his support of Japanese expansion into Asia – surely ironic in a postwar context. But the mise-en-scène, like the irony, is not wholly of Ozu's and Ikeda's making. A news photo from 1946 (fig. 183) is captioned 'Homeless boys climb on statue of Saigo in Ueno Park.' By returning the 1947 audience to the world that awaits them outside the theatre, the film presents practical material to test Otane's lesson of kindness. It also ends on an image that echoes the film's first line from Tamekichi's misleading monologue, a poetic notion that also anticipates the photography scene: 'Even the moon is shadowed once in a while, let alone small human beings who are easily shadowed into darkness.'

183. A news photo of 1946 showing homeless boys at the statue of Saigo in Ueno Park. The statue was a favorite gathering spot for war orphans.

If Ozu had made only this seventy-two minute film, he would have to be considered one of the world's great directors.

1948

Kaze no naka no mendori
A Hen in the Wind

Shochiku Ofuna studio. Script: Ryosuke Saito, Yasujiro Ozu. Cinematography: Yuharu Atsuta. Lighting: Haruo Isono. Art director: Tatsuo Hamada. Music: Sonji Ito. Editing: Yoshiyasu Hamamura. Cast: Shuji Sano (*Shuichi Amamiya*), Kinuyo Tanaka (*Tokiko*), Chieko Murata (*Akiko Ida*), Chishu Ryu (*Kazuichiro Satake*), Takeshi Sakamoto (*Hikozo Sakai*), Eiko Takamatsu (*Tsune*), Reiko Mizukami (*Orie Noma*), Chiyoko Ayatani (*Fusako Onoda*). 2,296 meters. Surviving prints: 84 min. Released 20 September 1948. Script, negative, and prints in existence.

While awaiting her husband's return from the war, Tokiko must prostitute herself in order to pay their son's hospital bill. Upon Shuichi's return, she tells him what she has done. In anger and shame, Shuichi asks for the details, then rapes her. He visits the brothel and meets Fusako, who is supporting her family through prostitution. After talking with his boss Satake he returns to Tokiko, but he is still furious and knocks her downstairs. Upon seeing her pain, he finds the strength to put the past behind them and promises her they will start again.

Little circulated and rarely shown, *A Hen in the Wind* is one of Ozu's least-discussed postwar films. This may also be traceable to a sense that it is not typical. For one thing, its story seems close to a 'Mizoguchi' idea, one that might have formed a subplot in *Yoru no onnatachi* (*Women of the Night*, 1948). It also seems an 'Occupation' film, dealing explicitly with the social problems of a conquered country and projecting an optimism for future rebuilding. In this respect, it echoes the moralistic endings of many works of its time, such as Kinoshita's *Osone-ke no asa* (*Morning for the Osone Family*, 1947) and Kurosawa's *Subarashiki nichiyobi* (*One Wonderful Sunday*, 1947). Yet Ozu's film deserves to be better known – partly for its unusual treatment of its conventional material, and partly for the ways in which it lays out many stylistic choices that would become common in subsequent works.

Derived from a story by Shiga Naoya, Ozu's and Saito's script was criticized as an attempt, like *Morning for the Osone Family*, Kozaburo Yoshimura's *Anjo-ke no butokai* (*Ball at the Anjo House*, 1947), and Kurosawa's *Waga seishun ni kui nashi* (*No Regrets for Our Youth*, 1946), to reject the past unproblematically. But Sato has suggested that *A Hen in the Wind* asked a genuinely difficult question: What did Japan lose in losing the war? The answer, he says, is the vaunted 'purity' that was central to wartime definitions of the Japanese spirit. Tokiko's becoming a prostitute symbolizes a loss of national purity. Shuichi's violence toward her becomes emblematic of the ingrained brutality of the war years, demonstrating that he has lost the noble purpose that had been used to justify the war. The film's lesson, Sato concludes, cuts deeper than those contemporary films that sloughed blame off onto villainous militarists and weak-willed collaborators. Ozu's film urges the ordinary viewer to forget the loss of national and personal purity. Instead of patriotic speeches, the film ends with a quiet resolve to ignore past mistakes and to face the future with an 'impure' but realistic hope.[73] Sato's account is persuasive. It explains a striking difference in tone between Ozu's film and those like Kinoshita's, Kurosawa's and Yoshimura's, and it is consistent with that refusal of transcendental solutions and that justification of human-scale compromise that one finds so often in Ozu. Yet we need also to consider how this thematic effect is achieved through narrative structure and narrational process.

Ozu builds his plot around a female/male split. The first half of the film centers on Tokiko, depicting Hiroshi's illness, her one night of prostitution, and the reaction of her friend Chieko. The last of these eleven scenes shows Tokiko, Hiroshi, and Chieko on a picnic. During this idyll, the two women recall the past, citing the turbulence of the war years and their 1930s dreams of Westernization. (Tokiko had wanted a house, an airedale, and a Max Factor compact.) As in *Record of a Tenement Gentleman*, Ozu's typical nostalgia for childhood gets superimposed upon the memory of prewar life. The postwar equivalents of such American references are the tawdry posters in the room of Orie, the woman who lures Tokiko into prostitution: *Love Letters* (1945), *Kiss and Tell* (1945), and *The Green Years* (1946). (As in *A Mother Should Be Loved*, Ozu seems to be using his beloved American cinema in a moralizing spirit, letting the films' titles suggest Orie's frivolity and anticipate Tokiko's fall.) The aim of this first half is to make us wholly aware of Tokiko's motives and feelings. As if the purpose of curing her son were not sufficient grounds for her taking up Orie's offer, the narration absolves her by showing only her customer, not Tokiko herself, after the sexual act, and by having him remark that she 'was no good, couldn't make it.'

When the women and Hiroshi return from the picnic, they find that at last Shuichi has returned from the war. The film now 'starts over', recycling elements from the first half but putting Shuichi at the center of events. After a celebration that night, Tokiko tells him she has prostituted herself. Thereafter, the plot alternates brief scenes of Tokiko with much longer scenes depicting Shuichi's anguished reaction. These create sombre parallels with Tokiko's half of the film: he visits the brothel she had worked in, and he has his own picnic by the river with Fusako, one of the brothel's girls. In addition, there are parallels within the second part: two scenes showing Shuichi and his boss Satake in their office, and two crucial scenes of violence in the couple's apartment. Most important is the shift in the film's 'center of consciousness'. If the first half put Tokiko's financial and moral problem at its center, this half constitutes a psychological study of the male's response. (Here Ozu diverges from what Mizoguchi would have done.) Melodrama tends to create an omniscient range of knowledge so as to maximize our awareness of errors of understanding and judgment. In the second half, we watch Shuichi misjudging Tokiko and gradually learning what we already know. But, as in melodrama generally, characters' knowledge does not automatically govern their emotions. Shuichi cannot forgive his wife. By the waterside, he offers to help Fusako find a job, but such kindness cannot be extended to Tokiko.

Should anyone criticize the film as wholly a justification of masculine self-pity, the second office scene is there to forestall such easy responses. While whores cavort in a cabaret in the background, Satake asks why Shuichi can forgive a stranger but not his wife. Shuichi says that his feelings prevent it. Satake the *raisonneur* answers: 'You've got to change your feelings with your will power. . . . Forget it as soon as you can.' At their apartment, Shuichi pushes Tokiko away from him, and she falls downstairs. He rushes to see if she is hurt, but he can only stand at the top of the stairs in a funk, then return to his cushion as she crawls painfully back up to him. Her masochism and his paralysis of will make this an excruciating scene to watch. Finally, when she begs him to hit her and express his hate, he simply extends his love. 'Let's forget it. It was just a mistake. . . . We must overcome it. We must love more deeply.' Only by seeing his wife as pitiable can he offer to change his feelings. The final embrace unites the traditional, stoically suffering Japanese woman and Ozu's typical diffident, confused man. As in the 1930s films, the male falters, scraping by on good intentions and the strength of his woman – shown, during the embrace, as a pair of hands knotted firmly behind his back, as if in prayer.

Stylistically, *A Hen in the Wind* picks up devices already latent in *What Did the Lady Forget?* and crystallizes them into fixed patterns that will dominate Ozu's postwar work. Music is now constantly present, both rising up within scenes and linking them. (Only three of twenty-two scenes lack nondiegetic music, and one of those contains diegetic music.) The twanging Hawaiian guitar of *What Did the Lady Forget?* returns to create a wrenching change of tone, when it underscores Tokiko's sob in her mirror and leads into shots of the bed she has shared at the brothel. Similarly, *A Hen in the Wind* displays the most common way in which Ozu will 'process' a scene in his late films: establishing shot; 'incorrect' shot/reverse-shot; reestablishing shot, either from the initial angle or 180 degrees to it; more shot/reverse-shots; another reestablishing shot, either from the initial angle or 180 degrees to it. At either end of the sequence stand one or more shots of indeterminate spaces, sometimes symmetrical in what they show, more often not. Whereas this schema can be found to some degree in the earlier films, it becomes every late film's intrinsic norm. Against this norm, however, certain particular strategies become salient, and they deserve a brief look.

The photographic quality of the film has a crispness of definition that is absent from Ozu's previous talkies. (Perhaps he started to use arc lighting and the improved Eastman black-and-white stocks.) The new sharpness of detail permits him to create unprecedented nuances of gesture and framing. For instance, his perfect matches on action can be realized on the very edges of the frame, as when the mah-jongg scenes rely on exact movement matches of players' hands (p. 112, figs. 15–16). With a greater image definition available, Ozu need not shoot close-ups of transitional objects; he can film in long-shot but use the gray scale and image composition to make the object prominent. For example, when Shuichi returns, the landlord's wife offers her last bottle of

184.

185.

sake to the couple. Tokiko tiptoes upstairs and sets it on the left edge of the staircase. In the next scene, after two shots, it sits on a step on the right side of the frame, seen in a longish shot (fig. 184). The next morning, as Chieko comes down the street, the bottle has traveled to the house stoop, visible in the left middle ground (fig. 185). The peregrinations of this bottle anticipate the adventures of towels, buckets, bottles, cups, and chopsticks in subsequent works. Finally, the crisper image permits Ozu to vary setups minutely. When Tokiko tells Shuichi of her prostitution, the reestablishing shot is slightly darker, signalling the shift to a sombre mood. (See also the example cited on p. 129.) Such slight differences will of course be part of Ozu's parametric strategy in later films.

A sequence that concisely illustrates Ozu's new exploitation of the nuances of photography and framing is the harrowing confrontation between Shuichi and Tokiko after she has told him about her prostitution. In the course of the scene, he throws a can at her, and it rolls down the staircase – prefiguring what will happen to her in the parallel sequence. He rapes her, then sits brooding angrily before stalking outside. This intensely emotional action is presented with an astounding stylistic rigor, forming a compendium of Ozu's characteristic tactics. At the start, Tokiko sits forlornly, seen in three shots (the second 90 degrees to the first, the third 45 degrees to the second). The last shot is held until Shuichi enters in the rear and sits (fig. 186). Cut in to Shuichi, turned three-quarters away (fig. 187). The cut to Tokiko violates continuity for the sake of a graphic match (fig. 188). Shuichi turns and orders her to come to him. She turns to face him (fig. 189). Ozu uses this new

186.

187.

188.

189.

190.

191.

192.

193.

194.

195.

196.

197.

198.

position to create a new graphic match in a cut to Shuichi. Cut to a re-establishing shot, not quite identical to the establishing framing (fig. 190). After he throws the can at her, he drags her to him and rapes her. Ozu cuts away to the stairs with the can visible at the foot, then to the Sakai family in bed, then back to the stairs. In the next shot Shuichi is sitting upright (fig. 191), and Ozu cuts 180 degrees to present a medium close-up of him as a shadow flits across his cheek (fig. 192). Ozu cuts to the lamp, a dragonfly fluttering on it (fig. 193). Cut to a shot of Tokiko, paralleling the initial one of her husband (fig. 194) and then to a 180-degree closer view of her (fig. 195). After another shot of Shuichi, Ozu at last presents an establishing shot (fig. 196). By delaying the establishing shot (as he had not done earlier), Ozu strengthens the impact of its being much darker than the initial framing (fig. 186). Ozu's new photographic range lets him present the minute changes of cushions in the lower parts of figs. 186 and 190, the climactic chiaroscuro in fig. 196, and even the shadow of a dragonfly.

In one more respect does *A Hen in the Wind* set the terms for Ozu's subsequent work. Its organization of intermediate spaces repeats a limited number of motifs of locale. (To some extent it recalls *Inn in Tokyo*.) The first scene constitutes the matrix from which most intermediate spaces will be selected. Outside, we start with an extreme long-shot of a street (fig. 197), then a view of the tanks, then a shot of houses with laundry, and finally a street. In nine later scenes, we will see variant framings of either the tanks or of the laundry in relation to them. The first scene also introduces us to the family's apartment in Tokiko's absence, and Ozu is at pains to establish the stairs, an architectural feature that his films normally suppress. The stairway, filmed squarely at several points, will 'pay off' in the brutal shot of Tokiko tumbling down it. The film's ending buckles the pattern shut, albeit not as neatly as does the exact symmetry of *Days of Youth*. The shot of the houses and laundry is dropped, and the order is changed: first a shot of the tanks, then the street on which Hiroshi plays, and finally a return to the establishing long-shot. But even here Ozu's pursuit of nuance is unflagging. The last shot of the tanks is a reversal of the first one, and the two women in the last shot have gained an umbrella since the film started (fig. 198). The just-noticeable differences of Ozu's late parametric style are now in place.

1949

Banshun

Late Spring

Shochiku. Story: Kazuo Hirotsu, *Chichi to musume* ('Father and Daughter'). Script: Kogo Noda, Yasujiro Ozu. Cinematography: Yuharu Atsuta. Art director: Tatsuo Hamada. Lighting: Haruo Isono. Editing: Yoshiyasu Hamamura. Music: Senji Ito. Cast: Chishu Ryu (*Shukichi Somiya*), Setsuko Hara (*Noriko*), Yumeji Tsukioka (*Aya Kitagawa*), Haruko Sugimura (*Masa Taguchi*), Hohi Aoki (*Katsuyochi*), Jun Usami (*Shoichi Hattori*), Kuniko Miyake (*Akiko Miwa*), Masao Mishima (*Jo Onodera*), Yoshiko Tsubouchi (*Kiku*). 12 reels, 2,964 meters. Surviving prints: 108 min. Released 19 September 1949. Script, negative, and prints in existence.

Noriko happily looks after her father Professor Somiya and enjoys the company of her friends. But Somiya and his sister Masa trick Noriko into thinking that he is going to remarry. Distraught, she agrees to meet Satake, a possible husband. Although she likes him, she resents her father's remarriage and hates the thought of leaving him. He persuades her that she will have a happy marriage if she works at it. After her marriage, Somiya comes home to an empty house.

Critics who see Ozu as preserving Japanese tradition in the face of modernization might seem to have strong evidence in *Late Spring*. No other Ozu film is so saturated with the iconography of a certain 'Japaneseness' – the tea ceremony, Zen gardens, temples, noh drama, the landscape around Kyoto, the seasonal cycle referred to in the title. Yet this iconography is used for a specific ideological purpose: to show that Japanese tradition can be reconciled with the new liberalism of the Occupation era. (In this respect it resembles Mizoguchi's *Sansho Dayu* (*Sansho the Bailiff*), 1954). Once more 'Japaneseness' is redefined.

The script's ideological project has been discussed at length by Kristin Thompson,[74] so I will simply summarize and develop some major points. In the context of the postwar constitution, new marriage laws, and changes in the post-Meiji family structure, *Late Spring* takes a liberal view of family relations and marriage. Aunt Masa represents very traditional values, but most other characters are identified with progressive views: Aya, the divorcee; Onodera, the widower who remarries; and especially Professor Somiya, the father who emphasizes marrying for love and happiness, not for perpetuation of the *ie*. (There is no emphasis on having children to maintain the family.) Somiya is portrayed as kind and humane, wholly different from the tyrannical patriarch of tradition. He brings Aya and Noriko tea, allows Noriko to boss him, and expresses deep emotional attachment to his daughter. Alone with Onodera, he pities her for what she suffered in the war. Significantly, in Kyoto he remarks that a son is better than a daughter – *not* for the traditional reason that daughters are *kane kui mushi* ('money-eating insects') but because daughters create more regret: 'If they're unwed, you worry, but if they do marry you feel let down.' But Onodera reminds him that 'we married grown-up ones too.' Ironically, Noriko is more old-fashioned than her father, insisting that he could not get along without her and resenting the idea that a widower might remarry. Unlike the youngest Toda siblings, she clings to an outmoded notion of propriety.

It is principally Somiya who redefines Japanese tradition. He is introduced talking with his assistant Hattori about Friedrich List, the German-American economist who inspired much Meiji policy: the dialogue characterizes Somiya as both a traditionalist and a liberal. Whereas Noriko's tea ceremony forms a social occasion, the father is a genuine connoisseur of noh and he savors the gardens and buildings of Kyoto. In the climactic scene at the end of the Kyoto interlude, he portrays Noriko's marriage as like his own, a gesture which at once makes hers traditional and his progressive. It is important that Noriko must be tricked into marrying: this father will not simply order her to marry. The Ozu father, in the 1930s deprived of traditional parental power, recovers his authority, but one in which tradition is redefined. *Late Spring* presents a new father-figure, as mild as Mr Toda and as selfless as Horikawa in *There Was a Father*, but now wise in the recognition of freedom of choice and the need for mutual happiness in marriage. And this wisdom is represented not as enforced Occupation policy but as inherently and spontaneously Japanese. Thus at the film's end Ozu can still depict the self-sacrificing parent as solitary, in a fashion analogous to the epilogue of *The Only Son*. This convention of the 'parent-film' can be accommodated to new political needs.

The blind spot in all this, of course, is that Noriko must marry. The film assumes, along with its original audience, that since she is getting into her middle twenties (the 'late spring' of the title), it is time she found a husband. Given this assumption, Masa and Somiya's ploy seems justified. Today we find this outrageous; but in a decade's time Ozu's films would have changed on this point too, as the finale of *End of Summer* makes clear. In any event, the manner of planning Noriko's marriage – through an *o-miai*, or arranged meeting – would also seem a reconciliation of tradition with modernity and liberalism (Somiya assures her that she's free to decline, and she turns out to like Satake – who resembles Gary Cooper).

Since Thompson also discusses how the film's style exemplifies many of the strategies I have been outlining in this book, I need not go into detail about its staging, framing, cutting, and so on. Instead I will confine myself to outlining the film's four-part structure and commenting on certain aspects of dramaturgy and style.

1) *Hattori as a marriage prospect* (Scenes 1-12)
The early scenes introduce the characters in a leisurely fashion, establishing the domestic routine of Noriko and her father while also setting up the crucial parallels: Aya, Noriko's working friend; and Onodera, who has a daughter like Noriko. At scene 7, the possibility of a romance between Noriko and Hattori is

raised during a biking scene that ends with an amiably flirtatious conversation by the sea. But the narration has concealed crucial information from both Somiya and us, so that when he suggests Hattori as a possible husband, both he and we are surprised to learn that Hattori is engaged. (The implication is that Noriko knew this well before the bike outing.) Still there is a 'recoil' effect, for soon Hattori is meeting Noriko at a coffeeshop and inviting her to a concert. Perhaps then he is a romantic possibility after all? Ozu cancels this by showing him at the concert alone, while Noriko walks home. There she meets Aya, and the two cheerfully discuss their married friends.

The opening scene is tantalizing in its non-expository qualities. Set in a room at Kenchoji, one of the five main temples in Kamakura, it introduces Noriko, her aunt Masa, and Mrs Miwa at a tea ceremony that is more a social occasion than a religious one. (Noriko and Masa chat about torn trousers and other prosaic details that the true Zen adherent would scour out of mind.) The scene also prepares us for several aspects of the film's narrational norm. Ozu's repeated cutaways to details of setting cover ellipses in the ceremony and play with our expectations about when the scene will end. The principal musical motif runs throughout the sequence. Significantly too, the scene begins at the railroad station, where the characters *aren't*. A later scene will do exactly the same thing, showing the train station *before* showing them already on the train hurtling toward Tokyo. (Here again, characters will change places unexpectedly during the cutaways.) In Tokyo, Onodera and Noriko discuss going to an art exhibit; cut to a sign for the exhibit, then to the steps of the art gallery; cut to the two in a bar, after they've gone to the exhibit. Noriko's absence from Hattori's concert is handled in parallel fashion, with a cut to the lobby of the concert hall and a cut in to the poster acting as 'placing' shots for a scene that never takes place.

The opening scene also establishes that in this film the intermediate spaces will not consist of close-ups of objects but rather of signs and land-scapes. The first four shots move in dominant/overtone fashion from the Kamakura station sign to railroad tracks and a train signal before showing the temple roof. Later, the Hattori building dominates a Ginza landscape, and signs for the art gallery and the bar are salient during the scene of Noriko's and Onodera's outing. The 'false' concert scene is marked as an intermediate space by thirty seconds' dwelling on the lobby and sign. During Noriko's bicycle outing with Hattori, Ozu lingers on traffic signs and a Coca-Cola advertisement as well as on the seascapes they pass.

199.

Finally, the opening scene introduces a tree-motif (fig. 199) that will reappear when Noriko leaves Hattori and walks down the street. Perhaps this organic image embodies the parallel of a season with Noriko's time of life.

2) *Aunt Masa's prospect and Somiya's possible remarriage* (Scenes 13-22)
Now that Hattori is ineligible, the plot has 'run down' and must be restarted. In scene 13, Aunt Masa provokes Noriko by suggesting she marry. To her response that her father could not take care of himself, Masa suggests that he marry the widowed Mrs Miwa. Now a dramaturgy of character reaction and development takes over. Noriko is shocked. The next five scenes essentially

repeat and intensify the rhythm that this scene initiates. Somiya and Noriko go to the noh play, and the sight of Mrs. Miwa there disturbs her deeply. She coldly separates from her father on the street. At Aya's, she is too distressed to eat, and when Aya suggests that she get married, she leaves distraught. Finally, at home that night, she questions Somiya and he half-lies to her about his remarriage. At last she breaks down and cries. A week later, prodded by Aya and pursued by Masa, Noriko grimly agrees to marry the suitor.

Despite the psychological linearity of the plotting, however, it is difficult to say exactly what makes Noriko consent. Her crucial period of decision is covered by a scene in which Masa and Somiya discuss the likelihood of acceptance and a bantering scene in which Aya and Noriko discuss her prospect. The ultimately mysterious cause of her acceptance is a device which Ozu would utilize in subsequent films.

This section ranges over a considerable time span, with gaps signalled only retrospectively. Hattori's marriage is alluded to by the wedding portrait that is delivered to Noriko's and Somiya's home. At the micro-level, Noriko's visit to Aya is flagrantly compressed or ellided in a sequence which alternates brief shots of her with shots of Aya's clock, successively reading 3.48, 3.52, and 4.00. At the larger level, despite ellipses the critical action takes place on two days: the day of the visit to the noh, Noriko's call on Aya, and her confrontation with her father; and a day a week later when she comes home from Aya's and finally consents to marry.

200.

Each day has its 'purely Japanese' prototype, like that of the tea ceremony in the first part. During the second day, Masa and Somiya pass a temple, where she finds a purse she will keep as a good omen of Noriko's decision. The noh scene, in a sense the centerpiece of this part, alternates views of Somiya immersed in the performance with shots of Noriko, wounded by the sight of Mrs Miwa. The play itself, *Morikawa*, presents an explicit parallel in its depiction of an aristocratic woman driven into a frenzy by the memory of a lost lover. The scene ends with a bold stroke. Ozu cuts to a leafless tree outside (fig. 200), a shot which recalls noh tradition (a stylized painted pine is part of a noh set) and which picks up the tree-motif from the first part; on the soundtrack, the noh performance continues, mingling for a while with the nondiegetic motif of the film's score. This remarkable shot not only serves as a transition out of the theatre but also privileges the noh scene as the turning point of Noriko's emotional response.

3) *Kyoto interlude* (Scenes 23-27)

This section alternates two typically Ozuian idylls with three scenes between father and daughter in their hotel room. In the course of these, Noriko sees that Onodera's remarriage is not as repugnant as she had thought, but she still longs not to leave Somiya. As they pack to leave, Somiya tells her that his life is ending and she must start hers with a husband. The two must strive for happiness in marriage. She acquiesces.

Each of the stunning Kyoto scenes is worthy of detailed analysis, but briefly we can notice how Ozu heaps up iconography of 'Japanese tradition'. Kyoto is introduced through contiguity shots of pagoda roofs, the dominant element in the precinct's architecture. A trip to the Kiyomizudera (the Temple of Clear Water) culminates in imagery of dripping water that echoes Shinto and Buddhist purification rituals, ironically contrasting with Noriko's claim that Onodera is 'unclean' (fig. 201). That night, in their room, as Somiya sleeps and Noriko stares upward, Ozu cuts away to a shot of a vase and a shoji on which bamboo branches are silhouetted – a cliché of 'Japaneseness'. (For more on this scene, see p. 117.) Later, Somiya and Onodera sit at the Ryoanji garden and discuss the inevitability of children leaving home. Ozu's cutting plays a vast game with the huge rocks and whorls of sand, which, traditionally representing the sea and islands, hark back to Kamakura's ocean front. The first pair of scenes juxtaposes Noriko's sense of propriety with a landscape or object that embodies tradition in distilled form; in the third scene mentioned, the sand at Ryoanji links the old men to the absolute purity of the Japanese spirit, as embodied in the earliest Zen garden. The film's late-arriving motif echoes the traditional cast of the other scenes: the first Kyoto sequence ends with Noriko glimpsed in her dresser mirror (fig. 202), before Ozu cuts to a hillside dense with trees, repeating the motif that has been associated with her throughout.

201.

4) *Marriage preparations and aftermath* (Scenes 28–30)

Several elements and strategies unite in this last part. Noriko's bentwood armchairs, heavily emphasized during her talk with Aya and reemphasized when she spurns her father after the noh play, are now downstairs, occupied by Hattori and Somiya. Noriko, in her wedding garb, bids a grateful farewell to her father. The mirror returns, as the place where father's and daughter's glances cross but also as the vessel which, at the scene's end, reflects her empty room (fig. 203).

202.

Just as we never see Hattori's bride, so we never see Noriko's groom, let alone the wedding: the elliptical narration now concentrates on Somiya. He takes Aya to his favorite bar and tells her he doesn't intend to remarry. The bar scene ends with an echo of the classroom scene in *The Only Son*: Ozu cuts away from Aya and Hattori to the empty tavern, and then the lights go out, soundlessly. The shot not only creates a retrospective ellipsis during which the customers leave, but it looks forward to the bleak solitude of the final scene.

Hattori comes home, passing through a corridor marked by the absence of Noriko (her sewing machine is gone). He takes off his coat – something the dutiful woman should do for him – and sits in one of her armchairs. As he peels the apple, the main musical motif swells up and Ozu films him in shots which parallel (through inversion) the earlier views of Noriko in her room, weeping after he implied he would remarry. A final cut back to the waves recalls the bike ride along the shore and, more connotatively, the idyll at Ryoanji, when Somiya had expressed regrets about Noriko's leaving.

203.

In many ways, as the first postwar product of the Ozu-Noda collaboration, *Late Spring* would become the major prototype of the 1950s and 1960s work. Sato has suggested that after the initial failure of *A Hen in the Wind*, Noda steered the director to a middle-class milieu reminiscent of *Brothers and Sisters of the Toda Family*, his biggest success.[75] *Early Summer*, *Tokyo Story*, *Late*

Autumn, and especially *An Autumn Afternoon* can be seen as variants of *Late Spring*. Now also appears the split between older critics who admire Ozu's 'traditional' beauty and younger ones who charge him with a failure to face social reality. More exactly, *Late Spring* introduces not Ozu the anguished conservative mourning the loss of a way of life but rather Ozu the liberal who acknowledges the need for change, though he regrets the damage it will cause. Stylistically, the film crystallizes intrinsic norms that will prove central to the late films – even though those films will themselves deviate creatively from them. Finally, in Noriko Ozu gives us a new, enigmatic heroine. His narration ellides key events and withholds important information about her state of mind. As ever, characterization becomes subordinate to the overall narrational design of the film.

1950

Munekata shimai
The Munekata Sisters

Toho/Shintoho. Story: Jiro Osaragi. Script: Kogo Noda, Yasujiro Ozu. Cinematography: Joji Ohara. Art director: Tomoo Shimogawara. Editing: Toshio Goto. Cast: Kinuyo Tanaka (*Setsuko*), Hideko Takamine (*Mariko*), Ken Uehara (*Hiroshi Tashiro*), Sanae Takasugi (*Yoriko Mashita*), Chishu Ryu (*Tadachika Munekata*), So Yamamura (*Ryosuke Mimura*), Tatsuo Saito (*Professor Uchida*). 3,080 meters. Surviving prints: 112 min. Released 25 August 1950. Script, negative, and prints in existence.

Setsuko is struggling to make a success of a bar in Tokyo and to rehabilitate her ill and drunken husband Mimura. Her sister Mariko discovers that the antique dealer Hiroshi had once been in love with Setsuko. She alternates between pursuing Hiroshi herself and trying to rekindle his romance with her sister. Relations between Setsuko and Mimura deteriorate and the bar fails. Mimura dies in a drunken stupor. Although Setsuko and Hiroshi love one another, she refuses to marry him. She and Mariko return to Kyoto, where their father is slowly dying.

The Munekata Sisters has the aura of a prestigious project. The Shintoho ('New Toho') company had been formed in 1947, and during its brief heyday it sought famous directors whom it hoped would guarantee success. The firm produced three films by Naruse, most notably *Okasan* (*Mother*, 1952), and Mizoguchi made both *A Picture of Madame Yuki* (1950) and *Saikaku ichidai onna* (*Life of Oharu*, 1952) there. By all accounts, Shintoho offered Ozu a tempting contract but insisted on choosing the story and the performers. The vehicle was a serialized novel by Jiro Osaragi, a popular writer who had recently served as a counsellor to the government. Although Ozu claimed to have enjoyed the project, he also remarked that adapting a novel did not sit well with him, since he had to find an actor who suited the story rather than write an original story around an actor.[76] The result was a cast consisting of some of the biggest stars in the Japanese cinema, but including performers with whom Ozu had never worked extensively. (Ken Uehara had a walk-on shot in *What Did the Lady Forget?*, while Hideko Takamine had as a child performed in some of his early efforts.)

For many critics the lack of control accorded to Ozu is responsible for the film's obvious failings. David Owens has concisely summed them up: 'This melodramatic story suffers from too schematic a division between tradition and modernity, too self-conscious an effort to depict the gulf between pre-war and post-war Japan.'[77] The melodramatic devices – two sisters in love with the same man, a drunkard's sudden death, a woman's noble repudiation of her love – did not go unnoticed by Ozu himself. Unlike *Late Spring*, he remarked in 1950, this was a 'very heavy' script; he hoped, however, to 'direct it very lightly.'[78] Yet certainly the script tugs against this, showing as perhaps no other film does the limits of Ozu's style when confronted with a linear plot. The oblique opening, in which we see Professor Uchida lecturing on cancer before we are introduced to Setsuko, takes on an uncharacteristically simple significance when we learn that her father has the disease. After a lengthy series of expository scenes, the conflicts emerge when Hiroshi offers to loan Setsuko money to keep her bar going. There follows a string of emotionally explicit quarrels – between the sisters, between Mariko and Hiroshi, between Setsuko and her husband. During the last night in which the bar is open, Mimura smashes glasses in the bar mirror. Later that night, he quarrels with Setsuko, slaps her fiercely, and leaves. When he eventually staggers home and collapses from heart failure we get, for the only time in any Ozu film, a woman's scream. Ozu's camera and cutting techniques are as rigorous as ever, but *The Munekata Sisters* shows the extent to which the functioning of his style depends upon a more static, diffuse sort of syuzhet organization. It is not too farfetched to see the script as being perfectly suitable for Sirk – as, say, *Late Spring*'s script could not be.

In addition, Owens rightly points out the heavy-handedness of the film's thematic oppositions. The plot is organized around one *topos* common in Japanese popular culture since the 1920s – the pairing of two women, usually sisters, one of them representing tradition, the other representing modernity. In one scene, an argument brings out all the clichés. Mariko says Setsuko's way of thinking is outdated, and Setsuko replies: 'Really lovely things never grow old. This new way of thinking of yours amounts to no more than shortening your skirts when others do or dyeing your hair if that's all the fashion.' Mariko can only reply that they belong to two different generations.

There is a related difficulty with the film – its use of 'Japaneseness'. The plot shifts from one picturesque locale to another – from Yakushiji Temple near Nara to the Moss Temple in Kyoto, from bars in Tokyo to an antique shop in Kobe to a mountain villa in Hakone. There is an 'applied' quality to the idyllic moments, as when at her father's home Mariko hears a nightingale. The general point is made with crushing explicitness when old Munekata echoes

Setsuko's views: 'So very pleasant seeing traditional Japanese things.' The use of the Yakushiji Temple as the site of Hiroshi's hoped-for reconciliation with Setsuko seems especially precious, in that the temple is identified with the god of healing. The iconography of Japanese tradition supports a nostalgia for the past that is quite free of the postwar liberalism of *Late Spring*. Talking with Hiroshi, Mariko recalls prewar scenes of the seashore and of the Imperial Palace Theatre. That Hiroshi deals in antiques and that the father is dying of cancer only reinforce a simple sentimentalization of the past, giving the film little of the dynamic relation of the past to contemporary life that we find in *Record of a Tenement Gentleman* or *A Hen in the Wind*. In this film, Ozu comes close to being what he is often called – a mourner for a lost tradition.

Sato has sought to defend the film as dealing in an enlightening way with the inadequacies of postwar men.[79] Yet the whole narrational shape of the film runs against this. The passive Hiroshi (Uehara's *nimaime*, or 'sensitive' type, seen also in *Madame Yuki*) and the intemperate Mimura are seldom shown except in relation to the women. Scenes alternate in being developed around Setsuko or Mariko, with the younger sister coming to dominate the film's middle portion. It is in fact Mariko's growing narrational presence that gives Setsuko what little depth she has. Seen less frequently and more from without, Setsuko is capable of the sort of enigmatic action that we find in *Late Spring*'s Noriko and in later Ozu heroines. Why does Setsuko repel the man whom she had agreed to marry? But soon enough in the coffee shop she explains that she has accepted the difference between herself and her sister and thus remains true to herself. This final explanation, as well as the last scene in which the two sisters savor a mutual appreciation of the Kyoto mountainside, leaves the film locked in the static reiteration of commonplace oppositions: tradition and modernity, past and present.

Which is to say that although it is rigorous, *The Munekata Sisters* forgets to play. True, there are some minor moments. Mimura is introduced wearing an eyepatch, which recalls Tomio in *Passing Fancy*. A shot of Mariko includes Nipper, featured as prominently as in *Dragnet Girl* (fig. 204). The inscription in the Accacia Bar – 'I drink upon occasion, and sometimes upon no occasion' – comes from *What Did the Lady Forget?* Most of the familiar stylistic devices appear, including a strikingly minimal establishing shot (Mimura at his desk, with only his foot indicating his presence, fig. 205) and a use of depth staging and selective focus during the quarrel of Setsuko and Mimura. Most interesting, perhaps, is the handling of the parallel scenes at Yakushiji Temple, first with the two sisters and then, near the film's close, with Setsuko and Hiroshi. The first scene opens with a low-angle shot of the pagoda, then three shots of the women sitting on the steps (figs. 206–208), the second about 135 degrees to the first shot, the third 90 degrees to the second. At the scene's end, as the sisters leave, the camera holds on the empty yard and then arcs slowly leftward, as if mimicking the movement through space that the initial cutting had executed. In the later sequence, a different view of the pagoda introduces the action. Hiroshi and Setsuko enter in a different extreme long-shot (fig. 209), this one shifted rightward about 90 degrees to its mate in the earlier scene. The couple walk to the porch and then sit and talk (figs. 210–211) – these two shots almost exactly replicating the earlier ones. After Setsuko has

204.

205.

206.

207.

208.

209.

210.

211.

212.

213.

told him she cannot remarry, she runs off, leaving Hiroshi in a shot that echoes the beginning and ending of the first scene (fig. 212). Ozu will supply a reaction shot of Hiroshi, but only after a shot recalling an earlier composition and marking Setsuko's absence (fig. 213). The scene concludes with a framing of the pagoda that replicates the shot that began the *first* scene. But this mild permutational pattern frames two scenes in which the characters recall a picnic before the war and in which the dramatic issues are starkly spelled out.

1951

Bakushu
Early Summer

Shochiku. Script: Kogo Noda, Yasujiro Ozu. Cinematography: Yuharu Atsuta. Art director: Toshio Hamada. Lighting: Itsuo Takashita. Editing: Yoshiyasu Hamamura. Music: Senji Ito. Cast: Setsuko Hara (*Noriko*), Chishu Ryu (*Koichi*), Chikage Awajima (*Aya Tamura*), Kuniko Miyake (*Fumiko*), Ichiro Sugai (*Shukichi*), Chieko Higashiyama (*Shige*), Haruko Sugimura (*Tami Yabe*), Ryukan Nimoto (*Kenkichi Yabe*), Zen Murase (*Minoru*), Isao Shirosawa (*Isamu*), Shuji Sano (*Sotaro Satake*). 3,410 meters. Surviving prints: 125 min. Released 3 October 1951. Script, negative, and prints in existence.

The Mamiya family hosts a visit from their grandfather's brother. At the suggestion of Noriko's boss Satake, the family investigate her marrying a successful middle-aged businessman. In the meantime, Noriko's older brother Koichi assigns his assistant, their neighbor Yabe, to a hospital post in Akita. One evening, Yabe's mother blurts out that she has always hoped that Noriko would marry Yabe. Abruptly Noriko agrees to do so. The Mamiyas object and pressure Noriko to change her mind, but she remains committed. Only after a farewell photography-portrait session does Noriko break down in tears. Lacking her contribution to the household income, the family dissolves and the grandparents go to live with Uncle.

'The unity of a work,' writes Yuri Tynianov, 'is not a closed symmetrical whole, but an unfolding dynamic integrity; between its elements stands, not the static sign of equation and addition, but always the dynamic sign of correlation and integration.'[80] A poetics of cinema must recognize that various tendencies in a film struggle with one another, and this struggle is played out in the perceptual, affective, and cognitive activities of the spectator. Any Ozu film could illustrate this, but *Early Summer* is an especially apt case, for here a predominant stability of structure and style sets off various decenterings and autonomous patterns of variation.

At a macrostructural level, *Early Summer* exhibits a remarkable coherence, considering the number of characters it depicts. The Mamiya family is not particularly large:

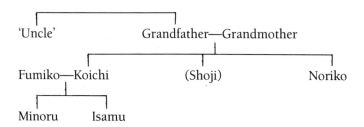

But if one adds all the friends, co-workers, and neighbors who appear, the cast of characters rises to nineteen, each distinctly individualized. (Mr Manabe, the suitor whom we never see, should perhaps be added to this total.) The film binds these characters together into a plot consisting of three large 'acts': the Uncle's visit; finding Noriko a husband; and the family's reaction to her marriage plans. Each part contains one idyll (the visit to the Great Buddha, the grandparents' day in the park, Noriko and Fumiko walking along the seashore).

In the first act, a round of daily routines – breakfast, commuting, office work, a restaurant meal – is linked to the family's preparations for Uncle's arrival. His visit thus motivates one of the most informative expository stretches in any Ozu film. By the time he is ready to leave, every character has been introduced, the family's daily life has been fully depicted, and the issue of Noriko's marriage has been broached – not only by Uncle but by her boss Satake, who has a prospect. Yet such exposition is 'tight' only by Ozu's standards. The first act expands the more concentrated exposition of the Hollywood film into about forty minutes of leisurely foreshadowing and character delineation. (An American family-film like *Meet Me in St Louis* offers an interesting contrast, although even its exposition is less concentrated than that in many Hollywood films.) In this first act, causality is less important than sheer temporal succession.

The last bit of the last scene of act one, in which Fumiko and Noriko are in the kitchen discussing marriage prospects, initiates the next major part, which has a strong causal impetus. Most of the scenes revolve directly around Noriko's marriage. Koichi and Fumiko investigate Satake's prospect; Noriko and her friend Aya banter with their married girlfriends; the grandparents muse on the prospects of losing Noriko. Even the brothers' tantrum over toy train tracks affects this line of action, since Noriko and Yabe are brought together in the search for the boys. A secondary line of causal action involves Koichi's appointing Yabe to a distant hospital in Akita. Act two draws these lines of action together in Noriko's sudden acceptance of the impromptu marriage proposal made by Yabe's mother.

The last act consists principally of reactions and effects. Like the first part, this is less tightly causal. The principal 'action' involves getting the family to accept Noriko's decision – which they do, mysteriously and without indicated reason. (Poor Yabe is so secondary to this process that we never see him after he gets the news he will marry Noriko, a prospect he does not seem to greet with joy.) The last scene, of the grandparents living with Uncle in Yamato, is both an epilogue and a parallel to the first scene, as we shall see later.

The film exhibits 'classical' unity at a more fine-grained level as well. Act one freely interweaves secondary characters such as Satake, Aya, and Tami, who encounter the principal characters in various settings. As the film develops, a similar interweaving of motifs (cake, expenses, 'old maids') ensues. Many scenes are knit together by the Hollywood devices of daily routines and explicit appointments. Ozu will link sequences by conventional dialogue hooks, as when Koichi tells his neighbor that his house is filled with kids and we then cut to the kids. Ozu also uses several sound bridges, such as the kabuki performance heard first in the theatre, then on the radio; or the clacking windvane from one scene that has already been 'sneaked in' at the end of the previous sequence. Even the occasionally jarring sonic cut, when a sliding door is followed by the blast of train wheels, appeals to the norm of a dynamic continuity.

The film's overall narrative and stylistic coherence forms a backdrop against which more eccentric processes stand out. Classical Hollywood procedures constitute a set of intrinsic norms that can be qualified or negated by dynamic narrational strategies. Most obviously deviating from the film's rigorous macrostructure is the psychological and thematic treatment of Noriko's decision to marry Yabe. The elliptical handling of Noriko's attitude begins in act two: the narration dwells on Koichi and Fumiko's plot to ask her about marrying, but then neglects to present her reaction to the offer. Later, the narration suppresses information about Noriko's attitude to Yabe. In the first act, while he and Noriko wait for a train, he is established as an acquaintance. For some time thereafter, though, no particular relation between the two is implied. When Minoru and Isamu run off, she calls at Yabe's and they set out to find the boys. The narration does not show their search, moving instead to a neighbor's home in which Koichi gets the news that his sons were found. The omission is important for two reasons. Initially, by not showing any interpersonal development, the narration implies that there was none. In retrospect, however, Noriko's decision to marry Yabe raises the possibility that during their search for the boys something of moment did affect her feelings toward him.

The third act's gaps involve other factors as well, such as the suppression of Noriko's meeting with Mr Manabe and the concealment of the factors that change the family's attitude toward the marriage; but most gaps still center on Noriko's motive. In explanation, she says she suddenly felt that she'd be happy with Yabe; she tells Aya she feels safe with him. But Yabe is now shouldered out of the plot, so we get no scenes in which the couple share their feelings. Even their marriage, a major causal event, is skipped over, represented *in absentia* by the bridal procession through the barley fields in the epilogue. The uncertainty about Noriko's motivation shapes stylistic factors as well. When Mrs Yabe 'proposes' to Noriko, Ozu uses two abnormally long takes (thirty-six and fifty-three seconds respectively) to conceal Noriko's reaction: she sits facing away from us as Mrs Yabe beseeches her to marry her son (fig. 214). An 'art-cinema' interpretation might take Noriko's acceptance as a realistic depiction of the unpredictability of human action, but a poetics of cinema can explain such a depiction, realistic or not, as produced by narrational omissions that work against an initially and classically 'replete' body of information.

214.

Noriko's action also involves a decentering of any simple thematic unity which we might attribute to the film. At first glance the film's ideological oppositions seem much more stark than that in *Late Spring*. On one side is a 'Japaneseness' embodied in such clichés of tradition as the Chinese scroll painting which Uncle brings as a present, a bird calling in the garden, the Grand Buddha of Kamakura, the kabuki theatre, and the Boys' Day celebration. The grandfather is most closely identified with this theme. He keeps birds, paints ceramics, and savors old prints and kabuki. The narration dwells on him, moving from the others at work in town to show him at home, trimming his grandson's toenails and tolerantly accepting the boy's selfishness. At crucial moments, he injects comments that argue for acceptance of the inevitable. He smiles serenely as he discusses his missing son Shoji: 'There's no hope now.' In the park, he warns his wife not to ask for too much. Most crucial is the scene in act three which shows his placid resignation. Going out to get birdseed, he waits by a crossing for the train to pass, and as he waits he lifts his head, smiling slightly. If the train has come to be associated with the commuters Noriko and Koichi, and thus the modern life of Tokyo, Grandfather may be taken to incarnate the capacity of Japanese tradition to accept whatever changes life may bring.

On this reading, Noriko would embody the 'modernity' principle. She and her friends are linked to the train, the Tokyo cityscape, the office, Ginza coffeeshops, and a café with a pseudo-Matisse mural. Aya had once expected that Noriko would lead a Westernized life, complete with Coca-Cola in the refrigerator. And indeed, Noriko's modernity seems demonstrated by her marriage decision. Although the transgression may not be apparent to Western audiences today, it is flagrant. Acting on impulse and deciding without consultation, she refuses her family any right to participate in choosing her husband. She ignores all the family's negotiations with Mr Manabe, thus exposing them to great embarrassment. She picks not a wealthy older man but a widower with a child and a job in a distant province. She puts Yabe in an awkward situation by giving him no voice in the matter. In sum, she flies in the face of tradition.

But things are not so simple. The grandfather, representative of tradition, exercises no authority over his daughter; it is the sour Koichi, who thinks that postwar women are impudent, who presses his sister into an arranged marriage. And this grandfather does not possess the equability of Somiya in *Late Spring*; he is shocked and saddened by Noriko's impulsive act. As for her, she is not the simple rebellious postwar girl. In a crucial scene in a coffeeshop, Yabe is identified with his boyhood friend, Noriko's missing brother Shoji. Later we learn that Yabe, Shoji, Noriko, and Aya had hiked together before the war. The narration's elliptical presentation of Noriko's decision thus hints that it is a deeply conservative one: to marry the boy next door, who works as an assistant to one brother and who grew up with the other. Marrying Yabe is like marrying within the family. Yet this is still far from a simple lapse into the familiar. There is an insistent motif of risk: Aya says that hoping for happiness is like hoping to win at the racetrack; Koichi claims that Mr Manabe is the best Noriko can hope for. And marrying Yabe dislocates the 'traditional' family while dispatching both Noriko and her parents to a rural world far more traditional than the one they inhabit in Kamakura. Where *Late Spring* promises a synthesis of modernity and tradition, *Early Summer* posits a fragile modernity, one which recognizes that a 'love match' is still chancy and which may spring from a desire to recapture a prewar innocence.

At the level of local texture, the intrinsic norms of continuity are contested by a variety of transitions. There are, of course, images of intermediate spaces, such as the variations upon the shots of office buildings and street lamps (figs. 215–216). There is the 'empty' shot of the theatre box after the kabuki play

215.

216.

217.

218.

has ended. There are also ambiguously placed shots, such as that showing the corridor and a dresser's drawers, which may belong either to the portrait scene or to the meal scene. More than usual in Ozu, however, we find transitions based on a play between cues for continuity and those for discontinuity. Sometimes Ozu will imply continuity only to disconfirm it. Grandmother looks up, and we hear the clacking of a windvane; cut to a shot of carp kites flying, signalling 'Boys' Day'; but it is possible that she is not seeing this. (See p. 133.) (The continuity is also thematic, since the grandparents have just been discussing their lost son.) The continuity/discontinuity tactic becomes a source of wry stylistic humor when Ozu matches the gesture of Noriko and Aya drinking with that of the grandparents eating in the park – complete with a 90-degree shift in angle (p. 133, figs. 81–82). Ozu will also make us wait to confirm our hypotheses about continuity. A restaurant scene begins with a corridor, down which a waitress walks (fig. 217). The next shot (fig. 218), with its prominent vacant spaces, suggests that the waitress will come into the room. She never does. Later the viewer can take the shot as conveying, very obliquely, the information that (a) the kabuki play is being broadcast on the radio in the upper left (an aural continuity link to the prior scene); (b) Noriko and Aya are listening to it (their legs are in the foreground); and (c) their companion Takaka has left the room, vacating the spot on which the composition centers. From the assumption of continuity to a momentary but salient discontinuity we retrospectively construct a new, more comprehensive continuity.

Such transitions parody the neat 'hooks' from scene to scene that are so prominent in earlier portions of the film. Similar in function are the outrageous camera movements that mark the beginning and ending of several scenes. The most famous example occurs near the film's end, when the camera tracks back from Aya and Noriko as they walk down a corridor. The narration cuts to a forward tracking movement that for an instant seems to be their POV – only to reveal it as an 'objective' shot of the corridor of the Mamiya family home. This false POV movement is foreshadowed much earlier when the camera tracks to follow Noriko and then the narration cuts to a movement gliding through the empty kabuki theatre. Throughout the film, the camera movements are rectilinear, framing a hospital scene by two rightward movements or tracking forward or back. A good instance of the playful use of camera movement comes when Ozu tracks in on a close-up of a broken breadloaf and continues the movement forward in the next shot, following Minoru and Isamu as they wander petulantly along the sea wall – a cut on the idea of 'twoness'. As the film progresses, the axes of camera movement (in/out, left/right) are increased. The beach idyll begins with a placing shot of a sand dune and then presents the most stupendous camera movement in Ozu's career: a perfectly perpendicular rising which reveals Noriko and Fumiko as two almost identical columns in a rippling expanse of sand (fig. 219). So rigid is the upward movement and so absolutely does the framing refuse the conventional high angle of the ordinary crane shot that we seem to be watching, from a fixed point, the rotation of the earth. As a parody of the classical 'establishing' crane shot, a codified rhetorical flourish, Ozu's shot is certainly worth the three days it took to make.[81]

219.

220.

221.

222.

The dynamic way in which a stability of structure and style is counter-posed to a gap-ridden, sometimes playful violation of expectations is especially evident in the epilogue, which depicts the grandparents at Uncle's home in Yamato. In placement and detail, the scene echoes the opening sequence, and the contrasts are marked. Instead of opening shots anchored 'inside' the family's home, we get a series of shots that frame the house against mountains and fields. A cheerful, cramped family bustling to a music-box version of 'There's No Place Like Home' has been replaced by three sombre old people in a space much too big for them. In both scenes, the grandfather becomes a central figure. He is given a commentative and reflective role throughout, and he is singled out for stylistic emphasis. In the first scene, an across-the-line cut-in is matched on Grandfather's act of drinking. In this scene, a symmetrically reversed cut-in parallels that moment. This epilogue contains other echoes too. The lingering shot of Grandmother recalls the shot of her that closed the scene concerning their missing son, while the shots of the fields of grain also echo a motif associated with him – the corn which he sent to Yabe from China and which Noriko wants as a keepsake.

223.

It might seem perverse to find in this symmetrical scene traces of Ozu's decentering, but they are there. The opening of the scene presents three establishing shots (figs. 220–222); the scene ends with three shots too, but they constitute a variant series of the first three (figs. 223–225). The elliptical quality of the film's narration is brought home in the glimpse of the bridal procession, which stands in for Noriko's offscreen wedding. And the last shot (fig. 225), which tracks rightward in an arc, keeps the homes fixed in the center while the fields of grain flow past. This shot parallels the film's first image, of waves at Kamakura, thus creating a poetic metaphor and an ironic contrast. It also forms the horizontal counterpart of the vertical crane shot at the beach (fig. 219). Thus the last image, accompanied by the return of the children's choir used in the opening credits, finally anchors the title – correctly translated, not 'Early Summer' but *The Barley-Harvest Season*. The shot uses an utterly and specifically cinematic device to freshen up the clichéd theme of momentary change within overarching stability. And it supplies a climax to the film's additive stylistic development, its 'unfolding dynamic integrity'.

224.

225.

Ochazuke no aji
The Flavor of Green Tea over Rice

Shochiku. Script: Kogo Noda, Yasujiro Ozu. Cinematography: Yuharu Atsuta. Art direction: Tatsuo Hamada. Lighting: Itsuo Takashita. Editing: Yoshiyasu Hamamura. Music: Ichiro Saito. Cast: Shin Saburi (*Mokichi Satake*), Michiyo Kogure (*Taeko*), Koji Tsuruta (*Noboru*), Chishu Ryu (*Sadao Hirayama*), Chikage Awajima (*Aya Amamiya*), Keiko Tsujima (*Setsuko*). 12 reels, 3,156 meters. Surviving prints: 116 min. Released 1 October 1952. Script, negative, and prints in existence.

Bored with her marriage to the executive Mokichi, Taeko runs off to a spa with her friends. The Satakes' niece Setsuko refuses to participate in an arranged marriage, calling it feudalistic and reminding Taeko that her marriage has turned out badly. When Setsuko flees from an *o-miai* meeting, she tags along with Mokichi and the raffish office worker Noboru. Taeko discovers Mokichi's role in Setsuko's rebellion and after a mild quarrel with him, she leaves to be alone. Mokichi is abruptly dispatched to Uruguay, but he cannot contact Taeko before he flies off. His plane turns back, however, and he finds her waiting for him. Over a shared meal of *ochazuke*, simple rice with green tea, Taeko realizes the virtues of Mokichi's relaxed and simple mode of life.

About two-thirds of the way through *The Flavor of Green Tea over Rice*, Taeko is shown riding in the rear car of a train racketing over a trestle and bound for Nagoya. She has quarreled with her husband Motoki and wants to go away for a while. In the course of the scene, she does nothing but sit impassively, silent. Few directors would, I think, spend almost ninety seconds and nine shots on such an inert scene. Yet because it performs many functions in Ozu's characteristic strategy of filmmaking, the sequence offers several convenient ways into the film's overall design.

The scene marks a major turning point in the film's plot structure. The film is more loosely constructed than *Early Summer*, with often little more than appointments hooking scenes together. Many plot elements – such as Setsuko's escapade and the false scolding scene, and the wives' final roundtable discussion – are lifted directly from *What did the Lady Forget?*. The plot is fundamentally motivated by Taeko's boredom with her marriage, a state established in the first nine scenes when she fibs to Motoki and carouses at a spa with her friends. The second part of the syuzhet revolves around Setsuko's *o-miai*, a line of action imbricated with the marital situation of her aunt and uncle not only by virtue of their intervention in her family quarrel but also by the fact that she uses the disintegration of their marriage as proof of the futility of arranged matches. After Setsuko's *o-miai* fails and Taeko discovers

Motoki's role in it, the film's third section returns to the couple and their 'cold war'. Their awkwardness together and their discussion of their different tastes lead directly to Taeko's train journey, which she justifies in a note to him: 'I want to have my own way for a while.' Her solitude in the observation car at once expresses her self-centered reflection on her marriage and contrasts with the cheerful train journey to the spa with her friends. Taeko's impassive meditation during the train ride also foreshadows her reaction to Motoki's absence, when she sits silently at his desk looking at his cigarettes and later lies quietly on her bed. The act of thinking – so rarely represented in Hollywood films (recall Ozu's admiration for pensive moments in Wyler and Ford – p. 85) – prepares the way for Taeko's change in character when, at the plot's climax, the problem of her boredom will be solved by their shared meal of green tea over rice.

More generally, the train scene links up with Ozu's portrayal of Taeko's marriage and the class mores she represents. In Ozu's recasting of his 1939 home-front script (see pp. 280–1), he has brought the story closer to the satiric tone of his social comedies. Taeko, daughter of a wealthy businessman, is presented as wilful and spoiled, whereas Motoki is gradually characterized as more earthy and informal. The difference is underlined by their quarrel just before the train scene, when the two discuss varying tastes. (Her insistence that she will always travel first class motivates her solitude in the observation car.) Ozu's satire also hints at the inconsistencies in the upper bourgeoisie's lifestyles. Taeko always wears kimono but has a completely Western boudoir and sleeps in a four-poster bed. Motoki usually wears a business suit but sleeps in traditional fashion, in bedding on the floor. The plot respects the postwar split between the sexes: the male goes out at night with his associates, the wife spends the day with her friends, and as a couple they do very little together. A group of women alone may lapse into bawdy behavior and caustic repartee, as when during their stay at the inn the married women personify their husbands as thick-headed carp. Other touches, such as the caricature of Setsuko's insipid suitor and the dwelling on the recent craze for pachinko, contribute to the film's satire. A scene at a baseball game echoes the racetrack sequence in Lubitsch's *Lady Windermere's Fan* (1925). Most quietly savage of all is the lengthy, climactic scene in which Taeko and Motoki search for food, completely at a loss in their own kitchen: the bourgeoisie alienated from the most basic acts of life in a way, say, that the Mamiyas in *Early Summer* never are.

Narrationally, the film moves from a concentration on Taeko to a focus on Motoki, who is revealed to be less thick-headed than his wife thinks. The shift reveals a characteristically Ozuian commitment to Motoki's values. He is contrasted with Aya's emasculated husband Kyoichiro, who slinks around with a mistress and must ask his wife for spending money. During Motoki's trip to Uruguay and later, during their nocturnal meal of rice and tea, Taeko learns to appreciate his modest tastes. Later it is revealed that he has always seen through her lies, but in his casual way he had simply ignored them. Furthermore, Motoki is connected by causality and parallelism to the subplot involving Setsuko's arranged marriage. He tries to mediate between his wife's traditional demands for Setsuko's *o-miai* and Setsuko's justifiable lack of interest. Significantly, Motoki's younger parallel is the aspiring executive Noboru, 'the carefree', who tells Setsuko he likes simple things. Ideologically, it is a cliché to make a rich executive have cheap tastes; put his wealth aside and he becomes an ordinary chap. In accordance with this, Motoki's wartime nostalgia is both correct as per Occupation standards ('I want no more war at all') and redolent of a 'typically Japanese' sense of nature: he recalls the beauty of the coconut groves and the Southern Cross. Motoki is the first of Ozu's line of middle-aged businessmen who, amidst the relative comfort of the 1950s and 1960s, are moved by music and memories to recall the war days as oddly placid. Played by Shin Saburi, the happy-go-lucky Shojiro of *Toda Family* and Shochiku's equivalent of James Stewart in many a wartime product, Motoki becomes the model of the unpretentious postwar citizen. Ozu blunts the ideological point with comedy: Motoki's ineffectual handling of the Setsuko affair, his befuddlement by pachinko, and especially the goofy attitude which he inspires in Taeko at the end: 'Now his most loathsome points begin to fascinate me.'

By now motivic unity is to be expected in an Ozu film. During Motoki's reunion with his war buddy Hirayama, they recall the old North Bridge in Singapore – a motif which links up with the bridge that Taeko's train rattles along during her trip to Nagoya. This is Ozu's vehicle-film: two train-trips, a plane trip, and a dynamic opening scene in a car (which recalls the start of *What Did the Lady Forget?*). Motifs of place, such as Motoki's desk at his office and the radio cabinet and dining table at home, are invoked to set up a scene quickly. The omniscient narration establishes the couple's cabinet area long before it is actually inhabited, since two crucial meal scenes will occur there much later. Similarly, Motoki's table at home becomes his refuge from Taeko's scoldings, then much later serves as a reminder of him to her. It is chiefly through motifs of food that Motoki is paralleled not only to the ravenous Noboru but also to the maid Fumi, whose country relatives eat as noisily as her master does.

226.

Taeko's train scene is also exemplary for its measured control of tempo. While its découpage is not as symmetrically strict as that in other similar sequences, the sequence's shots vary within relatively narrow bounds. Two shots run seven seconds each, two run nine seconds, two run eleven seconds, two run twelve seconds, and one – a medium shot of Taeko reflecting – lasts fourteen seconds. The measured pacing is all the more prominent by virtue of the fact that there is no dialogue or movement to motivate shot changes; each cut is arbitrary in its timing. In the film as a whole, Ozu smoothes out the tempo chiefly by means of transitional shots of characters walking through corridors, either in an office building or at the Satakes' home. (This is another tactic seen in rudimentary form in *What Did the Lady Forget?*; pp. 276–7.)

227.

The 'flattening' of tempo thereby achieved can function as an intrinsic norm. For example, in the fourth scene, a series of three shots shows Fumi pattering through the house on her duties; three more shots show Taeko coming to greet Motoki as he returns home; and three more show the couple retracing Taeko's steps. The norm soon gets disrupted when, without any corridor shots, Setsuko simply enters the room. Such minute deviations in tempo can also accentuate the drama's development. During Taeko's and

324

228.

229.

230.

231.

232.

233.

Motoki's cold war in the third part, there are *no* shots showing them walking in corridors, only elliptical cuts of them leaving one room and entering another. Once they are separated, however, corridor shots return, depicting Motoki wandering through the house in Taeko's absence or showing Taeko and her friends in the house while he is away. When Satake returns from his aborted plane trip, the narration parallels his return home in scene 4 by following Taeko through two corridor shots and then taking the couple through two more. When the couple decide to fix a snack, two more corridor shots take them to the kitchen. Even before their reconciliation is achieved, the narration has prepared for it by (differentially) resettling into the domestic tempo of the beginning.

234.

The train scene constitutes a node in the narration's characteristic use of other film techniques. The sequence starts with two jarring intermediate spaces: the railroad track seen from the rear platform (fig. 226) and a rearward cut to the inside of the rear observation car (fig. 227) which still leaves Taeko offscreen. Cut to a medium-shot of her, pensive (fig. 228). Cut to a long-shot of her (fig. 229) which 'answers' fig. 227 by leaving the table and vase offscreen. Another medium-shot of her (fig. 230) reveals the long-shot to have been an arbitrary rhythmic interruption, since she neither moves nor changes expression. As a deafening clatter announces the train's crossing of the trestle, Ozu returns to the longer view of the car (fig. 231) and we watch the bridge race into the distance. Cut back to Taeko, as before (fig. 232). A new shot, parallel to that which opened the scene, puts us back on the platform, watching gridwork contract around the vanishing point (fig. 233). But the symmetry is broken, the scene continues for one more shot: a cut takes us back inside the car for a final view of the table, flowers, and doors (fig. 234). Lest a critic try to read the scene as conveying something *about* Taeko – that, say, the rushing retreat of the tracks symbolizes her regret at leaving home – we should recall that we do not know, and will never know, what she is thinking now. Rather, stylistic patterning uses a hiatus in the narrative in order to come forward. In its gradual revelation of contiguous spaces, its permutational shifts, its play upon abstract compositional forms and movements, and its expansion of scenographic elements far beyond causal needs, the scene typifies the parametric tendencies of Ozu's narration. And it includes, as usual, a comically eccentric detail: the legs and feet of another passenger (fig. 229) who will be resolutely ignored throughout the sequence.

235.

In its obstinate refusal to show us what Taeko sees, the scene also exemplifies one moment of the film's point-of-view continuum. The first scene plays on optical POV from a moving car as Taeko and Setsuko ride down the Ginza, with the shots out the car windows sometimes correlating and sometimes not correlating with the passengers' glances. During the train trip to the spa, the narration makes deliberately ambiguous the characters' placement in relation to views of the passing landscape (fig. 235). The spa visit is itself bracketed by Ozu's characteristic 'unclaimed' establishing shots from windows. (See pp. 116, 132.) Such dislocation of POV patterns are similar to the film's bold use of intermediate spaces. Taeko's train journey foregrounds this device by making five out of nine shots cutaways. Earlier, during the spa scene, a cutaway to the pond outside creates a false scene ending. A cutaway from Hirayama's wartime song to the empty, darkened pachinko parlor is even more temporally uncertain, since when Hirayama started singing the parlor was apparently still open and busy. The film also initiates Ozu's 'false' dialogue hook, whereby character dialogue sets up the expectation of seeing someone somewhere else and the narration obligingly cuts to this new spot only to reveal that the character in question is *not* there. Here a cut to Motoki's vacant desk in his office becomes, retroactively, another intermediate space wedged into the succession of scenes.

In *Green Tea*, the issue of intermediate spaces leads necessarily to the film's most outrageous stylistic device – its camera movements. This is a complicated matter. On one dimension, there are camera movements which arise from the movement of a vehicle, such as the opening scene's shots through car windows or later shots from trains, such as those during Taeko's trip. Along another dimension, we can distinguish between those camera movements which follow character movement (such as the last scene's track back to follow Setsuko and Noburo walking down the street) and those which do not (such as the movement down the aisle of the kabuki theatre, a repetition of a movement from *Early Summer*). Along yet another dimension, there are the obliquely-angled movements, such as those just mentioned, as opposed to perfectly linear, forward or backward movements. In a sense, the railroad-track shots of Taeko's train journey exemplify the latter, but the most striking instances are those short, frequent track-ins or track-outs in relation to

326

intermediate spaces in the settings. There is, finally, the question of timing – *when* in the shot's progress the camera movement starts.

The narration uses these rigorously distinct options as a basis for playful parametric variation. At the start of a scene, the camera will already be tracking back across a set; or after the characters leave, the camera will suddenly glide forward, toward no particular target. In the fourth scene, as Taeko and Motoki walk down the corridor, the camera tracks back to follow them as they advance. A 180-degree cut to a forward-tracking shot creates a wrenching kinesthetic effect as the couple walk away from us. (The effect harks back to similar cuts in *That Night's Wife*.) But then the couple go out of the corridor and for two seconds the forward track continues, turning the corridor into a fleeting intermediate space. A subsequent variant is to allow the characters to walk out of sight into the distance and then start to track slowly forward, creating the most perversely fruitless of 'following shots'. (At this rate we will never catch up.) While there is symmetry and inversion among some of these movements, on the whole they can be understood only as abstract spatial markers, born of a rigid grid of differences and exhaustively deployed across the film, wielded by a narration that can flaunt its parametric operations.

The playfulness of these operations is evident not only in the train sequence but also in the last scene, when Noburo and Setsuko walk along the street. Narratively, certain parallels emerge: he has already been likened to Motoki, and now Setsuko's poutiness echoes Taeko's wilfulness. As she flees from him, the camera keeps its distance, allowing her to hide in a guard's stall and push him out. He pursues her into the distance, and the camera unseats itself and inches forward for ten seconds before the fade-out. As a satiric alternative to the clichéd track-back final shot, this works quite well; but since the earlier 'mistimed' camera movements were applied only to Taeko or Motoki, it reinforces the narrative parallels as well. Ozu would never again employ such flagrant camera movements, but it is characteristic of him to subject them to rigorous, semi-abstract organization.

1953

Tokyo monogatari
Tokyo Story

Shochiku. Script: Kogo Noda, Yasujiro Ozu. Cinematography: Yuharu Atsuta. Art direction: Tatsuo Hamada. Lighting: Itsuo Takashita. Editing: Yoshiyasu Hamamura. Music: Kojun Saito. Cast: Chishu Ryu (*Shukichi Hirayama*), Chieko Higashiyama (*Tomi*), Setsuko Hara (*Noriko*), Haruko Sugimura (*Shige Kaneko*), Nobuo Nakamura (*Kaneko*), So Yamamura (*Koichi*), Kuniko Miyake (*Ayako*), Kyoko Kagawa (*Kyoko*), Eijiro Tono (*Sanpei Numata*), Shiro Osaka (*Keizo*), Zen Murase (*Minoru*), Mitsuhiro Mori (*Isamu*). 14 reels, 3,702 meters. Surviving prints: 135 min. Released 3 November 1953. Script, negative, and prints in existence.

Leaving their youngest daughter Kyoko in Onomichi, Shukichi and Tomi Hirayama visit their son Koichi and daughter Shige in Tokyo. They find them busy and a little callous. It is Noriko, widow of their son Shoji, who offers them genuine hospitality. Koichi and Shige send their parents on a trip to the spa at Atami, but homesickness and the noisy resort atmosphere make the couple depart. Arriving unexpectedly in Tokyo, they have no place to stay. They separate, Tomi going to sleep at Noriko's while Sukichi goes out drinking with old friends. Eventually they set out for home, only to be forced to stop in Osaka when Tomi falls ill. Shortly after they return to Onomichi, she dies. The children, initially grief-stricken, hasten back to Tokyo. Only Noriko stays on to help. As she leaves, Shukichi thanks her, urges her to remarry, and gives her his wife's watch.

Tokyo Story has long been regarded as quintessential Ozu and is often considered his masterpiece. It was a great popular success in Japan, and it was the Ozu film that aroused interest among American critics upon its release in 1972. (Unfortunately, it does not survive in good condition: the original negative was destroyed by a laboratory fire, and the internegative struck from positive prints does not render the chiaroscuro that Ozu and Atsuta sought.[82]) In certain respects the film can stand as typical Ozu, but in others it is an unusual work, particularly in view of its immediate predecessors.

The film is characteristic in its recycling of earlier material. The rural parents' visit to Tokyo is an Ozu motif that stretches back to *Dreams of Youth*. The parents' belief that their children are 'better than average' echoes that of the old Hirayamas in *Early Summer* (though here the phrase works more as solace than as accurate judgment). A gag involving rude children and a lumpy bag is lifted from *Early Summer*'s bread-kicking scene. In recasting McCarey's *Make Way for Tomorrow*, which Ozu had not seen but Noda had, *Tokyo Story* continues Ozu's 1930s habit of borrowing from American cinema. (In addition, the boy Minoru whistles the theme from *Stagecoach*.) *Brothers and*

Sisters of the Toda Family is another obvious source, evoked in the theme of the good siblings and the plot device of shuttling the parents from household to household. In its generally sombre tone, *Tokyo Story* is reminiscent of *There Was a Father* – another film in which Ryu plays an aging father. As usual, there are nostalgic scenes looking back to the prewar period, as when characters linger over memories of visits to Kamakura, a childhood view of fireworks, or a drunken night on the town.

In its plot structure, *Tokyo Story* resembles *The Only Son*, but with the confrontations left out. *Tokyo Story*'s immediate predecessors contain much stronger causal lines. In *Early Summer*, for instance, a Tokyo visit from a provincial relative serves as an expository mechanism before the plot moves to the central intrigue involving Noriko's marriage. Here Ozu and Noda present an episodic, leisurely survey of the extended family, structured around journeys that link Onomichi, Tokyo, Atami, and Osaka. Variety is created by shifts from one picturesque locale to another and by the gradual revelation of every family member's routines, both at home and at work. Note, for instance, how the parents' first stopover in Osaka en route to Tokyo is simply omitted from the syuzhet, so that we meet the youngest son Keizo only after the mother's illness on the way back home has forced them to stay with him again. In two comparatively late scenes, one of Keizo at work and one of Shukichi and Tomi in his room, we finally get information about this last family member. (This delay also has important effects on how we judge his character, as I shall suggest shortly.) Very late, the plot implies that all the traveling may have brought on Tomi's death; only here does a fairly loose causality enter to bind the film together.

What serves this binding function at the more local level are long- or short-term appointments, plans, and 'hooks'. Upon his arrival in Tokyo, Shukichi announces that he will look up Hattori; thirteen scenes later, he does. Near the end of a scene someone will refer to a trip or an outing, and the next scene will present it. The several scenes following the visit to Atami, all taking place within twenty-four hours in Tokyo, are linked as accounts of Shukichi's night out with his pals and of Tomi's overnight stay with Noriko. Just as the film plays down causality and overt conflict, so does it omit deadlines. In the early and middle portions, the only touches of 'drama' are the fleeting premonitions of Tomi's death – once during her outing with Isamu, once in her dizziness on the Atami sea-wall, and in several conversations.

The slackening of causality allows the film to make thematic material particularly salient. Like Ozu's other popular masterpiece *I Was Born, But . . .*, *Tokyo Story* leans to the didactic side. One element is crystallized in a proverb near the film's end: 'Be kind to your parents while they're alive.' This is set against the possibility of kindness extended by unrelated people, such as Noriko, and even Shige's husband Kaneko. There is also the Ozu motif of parental disillusionment, seen in the echoes of *The Only Son* and *Early Summer*. This theme gets absorbed into a more cosmic sense that life will always fall short of expectations. In the stunning final dialogue between Kyoko and Noriko – one of the most famous scenes in all of Ozu's work – the younger girl denounces her siblings' selfishness. Noriko replies that it's inevitable:

>*Kyoko*: Isn't life disappointing?
>*Noriko* (smiling): Yes, it is.

Such explicit discussions of piety, kindness, and the nature of life may invite us to see this as a fairly schematic tale. As Ozu remarked, 'This is one of my most melodramatic pictures.'[83] Yet it is not even as much a parable as is *I Was Born, But . . . . Tokyo Story* uses characterization, as revealed through narrative structure and narrational processes, to enrich and qualify its stark thematic oppositions.

Let us start with the apparently sharp contrast between Shige and Noriko. As Dennis Konshak points out, characterization of the two women starts in the second scene, when both greet the arriving parents. Right after Noriko remarks that Tomi hasn't changed, Shige says she's gotten fatter.[84] Throughout the action, Shige is treated as a penny-pinching, sharp-tongued killjoy, the prototype of the uncaring daughter. Yet according to Sato this portrait is not a savage one; certain scenes we might take as damning – such as her telling her customers that her parents are just friends from the country, or her bringing her mourning-clothes to Onomichi – can be regarded as comic.[85] This would make the long-held take in which, muttering, she prepares to put her drunken father to bed a humorous high point of the film. By contrast, our first impression of Noriko is that of unblemished goodness. Her star image (Hara was known as the 'eternal virgin'), her cramped working-class lifestyle, her very formal speech to her in-laws, and in the arrival scene her late appearance – all set Noriko off from the main family. It is she, however, who delivers the ultimate news to Kyoko that life is disappointing. This raises a muted question about Noriko's character: does this verdict stem from *akirame*, resignation in the face of destiny, or from a more immediate source? The plot has an answer, but before we consider it we might glance at a family member who is usually neglected, even by critics who put characterization at the center of their interest.

The youngest son Keizo is introduced quite late, only after the parents are returning from Tokyo. Postponing the presentation of Keizo allows us to scrutinize him for any sign of the narrowness and ingratitude of Koichi or Shige, or the spontaneous kindness of Noriko. The results are mixed. At his railroad office he tells his co-worker of the parents' unexpected stop and calls it a nuisance. But his colleague reminds him of the filial-piety proverb, and Keizo says with a smile, 'That's right. "No one can serve his parents beyond the grave".' The possibility that he may be a complex figure is confirmed when he leaves Tomi's funeral to sit outside because, as he puts it, burning incense won't make up for his deficits as a son. As he wanders back to the ceremony, he murmurs: 'No one can serve his parents beyond the grave.' Yet even this burst of self-recrimination is not definitive, for later, in the restaurant, he withdraws his offer to stay with his father and plans to leave with Shige and Koichi. Standing halfway between the Tokyo kinfolk and the stronger commitment of Kyoko and Noriko, Keizo reminds us of the gradations in all the characters.

These gradations give the theme a social dimension that is usually not mentioned in relation to the film. What has made the older children so callous? Partly their nuclear families, which count for more than the *ie*, but also their overriding commitment to their jobs – Koichi's medical practice and Shige's hairdressing business. Shukichi's old crony Numata says that his son is a failure; like Ryosuke in *The Only Son*, the son claims that Tokyo is so big that one cannot get ahead. Shige and Koichi have been changed by the Tokyo rat race, while Noriko is at least temporarily content to be simply an 'office lady', and Kyoko can live at home and teach elementary school. Keizo is once again an intermediate case, without the bourgeois aspirations of his Tokyo brother and sister but still putting in his time in the office even while his mother is ill. This is a 'Tokyo story' in that the city shapes characters' temperaments. In recognizing how the children have changed since childhood in Onomichi, Shukichi seems to have arrived at the reconciliation Otsune may or may not achieve in *The Only Son*, for he tells Numata (in an echo of the grandfather in *Early Summer*) that they mustn't expect too much.

A still more delicate shading is given Noriko's character during the penultimate scene, in which the source of her verdict on life's disappoint-ments is suggested. After Shukichi has reiterated his wife's advice that Noriko forget Shoji, he thanks her and calls her a good woman. It is then that Noriko, like Keizo, criticizes herself. She has not been the dutiful widow; she *has* forgotten Shoji. 'There are days when I don't think of him at all.' Like the niece in *What Did the Lady Forget?*, the youngest Toda siblings, and the daughter in *Late Spring*, Noriko is more conservative than her elders. Under the idealized *ie* system, a widowed daughter-in-law would be taken in by the main family; but that system is dead, and Noriko must find another way of living. Having no career to occupy her time, feeling that she should not remarry, she finds her life hanging in desperate uncertainty: 'The days pass and nothing happens. I feel a kind of impatience. My heart seems to be waiting – for something. Oh yes, I'm selfish.' The traditionally proper attitude of a young widow is at war with her wishes. Shukichi gently waves away her self-recrimination. Just as Somiya in *Late Spring* urged his daughter not to waste her life with him, Shukichi tells Noriko to feel no remorse about remarrying. Ozu's Occupation-tinted liberalism is an undercurrent throughout the scene, as Shukichi repeats that Noriko is a good woman, 'an honest woman'. He gives her Tomi's watch and virtually bids her farewell, as if she were an unmarried daughter leaving the family. What makes her goodness finally plausible is her honesty, her uncertainties, and her demanding standards. In the film's final moments, the script introduces an equally honest modesty into Shukichi's personality, through the same device of self-recrimination. Earlier, in the vigil scene and in the dawn afterward, Shukichi is presented as having passed through grief. Now the serenity of his dawn-greeting scene is qualified by his remark to the neighbor woman: 'If I had known things would come to this, I'd have been kinder to her.' By making even the most virtuous people clear-sighted about their own shortcomings, Ozu's plot nuances the stark oppositions in the film's thematic material.

This discreet manipulation of fabula data is characteristic of *Tokyo Story*'s narration. In many respects, the film is one of Ozu's most conservative, making its rigors quite 'flat' and banishing playfulness almost completely. The sort of steady pace we observed in the corridor shots of *The Flavor of Green Tea*

236.

237.

238.

239.

over Rice now dominates the entire film. Against the sober background of more or less standard optical POV, *donden* cutting, and deep-space compositions recalling those of the family in *Early Summer*, certain picturesque moments stand out, such as the way the fallen Tomi curls her body within the arc of the distant island (fig. 236). Most remarkably, the film frequently does not utilize contiguous elements for intermediate shots between scenes of narrative action. But the film's stylistic texture is in fact woven out of a rigorous development of such spaces, as well as a patterned use of sound. Both tactics create a growing fluidity and emotional sweep as the film goes on. In the early portions of the film, landscape shots are used in a quite traditional manner to establish the locales (Onomichi, the Koto area of Tokyo, Shige's beauty parlor). There is almost none of the dominant/overtone interplay we find in previous Ozu works, and only one transition – that between scene 2, which ends with Minoru's empty desk and a shot of him playing on the hill, and scene 3, which starts with him studying in his father's office – creates a brief dynamic of presence and absence. Similarly, in the early stretches music does not link scenes; it will either start jarringly or simply give way to traffic or a noisy party. However, at the end of the ninth scene, Ozu begins to develop stronger visual links between scenes. Noriko fans Tomi and Shukichi; cut to Koichi and Shige fanning themselves. At the end of that scene, cut from Koichi and Shige, still fanning, to women sitting on the Atami sea-wall, fanning. The Atami sequences are rendered cohesive by the film's first notable visual permutations: three views of the sea, punctuating phases of their stay (figs. 237–239).

Upon the couple's return to Tokyo, music becomes more of a continuity factor. It links the scene of their return to that of their rest in the park, as well as leading from Noriko's apartment to Shige's shop. By the time the couple leaves, we have a genuine dominant/overtone passage as well, sidling through a train station waiting room. Finally, as the plot winds down, the narration begins to create intermediate spaces out of properly causal ones. At Noriko's office, at Koichi's home, at the Onomichi home – more and more Ozu does not cut away when a character leaves the shot, letting the space stand empty for some moments. During Tomi's death, a scene starts with a moth batting against a lamp (an echo of *There Was a Father* and *A Hen in the Wind*); at her funeral, Ozu can transform Keizo's POV shots of the graveyard into pure intermediate images. We have already seen (p. 55) the film's systematic use of different sorts of offscreen sound; this too lends a sense of developing unity to the final portions. The film's epilogue[86] can return to the landscapes of the prologue, now no longer atmospheric 'placing' shots but images and sounds charged with narrative connotations: the train that carries Noriko echoing the locomotive noise that recurs throughout the film, the view of the boats recalling the rhythmic chuggings, hammerings, drillings, and cicadas' chitterings we have heard throughout the film. The final images of Onomichi harbor remain suspended between being Shukichi's point of view and constituting a grand, omniscient rhyme with the prologue.

Tokyo Story has invited such a range of moral and spiritual interpretation that we might usefully remember in closing that it is typical of Ozu's works in arising from immediate concerns of his historical moment. The shots of

Tokyo construction were topical during the postwar building boom. Contemporary observers remarked that postwar economic organization was eroding the traditional *ie* system, and care of the elderly became a more pressing problem. A popular book of the early 1950s was called *Children Who Do Not Look After Their Parents*.[87] Even at their most evocative, Ozu's films are always referential.

Tokyo Story (production still)

1956

Soshun

Early Spring

Shochiku. Script: Kogo Noda, Yasujiro Ozu. Cinematography: Yuharu Atsuta. Art direction: Tatsuo Hamada. Lighting: Masao Kato. Editing: Yoshiyasu Hamamura. Music: Kojun Saito. Cast: Chikage Awajima (*Masako Sugiyama*), Ryo Ikebe (*Shoji*), Keiko Kishi (*Chiyo Kaneko*), Teiji Takahashi (*Taizo Aoki*), Chishu Ryu (*Kiichi Onodera*), So Yamamura (*Yutaka Kawai*), Haruko Sugimura (*Tamako*), Takako Fujino (*Terumi Aoki*), Masami Taura (*Koichi Kitagawa*), Kumeko Urabe (*Shige Kitagawa*), Kuniko Miyake (*Yukiko Kawai*). 16 reels, 3,956 meters. Surviving prints: 144 min. Released 29 January 1957. Script, negative, and prints in existence.

Shoji, a young office worker, is drawn into an affair with 'Goldfish', a typist among his group of commuting friends. This leads to his eventual separation from his wife Masako. At the same time, Shoji decides to accept a transfer to one of his firm's rural outposts. Masako comes to join him, and they are reconciled.

The mid-1950s saw important changes in the Japanese film industry, and *Early Spring* bears some traces of them. Although theatre attendance had risen close to one billion and Japanese films had won increasing acclaim on the international scene, Shochiku was becoming increasingly embattled. New genres, such as science fiction, rock-and-roll musicals, and erotic films, made home dramas look old-fashioned. The demand for double-feature programs strained the firm's production capacity. In 1955–56, for the first time in decades, Shochiku's profits fell into second place, behind the new Daiei.[88] Under Kido's leadership, the studio tried various tactics. It offered mildly scandalous products of its own, while at the same time Kido sought to update the Ofuna-flavor film. Both *Early Spring* and its successor, *Tokyo Twilight*, seem to embody something of these efforts: more melodramatic in their plots, using more explicitly sexual intrigues, they suggest attempts to modernize the *shoshimin-geki*. Big stars, most of them young, make *Early Spring* a self-consciously 'youth-oriented' film. Despite a shift in the 'feasible subset' of choices, however, Ozu continues to recast characteristic themes, narrative structures, and narrational strategies.

Various thematic materials carry over from earlier works. There are by-now obligatory scenes recalling pre-1946 life. (The film's title may also be an oblique and ironic reference to *Early Spring*, a 1942 collection of patriotic essays by Naoya Shiga.) The reunion of Shoji's war buddies explicitly recalls the 1930s, not only in their reminiscences of eating dog-meat sukiyaki in China but also in particular echoes of Ozu's earlier films. The men's chant recalls the cheerleading of *I Flunked, But . . .* and *Where Now Are the Dreams of*

Youth?, and one of the two pals who goes home with Shoji is played by Hideo Mitsui, a star of *Dragnet Girl*, *Story of Floating Weeds*, and other pictures. The men's drunken ineffectuality recalls the fallen male figure of Ozu's early work, and their nostalgic reminiscences are neatly undercut by Masako's comment: 'With soldiers like that, no wonder Japan lost the war.' The film also exploits a Tokyo nostalgia that echoes the end of *Tokyo Chorus* and *What Did the Lady Forget?*. The train motif makes the final scenes at Seta Bridge and in Mitsuishi parallel to the Tokyo and Kamata ones. At the film's end, when Shoji and Masako look out at the bleak smokestacks of the industrial town, they agree that three years will pass quickly, but then he points out that by taking that train they could be in Tokyo tomorrow.

These recurrent elements are subordinated to two major 'semantic fields'. One involves marriage, as embodied in the domestic difficulties of Shoji and Masako. This constitutes one line of action. It is initiated in the couple's bored routine of awakening in the first scene, continues through Shoji's taking Masako for granted and her increasing indifference to him, intensifies with Shoji's neglect of their son's death-anniversary, and climaxes with her discovery of his infidelity. The action is not resolved until the last scene, when Masako comes to join him in Mitsuishi and they determine to start afresh there. In this respect, the plot resembles that of *What Did the Lady Forget?*, *A Hen in the Wind*, and *The Flavor of Green Tea over Rice*, each of which ends with an estranged couple seeking to create a better marriage. Through a series of parallels across the film, the Sugiyamas' marriage is echoed in that of their immediate neighbors, in that of Shoji's pal Aoki, in that of the widow Saeko, and in that of Masako's mother. The parallels allow the plot to voice a range of attitudes toward marital infidelity, ranging from Shoji's co-workers' somewhat self-righteous condemnation to Masako's mother's counsel of benign neglect. Significantly, it is a bachelor – Shoji's mentor Onodera, played by Chishu Ryu – who may help reunite the couple for a second chance.

'I wanted,' Ozu remarked, 'to portray what you might call the pathos of the white-collar life.'[89] This constitutes the second semantic field mobilized by the film. The band of young commuters to which Shoji belongs was modeled upon neighbors of Noda to whom he introduced Ozu.[90] *Early Spring* establishes its referentiality in its second scene, a quiet montage of suburban workers converging upon the train station. The sequence is reminiscent of 1930s Japanese urban dramas, especially Ozu's own *Walk Cheerfully* and *Dragnet Girl*, and of European 'city symphonies'. The company milieu also creates a causal pressure: in a device already exploited in *Early Summer* and *Green Tea*, Shoji is transferred, which intensifies his dramatic crisis. At the same time, the thematic implications of the salaryman lifestyle are brought out early when two workers in Shoji's office look down from their window and comment on the flood of commuters. As we have seen (p. 35), this was no less a contemporary commonplace than the salaryman clichés of the 1920s and 1930s. One American sociologist reported during the 1950s that the new salaryman became a popular identification figure: he 'mediates the direct impact of Westernization and industrialization by offering a model of life which is modest enough to be within the range of realistic hopes and modern enough to be worthy of their highest aspirations.'[91]

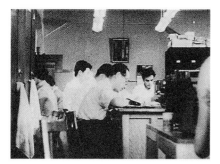

240.

241.

Yet Ozu's film assembles a range of comments which, at intervals through the plot, criticize the salaryman ethos. Near the end of the first day, Onodera says to his self-employed friend Kawai: 'Sometimes I just hate my work.' Shoji turns aside his war buddies' envy of his white-collar job by reminding them that they have skills: 'If I'm fired, I starve. . . . Salaried workers are a dime a dozen.' A scene of Shoji's commuting pals compaining about their lives is immediately followed by a scene in which the sickly Miura longingly imagines going back to work, and then recalls first seeing the company on a school excursion. An ironic image of the company man, Miura kills himself with an overdose of sleeping powder. At his funeral, Kawai remarks that Miura's naive loyalty was traceable to his being a bachelor. 'Disillusionment comes quickly if one has a wife and children. Babies come faster than a raise.' Near the film's end, as Shoji is about to leave Tokyo on a company transfer, the theme is generalized still more. An old man whom he meets at Kawai's bar says that he has nothing to look forward to in retirement: his pension won't finance his opening a stationery shop. 'I've worked thirty-one long years to find that life is an empty dream.' To this emblem of what awaits Shoji, Ozu and Noda add Kawai's remark that the home of Finance Minister Ikeda – once the nation's 'No.1 Salary Man' – is now rundown and forgotten. Those critics who see Ozu's postwar films as lacking social bite should recall such explicit discussions, as well as the visual portrayal of office life as a series of perspective views of files, lockers, desks, and machinery (fig. 240), and the shots which literalize the nickname *madogiwa-zoku*, 'workers who sit by the windows' (fig. 241).

Not only Shoji but two other characters serve to link the worlds of marriage and work. Shoji has his affair with Chiyo Kaneko, or 'Goldfish', who works in a typing pool and is one of his fellow commuters. Normally Shoji keeps his home life separate from his work, but his pals' quizzing of Goldfish about Shoji leads her to burst into his household to see him, thus confirming Masako's suspicions and leading her to leave him. It is another mediating figure, the widower Onodera, who helps heal the breach. As both a senior employee and a friend of the family, he can spend the night with the couple and advise Shoji about work. At the start of the film, he is what Shoji will become, an exile working in the provinces. Near the end, on the Seta bridge, he tells Shoji that because a company can be 'a cold thing', married life is precious. Onodera's subsequent letter to Masako may have affected her decision to rejoin her husband. At the level of ideological work, Onodera justifies a resignation to the impersonality of the office worker's life: one needs a loving marriage in order to be 'carefree'. Here, individuality gets defined in a 'privatist' way, as appropriate only at the level of friends and family. (See p. 169.) Onodera also titles the film when at Lake Biwa he remarks that young men are in 'the spring time of life'.

To summarize subjects and themes so baldly is of course to falsify the dynamic process of the film, its play of narrative structure and narration. Ozu's longest surviving film, *Early Spring* employs no fewer than forty-three scenes to depict the salaryman's domestic and office life. The first seven scenes, in what may constitute a leisurely replay of the lost *Life of an Office Worker*, establish a day's routines – commuting, arrival at the office, work,

1956

336

lunch break, after-work drinks, and returning home. ('I tried to avoid any-thing that would be dramatic and to accumulate only casual scenes of everyday life in hopes that the audience would feel the sadness of that kind of life.'[92]) This first part is also broadly expository, mentioning Miura and the Sugiyamas' dead son. As in *Early Summer*, an early visit from an older person (here, Onodera) prepares for his role in the final portion.

These initial scenes, all occurring on a single day, center fairly closely on Shoji. But then the syuzhet's range of knowledge widens. After the Sunday hike, the middle portion of the film juxtaposes Shoji's love affair with other actions: Masako at home or with her friends, various members of the commuting gang with their friends or families. (This sort of alternating treatment is foreshadowed in miniature during the first scene, which wedges brief vignettes of the neighbors' life into the portrayal of Shoji and Masako's routine.) The Balzacian breadth of the film's depiction of the salaryman life arises from this strategy of interspersed episodes. At the film's first major climax, scene 32, the plot carries the alternating tactic down to the shot-by-shot level. Masako has discovered the affair with Goldfish. The narration crosscuts Masako downstairs with Shoji upstairs, ending the scene in typically Ozuian symmetries. After this scene, when Shoji and Masako separate, they are juxtaposed through crosscutting (scenes 35, 36, 37), through just missing one another in one locale (scene 38), and most sharply, through a cut from scene 38 to 39 that juxtaposes them in a false shot/reverse-shot. The last five sequences balance the first eight in refusing crosscutting and adhering to Shoji's actions – visiting Kawai, celebrating with his friends, visiting Onodera, working in Mitsuishi, and finally dis-covering Masako at his flat. Throughout, when the causal action does not propel the juxtaposition of scenes, there are always appointments and 'hooks' to create a local cohesion between episodes.

The alternation of episodes featuring different characters proceeds from Ozu's characteristically unrestricted narration, but it also cooperates with that narration's tendency to create many informational gaps. (See pp. 69-70.) One effect of this is to yield very oblique handlings of melodramatic clichés. For example, instead of presenting Masako's discovery of Shoji's lipstick-stained handkerchief directly, in scene 18, the narration presents her recounting of it to her mother, much later, in scene 26. Masako's visit to her dead son's grave, a sure-fire Ofuna tearjerker, is built up strenuously, and then ellided, replaced by a semi-comic scene involving Aoki, his pregnant wife, and a dog. Miura, Shoji's stricken colleague, is mentioned throughout – indeed, Shoji uses him as an alibi for infidelity – but we do not see him until scene 29. Similarly, when Shoji and Goldfish ride the truck during the hike, the scene ends abruptly, with a moving shot from the truck. Denied any access to the rest of the hike, we can only speculate on what might have happened between them.

More generally, the central love affair is handled through ellipsis and refraction. After the initial night (scenes 15–17), we do not see the couple alone together again, so for a time it is unclear whether the affair continues. The only evidence we have is second-hand: Masako's observation that Shoji now comes home early, and the co-workers' gossip about seeing him walking with Goldfish. But the former might simply reflect his contrition after one night's wrong step, and the latter, as Goldfish herself points out, is not damning. Because of the narration's reticence on the matter, we come to accept Shoji's guilt simply because everyone else does. As a result, we are shifted between an omniscient range of knowledge that encourages us to note parallels and ironies and a more suppressive, gap-ridden presentation that encourages us to suspend conclusions and rethink assumptions.

In its less playful aspect, this narration serves an external view of character, and the gaps contribute to making the three central characters psychologically indeterminate. Critics' accounts of Shoji's mental states and motivations do not come to grips with the fact that the narration simply gives us no clear or particular cause for his fling with Goldfish. The effect, as in *The Only Son*, is to make him more of an illustrative type, the young office worker simply bored and discouraged with his lot. At the film's end, when we learn that in Mitsuishi he now reads incessantly, we may sense a character change of sorts, but even this is qualified: he says there's nothing else to do. As for Goldfish, another puzzle persists. When she learns that Shoji is leaving, she confronts him tearfully, accuses him of escaping, and slaps his face. The next time we see her, at his farewell party, she wishes him well and smilingly offers to shake hands. What has led to this change of heart? We will never find out. A similar question arises with respect to Masako's reconciliation with Shoji. She arrives at Mitsuishi, ready to start anew, but nothing in particular – Shoji's letter, Onodera's letter, or even the eventual pressure of her mother's advice – is credited with softening her attitude. By virtue of its expansive scope, its insertions of scenes featuring peripheral characters, and its calculated suppressiveness, *Early Spring* keeps us resolutely outside its protagonists, leaving gaps in the syuzhet to the very end.

Less seriously, the mixture of unrestricted sweep and gap-creating tendencies produces Ozu's typical decenterings and deceptions. A scattered series of unmotivated tracking shots generates comic expectations akin to the more elaborate systems in *Early Summer* and *Green Tea*. The squared-off layout of Shoji's office creates stunningly ambivalent right-angled cuts. Including so many scenes allows Ozu to build parametric variations in every locale. As in *Tokyo Story*, intermediate spaces consist not of objects but of landscapes, and these will be exploited for many jarring transitions. Masako looks out a window; cut to a towering advertising sign; cut to Goldfish walking with Shoji. The sign functions first as an ambiguous POV shot, then as an establishing shot by virtue of contiguity. Even more vivid are two complementary misleading cutaways. At the end of the first scene of Shoji and his pals playing mah-jongg, the narration cuts to the apartment-house corridor, where the scene had begun. But this is a false scene ending, for then we cut back to them playing and singing. Only then does the scene end – without another shot of the corridor. The same cheating of expectations is at work in a parallel sequence that introduces Shoji's job at Mitsuishi. After five shots of smokestacks, the narration cuts inside the company office, with workers busy at their desks. We might expect the story action to begin, but then another cut takes us outside the office to show the building in extreme long-shot. So far, the scene resembles that at the start of *The Only Son* (see pp. 136–7), and we might expect that now we will be moved to another time and place. No: Ozu cuts back inside the building, to the office where Shoji and another clerk comment on the heat. *Then* the scene, such as it is, is over, and the narration cuts back outside for more landscape shots. The play of symmetry with asymmetry, of continuity with contiguity, and the requirement that we recall shots invites us to attend to composition and découpage for their own sakes, as a stylistic pattern running alongside the exigencies of subject, theme, and action.

1957

Tokyo boshoku
Tokyo Twilight

Shochiku. Script: Kogo Noda, Yasujiro Ozu. Cinematography: Yuharu Atsuta. Art direction: Tatsuo Hamada. Lighting: Akira Aomatsu. Music: Kojun Saito. Editing: Yoshiyasu Hamamura. Cast: Setsuko Hara (*Takako Numata*), Ineko Arima (*Akiko Sugiyama*), Chishu Ryu (*Shukichi Sugiyama*), Isuzu Yamada (*Kisako Soma*), Teiji Takahashi (*Noburo Kawaguchi*), Masami Taura (*Kenji Kimura*), Haruko Sugimura (*Shigeko Takeuchi*), So Yamamura (*Seki Sekiguchi*), Kinzo Shin (*Yasuo Numata*), Kamatari Fujiwara (*noodle vendor*), Nobuo Nakamura (*Sakae Aiba*). 15 reels, 3,841 meters. Surviving prints: 141 min. Released 30 April 1957. Script, negative, and prints in existence.

Shukichi Sugiyama's elder daughter Takako has left her husband and come to stay with him. Her sister Akiko is pregnant and searches for her lover Kenji. She ends up having an abortion. In the meantime, both daughters find out that their mother Kikuko, whom they believed dead, has returned to Tokyo. Years before, she had abandoned their father for another man. Devastated, Akiko commits suicide. As Kikuko and her husband leave Tokyo, she waits in vain for Takako to see her off at the station. Takako decides to return to her husband and try to make their marriage work.

Like *Story of Floating Weeds*, *Tokyo Twilight* represents a case of sharp internal struggle. Most generally, the film's frankly melodramatic materials and devices clash with the Ozuian penchant for suggestion and abstract structure. More specifically, there is the struggle between the youth-centered plot line and the emphasis placed on the role of the old. The unease which some critics have felt toward the film is due in part to such tensions; the praise which at least one critic accords the film arises from playing them down.[93]

Tokyo Twilight makes melodrama its dominant. As in *Story of Floating Weeds*, a secret about a parent is kept from a child. As in *The Munekata Sisters*, a good wife is abused by an alcoholic husband. There is the shock of an

339

unsavory discovery, as in *A Mother Should Be Loved* and *A Hen in the Wind*, followed by a suicide, as in *Woman of Tokyo*. This film adds still more sensational elements: a mother who runs off with her husband's subordinate, a daughter who must have an abortion. These ingredients are reinforced by the bleak and sombre settings: cramped households, seedy bars, a mah-jongg parlor, a chilly noodle shop, grey Tokyo streets. This is Ozu's only postwar film to take place in the dead of winter, and the characters huddle around stoves as if the cold were seeping through the walls. The film begins at twilight, and the scenes that ensue make it Ozu's darkest work since *That Night's Wife*, with nearly all the major action occurring at night or in shadowy interiors. (In many respects the film is akin to Naruse's postwar work.) For once there is not a trace of humor: the denizens of the Etoile bar and the skinny suspect at the police station are not comic but grotesque. Nothing must distract from the grim tone of the unfolding plot complications.

That unfolding begins almost immediately. Other 1950s Ozu films gradually introduce characters in everyday contexts, but *Tokyo Twilight* launches into a crisis in its second sequence. Shukichi comes home to find that Takako has left her husband, who is drinking heavily and beating the baby Michiko. The pressure mounts through a series of shocking revelations, volatile confrontations, and emotional outbursts. As Akiko searches for her lover Kenji, she begins to suspect that Kikuko is her mother. After Akiko is brought to the police station, there is a family quarrel, in which Shukichi denounces her ('You're no child of mine') and Akiko says she's not wanted ('I should never have been born'). When Akiko staggers in from her abortion, she bursts into tears at the sight of Michiko. As if all this weren't strong enough, as Takako puts her sister to bed she tries to cheer her up by discussing marriage prospects, which brings Akiko to tears again. Once Akiko learns Kikuko's secret, she becomes driven to know if Shukichi is indeed her father, and although everyone insists that he is, she refuses to believe them. A tearful encounter with Kikuko ends with Akiko running out shouting, 'I hate you'. Coming to the mah-jongg parlor in her mourning clothes, Takako coldly tells her mother that Akiko is dead and adds: 'You're to blame', before walking out. This leads Kikuko to bring flowers to the home and, after she has left, Takako, who has not spoken a word to her, breaks down weeping.

As in *The Munekata Sisters*, such explicitly emotional scenes deform Ozu's characteristic narrational tactics. Omniscience is now used for the codified generic purpose of giving the spectator a wide range of knowledge and permitting the emergence of irony and pity.[94] (Compare the permanent gaps left by the omniscience of *Late Spring* and *Early Spring*.) The chance encounter now becomes the unfortunate coincidence necessary to create high-pitched crises: Shukichi learns of Akiko's financial trouble by meeting a pal in a pachinko parlor, while at the climax Kenji happens into the café in which the despairing Akiko has just inquired about him. Ozu's elliptical narration skips over the moment when Akiko tells Kenji she is pregnant, but it will not conceal from us his evasive reaction. The obligatory nostalgia scenes are transformed into crucial expository passages involving Kikuko's past. Intermediate spaces become charged with fatalistic meaning, as when the scene of Akiko's suicide begins with a shot of a 'Danger' sign. How far we have traveled from the playful disorientation of the 1930s transitions is evident from a single, moralizing cut from Akiko going in for her abortion to a shot of Michiko toddling at home. A prosaic detail such as Kikuko at the station wiping the train window becomes another touch of pathos. And even opaque establishing shots, such as those of Shukichi and Aunt Shige at the restaurant (fig. 242) enter into the film's severe graphic design of verticals that slice off bodies and constrict the human figure. Thus while Takako cries after her mother leaves, we cut from a frontal view (fig. 243) to a ninety-degree view that stresses upright lines (fig. 244).

242.

But some aspects of form struggle against the film's melodramatic dominant. Cutaways and transitions seek to create parametric structures, most notably in the handling of the spaces contiguous to Kikuko's mah-jongg parlor and Gihei's noodle shop. In one scene, as Akiko is about to confront her father, his hat sways on its peg, recalling the transitional shot of the hat in scene 1. A more subtle parametric pattern is at work in the framing of the father seated at home, where from scene to scene, a rear view of his head and shoulders minutely shifts his relation to the verticals of the shoji.

243.

Ozu also tries to dedramatize the material. There is comparatively little nondiegetic music, and that usually brief. The most prominent music, a jaunty vibraphone tune, is equivocal as to its diegetic status, and its cheerfulness works ironically against the pathetic situations. (The same tune functioned in a similar capacity during the funeral of Miura in *Early Spring*.) After Akiko slaps Kenji and rushes out into the night, the narration self-consciously stays with him inside the noodle shop, even after Gihei has gone out to investigate. Similarly, Akiko's hospital scene is temporarily deflated by following Gihei out to the main lobby. But then the narration returns to the sickroom for Akiko's repentance, and we are back to the Shochiku deathbed scene beloved by Kido since the early 1930s. Again, Ozu seeks to stiffen the pathos by cutting to a clock (a 6.6 second shot), then to the yawning nurse crouched by her heater (12.5 seconds), and back to the clock (12.5 seconds). But once more the tactic backfires, as the reiteration of the clock easily becomes readable as a cliché of suspense and as a symbol of the ebbing of Akiko's life. Ozu reflected on the problem of lowering the film's emotional temperature: 'Whenever I try to handle that high a volume, somehow vibrations always appear. . . . Possibly my "octave" was too low; it should have been higher.'[95]

244.

The plot structure also seeks to check the melodramatic pressures by making the father's role fairly prominent. The first four scenes follow Shukichi through an evening and a day, so that initially it might seem that the story is about him. But the syuzhet's focus shifts to Akiko's search for Kenji, and a long central section traces her misadventures before returning home for a quarrel with Shukichi and Takako. The plot's third section alternates scenes involving the father and scenes involving his daughters. The focus of action then shifts to Kikuko — reacting to Akiko's death, bringing flowers to the family, and waiting at the train for Takako. The film's last scene returns to Shukichi, showing him dressing and leaving for work. To some extent, then, the old man's story frames that of his wife and daughters. This explains Ozu's otherwise puzzling claim that the film is about him.[96] Although he is a secondary character, the syuzhet does use Shukichi as a means of containing the emotional ups, downs, and twists of the women's lives. In the penultimate scene we can watch this containment seek to wrench the plot around.

Takako has not gone to meet her mother at the train, and she goes in to Shukichi. She tells him that she will return to Numata and try to make the marriage succeed. 'I don't want Michiko to feel the way Akiko did.' Now the previously severe Shukichi, who had called Akiko no daughter of his, becomes a beneficent father – urging Takako to go see her mother off, encouraging her to make her marriage work. The film becomes a reprise of *Late Spring* when Takako asks her father how he will manage alone. He assures her that he'll rehire the maid. He then goes to pray before Akiko's altar. After a film full of ineffectual, cruel, and hapless men, the figure of the stoic, solitary father is brought back – as if, after *Late Spring* and *Tokyo Story*, this sufficed for closure. (That the father is played by Ryu and the daughter by Hara of course gives the scene added weight.) This sequence thus marks the shift back to Shukichi as a framing pressure for the plot and enables the film to end by showing him leaving for work. There is even a gestural touch akin to the apple-peeling at the end of *Late Spring* and the fanning in *Tokyo Story*, but one as heavily motivated as almost everything else in the film. Shukichi finds Michiko's rattle, a toy which had figured prominently in two earlier scenes. *Tokyo Twilight* may have begun at dusk, but it ends in bright morning sunshine.

It is likely that the film's somewhat sensational material arose from a reaction to the current success of the 'sun tribe' (*taiyozoku*) youth movies and from charges that Ofuna films, especially Ozu's, were increasingly out of touch with life.[97] Upon its initial release, *Tokyo Twilight* attracted much adverse comment and wound up as number nineteen on the annual *Kinema Jumpo* poll. As no Ozu film since *The Only Son* had failed to rank in the top ten, he was shocked and hurt, and both he and Noda regarded the film as a failure. It remains an instructive case of the consequences of Ozu's 'raising his octave'. Noda put it another way: 'It's meaningless to try to express existing things realistically.'[98]

1958

Higanbana
Equinox Flower

Shochiku. Story: novel by Ton Satomi. Script: Kogo Noda, Yasujiro Ozu. Cinematography: Yuharu Atsuta. Art direction: Tatsuo Hamada. Music: Kojun Saito. Lighting: Akira Aomatsu. Editing: Yoshiyasu Hamamura. Agfacolor. Cast: Shin Saburi (*Wataru Hirayama*), Kinuyo Tanaka (*Kiyoko*), Ineko Arima (*Setsuko Hirayama*), Keiji Sata (*Masahiko Taniguchi*), Teiji Takahashi (*Shotaro Kondo*), Miyuki Kuwano (*Hisako Hirayama*), Chishu Ryu (*Shukichi Mikami*), Chieko Naniwa (*Hatsu Sasaki*), Fumio Watanabe (*Ichiro Naganuma*), Nobuo Nakamura (*Toshihiko Kawai*). 14 reels, 3,225 meters. Surviving prints: 120 min. Released 7 September 1958. Script, negative, and prints in existence.

Businessman Hirayama and his wife Kyoko have two unmarried daughters. While interceding for his friend Mikami, whose daughter Fumiko has moved in with her boyfriend, he also serves as advisor for Mrs Sasaki, a Kyoto innkeeper, and her daughter Yukiko. But then Hirayama's daughter Setsuko wishes to marry a young man he has never met, thereby flouting the family's plan for an arranged marriage. Hirayama is tricked into giving his consent to Setsuko's marriage. He attends the wedding under protest and afterwards stubbornly withholds his blessing. Finally, persuaded by Mikami and the Sasakis, he takes a train to visit the couple.

Saito's music may be slightly passionate, but the credits – black, white, and red characters jumping about a subdued brown ground – announce that this will be a lighter film than *Tokyo Twilight*. The ensuing action bears the impression out, with its satire (the bootlicking salaryman), pure comedy, and deep irony. The narration will also be far more self-consciously playful than in the previous film. There will be games with optical POV (the scene discussed on pp. 114–115) and with just-noticeable differences, as when in the last scene a setup down the aisle of a train is altered by the slight protrusion of an elbow. Shochiku's studio logo, depicting the colorful effects of a sunrise on Mount Fuji, will be cited in a painting seen down a hotel corridor. Establishing shots will be displaced: the second visit to the Luna Bar is prefaced by an establishing shot of a large RCA Victor sign (p. 112); only in the last scene in the Hirayama home is there an attempt to indicate the neighborhood. In particular, color will come forward as a striking element of visual design. Color film allows Ozu to highlight glasses and crockery in front of the characters and to show every glass as containing liquid at exactly the same level – as if more than a few viewers in the world would catch the joke (fig. 245). The color scheme of the credits becomes a doubly humorous gesture – anticipating the traditional bridal outfit as well as the hues of a railroad sign in the first scene that warns, 'Strong Winds Expected'.

245.

The narration thus creates a light attitude toward the serious center of the plot, Hirayama. In a reversal of *Late Spring* and *Late Autumn*, he clings to his daughter and opposes her marriage. Hirayama becomes the protagonist in the second scene, when he rises to praise the bride and groom's love match, which he contrasts to the 'unromantic and prosaic' arranged marriage he shares with Kyoko. But when he returns home that night his bad faith is revealed: he plans to arrange Setsuko's marriage against her will. From this scene on, the central conflict between himself and his wife and daughter will be marked by this struggle between modern and traditional attitudes. Late in the film, faced by Kiyoko's charge of inconsistency, he answers that life is a sum total of inconsistencies. The Hirayama drama will have two phases: getting him to allow Setsuko to marry Taniguchi, and reconciling him to the fact that she acted without consulting him. The first stage ends with Yukiko's trick; the second phase, reminiscent of that undergone by the family in *Early Summer*, is continued beyond the film's final scenes. By restricting stretches of the action to what Hirayama knows, the narration can let Yukiko trick the audience too. And even though Hirayama is not the film's center of consciousness, when the narration detours to follow other characters (Yukiko, Setsuko, Kondo, etc.) they invariably lead back to him.

As the plot's causal spine, the Hirayama line of action is accompanied by a welter of parallels, and these are more prominent than in most postwar Ozu films because some affect the main line of action strongly. Out of several subsidiary parallels, most notably that involving Kawai and his daughter, who is married off as the film begins, there emerge two pairs of anxious parents and restless daughters. Mikami's daughter Fumiko has left home to live with a cabaret pianist; Mrs Sasaki strives to find a good husband for Yukiko. These parallels have three main functions. First, they work to retard the Hirayama plotline, especially early in the film before the trouble with Setsuko finally breaks out. The expository portion of *Equinox Flower* consists of introducing Hirayama and his family by means of their relation to the Mikami and Sasaki families. In the second place, these parallels reinforce the split in Hirayama's attitude, allowing him to play the concerned father to Mikami and to present a liberal face to Yukiko. The third function of these parallels is causal. Acting as an intercessor for Mikami and a confidante for Yukiko, Hirayama improves their situations relatively little, but he certainly learns from them. After Hirayama sees Fumiko and her boyfriend in a noodle restaurant, he returns home to ask Setsuko if she has slept with her boyfriend. At the very end, as we shall see, the improvement in the relation between Mikami and Fumiko, and the concerted coaxings of Mrs. Sasaki and Yukiko, impel Hirayama toward a reconciliation with his own child. This is a more economical and classical use of parallelism than is usual for Ozu: it unifies the film and emphasizes the conflict.

The conservative application of parallels is echoed to some extent in the film's use of time, which includes, for once, a deadline. But the narration's handling mutes the suspense. Taniguchi's transfer to Hiroshima, which necessitates a quick proposal, is announced early on, but then dropped and revived only the day before he must leave. Otherwise, the film is elliptical in ways that Ozu has made his own. A funeral is anticipated but not shown. The

246.

247.

248.

249.

narration skips over Mikami's third visit to Hirayama, Taniguchi's second visit to the home, Kyoko's request that Kawai act as go-between, and the investigation of Taniguchi's background. As the plot progresses, the narration becomes steadily more elliptical – not only do we not see the wedding (after *Late Spring* and *Early Summer*, this is a predictable omission), but Taniguchi drops out of the film about halfway through, and we are denied any glimpse of Setsuko in the film's finale. The ellipses answer to the pressures of various narrative goals, such as the confinement to Hirayama's range of knowledge, the foregrounding of parallels, and, as we shall see shortly, a final thematic emphasis.

250.

Because of the film's shifting plotlines and elliptical narration, parametric variations often function partly to indicate the passage of time. Our introduction to Hirayama's office comes with a shot of clerks working while men wash windows; fifteen scenes later, there are no window-washers. Most prominent are the red objects dotted around the Hirayama home –table, radio, chair-cushion and teakettle. The amaryllis – the equinox flower of the title – puts out clusters of red blossoms. The cushion and teakettle function at once as props to be permuted within shots, as indices of changing narrative situations, and as pure spots of color. 'I wanted to highlight red here and there. Red turns out magnificently on Agfa film.'[99]

251.

The first scene in the household picks up the credits' color play. An oblique shot from one room to another features a white vase and a red teakettle (fig. 246); cut to a vase with red and white flowers next to red-wrapped gifts; cut to a red table against white walls, with Kyoko in the background. Almost every later scene in the Hirayama home includes the red teakettle and the red cushion of the hallway chair – sometimes only on the side of a shot or out of focus in the distance (fig. 247). Often something has changed. The teakettle will be gone, or joined by an orange cup (fig. 248). One scene's dominant/overtone play creates an intensified parametric 'node': a long-shot of the chair (fig. 249); a long-shot of Kyoko, with the teakettle in the lower rear center (fig. 250); a medium-shot of Kyoko with the chair in the background (fig. 251). As usual, such additive variation can create a kind of purely pictorial suspense about what the next variation will be. The late scene of the party of Kyoko and her daughters starts by replacing the teakettle with a tea-chest (fig. 252). Eventually the teakettle makes its entrance, yet the chair is, for once, not

252.

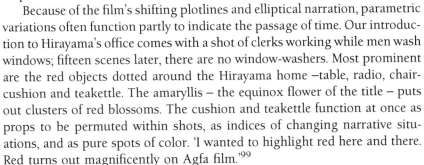

253.

254.

255.

shown. It is reserved, so to speak, for our last visit to the house. After Kyoko has hung up the phone, happy with the news that her husband will visit Setsuko, she goes and sits (for the first time) on the chair-cushion (fig. 253). But now where is the red teakettle? Ozu cuts from a medium-shot of Kyoko (fig. 254) to a shot of clothes flapping on a line, a bright red shirt stretched across it (fig. 255). We have seen this area before, but now it serves as a final resting spot for the red accents that have migrated around the space.

What leads up to that final phone call concerns more than Hirayama's attitude toward romantic marriages. *Equinox Flower* revives the theme of the loss of masculinity, setting its hero's decline against the quiet but assured authority of the father in *Late Spring* and the husband in *Flavor of Green Tea over Rice*. Although set in summer, this is a film of autumn, the time when the equinox flower blooms. Characterized as a wilful, often petty and tyrannical father, Hirayama remains powerless. His daughters will do as they please, preferably with his consent but if necessary without it. On the domestic front, Hirayama loses every battle except that of shutting off the radio. Moreover, his resentment of Taniguchi may be tinged with rivalry. As Ozu puts it, 'When his daughter is taken by another man, the father is jealous and he feels something physical and primitive.'[100] He retreats to the world of his peers – other businessmen with families of their own. Early in the film, out drinking after Kawai's daughter's wedding, Hirayama and his two pals briefly recall the war years and speculate that strong men sire daughters rather than sons. The fantasy of masculine achievement culminates in a reunion at Gamagori and initiates the film's final phase.

The ceremonial quality of the alumni gathering makes it stand in for the wedding we never see, but unlike a marriage, this gathering represents a vanished past. After desultory comments about raising children, the men listen raptly to Mikami's recitation of the farewell poem by Masashige Kusunoki. Masashige was a warrier chieftain of the fourteenth century who fought for an imperial restoration and committed suicide in the face of impossible odds. Over the centuries Masashige became the legendary prototype of fidelity to the emperor, and in the prewar era he was the model for Japanese youth, the incarnation of the samurai ethos, 'the paragon of failed loyalist martyrs'.[101] Before Mikami recites, he reflects that the poem 'doesn't quite fit this age', and indeed it is wholly about manliness, obedience to father and emperor, and the eternal veneration that awaits the fallen fighter. Then the men sing a wartime tune about the parting of Masashige from his son, a patriotic school song so popular that the Occupation banned it.[102] During Hirayama's idyll with his wife and daughters, Kyoko had confessed her fond memories of the war years, for then the family was together. Hirayama had then responded that he didn't like wartime, since commodities were scarce and people were arrogant. But this reunion's indulgence in nostalgia presents a different picture: a generation of executives who may play golf and drink American whiskey but who also imagine themselves the descendants of samurai and who ache for a past that promised glory.

This vision of masculine pride is brought back to earth in the film's last scenes. In an idyll parallel to the one with his family, Hirayama learns that Mikami is starting to patch things up with his daughter. In Kyoto, Hirayama visits the Sasakis and, adopting the role of paternal advisor once more, tells Yukiko to marry. But again his dignity is deflated as mother and daughter compel him to visit Setsuko in Hiroshima. The last scene shows him on a train, resigned to reconciliation, murmuring the Masashige song. As Mikami has told Hirayama, 'Ever with us are the dreams of our youth.' The proverbial phrase refers not only to the characters' pasts but to the 1928 Ozu film. If the title of *Dreams of Youth* anticipated the vantage point from which its action would be viewed nostalgically, *Equinox Flower* occupies that point and looks back to a past reconstructed, as often in Ozu, through popular memory, out of catchphrases, school songs, poems, and movies. (The very presence of Shin Saburi and Kinuyo Tanaka helps recall Ozu's 1930s cinema.) In his 1950s films, Ozu's comic-pathetic theme of the decline of paternal authority takes on a new historical dimension; and *Equinox Flower* manages to expose that historicity, treat it sympathetically, and yet keep it framed in irony.

1959

Ohayo

Ohayo (aka *Good Morning*)

Shochiku. Script: Kogo Noda, Yasujiro Ozu. Cinematography: Yuharu Atsuta. Art direction: Tatsuo Hamada. Lighting: Akira Aomatsu. Music: Toshiro Mayuzumi. Editing: Yoshiyasu Hamamura. Agfa-Shochikucolor. Cast: Keiji Sata (*Heichiro Fukui*), Yoshiko Kuga (*Setsuko Arita*), Chishu Ryu (*Keitaro Hayashi*), Kuniko Miyake (*Tamiko*), Haruko Sugimura (*Kikue Haraguchi*), Koji Shigaraki (*Minoru*), Masahiko Shimazu (*Isamu*), Hajime Shirata (*Kozo*), Haruo Tanaka (*Haraguchi*), Eiko Miyoshi (*Grandma Haraguchi*), Toyo Takahashi (*Shige Okubo*), Masuo Fujiki (*Zen*), Eijiro Tono (*Tomizawa*), Teruko Nagaoka (*Mrs Tomizawa*). 7 reels, 2,570 meters. Released 12 May 1959. Surviving prints: 94 min. Script, negative, and prints in existence.

In a neighborhood buzzing with gossip and trifling intrigues, a ne'er-do-well couple have a television set that attracts the local boys. Two of them, Minoru and Isamu, insist that their parents buy them one. Their demand denied, the boys go on a 'silence strike', refusing to speak. When this gets them into trouble at school, the boys flee from home. Found by their tutor Fukui, they return home to find a TV set waiting for them. The boys happily set out for school and resume their game of learning to fart on command.

> Letting rip a fart –
> It doesn't make you laugh
> When you live alone.
>
> Senryu poem

If we regard Ozu as primarily a masterful delineator of human character, *Ohayo* can seem only a diverting minor work. But if we pay attention to the film's mixture of topical material, plot devices, themes, spaces, and farts, we can find it no less rich than *Late Spring* or *Early Summer*. The critic's tendency to rate pathos more highly than comedy must be checked, especially in discussing a film as brazenly odd as this.

Ohayo's roots go back to the 1930s. The gags involving a pushy peddler and his upright confederate who follows in his wake to sell salesman-detection bells are reminiscent of *nansensu* episodes, as is the shot of the 'disreputable' couple coming home from work miming a jazz performance. Most obviously, the film resembles *I Was Born, But...*, not only in one of its central plot devices – two sons go on strike – but also in such particulars as a sinister gag with a cleaver. Yet *Ohayo* remains firmly a film of the 1950s. Plot devices, such as the way in which the boys' escape brings the sister Setsuko together with the tutor Fukui, hark back to *Early Summer*, and the drunken mutterings of the retired salaryman Tomizawa are lifted almost intact from *Early Spring*. Topical references are likewise strongly fixed. What pachinko was to *The Flavor of*

Green Tea over Rice, television is to *Ohayo*; just as the pachinko-parlor owner opined that the game would invite 'national decay', so the current cliché that 'terebi' would produce 'a land of a hundred million idiots' becomes the source of some one-liners in the Ukiyo-e *saké* shop. By making *sumo* the object of the boys' interest, the film refers to the social fact that the Japanese television boom of the 1950s was spurred by a wrestling craze. In addition, the use of bribes to get the boys to study reveals traces of the growing pressure on schoolchildren to prepare for the 'exam hell' of university admissions. And while the blocks of lower middle-class tract homes surrounded by industrial flats recall the landscape of Ozu's 1930s work, the idea of rendering the everyday doings of a neighborhood may owe something to Yasunari Kawabata's popular 1954 newspaper serial, *Tokyo no hito* (*Tokyo People*).

The film is a model of comic construction. In the first third, the Setsuko-Fukui romance is hinted at and the boys' appetite for television is established, but the main focus falls on the boys' farting game and, principally, the fuss over the Women's Association dues. Mrs Haraguchi, the block leader, asserts that she hasn't received the club dues, so the neighbors suspect that Mrs Hayashi has pocketed them. It is eventually revealed that Mrs Haraguchi's mother has forgotten to forward the dues to her daughter. This slender string of incidents, based upon classic comic devices like accident and misunderstanding, is initiated, prolonged, and resolved in the first seven scenes. The eighth scene, during which Hayashi encounters old Mr Tomizawa in the bar, might seem to be sheer breathing space, but in introducing Tomizawa's search for a job it lays the ground for the resolution of the problem which will dominate the rest of the film. Told to be quiet, the Hayashi boys Minoru and Isamu embark on their silence strike. In traditional comic fashion, this reopens the neighborhood-gossip plotline. When the boys pass Mrs Haraguchi without speaking, she infers that their mother bears her a grudge about the dues. She proceeds to stir up gossip against Mrs Hayashi. The boys' flight from the household brings the action to a crisis, which is resolved when it is revealed (to us and to them) that their parents have bought a TV from Mr Tomizawa, who now sells appliances. Two final comic twists – the fact that the boys now cheerfully speak to Mrs Haraguchi (thus giving rise to a new round of gossip) and the return of Kozo Haraguchi's inability to fart on cue – close the film.

Because of its concentration on neighborhood life, the film presents this comic action in ways that are fresh for Ozu. Certain scenes are very long, interweaving lines of action by means of crosscutting and 'overlapping' character trajectories. For instance, the first scene introduces neighborhood life by starting with Mrs Okubo, a comparatively minor character. She is visited by Mrs Tomizawa. While the two talk, Mrs Haraguchi drops in, and when she leaves, the narration follows her. After Mrs Okubo's son passes her, we follow him back to his home and then out to summon Kozo. Then we cut back to Mrs Okubo, still talking with Mrs Tomizawa. When the latter leaves, we follow her out until her path crosses that of Kozo, whom we pick up on his way to visit the shady couple who own the television. At their house, the boys call next door to the Hayashis, and the narration finally moves to the plot's main family. Avoiding his characteristic 'empty' intermediate spaces, Ozu creates a concentrated exposition by adapting the contiguity principle to a crisscrossing of characters' paths reminiscent of Tati. Nearly every scene in the neighborhood displays this dense weave of adjacent actions, which is especially apt for evoking the spread of gossip and the piling-up of misunderstandings. Crosscutting between locales is, in addition, often governed by a more subtle comic innovation: a shot of one person, seated or standing, will give way to a similarly-scaled shot of another person, in the same posture but observed from another angle.

Ohayo's comic bent also reshapes several of Ozu's basic thematic commonplaces. In buying the TV set, Mr and Mrs Hayashi do not simply yield to the boys. They are presented as undergoing a degree of sacrifice, since Mrs Hayashi wants a washing machine. The excuse is that of *The Only Son*: now the boys must study harder. Moreover, old Mr Tomizawa, the cashiered salaryman, is presented as an explicit parallel to the Hayashis. (One tip-off is the shot of a boiling teakettle as Hayashi sits pondering Mr Tomizawa's situation.) The parents buy the TV set from him partly to ease a plight which could, in a few years, become their own (an echo of Ryosuke's kindness to his widowed neighbor in *The Only Son*). There is also, of course, the theme of the decline of paternal authority. Early in the film, the two boys throw a tantrum that foreshadows their later rebellion. Hayashi comes home and emerges from the bathroom to ask who spilled the tooth powder. The boys casually ignore him. Later, when the boys demand a TV, Mrs Hayashi threatens them with discipline from their father, but they defy him. Significantly, the father tells the boys to stop chattering 'like a woman'. (Earlier in the film Mrs Haraguchi had asked Mrs Hayashi not to circulate news of the dues mishap: 'You know how women talk.') The boys parody the notion of the strong and silent male by taking it literally and turning it against the adults. At the end, the father gives in to their demands and remains ineffectual. As the boys rejoice over the TV, Hayashi tells them to quiet down, but Isamu says that he doesn't mean it; Ozu cuts to a shot of Hayashi, drawn up in a burlesque of a ferocious kabuki frown. Isamu's response is to whip out imaginary pistols and blast away.

I have mentioned Tati, whose influence may also be apparent on the soundtrack. Mayuzumi's score, very different from the usual work of Kojun Saito, strives both for a self-consciously comic quality and an impersonal sprightliness reminiscent of muzak. The farting motif is well integrated into the track as well. At the outset, when the game is introduced, the boys' success at breaking wind is indicated by the pitch of the result: highest for Isamu, deeper for Minoru. During one morning's exercise, Mr Okubo's flatulent outbursts rhythmically punctuate not only his knee-bending but also the music that accompanies it. (He is so proficient, his son explains, because he works for the gas company.)

The fart (*onara*, or *hé*) is a staple of Japanese art and literature, celebrated in scrolls depicting farting contests and in senryu poems such as the one quoted above. It may be relevant to *Ohayo* that there are now farting contests on Japanese television, and that a genre of children's comics is devoted to farting.[103] But in *Ohayo* the farting gags are bound to a satiric treatment of human language. From the start, the film interrogates two of language's dimensions, pragmatics and semantics. The schoolboys use English to deceive their parents. Zen recites it to appear that he's studying; Minoru lapses into it to baffle his mother; Isamu says, 'I love you' on any occasion. The crucial equivalence between farting and language occurs in the second scene, when Fukui taps Kozo's forehead and asks for a translation; the boy farts automatically. The boys explain that Mr Okubo is very good at it. Cut to him at home, farting. His wife appears: 'You called me?' She leaves. He farts again. Again she returns, asking what he wants. This time he asks a question. Already, the semantic content of language is equated with vulgar, meaningless sound, and humans' pragmatic context treats every stray noise as an attempt at deliberate communication.

This motif comes to the fore in the family quarrel about the boys' endless demands for a 'terebi'. Minoru complains that grownups talk too much as well: 'Hello. Good morning [*ohayo*]. A fine day. Where to? Just a ways. Is that so? – Just a lot of talk'. He objects to what Jakobson, following Malinowski, calls the 'phatic' function of language: 'messages primarily serving to establish, to prolong, or to discontinue communication.'[104] Giving up language in protest, however, the boys surrender *all* linguistic functions, including the referential. So they must invent their own sign system, consisting of a hand gesture, handshakes, and farting. The comic results show that these signs are vague, ambiguous, and hence unsuitable for communicating. Still, awareness of language's arbitrary social functions is no guarantee of communicative dexterity. Setsuko and Fukui agree that the boys don't understand how small talk 'acts as a lubricant in this world.' Yet Fukui's sister points out that 'important talk is difficult,' and that Fukui can't tell Setsuko he loves her: 'You talk only of weather and work.'

The theme of the inadequacies of language thus reaches a double denouement. Once the boys get their TV, they resume talking – and again, too much. When Hayashi orders them to pipe down, Isamu looks beyond his words: 'He's lying. His face says so. He's smiling.' It is as if the boys' crude semiotic system has sensitized them to nonverbal cues. (Or, since we never see Hayashi's face during Isamu's line, perhaps the boy has *mis*read the cue.) Later, at the railroad station, Fukui and Setsuko greet each other with a term that now suffices on its own to parody social exchange: 'Ohayo.' They go on to discuss the weather and cloud formations in banalities that perfectly exemplify the phatic function as 'a profuse exchange of ritualized formulas.'[105] Adults may use the phatic function to avoid transmitting meaning.

The film's comic treatment of plot construction and thematic material is enhanced by some of Ozu's most elegant experiments in playful rigor. Sato calls this tendency 'describing the inconsequential in a very strict fashion'.[106] Simple temporal regularities – six distinct days, from Wednesday afternoon to Monday morning – permit the syuzhet to present variations on activities occurring at different times of day. Spatially, the film treats the neighborhood as a grid of rectangular houses, to be filmed from the street in strict 90- and 180-degree orientations. The plot concentrates on five households (an echo of the fact that older city districts were organized in *gonin-gumi*, or five-household groups), but Ozu's manner of filming makes it quite difficult to reconstruct the exact layout of homes. Sometimes he uses the edge of a row of

Towers and Laundry

Houses and Fence

Down Street to Hill

Closer View of Hill

Hillside

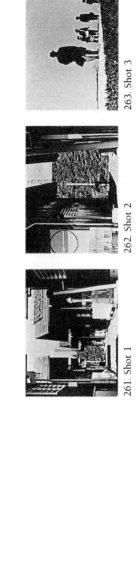

256. Shot 1

257. Shot 2

258. Shot 3

259. Shot 4

260. Shot 5

261. Shot 1

262. Shot 2

263. Shot 3

264. Shot 1

265. Shot 2

266. Shot 1

Scene 1:
Wednesday
(beginning
of film)

Scene 5:
Thursday

Scene 10:
Friday

Scene 13:
Saturday

269. Shot 1

271. Shot 32

270. Shot 2

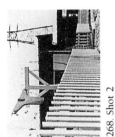

268. Shot 2

267. Shot 1

272. Shot 8

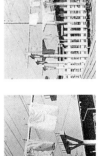

273. Shot 9

Scene 17:
Sunday

Scene 22:
Monday
(beginning)

(end)

Scene 23:
Monday
(end of film)

Permutational Variants in Landscape Shots in *Ohayo*

353

houses to prevent our determining which house a character leaves or enters. At other moments he films one house through the doorway of another, as in *Record of a Tenement Gentleman*. The somewhat confusing nature of the geography is laid bare when, after a hard night's drinking, Mr Tomizawa staggers in to the wrong house and assumes that the Hayashi family is visiting his wife.

The film's playfulness reaches a climax in its presentation of adjacent landscapes. We have already noticed whimsically nuanced gags like the shots discussed on p. 129, in which a distant electrical tower vanishes and reappears between the gaps in the roofs. But this visual motif is part of a larger parametric pattern. (See chart, pp. 352-3.) Each new day is introduced by shots of areas of the neighborhood. The possibilities are laid out at the film's dominant/overtone beginning (shots 1-5, figs. 256–260). This takes us from power towers through a street to a hillside. The beginning of the next day omits the first two shots and presents variants on the last three. (See scene 5, shots 1–3, figs. 261–263). (Admirers of Ozu's fastidiousness might observe how the placement of shadows distinguish this morning from yesterday afternoon.) Friday begins in an even more concise fashion (scene 10, shots 1-2, figs. 264–265), creating another visual gag: Mrs Haguchi's mother seems to be praying to the electrical tower. Finally, all that is necessary to introduce the Saturday exercise session is a single shot of the hillside (scene 13, shot 1, fig. 266).

Now the parametric play varies. Scene 17 starts with a long-shot of a row of homes and a closer view emphasizing laundry (figs. 267–268). These form two variants of shot 2 in scene 1 (fig. 257). (Shot 2 also prepares for the strong graphic match discussed on p. 123.) The plot's last day (scene 22) opens with a shift in shot order: first the hillside (fig. 269), then the extreme-long-shot view of the street (fig. 270). Not until the scene's very end, at shot 32, does the 'missing' view of this area appear (fig. 271). The film concludes with two landscape shots: the first a variant of the fence-and-laundry setup (fig. 272), the last a closer view of the laundry (fig. 273). Thus the two last scenes repeat, in scattered and reshuffled fashion, the five setups that opened the film.

Like the opening tracking shot of *Walk Cheerfully*, this ingenious permutational play, in its recasting of expectation and triggering of surprise, is a source of humor. We will never grasp the complete range of Ozu's work if we do not see comedy in the very texture of his style, in its play between unnecessary rigor and outlandish deviation. In other words: No less amusing than the last shot of Kozo's oft-washed underwear hanging on the line (fig. 273) is the fact that this framing is a 180-degree 'reverse shot' of fig. 256, the long-shot that opened the film ninety-four minutes earlier.

Ukigusa
Floating Weeds

Daiei. Script: Kogo Noda, Yasujiro Ozu. Cinematography: Kazuo Miyagawa. Art direction: Tomoo Shimogawara. Music: Kojun Saito. Lighting: Sachio Ito. Agfacolor. Cast: Ganjiro Nakamura (*Komajuro Arashi*), Machiko Kyo (*Sumiko*), Ayako Wakao (*Kayo*), Hiroshi Kawaguchi (*Kiyoshi Homma*), Haruko Sugimura (*Oyoshi*), Hitomi Nozoe (*Aiko*), Chishu Ryu (*the theatre owner*), Koji (Hideo) Mitsui (*Kichinosuke*), Haruo Tanaka (*Yatazo*), Yosuke Irie (*Sugiyama*), Hikaru Hoshi (*Kimura*), Mantaro Ushio (*Sentaro*), Kumeko Urabe (*Shige*). 9 reels, 3,259 meters. Surviving prints: 119 min. Released 17 November 1959. Script, negative, and prints in existence.

274.

After Komajuro's kabuki troupe arrives at a seaside town, his mistress Sumiko learns that his common-law wife and their son Kiyoshi are living there. Komajuro warns Sumiko not to tell his son, but she induces Kayo, another performer, to seduce the boy. When Komajuro finds out, he berates Sumiko and Kayo. In the meantime, the troupe has collapsed. Kiyoshi runs off with Kayo but returns. He tells Komajuro to leave them alone, and the old actor apologetically does so, leaving Kayo behind. At the train station, Komajuro encounters Sumiko and they travel on together.

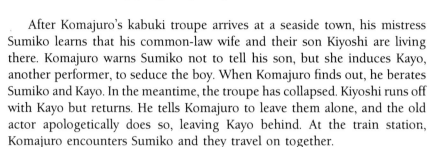

275.

Masaichi Nagata, Mizoguchi's producer and president of Daiei, had often asked Ozu to make a film for him. By shooting *Ohayo* in early spring, Ozu met his annual obligation to Shochiku and was available. He turned to a remake of *Story of Floating Weeds*, originally planned for Shochiku but postponed. Ozu and Noda moved the locale to the seashore, and instead of calling it *Daikon* ('Radish Actor') they shortened the original title to *Floating Weeds*.[107] Kazuo Miyagawa, Mizoguchi's habitual cinematographer in the postwar years, produced lustrous color images that confirm his great skill at handling chiaroscuro.

Except for touches which reflect the new sexual mores of post-1955 Japanese films, the finished work might as well take place in the 1930s. No automobiles, television, or hula hoops identify the period as contemporary. The notion of a traveling kabuki troupe, a commonplace of prewar cinema, was anachronistic in 1959. The troupe's show is accompanied by scratchy pop records of the early Showa era, and Komajuro's son Kiyoshi is studying for success as assiduously as any 1930s lad. The opening scenes' use of the lighthouse (figs. 274–275; see also p. 135) reworks an iconographic device seen in *First Steps Ashore* (1932) (figs. 276–277) and Part 2 of *Minami no kaze* (*South Wind*, 1940) (fig. 278). The film thus has no need for its characters to recall the prewar era, since its material and stylistic texture make it nostalgic through and through.

Part of the archaic flavor of the film is of course due to its being a fairly close remake of *Story of Floating Weeds*. The first seven scenes take place on a single Saturday, laying out all the prior story information and culminating in the first night's performance. The rest of the syuzhet is built around three melodramatic climaxes: a confrontation at Oyoshi's café after Sumiko has

276. *First Steps Ashore*

277. *First Steps Ashore*

278. *South Wind*

learned Komajuro's secret; a scene in the empty theatre, when he beats Kayo and Sumiko after learning of their plot; and a confrontation of father and son, during which Komajuro leaves. As in the earlier film, paternal authority ebbs away. An epilogue reunites Komajuro and Sumiko as two of a kind, both floating weeds.

There are, however, important revisions in the second version. Many small changes spring from the new milieu, so that the actors' clothes-washing in the first film is replaced by a day baking on the beach. The original plot has been stretched to include a leisurely exposition typical of Ozu's postwar work, a comic subplot involving the romantic dalliance of three actors in the troupe, a more dilatory handling of Sumiko's discovery of Komajuro's secret life, more frequent visits of Komajuro to his wife, and more explicit treatment of Kiyoshi's affair with Kayo. In addition, some scenes, such as the protagonist's confrontation with his woman outside the café, are handled more elliptically in the silent version. The result is a film over half an hour longer than the first version, and one less sharp in its depiction of the central situation. The central characters are similar in both films, but the old actor and his son are considerably more prominent in the first version. Sometimes the 1959 film lightly cites *Story of Floating Weeds* – by having Hideo Mitsui (the son in the early film) play a lustful actor in the troupe, by a shot of a bicycle that recalls the bike in the 1934 film, by the fluttering shreds of paper that fall during the theatre scenes, and by the posters which turn up unexpectedly all over town.

A detailed stylistic comparison of the two versions is impossible here; we can simply note the constancy of basic principles and the shift in some particular tactics. Each film cuts more rapidly than was normal in its day: the average shot lasts 5.2 seconds in *Story of Floating Weeds*, 7.5 seconds in *Floating Weeds*. At some points, the cutting pace of the two films is quite comparable. In the first dialogue between Komajuro and Kiyoshi, the shots average five seconds each, and one shot of Kiyoshi saying 'Okay' is only twenty-seven frames long. Ozu was aware that his late 1950s films were speeding up their editing.[108] Some cutting schemata have not changed in twenty-five years. Compare the 180-degree match-on-action of the protagonist's first entry into his wife's café, seen through a neighbor's doorway (figs. 279–282). (These shots incidentally show that Ozu was right in suggesting that his later camera position was not as low as it had once been.) The outrageous play with oblique eyelines returns occasionally in the later version, most notably in the scene of two actors drinking in the *sake* bar, in which the angle of each one's glance gives the lie to any notion that they might be looking at one another. The use of depth is likewise comparable, as in the way that Oyoshi's café becomes a zigzagged space with marked foregrounds (fig. 283).

Yet there are also important differences – or rather, novelties, extensions, and variants. The relatively straightforward *donden* cutting of the early version uses consistently oblique body, face, and eyeline (see pp. 90–91). The remake uses more ambivalent frontality to make character positions more equivocal, as in the four-way conversation early in the film during which a character's body slants sharply one way, the face tilts in another direction, and the eyes in yet another. *Story of Floating Weeds* lays out the troupe's loft as a circular

279. *Story of Floating Weeds*

280. *Story of Floating Weeds*

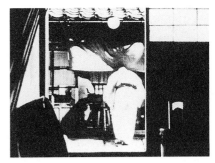

281.

282.

space, sometimes by means of overlapping figures and backgrounds, sometimes by means of the boy Tomibo, whose glance swivels around the room. *Floating Weeds*, on the contrary, slices the loft into two halves, filmed invariably in 180-degree and opposed setups, so that a pair of legs (see p. 100) or a movement serves as a reference point across the cut. This tactic lets Ozu use less fragmentary editing and more encompassing long-shots of the troupe. Sound also enables him to make some changes. As in *Story of Floating Weeds*, a sudden rainstorm spoils a performance, but now it is presented on the soundtrack, as a metallic drilling.

Whereas the first version is built upon a tension between unpredictable style and sacred material, *Floating Weeds* vividly displays Ozu's interplay of rigor and playfulness. The plot structure is 'geometricized' to a much greater extent than in the early film, carrying on the tendencies of *Inn in Tokyo*. The first seven scenes form a unified section not only as exposition but also as a matrix for subsequent development. Scenes 8–14 'recycle' and permute the locales or situations of the initial set:

1. Seashore and post office.

2. Boat: Sumiko assembles the troupe.
3. *Sake* bar: Kichi calls on Katsuko.
4. Barber's shop: an actor calls on Aiko.

5. Theatre: the troupe unpacks.

6. Café: Komajuro calls on Oyoshi and Kiyoshi.
7. Theatre: the first night's performance.

10. Seashore: Komajuro and Kiyoshi fish.
12. Sumiko questions Zensho.

8. *Sake* bar: Kichi and Katsuko after a night of pleasure.
9. Barber's shop: the actor calls on Aiko and gets a shave from her mother.
11. Theatre: Koma tells Sumiko of Komajuro's fishing.
14. Café: Koma plays chess with Kiyoshi.
13. Theatre: the next day's performance.

The repetitions are marked by parallel motifs, such as the lighthouse and the boat engines in 1 and 10, the shaving gag in 4 and 9, particular shot compositions in 6 and 14, and comparable actions, such as peering out from

283.

backstage in 7 and 13. The rest of the plot recycles the matrix again and again, creating new parallels: Kayo's visit to the post office (scene 16, echoing scene 1), a third, even more feeble performance (scene 15, echoing 7 and 13), a brief scene in the actors' loft after the show has closed (scene 19, echoing 5 and 11), a scene of Komajuro brooding at Oyoshi's (scene 21, strongly similar to scene 6), and so on. Add to this a rigorous patterning of the soundtrack, in which cicadas, crickets, rain, boat engines, locomotives, drums and flutes, and the offscreen hammering of an artisan create a constant, throbbing pulse for almost every scene. In the course of the film, the final train scene is carefully foreshadowed by offscreen train whistles.

Transitions loosen up such patterning, through the sort of perceptual play that *Story of Floating Weeds* generally lacks. Whereas the first version uses an emptied long-shot to 'cover' Kihachi's slapping of Otaka, *Floating Weeds* cuts away to a shot of the garden, echoing the scene's opening and suggesting that the scene might be over. The narration cuts to an empty street, a kabuki poster in the distance; and then cuts to a shot of Sumiko and Komajuro resuming their quarrel. The sense of a 'false' scene ending is thus much stronger, and more disorienting, in the later film. After the quarrel in the rain, the next shots of the theatre appear while offscreen an actor declaims: 'Silence – cease your clamor.' The second visit to Oyoshi's home (scene 14) uses omniscient narration to take us where the characters aren't – starting at the ground floor and sidling upstairs. A shot initially marked as an optical POV will become a cutaway with which to end a scene. While the actors sell off their goods, cheerful vibraphone music runs along nondiegetically. Most outrageously, one scene ends with the drone of an airplane offscreen and the next starts with a shot of the theatre, a bird wheeling in the sky as the drone continues – a Tati-like gag in which it is virtually impossible not to attribute the sound to the bird.

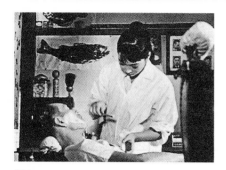

284.

285.

The same undercutting of rigor by unexpected changes can be found in the opening movement from the lighthouse to the post office (see pp. 135–6). By holding a composition, Ozu makes certain opaque long-shots shift into the graphic realm. He can play jokes by crossing the 180-degree line, as when the first barber-shop scene uses the frameline to dismember customers (figs. 284–285). And, as in *Equinox Flower* and *Ohayo*, color games emerge. Consider the transition from the rain-soaked quarrel to the theatre. The narration cuts from the street, seen in long-shot with a poster in the distance, to a corner, a hanging lamp and a pillar bearing a white placard in black characters. Cut to another placard, in red characters; as an overtone, the poster of the first shot appears in the background. The graphic jumps between red, white, and black recall the dancing written characters of the credit sequence.

Lest this last point seem to betray excessive finesse, we can end by looking briefly at the second climax, the confrontation between Komajuro and two women in the deserted theatre. The narration punctuates this violent double climax with a motif set up earlier, the scraps of white paper that flutter down from the rafters; the image connotes evanescence, linking to the drifting weeds of the title and recalling the cliché of cherry blossoms. Across this emotional structure Ozu lays an astoundingly stringent pattern of staging and editing.

Komajuro confronts Kayo in frontal compositions. He grabs and slaps her, and they swing around so that each still faces one another. Reverse-shots reveal them with places changed. A 90-degree cut shows Komajuro grabbing her, swinging her ninety degrees and twisting her arm. Then he swings her a further ninety degrees, until she admits that Sumiko planned for her to seduce his son. He releases her, and after more frontal medium-shots, Ozu cuts 180 degrees so that the characters' positions are again reversed and Komajuro is in the foreground once more. Kayo leaves to fetch Sumiko. When Sumiko enters, she faces Komajuro exactly as Kayo had. He rushes to her and slaps her several times. As he starts to leave, he pushes her away so that they face off in spots 180 degrees opposite to those in which they had started. In the Kayo encounter, two attacks, two exact exchanges of position; in the Sumiko encounter, one attack, one exact change of position; in both episodes, a rotation of figures as precisely plotted as dance steps. And throughout the entire scene, the red and black placards – sometimes on either edge of the frame, sometimes in the background – serve as minute measurements of the shifts in position. The unpredictable reappearances of these placards offset the geometrical rigor of the staging, anchoring the shots but also providing flecks of color that participate in a more nuanced, open-ended parametric play.

1960

Akibiyori
Late Autumn

Shochiku. Story: novel by Ton Satomi. Script: Kogo Noda and Yasujiro Ozu. Cinematography: Yuharu Atsuta. Art direction: Tatsuo Hamada. Music: Kojun Saito. Lighting: Kenzo Ishiwatari. Editing: Yoshiyasu Hamamura. Agfa-Shochikucolor. Cast: Setsuko Hara (*Akiko Miwa*), Yoko Tsukasa (*Ayako*), Mariko Okada (*Yuriko Sasaki*), Keiji Sata (*Shotaro Goto*), Shin Saburi (*Soichi Mamiya*), Sadako Sawamura (*Fumiko*), Miyuki Kuwano (*Michiko*), Masahiko Shimazu (*Tadao*), Chishu Ryu (*Shukichi Miwa*), Ryuji Kita (*Seiichiro Hirayama*), Shinichiro Mikami (*Koichi*), Nobuo Nakamura (*Shuzo Taguchi*), Kuniko Miyake (*Nobuko*), Yuriko Tashiro (*Yoko*), Koji Shigaragi (*Kazuo*), Fumio Watanabe (*Tsuneo Sugiyama*), Akako Senno (*Shigko Takamatsu*). 11 reels, 3,518 meters. Surviving prints: 129 min. Released 13 November 1960. Script, negative, and prints in existence.

Akiko Miwa and her daughter Ayako live happily together. Three businessmen, old friends of the family, decide to help Ayako get married. She resists. They then try to get Akiko to marry one of their number, the widowed Professor Hirayama. She declines, but Ayako is misled into thinking that her mother wishes to remarry and she is an obstacle. In the midst of these family tensions, Ayako's friend Yukiko intervenes and orders the men to desist. In the meantime Akiko and Ayako are reconciled and take a trip to a spa. Upon their return, Ayako marries. Akiko is left alone.

Throughout 1960, Japan was shaken by a storm of protest against the renewal of the Japanese-American Security Treaty. In January there was a violent clash between students and police at Haneda airport as Prime Minister Kishi set off for the United States. In June, before the Diet was to approve the treaty, over ten thousand students demonstrated, and one young woman was killed. The treaty was ratified. In October, a seventeen-year-old right-wing fanatic assassinated a Socialist leader on national television and later committed suicide in jail. It was in this climate that Oshima made his brilliant, brooding *Nihon no yoru to kiri* (*Night and Fog in Japan*, released October 1960). Only the most dedicated reflection-theorist could find traces of this tumult in *Late Autumn*; Sato has recalled seeing the film as utterly insular, portraying a tranquil society that no longer existed.[109] Ozu's 'Japaneseness' was nonetheless more acceptable than Oshima's: Shochiku withdrew *Night and Fog* after the assassination. Yet, for all its refusal of contemporary issues, *Late Autumn* continues Ozu's own exploration of Japan's past through the interaction of old and young, male and female. Like *Early Spring*, *Equinox Flower*, and *Floating Weeds*, it bears some trace of the 'youth cult' films of the late 1950s; it also continues to mock male vanity and to juxtapose the bland comfort of the postwar era with memories of what went before.

The film's plot is based on an alternation of two problems: marrying off Ayako and marrying off her mother Akiko. After an unusually concentrated exposition (the first two scenes on Miwa's death anniversary), the trio of middle-aged men set out to find a match for the daughter. Other friends, such as Akiko's superior at a sewing school, also try to help. But when Ayako announces that she won't marry, the action is at an impasse. The men now hatch the idea of marrying Akiko to one of them, the widower Hirayama. This intrigue leads to quarrels and misunderstandings. Again the issue shifts, and the men plot to get Ayako wed to Goto, her new boyfriend. They succeed.

Or do they? The oscillating syuzhet is rendered somewhat 'eccentric' by a narration which concentrates on one character or group for a block of scenes and then switches to another character for another block. The early part of the film concentrates on the matchmaking men; not until the seventh scene do we see Ayako's life with her mother. There follows a series of scenes tracing the shared life of mother and daughter. After Ayako tells Mamiya she won't marry, the narration switches to another string of scenes restricted to the men as they pursue the Hirayama possibility. This leads to a block of episodes organized around Ayako, who is shocked and angered by the idea of her mother's remarrying. The narration switches again: four scenes now concentrate upon Ayako's friend Yuriko, who assails the men for their meddling but then agrees to help Ayako marry. Another pair of scenes portrays the reconciliation of Akiko and Ayako during their trip. A scene with the wedding photographer draws all the major characters together; the next scene, an explicit parallel to the second one, shows the three men celebrating their success; the last scene shows Akiko alone. This circuitous, shuttling narration lets certain key questions, such as exactly what makes Ayako marry Goto, go unanswered. Because the narration elides their courtship and decision to marry, we cannot be sure that her marriage is caused by the matchmaking outsiders. Once more, the Ozu heroine becomes opaque. Other major pieces of action are kept offscreen, such as the role of Sugiyama in acting as a go-between, and the reconciliation of Ayako and Akiko. The film's narration here resembles that of Welles' *Magnificent Ambersons* (1942), in which crucial events are elided in favor of a concentration on the reactions of subsidiary characters.

The 'block-construction' of the syuzhet has an effect on Ozu's customary use of parallelism. Early in the film several parallel characters are introduced. Taguchi's carefree daughter, who constantly leaves her husband, and Mamiya's daughter Michiko might seem to be ripe for the sort of lengthy exploitation which Fumiko receives in *Equinox Flower*. But here the parallels are not developed at all. Even the pairing of Taguchi's and Mamiya's wives, both of whom tease their husbands with the same gags, creates comic highlighting, not large-scale plot architecture. The most telling parallels are those of situation, as when Yuriko tells Akiko that she should remarry so that Ayako won't have to support her in old age – an echo of what Hirayama's son had said in urging him to remarry.

The keenest comic parallels are reserved for the interfering men, each of whom has an impudent son or daughter. Running gags, such as Taguchi's and

Mamiya's ganging-up on Hirayama, or Hirayama's ill-timed rushes to the toilet, or the joke about the itch he needs to scratch, make the group into three ruminative stooges. All of them yearn for Akiko, and Ozu uses the fact that she has given two of them pipes to create one of his funniest and most merciless pieces of acting-in-unison, again at Hirayama's expense (see p. 85). The trio are treated ironically as well. When Taguchi announces with a wise air that as one gets older, one appreciates plain food, Hirayama deflates him: 'Like steak and pork tonkatsu?' Yuriko's stinging indictment of their meddling makes them cower and renders their businessman's suavity feeble. They are insulted by their sons and mocked by their wives. In their final scenes, oblivious to the distress their intrigues have caused, they can savor the fun they had along the way. Mamiya can even pontificate: 'It's people who tend to complicate life. Life itself is simple' – this after the complications *they* created, and just before one of them asks: 'What'll we do now?' Ozu underscores their frivolity by cutting straight from Taguchi's remark, 'Yeah, sure was fun,' to Akiko's formal kimono hanging at home, as she prepares for bed.

In their careless mischief, the three businessmen recall the college boys of Ozu's silent films. The men's recollection of their campus days – patronizing a drugstore in order to glimpse the young Akiko – resemble the scene in the 'Blue Hawaii' coffee bar of *Where Now Are the Dreams of Youth?*. Throughout *Late Autumn*, brand-name condiments (French's mustard, Lea & Perrin's Worcestershire sauce) get emphasized as much as Sunkist raisins and Libby's asparagus were in the 1920s and 1930s films. That Mamiya is played by Shin Saburi evokes the 1930s atmosphere, and his late arrival at the death-anniversary ceremony beomes a precise reference to *Brothers and Sisters of the Toda Family*. Thus does the Ofuna flavor become 'historicized'. Overall, the film's movement from comedy (the trio's machinations) to a chastened pathos (the problems of mother and daughter) is reminiscent of Ozu's earliest work.

A comparable, if less comic, nostalgia envelops the female characters. Mamiya's daughter sings the Waseda fight song, evoking *Days of Youth*; Mrs Taguchi recalls being infatuated with Girls' Opera. Ayako and Yuriko wave from rooftops to a newly wed couple in a passing train, as the friends had at the end of *Where Now Are the Dreams of Youth?*. Mariko Okada, who plays Yukiko, is the daughter of Tokihiko Okada, star of some of Ozu's 1930s films, while Miyuki Kuwano, who plays Mamiya's daughter, is the daughter of Michiko Kuwano, the insolent *moga* of *What Did the Lady Forget?*. In its basic story, *Late Autumn* is a revision of *Late Spring*, with Akiko (played by Hara, the daughter in the earlier film) taking the father's role and Ayako upset by an 'unclean' remarriage. As in the earlier film, the climax occurs during an excursion; but here the parent tells the child that the remarriage will not take place. 'You mustn't think that I lied to force you into marriage.' Akiko's advice lacks the didactic quality of that of Somiya in *Late Spring*, emerging as simply the consequence of their relationship and not the exhibition of a new liberalism. And in place of the grave 'Japaneseness' of the earlier film's Kyoto passages there is now nostalgia: Akiko asks if Ayako recalls living in Ikaho during the war; the schoolgirls on their excursion remind Ayako of her school trips and the sadness of the last night. There is, however, in both films the

286.

287.

288.

anticipation of future recollection; echoing Somiya, Akiko remarks: 'I'll always remember eating here together.'

The relationship of Akiko and Ayako, presented obliquely by the block-patterned narration, uses correspondingly more intangible and evanescent motifs than the pipes and dialogue that define the comic trio of businessmen. The shimmering reflections of water on the temple wall in the first scene and in the restaurant in the second scene return late in the film during the Ikaho excursion. In the two women's apartment, a red-and-blue striped towel skitters around in the background of certain shots; at one point it becomes part of a robust batch of stripes on a parcel and cups as well (fig. 286). The striped towel returns during the Ikaho spa scene, but, during Akiko's last scene at home, it is no longer visible. Is it packed away? Has Ayako taken it on her honeymoon? (In a sense, the last scene's cutaways to Akiko's formal kimono make this a causally charged substitute for the towel.) Staging patterns also compare phases of the relations between mother and daughter. After their quarrel, a *sojikei* shot puts daughter and mother in tense silence (fig. 287); at the spa, Ayako breaks down at the thought of leaving her mother (fig. 288).

As all these comparisons suggest, one effect of the 'block' narration is to juxtapose the private mother-daughter relationship to the outsiders' machinations. The very first scene begins with the three jolly businessmen joking at Miwa's death anniversary. Eight shots go by before Ozu reveals that Akiko and Ayako are also present, observing their friends with wry tolerance. The resulting mixture of tone – comic for the men and their wives, more lyrical for Akiko and Ayako – is carried through to the end, when Ozu cuts from the men's celebration to Akiko's quiet, smiling resignation. Autumn is in the poetic tradition the 'sad season', the period during which one meditates on life. Yet *Akibiyori* is not exactly 'late autumn' but rather, 'bright autumn weather' or 'a lovely autumn day'. The very title announces the film's fusion of humor and sadness.

The complexity of tone is also carried by the style's unusually sharp juxtaposition of rigor and playfulness. *Late Autumn* is one of the most outrageously sporting of Ozu's postwar works, in the same class as *Ohayo* and *An Autumn Afternoon*. Here he relies on our knowledge of his earlier films in order to undermine our predictions about stylistic patterning. A scene will start with what appears to be the most oblique establishing shot possible (fig.

363

289.

290.

289). What then seems to be a ninety-degree cut takes us to Mamiya and Akiko at a table (fig. 290). Unfortunately, the first shot is not an establishing shot at all, since it shows a different area of the restaurant. The beer bottle is for once not a spatial anchor but a pure distraction. (In case we missed this at the outset, the scene's ending cuts away from the couple to show the initial framing, now with the beer bottle gone.)

Throughout the film, the narration creates a play on Ozu's normal transitions. There is comparatively little priming of when the scene will end, so that the quarrel of mother and daughter lapses into silence and then is cut abruptly off by the next scene. Ozu can use a shot-change unlike anything seen before in his work, as when he cuts from a long-shot of a waitress advancing to an extreme long-shot of Akiko and Ayako coming down the corridor of their apartment house. An extremely tricky scene opening involves a cut to an office door, seen from inside. Nothing happens. Cut to the hall outside, with Hirayama approaching. Cut to Hirayama entering the office, seen from the inside. Twelve scenes later, another scene starts on this door, but then cuts to Mamiya at his desk. The playfully misleading insert has been reinserted into a rigorous pattern. There are startling sound transitions as well. At a restaurant Mamiya calls to a waitress and we hear 'Hai' from offscreen. Cut to a corridor, with a young woman bearing a tray and entering a room; but she is no waitress, only his daughter, and we are now at Mamiya's home. 'Hai,' she says, setting down the *sake*. In another scene, when Ayako and Yuriko walk away from the rooftop rail, their high heels make sharp clicking sounds; cut to a street, with another young woman in high heels walking in the same rhythm. Most jarring of all the sonic manipulations is the conclusion to Ayako's fierce outburst to her mother. 'It's filthy! I'd never agree!' She storms out. The shot holds on the door, and cheerful, bouncy muzak starts on the soundtrack.

A similarly playful recognition of Ozu's normal stylistic commitments seems to underlie the game of presence and absence initiated in the film's first scene. The first shot inside the temple shows the ceremonial gong isolated. When the ceremony is announced, the visitors leave the reception room and Ozu dwells on its emptiness. Cut to the temple, the space of the first shot now filled by the guests. In the course of the next three shots an absence is again marked by the spacing of the figures. Mamiya arrives and passes through the reception room. A 'master shot' of the celebrants, with the gong in the foreground, shows him filling the gap. After he has joined his cronies, Ozu cuts back to the reception room, as if seeking traces of his passage through the earlier shot. The scene is over. Its rigorous stasis contrasts sharply with the nervous aggressivity of Oshima's incessantly panning camera in *Night and Fog in Japan*. Even Ozu's youngsters, on a mountain hike or writing dutiful notes home, are fixed in an abstract pattern that presents slight variants and just-noticeable differences. Oshima's florid *plans-sequences* and theatrical strokes aim to render the political convulsions of 1960, but Ozu, committed to his characters' nostalgia, his earlier films, and a more parametric art, creates a quiet permutational play that makes its agents counters in a game of space.

1961

Kohayakawake no aki
The End of Summer

Takarazuka Eiga/Toho. Script: Kogo Noda, Yasujiro Ozu. Cinematography: Asakazu Nakai. Art direction: Tomoo Shimogawara. Lighting: Choshiro Ishii. Music: Toshiro Mayuzumi. Editing: Koichi Iwashita. Agfacolor. Cast: Ganjiro Nakamura (*Manbei Kohayakawa*), Setsuko Hara (*Akiko*), Yoko Tsukasa (*Noriko*), Michiyo Aratama (*Fumiko*), Keiji Kobayashi (*Hisao*), Masahiko Shimazu (*Masao*), Hisaya Morishige (*Eiichiro Isomura*), Chieko Naniwa (*Tsune Sasaki*), Reiko Dan (*Yuriko*), Haruko Sugimura (*Shige Kato*), Daisuke Kato (*Yanosuke Kitagawa*), Kakyu Sazan (*the chief clerk*), Chishu Ryu (*a farmer*). 7 reels, 2,815 meters. Surviving prints: 103 min. Released 29 October 1961. Script, negative, and prints in existence.

While the Kohayakawa family sets about running its *sake* business, arranging to marry off its youngest daughter Noriko, and exploring the possibility of helping the widowed daughter-in-law Akiko marry, the head of the family is behaving oddly. Old Manbei sneaks out daily to visit Tsune, a former mistress. This upsets his daughter Fumiko, who criticizes the old man. When he has a sudden heart attack, however, recriminations are set aside. He recovers and resumes his philandering. Soon he is stricken again, and his death brings a resolution: Noriko will marry the man of her choice, while Akiko will stay as she is.

The Kohayakawa family

Tsune = Manbei = (wife)   Shige   Sezo   (wife) = Yanosuke Kitagawa

?

Yuriko

Akiko = son   Fumiko = Hisao   Noriko

Minoru   Masao

The Autumn of the Kohayakawa Family, as the film is called in Japanese, takes on a major subject of both Western and Japanese literature of the last century: the decline of the extended bourgeois family. As the family tree shows, the Kohayakawas constitute the most vast *ie* in all of Ozu's work. The family epitomizes 'tradition', both because it owns its own small firm and because the oldest member Manbei was adopted into it in order to carry on the line. As the film progresses, the brewery's fortunes dwindle until at the end the elder son is contemplating selling out to a big company. In all these aspects, the film captures an authentic historical process: after the war, sixty per cent of the working population was involved in middle-class family enterprises. But by the time Ozu was making *The End of Summer*, most such businesses had vanished and the *ie* was splitting into nuclear families, with the father (and often the mother) working outside the home and grandparents living elsewhere. Like most of Ozu's films, this is concretely referential; but as in *Floating Weeds*, its 'present' is anachronistic, already a nostalgic refraction and displacement that appeals to the audience's popular memory of the past.

Correspondingly, the film owes a great deal to commonplaces in Ozu's earlier works. He had treated the breakdown of a family decades before, notably in *A Mother Should Be Loved* and *Brothers and Sisters of the Toda Family*. The handling of Noriko's love match – she is encouraged to marry the man of her choice – goes back to the liberalism of the Occupation films, especially *Early Summer*, and it had become a strong motif thereafter, as in *Equinox Flower*. The motif of the solitude of the widow or widower dates from at least the final (lost) scene of *A Mother Should Be Loved*. The coldness of relatives had been dealt with in *Toda Family* and *Tokyo Story*. The film also exudes a self-consciousness about dealing with such traditional subjects as the *ie*, as in the gag involving the old clerk who still can't sort out all the kinship relations and gives up, saying only, 'The Kohayakawa family is complicated.' The reworking of postwar historical material follows the principles established much earlier in Ozu's career and in the Meiji and Taisho fiction of his youth. (See pp. 147–53.)

The same familiarity greets us in the plot construction. The initial plot-lines involve Akiko's remarriage, possibly to the appallingly snazzy Mr Isomura, and Noriko's resistance to an arranged marriage. (Her real love Teramoto, like other suitors in postwar Ozu, is abruptly transferred to a remote town.) Here, however, these two lines of action, so central to *Late Autumn* (whose analogous roles are played by the same actresses), turn out to be secondary. The main plotline centers on Manbei's relation to the family and to his mistress Tsune. (The echo of *Floating Weeds* is obviously strengthened by having Ganjiro Nakamura in both parts.) Manbei's intrigue, his sudden illness, his equally sudden recovery, and his death occupy the bulk of the film. Akiko and Noriko's problems return and get resolved during his funeral. As in other male-centered Ozu works, the parallels often stress changes in Manbei's situation. He falls ill at home but dies at Tsune's; his pursuit by a junior clerk is paralleled to his later evasion of his family during a game of hide and seek. The richest cluster of parallels occurs on three occasions at which the family gathers: the mother's death anniversary, the family at home after Manbei's recovery, and the final funeral scene. Each employs crosscutting (a technique Ozu rarely uses) to move concisely from one knot of characters to another. Thus at the death anniversary, Akiko and Noriko squat by the river to discuss their problems, and on the hillside at Manbei's funeral (in shots and cuts symmetrical with those in the early scene) they squat again to consider how they will meet the future.

Standing more or less at the film's center, Manbei's adventures introduce a

291.

292.

293.

new twist into the Ozu commonplace of the dissolution of male authority. After the pitiful old salarymen of *Early Spring* and *Ohayo*, we have now a development beyond the college-boy irresponsibility of *Late Autumn*: a very old man who behaves like a carefree child. In Manbei, paternal authority has become infantile self-gratification. He sneaks out while playing a game with his grandson, and he delights in catching his clerk tailing him. At Tsune's, he lapses into the simple contentment of a man catered to by his woman, and he heedlessly promises Yuriko a mink stole he will never provide.

The film's geography strengthens the sense of an old man's relapse into youth. There is the modern city of Osaka, with its office buildings and its 'New Japan' sign. There is the family brewery in Fushimi, outside Kyoto, with its cicadas and paper lantern. And there is Tsune's inn, in an old quarter of Kyoto, where time has all but stood still. A stone lantern commands her garden. One hears from the neighborhood the plucking of a shamisen or the rapping of a barrel-maker's hammer. Here Tsune and Manbei talk of a tea shop they once knew, a snow viewing, their first night of love, and a firefly chase (an echo of a celebrated scene in Tanizaki's novel *The Makioka Sisters*). As usual in Ozu, characters' memories of the 1930s and 1940s shade off into echoes of 1930s and 1940s films. Even the dissonance which Ozu introduces – Yuriko the postwar girl, plump in her pink frock – becomes the icon of 'modernity-within-tradition' that only updates the *moga* of prewar cinema. The plot thus makes it fitting that Manbei dies in this island of nostalgia, and that one shot of Hisao lifting the veil from the body echoes the many off-center death scenes from Ozu's films decades before (fig. 291; see pp. 232, 294–5).

These narrative and thematic constructs are rendered in somewhat more explicit fashion than is usual for Ozu. Shot for Toho, *The End of Summer* is afflicted with a heavy-handed score that is either hyperdramatic or floridly lyrical, often mickey-mousing in a self-consciously cute way. In dramatic terms, the parody of the businessman, the chortling bow-tied Isomura, is broader than anything in prior works. Even Ozu's graphic matches are stark and simplified (figs. 292–293). The last three shots, which dwell on crows and cemetery stones while Mayuzumi's score pumps ominously in the background, come perilously close to banality.

Yet no Ozu film leaves pictorial qualities wholly unexplored. The scraps of betting receipts that drift down from the racing stands recall cherry blossoms, Hiroshige designs, and the white shreds that sift down from the rafters of the old theatre in both versions of *Story of Floating Weeds*. Most consistently exploited in this film are the circular forms associated with the Kohayakawa brewery. The firm is introduced by three shots of barrels (figs. 294–296); taken together, the compositional vectors of the shots yield an impression of contiguity, a sense of moving along a single row. Moreover, the firm's trademark is a central circle orbited by eight smaller ones (see p. 119, fig. 42). Depending on the lighting conditions and the background color, this family crest can change dramatically in hue. Later in the film, we return to shots of the barrels, with their ellipsoid forms now echoed by parasols ranked along them (figs. 297–298) – and one parasol bears the logo. (As we have already seen, the crest is another of those diagrams of the geometry of Ozu's 360-degree space.) The significance of purely abstract design in the film is laid bare in the scenes in the gallery where Akiko works; at one point, the narration cuts from a landscape painting to the hills of Arashiyama, where the family goes for an outing.

Manbei's sprightliness is matched by certain aspects of the film's narration. One intermediate shot juxtaposes a Kyoto temple with a TV antenna in the foreground. More systematically, Ozu playfully inverts the two pursuit scenes. The first, in which Manbei is trailed by the junior clerk, is cut with correct screen direction, so that the pursuit is always intelligible. Later, however, during the game, Ozu violates screen direction, making Manbei's frame entrances so confusing that the audience must play its own hide-and-seek game with the protagonist. Ozu also makes teasing use of eyelines, as when at Teramoto's farewell party, the young man is shown looking left (toward where Noriko sits) and then looking away, followed by a shot of her looking right, and then away – leaving us to wonder if, offscreen, the glances meet or miss. Ozu exploits a blue-green lantern in the family home for parametric purposes, at the start of the scene in which Manbei collapses (figs. 299–301), and then in an interplay with the family crest as we return to the sickbed (figs. 302–303). (Note too that the lantern ceases to act as a pivot for the final shot, when the family is in another room.)

Most memorable of all is the sadistic way in which the narration misleads the audience during an emotional high point that explicitly negates the grandmother's death scene in *Tokyo Story*. Noriko chops ice, having told the visitors that they cannot expect a change in Manbei's condition until dawn. Cut to dawn's shadows on a wall. Cut to more shadows. Then cut to a graveyard, the first explicit clue. After a shot of a street, we get a brief scene of Noriko weeping. Cut to the empty room by the garden. Then a brief scene of the two clerks talking about how sudden it all is and discussing Manbei in the past tense. After a lot more of this, we finally learn that he has not died after all. Indeed, he soon waddles out of his room to relieve himself, farting cheerfully. This amplification of *Passing Fancy*'s deathbed scene is only one indication of the fundamental continuity of narrational attitude between Ozu's prewar and postwar works.

294.

295.

296.

297.

298.

299.

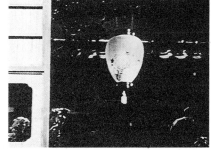

300.

301.

302.

303.

1962

Samma no aji
An Autumn Afternoon

Shochiku. Script: Kogo Noda, Yasujiro Ozu. Cinematography: Yuharu Atsuta. Art direction: Tatsuo Hamada. Music: Kojun Saito. Lighting: Kenzo Ishiwatari. Editing: Yoshiyasu Hamamura. Agfa-Shochikucolor. Cast: Shima Iwashita (*Michiko Hirayama*), Chishu Ryu (*Shuhei Hirayama*), Keiji Sata (*Koichi*), Mariko Okada (*Akiko*), Shinichiro Mikami (*Kazuo*), Teruo Yoshida (*Yutaka Miura*), Noriko Maki (*Fusako Taguchi*), Nobuo Nakamura (*Shuzo Kawai*), Kuniko Miyake (*Nobuko*), Eijiro Tono (*Sakuma, the 'Gourd'*), Haruko Sugimura (*Tomoko*), Daisuke Kato (*Yoshitaro Sakamoto*), Ryuji Kita (*Shin Horie*), Miseyo Tamaki (*Tamako*), Kyoko Kishida (*the bar hostess*). 9 reels, 3,087 meters. Surviving prints: 113 min. Released 18 November 1962. Script, negative, and prints in existence.

The aging salaryman Hirayama is goaded by his pals Kawai and Horie into finding a husband for his daughter Michiko. The need to do so is driven home to him by the pathetic state into which his old teacher Sakuma has fallen; he clung to his daughter, who now is too old to marry. Hirayama tries to arrange that Michiko marry the man of her choice, the young salaryman Miura; but he is already engaged. With the support of his son Koichi and his wife, Hirayama finds a prospect through Kawai. After the wedding, Hirayama drowns his sorrows in a bar. At home, his younger son Kazuo warns him to cut down on his drinking and he starts to face life without his daughter.

Critics, especially auteur critics, tend to take an artist's last work as a summing up, the goal toward which every other work has moved. The impulse is hard to resist with respect to *An Autumn Afternoon*. Here is Chishu Ryu, front and center as he has been in no Ozu film since *Tokyo Story*; how can he not be Ozu's alter ego, brought back for a final encompassing statement? Here too are many familiar faces – players from films from *Toda Family* onward. And here, surely, is Ozu's last meditation on resignation to change, on the inevitable dissolution of the family, on the ultimate loneliness facing every individual.

Actually, all this is not entirely plausible. Ozu was told to avoid borrowing actors from other studios; hence the Shochiku stock company and the centrality of Ryu.[110] Moreover, a close look at the film suggests that while it owes a good deal to prior works, in its characterization of young people and especially women, it constitutes a departure, not a repetition. Finally, it is significant that the narration observes the protagonist with more detachment than would be expected of the sympathetic study of solitude we get in, say, *Late Autumn*. The English-language title itself perhaps slants too much toward sombreness. The original title is 'The Taste of *Samma*'; it does evoke the brief season in late summer when *samma*, a variety of mackerel, is at its most savory, but the phrase is also appropriate for a movie that revolves around eating and drinking and that features a scene in which an old man, confessing that he leads a lonely life, discovers the succulence of sea-eel.

The exposition is unusually concise for a late Ozu film. The first two scenes spell out the father/daughter problem, prepare for the class reunion, and establish certain narrational norms, such as elliptical indirect transitions. (See the baseball-park decoy, discussed on p. 131.) Such a compressed exposition lets Ozu move immediately to retardatory episodes, chiefly one clump of scenes involving the Gourd and another around Koichi's and Akiko's borrowing of money to fulfill their consumer dreams. Not until scene 18 is Hirayama convinced to take action about getting Michiko married; after Miura is explored as a possibility, five scenes later she is lined up with Kawai's prospect; and immediately she is shown in her wedding dress. As in *Late Spring*, we never see her husband, or the marriage ceremony. All the material around her courtship and marriage is elided, as if squeezed out by the extensive parallels and delaying maneuvers of the film's first hour. The result is to throw the emphasis upon Hirayama, and to a lesser extent Koichi and Akiko. As in other late films, Ozu usually links his scenes by 'character contiguity', whereby a secondary figure in one scene becomes the main character of the next.

The film swarms with parallels of character and setting, but the central one is that which likens Hirayama's situation to that of other fathers' relation to their daughters. In the very first scene, we learn that Hirayama's subordinate Miss Taguchi will marry; that his secretary is unmarried but supports her father; that Hirayama's friend Kawai has found a prospect for Michiko; and that Professor Horie has married a young girl near his daughter's age. Later in the film, Hirayama learns that Sakamoto, his subordinate during the war, has married off his daughter. Most explicit of all is the elaborate parallel drawn between Hirayama and his old teacher Sakuma, nicknamed 'the Gourd.' The lengthy episodes around the Gourd present a cautionary tale: he clung to his daughter Tomoko, and she became too old to marry. Time and again Kawai warns Hirayama that he and Michiko will end up the same way. Ozu stresses the solitary unhappiness of the Sakumas in two scenes that linger on them after others have gone; the medium-shots of the weeping Tomoko (end of scene 7) and the despondent Gourd (end of scene 9), each sitting on a stool in their cheap noodle shop, seem to confirm the Gourd's drunken pronouncement that in the end everyone is alone.

The other stretches of retardatory material involve Hirayama's son Koichi and his wife Akiko. Here Ozu is able to present in brief compass a portrayal of the younger generation and the new salaryman culture. Unlike the anachronistic portrayal of a family business in *The End of Summer*, the scenes in and around Koichi's and Akiko's apartment stress current commodity worship. She wants money for a refrigerator while Koichi, like the little boys who crave balls and mitts in early Ozu, sulks because he can't buy golf clubs. (A scene on the office driving range nicely evokes his urge to caress the objects that are out of his financial reach.) Two shots of a neighbor's apartment emphasize the three electrical treasures of postwar life – refrigerator, vacuum cleaner, and television. Koichi and Akiko have an electric rice cooker and eat hamburger and tomatoes. They borrow from Hirayama but ask for more than they need so as to get other commodities. It would be wrong, I think, to see Ozu's treatment as more than a satiric jab at contemporary lifestyles; it is no more a denunciation of 'Westernization' than is his affectionate mockery of movie posters and pipes in his early films. There is satire as well in his characterization of Koichi, a timid and spoiled husband who at one point dons an apron. Akiko is a tough, no-nonsense wife who orders Koichi to make his bed, criticizes him for coming home tired, refuses to let him buy golf clubs, makes fun of his name, and snatches Hirayama's loan from Michiko before he can raise a protest. Yet she is never judged as harshly as, say, the self-centered Shige in *Tokyo Story* is – who, as we saw, also supplies comic moments.

Just as it would be reassuringly simple to judge the contemporary salaryman's world as mercenary and soulless, so the critic's task would be easier if longing for the past were presented wholly as a warm haze. Like most of Ozu's late works, *An Autumn Afternoon* includes many scenes steeped in nostalgia. The Gourd's reunion evokes middle-school memories running back forty years. Hirayama's meeting with Sakamoto recalls the war and postwar years. In Torys Bar Hirayama finds a hostess who reminds him of his dead wife. Hirayama tells Koichi he was twenty-six when he was born, which sets the son to counting on his fingers. Most concrete is the use of 'Gunkan machi', the 'Warship March', which Sakamoto plays on the jukebox in Torys and to which he marches and salutes. Although composed in 1897, it was one of the biggest hits of the 1930s. (Interestingly, the early 1960s saw a revival of old popular songs. The Warship March became a staple background tune in the sort of pachinko parlor shown in *Green Tea*.) As usual the nostalgia is not only for the historical period but for earlier Ozu films. At the reunion, the Gourd reports on the health of 'The Badger' – a reference to the name of a teacher in *Days of Youth* and to the protagonist of *There Was a Father*. The stylistic handling of the two Warship-March renditions in Torys Bar, with their cutaways to hanging lamps, recalls inserts of ceilings, fans, and lights in *Where Now Are the Dreams of Youth?*, *Passing Fancy*, and *The Only Son*. The use of 'music-box' renditions of 'Annie Laurie' recalls such popular Western tunes as 'Old Black Joe' in *The Only Son* and 'Home Sweet Home' in *Early Summer*.

But before we see the present as inevitably a corruption of that past for which the old men yearn, we should notice how, as in *Equinox Flower*, nostalgia is qualified and criticized, often by the very characters who indulge in it. The Gourd's drunken pronouncement that 'Human beings have melted away since the war' is 'placed' by the commonsensical comments of the salarymen who entertain him. In a moment of sharp comedy, Sakamoto fantasizes Japan's winning the war, with Westerners wearing wigs and playing samisens while chewing gum. Hirayama replies: 'It's lucky we lost.' The same note is struck when, as the Warship March booms out, two strangers at the bar imitate officers repeating by radio that the Imperial Forces were wiped out. Ozu manages to make us feel the intensity of nostalgia while maintaining some ironic distance on it.

The same sort of distance is taken upon Hirayama's situation itself. The

Gourd parallel is both negative (don't let your daughter waste her life serving you) and positive, in that as the film goes on Hirayama declines into the drunken sentimentality displayed by his teacher. In Torys Bar, Hirayama can drift into a nostalgic dream of military glory and obedient womanhood, with the bar madam resembling his wife, her solicitude contrasting with the astringency of Akiko and the independence of Michiko. Celebrating at Kawai's after the wedding, he makes drunken pronouncements about children ('Not worth the trouble of bringing them up') which recall the Gourd's. He visits Torys Bar sunk in self-pity, telling the hostess he's been to 'a funeral – more or less'. Significantly, *An Autumn Afternoon* contains no scenes of shared family life, no idyll or outing showing parent and child in harmony with nature. There is thus no context for what Hirayama claims to have lost; his family life consists of his returning late from a night on the tiles, Michiko waiting to make his meal, and Kazuo's offhanded selfishness. That Hirayama's despondency is somewhat self-indulgent is also suggested by the way that the celebration scene at Kawai's lingers on the other men's reactions. Kawai remarks: 'The first night after losing your girl is hard' – implying that Hirayama will get over it as Kawai and Horie have. Thus the last scene may signal Hirayama's delayed recognition of how much Michiko's leaving will change his life. Yet at the same time a broader view is signalled by the music. A bouncy nondiegetic rendition of the Warship March takes us up to Michiko's room, associating the daughter's absence with Hirayama's memory of his wartime life, his fascination with the bar hostess, and his recollection of his wife. It is an ironic, 'external' insight which Hirayama cannot share.

I am claiming, then, that the film's organization and stylistic texture suggest an implicit meaning that mitigates any endorsement of Hirayama's solitary and nostalgic despondency. I would also claim that as part of its symptomatic meaning, the film wrestles with an ideological problem crystallized in the figure of Michiko. A stern mistress of the house who tells her father and brother to do the dishes, she is far from the stereotyped passive Japanese woman. If Ozu's previous films were not enough, *An Autumn Afternoon* alone should suffice to disprove glib claims that his women are docile creatures. Michiko is sharp-tongued, even defiant; she is the first Ozu daughter to tell her father not to push her around. She also receives the oblique narrational treatment afforded the heroines of *Late Spring*, *Early Summer*, *Equinox Flower*, and other films. The narration's concentration upon Hirayama, Koichi, and the Gourd means that we virtually never see Michiko with her friends or at her job. Unlike earlier heroines, she confides in no one. True, after visiting Koichi she discusses husbands with Miura, and in retrospect this brief scene on a train platform becomes a hint that she is romantically interested in him; but this information is actually provided through a conversation between Koichi and Hirayama.

Once Miura is found to be engaged, Michiko is left without a marriage prospect. Now, in a blatantly ideological maneuver, the narrational focus shifts completely to Hirayama. We never learn of Michiko's desires, and she becomes the passive object to be married off. In a stunning ellipsis, Ozu cuts from Hirayama arranging an *o-miai* to the day of the wedding itself. The narration has it both ways: because Michiko is initially characterized as independent, the viewer can assume that she would not have submitted to the arranged marriage if she hadn't found the candidate somewhat attractive; but by eliding the courtship and giving us no access to her attitudes, the narration portrays the marriage as the immediate result of Hirayama's efforts, hastening us along to explore the action's *real* effects – on him. One can argue that the Michiko mystery emerges as a 'structuring absence' in the one moment we see her alone: having heard of Miura's engagement, she sits at her desk alone, twisting a tape measure around her fingers. Unlike many Ozu heroines, she is not crying. What she is thinking will never be revealed.

The opacity of Michiko's final actions seems all the more vivid against the background of the film's narrational repetitions. Seldom has an Ozu film so explicitly set up a matrix of characters, actions, locales, and motifs and rigorously recycled them. A survey of one day establishes the pattern of office work/nighttime carousing/return home (scenes 1-4); the syuzhet starts over again and pushes the same pattern through the Gourd-plot (scenes 6–12). After a digression into the Koichi-Akiko plot (scenes 13–15), the rhythm starts once more with Hirayama back at his office (16), going out on the town with Kawai and the Gourd (17) and returning home (18). Once the Michiko plot is firmly launched, Ozu varies the pattern, but by now the template is well established and scenes are slotted in firmly as repetitions and variants of earlier ones.

Threading through such geometrical patterning are the recurrent motifs, such as the running gag about Horie's marriage to a young woman. (The Garden of Forking Paths again: Ryuji Kita, who played the professor rebuffed by Akiko in *Late Autumn*, now gets a wife.) Ozu can treat these playfully because the recycling of episodes 'naturally' creates ellipses which can be suppressed. Thus in one scene, Kawai and Hirayama fool both the waitress and the viewer into thinking Horie has died. Later the same trick is pulled when Hirayama is told that Michiko is shut out because Horie has a bride for Kawai's prospect. Because of our restriction to Hirayama's range of knowledge and our assumption that the film will play down its ellipses, we are duped exactly as he is. In a sense, this play with ellipsis forms a temporal counterpart to the film's numerous jokes on offscreen space, so reminiscent of the sudden or withheld frame entrances in Ozu's college comedies.

The film's highly playful narration recalls the early films' flashiness in other ways. The credits replace the standard burlap backing with gorgeously tinted stalks of grass – designs which echo the cartoon titles of Ozu's earliest work. The silver, white, and red colors dominating the opening shots prefigure the hues of Michiko's bridal costume.[111] The just-noticeable differences of the early style are, so to speak, more noticeable here. Spinning ventilators (a Shochiku trademark since the 1930s) are visible outside Michiko's window. The oblique introduction of Hirayama in the first five shots (see pp. 106–7) is a masterpiece of dominant/overtone construction, with the smoke from the chimneys serving as an evocative overtone akin to that of the smoke in the penultimate scene of *Woman of Tokyo* (see pp. 242–3). Seldom since the war has Ozu dared to match movement with such graphic boldness as in his cut from Hirayama to Kawai drinking (p. 110, figs. 7-8). And rarely has he used

304.   305.   306.

objects as independent elements so geometrically as in the shots that take us
from outside a restaurant to an interior (with plastic pails as the link),
through the upstairs, introducing beer bottles (fig. 304) and a soy-sauce
bottle (fig. 305); to Koichi and Miura eating, framed by a beer bottle and a
soy-sauce bottle (fig. 306; are these the ones seen in the previous shot?); and
finally to a lengthy series of frontal shots, graphically matched with an
exactitude that extends, outrageously, to the label on the beer bottles, but
which in a spirit of perverseness now shuttles another soy-sauce bottle across
the frame (figs. 307–308). The audacity of this sequence recalls the sprightly
shot combinations of such silent work as *Walk Cheerfully* and *The Lady and the
Beard*.

307.

The playfulness extends to the film's transitions. Most scenes are linked by
intermediate spaces on at least one 'side' of the scene-change, and there is
usually music as a cue for a scene's start or stop. Ozu will make a transition on
two café signs, or link Koichi swinging his golf club in his apartment to a shot
of a ball hitting a target on a driving range. As usual, an abrupt 'montage'
effect can arise from the clash of two kinds of music. (See, for example, the
first shift to Torys Bar.) The first inter-scene transition, involving the false
expectation that Kawai has gone to a baseball game (see p. 131) is the film's
most flagrant, though not its most complicated: an outlandish play of absence
and presence so early in the film alerts us to the more nuanced transitions that
will follow. One set of these, involving the permutations around the signs on
the street of Torys Bar, has already been discussed (pp. 127–8). Another
subtle set involves the Hirayama home.

308.

Unlike *Late Spring* and *Early Summer*, *An Autumn Afternoon* delays showing
us the environs of the home until the limousines are outside to take the family
to Michiko's wedding. Throughout the bulk of the film, every scene in the
house is introduced by a long-shot down the hallway toward the main door. In
the first two scenes at home, Hirayama is shown coming in and being greeted
by Michiko. In the third scene, he enters but Michiko does not. In the three
remaining scenes taking place at home, the hall shot shows no one entering; it
serves as an 'empty' space to introduce the locale. Corresponding to this
development is a progression during which we explore more of the house. In
the fourth home scene – the first one to begin with an empty frame – the
narration follows Hirayama going upstairs to Michiko, anxious in her room. In
the next scene at home, we again follow Hirayama upstairs to see Michiko as a

bride, and the narration self-consciously lingers there after the family has left, in order to show new details of the room and reveal a view out the window. In the last scene, Hirayama sits feebly rocking downstairs, but a series of shots takes us down the hall, up the stairs, and to the empty room before bringing us back to Hirayama, now standing at the foot of the stairs, as if he had only just caught up with the 'authorial' commentary.

In a similar fashion, the endings of the home scenes establish a pattern that comes to culmination in the film's final shot. The first home scene closes with Michiko in the kitchen. The second ends with Hirayama washing up alone in the bathroom, seen from the corridor as in the kitchen shot. The third scene ends with Hirayama sending Kazuo off to eat in the kitchen ('Take care of yourself') before he slowly undresses in medium-shot and a solo violin creeps in on the soundtrack. The fourth home scene ends with a shot of Michiko alone in her room, twisting the tape measure. In the fifth scene, the camera lingers on Michiko's room in the fashion already described, as if space had finally been emptied out. The film ends with a shot of Hirayama, who stands staring agonizingly up the stairs and then totters to the distant kitchen to pour himself some tea. The film's final scene thus condenses aspects of all the earlier endings: the tour of the upstairs (a doubling of home scenes four and five), a medium-shot of Hirayama alone underscored by the violin phrase (scene three), a framing of Hirayama at a distance (the second home scene), and a view of a figure in the kitchen (the first home scene). To the recycling of routines and locales, and the variants of repeated shot-rows, there corresponds a series of 'pre-endings' that climax in an image made evocative by its rigorously patterned context.

An Autumn Afternoon is not, then, a testament. Like Ozu's other works, it is a complex reworking of strategies derived from earlier films, as well as an attempt to try new things. It is another manifestation of an aesthetic system whose rigor, breadth of detail, and suppleness of variation give it a simplicity and richness unparalleled in the history of the cinema. His next film, for which he completed only notes, was to have brought back Tadao Ikeda, the scriptwriter of the 1930s, to work with Noda. It was to center on a man who gets cancer and who has a daughter about to get married. Once more we find a minimal variant on a preestablished pattern. But the film's innovation would have reflected more explicitly than ever before a life steeped in the love of cinema. The film's characters would have been movie performers, and the title was to be *Radishes and Carrots*, Ozu's favorite slang for poor actors. One might be tempted to consider this unfinished film (a version of which was directed by Ozu's pupil Minoru Shibuya) a summing up, were it not for the fact that when Ozu died there was no evidence of flagging powers: *An Autumn Afternoon*, despite its concern with aging, is in form and attitude a young man's work.

Appendix

Some Quantitative Aspects of Ozu's Films

Film	Length in feet (16mm except as noted)	Number of scenes (not incl. credits)	Number of shots (incl. credits)	Number of titles (and per cent)	Average shot length feet (seconds)
Days of Youth	3696	33	1371	129 (9%)	2.7 (4.5)
Walk Cheerfully	3441	24	1075	151 (14%)	3.2 (5.3)
I Flunked, But. . .	2304	15	619	70 (11%)	3.7 (6.2)
That Night's Wife	2345	24	680	54 (8%)	3.5 (5.7)
The Lady and the Beard	2680	15	809	108 (13%)	3.3 (5.5)
Tokyo Chorus	3242	15	1086	144 (13%)	3 (5)
I Was Born, But . . .	3217.5	16	1348	161 (12%)	2.4 (4)
Where Now Are the Dreams of Youth?	3065.5	20	1155	186 (16%)	2.7 (4.5)
Woman of Tokyo	1671	12	640	120 (18%)	2.6 (4.4)
Dragnet Girl	3607.5	26	1457	293 (20%)	2.4 (4)
Passing Fancy	3707	23	1479	393 (27%)	2.5 (4.1)
A Mother Should be Loved	2557.5	16	796	197 (25%)	3.2 (5.3)
Story of Floating Weeds	3085.5	21	982	266 (27%)	3.1 (5.2)
Inn in Tokyo	2863	22	1056	303 (29%)	2.7 (4.5)
The Only Son	2966	20	532		5.6 (9)
What Did the Lady Forget?	2554	22	373		6.9 (11.5)
Brothers and Sisters of the Toda Family	3753	19	468		8 (13.3)
There Was a Father	3128	31	353		8.9 (14.8)
Record of a Tenement Gentleman	2559.5	16	423		6 (10)
A Hen in the Wind	7494.5*	21	541		13.9* (9)
Late Spring	3859.5	30	672		5.7 (9)
The Munekata Sisters	4024.5	29	684		5.9 (9.5)
Early Summer	4482.5	36	765		5.9 (9.5)
Flavor of Green Tea over Rice	4162.5	30	877		4.7 (8)
Tokyo Story	4855	33	786		6.2 (10.2)
Early Spring	5178	43	872		5.9 (9.5)
Tokyo Twilight	5044	32	10_4		4.9 (8)
Equinox Flower	4320	28	1032		4.2 (7)
Ohayo	3369.5	24	819		4.1 (7)
Floating Weeds	4252	30	963		4.4 (7.5)
Late Autumn	4618.5	36	1121		4.1 (7)
End of Summer	3677.5	24	892		4.1 (7)
An Autumn Afternoon	4036	27	975		4.1 (7)

*35mm length

Notes

Introduction

1. Readers interested in more detailed and abstract arguments should consult David Bordwell and Kristin Thompson, *Film Art: An Introduction* (New York: Knopf, 1985); David Bordwell, Janet Staiger, and Kristin Thompson, *The Classical Hollywood Cinema: Film Style and Mode of Production to 1960* (New York: Columbia University Press, 1985); and David Bordwell, *Narration in the Fiction Film* (Madison: University of Wisconsin Press, 1985).

PART I

Chapter 1

1. Donald Richie, *Ozu* (Berkeley: University of California Press, 1974), pp. 195–6.
2. See, for instance, Deke Dusinberre, 'Yasujiro Ozu, Master of Moods', *The Movie* no. 46 (1980): p. 916.
3. Jean-Paul Sartre, *Search for a Method*, trans. Hazel E. Barnes (New York: Vintage, 1980), p. 56.
4. Boris Tomashevsky, 'Literature and Biography', in *Readings in Russian Poetics*, ed. Ladislaw Matejka and Krystyna Pomorska (Cambridge, MA: MIT Press, 1971), p. 55.
5. Robert C. Allen and Douglas Gomery, *Film History: Theory and Practice* (New York: Knopf, 1985), pp. 67–108.
6. See Bordwell, *The Films of Carl-Theodor Dreyer* (Berkeley: University of California Press, 1981), pp. 9–24.
7. Quoted in *Ozu Yasujiro wo yomu* [Reading Yasujiro Ozu] (Tokyo: Firuma Atosha, 1982), p. 37.
8. Tadao Sato, *Ozu Yasujiro no geijutsu* [The Art of Yasujiro Ozu] vol. 2 (Tokyo: Asahi Shinbunsha, 1979), pp. 211–14.
9. Shimba Iida, 'Talking about People: Yasujiro Ozu', *Film* [UK] no. 36 (Summer 1963): p. 9.
10. Quoted in Sato, *Ozu no geijutsu* vol. 2, p. 67.
11. 'Ozu on Ozu: The Talkies,' *Cinema* [USA] vol. 6, no. 1 (1970): p. 4.
12. Quoted in *Ozu wo yomu*, p. 39.
13. Iida, 'Talking about People': p. 9.
14. Komatsu Kitamura, quoted in Tadao Sato, *Ozu Yasujiro no geijutsu* vol. 1 (Tokyo: Asahi Shinbunsha, 1978), pp. 195–6.
15. Quoted in *Ikite wa mita keredo* [*I Lived, But . . . : A Biography of Yasujiro Ozu*], film produced by Shochiku Ltd., 1984.
16. On the many meanings of *edokko*, see Kohiro Yuchiro, 'Edo: The City on the Plain', in *Tokyo: Form and Spirit*, ed. Mildred Friedman (Minneapolis: Walker Art Center/New York: Abrams, 1986), p. 44.
17. Yasujiro Ozu, 'How I Became a Film Director', in *The Masters of Japanese Cinema*, ed. and trans. Leonard Schrader (unpub. ms., Pacific Film Archive, n.d.), p. 242.
18. Tadao Sato, 'The Art of Yasujiro Ozu (6)', *The Study of the History of the Cinema* no. 9 (1977): p. 96.
19. *Ozu wo yomu*, p. 19.
20. Shinbi Iida, 'Filmmaking in America and Japan', in L. Schrader, ed., *Masters*, p. 241.
21. Shinbi Iida, Fuyuhiko Kitagawa, and Seiji Mizumachi, 'Entertainment and the Eighth Art', in L. Schrader, ed., *Masters*, p. 228.
22. *Ozu wo yomu*, p. 59.
23. Quoted in *Ozu wo yomu*, pp. 19–20.
24. Tadao Sato, 'The Art of Yasujiro Ozu (7)', *The Study of the History of the Cinema* no. 10 (1977): p. 94.

25. Sato, *Ozu no geijutsu* vol. 2, p. 13.
26. Hideo Tsumura, 'In morte di Yamanaka Sadao [1938]', in *Schermi giapponesi* vol. 1 (Venice: Marsilio, 1984), p. 28.
27. Richie, *Ozu*; Paul Schrader, *Transcendental Style in Film: Ozu, Bresson, Dreyer* (Berkeley: University of California Press, 1972), pp. 17–55.
28. Noël Burch, 'Three Early Films', in *Yasujiro Ozu: A Critical Anthology*, ed. John Gillett and David Wilson (London: British Film Institute, 1976), pp. 35–7.
29. Akira Iwasaki, 'Ozu and Japanese Film', in L. Schrader, ed., *Masters*, pp. 290–3.
30. P. Schrader, *Transcendental Style*, p. 46.
31. 'Ozu on Ozu: The Talkies': p. 3.
32. Shinbi Iida and Akira Iwasaki, 'A Talk with Ozu', *Cinema* [USA] vol.6, no. 1 (1970): p. 40.
33. 'Ozu on Ozu: The Silents', *Cinema* [USA] vol. 7, no. 3 (Winter 1972–3): p. 24.
34. See P. Schrader, *Transcendental Style*, pp. 18–19.
35. Kristin Thompson, 'Notes on the Spatial System of Ozu's Early Films', *Wide Angle* vol. 1, no. 4 (1977): pp. 8–17.

Chapter 2

1. Roman Jakobson, 'The Dominant', in Matejka and Pomorska, eds., *Readings in Russian Poetics*, p. 87.
2. Erik Olin Wright, *Class, Crisis and the State* (London: New Left Books, 1978), p. 23.
3. Donald Kirihara, 'A Reconsideration of the Institution of the Benshi', *Film Reader* no. 6 (1985): p. 48.
4. For further discussion, see David Bordwell, 'Our Dream-Cinema: Western Historiography and the Japanese Film,' *Film Reader* no. 4 (1979): p. 51.
5. Shiro Kido, *Nihon eiga den: Eiga seisakusha no kiroko* [A Japanese Film Biography: Chronicle of a Film Producer] (Tokyo: Bungei Shinju, 1956), pp. 39–40.
6. Ibid.
7. Joseph L. Anderson and Donald Richie, *The Japanese Film: Art and Industry*, expanded ed. (Princeton: Princeton University Press, 1982), pp. 53–4.
8. Kido, *Nihon eiga den*, p. 256.
9. See Sato, 'Art of Ozu (7)': pp. 91–2.
10. 'Ozu on Ozu: The Silents': p. 22.
11. Tadao Sato, 'The Art of Yasujiro Ozu (8)', *The Study of the History of the Cinema* no. 11 (1978): p. 96.
12. These categories and labels are my own. I choose the term 'calligraphic' in order to emphasize the fluid, gestural qualities of technique used here. The 'pictorialist' tag should suggest that this style relies upon the shot as a complex and developing composition, in contrast to the 'piecemeal' style, which breaks a scene into comparatively simple and static shots. I discuss these styles and others at greater length in a forthcoming study of style in Japanese cinema of this period.
13. For a discussion of Mizoguchi's use of this style, see Bordwell, 'Mizoguchi and the Evolution of Film Language', in Stephen Heath and Patricia Mellencamp, eds., *Cinema and Language* (Frederick, MD: University Publications of America, 1983), pp. 107–15.
14. Noël Burch, *To the Distant Observer: Form and Meaning in the Japanese Cinema* (Berkeley: University of California Press, 1979), p. 148.
15. Audie Bock, *Japanese Film Directors* (Tokyo: Kodansha, 1978), p. 105.
16. Anderson and Richie, *Japanese Film*, pp. 287–8.
17. Tadao Sato, *Currents in the Japanese Cinema*, trans. Gregory Barrett (Tokyo: Kodansha, 1982), p. 192.
18. Tadao Sato, 'The Art of Yasujiro Ozu (1)', *The Study of the History of the Cinema* no. 4 (1974): p. 92.
19. Marvin Zeman, 'The Serene Poet of Japanese Cinema: The Zen Artistry of Yasujiro Ozu', *The Film Journal* vol. 1, nos. 3–4 (Fall–Winter 1972): pp. 62–71.

20. P. Schrader, *Transcendental Style*, p. 49.
21. Richie, *Ozu*, pp. 51–2.
22. Ibid., p. 256.
23. Shuichi Kato, *A History of Japanese Literature*, vol. 1: *The First Thousand Years*, trans. David Chibbett (Tokyo: Kodansha, 1979), pp. 20–2.
24. Tatsuo Arima, *The Failure of Freedom: A Portrait of Modern Japanese Intellectuals* (Cambridge, MA: Harvard University Press, 1969), pp. 7–13.
25. See Makoto Ueda, *Literary and Art Theories in Japan* (Cleveland: Case Western Reserve University Press, 1967), for a detailed survey. Cf. Burch, *Distant Observer*, pp. 25–53.
26. P. Schrader, *Transcendental Style*, pp. 27–35.
27. Shigehiko Hasumi, *Kantoku Ozu Yasujiro* [Director Yasujiro Ozu] (Tokyo: Chikuma Shobo, 1983), passim.
28. Raymond Williams, *The Long Revolution* (Harmondsworth: Penguin, 1965), pp. 67–70.
29. See Kokusai Bunka Shinkokai, *Introduction to Contemporary Japanese Literature* (Tokyo: Kokusai Bunka Shinkokai, 1939), p. xlii.
30. J. Thomas Rimer, *Modern Japanese Fiction and Its Traditions: An Introduction* (Princeton: Princeton University Press, 1978), p. 165.
31. Miriam Silverberg, 'Nakano Shigehara's Reproduction of Taisho Culture', unpub. ms.
32. Yasuzo Masumura, *Profilo storico del cinema giapponese*, trans. Guido Cincotti (Rome: Bianco e nero, 1955), p. 20.
33. Anderson and Richie, *Japanese Film*, pp. 323–4.

Chapter 3

1. Quoted in Edward Seidensticker, 'Tanizaki Jun-ichiro, 1886–1965', *Monumenta Nipponica* vol. 21, nos. 3–4 (1966): p. 255.
2. Victor Shklovsky, *Résurrection du mot; Littérature et cinématographe*, trans. Andrée Robel (Paris: Lebovici, 1985), pp. 93–101; Yuri Tyniyanov, *The Problem of Verse Language*, trans. and ed. Michael Sosa and Brent Harvey (Ann Arbor: Ardis, 1981), pp. 31–47.
3. Shklovsky, *Résurrection*, p. 96.
4. Harris I. Martin, 'Popular Music and Social Change in Prewar Japan', *The Japan Interpreter* vol. 7, nos. 3–4 (Summer-Autumn 1972): p. 334.
5. Siegfried Kracauer, *Die Angestellten* (Frankfurt am Main: Suhrkamp, 1980).
6. Ezra F. Vogel, *Japan's New Middle Class*, 2nd ed. (Berkeley: University of California Press, 1971), p. 268.
7. Kita Genji, *The Guardian God of Golf and Other Humorous Stories*, trans. Hugh Cortazzi (Tokyo: Japan Times, 1972).
8. Carol Gluck, *Japan's Modern Myths: Ideology in the Late Meiji Period* (Princeton: Princeton University Press, 1985), pp. 187–9.
9. Dore, *City Life*, pp. 111–17.
10. Sato, *Ozu no geijutsu* vol. 2, pp. 145–7.
11. See Akira Fujitake, 'The Formation and Development of Mass Culture', *The Developing Economies* vol. 5, no. 4 (December 1967): p. 781.
12. Dore, *City Life*, pp. 255-67.
13. H. D. Smith, 'Tokyo as an Idea: An Exploration of Japanese Urban Thought until 1945', *Journal of Japanese Studies* vol. 4, no. 1 (1978): pp. 53–5.
14. Henry DeWitt Smith II, 'The Tyranny of Tokyo in Modern Japanese Culture', in *Studies on Japanese Culture* vol. 2 (Tokyo: PEN Club, 1973), pp. 367–9.
15. Quoted in Edward Seidensticker, *Low City, High City: Tokyo from Edo to the Earthquake* (New York: Knopf, 1983), p. 15.
16. Miriam Beard, *Realism in Romantic Japan* (New York: Macmillan, 1930), pp. 222–5.
17. Quoted in Edward Seidensticker, *Kafu the Scribbler: The Life and Writings of Nagai Kafu, 1879-1959* (Stanford: Stanford University Press, 1965), p. 33.

18. Earl H. Kinmonth, *The Self-Made Man in Meiji Japanese Thought: From Samurai to Salaryman* (Berkeley: University of California Press, 1981), pp. 55–8, 331–9; Gluck, *Modern Myths*, pp. 21–38, 206–9; and Oka Yoshitake, 'Generational Conflict after the Russo-Japanese War', in *Conflict in Modern Japanese History*, ed. Tetsuo Najita and J. Victor Koschmann (Princeton: Princeton University Press, 1982), pp. 197–200.

19. Gluck, *Modern Myths*, pp. 281–5.

20. M. Y. Yoshino, *Japan's Managerial System: Tradition and Innovation* (Cambridge, MA: MIT Press, 1968), p. 57.

21. Tadashi Fukutake, *The Japanese Social Structure: Its Evolution in the Modern Century*, trans. Ronald P. Dore (Tokyo: University of Tokyo Press, 1982), p. 213.

22. Kazuo Miyagawa, *Watashi no eigajinsei rokujunen* [Sixty Years of My Life in Films] (Tokyo: PHP Kenkyusha, 1985), pp. 92ff.

23. Richie, *Ozu*, p. 1.

24. 'Ozu on Ozu: The Talkies': p. 4.

25. Yann Tobin, 'Pourquoi l'eau de mer est-elle salée?', *Positif* no. 237 (December 1980): pp. 32–4.

26. Takeo Doi, *The Anatomy of Dependence*, trans. John Bester (Tokyo: Kodansha, 1981), p. 153.

27. Sato, *Currents*, pp. 131–8.

28. Joan Mellen, *The Waves at Genji's Door: Japan through its Cinema* (New York: Pantheon, 1976), p. 152.

29. 'Ozu on Ozu: The Talkies': p. 5.

30. Sato, *Ozu no geijutsu* vol. 2, pp. 129–30.

31. 'Ozu on Ozu: The Talkies': p. 4.

32. Cited in Alain Berque, *Vivre l'espace au Japon* (Paris: Presses Universitaires de France, 1982), p. 162.

33. Smith, 'Tokyo as an Idea': pp. 71–2.

34. John W. Dower, 'Ways of Seeing, Ways of Remembering: The Photography of Prewar Japan', in Japan Photographers Association, *A Century of Japanese Photography* (New York: Pantheon, 1980), p. 17.

35. See William H. Coaldrake, 'Order and Anarchy: Tokyo from 1868 to the Present', in Friedman, ed., *Tokyo: Form and Spirit*, p. 69.

36. Mitsuko Nakamura, *Contemporary Japanese Fiction 1926-1968* (Tokyo: Kokusai Bunka Shinkokai, 1969), p. 15.

37. Dore, *City Life*, pp. 79–80.

38. Etsuo Kaji, 'The Invisible Proletariat: Working Women in Japan', *Social Praxis* vol. 1, no. 4 (1973): p. 384.

39. G. C. Allen, *Appointment in Japan: Memories of Sixty Years* (London: Athlone Press, 1983), p. 18.

40. For a somewhat different interpretation of the train motif, see Richie, *Ozu*, p. 14.

Chapter 4

1. Quoted in Richie, *Ozu*, p. 188.

2. Bordwell, *Narration*, pp. 49–61.

3. Jonathan Rosenbaum, 'Ozu at the Cinémathèque', in Gillett and Wilson, eds., *Ozu: A Critical Anthology*, p. 34.

4. Meir Sternberg, *Expositional Modes and Temporal Ordering in Fiction* (Baltimore: Johns Hopkins University Press, 1978), pp. 183–235.

5. Richie, *Ozu*, pp. 39–48.

6. Quoted ibid., p. 46.

7. Ibid., pp. 20–8.

8. André Tournès, 'Découvrir Ozu', *Jeune cinéma* no. 123 (December 1979–January 1980): p. 18.

9. Victor Shklovsky, *Sur la théorie de la prose*, trans. Guy Verret (Lausanne: L'Age d'homme, 1973), p. 87.

10. 'Ozu on Ozu: The Silents': p. 24.

11. Akira Iwasaki, 'Ozu and Japanese Film', in L. Schrader, ed., *Masters*, p. 291.

12. Roland Barthes, 'Action Sequences', in Joseph Strelka, ed., *Patterns of Literary Style* (University Park: Pennsylvania State University Press, 1971), pp. 5–14; Jean Matter Mandler, *Stories, Scripts, and Scenes: Aspects of Schema Theory* (Hillsdale, New Jersey: Erlbaum, 1984).

13. Tadao Sato, 'Rising Sons', *American Film* vol. 11, no. 3 (December 1985): p. 60.

14. Richie, *Ozu*, pp. 15–16.

15. Jorge Luis Borges, *Labyrinths: Selected Stories and Other Writings*, ed. Donald A. Yates and James E. Irby (New York: New Directions, 1964), p. 26.

16. Quoted in Sato, *Ozu no geijutsu* vol. 2, p. 85.

17. Richie, *Ozu*, p. 24.

18. See Bordwell, *Narration*, pp. 9–12.

19. Sato, 'Art of Ozu (7)': p. 93.

20. See Anderson and Richie, *Japanese Film*, p. 46; Kikuo Yamamoto, '"Ames sur la route" et la spécificité du cinéma japonais', in *Le cinéma japonais de ses origines à nos jours*, ed. Hiroko Govaers (Paris: La Cinémathèque Française/La Fondation du Japon, 1984), p. 119.

21. *Ozu wo yomu*, p. 25.

22. 'Ozu on Ozu: The Silents': p. 24.

23. Kojun Saito, quoted in Norio Nishijima, Yasuo Horikiri, and Michihiro Maekawa, eds., *Libro Cinematheque Ozu Yasujiro: Tokyo Monogatari* (Tokyo: Riburopoto, 1984), p. 259.

24. See Bordwell et al., *Classical Hollywood Cinema*, pp. 79–82; and Bordwell, *Narration*, p. 83.

25. Richie, *Ozu*, pp. 23–36, 71–2.

26. *Ozu wo yomu*, p. 34.

27. Michael Wood, 'Goriot in Tokyo', *New York Review of Books* (12 June 1975): p. 36.

28. Burch, *Distant Observer*, p. 183.

29. Sato, *Ozu no geijutsu* vol. 1, p. 214.

30. I thank David Owens for pointing out this word play to me.

31. Quoted in Richie, *Ozu*, p. 189.

Chapter 5

1. Marcel Benabou, 'Rule and Constraint', in *Oulipo: A Primer of Potential Literature*, trans. and ed. Warren F. Motte, Jr. (Lincoln: University of Nebraska Press, 1986), p. 41.

2. See Bordwell, *Narration*, pp. 274–310.

3. Yoshitaka Yoda, 'Souvenirs', *Cahiers du cinéma* no. 169 (August 1965): p. 34.

4. See Richie, *Ozu*, pp. 74–7, 96, 100.

5. Chishu Ryu, 'Yasujiro Ozu', *Sight and Sound* vol. 33, no. 2 (Spring 1964): p. 92.

6. Ibid.; Kogo Noda, 'Ozu's Way of Working', in L. Schrader, ed., *Masters*, p. 273.

7. Audie E. Bock, *Mikio Naruse: Un maître du cinéma japonais*, trans. Roland Cosandry and André Kaenal (Locarno: Thirty-Sixth Film Festival, 1983), p. 12.

8. 'Témoignages sur l'art de Yasujiro Ozu', *Cinejap* no. 2 (Spring 1979): p. 24.

9. Hasumi, *Kantoku Ozu*, p. 200.

10. Atsuta, quoted in *Tokyo-Ga* (1985), a film by Wim Wenders.

11. Ibid.

12. Shigehiko Hasumi, 'Interview de Yuharu Atsuta', in Hiroko Govaers, ed., *Le cinéma japonais de ses origines à nos jours*, Part Two (Paris: La Fondation de Japon/Kawakita Memorial Film Institute, 1984), p. 80.

13. Atsuta, quoted in *Tokyo-Ga*.

14. Hasumi, 'Interview', p. 83.

15. Tadao Sato, 'The Art of Yasujiro Ozu (4)', *The Study of the History of the Cinema* no. 7 (1975): pp. 84–6.

16. Richie, *Ozu*, p. 176.

17. See for examples David Bordwell, *French Impressionist Cinema: Film Culture, Film Theory, and Film Style* (New York: Arno Press, 1980), pp. 195–207.

18. Hasumi, 'Interview', p. 81.

19. *Ozu wo yomu*, pp. 21–2.

20. Ibid., pp. 36–7.

21. Sato, *Ozu no geijutsu* vol. 2, pp. 235–6; Rosenbaum, 'Ozu at the Cinémathèque', p. 34.

22. Hasumi, 'Interview', p. 82.

23. Bordwell, *Narration*, pp. 7–12.

24. 'Ito Daisuke on Ozu', in L. Schrader, ed., *Masters*, p. 311.

25. This speculation gains some support from a 1954 interview in which Ozu explains that when filming the Japanese house, one must shoot from a low point, and he adds a reference to still photography: 'When I'm using a Rollei [the prototypical twin-lens camera], I would look from above, but when using a Leica, I would look from below [that is, one would have to crouch to get that camera's lens to a comparably low level].' (Quoted in *Ozu wo yomu*, pp. 36-7.)

26. 'Témoignages': p. 18.

27. Kido, *Nihon eiga den*, p. 76.

28. 'Dialogue on Film: Masahiro Shinoda', *American Film* vol. 10, no. 7 (May 1985): p. 13.

29. Ibid.

30. Jonathan Culler, 'Making Sense', *20th Century Studies* no. 12 (December 1974): p. 33.

31. Kristin Thompson, *Breaking the Glass Armor: Neoformalist Film Analysis* (Princeton: Princeton University Press, 1988), Chapter 12.

32. See Hasumi, 'Interview', p. 81; 'Témoignages': p. 19.

33. Shinbi Iida and Akira Iwasaki, 'A Talk with Ozu', *Cinema* [USA] vol. 6, no. 1 (1970): p. 8.

34. *Ozu wo yomu*, pp. 36–7.

35. 'Témoignages': p. 23.

36. Kido, *Nihon eiga den*, pp. 76–7.

37. Renato Berta, 'A la recherche du regard: Entretien avec Yuharu Atsuta', *Cahiers du cinéma* no. 378 (December 1985): pp. 43–4, 46.

38. Richie, *Ozu*, p. 125.

39. Sato, 'Art of Ozu (4)': pp. 94–5.

40. Ibid.: p. 96.

41. 'Témoignages': p. 23; Hasumi, *Kantoku Ozu*, p. 220.

42. Richie, *Ozu*, p. 127.

43. Hasumi, *Kantoku Ozu*, p. 222.

44. 'Témoignages': p. 24.

45. Iida and Iwasaki, 'Talk with Ozu', p. 7.

46. *Ozu wo yomu*, p. 39.

47. Ibid.

48. Berta, 'A la recherche': pp. 44, 46.

49. Ryu, 'Yasujiro Ozu': p. 92.

50. Hasumi, *Kantoku Ozu*, p. 212.

51. Sato, *Ozu no geijutsu* vol. 1, pp. 235–7.

52. Sato, *Ozu no geijutsu* vol. 2, p. 64.

53. Ibid., p. 231.

54. Quoted in Richie, *Ozu*, p. 258.

55. Quoted ibid., p. 147.

56. Quoted ibid.

57. Ryu, 'Yasujiro Ozu': p. 92.

58. Sato, *Currents*, p. 191.

59. Tadao Sato, 'The Art of Yasujiro Ozu (1)', *The Study of the History of the Cinema* no. 4 (1974): p. 94.

60. Tadao Sato, 'The Art of Yasujiro Ozu (3)', *The Study of the History of the Cinema* no. 3 (1975): p. 95.

61. Quoted in *Tokyo-Ga.*

62. Burch, *Distant Observer*, p. 174; italics in original.

63. Quoted in E. H. Gombrich, *The Sense of Order: A Study in the Psychology of Decorative Art* (Ithaca: Cornell University Press, 1979), p. 96.

64. Hasumi, *Kantoku Ozu*, p. 247.

65. 'Témoignages': p. 19.

66. Shinbi Iida et al., 'Entertainment', pp. 224–7.

67. Sato, *Ozu no geijutsu* vol. 1, p. 175.

68. 'Ozu on Ozu: The Talkies': p. 3.

69. See Bordwell et al., *Classical Hollywood Cinema*, pp. 25–9; cf. Richie, *Ozu*, pp. 162–4.

70. Cf. ibid.

71. See Bordwell et al., *Classical Hollywood Cinema*, pp. 63–9; Bordwell, *Narration*, pp. 156–204.

72. Sato, *Currents*, p. 189.

73. Burch, *Distant Observer*, p. 159.

74. Ibid.

75. Ibid., pp. 159–60.

76. See Bordwell, *Narration*, pp. 9–12, 99–146.

77. Burch, *Distant Observer*, p. 174.

78. Quoted in Richie, *Ozu*, pp. 152–3; cf. Tadao Sato, 'The Art of Yasujiro Ozu (8)', *The Study of the History of the Cinema* no. 11 (1978): p. 94.

79. Hasumi, 'Interview', p. 83.

80. Hasumi, *Kantoku Ozu*, p. 220.

81. Hasumi, 'Interview', p. 83.

82. See Barry Salt, *Film Style and Technology: History and Analysis* (London: Starword, 1983), p. 285; Edward Dmytryk, *On Film Editing* (Boston: Focal Press, 1984), pp. 24–33.

83. Cited in Sato, *Ozu no geijutsu* vol. 2, pp. 68–70.

84. Berta, 'A la recherche': p. 46.

85. *Ozu wo yomu*, p. 341.

86. For an overview of the 'mental rotation' literature, see Roger N. Shepard and Lynn A. Cooper, *Mental Images and Their Transformations* (Cambridge, MA: MIT Press, 1982).

87. See Edward Branigan, 'The Space of *Equinox Flower*', *Screen* vol. 17, no. 2 (Summer 1976): pp. 93–5.

88. Julian Hochberg and L. Gellman, 'The Effect of Landmark Features on Mental Rotation Times', *Memory and Cognition* no. 5 (1977): pp. 24–5.

89. The mention of contiguity should not imply that I think Ozu's space is somehow 'metonymic' rather than 'metaphoric'. In my view, this opposition has been used by film and literary theorists in far too loose and casual a fashion. (See Maria Ruegg, 'Metaphor and Metonymy: The Logic of Structuralist Rhetoric', *Glyph* no. 6 (1979): pp. 141–57.) I would hope that this discussion of Ozu's contiguity cues will show that a poetics sensitive to a continuum of devices, structures, functions, and processes can reveal more than can a semiotics based on all-inclusive binary distinctions.

90. Cf. Burch, *Distant Observer*, pp. 158–9.

91. See Seymour Chatman, *Story and Discourse: Narrative Structure in Fiction and Film* (Ithaca: Cornell University Press, 1978), p. 212; Bordwell, *Narration*, pp. 66, 125–6.

92. See Bordwell et al., *Classical Hollywood Cinema*, pp. 25–9.

93. 'Ozu on Ozu: The Silents': p. 24.

94. Quoted in Sato, *Ozu no geijutsu* vol. 1, p. 81.

95. See Schrader, *Transcendental Style*, p. 29; Anderson and Richie, *Japanese Film*, pp. 132, 160.

96. Richie, *Ozu*, p. 56.
97. Ibid., p. 170.
98. Tom Milne, 'Flavour of Green Tea over Rice', *Sight and Sound* vol. 32, no. 4 (Autumn 1963): p. 184.
99. Kathe B. Geist, 'Yasujiro Ozu: Notes on a Retrospective', *Film Quarterly* vol. 37, no. 1 (Fall 1983): p. 6.
100. Burch, *Distant Observer*, p. 162.
101. Ibid.
102. Ibid., p. 160.
103. Ibid., p. 172.
104. Ibid., p. 166n.
105. Ibid., p. 293.
106. Ibid., p. 170.
107. Ibid., p. 293.

Chapter 6

1. Quoted in *Ozu wo yomu*, p. 41.
2. See his discussion of graphic matches between igloos and faces in *Izbrannye proizvedeniya v chesti tomakh* [Selected works in six volumes], vol. 2 (Moscow: Iskusstvo, 1964), p. 375.
3. Sato, *Ozu no geijutsu* vol. 1, p. 82.
4. Shinoda, 'Dialogue on Film': p. 12.
5. Richie, *Ozu*, pp. 112–13.
6. Branigan, 'Space of *Equinox Flower*': p. 100.
7. Edward R. Branigan, *Point of View in the Cinema: A Theory of Narration and Subjectivity in Classical Film* (New York: Mouton, 1984), p. 105.
8. Ibid., pp. 106–8.
9. Ibid., p. 108.
10. Ibid., p. 114.
11. Dennis J. Konshak, 'Space and Narrative in *Tokyo Story*', *Film Criticism* vol. 4, no. 3 (Spring 1980): p. 39.
12. P. Schrader, *Transcendental Style*, pp. 49–51.
13. Richie, *Ozu*, p. 174.
14. Ibid. In an earlier discussion of this sequence, Richie is explicit: 'By seeing what she sees (a vase alone, solitary, beautiful) we can more completely, more fully comprehend and *hence* feel what she herself is feeling.' See Donald Richie, 'Yasujiro Ozu, *Film Quarterly* vol. 17, no. 2 (Winter 1963–4): p. 16.
15. I am indebted to Kyoko Hirano for this information, derived from her investigation of scripts submitted to the Civil Information and Education Section, 12 April 1949 and 10 September 1949. The finished draft of the script is available as *Printemps tardif*, trans. M. and E. Wasserman (Paris: Publications orientalistes de France, 1986). The scene in question is on p. 41; Noriko is described as staring fixedly at the ceiling, and there is no mention of the vase.
16. For further discussion of this scene, see Thompson, *Breaking the Glass Armor*, Ch. 12.
17. See Bordwell, *Narration*, pp. 274–310.
18. The shots are reproduced in color in Bordwell and Thompson, *Film Art*, between pages 146 and 147.
19. Branigan, 'Space of *Equinox Flower*': pp. 77–80.
20. See Roman Jakobson and Morris Halle, *Fundamentals of Language* (The Hague: Mouton, 1971) pp. 90–2; Donald Rice and Peter Schofer, *Rhetorical Poetics: Theory and Practice of Figural and Symbolic Reading in Modern French Literature* (Madison: University of Wisconsin Press, 1983), pp. 3–15.
21. Cited in Mansuku Itami, 'A propos de l'adaptation cinématographique des oeuvres littéraires,' in Govaers, ed., *Le cinéma japonais de ses origines*, p. 123.

22. Cf. Alain Bergala, 'L'homme qui se lève', *Cahiers du cinéma* no. 311 (May 1980): p. 29.

23. Branigan, 'Space of *Equinox Flower*': pp. 83–5.

24. Roland Barthes, *Critical Essays*, trans. Richard Howard (Evanston: Northwestern University Press, 1972), pp. 20–1.

25. See Bordwell, *Narration*, pp. 274–9.

26. Thompson, *Breaking the Glass Armor*, Ch.12.

27. See Jean Starobinski, *Words upon Words: The Anagrams of Ferdinand de Saussure* (New Haven: Yale University Press, 1979).

28. Hasumi, *Kantoku Ozu*, pp. 210–11.

29. See Kristin Thompson and David Bordwell, 'Space and Narrative in the Films of Ozu', *Screen* vol. 17, no. 2 (Summer 1976): pp. 41–73; Sergei Eisenstein, *Film Form*, trans. Jay Leyda (New York: Meridian, 1957), pp. 75–83.

30. The following stills are reproduced in reverse in Burch, *Distant Observer*, p. 177.

31. Geist, 'Notes', pp. 5–6.

32. Joël Magny, 'Le printemps d'Ozu', *Cinéma 81* no. 265 (January 1981): pp. 18–20, 24.

33. Sato, *Currents*, p. 188.

34. See Bordwell, *Narration*, pp. 21–6.

35. Bergala, 'L'homme', p. 25.

36. See Emile Benveniste, 'L'appareil formel de l'énonciation,' in *Problèmes de linguistique générale* vol. 2 (Paris: Gallimard, 1974), pp. 81–5; Catherine Kerbrat-Orecchioni, *L'énonciation: De la subjectivité dans le langage* (Paris: Armand Colin, 1980), pp. 28–35; Bordwell, *Narration*, pp. 21–6.

37. Bergala, 'L'homme', pp. 26–8.

38. Ibid., p. 30.

39. Bordwell, *Narration*, pp. 9–15.

40. See ibid., pp. 278–9.

41. Noël Burch, 'Fritz Lang: German Period', in *Cinema: A Critical Dictionary*, vol. 2, ed. Richard Roud (New York: Viking, 1980), pp. 583–99.

42. Burch, *Distant Observer*, p. 156.

43. See Thompson and Bordwell, 'Space and Narrative'; Branigan, 'Space of *Equinox Flower*'; Thompson, 'Notes'.

44. On the perceptual and cognitive sources of evocative symbolic readings, see Dan Sperber, *Rethinking Symbolism*, trans. Alice L. Morton (Cambridge: Cambridge University Press, 1975), pp. 85–144.

45. 'Shindo Kaneto on Ozu', in L. Schrader, ed., *Masters*, p. 317.

46. Nyozekan Hasegawa, *The Japanese Character: A Cultural Profile* (Tokyo: Kodansha, 1982; orig. 1938), pp. 127–8.

Chapter 7

1. 'On Literary Evolution', in Matejka and Pomorska, *Readings in Russian Poetics*, p. 67.

2. Earl Miner, *Japanese Linked Poetry* (Princeton: Princeton University Press, 1979), p. 59.

3. Donald Keene, *World within Walls: Japanese Literature of the Pre-Modern Era 1600—1867* (New York: Grove, 1976), pp. 21–37.

4. Berque, *Vivre l'espace*, pp. 78–9. See also David Pollack, *The Fracture of Meaning: Japan's Synthesis of China from the Eighth through the Eighteenth Centuries* (Princeton: Princeton University Press, 1986), pp. 209–13.

5. Earl Miner, *An Introduction to Japanese Court Poetry* (Stanford: Stanford University Press, 1968), p. 20.

6. Miner, *Linked Poetry*, p. 78.

7. Makoto Ueda, *Matsuo Basho* (Tokyo: Kodansha, 1982), p. 165.

8. Ibid., p. 156.

9. Quoted in Teiji Itoh, *Space and Illusion in the Japanese Garden*, trans. Ralph Friedrich and Masajiro Shimamura (New York: Weatherhill/Tankosha, 1973), pp. 48–9.

10. Berque, *Vivre l'espace*, pp. 122–3.

11. See Richard B. Pilgrim, *Buddhism and the Arts of Japan* (Chambersburg, Pennsylvania: Anima, 1981), pp. 49–56.

12. Gunter Nitschke, '"Ma": The Japanese Sense of "Place" in Old and New Architecture and Planning', *Architectural Design* vol. 36 (March 1966): pp. 117ff; and Berque, *Vivre l'espace*, pp. 118–47.

13. Ibid., p. 65.

14. Donald Keene, *Japanese Literature: An Introduction for Western Readers* (New York: Grove, 1955), pp. 46–7.

15. Irmela Hijiya-Kirschnereit, 'The Concepts of Tradition in Modern Japanese Literature', in *Tradition and Modern Japan*, ed. P. G. O'Neill (Tenterden, Kent: Norbury, 1981), p. 210.

16. See Earl Miner, *Japanese Poetic Diaries* (Berkeley: University of California Press, 1969), p. 9.

17. These genres are usefully surveyed in J. Thomas Rimer, *Modern Japanese Fiction and Its Tradition: An Introduction* (Princeton: Princeton University Press, 1978), pp. 62–79.

18. See Keene, *World within Walls*, pp. 396–435, and Robert W. Leutner, *Shikitei Sanba and the Comic Tradition in Edo Fiction* (Cambridge, MA: Harvard University Press, 1985).

19. Keene, *Japanese Literature*, pp. 18–20.

20. Donald Keene, *Dawn to the West: Japanese Literature in the Modern Era: Fiction* (New York: Holt, Rinehart and Winston, 1984), pp. 138–9.

21. Faubian Bowers, *Japanese Theatre* (Rutland, Vermont: Tuttle, 1974), p. 210.

22. Cf. Burch, *Distant Observer*, pp. 67–72.

23. Makoto Ueda, *Modern Japanese Writers and the Nature of Literature* (Stanford: Stanford University Press, 1976), p. 208.

24. Masao Miyoshi, *Accomplices of Silence: The Modern Japanese Novel* (Berkeley: University of California Press, 1974), p. xii.

25. Ueda, *Modern Japanese Writers*, pp. 131–3; see also Noriko Mizuta Lippit, *Reality and Fiction in Modern Japanese Literature* (White Plains, New York: M. E. Sharpe, 1980), pp. 55–65.

26. Katai Tayama, *The Quilt and Other Stories*, trans. Kenneth G. Henshall (Tokyo: University of Tokyo Press, 1981), p. 96.

27. Shimazaki Toson, *The Family*, trans. Cecelia Segawa Seigle (Tokyo: University of Tokyo Press, 1978), p. 104.

28. Miyoshi, *Accomplices*, p. xi.

29. Anderson and Richie, *Japanese Film*, pp. 21–34; Peter B. High, 'The Dawn of Cinema in Japan', *Journal of Contemporary History* vol. 19, no. 1 (1984): pp. 23–57.

30. Earl Ernst, *The Kabuki Theatre* (Honolulu: University of Hawaii Press, 1974), pp. 69, 251–2; Sato, *Currents*, p. 20.

31. Bordwell, 'Dream-Cinema', pp. 46–7.

32. Burch, *Distant Observer*, pp. 25–34.

33. Keene, *Dawn to the West*, p. 747.

34. Nitschke, '"Ma"': p. 155.

35. Laurence Smith, *The Japanese Print since 1900: Old Dreams and New Visions* (London: British Museum, 1983), p. 10. See also Mitsuko Sakamoto, 'The Westernizing of "Ukiyo-e" at the End of the Tokugawa Era', and Muneshige Narasaki, 'Western Influence and Revival of Tradition in "Ukiyo-e"', in Society for Study of Japonisme, *Japonisme in Art: An International Symposium* (Tokyo: Committee for the Year 2001 and Kodansha, 1980), pp. 18–25 and 313–22.

36. Minoru Harada, *Meiji Western Painting*, trans. Akiko Murakata (New York: Weatherhill/Shibundo, 1974), pp. 49–51, 71–80.

37. Ibid., p. 121.

38. Smith, *Japanese Print*, pp. 16–19.

39. Kokusai Bunka Shinkokai, *Introduction*, pp. 273–4.

40. Matsuo Kishi, 'Ozu Yasujiro', in *Nihon eiga kantoku* [Encyclopedia of Japanese Film

Directors], supplement to *Kinema Jumpo* no. 698 (24 December 1976), pp. 104–5.

41. See Bordwell et al., *Classical Hollywood Cinema*, pp. 25–33.

42. Kishi, 'Ozu', p. 105.

43. Keene, *World within Walls*, p. 14.

44. The standard discussion of this in English is Ruth Benedict, *The Chrysanthemum and the Sword: Patterns of Japanese Culture* (New York: New American Library, 1974; orig. 1946), pp. 222–7.

45. Sato, *Ozu no geijutsu* vol. 1, p. 226.

46. See Bordwell, *Narration*, pp. 178–86.

47. Sato, *Ozu no geijutsu* vol. 1, pp. 229–33.

48. Iida et al., 'Entertainment', p. 219.

49. See Thompson, 'Notes': p. 12.

50. Shklovsky, *Théorie de la prose*, p. 265.

51. Quoted in Sato, *Ozu no geijutsu* vol. 2, p. 105.

52. Sato, *Currents*, p. 190.

Chapter 8

1. Tadao Sato, 'The Art of Yasujiro Ozu (2)', *The Study of the History of the Cinema* no. 5 (1974): p. 84.

2. Jon Elster, *Ulysses and the Sirens: Studies in Rationality and Irrationality*, rev. ed. (Cambridge: Cambridge University Press, 1984), p. 113. See also Jon Elster, *An Introduction to Karl Marx* (Cambridge: Cambridge University Press, 1986), pp. 25–31; and Christopher Cherniak, *Minimal Rationality* (Cambridge, MA: MIT Press, 1986), pp. 3–76.

3. For a discussion of this concept, see I. C. Jarvie, *Concepts and Society* (London: Routledge and Kegan Paul, 1972).

4. Jon Elster, *Sour Grapes: Studies in the Subversion of Rationality* (Cambridge: Cambridge University Press, 1983), p. 80.

5. Jon Elster, *Making Sense of Marx* (Cambridge: Cambridge University Press, 1985), p. 4. See also Elster, *Introduction*, pp. 22–5.

6. Quoted in Hasumi, *Kantoku Ozu*, pp. 205–6.

7. *Ozu wo yomu*, p. 23.

8. William K. Wimsatt and Monroe C. Beardsley, 'The Intentional Fallacy', in Wimsatt, *The Verbal Icon: Studies in the Meaning of Poetry* (Lexington: University of Kentucky Press, 1954), pp. 3–18.

9. Elster, *Making Sense*, p. 18. See also John Roemer, '"Rational Choice" Marxism: Some Issues of Method and Substance', in Roemer, ed., *Analytical Marxism* (Cambridge: Cambridge University Press, 1986), pp. 191–201.

10. Elster, *Ulysses*, p. x.

11. *Ozu wo yomu*, p. 33.

12. J.-P. Berthomé, 'Fleurs d'équinoxe', *La Saison Cinématographique 1969*, p. 134.

13. Donald Keene, 'The Barren Years: Japanese War Literature', *Monumenta Nipponica* vol. 33, no. 1 (Spring 1978): pp. 68–79.

14. Sato, *Ozu no geijutsu* vol. 2, pp. 101–2.

15. Hasumi, *Kantoku Ozu*, pp. 207–8.

16. *Ozu wo yomu*, p. 121.

17. Sato, *Ozu no geijutsu* vol. 2, p. 87.

18. Quoted in *I Lived, But . . . .*

19. Ibid.

20. Quoted in Kishi, 'Ozu', p. 105. This letter was not published until after the war.

21. Quoted in *Ozu wo yomu*, pp. 28–9.

22. Quoted ibid., p. 30.

23. *Kokutai no Hongi: Cardinal Principles of the National Entity of Japan*, trans. John Owen

Gauntlett and ed. Robert King Hall (Cambridge, MA: Harvard University Press, 1949), p. 87.

24. See Ueda, *Literary and Art Theories*, pp. 218–35; Earl Miner, 'Toward a New Conception of Classical Japanese Poetics', *Studies on Japanese Culture*, vol. 1 (Tokyo: Japan PEN Club, 1973), pp. 100–9.

25. Shinji Iida, 'Filmmaking in America and Japan', in L. Schrader, ed., *Masters*, p. 241.

26. Kishi, 'Ozu', p. 105.

27. Sato, *Ozu no geijutsu* vol. 2, p. 37.

28. Ibid., pp. 75, 22.

29. Akira Iwasaki, 'Ozu and Japanese Film', in L. Schrader, ed., *Masters*, pp. 290–3.

30. Kido, *Nihon eiga den*, p. 75.

31. Quoted in Tadao Sato, 'The Art of Yasujiro Ozu (5)', *The Study of the History of the Cinema* no. 8 (1976): pp. 90–1.

32. Quoted in Sato, *Ozu no geijutsu* vol. 2, p. 80.

33. See Beard, *Romantic Japan*, pp. 169–81.

34. R. P. Dore, *City Life in Japan: A Study of a Tokyo Ward* (Berkeley: University of California Press, 1967), pp. 11–13.

35. Michio Morishima, *Why Has Japan 'Succeeded'?: Western Technology and the Japanese Ethos* (Cambridge: Cambridge University Press, 1982), pp. 168–9.

36. See Nago Nichikawa, 'Occidentalisation et "Retour au Japon"', *Corps écrit* no. 17 (1986): pp. 81–90.

37. Junichiro Tanizaki, *In Praise of Shadows*, trans. Thomas J. Harper and Edward G. Seidensticker (New Haven: Leete's Island Books, 1977), p. 42.

38. See Seidensticker, 'Tanizaki Jun-ichiro', pp. 252–3.

39. See Robert Cohen, 'Toward a Theory of Japanese Narrative', *Quarterly Review of Film Studies* vol. 6, no. 2 (Spring 1981): pp. 198–200; Burch, 'Approaching Japanese Film', p. 95.

40. Doi, *Anatomy of Dependence*, pp. 65–100.

41. Sato, *Ozu no geijutsu* vol. 2, pp. 34–8.

42. Sarah Hamilton Nolte, 'Individualism in Taisho Japan', *Journal of Asian Studies* vol. 43, no. 4 (August 1984): pp. 670–80.

43. Burch, *Distant Observer*, p. 262.

44. Sato, *Ozu no geijutsu* vol. 2, pp. 72–8.

45. Pierre Macherey, *A Theory of Literary Production*, trans. Geoffrey Wall (London: Routledge and Kegan Paul, 1978), p. 155.

46. Editors of *Cahiers du cinéma*, 'John Ford's *Young Mr. Lincoln*', in *Screen Reader*, ed. John Ellis (London: SEFT, 1977), p. 116.

47. For an elaboration of the performance metaphor, see Terry Eagleton, *Criticism and Ideology: A Study in Marxist Literary Theory* (London: New Left Books, 1976), pp. 64–70.

48. Quoted in *I Lived, But* . . . .

49. Sato, *Ozu no geijutsu* vol. 2, pp. 206–8.

50. Agnes Heller, *Everyday Life*, trans. G. L. Campbell (London: Routledge and Kegan Paul, 1984); Fiona Mackie, *The Status of Everyday Life: A Sociological Excavation of the Prevailing Framework of Perception* (London: Routledge and Kegan Paul, 1985); and Michel de Certeau, *The Practice of Everyday Life*, trans. Steven F. Rendall (Berkeley: University of California Press, 1984).

51. Fredric Jameson, 'Reification and Utopia in Mass Culture', *Social Text* no. 1 (Winter 1979): p. 144.

52. Stanley Aronowitz, 'Film: The Art Form of Late Capitalism', *Social Text* no. 1 (Winter 1979): p. 122.

53. Ibid.

54. Macherey, *Literary Production*, p. 91.

55. See ibid., p. 162.

56. See also in this connection Fredric Jameson's *The Political Unconscious: Narrative as a Socially Symbolic Act* (Ithaca: Cornell University Press, 1981), which adopts an explicitly thematic approach, refusing 'much of formal or stylistic, purely textual analysis' (as if all these were synonymous) in favor of 'the various types of "strong" rewritings implied by interpretations that identify themselves as such and wear a particular label' (p. 59). The emphasis on thematization is curious in a tradition that owes so much to Herbert Marcuse, whose utopian socialism puts a neo-Kantian emphasis on the role of form. See Marcuse, *The Aesthetic Dimension: Toward a Critique of Marxist Aesthetics* (Boston: Beacon Press, 1978), pp. 8–21.

57. I borrow the term 'finalist' from Tzvetan Todorov, *Symbolisme et interprétation* (Paris: Seuil, 1978), pp. 160–1. My criticism of the limitations of the symptomatic approach raises more basic theoretical issues – about the adequacy of the analogy between the text and the discourse of the psychoanalytic patient; about whether this approach, which appeals so frequently to the social basis of perception, has got a theory of perception (rather than speculatively hopeful snippets from the *Grundrisse*); about whether every piece of cultural production is riven by contradiction or whether this occurs only in the domain of what Althusser calls 'real art'; about whether the text's unconscious displays true contradictions (which are inescapable) or whether it displays only incompatibilities or inconsistencies (which are thus corrigible, perhaps through 'better scriptwriting'); about what specific social-historical processes could cause textual displacement. In all, there is a genuine debate here, between a historical poetics grounded in a perceptual-cognitive model of mind and a psychoanalytic semiotics grounded in a drive-theory of mind. I try to take up these issues in a work in progress on the practice of film interpretation.

58. Yomishi Kasahara, 'Fear of Eye-to-Eye Confrontation among Neurotic Patients in Japan', in *Japanese Culture and Behavior: Selected Readings*, ed. Takie Sugiyama Lebra and William P. Lebra (Honolulu: University Press of Hawaii, 1974), p. 402.

59. Ibid., p. 397; Berque, *Vivre l'espace*, pp. 184–6.

60. Cf. Tadao Sato, 'Le point du regard', *Cahiers du cinéma* no. 310 (April 1980): pp. 5–6.

61. Hasumi, *Kantoku Ozu*, p. 134.

62. John Fiske, 'Television and Popular Culture: Reflections on British and Australian Critical Practice', *Critical Studies in Mass Communication* vol. 3 (1986): pp. 209–13.

63. Kido, *Nihon eiga den*, p. 74.

64. Sato, *Ozu no geijutsu* vol. 1, p. 262.

65. Tsuneo Hazumi, *Eiga gojunen-shi* [Fifty-Year History of Film] (Tokyo: Masu Shobo, 1942).

66. *Ozu wo yomu*, p. 37.

67. See Sato, *Ozu no geijutsu* vol. 2, pp. 176–7.

68. Quoted in Jan Dawson, *Wim Wenders*, trans. Carl Wartenberg (New York: Zoetrope, 1976), p. 10.

69. Quoted ibid., p. 8.

70. Fiske, 'Television': pp. 204–8.

71. Apart from brief and unsubstantiated claims that spectators have assimilated something called the 'classic realist text'. See Bordwell, *Narration*, pp. 18–20.

72. Ibid., pp. 149–55.

73. In Yoji Yamada's 1986 *Kinema no tenchi* (*Final Take: The Golden Days of Movies*), made to celebrate the fiftieth anniversary of the opening of Shochiku's Ofuna studio, a director obviously modeled on Ozu helps a young woman become a star. Treating Ozu as the preeminent director of Shochiku's golden age would seem to establish him as a representative of Japanese classicism.

74. See, for instance, Don Willis, 'Yasujiro Ozu: Emotion and Contemplation', *Sight and Sound* vol. 48, no. 1 (Winter 1978/79): p. 44.

75. See Eric Rentschler, *West German Film in the Course of Time: Reflections on the Twenty Years Since Oberhausen* (Bedford Hills, New York: Redgrave, 1984), pp. 169, 176–7;

Inez Hedges and John Bernstein, 'History, Style, Authorship: The Question of Origins in the New German Cinema', *Journal of Contemporary History* 19 (1984): pp. 179–82; Tamara Evans, 'The Silence of Ideology and the Ideology of Silence in Peter Handke's *The Left-Handed Woman*', *Persistence of Vision* no. 2 (Fall 1985): p. 47. The art-cinema interpretive strategies underpinning such readings are discussed in Bordwell, *Narration*, pp. 228–33.

76. Noël Burch, *Theory of Film Practice*, trans. Helen R. Lane (New York: Praeger, 1973), pp. 25, 54.

PART II

1. Sato, *Ozu no geijutsu* vol. 1, pp. 157–9.
2. Ibid., pp. 164–5.
3. *Ozu wo yomu*, p. 44.
4. Richie, *Ozu*, p. 204.
5. *Ozu wo yomu*, p. 53.
6. Sato, *Ozu no geijutsu* vol. 1, p. 166.
7. *Ozu wo yomu*, p. 63.
8. Sato, *Ozu no geijutsu* vol. 1, pp. 176–7.
9. *Ozu wo yomu*, p. 67.
10. Sato, *Ozu no geijutsu* vol. 1, pp. 188–9.
11. Ibid., pp. 182–6.
12. 'Ozu on Ozu: The Silents': p. 24.
13. See Bordwell, *Dreyer*, pp. 62–3, 121–4, 147–58.
14. 'Ozu on Ozu: The Silents': p. 24.
15. *Ozu wo yomu*, p. 83.
16. Sato, *Ozu no geijutsu* vol. 1, p. 196.
17. Ibid., pp. 202–3.
18. Ibid., p. 214.
19. Ibid., pp. 214–16.
20. *Ozo wo yomu*, p. 95.
21. Sato, *Ozu no geijutsu* vol. 1, pp. 254–8.
22. 'Ozu on Ozu: The Silents': p. 24.
23. Sato, *Ozu no geijutsu*, vol. 1, p. 258.
24. Ibid., p. 261.
25. Tadao Sato, 'The Comedy of Ozu and Chaplin: A Study in Contrast', *Wide Angle* vol. 3, no. 2 (1979): p. 53.
26. See for example Tobin, 'Pourquoi l'eau de mer. . .?': p. 33.
27. Sato, *Ozu no geijutsu* vol. 1, pp. 275–6.
28. Ibid., p. 276.
29. Ibid., pp. 273–4.
30. Ibid., p. 278; *Ozu wo yomu*, p. 125.
31. Discussion of *Woman of Tokyo* occupies pages 162–73 of Burch, *Distant Observer*.
32. Burch, *Distant Observer*, p. 167.
33. See Bordwell, *Narration*, pp. 110–13.
34. Burch, *Distant Observer*, p. 170.
35. See Richie, *Ozu*, pp. 112–13, and J. Hoberman, 'Japant-Garde Japanorama', *Artforum* vol. 24, no. 2 (October 1985): pp. 97–8.
36. Kishi, 'Ozu', p. 104.
37. Sato, *Ozu no geijutsu* vol. 1, pp. 224–5; 'Ozu on Ozu: The Silents': p. 24.
38. Alain Bergala, '*Coeur capricieux*', *Cahiers du cinéma* no. 311 (May 1980): p. 35.
39. Richie, *Ozu*, pp. 22–4; Burch, *Distant Observer*, p. 183.
40. 'Ozu on Ozu: The Silents': p. 24.

41. Macherey, *Literary Production*, pp. 41–2.

42. Sato, *Ozu no geijutsu* vol. 2, pp. 18–20.

43. 'Ozu on Ozu: The Silents': p. 24.

44. Sato, *Ozu no geijutsu* vol. 2, p. 13; Nagisa Oshima, *Ecrits 1956—1978: Dissolution et jaillissement*, trans. Jean-Paul Le Pape (Paris: Gallimard, 1980), p. 21.

45. Thompson, *Breaking the Glass Armor*, Ch. 12.

46. 'Ozu on Ozu: The Silents': p. 24.

47. Quoted in Dore, *City Life*, pp. 199–200.

48. 'Ozu on Ozu: The Talkies': p. 3.

49. Burch, *Distant Observer*, p. 178.

50. Hasumi, 'Interview', p. 80; see also 'Ozu on Ozu: The Talkies': p. 3.

51. David Owens, '*What Did the Lady Forget?*' program notes for Ozu retrospective, Japan Society of New York, 17 and 19 November 1982, n.p.

52. Ben-Ami Shillony, *Politics and Culture in Wartime Japan* (Oxford: Clarendon Press, 1981), p. 145.

53. See, for detailed chronicles, Richard H. Mitchell, *Thought Control in Prewar Japan* (Ithaca: Cornell University Press, 1976) and *Censorship in Imperial Japan* (Princeton: Princeton University Press, 1983).

54. See Shillony, *Politics and Culture*.

55. Sato, *Ozu no geijutsu* vol. 2, pp. 96–7.

56. Hasumi, 'Interview', p. 82.

57. Joan Mellen, *The Waves at Genji's Door: Japan through its Cinema* (New York: Pantheon, 1976), pp. 154–6.

58. Thomas R. H. Havens, *Valley of Darkness: The Japanese People and World War Two* (New York: Norton, 1978), p. 10.

59. Ibid., p. 29.

60. Sato, *Ozu no geijutsu* vol. 2, p. 100.

61. Hazumi, *Eiga gojunen-shi*, pp. 435–6.

62. 'Ozu on Ozu: The Talkies': p. 3.

63. For an account of the affair, see Jay Rubin, *Injurious to Public Morals: Writers and the Meiji State* (Seattle: University of Washington Press, 1984), pp. 263–5.

64. Mellen, *Genji's Door*, pp. 156–9.

65. See Havens, *Valley of Darkness*, p. 69.

66. John Dower, *War without Mercy: Race and Power in the Pacific War* (New York: Pantheon, 1986), p. 230.

67. *Kokutai no Hongi*, p. 97.

68. Ibid.

69. Sato, *Ozu no geijutsu* vol. 2, pp. 72–6.

70. *Ozu wo yomu*, p. 31.

71. Burch, *Distant Observer*, pp. 180–2.

72. Shinoda, 'Dialogue on Film', p. 13.

73. Sato, *Ozu no geijutsu* vol. 2, pp. 107–13.

74. Thompson, *Breaking the Glass Armor*, Ch. 12.

75. Sato, *Ozu no geijutsu* vol. 2, pp. 114–16.

76. 'Ozu on Ozu: The Talkies': p. 4.

77. David Owens, '*The Munekata Sisters*', program notes for Ozu retrospective, Japan Society of New York, 24, 26–28 November 1982, n.p.

78. Iida et al., 'Entertainment', pp. 233–4.

79. Sato, *Ozu no geijutsu* vol. 2, pp. 121–3.

80. Yuri Tynianov, 'Rhythm as the Constructive Factor of Verse', in Matejka and Pomorska, *Readings in Russian Poetics*, p. 128.

81. Hasumi, 'Interview', p. 82.

82. Hasumi, *Kantoku Ozu*, p. 202.

83. 'Ozu on Ozu: The Talkies': p. 4.

UNIVERSITY OF MANCHESTER LIBRARY

84. Konshak, 'Space and Narrative in *Tokyo Story*': p. 33.
85. Sato, *Ozu no geijutsu* vol. 2, p. 169.
86. The sequence I am describing is presented in stills in Richie, *Ozu*, pages 84–7. There, however, they are arranged in jumbled order. Starting at the bottom of the left-hand column, with the long-shot of the school, and reading down the succeeding columns, the reader should find them representing these shots: 1, 2, 3, 4, 6, 10, 7, 8, 15, 5, 11, 12, 13, 14, 16, 17, 18. Shot 9, a high-angle view of empty railroad tracks, is missing from Richie's layout.
87. Dore, *City Life*, p. 134.
88. Anderson and Richie, *Japanese Film*, p. 249.
89. 'Ozu on Ozu: The Talkies': p. 4.
90. Sato, *Ozu no geijutsu* vol. 2, p. 116.
91. Vogel, *New Middle Class*, p. 268.
92. 'Ozu on Ozu: The Talkies': p. 4.
93. Mellen, *Genji's Door*, pp. 322–6.
94. Bordwell, *Narration*, pp. 70–3.
95. *Ozu wo yomu*, p. 38.
96. 'Ozu on Ozu: The Talkies': p. 5.
97. Anderson and Richie, *Japanese Film*, pp. 264–7, 287–8.
98. Sato, *Ozu no geijutsu* vol. 2, p. 124.
99. Iida and Iwasaki, 'A Talk with Ozu': p. 7.
100. Ibid.
101. Ivan Morris, *The Nobility of Failure: Tragic Heroes in the History of Japan* (New York: Holt, Rinehart and Winston, 1975), p. 106.
102. Ibid., pp. 131–2.
103. Frederick L. Schodt, *Manga! Manga! The World of Japanese Comics* (Tokyo: Kodansha, 1983), pp. 29–31.
104. Roman Jakobson, 'Concluding Statement: Linguistics and Poetics', in *Style and Language*, ed. Thomas A. Sebeok (Cambridge, MA: MIT Press, 1960), p. 355.
105. Ibid.
106. Sato, *Ozu no geijutsu* vol. 2, p. 185.
107. Ibid., pp. 20–1; *Ozu wo yomu*, pp. 39–40.
108. 'Ozu on Ozu: The Talkies': p. 5.
109. Sato, *Ozu no geijutsu* vol. 2, p. 180.
110. *Ozu wo yomu*, pp. 40–1.
111. See Bordwell and Thompson, *Film Art*, pp. 146–7, for color illustrations.

Bibliography

ANDERSON, Joseph L., and Donald RICHIE. *The Japanese Film: Art and Industry*. Expanded edition. Princeton: Princeton University Press, 1982.

ANDERSON, Lindsay. 'Two Inches off the Ground.' *Sight and Sound* vol. 27, no. 3 (Winter 1957-8): pp. 131-60.

BEARD, Miriam. *Realism in Romantic Japan*. New York: Macmillan, 1930.

BEASLEY, W. G. *The Modern History of Japan*. Second ed. New York: Praeger, 1975.

BENEDICT, Ruth. *The Chrysanthemum and the Sword: Patterns of Japanese Culture*. New York: New American Library, 1974.

BERGALA, Alain. '*Coeur capricieuse*.' *Cahiers du cinéma* no. 311 (May 1980): pp. 34-5.

———— 'L'homme qui se lève.' *Cahiers du cinéma* no. 311 (May 1980): pp. 24-30.

———— 'Retrospective Ozu à la Cinémathèque.' *Cahiers du cinéma* no. 311 (May 1980): pp. 32-9.

———— '*Tokyo-Ga* de Wim Wenders.' *Cahiers du cinéma* no. 374 (July-August 1985): p. 46.

BERQUE, Augustin. *Vivre l'espace au Japon*. Paris: Presses Universitaires de France, 1982.

BERTA, Renato. 'A la recherche du regard: Entretien avec Yuharu Atsuta.' *Cahiers du cinéma* no. 378 (December 1985): pp. 42-7.

BERTHOME, J. P. '*Choeur de Tokyo*.' *La saison cinématographique 1969*: p. 63.

———— '*Fleurs d'equinoxe*.' *La saison cinématographique 1969*: pp. 134-5.

BEZOMBES, Renaud. '*Le goût du saké, Fin d'automne*.' *Cinématographe* no. 41 (November 1978): pp. 74-5.

———— 'Jardin Zen.' *Cinématographe* no. 57 (1980): pp. 29-32.

BIETTE, Jean-Claude. '*Le goût du saké* (Ozu Yasujiro).' *Cahiers du cinéma* no. 296 (January 1979): pp. 41-3.

BOCK, Audie E. *Japanese Film Directors*. Tokyo: Kodansha, 1978.

———— *Mikio Naruse: A Master of the Japanese Cinema*. Chicago: The Film Center of the School of the Art Institute, 1984.

———— *Mikio Naruse: Un maître du cinéma japonais*. Trans. Roland Cosandry and André Kaenal. Locarno: Thirty-sixth Film Festival, 1983.

———— 'Ozu Reconsidered.' *Film Criticism* vol. 8, no. 1 (Fall 1983): pp. 50-3.

BONNET, Jean-Claude. 'A la découverte d'Ozu.' *Cinématographe* no. 35 (February 1978): pp. 23-4.

BONNET, Jean-Claude and Renaud BEZOMBES. 'Le Japon de Yasujiro Ozu.' *Cinématographe* no. 52 (November 1979): pp. 56-8.

BORDWELL, David. 'Ozu, Yasujiro.' In Christopher Lyons, ed. *The International Dictionary of Films and Filmmakers*. Vol. II: *Directors/ Filmmakers*. Chicago: St. James Press, 1984, pp. 397-8.

BOURGET, Eithne. 'Les rites de la communication et du silence (sur *Ohayo*).' *Positif* no. 205 (April 1978): pp. 37-9.

BOWERS, Faubian. *Japanese Theatre*. Rutland, Vermont: Charles E. Tuttle, 1974.

BOYERS, Robert. 'Secular Vision, Transcendental Style: The Art of Yasujiro Ozu.' *Georgia Review* vol. 32, no. 1 (Spring 1978): pp. 63-91.

BRANIGAN, Edward R. *Point of View in the Cinema: A Theory of Narration and Subjectivity in Classical Film*. New York: Mouton, 1984.

———— 'The Space of *Equinox Flower*.' *Screen* vol. 17, no. 2 (Summer 1976): pp. 74-105.

BREWSTER, Ben. '*Soshun (Early Spring)*.' *Monthly Film Bulletin* no. 511 (August 1976): pp. 177-8.

BROSSARD, Jean-Pierre, ed. *Introduction à Yasujiro Ozu*. Locarno: Cinediff, 1979.

BURCH, Noel. 'Approaching Japanese Film.' In Stephen Heath and Patricia Mellencamp, eds. *Cinema and Language*. Frederick, Maryland: University Publications of America, 1983.

———— *To the Distant Observer: Form and Meaning in the Japanese Cinema*. Rev. and ed. Annette Michelson. Berkeley: University of California Press, 1979.

BARUMA, Ian. *Behind the Mask: On Sexual Demons, Sacred Mothers, Transvestites, Gangsters, Drifters, and Other Japanese Cultural Heroes*. New York: Pantheon, 1984.

CHEVALLIER, Jacques. '*Voyage à Tokyo*.' *La Saison cinématographique 1978*: p. 335.

CIMENT, Michel. 'Le cinéma japonais à l'heure (tardive) de la déconstruction (sur un livre de Noël Burch).' *Positif* no. 225 (December 1979): pp. 48-50.

———— 'Sur les yeux d'occident.' *Positif* no. 205 (April 1978): pp. 30-6.

———— 'Le cinéma muet japonais.' *Le cinéma* no. 136 (September 1984): pp. 2712-15.

COHEN, Robert. 'Toward a Theory of Japanese Narrative.' *Quarterly Review of Film Studies* vol. 6, no. 2 (Spring 1981): pp. 181-200.

COLEMAN, Francis X. '*Tokyo Story*: The Virtues of Mannered Simplicity.' In Philip Nobile, ed. *Favorite Movies: Critics' Choice*. New York: Macmillan, 1973, pp. 202-12.

COLPART, Giles. '*Goût du saké*.' *La saison cinématographique 1979*: pp. 150-1.

DANEY, Serge. 'Et pourtant nous sommes nés.' *Cahiers du cinéma* no. 311 (May 1980): pp. 33-4.

———— 'Notes nippones.' *Cahiers du cinéma* no. 343 (January 1983): pp. 26-34.

DAWSON, Jan. *Wim Wenders*. Trans. Carla Wartenberg. New York: Zoetrope, 1976.

'Dialogue on Film: Masahiro Shinoda.' *American Film* vol. 10, no. 7 (May 1985): pp. 10-13.

DOI, TAKEO. *The Anatomy of Dependence*. Trans. John Bester. Tokyo: Kodansha, 1981.

DORE, R. P. *City Life in Japan: A Study of a Tokyo Ward*. Berkeley: University of California Press, 1967.

DOWER, John W. *War without Mercy: Race and Power in the Pacific War*. New York: Pantheon, 1986.

DUSINBERRE, Deke. '*Tokyo Story*.' *The Movie* no. 46 (1980): pp. 918-19.

———— 'Yasujiro Ozu, Master of Moods.' *The Movie* no.46 (1980): pp. 915-17.

ERNST, Earle. *The Kabuki Theatre*. Honolulu: University Press of Hawaii, 1974.

EYQUEM, Olivier. 'Métamorphoses de l'enfant-roi (Ozu dans les années trente).' *Positif* no. 237 (December 1980): pp. 26-31.

FARBER, Manny. 'Film [*End of Summer*].' *Artforum* vol. 8, no. 10 (June 1970): p. 94.

FRIEDMAN, Mildred, ed. *Tokyo: Form and Spirit*. Minneapolis: Walker Art Center/New York: Abrams, 1986.

FUJITAKE, Akira. 'The Formation and Development of Mass Culture.' *The Developing Economies* vol. 5, no. 4 (December 1967): pp. 767-82.

GEIST, Kathe B. 'Yasujiro Ozu: Notes on a Retrospective.' *Film Quarterly* vol. 37, no. 1 (Fall 1983): pp. 2-9.

———— 'Narrative Style in Ozu's Silent Films.' *Film Quarterly* vol. 40, no. 2 (Winter 1986-87): pp. 28-35.

GILLETT, John and David WILSON, eds. *Yasujiro Ozu: A Critical Anthology*. London: British Film Institute, 1976.

GLUCK, Carol. *Japan's Modern Myths: Ideology in the Late Meiji Period*. Princeton: Princeton University Press, 1985.

'*GOSSES de Tokyo*.' *Le cinéma* no. 136 (September 1984): pp. 2716-17.

GOVAERS, Hiroko, ed. *Le cinéma japonais de ses origines à nos jours*, 1984. Paris: Cinémathèque Française/ La Fondation du Japon, 1984.

GRAFE, Frieda. 'Der Herbst der Familie Kohayagawa.' *Filmkritik* no. 12 (November 1968): pp. 788, 790.

———— 'Spätherbst.' *Filmkritik* 11 (October 1967): pp. 577-8.

GUERIN, William K. 'Ford, Ozu, et nous.' *Cinéma 81* no. 266 (February 1981): pp. 28-33.

HALLIDAY, Jon. *A Political History of Japanese Capitalism*. New York: Pantheon, 1975.

HANE, Mikiso. *Peasants, Rebels, and Outcastes: The Underside of Modern Japan*. New York: Pantheon, 1982.

HAPONEK, Jean. 'Autumnal Ozu: *The End of Summer.' Filament* no. 4 (1984): pp. 22-7.

HASUMI, Shiguehiko. 'Interview de Yuharu Atsuta.' In Hiroko Govaers, ed. *Le cinéma japonais de ses origines à nos jours*, Part 2. Paris: Fondation du Japon/ Kawakita Memorial Film Institute, 1984, pp. 79-83.

———— *Kantoku Ozu Yasujiro* [Director Yasujiro Ozu]. Tokyo: Chikuma shobo, 1983.

HAZUMI, Tsuneo. *Eiga gojunen-shi* [Fifty-Year History of Film]. Tokyo: Masu shobo, 1942.

HIRANO, Kyoko. 'American Censorship Policy on Prohibited Film Subjects in Japan: 1945-1952.' Unpublished paper, 4 September 1985.

———— 'Samma no Aji.' In Christopher Lyon, ed. *The International Dictionary of Films and Filmmakers*, vol. 1: *Films*. Chicago: St. James Press, 1984, p. 408.

HOBERMAN, J. 'Japant-Garde Japanorama.' *Artforum* 24, 2 (October 1985); pp. 97-101.

HOLTHOF, Marc. 'Ozu's Reactionary Cinema.' *Jump Cut* no. 18 (August 1978): pp. 20-2.

IIDA, Shinbi. 'Talking about People: Yasujiro Ozu.' *Film* (UK) no. 36 (Summer 1963): pp. 8-10.

IIDA, Shinbi and Akira IWASAKI. 'A Talk with Ozu.' *Cinema* (USA) 6, 1 (1970): pp. 7-8.

———— 'Entretien avec Yasujiro Ozu.' *Positif* no. 214 (January 1979): pp. 39-40.

IROKAWA, Daikichi. *The Culture of the Meiji Period*. Trans. and ed. Marius B. Jansen. Princeton: Princeton University Press, 1985.

IMAMURA, Taihei. 'The Japanese Movie and Way of Thinking.' *Science of Thought* 2 (1956): pp. 1-49.

IWASAKI, Akira. 'The Japanese Cinema.' *Film* (UK) 10 (November-December 1956): pp. 6-10.

———— *Nihon eiga sakka-ron* [Japanese Film Directors]. Tokyo: Chuokoron Sha, 1958.

KATO, Hiroshi. *Eiga kantoku: Yamanaka Sadao* [Film Director Sadao Yamanaka]. Tokyo: Kinema Jumposha, 1985, pp. 186-200.

KEENE, Donald. *Dawn to the West: Japanese Literature in the Modern Era: Fiction*. New York: Holt, Rinehart, and Winston, 1984.

———— *Japanese Literature: An Introduction for Western Readers*. New York: Grove, 1955.

———— *World within Walls: Japanese Literature of the Pre-Modern Era 1600-1867*. New York: Grove Press, 1976.

KIDO, Shiro. *Nihon eiga den: Eiga sesakuska no kiroku* [A Japanese Film Biography: Chronicle of a Film Producer]. Tokyo: Bungei-Shunju-Sha, 1956.

KINMONTH, Earl H. *The Self-Made Man in Meiji Japanese Thought: From Samurai to Salary Man*. Berkeley: University of California Press, 1981.

KISHI, Matsuo. 'Ozu Yasujiro.' In *Nihon eiga kantoku zenshu* [Encyclopedia of Japanese Film Directors], supplement to *Kinema Jumpo Zokan* no. 698 (24 December 1976): pp. 103-5.

KOKUSAI Bunka Shinkokai, ed. *Introduction to Contemporary Japanese Literature*. Tokyo: Kokusai Bunka Shinkokai, 1939.

KONSHAK, Dennis J. 'Space and Narrative in *Tokyo Story.' Film Criticism* vol. 4, no. 3 (Spring 1980): pp. 31-40.

KORNHAUSER, David. *Urban Japan: Its Foundations and Growth*. London: Longmans, 1976.

LANG, Robert. 'Toward an Evaluation of the Films of Yasujiro Ozu.' *Columbia Film Review* vol. 1, no. 1 (November 1982): pp. 8-10.

LI, H. C. 'Tokyo Story/ New York/ 1972: Ozu's Impact on America.' Paper delivered at Japanese Studies Association of Australia, 18-21 May 1983.

LIPPIT, Noriko Mizuta. *Reality and Fiction in Modern Japanese Literature*. White Plains, New York: M. E. Sharpe, 1980.

LOCKWOOD, William W. *The Economic Development of Japan*. Expanded ed. Princeton: Princeton University Press, 1968.

LOVELL, Alan. 'The Craftsmanship of Yasujiro Ozu.' *Peace News* (30 October 1962): p. 11.

MACHEREY, Pierre. *A Theory of Literary Production*. Trans. Geoffrey Wall. London: Routledge and Kegan Paul, 1978.

MAGNY, Joël. 'Le printemps d'Ozu.' *Cinéma 81* no. 265 (January 1981): pp. 16-27.

———————— 'Quelle nostalgie?' *Cinema 79* no. 252 (December 1979): pp. 60-2.

MARTIN, Harris I. 'Popular Music and Social Change in Prewar Japan.' *The Japan Interpreter* vol. 7, nos. 3-4 (Summer-Autumn 1972): pp. 332-52.

MARTIN, Marcel. *'Voyage à Tokyo.'* *Ecran* no. 66 (February 1978): pp. 58-9.

MASSON, Alain. 'Bien définir et bien peindre (sur *Le goût du saké* et *Fin d'automne*.' *Positif* no. 214 (January 1979): pp. 30-7.

———————— 'La netteté est l'ornement de la justesse (sur Yasujiro Ozu).' *Positif* no. 239 (February 1981): pp. 2-12.

MASUMURA, Yasuzo. *Profilo storico del cinema giapponese*. Trans. Guido Cincotti. Rome: Bianco e nero, 1955.

MEARS, Helen. *Year of the Wild Boar*. Philadelphia: Lippincott, 1942.

MELLEN, Joan. *The Waves at Genji's Door: Japan through its Cinema*. New York: Pantheon, 1976.

MILNE, Tom. 'Flavour of Green Tea over Rice.' *Sight and Sound* vol. 32, no. 4 (Autumn 1963): pp. 182-186, 206.

MINER, Earl. *An Introduction to Japanese Court Poetry*. Stanford: Stanford University Press, 1968.

———————— *Japanese Linked Poetry*. Princeton: Princeton University Press, 1979.

———————— Ed. *Principles of Classical Japanese Literature*. Princeton: Princeton University Press, 1985.

MITCHELL, Richard H. *Thought Control in Prewar Japan*. Ithaca: Cornell University Press, 1976.

———————— *Censorship in Imperial Japan*. Princeton: Princeton University Press, 1983.

MIYAGAWA, Kazuo. *Watshi no eigajinsei rokujunen* [Sixty Years of My Life in Films]. Tokyo: Kenkyusha, 1985, pp. 92-103.

MIYOSHI, Masao. *Accomplices of Silence*. Berkeley: University of California Press, 1974.

MONTY, Ib. 'Ozu hans lif og hans film.' *Kosmorama* no. 127 (Autumn 1975): pp. 239-41.

MURAKAMI, Hyoe and Edward G. SEIDENSTICKER, eds. *Guides to Japanese Culture*. Tokyo: Japan Culture Institute, 1977.

NAKAMURA, Mitsuo. *Contemporary Japanese Fiction 1926-1968*. Tokyo: Kokusai Bunka Shinkokai, 1969.

NAKAMURA, Takafusa. *Economic Growth in Prewar Japan*. Trans. Robert A. Feldman. New Haven: Yale University Press, 1983.

NIOGRET, Hubert. '"Introducing: Yasujiro Ozu," ou pour la première fois à l'ecran.' *Positif* no. 203 (February 1978): pp. 3-13.

———————— 'Quelques familles japonaises: Sur une retrospective à la Cinémathèque Française.' *Positif* no. 267 (May 1983): pp. 12-13.

NISHIJIMA, Norio, Yasuo HORIKIRI, and Michihiro MAEKAWA, eds. *Libro Cinematheque Ozu Yasujiro: Tokyo Monogatari*. Tokyo: Riburopoto, 1984.

NITSCHKE, Gunter. '"Ma": The Japanese Sense of "Place" in Old and New Architecture and Planning.' *Architectural Design* vol. 3 (March 1966): pp. 117-56.

O'NEILL, P. G., ed. *Tradition and Modern Japan*. Tenterden, Kent: Paul Norbury, 1981.

OSHIMA, Nagisa et al. *Nihon eiga o yomu: Paionia tachi no isan* [Reading Japanese Film: Heritage of the Pioneers]. Tokyo: Dagero Shuppan, 1984.

OZU, Yasujiro. 'Eiga no aji; Jinsei no aji' [The Flavor of Cinema; The Flavor of Life]. *Kinema Jumpo* no. 273 (10 December 1960): p. 35.

———————— 'Ozu on Ozu: The Silents.' *Cinema* (USA) vol. 7, no. 3 (Winter 1972-73): pp. 22-4.

———————— 'Ozu on Ozu: The Talkies.' *Cinema* (USA), vol. 6, no. 1 (1970): pp. 3-5.

———————— *Ozu Yasujiro sakuhinshu* [Scenarios of Yasujiro Ozu]. Ed. Kazuo Inoue. Four volumes. Tokyo: Ripushobo, 1983.

OZU, Yasujiro and Tadao IKEDA. *Todake no keimai hoka: Shinario: Chichi araki, Todake no keimai* [Brothers and Sisters of the Toda Family and Other Writings: Scripts: There Was a Father; Brothers and Sisters of the Toda Family]. Tokyo: Aoyama Gakuin, 1943.

Ozu, Yasujiro and Kogo Noda. *Ochazuke no aji hoka: Shinario: Ochazuke no aji, Bakushu, Banshun* [Flavor of Green Tea over Rice and other writings: Flavor of Green Tea over Rice, Early Summer, Late Spring]. Tokyo: Aoyama Gakuin, 1952.

———— 'Tokyo Story.' In Howard Hibbett, ed. *Contemporary Japanese Literature: An Anthology of Fiction, Film, and Other Writing Since 1945.* New York: Knopf, 1977, pp. 189-237.

———— *Crépuscule à Tokyo; Début d'été; Le goût du saké; Printemps tardif; Le voyage à Tokyo.* Trans. M. and E. Wasserman. Paris: Publications orientalistes de France, 1986.

Ozu Yasujiro hito to geijutsu [Ozu's Nature and His Works]. *Kinema Jumpo* no. 1173 (February 1964).

Ozu Yasujiro meisaku eiga ongaku shu [Ozu Yasujiro Memorial Album: Music from His Masterpieces]. Tokyo: Japan Crown, 1972. GW-5233. Phonograph record.

Ozu Yasujiro no sekai [The World of Yasujiro Ozu]. Tokyo: Japan Victor, 1972. SJV-1140-1M. Phonograph records.

Ozu Yasujiro wo yomu [Reading Yasujiro Ozu]. Tokyo: Firuma Atosha, 1982.

Paini, Dominique. 'Notes de parcours.' *Cinéma 81* no. 265 (January 1981): pp. 6-10.

———— 'Ozu: un japonais à Paris.' *Cinéma 79* no. 243 (March 1979): p. 58.

Philippe, Jean-Claude. 'Ozu Yasujiro.' *Dossiers du cinéma: Cinéastes I.* Paris: Castermann, 1971.

Pinguet, Maurice. 'Le temps de l'amour et de la révolte.' *Les Nouvelles littéraires* no. 2622 (9-16 February 1978): p. 11.

———— 'Le regard d'un peintre: Jean Degottex.' *Cinéma 81* no. 266 (February 1981): pp. 36-8.

Richie, Donald. *Ozu.* Berkeley: University of California Press, 1974.

———— 'Viewing Japanese Film: Some Considerations.' *East-West Film Journal* vol. 1, no. 1 (December 1986): pp. 23-35.

Rimer, J. Thomas. *Modern Japanese Fiction and Its Traditions: An Introduction.* Princeton: Princeton University Press, 1978.

Rosenbaum, Jonathan. 'Richie's Ozu: Our Prehistoric Present.' *Sight and Sound* vol. 44, no. 3 (Summer 1975): pp. 175-9.

Ryu, Chishu. 'Reflections on My Mentor.' *Cinema* (USA) vol. 6, no. 1 (1970): p. 6.

———— 'Yasujiro Ozu.' *Sight and Sound* vol. 33, no. 2 (Spring 1964): p. 92.

Sato, Tadao. 'The Art of Yasujiro Ozu.' *The Study of the History of the Cinema* no. 4 (1974): pp. 80-96; no. 5 (1974): pp. 81-96; no. 6 (1975): pp. 85-96; no. 7 (1975): pp. 84-96; no. 8 (1976): pp. 84-96; no. 9 (1977): pp. 88-96; no. 10 (1977): pp. 91-6; no. 11 (1978): pp. 91-6.

———— 'The Art of Yasujiro Ozu.' *Wide Angle* vol. 1, no. 4 (1977): pp. 44-8.

———— 'The Comedy of Ozu and Chaplin: A Study in Contrast.' *Wide Angle* vol. 3, no. 2 (1979): pp. 50-3.

———— *Currents in Japanese Cinema.* Trans. Gregory Barrett. Tokyo: Kodansha, 1982.

———— *Ozu Yasujiro no geijutsu* [The Art of Yasujiro Ozu]. Two volumes. Tokyo: Asahi Shinbunsha, 1978-9.

———— 'Le point de regard.' *Cahiers du cinéma* no. 310 (April 1980): pp. 5-10.

———— 'Rising Sons.' *American Film* vol. 11, no. 3 (December 1985): pp. 58-62, 78.

Satomi, Jun et al., ed. *Ozu Yasujiro hito to shigoto* [Yasujiro Ozu: The Man and His Work]. Tokyo: Banyusha, 1972.

Schrader, Leonard, ed. and trans. *The Masters of Japanese Film.* Unpublished ms., n.d. Pacific Film Archive, Berkeley, California.

Schrader, Paul. *Transcendental Style in Film: Ozu, Bresson, Dreyer.* Berkeley: University of California Press, 1972.

Seidensticker, Edward. *Low City, High City: Tokyo from Edo to the Earthquake.* New York: Knopf, 1983.

Shillony, Ben-Ami. *Politics and Culture in Wartime Japan.* Oxford: The Clarendon Press, 1981.

SMITH, H. D. 'Tokyo as an Idea: An Exploration of Japanese Urban Thought until 1945.' *Journal of Japanese Studies* vol. 4, no. 1 (1978): pp. 45-80.

SMITH, Larry. 'Yasujiro Ozu: An Appreciation.' *Take One* vol. 4, no. 9 (May 1975): pp. 8-9.

SMITH, Robert J. *Japanese Society: Tradition, Self, and the Social Order*. Cambridge: Cambridge University Press, 1983.

Studies on Japanese Culture. Two volumes. Tokyo: Japan P.E.N. Club, 1973.

TAKAHASHI, Osamu. *Kenrantaru kagee—Ozu Yasujiro* [Dazzling Shadowgraph: Yasujiro Ozu]. Tokyo: Bungei Shunjun, 1982.

TANIZAKI, Jun'ichiro. *In Praise of Shadows*. Trans. Thomas J. Harper and Edward G. Seidensticker. New Haven: Leete's Island Books, 1977.

——— 'Témoignages sur l'art de Yasujiro Ozu.' *Cinejap* no. 2 (Spring 1979): pp. 16-27.

TESSIER, Max. 'Entretien avec Chishu Ryu.' *L'avant-scène du cinéma* no. 204 (15 March 1978): p. 6.

——— '*Le goût du saké; Fin d'automne*.' *Ecran* no. 75 (December 1978): pp. 56-8.

——— *Images du cinéma japonais*. Paris: Veyrier, 1981.

——— *Yasujiro Ozu. Anthologie du cinéma* no. 64 (July-October 1971).

——— 'Yasujiro Ozu et le cinéma japonais à la fin du muet.' *Ecran 79* no. 86 (December 1979): pp. 30-7.

THOMPSON, Kristin. 'Notes on the Spatial System of Ozu's Early Films.' *Wide Angle* vol. 1, no. 4 (1977): pp. 8-17.

THOMPSON, Kristin and David BORDWELL. 'Space and Narrative in the Films of Ozu.' *Screen* vol. 17, no. 2 (Summer 1976): pp. 41-73.

TOBIN, Yann. 'Pourquoi l'eau de mer est-elle salée?' *Positif* no. 237 (December 1980): pp. 32-5.

TOURNES, André. 'Découvrir Ozu.' *Jeune Cinéma* no. 123 (December 1979–January 1980): pp. 14-21.

TUCKER, Richard. *Japan: Film Image*. London: Studio Vista, 1973.

UEDA, Makoto. *Literary and Art Theories in Japan*. Cleveland: Press of Case Western Reserve University, 1967.

VASEY, Ruth. 'Ozu and the noh.' *Australian Journal of Screen Theory* no. 7 (1980): pp. 88-102.

VOGEL, Ezra F. *Japan's New Middle Class*. Second ed. Berkeley: University of California Press, 1971.

Voyage à Tokyo [Découpage of *Tokyo Story*]. *L'avant-scène du cinéma* no. 204 (15 March 1978).

WILLIS, Don. 'Yasujiro Ozu: Emotion and Contemplation.' *Sight and Sound* vol. 48, no. 1 (Winter 1978-9): pp. 44-9.

WOOD, Michael. 'Goriot in Tokyo.' *New York Review of Books* (12 June 1975): pp. 36-7.

WOOD, Robin. '*Tokyo Story*.' *Movie* no. 13 (Summer 1965): pp. 32-3.

——— 'Yasujiro Ozu: Record of a Cinema Gentleman.' *The Economist* (30 June 1984): p. 82.

ZEMAN, Marvin. 'The Serene Poet of Japanese Cinema: The Zen Artistry of Yasujiro Ozu.' *The Film Journal* vol. 1, no. 3-4 (Fall-Winter 1972): pp. 62-71.

Index

401

INDEX

UNIVERSITY OF WINCHESTER
LIBRARY